# BEAUTIFUL BRITISH COLUMBIA

## TRAVEL GUIDE

# BEAUTIFUL BRITISH COLUMBIA TRAVEL GUIDE

**Editor-in-Chief**
Bryan McGill
**Executive Editors**
Cheryl Coull, Anne Mayhew
**Graphic Designer**
Noreen Dennis/Dennis & Struthers Communications

**Writers and Researchers:**
*Vancouver Island* Cheryl Coull, Bruce Obee.
*Southwestern British Columbia* Anne Mayhew, Bryan McGill.
*Okanagan-Similkameen* Cheryl Coull, Allan Coyle, Anne Mayhew, Bryan McGill.
*Kootenay Country* Cheryl Coull, Anne Mayhew.
*High Country* Bryan McGill, Bruce Obee.
*Cariboo-Chilcotin* Anne Mayhew, Rosemary Neering.
*North by Northwest* Cheryl Coull, Jim Stirling.
*Peace River-Alaska Highway* Jim Stirling.
*British Columbia Rockies* Anne Mayhew.
*Alberta Rockies* Doug Leighton, Anne Mayhew.

**Graphics Consultant:** Karen Hodgson.
**Editorial Assistant:** Anita Willis.
**Index:** Bruce Obee.
**Fact Checking:** Karen Gibbs, Sophronia Siu.
**Regional and Route Maps:** Rob Struthers/ Dennis & Struthers Communications.
**Photography:** Gunter Marx Photography (except where noted).
**Cover Design:** Ken Seabrook.
**Decorative Art:** Mary Scobie.

Published by Beautiful British Columbia, a division of Great Pacific Industries Inc., 929 Ellery Street, Victoria, British Columbia, Canada V9A 7B4. Phone 604-384-5456.

**President**
John L. Thomson.
**Director, Publishing and Manufacturing**
Tony Owen.

 To order the Beautiful British Columbia *Travel Guide*, call toll-free in Canada and the USA. 1-800-663-7611, or from Victoria and elsewhere 604-384-5456. Pacific Time. Fax: 604-384-2812.

Colour separations and film by WYSIWYG Graphics Inc., Vancouver. Printed in Canada by Ronalds Printing, Vancouver.

**Canadian Cataloguing in Publication Data**
Main entry under title: Beautiful British Columbia travel guide
Previously published as supplements to: Beautiful British Columbia magazine. Includes index.
ISBN 0-920431-16-X (spiral bound) – ISBN 0-920431-17-8 (pbk.)
1. British Columbia – Guidebooks.
I. McGill, Bryan. II. Beautiful British Columbia Magazine (Firm).
FC3807.B42 1994 917,1104'4 C94-910060-9
F1087.B42 1994

**Front Cover:** Highway 99 (Sea to Sky Highway) winds past Howe Sound into the Coast Mountains. Photograph by Chris Speedie/Image Finders.

**Inside Front Cover:** Rockies in winter, Kootenay National Park.
**Inside Back Cover:** Nuna Falls, Vermilion River, Kootenay National Park.

*Idaho Peak in the Selkirk Mountains, near Sandon Ghost Town.*

# BEAUTIFUL BRITISH COLUMBIA
## TRAVEL GUIDE

# A Guide to the Travel Guide

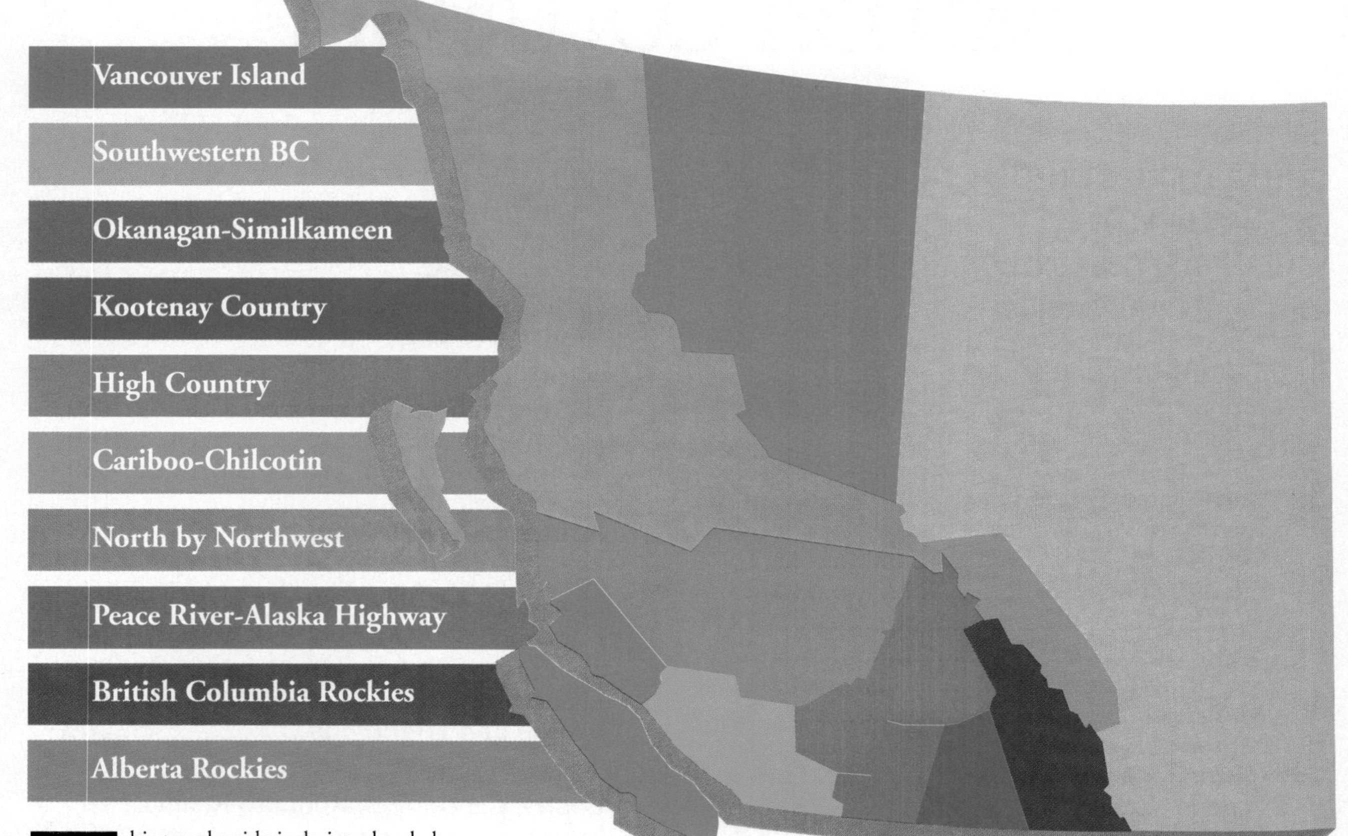


This travel guide is designed to help you have the best imaginable touring experience within British Columbia and the Alberta Rockies – the richest, most interesting, most rewarding, even the funniest. The essence of this guidebook lies in the *Logs*, with their item-by-item coverage of highways and byroads, with all the bits of local gossip and tips that come with the meal. Like *Ship's Logs* or *Pilot's Logs*, our *Travellers' Logs* go from *Here* to *There*. They're capsule journals to adventure.

All you have to know is which *Here* to *There* you want to "do." So this book is designed to be used at home first (or in the hotel, or at the campsite with a Coleman lantern). That is where you take a broad look at what you might want to explore, read introductions to the regions, check opening remarks that introduce each *Log*, see if it's the kind of road you want to travel, if you have the right vehicle, if it's what you feel like.

When you have pinpointed your trek, and chosen your route maps, then the book goes "on the road" right beside you.

ALL DISTANCES ARE NOT EQUAL! We admit right up front that our distances are only reasonably accurate. We found a welter of contradictions among current official and unofficial sources on distances between towns, cities, and other points on the maps. This was largely due to varying starting points, such as town borders (often unclear) and town centres. Whenever possible, we measured from city or town halls, or village offices, to gauge distances from town to town.

Also note that all odometers are not equal. It may be worth while to check yours out. And tire pressure influences the readings: low tire pressure makes for longer kilometres. With all these factors, the best we can say is that our distances are "approximately exact," but probably more exact over all than any other single source.

This travel guide is already famous for the number of telephone numbers listed.

Please note:

Area Code for British Columbia: 604.

Area Code for Alberta: 403.

With minor variations, we have stayed with regional divisions set up by the BC government, *High Country*, *North by Northwest*, and so on. These are arbitrary divisions, but they work, to an extent, and we felt it would be more helpful to the traveller if our *Travel Guide* tallied with the government infocentres and publications.

If at any time you become lost while travelling within BC, well, what a great opportunity – just collar the nearest resident. Locals are likely to be friendly and may know some good stories.

# ROUTE MAPS

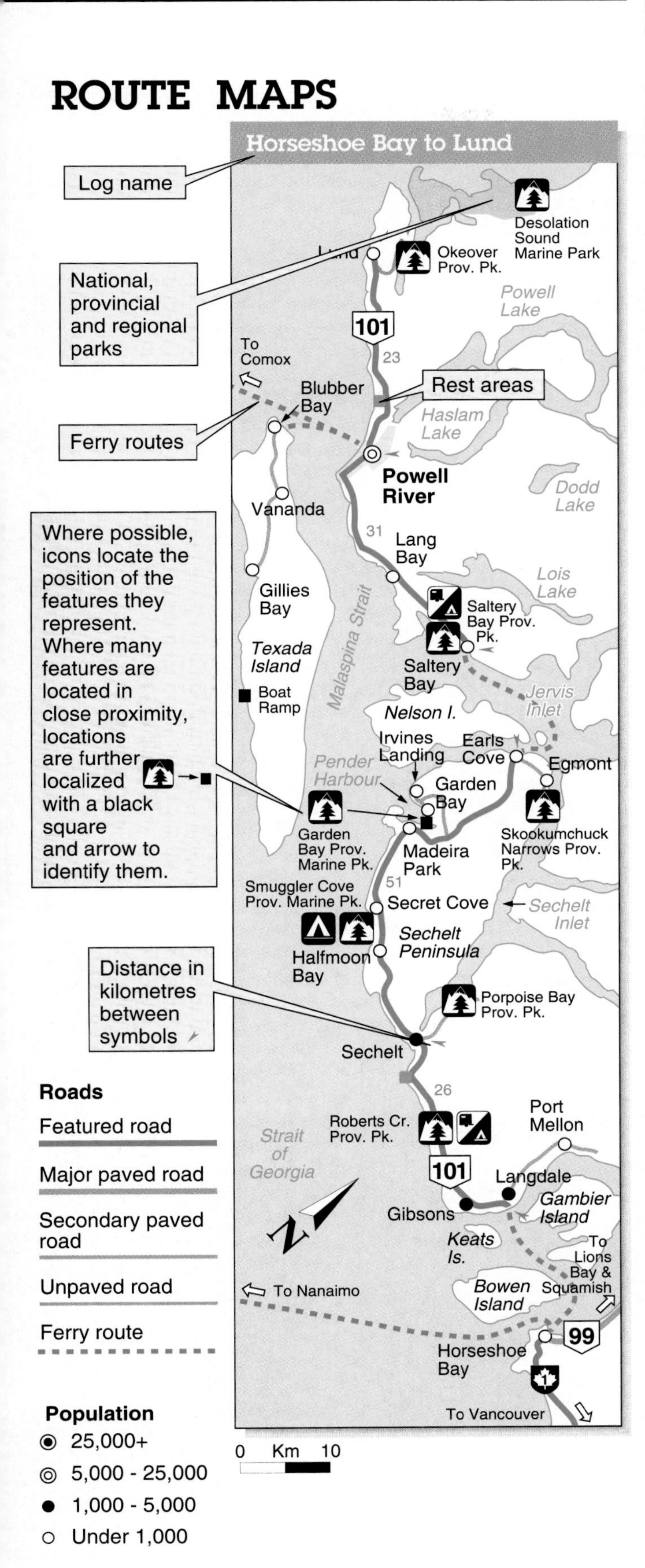


## From the Editor

We're on the road again with the fourth revised edition of our travel guide to British Columbia, now entitled, as befits its contents, the Beautiful British Columbia *Travel Guide*. We've spent two years updating, revising, expanding, and improving upon the third edition, published in 1990. With more than 60,000 copies of prior editions sold, this book is headed for BC's all-time best-seller list.

We are not hesitant to proclaim this is the most comprehensive, most useful, most readable, brightest, and smoothest guide to BC ever published. Right away, for those familiar with any of the last editions, you will notice a leap forward in the look of the book. The enhanced features include:

- Some 85 route maps, now in full colour, now easier to follow.
- A full map of British Columbia that introduces the *Travel Guide*. It gives you, at a glance, the big picture and shows you how the route maps connect to each other.
- New and bigger full-colour maps for each of the nine tourism regions of BC and for our Alberta Rockies section.
- A clearer and cleaner design. You should be able to glide through the *Travel Guide* effortlessly and happily find your way through the mazes of highways, roads, and streets in BC.
- New, more readable, more compact typography. This has allowed us to pack in more information, describing more than 4,000 points of interest along 40,000 kilometres of highway and byroad.
- A more comprehensive index that will allow you quick and easy access to the mountain of information we have amassed.

Above all, the book contains more exhaustive research than before. We count a quarter million words, the size of two fat novels. The narrative ranges from precise, when giving directions, to eloquent, when taking note of the landscape, to entertaining, when dealing with some of BC's bizarre or colourful persons and events, past and present.

Some route descriptions, or *Logs*, are much more detailed than previously, such as Hwy 101 up through the Sechelt Peninsula and the Sea-to-Sky Hwy (Hwy 99) from Vancouver through Whistler to the Interior. This latter route has taken on more significance in the intervening four years, thanks to the paving and upgrading of the old Duffey Lake Road. This has effectively made Hwy 99 a third major route – besides the Trans-Canada (Hwy 1) and the Coquihalla tollway (Hwy 5) – and a scenic one, at that, from the Lower Mainland directly into the Cariboo. The other notable highway advancement is the Coquihalla Connector (Hwy 97C). It branches off the Coquihalla tollway near Merritt and zips travellers smack into the heart of the Okanagan Valley, just south of Kelowna, shaving 90 minutes off driving from the coast, making it less than a four-hour trip.

Many editors, writers, researchers, mapmakers, graphic artists, and production technicians have toiled on the development of this guide since its 1988 start, but nobody more than its present executive editors, Cheryl Coull and Anne Mayhew. Both played a major role in pioneering the first edition, then Cheryl was executive editor again for the second, and Anne for the third. Each has been up and down many intriguing roads. Each has researched and written a great deal. Each has combed through this document repeatedly, rewriting, editing, proofing, and making sure it all came together as clearly as possible.

It must be remembered, though, BC is a wondrous labyrinth. Any good mirror of it, as we think this book is, should happily overwhelm any traveller.

Bryan

# Route Finder: Route Maps at a Glance

Boxes identify specific route descriptions or *Logs*, the regions, and the pages where they are to be found.

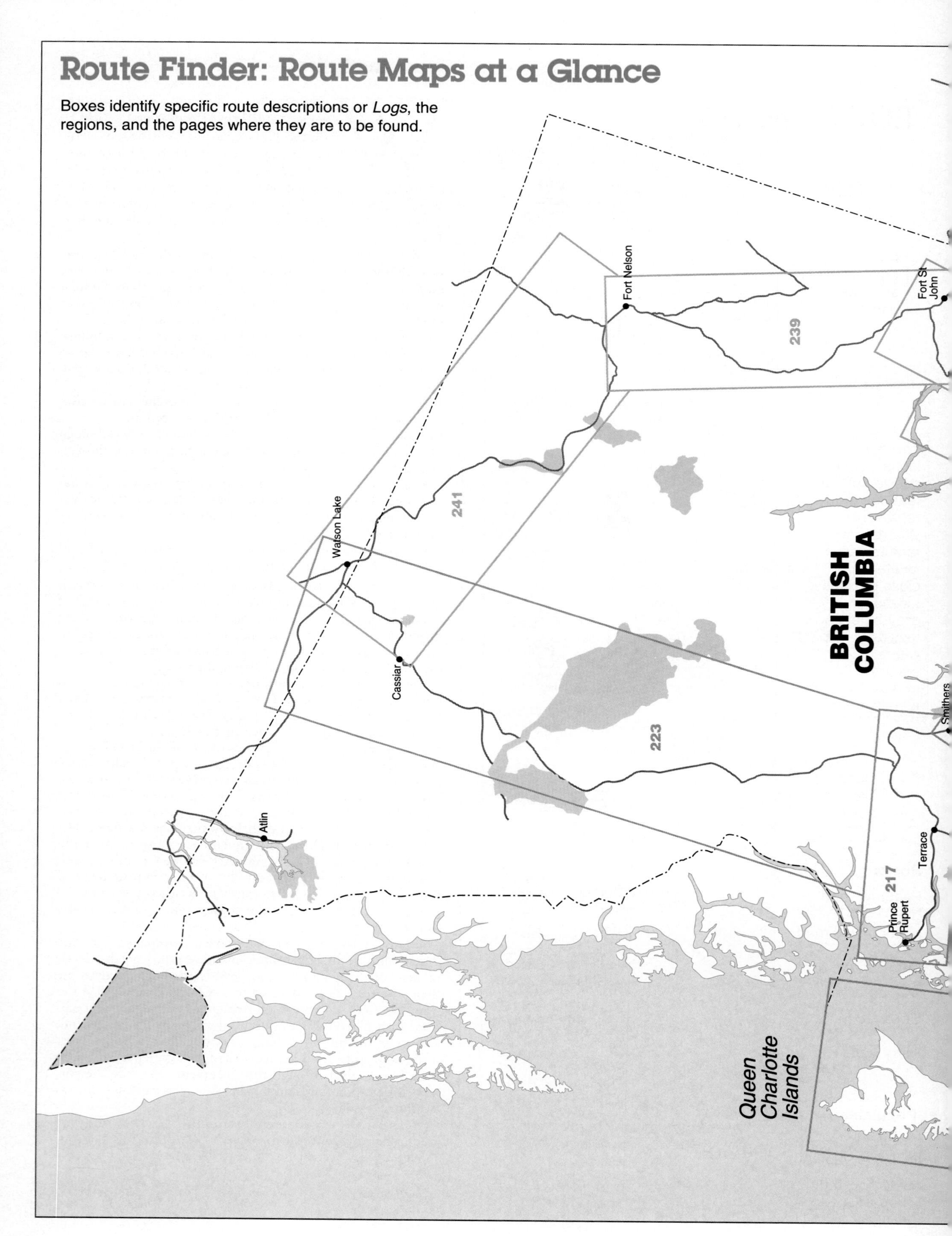

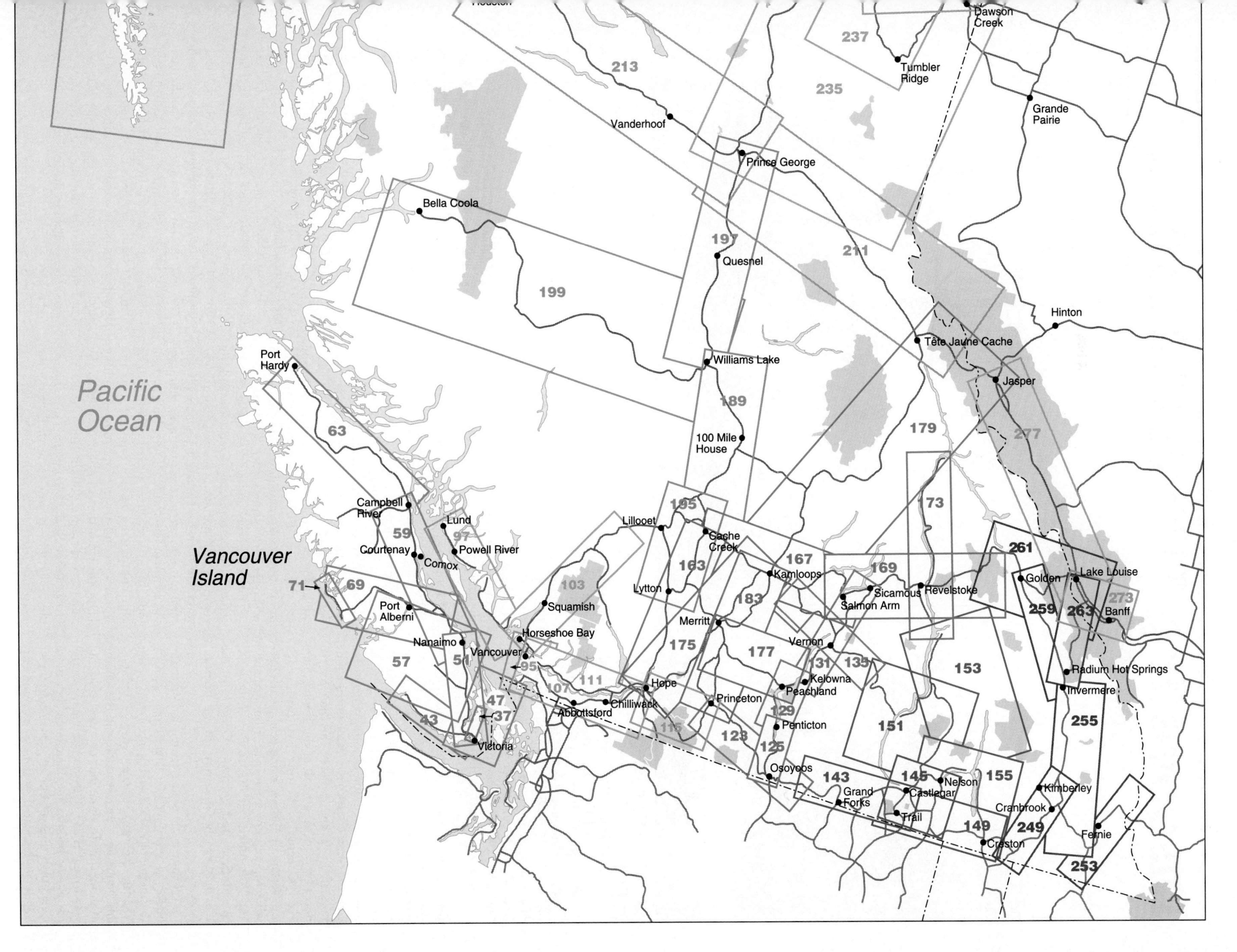
Dawson Creek
237
Tumbler Ridge
235
Grande Pairie
213
Vanderhoof
Prince George
Bella Coola
197
Quesnel
211
199
Hinton
Tête Jaune Cache
Port Hardy
Williams Lake
Jasper
Pacific Ocean
189
63
179
100 Mile House
277
173
195
Campbell River
Lillooet
Lund
Cache Creek
59
97
261
Courtenay
Powell River
167
169
Vancouver Island
Comox
163
Kamloops
Golden
Lake Louise
71
69
103
Lytton
Sicamous
Revelstoke
273
Port Alberni
Squamish
183
Salmon Arm
259
263
Banff
Merritt
Horseshoe Bay
Nanaimo
175
177
Vernon
57
51
Vancouver
135
153
95
131
Radium Hot Springs
107
111
Kelowna
Hope
Peachland
Invermere
47
Chilliwack
Princeton
43
37
Abbotsford
129
255
Penticton
151
Victoria
115
123
125
Osoyoos
143
145
Nelson
155
Grand Forks
Castlegar
Kimberley
Cranbrook
Trail
149
249
Creston
Fernie
253

# Discovering British Columbia

*Fort Victoria 1843, watercolour by Harry Heine. Historic Hudson's Bay Company steamer, SS* Beaver, *in foreground*

Two hundred years ago, in the sloop *Princesa Real*, Manuel Quimper sailed into the Strait of Juan de Fuca off the southern coast of Vancouver Island. On that fair day of June 23, 1790, he was guided into Sooke Harbour by three native canoes, landing in his Spanish longboat just across from Whiffin Spit, a few kilometres west of Victoria.

On June 23, two centuries later, with an abundance of high spirits, residents of the area marked the occasion with bicentennial festivities. This was one of a cluster of many bicentenaries in the Pacific Northwest, for Captain James Cook had arrived in 1778 (anchoring near Friendly Cove in Nootka Sound), to be followed by a succession of intrepid explorers. Captain George Vancouver came into Juan de Fuca in 1792, and explored the coast for the next two years. As a result of this timing, there always seems to be one two-hundredth anniversary or another being celebrated somewhere up and down the coast, from Nanaimo and Port Alberni in BC, to Port Townsend, Washington, and Portland, Oregon, in the US, marking the "discovery" of this beautiful land.

Of course 200 years is merely a drop in the bucket of time, and the larger cities of BC – the metropolis of Greater Vancouver, Greater Victoria, Kelowna, Prince George, Kamloops, and Nanaimo – are just toddlers in the scheme of things. In the thousands of years before BC was discovered, there existed here many nations of peoples speaking languages more varied than those of Europe, co-existing under highly sophisticated systems of government, managing local resources, and trading with neighbours.

To European eyes, this land may be young, but in most other terms, it is ancient.

From either perspective — BC is old or BC is young — much remains to be discovered. Travellers sometimes mistakenly believe "the New World" has relatively little to offer in the way of history and culture. Where are the cathedrals, the venerable artistic traditions, the fortresses? To eyes that gaze long enough, these things appear: the cathedrals are all around, in the ancient (albeit endangered) forests, and up high in the mountains where Thunderbird himself reigns. The arts can be found, in modern galleries, in tiny communities as evolving traditions, even on rocky outcroppings facing the sea, expressions of wonder dating back 10,000 - 13,000 years. There are fortresses too: fur-trade bastions from the early days of European occupation, and promontories up and down the coast, from which the First Nations defended themselves.

Beyond history and culture, the land itself remains to be explored. Even with today's complex transportation systems, with highways and back roads reaching apparently the remotest corners of the province, there are places where few people, if any, have ever set foot. BC is immense, a total of 948,600 sq km, comprising nearly one-tenth of the world's second largest country, stretching 1,300km from the American border to the Yukon, and nearly 900km from the Pacific Ocean to the Rocky Mountains. Furthermore, the topography is varied and challenging, the coastline itself so fraught with inlets and fjords, sounds and passages, that stretched out it would be some 27,000km long. And north to south, the province is striated by a series of rugged young mountain ranges (at 60 million years old, a mountain is geologically young), making east-west travel an adventure in any century.

## Mountains and Rivers

Three-quarters of BC lies 1,000m and more above sea level, a mountainous land from the Rockies in the east, to the two maritime ranges on the Pacific. Many people feel the coastal ranges are even more spectacular than the Rockies.

But that is not all. In between, lining up north-south in formidable succession to the Rockies, are the three parallel ranges of the Columbia Mountains: the Purcells, the Selkirks, and the Monashees. To the north is the Cariboo Range.

Between the Columbia Mountains and the Coast Mountains lies the rolling Interior Plateau, with its own complement of mountains and valleys, uplands and lowlands. This Interior Plateau, the rolling grasslands and sagebrush, spreads south across the border into the US. In the Okanagan, near Osoyoos, is Canada's only desert, home of Great Basin spadefoot toads, northern Pacific rattlesnakes, tiger beetles, scorpions, and other unlikely species. At the opposite end of the plateau, near Prince George, are some of the province's largest lakes – Babine, Stuart, François, Ootsa, and others.

For British Columbians, western Canada

begins at the Rockies. Here the Great Continental Divide splits the country, and the nation's rivers either flow away from BC, or run across the province to the Pacific. Mt Robson, at 3,954m the highest peak in the Canadian Rockies, is the birthplace of the Fraser, Canada's third longest river. From these mountains the Fraser runs a 1,370km course to the sea at Vancouver. It flows across the Interior Plateau, joined on the way by such tributaries as the Nechako, Chilcotin, and Quesnel rivers, until it meets the Thompson River at Lytton. From there it boils south through its infamous lower canyon. By the time it reaches the sea, the Fraser has drained an area of 230,000 sq km, nearly one-quarter of the province.

The northern half of the province offers a surprising mix of plateau, mountains, and prairies. The northern reaches of the Rockies turn diagonally northwest, so that the northeast corner of BC actually lies east of the big mountains and, with its grain elevators, chinooks and blizzards, is more closely associated with Alberta. West of the mountains lies a topographic oddity known as the Rocky Mountain Trench, a remarkable valley visible from space, 3 to 16km wide, extending 1,600km from the 60th parallel down to Montana. Williston Lake reservoir, the largest lake in BC, lies in the trench. The great Peace River flows from this lake towards the Mackenzie River delta, draining into the Arctic Ocean.

## Highest Mountains

The Coast Mountains are the highest in North America. Here, in the extreme northwest corner of BC, on the Alaska border, is Fairweather Mountain, at 4,663m the highest point in BC. Just north of BC, in the Yukon, is Mt Logan, at 5,959m the highest point in Canada. And near the northwest end of these coastal mountains is Alaska's Mt McKinley, at 6,194m the highest peak on the continent. Mt Waddington, south, is 4,016m.

## Islands

All of these ranges are part of the formidable Canadian Cordillera, one of the world's major mountain systems. They don't end at the Pacific Ocean: beyond the Coast Range are the Insular Mountains, rising from the sea as islands. The ranges of Vancouver Island, the largest North American island in the Pacific, rival the Rockies when you consider the vertical distance from sea bottom to the highest peak. Mt Golden Hinde, at 2,200m, is the centrepiece of Strathcona, BC's oldest provincial park. North of Vancouver Island, the Queen Charlottes, domain of the Haida peoples, are a cluster of more than 150 wild and misty isles on the westernmost edge of Canada. In all, 6,500 islands and islets lie off the mainland coast of BC.

## Explorers

This extraordinary diversity has challenged all who have searched for transportation routes from the Interior to the sea. Among the first was Captain George Vancouver, who wrote of the "innumerable pleasing landscapes" he discovered as he surveyed the north Pacific coast in the early 1790s. Vancouver, continuing Britain's futile search for a North West Passage to the heart of the continent, explored much of BC's coastline. One of his objectives was to determine whether the interior of the mainland could be reached by "arms of the sea, or by the mouths of large rivers." So he concentrated on the mainland coast, surveying many of the long, meandering inlets that penetrate the steep and forested slopes of the Coast Mountains.

Vancouver had visited the BC coast 14 years earlier with Captain James Cook, first British explorer to land on BC soil. Cook's expedition had returned to England with news of great profits to be made from the sale of sea otter pelts. By the time Vancouver returned, fur traders from Russia, America, Spain, and Britain were sailing established courses between North America and Canton. (The sea otters, at least in this area, were wiped out.)

While Vancouver was attempting to sail inland by sea, Alexander Mackenzie was trying to reach the sea from the eastern side of the Rockies. An employee of the North West Company, he'd heard from Cook's expedition of the lucrative coastal fur trade. In 1793 Mackenzie followed the Peace River across the Rockies, then travelled an amazing 400km downstream on the Fraser. He headed overland to the west, with the help of native guides, paddling to the sea through the Coast Mountains, on the Bella Coola River.

In 1808, Simon Fraser, another North West Company man, descended the river eventually named in his honour. In a harrowing 35-day down-river journey, he reached the mouth of the Fraser. However, he had believed himself to be travelling the Columbia, and his disappointment was intense when he discovered he had been struggling with the wrong river.

## Early Settlements

While Fraser was navigating his river, David Thompson, also of the North West Company, was exploring the headwaters of the Columbia River. He travelled the Columbia to the sea, confirming a route from the interior to the coast. Trading posts established on these and other routes formed the nucleus of the province's first European settlements. By the time Canada's two rival fur-trading firms – the North West Company and the Hudson's Bay Company – merged in 1821, the forts were surrounded by farms which supplied grain, produce, milk, and other agricultural goods to traders and travellers.

## Gold Rush

Farmers around Fort Victoria, built in 1843, supplied American whalers and Russian fur traders. Agriculture became a mainstay when the Royal Navy arrived in 1846 to survey surrounding waters and protect British subjects. Fort Victoria was well on its way to becoming a major seaport when Vancouver Island was declared a British colony in 1849, year of the California Gold Rush. When gold was discovered on the lower Fraser River in 1858, the same year the mainland colony of BC was established, Fort Victoria was inundated with fortune seekers.

*Detail of totem pole, Acous Peninsula, west coast of Vancouver Island.*

More than 25,000 men took $500,000 worth of gold from the lower Fraser, then abandoned the diggings to the more diligent Chinese by 1859. Reports of bigger nuggets farther north, in the Cariboo, lured miners away. The new colonial government, eager to provide access to developing areas, began building the Cariboo Road from Yale to Barkerville, which was completed in 1861. The Cariboo gold, however, was deep in the ground and expensive to retrieve. Many miners turned to trapping, road building, or farming.

More gold was discovered in 1865 on the Columbia River's Big Bend, north of Revelstoke. The colonial government helped, building a road from Cache Creek to Savona, on Kamloops Lake. From Savona, miners went by paddlewheeler and trail through the Thompson River system to, hopefully, the gold.

## EMERGENCIES 9-1-1

Dialing **9-1-1** will give you access to ambulance, fire, and police in many areas of the province. If you do not have immediate success with **9-1-1**, dial **0** for Operator — every operator is trained to handle your emergency calls. These and other emergency numbers are listed on the inside front covers of telephone directories for specific communities.

### Police

Some BC municipalities have their own police departments; many are policed by the Royal Canadian Mounted Police. Phone numbers are in the front of telephone directories.

### Health and Hospitals

Travellers from outside BC who have health insurance plans should ensure they are adequately covered before leaving home. Extra health insurance can be purchased from travel agents.

Hospitals in BC are listed in the yellow pages of telephone directories. People taking prescribed medicine should carry a copy of the prescription in case it needs refilling in BC.

### Tourist Alert

Urgent messages for travellers in BC can be given to local police. If your name appears in a newspaper, at an infocentre, or is broadcast on radio or television, contact the nearest police department.

### First Roads and Railways

Like the Fraser River gold rush, Big Bend fizzled within a year. By 1866, when Vancouver Island and BC were united, it was obvious that fur trading and gold mining could not form a stable economic base for a developing colony. So in 1873, two years after BC became a Canadian province, the provincial government embarked on a policy to encourage agriculture and logging. An integral part of the policy was construction of trunk roads linking industrial centres and markets.

Distances were great, costs were high, progress was slow. But roads gradually reached into much of southern BC. The frenzy subsided with the Canadian government's fulfillment of the promise which lured BC into Confederation, to build a railway joining the West with the rest of Canada. While construction crews laid track through the Rockies at Kicking Horse Pass, and through the Selkirks at Rogers Pass, others were building along the banks of the Fraser River from Port Moody, and up the Thompson River toward the Rockies. On November 7, 1885, the Canadian Pacific Railway became the nation's first transcontinental railway: at Craigellachie, near Shuswap Lake, "a plain iron spike welded East to West," the last spike.

Other railways, including the Canadian National, soon were laying track through the mountain passes and along the river corridors explored by early fur traders. Many of these new railway lines were used in conjunction with steamships. Roads lost their significance. In the notorious Fraser Canyon, portions of the Cariboo Road were severely damaged by the CPR and CNR around the turn of the century, yet the road wasn't reopened until 1926. It became fashionable to travel by train, and much of the nation's business was done in fancy dining cars and staterooms.

### BC's Highways Today

But the exploitation of BC's natural resources had begun and railways were not enough. Industries were developing – logging and sawmilling, mining for copper, zinc, silver, and other ores, agriculture, salmon fishing, tourism. The automobile age came to BC in the 1920s and road building continued. By the late '30s and early '40s, many old wagon roads were paved and new roads constructed. There was still more demand.

World War Two dampened road-building efforts, but the affluence that came after the war brought with it a huge increase in automobile ownership. There were 237,000 passenger vehicles registered in 1952, when BC's population was 1.3 million. (Today, with a population of 3.3 million people, there are 3 million passenger vehicles registered.) In the 1950s and '60s the government embarked on a major program of upgrading old roads and building new ones.

The first multi-laned highways were built, and ferries became an integral part of the BC highways system. By 1962 the Trans-Canada Highway had followed the CPR route through Rogers Pass. In 1964, the $25-million Port Mann Bridge, 2,104m long, was built over the Fraser River on the Trans-Canada.

Today, some of BC's 2,700 highway bridges are among the longest in the world. Snowsheds and long tunnels cover roads in the most forbidding terrain, and ferries remain a vital part of the highways system. Modern-day motorists have available to them some 42,500km of public highways, more than half of them paved (22,053km, to be exact).

Even with this vast network of roads, much of the province remains accessible only by water, air, or hiking trail. It seems that wherever you live in BC, the wilderness is close at hand. Not only the Rocky Mountains separate British Columbians from other Canadians: it is the accessibility of BC's outback, the ability to be constantly in touch with astounding natural features that draw people from around the globe.

## Crossing the Border

There are 22 points of entry for motorists travelling across the Canada-US boundary into BC. These are indicated on the regional maps. Details are also in the *Logs*. When crossing the border into Canada, US citizens should carry identification. People from other countries need passports. For info on Canada Customs regulations, contact: Public Relations Branch, 333 Dunsmuir St, Vancouver, BC, V6B 5R3. Call 666-0545; after 4:30pm and weekends or holidays, 666-0272; or 538-3610 for 24-hour information.

For travellers of the busy Douglas/Blaine crossing south of Vancouver, the Peace Arch Entry Project (PACE) provides time-saving lanes and Travellers Declaration Cards to approved applicants only. Applications must be picked up at the Douglas border crossing. For info: 535-9346.

### *By Boat*

If non-residents are entering BC by boat, there are many marine customs ports. Victoria and Vancouver are the largest, but Nanaimo, Courtenay/Comox, Campbell River, Sidney, Port Alberni, Powell River, Kitimat, Ucluelet, White Rock, Prince Rupert, Bedwell Harbour, and Stewart all have customs facilities. Waneta, on the Columbia River near Trail, can also process visitors arriving by boat.

### *Declaring Goods*

Laws concerning the amount of duty-free goods foreigners can take back to their home countries from Canada vary with each country. Americans returning home after more than 48 hours in Canada may take back $400 worth of goods without paying duty. If you've been in Canada less than 48 hours, the maximum duty-free amount is $25.

Sporting and outdoors gear, tape recorders, optical items, stereos, radios, musical instruments, typewriters, and other equipment for personal use should be declared when entering Canada.

### *Guns and Other Weapons*

Canada has strict laws concerning firearms and restricted weapons. In recent years BC provincial courts have imposed fines and ordered the confiscation of guns illegally carried into Canada from the US. Restricted weapons in Canada include revolvers, pistols, and fully automatic firearms. Rifles and shotguns normally used for hunting may not be brought into Canada, unless the owner intends to hunt.

Motorists who drive into Canada with guns are usually sent back to the US, where they can store their firearms with gun dealers in border towns. Those who arrive on Vancouver Island aboard ferries from the US must declare their guns, which are then sent back on the next US-bound ferry. Those failing to declare firearms are usually charged under Canadian law if a customs search turns up a weapon.

### Liquor

The legal drinking age in BC is 19. People crossing the BC-US border can carry up to 1.1 litres of spirits or wine, or 8.1 litres of beer or ale. Drinking alcohol in public places is prohibited in BC. Drinking is permitted in provincial campgrounds at your campsite, which is considered private. Impaired driving is a criminal offence.

### Pets

Dogs and cats older than three months coming from the US must be accompanied by a veterinary certificate stating the animal has been vaccinated for rabies during the previous three years. The certificate, which should describe the animal, must state the date of vaccination.

Travellers from the US may bring two pet birds into Canada, along with a written declaration that the birds have been in the owner's possession for the previous three months, and have not been in contact with other birds. Parrots require export permits before they can be taken out of the US. Any birds from countries other than the US will be destroyed at the border.

### Plants

The import of plants, including soil, is heavily regulated. All plants must be declared at the time of entry.

## METRIC SYSTEM

Sometimes travelling in Canada with its multitude of cultures is like visiting a foreign country – even for Canadians. Differences in language and habit don't make things any easier, but they do add an air of the exotic. Likewise with the metric system, introduced to make measuring easier. There are those of us here who have found it downright confounding. We offer you a fast way, and a slow way, to convert the measurements.

### Metric Quick Tricks:

- A centimetre (cm) is smaller than half an inch.
- A metre (m) is a bit bigger than a yard.
- A kilometre (km) is just over half a mile.
- A hectare (ha) is about two and a half acres.
- A kilogram (kg) is just over two pounds.
- To convert Celcius (C) to Fahrenheit, double it, and add 32 degrees.

### Exact Formulas for Converting Metric to Imperial*:

| | | | |
|---|---|---|---|
| **Length** | | | |
| **mm** (millimetres) | X | 0.04 | = inches |
| **cm** (centimetres) | X | 0.39 | = inches |
| **m** (metres) | X | 3.33 | = feet |
| **m** (metres) | X | 1.09 | = yards |
| **km** (kilometres) | X | 0.62 | = miles |
| **Area** | | | |
| **ha** (hectares) | X | 2.47 | = acres |
| **sq km** (square km) | X | 0.39 | = sq miles |
| **Weight** | | | |
| **g** (grams) | X | 0.035 | = ounces |
| **kg** (kilograms) | X | 2.2 | = pounds |
| **Volume (Imperial not US)** | | | |
| **mL** (millilitres) | X | 0.03 | = fluid ounces |
| **L** (litres) | X | 1.76 | = pints |
| **L** (litres) | X | 0.88 | = quarts |
| **L** (litres) | X | 0.22 | = gallons |

**Temperature**

**C** (Celcius) Multiply by 1.8, then add 32 to get Fahrenheit.

* **Remember:** An Imperial gallon is larger than a US gallon. A US gallon is 3.785 litres; a US quart is .946 litres. Rule of thumb: a US quart and a litre are almost the same; therefore, about four litres to the US gallon.

## Tourist Information

**British Columbia in General:** When planning a vacation in British Columbia, be sure to take advantage of the information services available. Call or write to the sources listed below for details on the province's scenic attractions, events, accommodations, parks, and recreation opportunities. The telephone area code is 604 throughout British Columbia.

**Discover British Columbia:** For free B.C. travel information and accommodations reservations from anywhere in North America, call toll-free **1-800-663-6000.** International callers and those in B.C.'s lower mainland, call **663-6000.**

**Tourism British Columbia:** Parliament Buildings, Victoria, BC, V8V 1X4. In the U.S., write: Box C-34971, Seattle, Washington, 98124-1971. In England, write: 1 Regent Street, London, England, SW1Y 4NS.

**Tourism Regions:** BC has nine official tourism regions, each administered by a tourism association that works with the provincial ministry to maintain standards. Tourism Association addresses and phone numbers are in the introduction to each region. The *Travel Guide* has based its regions upon these nine tourism regions.

**Specific Cities and Towns:** More than 150 communities throughout BC are members of the Travel Infocentre Network. They operate centres providing tourist information about their areas as well as the entire province. Most infocentres are conspicuous, often on main routes into towns, and some are staffed by certified travel counsellors. They can help reserve accommodation or tours. Infocentres are listed in the *Log* after details on the community. Many operate only in summer. For year-round information, mailing addresses and telephone numbers of infocentres and/or their parent Chambers of Commerce or local government offices are listed.

**Vancouver:** Infocentre, Plaza level, Waterfront Centre, 200 Burrard St, Vancouver, BC, V6C 3L6. 683-2000, from the US: 1-800-888-8835.

**Victoria (Vancouver Island):** Infocentre, 812 Wharf St, Victoria, BC, V8W 1T3. 382-2127.

**BC Provincial Parks in General:** BC Parks, 800 Johnson St, Victoria, BC, V8V 1X4. 387-5002.

**National Parks in General:** Canadian Parks Service, Information Services, Western Regional Office, Room 520, 220-4th Ave SE, Box 2989, Station M, Calgary, Alberta, T2P 3H8. 403-292-4401.

**Canada in General:** Tourism Canada, 235 Queen St, Ottawa, Ontario, K1A 0H5. 613-954-3940. Or 710-1175 Douglas St, Victoria, BC, V8W 2E1.

**Yukon Territories:** Tourism Yukon, Box 2703, Whitehorse, YT, Y1A 2C6. 403-667-5340.

**Alberta:** Alberta Tourism, Box 2500, Edmonton, AB, T5J 2Z2. Local calls: 403-427-4321, Fax: 403-427-0867. From across Canada and US: 1-800-661-8888.

## Accommodation and Camping

Throughout BC there's accommodation to suit every traveller. There are resort lodges with fireplaces and hot tubs or just the "basic skier's room." There are hotels, motels, hostels, family inns offering bed and breakfast (B&Bs). Even the campgrounds range from luxurious to rustic. Many facilities cater to specific activities, such as skiing, fishing, or horseback riding.

Visit or write specific infocentres or regional tourist associations for detailed listings and brochures, and for a free copy of the tourism ministry's *British Columbia Accommodations* guide, listing locations, phone numbers, and prices of hotels, motels, and campgrounds throughout the province. Whatever the season, whatever the region, it is wise to make reservations, especially with private campgrounds in popular areas.

### For the Hosteller

The Canadian Hostelling Association offers inexpensive year-round accommodation in many communities. Memberships are available at all hostels. Non-members are welcome, but overnight rates are higher. Contact Canadian Hostelling Association, BC Region, 1515 Discovery St, Vancouver, BC, V6R 4K5. 224-7177. **Vancouver Hostel:** 1515 Discovery St, Vancouver, BC, V6R 4K5. 224-2308. **Victoria Hostel:** 516 Yates St, Victoria, BC, V8W 1K8. 385-4511. **Whistler Hostel:** 5678 Alta Lake Rd, Box 128, Whistler, BC, V0N 1B0. 932-5492.

**Penticton Hostel:** 464 Ellis St, Penticton BC, V2A 2M2. 492-3992. **Kamloops's "Old Courthouse" Hostel:** 7 W Seymour St, Kamloops, BC, V2C 1E4. 828-7991.

**Vancouver YMCA:** 955 Burrard St, Vancouver, BC, V6Z 1Y2. 681-0221. **YWCA:** 580 Burrard St, V6C 2K9. 662-8188. **The University of British Columbia** also has summer housing May-Aug. During school year, a few one-bedroom suites are also available. Contact the UBC Conference Centre, 5961 Student Union Boulevard, Vancouver, BC, V6T 2C9. 822-1060.

On Vancouver Island, in Victoria, the **Universtiy of Victoria** has low-budget B&B accommodation early May-Aug. Write: University of Victoria, Housing and Conference Services, Box 1700, Victoria, BC, V8W 2Y2. 721-8395. The **YWCA**, in downtown Victoria, offers year-round accommodation for women. Write 880 Courtenay St, Victoria, BC, V8W 1C4, or call 386-7511.

In Nanaimo, **Malaspina College** has accommodation available May-Aug. Write Western Student Housing Ltd, 750 Fourth St, Nanaimo, BC, V9R 6C5, or call 754-6338.

For information on **Elderhostel** programs, see *Educational Holidays,* p. 22.

### Bed and Breakfast

Growing more popular is "B&B" accommodation in private homes, available in most centres, and some lovely rural spots, too. A delightful way to travel. Contact the British Columbia Bed and Breakfast Association, 276-8613. Local listings and infocentres can help with specific communities.

### Commercial Campgrounds

Many commercial tent, trailer and RV parks are located in or near communities, or outside populated areas. Some are in First Nations reserve communities, and most are in scenic settings such as on lake or ocean shores. Amenities vary from simple campsites with outhouses to full-service campgrounds with flush toilets and showers, electricity, laundries, sani-stations, stores, playgrounds, and games rooms. Check with infocentres or the tourism ministry's *British Columbia Accommodations* guide.

### Provincial, National Parks

There are 11,500 campsites in 184 BC provincial parks, usually in forests or on lakes, rivers, or ocean beaches. A small number have wilderness shelters or lodges; some have showers. But generally facilities are basic: flush or pit toilets, fireplaces, picnic tables, wood supply, water. In summer many offer nature walks and talks. Some offer wilderness walk-in camping only. Provincial marine parks are mainly accessible by boat.

Reservations are not taken for provincial campgrounds, and in summer it's wise to select your site early in the day. *Logs* indicate which campgrounds are frequently full, and give phone numbers for parks branch district offices so you can find out if campsites are still available. Overnight fee ranges from $6 to $15.50 and is generally collected between late spring and early fall. Some provincial campgrounds

**Continued page 14**

## HOLIDAYS IN BRITISH COLUMBIA

There are nine statutory holidays in BC. Many restaurants, shops, pubs, and other businesses, along with airlines, ferry, and transportation companies remain open on holidays. Banks, liquor stores, most offices, and many stores are closed. Boxing Day, Dec 26, is a recognized, but not a statutory holiday.

- New Year's Day: Jan 1.
- Good Friday: Late March, mid-April.
- Victoria Day: May 24 weekend (or close).
- Canada Day: July 1.
- BC Day: Early Aug.
- Labour Day: First Mon in Sept.
- Thanksgiving: Early Oct.
- Remembrance Day: Nov 11.
- Christmas: Dec 25.
- Boxing Day: Dec 26.

*Royal Canadian Mounted Police Musical Ride.*

# MAJOR BRITISH COLUMBIA EVENTS

*Abbotsford International Airshow, Lower Mainland.*

Local events are listed alphabetically by town or city in the introduction to each region. Do check them out. They give a flavour of an area, a glimpse of a different daily life... from horse racing at Kamloops' Sagebrush Downs, to Lumby's Chicken Flying Contest. There's a Yellowhead Loppett at McBride, Cabin Fever Days at Stewart, Mutton Bustin in Rock Creek, the Sandblast at Prince George, and an Eagle Count in Squamish. Everywhere, there are rodeos, regattas, sea queens, snowfests, logger-jogger days. Everything has a festival: strawberries, blueberries, blossoms, and borscht. Anything that can move is raced: bicycles, horses, skis, dogs, rafts, mini-sternwheelers, Canada geese (wooden ones), bathtubs, outhouses, and pigs (in Dawson Creek's Celebrity Challenge).

All these community events give you a chance to stop, have some fun, get to know the local people, and see what they do for work and pleasure. It's a wonderfully rich array of festivities.

Major annual events that attract people from all over BC and North America include:

- **Cariboo Cross-Country Ski Marathon:** Feb. 100 Mile House. Competitors from Canada and US.
- **The Brant Festival:** April. Celebrating the return of the small black goose. Thousands return, thousands celebrate. Many activities, including a Wild Goose Chase. Parksville-Qualicum.
- **The Cloverdale Rodeo:** May. The Big One. Rated No. 1 in North America.
- **Swiftsure Races:** Late May. Victoria. Some 350 sailboats participate.
- **Coombs Country Bluegrass Festivals:** Two of them, May and Aug.
- **Canadian International Dragon Boat Festival:** June. Racing on the waters of Vancouver's False Creek, with multicultural entertainment at Pacific Place Plaza of Nations on former Expo '86 site. Attracts 2,000 paddlers, over 100,000 spectators.
- **Victoria Folkfest:** End of June, Canada Day. At Royal BC Museum. Ethnic performances, food booths. Over 150,000 visitors!
- **Hedley Blast:** Mid-July. Largest country music festival in Pacific Northwest. Big names. Upwards of 20,000 camp on banks of the Similkameen River.
- **Annual Mission Indian Friendship Centre Powwow:** Early July. Mission. Native Indian dances draw participants from all over North America.
- **Williams Lake Stampede:** Early July. Cariboo Country's big stampede. Brahma bull riding, calf roping.
- **Vancouver Folk Music Festival:** Mid-July. At Jericho Beach. Music from Latin America, Asia, England, Eastern Europe. Ethnic food.
- **Vancouver Sea Festival:** Mid-July.
- **Nanaimo Bathtub Festival:** Mid-July. Tubs are raced from Nanaimo, Vancouver Island to Vancouver.
- **Sandcastle Competitions:** In Parksville, Vancouver Island, mid-July (attracts 40,000 people). Plus Christina Lake's, early Aug, the Lower Mainland's Harrison Hot Springs Sand Sculpture Classic, early Sept. Sculptures stay till Oct.
- **Earth Voice Festival:** Late July. A continuation of "Voices for the Wilderness" begun by Lower Mainland Mount Currie and Lytton First Nations communities to save the Stein Valley from logging. One of the largest open-air gatherings of its kind in North America. Now held on Seabird Island in the Fraser River.
- **Mile-High Symphony:** Early Aug. Vancouver Symphony Orchestra concert atop Whistler Mountain.
- **Abbotsford International Airshow:** Mid-Aug. Abbotsford Airport. Over 300,000 people.
- **Powwow Days:** Mid-Aug. Kamloops. Traditional native dances, food.
- **Kelowna Apple Triathlon:** Late summer.
- **Ironman Canada Triathlon:** Penticton. International qualifier. Late Aug.
- **Pacific National Exhibition (PNE):** Two weeks, late Aug-Labour Day. Vancouver. Street shows, rides, agricultural booths.

are open year-round, but access in winter may be blocked by snow. Mentally and physically handicapped people camp free of charge by showing a disabled access card. BC seniors may camp before June 15 and after Labour Day for a discount of 50 percent; otherwise the regular fee applies. A few campgrounds have group campsites, for which reservations are required.

There are four national parks in BC with camping facilities for RV and rustic campers. These are Pacific Rim, Kootenay, Yoho, and Glacier. Mt Revelstoke Park and South Moresby (Gwaii Haanas) Marine Park Reserve have only back-country camping facilities. Banff and Jasper parks in Alberta have RV and back-country campgrounds. Overnight fees range from $7.25 to $17.50, depending on time of year and type of campsite. Some are open year-round, some are free in winter. For more information, contact Heritage Communications, Canadian Parks Service, Information Services, Western Regional Office, Room 252, 220-4th Ave SE, Box 2989, Station M, Calgary, AB, T2P 3H8. 403-292-4401.

### Back to Basics

In BC it is legal to camp on Crown land as long as you are not in violation of any permit or lease and no special restrictions or fire closures are in effect. Off the beaten track, little-known campsites, some set aside by the BC Forest Service or forest companies, are scattered through the bush. In some outback areas of provincial parks, wilderness camping is allowed but open fires are prohibited.

Anyone is welcome to use these backwoods sites and simple respect for those who follow is expected. **Fire is a serious threat throughout BC** in summer, particularly in these outback sites; ensure that campfires are completely extinguished before going to bed or leaving a campsite for any period of time.

For information and maps of Forest Service recreation sites write the BC Forest Service, Recreation Section, 4595 Canada Way, Burnaby, BC, V5G 4L9. 660-7500. Or contact the Forest Service regional and district offices listed below.

*Travelling through the BC Rockies.*

**Vancouver Forest Region:** 4595 Canada Way, Burnaby, BC, V5G 4L9. 660-7500. District offices are in Campbell River, Port Alberni, Port McNeill, Duncan, Powell River, Rosedale, Hagensborg, Squamish, and Queen Charlotte City.

**Cariboo Forest Region:** 540 Borland St, Williams Lake, BC, V2G 1R8. 398-4345. District offices in Alexis Creek, Horsefly, 100 Mile House, Quesnel, Williams Lake.

**Kamloops Forest Region:** 515 Columbia St, Kamloops, BC, V2C 2T7. 828-4131. Offices in Clearwater, Kamloops, Merritt, Penticton, Lillooet, Salmon Arm, Vernon.

**Nelson Forest Region:** 518 Lake St, Nelson, BC, V1L 4C6. 354-6200. Offices in Castlegar, Grand Forks, Cranbrook, Golden, Invermere, Nelson, and Revelstoke.

**Prince George Forest Region:** 1011-4th Ave, Prince George, BC, V2L 3H9. 565-6100. Offices in Dawson Creek, McBride, Fort Nelson, Mackenzie, Fort St James, Prince George, Fort St John, and Vanderhoof.

**Prince Rupert Forest Region:** 3726 Alfred St, Bag 5000, Smithers, BC, V0J 2N0. 847-7500. District offices in Smithers, Dease Lake, Terrace, Hazelton, Burns Lake, Houston, and Prince Rupert.

## Transportation

Detailed information on how to get around and between BC's tourism regions — on coastal and inland ferries, airlines, buses, railways, by car or urban transit — can be found in the *Transportation* sections for each specific region. Many of these transportation systems are trans-regional. So, for example, information on mainland to Vancouver Island ferry routes appears under *Vancouver Island, Southwestern BC,* and *North by Northwest* regions. Information on BC Rail's service from Vancouver to Prince George appears under the regions through which the railway passes — *Southwestern BC, High Country, North by Northwest,* and *Alberta Rockies.*

Several bus (coach) lines link communities and regions of the province — so look in the *Transportation* section in the region you think you would like to start from, and go from there. Likewise with airlines. *Bon voyage.*

### Some Transportation Highlights

■ **BC Ferries:** One of the world's largest and most modern ferry fleets. This government-owned vehicle and passenger fleet has 40 ships, some carrying 2,000 people and nearly 500 cars at a time to 42 ports of call on the coast. The fleet links BC's mainland to Vancouver Island, the Gulf Islands, the Sechelt Peninsula, and the Queen Charlotte Islands.

■ **VIA Rail:** Canada's national rail service, linking Vancouver to Alberta to the rest of Canada. Includes the E&N (Esquimalt and Nanaimo Railway) linking Victoria, on southern Vancouver Island, to mid-island communities, and terminating in Courtenay.

■ **BC Rail:** A very scenic excursion from North Vancouver to Prince George (*North by Northwest*). From here it's possible to link up with VIA Rail's train west to Prince Rupert, or east to Jasper.

■ **Rocky Mountain Railtours:** Another very scenic excursion from Vancouver to Jasper, Banff, or Calgary in Alberta. Two days, with an overnight stay in Kamloops.

## Motoring

In many ways, driving is one of the easiest ways to travel in BC, especially if exploring beyond the Lower Mainland or Victoria on Vancouver Island.

While most BC residents are familiar with provincial and Canadian vehicle laws, visitors must make themselves aware of, and follow these regulations. Canadians drive on the right side of the road, as in the US, but use the metric system for distances and speed (see *Metric System, p.11*). The speed limit on highways is usually 80-100 kilometres per hour (km-h), and in cities and towns, 50km-h or less.

Drivers using industrial roads must remember that logging trucks and other working vehicles have the right-of-way. Restrictions may apply on industrial roads: some stipulate hours of use. Companies which maintain industrial roads usually post signs explaining regulations.

### Licences and Insurance

Foreign driver's licences are legal in Canada, but motorists coming from the US should check with their insurance companies about liability insurance for non-residents in Canada. If a car from outside BC is involved in an accident, call the nearest office of the Insurance Corporation of BC (ICBC).

### Fuels and Laws

All common fuels, including diesel, leaded and unleaded gasoline, are available and sold in litres. Propane is also available. Motorcyclists must wear helmets, and seat belts must be worn in vehicles. Impaired driving is a criminal offence in Canada, punishable by heavy fines, jail terms, and automatic driving suspensions. Refusing to take a breathalyser test is also an offence. The impairment level is .08 percent (80mg of alcohol in 100mL of blood).

### Maps and Road Conditions

Up-to-date road maps of BC are available from infocentres. For information on road conditions, call:

■ **Ministry of Transportion and Highways InfoLine:** From Vancouver: 525-HWYS (4997); Abbotsford: 855-4997; Whistler: 938-4997; Kelowna: 860-4997; Kamloops: 371-4997; Victoria: 380-4997; from all other areas of BC: toll-free 1-800-663-4997. BC Cellular subscribers: toll-free *4997 SEND. After dial-

**Continued page 16**

# British Columbia's Vital Statistics

### Total BC Population: **3,282,061**

BC comprises 12 percent of Canada's total population. BC is Canada's third most populated province. There are an average of 3.5 people per sq km in BC.

### Where the People Are

**Greater Vancouver 1,542,744**

Includes the cities of Vancouver, New Westminster, North Vancouver, Richmond, Surrey, Port Coquitlam, White Rock, Langley, and Port Moody; and the districts of Burnaby, Coquitlam, Delta, North Vancouver (both a city and a district), Langley, and West Vancouver.

**Greater Victoria 299,550**

Includes the cities of Victoria and Colwood, the district municipalities of Oak Bay, Esquimalt, Saanich, Central Saanich, North Saanich, Metchosin, and the townships of Sidney and View Royal.

### Other Large Centres

| | |
|---|---|
| **Kelowna** | **75,950** |
| **Prince George** | **69,653** |
| **Kamloops** | **67,057** |
| **Nanaimo** | **60,129** |

### BC's Measurements

BC comprises 10 percent of Canada's land surface, and is the third largest province in Canada.

**Total land area:** 929,730 sq km
**Freshwater area:** 18,070 sq km
**Coastline length:** 27,200 km

### Total Area of BC: **947,800 sq km**

### BC's Neighbours

Washington State, Idaho and Montana in the US border BC on the south for 640km; Alberta on the east for 1,545km; the Northwest Territories and the Yukon on the north for 1,062km; and Alaska on the northwest for 893km.

### Time Zones

Like other Canadian provinces, BC switches to daylight-saving time from the first Sunday in April to the last Sunday in October. There are also two time zones in BC. Most of the province is on Pacific Time, but as you move east toward the Rockies, time moves an hour ahead to Mountain Time. Alberta is also on Mountain Time. Specific points for time zone changes on major highways are indicated in the appropriate *Logs*.

There is also a maverick area in BC — stretching from Creston to Yahk — which refuses to change to daylight-saving time. You'll certainly learn about it if you go to Yahk (and back). There, it's Mountain Standard Time all the time.

### Emblem and Flag

In 1871, BC joined the Canadian Confederation. In 1906, King Edward VII approved the province's shield, which was designed by Reverend Arthur Beanlands. It shows the Union Jack on the shield's upper third, symbolizing the province's origin as a British colony. The bottom features a gold half-sun, symbolizing BC as Canada's most westerly province, imposed upon three wavy blue bars representing the Pacific. The shield is supported by a ram and a stag.

BC's motto, engraved on the shield, is *Splendor sine occasu* (Splendor Without Diminishment).

The provincial flag, duplicating the shield in the shape of a rectangle, was adopted by the government in 1960.

### Official Bird, Official Tree

LOUISE LAWRENCE

In 1988, the province named the obstreperous Steller's jay as BC's official bird, and the red cedar as the official tree. The jay, an intelligent rogue known for its bold food raids on campgrounds, won a popularity contest sponsored by the government. The red cedar, valued for its many uses, from totem poles and dugout canoes to saunas and sundecks, is a specimen of towering magnificence, growing more than 60m and able to live as long as a millenium, if it can avoid the chain saw.

### The Pacific Dogwood

This native tree, protected by law, became the provincial emblem in 1956. It is a resplendent tree, noted for its big white blossoms in spring, and red berries and brilliant foliage in fall.

### Official Stone and Tartan

BC jade, a nephrite jade usually dark green, is sold as jewelry throughout the province. The tartan, consisting of 128 different types of thread, was recorded in 1969 in the books of the Court of the Lord Lyon, King of Arms, Scotland.

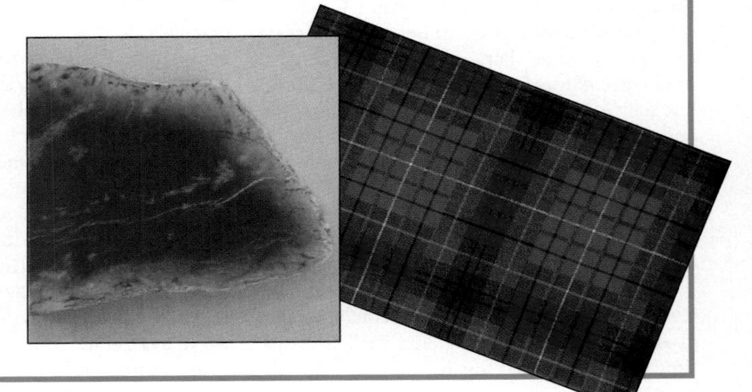

ing, be prepared to punch in 1, 2, or 3. A 24-hour recorded message gives info on **1)** coastal and major southern routes, including Okanagan and Kootenays; **2)** northern routes; **3)** Vancouver Island and Lower Mainland.

If you wish to speak with a representative of the ministry, phone 660-9770.

## Weather and What to Wear

Hot, cold, dry, wet: the weather in BC is as varied as the geography. Rule of thumb: the farther you are from the western side of a mountain range, the drier it will be. In general, the farther from the ocean, the greater the difference between high summer and low winter temperatures. The time you choose to travel, like the clothes you'll need to wear, depends on what you want to do. There is no wrong time to come – in each season there is something special to do. (See *Outdoors Activities.*)

### The Wet Coast?

At some places along BC's coast, rain falls in mythological proportions. The story is, people don't tan in BC, they rust.

The wettest weather station in North America is at Henderson Lake, near Ucluelet, on the outer coast of Vancouver Island, where weather systems from the Pacific dump a wonderful annual average of 6,550mm of rain onto thriving forests. Records from Henderson Lake show that on one December day in 1926 it rained more than 415mm. However, along significant parts of BC's coast rain does not fall in mythological proportions – though the myth does live on. In Vancouver, annual precipitation is substantially lower than much of Canada at 1,068.1mm. And the annual sunshine average is comparable at 1,931 hours. But still, lapel buttons proclaim: "I love Raincouver."

In Victoria, the umbrella is a mandatory item of executive fashion, just as gumboots are traditional for Gulf Islanders. But the truth of the matter is, here, on the leeward side of the Vancouver Island Mountains, one can only expect some 700-800mm of precipitation in a year. And Victoria gets more sunshine (2,100 hours a year) than anywhere else in Canada except the southern prairies. Victoria celebrates spring, in late February, with a week-long flower count.

BC's gentle year-round climate is one of the main reasons why people from Canada's cold and blustery east move here to what they call "Lotus Land." Parts of the southern coast might get damp (mainly in fall and winter), but they'll be neither hot and sticky, nor cold and snowbound. Winter weather, with an average high of 5 degrees C, rarely calls for more than a medium overcoat. Victoria is the only city in the country that has recorded an entire winter when the thermometer didn't drop below freezing.

Snow may fall on the towns and cities a few times a year, but it doesn't remain on the ground for long. Where it does stick is up in the mountains, making for some of North America's finest skiing conditions.

Along the province's northern coast, from the Queen Charlotte Islands and beyond, winter and summer temperatures are cooler than in the south, but the climate can still be characterized as mild. It is wet, though. Prince Rupert gets roughly twice as much rain as Victoria and Vancouver, and half the sunshine.

**To wear:** most people come for the outdoors and it's advisable to carry wet-weather gear year-round, particularly on the west coast. Hiking boots or high-topped rubber boots tend to get a lot of use at all elevations, and rubber beach shoes are handy for wading near rocky shores in summer. Bring your bathing suit. And, even in summer, a windbreaker. Also binoculars and day-pack.

### BC's 'Desert'

As you move farther from the coast and into the Interior valleys of southern BC, the seasons become more "defined." Hotter summers, colder winters. July and August temperatures average in the low 30s C, and occasionally rise above 40 degrees C. Mid-winter temperatures drop below 9 or 10 C. (That is still mild by most standards – Winnipeg averages 24 C.)

But, it's dry – scanty precipitation is the outstanding characteristic of the Okanagan-Similkameen and Thompson river valleys. The thriving orchards of the Okanagan Valley are heavily irrigated – other areas are left to sagebrush, cactus, and even rattlers. BC's only bit of desertlike landscape lies just north of the US border, near Osoyoos and Canada's only banana farm.

Don't forget your bathing suit – the golden beaches will beckon.

### The Unpredictable Mountains

Southeastern BC is dominated by the Monashees, Selkirks, Purcells, Rockies. A general rule: the higher you go, the cooler it gets.

In summer, the valleys (where you'll find most of the towns and cities) are comfortable, mid-30s C and lower. The lakes and rivers offer refreshing breezes, and if that isn't enough, a dip in their glacier-fed waters should be.

Weather can be quite localized and unpredictable in mountain country. Evening temperatures can drop up to 15 degrees below daytime levels, so even in summer warm clothing should be kept on hand. In summer, too, dramatic and wet lightning storms are not uncommon. Strong winds often come with them – don't be out in the middle of a lake.

Most places you'll be, mid-winter temperatures won't fall below 7 C. Precipitation falls mostly as snow. Mountain highways are constantly maintained: ploughed, sanded, and salted when necessary. A number of the highest highway passes, such as Kootenay Pass (el 1,774m) between Salmo and Creston, are occasionally deemed avalanche-hazard zones. In such cases they will be closed to traffic while avalanche control measures are taken. Closures may last a few minutes or a few days, and alternate routes, where possible, are suggested.

### The Great White? North

From central BC north, summers are short, winters long, and precipitation mostly light. The weather in any season gets cooler as you go north. Summers are mild – highs average 30 C around Prince George but drop to below 15 C by the time you get to the Peace River Valley. There are occasional sunbursts shooting temperatures 10-15 degrees higher. With or without heat waves, summer days may seem endless: there are 17 hours of daylight at summer solstice in Prince George; 19 hours in Atlin near the Yukon. Indian summers are some of the loveliest times of the year. Misty mornings give way to golden days and crisp evenings. In most northern areas, snow usually falls from September or October through April. In the high Rocky Mountain passes, a light snowfall in early August is not unusual. Winter nights are as long as summer days. And very cold temperatures drop to below 12 C in the province's centre; below 25 in the northern corners.

**To wear:** a bathing suit for heat waves and hot springs; clothing that puts a layer between you and the mosquitos that can be a nuisance anytime except mid-winter; and for winter you'll need heavy coats, scarves, warm gloves or mitts, and boots. Always bring an extra sweater.

### Weather Check

For a recorded daily report on Lower Mainland weather, call 664-9010. For areas outside the Lower Mainland, call 664-9032. Call 656-3978 for Victoria's weather recording, and for Nanaimo, 245-8877. Or call weather stations in Castlegar, Dease Lake, Hope, Kamloops, Kelowna, Penticton, Port Alberni, Port Hardy, Prince George, Revelstoke, Terrace, Victoria International Airport. See the phone book's blue pages under *Government of Canada, Weather Information.*

### Winter Weather Warnings

Warnings will be issued if the following conditions are expected:

■ **Heavy Snow:** 5cm on the coast, or 10cm in the Interior, or more, expected within 24 hours.

■ **Heavy Rain:** 50mm on the inner coast, 100mm on the west coast of Vancouver Island and the north coast, 25mm in the Interior, or more within 24 hours.

■ **Winds:** Over 65km-h or gusts over 90km-h expected.

■ **Freezing Rain or Drizzle:** "Icestorm" warnings will be given if condition is expected to last more than two hours.

## British Columbia's Parks

BC's national and provincial parks are admired by people from around the world. More than half of BC's "representative landscapes" are found in parks – caves and alpine meadows, mountain peaks, virgin rain forests, extinct volcanoes, paddling and portage routes, historic towns, Pacific islands, and the nation's highest waterfalls.

Together, five national and about 400 provincial parks and recreation areas comprise over five million hectares – nearly six percent of BC's total land area. These parks vary from little-known local beaches to vast tracts of mountains, forests, and waterways as large as 9,000 sq km. The national parks are: Pacific Rim, on Vancouver Island; Kootenay and Yoho, both in the Rockies; Glacier and Mt Revelstoke, both in High Country. There is also the South Moresby National Park Reserve, on the Queen Charlotte Islands. Here, the First Nations Haida people and the Canadian government are still trying to work out a mutually acceptable system of joint management.

Originally created to encourage tourism, BC's parks are major attractions for visitors and residents alike. More than 20 million people a year visit BC's provincial parks.

In a province whose economy is based on natural resource development, however, even parks are not immune to environmental controversy. BC's recreation areas are similar to parks except that other resource use such as mining may be permitted. In most cases the government allows this industry to honour old mineral or timber claims, many of which were granted before these parks were established. The recreation areas total 9,788 sq km – less than two percent of BC's total parkland. It is hoped that one day all BC parks will be free of industrialization. The newly announced Tatshenshini-Alsek Wilderness Park, in BC's northwest corner, is a hopefull sign. Here, nearly one million hectares have been spared from a mining scheme, and together with existing US and Canadian parks, is one of the largest international protected areas in the world.

The most popular parks are summer vacation spots for families. Nature activities, slide shows, interpretive hikes, outdoors demonstrations, even concerts and sports days are held in some parks during summer. Another exciting program is the "Community Astronomy Program." The HR MacMillan Planetarium and Gordon Southam Observatory's "star truck" visits the province's provincial and national parks during the summer, exposing stargazers to the moons of Jupiter, Ring Nebula, spiral arms of the Whirlpool Galaxy, and other wonders of clear night skies.

Handicapped BC residents camp free in provincial parks with a disabled access card. Apply at a BC Parks district office or at park headquarters. Several parks are set up for people in wheelchairs. Seniors camp at a discount of 50 percent before June 15 and after Labour Day. Full rate applies during peak season. See *Accommodation and Camping, p.12* for details on staying overnight in BC's parks.

Detail on specific parks is provided in the *Logs*. For more info: BC Parks, 800 Johnson St, Victoria, BC, V8V 1X4. 387-5002. National parks info: Western Parks Canada, 220-4th Ave SE, Calgary, AB, T2P 3H8. 403-292-4401.

*Peaks in the Bugaboos, East Kootenay.*

# BRITISH COLUMBIA'S MONSTERS

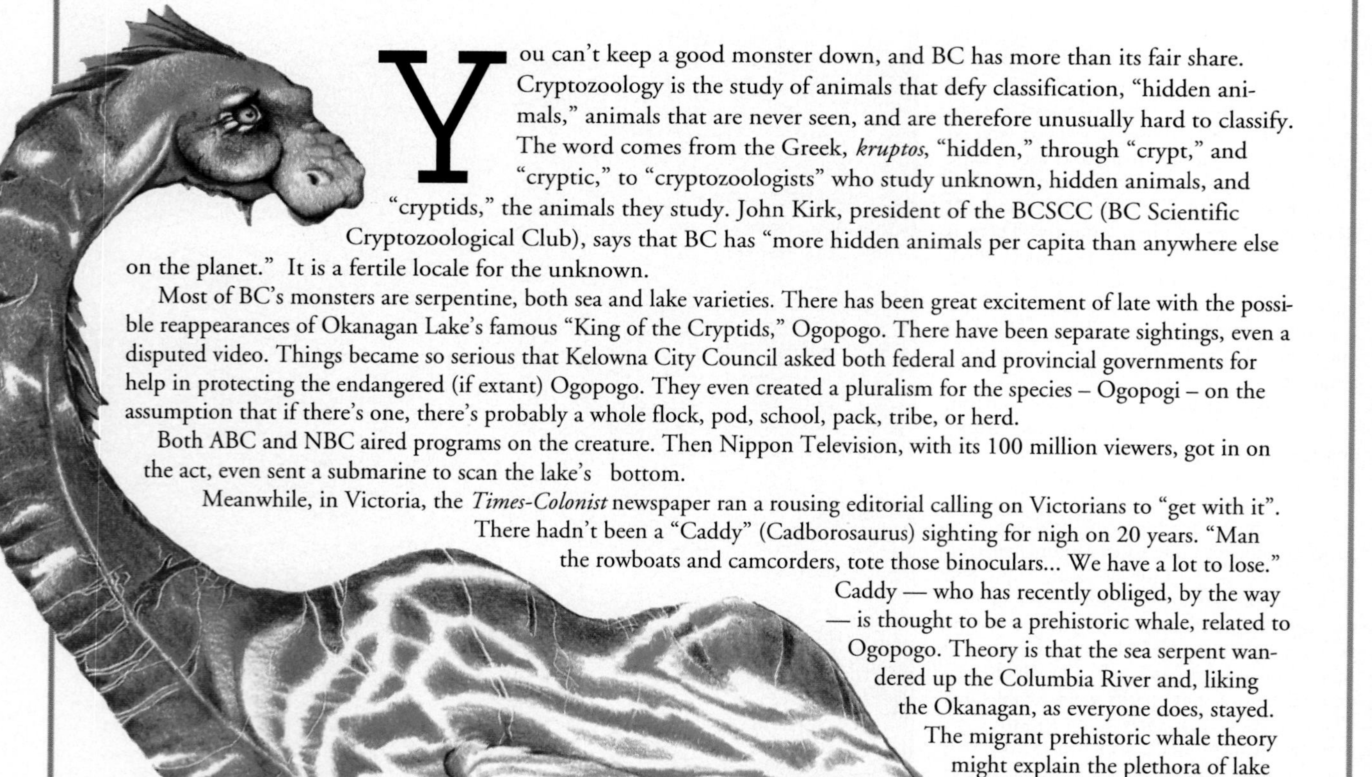

You can't keep a good monster down, and BC has more than its fair share. Cryptozoology is the study of animals that defy classification, "hidden animals," animals that are never seen, and are therefore unusually hard to classify. The word comes from the Greek, *kruptos*, "hidden," through "crypt," and "cryptic," to "cryptozoologists" who study unknown, hidden animals, and "cryptids," the animals they study. John Kirk, president of the BCSCC (BC Scientific Cryptozoological Club), says that BC has "more hidden animals per capita than anywhere else on the planet." It is a fertile locale for the unknown.

Most of BC's monsters are serpentine, both sea and lake varieties. There has been great excitement of late with the possible reappearances of Okanagan Lake's famous "King of the Cryptids," Ogopogo. There have been separate sightings, even a disputed video. Things became so serious that Kelowna City Council asked both federal and provincial governments for help in protecting the endangered (if extant) Ogopogo. They even created a pluralism for the species – Ogopogi – on the assumption that if there's one, there's probably a whole flock, pod, school, pack, tribe, or herd.

Both ABC and NBC aired programs on the creature. Then Nippon Television, with its 100 million viewers, got in on the act, even sent a submarine to scan the lake's bottom.

Meanwhile, in Victoria, the *Times-Colonist* newspaper ran a rousing editorial calling on Victorians to "get with it". There hadn't been a "Caddy" (Cadborosaurus) sighting for nigh on 20 years. "Man the rowboats and camcorders, tote those binoculars... We have a lot to lose." Caddy — who has recently obliged, by the way — is thought to be a prehistoric whale, related to Ogopogo. Theory is that the sea serpent wandered up the Columbia River and, liking the Okanagan, as everyone does, stayed. The migrant prehistoric whale theory might explain the plethora of lake serpents in BC, in 23 other Interior lakes including Kootenay, Harrison, Osoyoos, and Shuswap. But it's seriously doubted that any of these lakes could provide enough food for such a large mammal. Nor does the theory explain other monsters, such as the *slellucum* of Cultus Lake, a supernatural being in the form of a great bear which inhabited or inhabits the area – considered taboo – and is held responsible for the lake's fierce storms. Native legend also tells of a monstrous halibut, from which the Nimpkish people derived their name, which devoured canoes and caused a terrible riptide near Alert Bay on northern Vancouver Island.

Then there's the Sasquatch or "Bigfoot," around Harrison Hot Springs (Sasquatch Provincial Park). Also sightings in Manning Provincial Park.

If you see a Sasquatch, or any other monster for that matter, please report it immediately to local authorities. And if you think we jest, remember, when all is said and done, and the last snicker has been snuck, that nobody knows for sure. Any of these creatures might really exist.

*Portrait of Ogopogo by Mario Labonté.*

## Outdoor Activities

The following is a list of BC's best-loved outdoor activities. More information can often be found in the *Logs*. Check the *Index* for communities, parks, lakes, rivers, and other places listed below.

**Outdoor Recreation Council of BC:** Established to provide a central resource and info centre on outdoor recreation and education in BC. Close to 48 associations and groups are involved in the activities listed below, and a few others are Outdoor Recreation Council of BC members. The council has published 10 regional maps showing where to hike, horseback ride, launch boats, mountain climb, camp, view wildlife, and take advantage of BC's other recreational opportunities. Contact Suite 334, 1367 W Broadway St, Vancouver, BC, V6H 4A9. 737-3058. These maps are also available in many bookstores.

**Rentals:** For camping, climbing, boating, horseback riding, skiing – you name it – look in classified section of the telephone book, or ask at infocentres.

### Hiking and Walking

**Provincial and National Parks:** Some of the province's best hiking. Hundreds of options. Treks for the fit and experienced that take days or weeks to complete; yet often, in the same park, are easy walking trails taking just minutes or a few hours. Plan early – some popular trails have quota registration systems to reduce foot traffic. Maps are usually available in parks, also from Provincial Parks offices, national parks, infocentres, outdoors stores.

**BC's Most Famous:**

■ **West Coast (Historic Lifesaving) Trail:** 5-7 days, Vancouver Island. Trail open May-Sept. 52 hikers allowed in each day. Reservations must be made: 728-1282 for information. See *Parksville-Ucluelet*, p.70.

■ **Cape Scott Trail:** To tip of North Vancouver Island, beaches, lighthouse, history; one long day in.

■ **Alexander Mackenzie Grease Trail:** Cariboo-Chilcotin. Trace explorer's steps; 25 days.

■ **Naikoon Provincial Park East Beach Trail:** Queen Charlotte Islands, 5-7 days of beach walking.

■ **Local Trails:** Infocentres often have detailed maps for nearby trails.

■ **Beaches, Deer Trails:** On your own — watch for high tides and headlands, try not to get lost in the forest. Write Outdoor Recreation Council for safety info.

### Mountaineering and Rock Climbing

Though BC is one of the world's best climbing locations, there is as yet no central source of information on where, when and how to go, or on all the types of mountaineering and climbing possible.

**Federation of Mountain Clubs:** Suite 336-1367 W Broadway St, Vancouver, BC, V6H 4A9. Call 737-3053 for info on hiking, mountaineering and climbing courses. These can be holidays in themselves. Federation can also provide a list of mountain-oriented clubs. Visitors are welcome to join these groups for hiking, ski-mountaineering, climbing, and other excursions geared to mountain enthusiasts of all ages and abilities.

**Best Places:** Provincial and national parks in the Rockies, Selkirks, Purcells, Monashees, and Coast Range. The Rocky Mountains currently provide the most accessible high-peak climbing, but other ranges, such as the Coast Mountains offer fantastic fly-in wilderness climbing opportunities. The Mt Waddington area on the central coast is very popular for ski mountaineering.

**Famous Rocks to Climb:** The Stawamus Chief, and peaks in Tantalus Range near Squamish, a short distance from Vancouver; Zopkios Ridge (Coquihalla Highway); Bugaboo Provincial Park and Alpine Recreation Area in the Rockies.

**For More Information:** Write provincial parks listed here. Check bookstores for *A Guide to Climbing and Hiking in Southwestern BC* by Bruce Fairley, or *103 Hikes* by David & Mary Mackaree, and write the Federation of Mountain Clubs for lists of local organizations.

### Bungy Jumping

Plunging off a 50m bridge or a cliff with just an elastic bungy cord tied to your ankles. Bungy jumping is the latest BC craze to emerge from Down Under, but it traces back to simple transportation – swinging off vines in the South Pacific. The Bungy Zone in Nanaimo on Vancouver Island, the first legal bungy jumping organization in North America is famous for hosting "Naked Day," one chilly day in 1992 and again in 1993. Their claim: "No special clothing or skills required." Contact Bungy Zone, Box 399, Stn B, Nanaimo, BC, V9R 5L3. 753-5867.

Also,in the Okanagan-Similkameen, Penticton's Bungy World, operating from the highest bridge in Western Canada. Contact Bungy World, S-40, C-2, RR 2, Penticton, BC, V2A 6J7. 493-2626.

### Hang-Gliding

Closest thing to a bird's-eye view of BC.

**Best time:** Spring to early summer.

**Best Places:** Lower Mainland, Vancouver Island, Ashcroft, Cache Creek, Kamloops and Clinton in and around the Cariboo, Vernon and Falkland in the Okanagan, Sicamous in High Country, and Golden, in the Rockies. Many qualified instructors in these areas offer instruction and professional-assisted tandem rides. Various competitions. Contact the Hang Gliding Association of BC, 3595 Old Clayburn Rd, Abbotsford, BC, V2S 6S7. 854-5950(Canada), 734-3377(BC) or 980-9566.

### Hot-Air Ballooning

Passengers have exchanged wedding vows, held company picnics, filmed music videos, even shot a TV scene in a hot-air balloon – others just enjoy the view hundreds of metres up. Conditions best between spring and early fall. Three outfits in Southwestern BC: Fantasy Balloon Charters in Langley, 736-1974 or 530-1974; Pegasus Ballooning in Surrey, 531-3400. As well, Stardust Ballooning in Kelowna hosts the Balloon Rendezvous every Thanksgiving weekend. 868-8382 for more info.

*World free-style competition on Blackcomb Mountain, above Whistler Village.*

### Windsurfing

**Best Places:** Squamish and the Sunshine Coast, north of Vancouver, Jericho Beach in Vancouver and White Rock, all in Southwestern BC; Okanagan and Kalamalka lakes in the Okanagan, Shuswap Lake in High Country, and Elk and Nitinat lakes on Vancouver Island. Rentals available. For instruction, try Windsure Windsurfing School in Vancouver, 224-0615. Experts flock to the prime locale of Squamish – which means, aptly "Mother of the Wind."

## Horseback Riding

**Best Places:** Cariboo-Chilcotin, Cascade Mountains – Manning and Cathedral provincial parks are just a few hours from Vancouver, northern wilderness parks, Rocky Mountains, Okanagan-Similkameen. Ask at infocentres for list of stables, outfitters, riding camps. There are also more than a dozen guest ranches in BC; some offer a rustic ranch setting, others are full-facility resorts. Contact: BC Guest Ranchers' Association, Box 4501, Williams Lake, BC, V26 2V8. 392-2226.

## Cycling

**Bicycling Association of BC:** Suite 332-1367 W Broadway St, Vancouver, BC, V6H 4A9, call 737-3034 for info on routes, safety, equipment, restrictions. Send $3 or three international reply coupons for specific enquiries or requests for individual routing.

**Popular and Not-So-Hilly Routes:** Check *Logs* for Gulf Islands, Saanich Peninsula (Vancouver Island), Fraser Valley, Sunshine Coast, Okanagan Valley.

**Popular Mountain Routes:** Check *Logs* for Kootenay and Rocky Mountain regions.

**Tours:** Companies in Vancouver and New Westminster, Victoria on Vancouver Island, Nelson in the Kootenays, and Banff, Alberta. Write the Bicycling Association, and check with infocentres.

## Grey-Whale Watching

**Best Places From Land:** Pacific Rim National Park on Vancouver Island. Some 20,000 grey whales travel north along BC's west coast Feb-April in annual migration from Baja, California, to the Bering Sea. They pass by again, heading south, Sept-Oct. On clear, calm days you may see tails and flippers. On stormy days, you may see spume. Use binoculars. Park naturalists on hand. Some grey whales remain resident year-round. Visit Wickaninnish Centre for excellent displays. Whales can also be seen from North Beach on Graham Island in the Queen Charlotte Islands.

**From Sea:** Charters and tours depart from Vancouver and North Vancouver; and from Tofino and Ucluelet on Vancouver Island. Ask at infocentres.

## Killer-Whale Watching

**Best Places From Land:** Serendipity helps. Best time is early summer to early fall from shores in Haro and Johnstone straits, near Vancouver Island. About 30 pods, with a total population of some 400 whales, live year-round in waters between BC and Washington State.

**From Sea:** Pods of killer whales, also Dall's porpoises, occasionally spotted from BC Ferries in Active Pass through the Gulf Islands and more often through the Inside Passage. Charter operators offer very good chance of sighting. Ask at infocentres in Vancouver and North Vancouver in Southwestern BC, and on Vancouver Island at Victoria, Nanaimo, Port McNeill, Alert Bay, Port Hardy, Tofino, and Ucluelet. There is no infocentre in Telegraph Cove, but ask anyone there – it's one of the best spots.

*Whitewater rafting on the Thompson River.*

## Boating

BC has more than 27,000km of ocean coastline and 20,000 sq km of inland waters. There are more than 6,500 islands and islets. Season is basically year-round. Thousands of charter companies and rental outlets can recommend the best places to go. Ask at infocentres, or check phone books for listings.

**Transporting Boats into Canada:** Contact Canada Customs, 1001 W Pender St, Vancouver, BC, V6E 2M8. 666-0545.

Best Sailing and Cruising Places: Inside Passage, Jervis Inlet, Desolation Sound, Princess Louisa Inlet, Gulf Islands, Howe Sound, Queen Charlotte Islands. For instruction info, phone Sailing Association of BC at 737-3113.

**Best Canoeing and Kayaking Places:** Bowron Lakes Canoe Route and Tweedsmuir Provincial Park in the Cariboo; Broken Group Islands , Nitinat Lakes, Nootka Sound, Upper Campbell and Buttle lakes on Vancouver Island; Wells Gray Provincial Park in High Country; Powell River Canoe Route in Soutwestern BC; Queen Charlotte Islands. For detailed info on all types of canoeing and river kayaking, contact Canoe Sport BC, 1367 W Broadway St, Vancouver, BC, V6H 4A9. 275-6651. For sea kayaking contact Sea Kayaking Association of BC, 7955 161st Street, Surrey, BC, V3S 6H9, or call 597-1122.

**River Rafting:** There are some 30 outfitters ready to take groups or individuals along the same watery pathways that opened BC up to the explorers. Some of the best rivers: Fraser, Thompson, Tatshenshini-Alsek, Chilcotin, Chilliwack, Kootenay, Skeena, and the Nahanni River in the Northwest Territories. Contact Registrar of River Rafting in Victoria c/o BC Parks, 800 Johnson St, Victoria, BC, V8W 1X4. 387-4427.

**Houseboating:** On Shuswap Lake (over 300 houseboats for charter and 1,000km of navigable waterways) in High Country, also Okanagan Lake, Kootenay Lake, Takla Lake (*North by Northwest*).

## Fishing and Fish Watching

**Best Saltwater Fishing:** In the chuck around Campbell River. The tyee (trophy-sized chinook salmon) is the prize, often weighing more than 22kg. Also coho and spring salmon, lingcod and halibut. Other excellent fishing grounds are the Alberni Inlet, Rivers Inlet, and waters off Tofino and Ucluelet. All in Vancouver Island region. Best in spring, summer, fall.

**Best Freshwater Fishing:** Steelhead (feisty sea-run rainbow trout) at 3-10kg. Also cutthroat, Dolly Varden, kokanee (land-locked sockeye) and a number of varieties of trout,

*Coho salmon catch at Campbell River on Vancouver Island.*

especially rainbow. Anywhere there's a lake or river.

**What Tackle Where:** Ask Department of Fisheries and Oceans, Recreational Fisheries Branch, marina and sporting goods store operators, or anyone you see carrying a fish. Check the bookstore, too.

**Regulations:** Licences are required for all individuals sport fishing in tidal waters. Freshwater angling licences required for all persons aged 16 or over. Licences are sold in many sporting goods stores, department stores, marinas and government agencies. For specific info about tidal-water fishing regulations and conditions, contact Department of Fisheries and Oceans, 555 W Hastings St, Vancouver, BC, V6B 5G3. Call 666-0383 or 666-2268 for a 24-hour taped message of tidal water openings and closures. For non-tidal water fishing, contact Ministry of Environment, Fish and Wildlife Information, 780 Blanshard St, Victoria, BC, V8V 1X4. 387-9737.

**Fishing Camps:** Throughout province. Ranging from rustic to luxurious. Check infocentres, and Tourism BC's *Accommodations* guide.

**Fish Hatcheries:** More than 50 locations in BC to see salmon, sea-run trout, and freshwater trout. These include hatcheries, spawning channels, major spawning rivers. Most hatcheries are open to visitors, with tours on request. Hatcheries are listed in *Logs.* Salmon and sea-run trout facilities operate under the Federal Ministry of Fisheries and Oceans, 555 W Hastings St, Vancouver, BC, V6B 5G3. Trout hatcheries come under BC Ministry of Environment, 780 Blanshard St, Victoria, BC, V8V 1X4. See fish at stages of life cycle from egg to fingerling to spawning adult.

**Spawning Rivers:** Some of the best places to see late summer or early fall salmon runs are: the now-famous Adams River in High Country; Hells Gate Fishways in the Cariboo; Fulton River Spawning Channels, North by Northwest; Goldstream and Stamp Falls provincial parks on Vancouver Island. For more information: Department of Fisheries and Oceans, Suite 400, 555 W Hastings St, Vancouver, BC, V6B 5G3. 1-800-663-9333 or 666-0383.

## Skiing

BC lies within Canada's Cordilleran region, one of the major mountain systems of the world. The entire province consists of ranges, subranges, and high-elevation plateaus. Downhill, cross-country, heli-skiing, and powdercat skiing are well established. There are 35 full-facility downhill ski areas in BC, plus a few "family" hills with limited facilities. Some 30 cross-country or Nordic skiing destinations as well, plus countless local areas – anywhere where there's fresh air, scenery, snow, and enough space between the trees.

**Most Famous Downhill Ski Areas:** Whistler/Blackcomb and Grouse in Southwestern BC; Red Mountain and Whitewater in the Kootenays; Big White and Silver Star in the Okanagan; Mt Washington, Vancouver Island.

**Most Famous Cross-country Ski Areas:** Mt Washington on Vancouver Island; Whistler Mountain and Manning Park, Southwestern BC; Lac le Jeune, 108 Mile and The Hills, in the Cariboo. For downhill and cross-country, see *Ski Index* and *Logs.* Or write Tourism British Columbia, Parliament Buildings, Victoria, BC, V8V 1X4.

## Scuba Diving

BC's waters are said by *National Geographic* to be "the finest in the world second to the Red Sea." Best months for visibility are July/Aug-March. Prime time is Oct-Jan.

**Famous Diving Spots:** In Southwestern BC – Sunshine Coast, North Vancouver, Powell River. Around Vancouver Island – Barkley Sound, Race Rocks near Victoria, Saanich Inlet, Discovery Passage.

## Gold Panning

**You Might Find Gold:** In many of BC's creeks and rivers. In the Cariboo area, try Emory Bar at Emory Creek Provincial Park near Yale, the Gold Panning Recreational Reserve near Lytton, Lillooet; in the North by Northwest there's Kleanza Creek Provincial Park, Telegraph Creek, and Spruce Creek near Atlin; the Princeton area of the Okanagan; and Goldstream River in Goldstream Provincial Park on Vancouver Island. BC's resident gold-panning expert is Rossland native Bill Barlee: author, miner, historian, entrepreneur, and provincial cabinet minister. His best-selling books on gold panning, now out of print, are as precious and elusive as a gold nugget. But you can still catch Barlee reminiscing about the good old days on his nationwide TV series, *Gold Trails and Ghost Towns.* Or visit Barlee's private museum in Penticton, The Museum of the Old West.

**Regulations:** Hand-panning for gold is permitted everywhere in BC except placer (staked) claims or leases and most parks and aboriginal reserves. For info: Gold Commissioner, Mineral Titles Branch, 1810 Blanshard St, Victoria, BC, V8V 1X4. 952-0542. Or drop in on gold commissioner for mining division where you wish to pan.

## Caving

About 1,000 of BC's thousands of caves have been charted and explored. Most are on Vancouver Island, and most are undeveloped. Helmets, lights, appropriate footwear, and extreme caution are required.

**Most Famous Caves:** Nakimu Caves, Horne Lake Caves Provincial Park, Little Hustan Lake Caves Regional Park, Upana Caves Recreation Site, and Cody Cave Provincial Park. In the Rockies, Arctomys Cave near Mt Robson is -536m, the deepest cave system north of Mexico. The Yorkshire Pot complex at Crowsnest is almost 10km long.

**Tours:** At Horne Lake Caves Provincial Park and out of Gold River, Port McNeill, on Vancouver Island, and at Ainsworth, in the Kootenays.

**Recreational Caving:** Contact BC Speleological Federation, Box 733, Gold River, BC, V0P 1G0. 283-CAVE for info on federation members throughout BC.

**Commercial Caving:** Cave Guiding Association of BC, Box 897, Gold River, BC, V0P 1G0. 283-7144.

**Information:** BC Speleological Federation, Box 733, Gold River, BC, V0P 1G0. 283-CAVE for further info on caving as well as addresses for federation's 10 member groups. Also call North Vancouver Island Regional District 956-3301.

## Golfing

BC is a golfer's paradise, and among the few places on the continent to be selected by the Professional Golf Association as a golf tour destination. There are over 200 golf courses ranging from par 3's to challenging 18-hole championship courses.

**Best Places:** Fairmont and Radium Hot Springs, BC Rockies, and the Okanagan Valley. Because of the mild climates, you can golf year-round in Southwestern BC and Vancouver Island. Contact infocentres. Write Tourism British Columbia, 1117 Wharf St, Victoria, BC, V8W 2Z2. Call 1-800-663-6000 or 685-0032 in Vancouver.

## Hot Spring Soaking

**Famous Resorts and Developed Springs:** Ainsworth and Nakusp in the Kootenays; Albert Canyon, Fairmont, and Radium in the Rockies; Harrison in Southwestern BC; Lakelse, North by Northwest; Liard River, Alaska Hwy.

**Undeveloped for the Adventurous:** Halcyon, Halfway River, St Leon, in the Kootenays; Hot Springs Cove on Vancouver Island; Lussier, in the Rockies; Pemberton area, in Southwestern BC.

# Educational Holidays

Here are opportunities to stop and absorb the cultural and natural wealth of an area. Several colleges, cultural centres, and other institutions offer courses or experiences in subjects ranging from sketching to native culture. They vary from a few hours to a few weeks. You might be able to sign up on the spot, but it's recommended to call or write in advance.

■ **Elderhostel Canada:** For people over 60, and their companions. To receive a brochure of programs offered in some 50 BC communities: Elderhostel Canada, 308 Wellington St, Kingston Ont, K7K 7A7. 613-530-2222. A detailed seasonal catalogue is also available free on request (it's also in many libraries). One-week sessions include such courses as Island Artists at Work, Okanagan Archaeology, Forest Familiarization, Ski the Silvery Slocan, and Holistic Living. Average cost of $330 per person includes six nights accommodation, meals, classes, extracurricular activities. BC locations include Kaslo in the Kootenays, Galiano Island, Bamfield, Strathcona Park, Alert Bay, on Vancouver Island, the Queen Charlotte Islands, Mt Robson in the Rockies, Vancouver, and other exotic places. There are more than a quarter of a million participants worldwide each year.

■ **Kootenay Lake Summer School of the Arts:** Mid-summer. Box 422, Nelson, BC, V1L 5R2. 352-2402 or 352-7067. Beginner-to-advanced programs include visual arts, music, theatre, dance, massage, writing, cartooning, political theatre.

■ **Annual West Kootenay Women's Festival:** Mid-Aug. Vallican. 352-9916. Workshops, arts and crafts bazaar, music, children's activities. This is for women only; but children of both sexes are most welcome.

■ **Kaslo on the Lake Summer Festival of the Arts:** July-Aug. Kaslo. Through the Langham Cultural Centre. Box 1000, Kaslo, BC, V0G 1M0. 353-2661. Some 50 classes in visual, performing, and healing arts for all ages.

■ **Naramata Centre for Continuing Education:** Box 68, Naramata, BC, V0H 1N0. 496-5751. Week-long and weekend courses year-round. Self development, spiritual development, children, youth, young adult programs, and creative arts.

■ **Okanagan Summer School of the Arts:** Three weeks in July. School running for over three decades. Box 22037, Penticton, BC, V2A 8L1. 493-0390. Over 80 courses and nearly as many instructors, including world-class performers and artists. Mostly one-week courses, 15-25 hours per week in music, visual arts, theatre, dance, children's programs, fibre arts, computers, science camps. Day starts with tai chi. For all ages, all abilities.

■ **Island Mountain Arts (Summer School):** Late July. Box 65, Wells, BC, V0K 2R0. 994-3466. Week-long courses in visual and musical performing, and literary arts for children and adults.

■ **Nechako Valley Summer School of the Arts:** Box 1438, Vanderhoof, BC, V0J 3A0. 567-3030. Day and week-long art courses, late July-Aug.

Blue Sky *by Emily Carr, 1936. Art Gallery of Greater Victoria.*

■ **Atlin Centre for the Arts:** Mid-June to late Aug. Apply up to a year in advance: 19 Elm Grove Ave, Toronto, Ont, M6K 2H9. 416-536-7971 in Toronto, or 651-9693 in Atlin. Three- and four-week multi-disciplinary workshops: Art Through Experiencing, Idea and the Creative Process. Also writers' and photographers' workshops. Beautiful northern summer setting draws students "ready for risk taking" from all over the world.

■ **University of BC Museum of Anthropology:** See *Vancouver, p.86.* Native cultural workshops and excursions.

■ **University of Victoria:** Division of University Extension, Box 3030, Victoria, BC, V8W 3N6. 721-8451. Nature courses, seniors programs, BC heritage.

■ **Emily Carr College of Arts and Design Summer Program:** July-mid-Aug. Apply in advance to Part-time Studies, Emily Carr College of Arts and Design, 1399 Johnston St, Vancouver, BC, V6H 3R9. 844-3810. Three-week intensive beginner-advanced courses in visual arts, workshop weekends.

■ **Outward Bound Western Canada:** 109-1367 W Broadway, Vancouver, BC, V6H 4A9, 737-3093. Programs tpromote personal growth through a shared wilderness adventure. Mountaineering courses of 9-21 days in Coast Mountains north of Whistler. Ages 15-adult.

■ **Metchosin Summer School of the Arts:** Mid-July-Aug. Contact 911A Linden Ave, Victoria, BC, V8G 4G8. 598-1695. Lester B. Pearson College Campus at Pedder Bay. Intensive one- and two-week sessions in fine arts and crafts. Writing, ceramics, sculptural basketry, drawing. Also lectures, films, concerts. Lovely natural setting.

■ **Malaspina College:** Fall courses. 900 Fifth St, Nanaimo, BC, V9R 5S5. 753-3245. For Parksville/Qualicum: Box 42, Parksville, BC, V0R 2S0. 248-2096. From etching on glass to soapmaking, or an introduction to birds of Vancouver Island.

■ **Strathcona Park Lodge and Outdoor Education Centre:** Box 2160, Campbell River, BC, V9W 5C9. 286-8206. Outdoor summer camps, family excursions. For everyone. Also the COLT (Canadian Outdoor Leadership Training) Centre, with 100-day intensive programs developing water- and land-based outdoor skills, environmental awareness, and teaching ability in experiential education. For adults 19 and over. Call 286-2008 or 286-3122.

■ **Hollyhock Farm:** May-Oct. Box 127, Mansons Landing, Cortes Island, BC, V0P 1K0. 935-6465. Rest and relaxation retreats, workshops in the practical, creative, and healing arts.

## First Nations

Long ago, and just yesterday, the story of BC's First Nations was told as a romance and a tragedy.

The romance usually began with "Long ago." It described "one of the richest cultures on earth," flourishing on the gentle Pacific coast since time began, or at least since Raven, the Transformer, created the First People. Or, at least since 10,000-13,000 years ago, when anthropologists say the first First People travelled here from Asia, crossing a narrow strip of land bridging the Bering Sea.

The tragedy — "after white people came" — is usually marked by the year 1774 and the British Captain Cook's first encounter with the "Nootka" people off Vancouver Island's west coast. In this tale, entire communities were obliterated by smallpox, tuberculosis, venereal disease, violence, alcoholism and social and economic disruption delivered by the newcomers. Some west-coast aboriginal people named these ghostlike visitors *Mamaul-ney*, "people who live in boats," people who have no home. Others called them "people with wooden feet." In less than a generation they unravelled much that hundreds and thousands of generations had created.

But this story is more than romance and tragedy. BC's aboriginal peoples have their own voices and their own versions, their own roles in this, their story. There are more than 90,000 peoples of aboriginal descent in BC. They are divided into 11 major linguistic groups, and further divided into a multitude of dialects. There are currently 197 native bands or communities occupying some 350 reserves. Most of these bands are represented by the province's 33 tribal councils or governments.

Many of Christopher Columbus's "Indians" are reviving their own names: the Kwichsutaineuk-ha-wha-meese are on Gilford Island, the Mamaleleqala Qwe'Qwa'Sot-Enox live near Campbell River; the people of Vancouver Island's west coast are the Nuu-Chah-Nulth, not the Nootka, and those of northeastern Vancouver Island comprise the Kwakwaka'wakw, no longer the slightly more easily pronounced Kwakiutl.

Strengthened by their separate identities and stories, the leaders of BC's aboriginal communities are gathering to discuss mutual concerns. Committees representing Canada's aboriginal peoples are unyielding in their demand for changes that will ensure the survival of indigenous societies, their languages, and layer upon layer of knowledge and memory that may die if not safeguarded. That means secured access to lands and resources so aboriginal peoples can be self-sufficient and fiscally autonomous. It means self-government.

So, it is no longer possible or desirable to tell a simple tale of BC's aboriginal peoples. There are many stories to hear, and many storytellers. There is much for us all to learn.

If you look closely, you'll find aboriginal stories everywhere. On our shores and mountains and forests, among the ravens, eagles, whales, salmon. In our first industries – fishing, logging and mining – launched by the labour of the province's first workforce, aboriginal peoples. In the towns and cities that grew around those industries and that were, often, sites of aboriginal communities. In our modern railways and highways. Aboriginal peoples set those routes a thousand years ago, and much more recently, helped comprise the work crews that laid tracks and asphalt over them.

There are the poignant stories told by ancient totems in Ninstints on the Queen Charlotte Islands, now a UNESCO world cultural heritage site, stories told by greying totems in northern communities like Kitwancool, meaning "people of a small village." Depleted over a century ago by disease and warfare, Kitwancool is now reclaiming its former name, Gitanyow, "awesome warrior people." There are the stories told by newly carved totems, such as those along the busy streets of Duncan, on Vancouver Island. The "City of Totems" acknowledges the surrounding Cowichan people's role in that community's development.

In museums and galleries and book stores, grandiose and humble, up and down the province, there are stories and stories, beyond romance, beyond tragedy. Vancouver's UBC Museum of Anthropology and Victoria's Royal BC Museum are excellent starting points. Then, the sea-snail shaped Kwagiulth Museum at Cape Mudge on Quadra Island, the U'Mista Cultural Centre at Alert Bay, the 'Ksan village near Hazelton, the Queen Charlotte Islands Museum, and Prince Rupert's Museum of the North are just a few very significant others.

Aboriginal peoples are very much at the heart of our latest industry, tourism. Telling their stories through art and ceremony, guiding visitors through their land and seascapes. Offering another way of seeing. On the Queen Charlotte Islands the Haida people are working on a joint management plan for the fragile ecosystem encompassed by the new South Moresby Gwaii Haanas Marine Park Reserve, part of their traditional territory. In the Interior, the Kamloops Indian Band has built a 25ha cultural centre, featuring 3,000 year-old pit-house sites and a reconstructed Shuswap village. Duncan's Native Heritage Centre offers native foods, artistry, and theatre. The Annual Mission Indian Friendship Centre Powwow has been attracting aboriginal dancers to Southwestern BC from all over North America for two decades.

One story leads to another. Begin with the *Travel Guide's Logs* and events listings. Infocentres and museums will lead you to more, and beyond that, there is serendipity.

Remember though, that villages, old artifacts and new, even stories and songs, belong to the people who created them. We are being invited to share some of them, but it is a privilege that must be respected.

*Wet'suwet'en salmon fisherman on the Bulkley River near Moricetown.*

## Wildlife

There is no place in Canada with as many wild animal species as BC. Three-quarters of Canada's wildlife species – 120 mammals and nearly 300 birds – actually breed here. A checklist of vertebrates known to be found in BC, either living here or passing through, totals 143 mammals, 448 birds, 19 reptiles, and 20 amphibians. If we include the 453 species of fish, the total would come to 1,083 different species. Many of these can be seen from over 60 Wildlife Viewing Areas being set up throughout the province by a new BC Environment "Wildlife Watch" program. (For additional information on this program, contact BC Environment, Wildlife Branch, 780 Blanshard St, Victoria, BC, V8V 1X5. 387-9767. Or contact regional offices.)

Photographers, naturalists, and the naturally curious are attracted by everything from beavers to wolverines. There's big game – mountain goats, moose, caribou, bighorn sheep, deer, elk, wolves, cougars, grizzlies, black bears. Equally intriguing is the multitude of small creatures – fishers, badgers, porcupines, skunks, otters, mink, weasels, squirrels, chipmunks, turtles, toads, and shrews.

Most conspicuous are the birds, from tiny chickadees and kinglets to eagles and ospreys. More than a million birds migrate on the Pacific flyway and hundreds of thousands stop to nest. The wetlands of the province are inhabited by countless waterfowl divers and dabblers, trumpeter and whistling swans, snow geese, Canada geese, pelicans.

Off the coast, more than two dozen marine mammal species – sea lions, dolphins, seals, killer whales, humpback whales, porpoises – are seen regularly by beachcombers, boaters, and seashore hikers. Nearly all of the world's Pacific grey whales – about 20,000 – swim past the length of BC's coast in the spring and fall.

*Black bear cub.*

These northern waters are also being recognized as one of the premier diving areas of the world. Visibility can be phenomenal, and the colours have a startling clarity. There is giantism in many of the species: mussels so huge that one will make a chowder, and the world's largest sea urchin, the giant red, with a diameter over 18cm. The diver faces few dangers from the sea creatures themselves. Only one common jellyfish is poisonous, the lion's mane of Sherlock Holmes' notoriety. Wolf eels can be dangerous, but only if pestered; they can be quite gentle if treated with TLC. There are many species of shark in BC waters, including the large (up to 6m) primitive sixgill, but no recorded shark attacks. Theory is that cold water makes them more docile.

All five Pacific salmon species migrate far into the province's Interior. The Fraser, with its many tributaries, has the largest salmon runs in the world. As many as 300 million young salmon may migrate out of the river some years and more than 10 million may return to spawn.

Travellers in BC invariably encounter wildlife and places to watch for animals are noted in *Logs*. It's a pleasant privilege to capture these animals on film and, while most are harmless, a few mishaps involving wild animals and humans occur each year. Common sense and caution should be exercised when trespassing into a wild animal's domain.

### Beware the Bear

Black bears are occasionally bothersome in campsites and grizzlies can be a problem in the back country. Don't cook inside a tent. Lock your food in the trunk of a car. In the back country, food should be strung high in a tree a good distance from camp. Many parks provide information on how to avoid unfortunate encounters with bears.

### Cautious Cougars

Cougars, more timid than bears, are rarely seen by campers. But some, particularly old or sick animals, view small children and dogs as easy prey. Both cougars and bears, found in most parts of BC, normally avoid confrontations with humans. Make these animals aware of your presence by singing, shouting, or shaking a tin of pebbles.

Having said this, it is only fair to add that, while your chances of seeing a cougar in the wilderness are slight, come winter, cougars sometimes start moving around, especially south into Victoria. Usually a cougar or three per winter finds itself loping about the residential streets of that proverbially civilized town, and one winter, one made its way into the parkade of the venerable Empress Hotel. (Whenever possible, such vagrants are tranquillized and sent home.)

*Elk, or wapiti, wading in a river.*

### *Rattlers are Rare*

The northern Pacific rattlesnake, BC's only venomous snake, occurs in the desertlike south Okanagan Valley, and in the Interior dry belt as far north as Cache Creek. Unless you step on a rattlesnake, you're not likely to get bitten, but if you see one, give it a wide berth and keep your pets away from it.

### *Bugs and Buzzers*

Mosquitoes and blackflies, particularly in northern BC, are numerous in spring and summer when they breed. Your best defences are fly swatters and insect repellents.

Bees, hornets, and wasps usually sting only in self-defence. The pain and itching of a sting can be relieved by applying an ice pack or a paste of baking soda and cold cream.

Ticks are a hazard to people and pets, especially in dry areas. They attach themselves to the skin and draw blood through sharp beaks. Applying gasoline, kerosene, alcohol, or a hot match to a tick will force it to relax its jaws. Then you can gently lift it out.

### *Paralytic Shellfish Poisoning*

Shellfish collectors should be wary of red tides. This deadly phenomenon is caused by microscopic algae ingested by filter-feeding shellfish, such as mussels, oysters, or clams. These algae bloom in the sunlight, often giving the sea a tomato-soup appearance. Although harmless to shellfish, they produce some of the most toxic natural poisons on earth, causing muscular paralysis and possible death by asphyxiation in warm-blooded animals. If you eat contaminated shellfish you may feel a tingling in your lips and tongue, followed by a numbness in your toes and fingertips. Induce vomiting and call a doctor. Federal fisheries authorities monitor the coast areas and post warnings in contaminated areas. It is dangerous and illegal to harvest shellfish from these areas.

## ENDANGERED SPECIES

There are over 40 species of plants, birds, and animals in BC on a list produced by the Committee on the Status of Endangered Wildlife in Canada. Three animal species in BC are officially listed as "endangered" under the provincial Wildlife Act — the Vancouver Island marmot, the burrowing owl, and the sea otter.

G. PATRICK GREEN

*Vancouver Island marmots.*

The chocolate-coloured Vancouver Island marmot, which resembles a woodchuck, inhabits logged and alpine areas of the south island. A recovery team using radio-tagging is currently working to increase the existing marmot population of about 300. A recovery team also has been appointed to improve the survival chances of the pigeon-sized burrowing owl in the Okanagan, where fewer than 50 exist.

Sea otters, numbering now about 800 in BC, were re-introduced from Alaska in the late 1960s and early '70s. A small number inhabit Bajo Reef, near Nootka Sound, while most occupy the waters of Checleset Bay, an ecological reserve off northwest Vancouver Island.

P. LOWRIE

*Sea otters.*

The Dawson woodland caribou was once found in the Queen Charlotte Islands. Its status today is final: extinct. There is some good news: the white pelican has been taken *off* the endangered list. There are about 100 pairs breeding in a colony at Stum Lake, 65km west of Williams Lake. Their habitat is protected within White Pelican Provincial Park, and they are doing well.

## Orchids and Others

One of the rarest flowers in Canada (not endangered, but rare) is the waxy white, delicately scented phantom orchid (*Cephalanthera austiniae*). It is localized, and kept secret, in a few small areas of the Lower Mainland and southern Vancouver Island, and has official protection at Katherine Tye's "Sky Meadows," a 3ha property overlooking Cultus Lake in the Fraser Valley. The land, donated to the province, is now an ecological reserve. One of the most interesting orchids, the phantom is unique in the genus: it is saprophytic (lives off dead material), not parasitic.

The phantom orchid has been pictured here because most people will simply never get an opportunity to see one. There are, however, more than 500 *conspicuous* species of native wildflowers, flowers that you can reasonably expect to view. Indeed, BC is Canada's first province of flowers. Apart from the wildflowers, there are innumerable rushes, sedges, and so forth, as well as another 500 species of smaller flowering plants.

It is BC's extraordinarily diverse climate, from the snowy slopes of the Rocky Mountains to the warm, wet regions of the coast, to the boglands, the alpine meadows, the prairies, river valleys and the dry country between – that makes for this variety of flora unequalled anywhere else in Canada.

But before directing you to go wild, searching for blooms in the countryside, your attention should be drawn to the UBC Botanical Garden – Canada's oldest botanical garden – in Vancouver. This is a research garden rather than a show garden (although in places it is very showy). Its BC native plant section warrants special mention.

Should you be in Revelstoke mid-August, you might join the "Pilgrimage to Eva Lake," a 12km Canadian Parks Service hike to Mt Revelstoke to see wildflowers in bloom. Another special spot is Rhododendron Flats in Manning Park: come mid-June to see a spectacular display of rare wild Pacific rhododendrons. And for beautiful pink fawn-lilies (*erythronium revolutum*), visit the Honeymoon Bay Wildflower Ecological Reserve near Lake Cowichan on Vancouver Island, at the end of April.

ENID LEMON

*Phantom orchid.*

# Environmental Hot Spots

*Carmanah Valley giants, west coast of Vancouver Island.*

The winter 1989 issue of *Beautiful British Columbia Magazine* carried its first unbeautiful picture in 30 years of publishing. It was a shocking full-page photograph of a clearcut forest near the start of the Carmanah Valley on the west coast of Vancouver Island. Carmanah holds groves of giant centuries-old sitka spruce trees, one, the Carmanah Giant, towering 95m above the creek bank, is believed the tallest tree in Canada.

The Carmanah Giant lies at the edge of one of BC's ancient rain forests threatened by logging. In 1990, the BC government preserved the area surrounding the Giant, the lower half of the 6,700ha Carmanah Valley watershed, as parkland. Yet environmentalists claim that this decision only divides the biodiversity of the valley, leaving the protected portion vulnerable to adjacent industry. If widespread clearcutting were to continue in the upper Carmanah Valley, for example, the ecosystem of the entire watershed would be damaged.

Carmanah was the target of a nationwide protest; and now international attention has been focussed upon Clayoquot Sound, the Walbran Valley and on many other environmental hot spots in BC. Largely because of this attention, the provincial government has been working to resolve the opposing pressures of resource use and environmental preservation.

In 1992, BC's provincial government initiated a "protected areas strategy" that will double parks and wilderness areas by the year 2000 from 6 percent to 12 percent of BC's total area. Under this plan, the entire Khutzeymateen Valley has been designated a wildlife sanctuary, the first area in Canada to be protected specifically for grizzly bears.

As well, Robson Bight in the Johnstone Strait, off the northeast coast of Vancouver Island, has been recommended a protected habitat for killer whales. To preserve the area, the government called a moratorium on logging in the lower Tsitika Valley, but it is uncertain whether the initiative will halt the boat traffic off Robson Bight, where the orca now come to rub on the pebbled beach.

Increasingly, BC is a province where environmental concerns are in harmony with tourist demands. A UVic geography instructor, Dr David Duffus, has found, for example, that coastal whale watching is one of BC's most promising attractions worth millions of dollars annually. Visitors from all over the world converge on BC to experience the splendour of its natural environment. Obviously there had better be some environment left.

Although BC has begun to address its environmental crises, many areas remain threatened.

**Major areas of concern:** On Vancouver Island – the upper Carmanah Valley; the Clayoquot Sound area (dubbed "Clearcut Sound") near Tofino, which includes Meares Island, Flores Island, Megin Watershed, Sulphur Pass, Shelter Inlet, and the Clayoquot River; the Kyuquot area; Tahsish River (Roosevelt elk habitat); and Robson Bight and Tsitika River south of Telegraph Cove; in Southwestern BC – the contentious water fowl-preservation areas near Boundary Bay; in the Cariboo – the Stein Valley west of Lytton; North by Northwest – the Chilko Lake/Taseko River/Big Creek area and the Blue Lead Creek Watershed; the Stikine River, and the Kitlope watershed between Fiordlord Recreation Area and Tweedsmuir Provincial Park; in the Rockies – the Elk Valley, also threatened by mining. In the Queen Charlotte Islands, Ninstints on Anthony Island was declared a UNESCO world cultural heritage site in 1981. And after a long struggle, South Moresby was finally declared a national park reserve in 1987, but there are still outstanding mining concerns and Haida Nation land claims to work out, and logging continues. See *Index* for more details on many of these locations.

BC, with so much beauty to protect, is home to many highly organized environmental groups:

■ **Friends of Clayoquot Sound:** Box 489, Tofino, BC, V0R 2Z0. At 331 Neil St. 725-4218. 15 years ago, this grassroots group came together to prevent logging of Meares Island.

■ **Clayoquot Resource Centre:** 1314 Broad St, Victoria, BC, V8W 2A9. 383-7130.

■ **Greenpeace:** 1726 Commercial Dr, Vancouver, BC, V5N 3A4. 253-7701. This international organization originated in Vancouver.

■ **Sierra Club of Western Canada:** 314-620 View St, Victoria, BC, V8W 1J6. 386-5255. This first chapter of the Sierra Club in Canada was opened in Victoria in 1969. "Not blind opposition to progress, but opposition to blind progress" is their call. They also have a new storefront operation in Market Square, Victoria, called "Ecology House." Maps, recycled computer paper, and ecologically-sound products are available for sale.

■ **Western Canada Wilderness Committee:** 20 Water St, Vancouver, BC, V6B 1A4. 683-8220. Operating out of Vancouver with a Victoria chapter. The committee states that it is "not against all mining and logging everywhere. However, there are special areas of outstanding ecological significance that ... must be protected and preserved."

■ **Friends of Ecological Reserves:** Box 8477, Victoria, BC, V8W 3S1. 595-4813. Working province-wide to protect reserves already established, and to propose new ones. Reserves are unique ecosystems established by orders-in-council for study purposes, or to preserve rare or endangered plants, animals, and land formations. Volunteer wardens work with the government to monitor the reserves. Over a hundred reserves to date.

■ **Valhalla Wilderness Society:** New Denver, in the Kootenays. Box 224, New Denver, BC, V0G 1S0. 358-2449.

■ **The Nature Trust of British Columbia:** 808-100 Park Royal South, West Vancouver, BC, V7T 1A2. 925-1128. The only non-government organization in BC that buys ecologically-important land to be preserved, "for all of us forever."

# IMPORTANT BRITISH COLUMBIA TRIVIA

## BC Has the Longest, Widest, Shortest, the Most, and the Only

BC covers 952,263 sq km. It is Canada's third largest province, occupying 9.5 percent of the country, or .64 percent of the world's land surface. It nearly quadruples Great Britain; is two-and-a-half times the area of Japan; is bigger than any state in the US excluding Alaska; can encompass Washington State, Oregon and California combined, or Texas and Oklahoma, or France, West Germany, the Netherlands, Belgium, and Austria put together; only about 30 nations are larger – Egypt is a little bit bigger, Tanzania is a wee bit smaller.

## How We Got Our Name

BC's name arose from confusion, and it took no less than a queen to put it all straight. The word *Columbia* goes back to 1792 when Bostonian Captain Robert Gray renamed the big river the Spaniards called Rio de San Roque after his ship, *Columbia*. The lower part of the province (much of it drained by the Columbia) became known as Columbia Country. The upper part became New Caledonia, as named by explorer Simon Fraser. Meanwhile, Captain George Vancouver was busy giving various names to parts of the province, such as New Georgia and New Hanover.

In 1858, after observing that New Caledonia was also the name of a French colony elsewhere, and that there was a Columbia in South America, Queen Victoria decided on British Columbia as the best name for the vast colony.

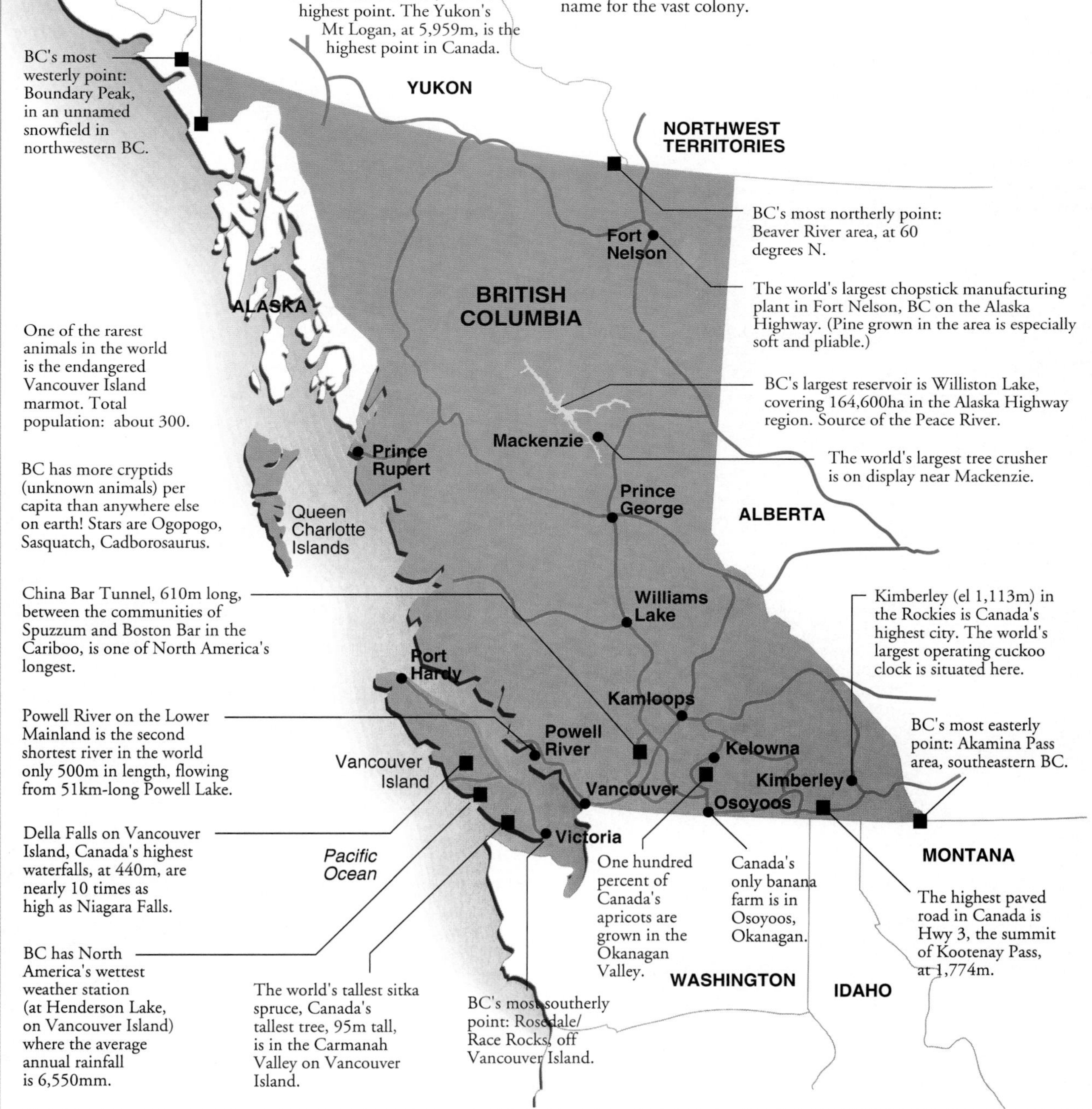

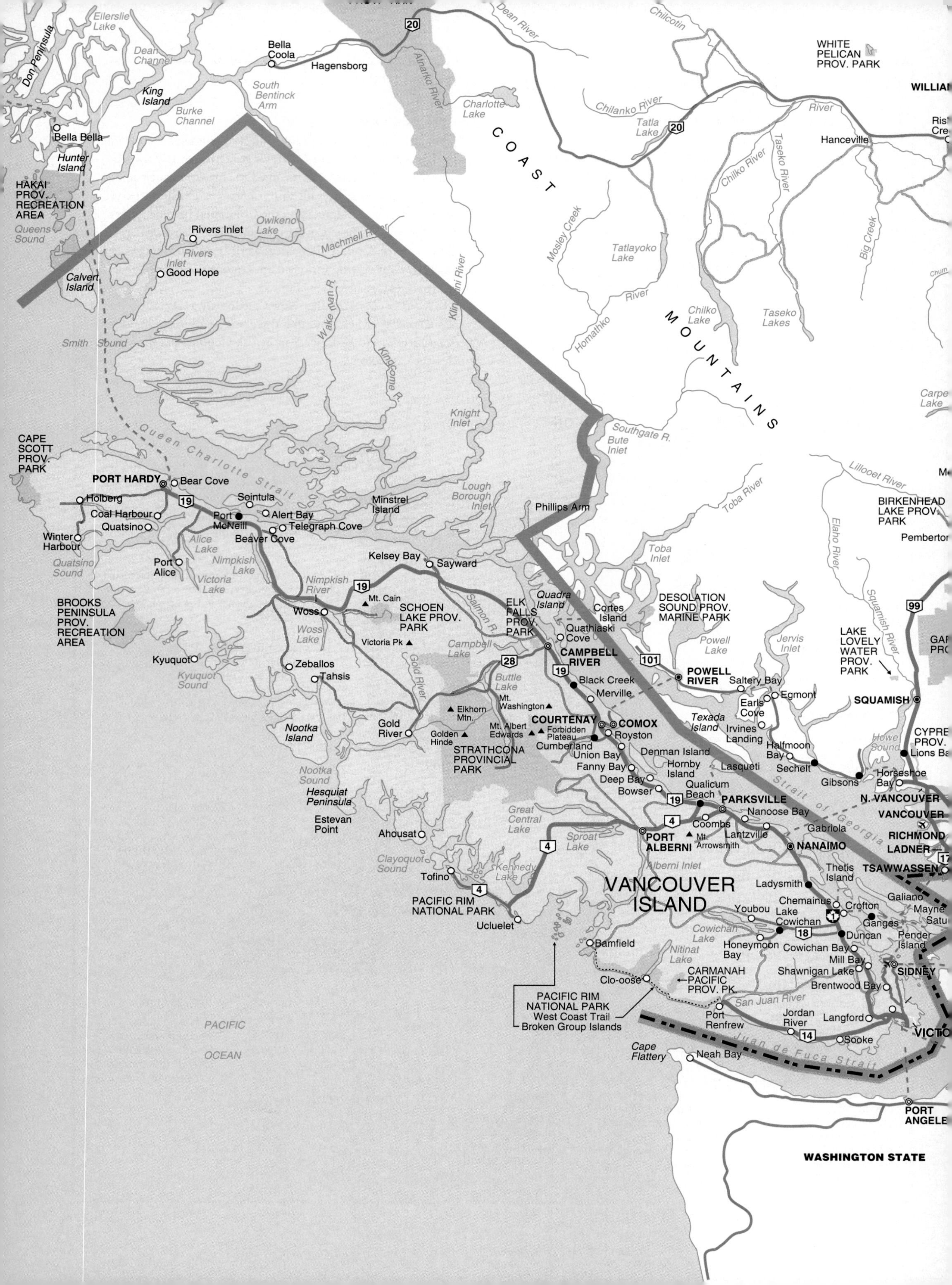

Bella Coola
Hagensborg
Bella Bella
Hunter Island
HAKAI PROV. RECREATION AREA
Calvert Island
Rivers Inlet
Good Hope
COAST MOUNTAINS
WHITE PELICAN PROV. PARK
Hanceville
Chilanko River
Tatla Lake
Charlotte Lake
Chilko Lake
Taseko Lakes
Tatlayoko Lake
Knight Inlet
Bute Inlet
Phillips Arm
CAPE SCOTT PROV. PARK
PORT HARDY
Bear Cove
Holberg
Coal Harbour
Quatsino
Winter Harbour
Sointula
Port McNeill
Alert Bay
Telegraph Cove
Beaver Cove
Minstrel Island
Port Alice
Kelsey Bay
Sayward
BROOKS PENINSULA PROV. RECREATION AREA
Woss
Mt. Cain
SCHOEN LAKE PROV. PARK
Victoria Pk
ELK FALLS PROV. PARK
Quadra Island
Cortes Island
Quathiaski Cove
CAMPBELL RIVER
DESOLATION SOUND PROV. MARINE PARK
Powell Lake
POWELL RIVER
Saltery Bay
Egmont
Earls Cove
Irvines Landing
Kyuquot
Zeballos
Tahsis
Black Creek
Merville
Mt. Washington
COURTENAY
COMOX
Royston
Cumberland
Union Bay
Fanny Bay
Deep Bay
Bowser
Denman Island
Hornby Island
Lasqueti
Texada Island
Halfmoon Bay
Sechelt
Gibsons
Horseshoe Bay
SQUAMISH
LAKE LOVELY WATER PROV. PARK
BIRKENHEAD LAKE PROV. PARK
Pemberton
Lions Bay
N. VANCOUVER
VANCOUVER
RICHMOND
LADNER
TSAWWASSEN
Nootka Island
Gold River
Elkhorn Mtn.
Golden Hinde
Mt. Albert Edwards
Forbidden Plateau
STRATHCONA PROVINCIAL PARK
Hesquiat Peninsula
Estevan Point
Ahousat
Tofino
Ucluelet
PACIFIC RIM NATIONAL PARK
Great Central Lake
Sproat Lake
Kennedy Lake
PORT ALBERNI
Mt. Arrowsmith
Qualicum Beach
PARKSVILLE
Coombs
Nanoose Bay
Lantzville
Gabriola
NANAIMO
Strait of Georgia
VANCOUVER ISLAND
Alberni Inlet
Ladysmith
Thetis Island
Chemainus
Crofton
Galiano
Mayne
Ganges
Youbou
Lake Cowichan
Duncan
Cowichan Lake
Honeymoon Bay
Cowichan Bay
Pender Island
Mill Bay
Shawnigan Lake
SIDNEY
Brentwood Bay
Bamfield
Nitinat Lake
Clo-oose
CARMANAH PACIFIC PROV. PK.
PACIFIC RIM NATIONAL PARK
West Coast Trail
Broken Group Islands
San Juan River
Port Renfrew
Jordan River
Langford
Sooke
Juan de Fuca Strait
Cape Flattery
Neah Bay
PORT ANGELES
WASHINGTON STATE
Queen Charlotte Strait
Smith Sound
Queens Sound
Quatsino Sound
Kyuquot Sound
Nootka Sound
Clayoquot Sound
PACIFIC OCEAN

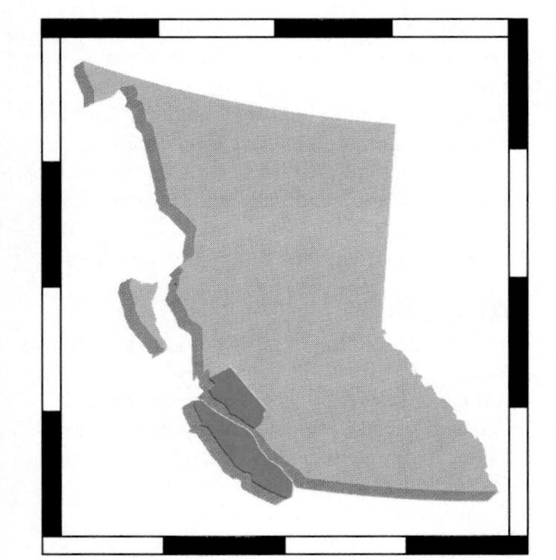

# Vancouver Island

## *Big, Beautiful, Incomparable*

*"To describe the beauties of this region, will, on some future occasion be a grateful task to the pen of a skillful panegyrist. The serenity of the climate, the innumerable pleasing landscapes, and the abundant fertility that nature puts forth, require only to be enriched by the industry of man with villages, mansions, cottages and other buildings, to render it the most lovely country that can be imagined."*

Captain George Vancouver (1757 – 1798)

Captain Vancouver's favourable description of the island that bears his name is not surprising. For natives and newcomers alike, the "serenity of the climate, the ... pleasing landscapes" that so impressed Vancouver two centuries ago, are still the island's most attractive attributes. What's interesting, however, is that this admiring portrayal was written by a man who for two decades had explored the shores of some of the world's most beautiful islands – Tahiti, New Guinea, the Canary Islands, Hawaii, New Zealand, the Solomon Islands, and West Indies. Yet it was the wild and intricate coast of Vancouver Island, the rain forests, rivers and mountains, that stirred his imagination.

The immensity of this island must soon have become apparent to the young captain as he explored the inside waters – between Vancouver Island and the mainland – in the spring and summer of 1792. At the end of summer he returned to Nootka Island, off Vancouver Island's west coast, where he'd landed 14 years earlier as a crewman with Captain James Cook. Neither Cook nor Vancouver at that time realized they'd come upon the largest North American island in the Pacific.

Vancouver's journey focused on the mainland shore, so he didn't travel every inch of the island's 3,440km coastline. But certainly he saw many of the harbours and headlands, the estuaries, islands, and inlets that today's sailors encounter as they circumnavigate Vancouver Island.

It would have been difficult for Vancouver to appreciate the incredible diversity of his newfound island without exploring the dense virgin forests. The mountains that form the backbone of Vancouver Island rival the Rockies when the vertical distance between peaks and foothills is considered. Mt Golden Hinde, at 2,200m the highest point, stands at the island's centre. High in these mountains, above forests of western red cedar and hemlock, Douglas fir and sitka spruce, profusions of wildflowers embellish alpine meadows. The glaciers and frigid lakes surrounding these meadows form the headwaters of countless watersheds streams and tributaries that flow through some 2,000 island lakes before reaching the sea. Not far from Mt Golden Hinde, in Strathcona Provincial Park, is Della Falls, 440m high, Canada's highest falls tumbling in three cascades from the cold, clear waters of a mountain lake.

Geographically, the differences between the east and west sides of the island are profound. While the western side of the mountains is penetrated by more than two dozen long, meandering inlets, the low-lying eastern side has only one – the famous Saanich Inlet. The west coast is the wild side of Vancouver Island, a rugged, often inhospitable place inhabited by the hale and the dauntless Westcoast settlements – Bamfield, Ucluelet, Tofino, Tahsis, Zeballos – are small compared to those on the other side. Almost all the island's major centres are spread along the east coast.

*Long Beach, Pacific Rim National Park, west coast of Vancouver Island.*

Thirty-three mammal species, from bats to beavers, inhabit the island. There are thousands of black bears, black-tailed deer, and Roosevelt elk, as well as cougars and timber wolves. At some higher elevations are small colonies of Vancouver Island marmots, an endangered subspecies – more rare than the giant panda – unique to the island.

More conspicuous are the birds, hundreds of thousands that migrate on the Pacific flyway in spring and fall. One hundred and fifty species stop here each spring to breed, thousands remain through winter. The seas surrounding Vancouver Island are home for 28 marine mammal species. Blubbery Steller's sea lions, sea otters, and playful dolphins patrol these waters with harbour and fur seals, porpoises, whales, and others.

# VANCOUVER ISLAND'S VITAL STATISTICS

## Where the People Are

**Greater Victoria** **299,550**

Includes the cities of Victoria and Colwood, the district municipalities of Oak Bay, Esquimalt, Saanich, Central Saanich, North Saanich, Metchosin, and the townships of Sidney and View Royal.

## Other Large Centres

| | |
|---|---|
| **Nanaimo** | **60,129** |
| **North Cowichan** | **21,373** |
| **Campbell River** | **21,175** |
| **Port Alberni** | **18,403** |
| **Courtenay** | **11,652** |
| **Comox** | **8,253** |
| **Port Hardy** | **5,082** |

## Vancouver Island's Total Population: 589,695

- Vancouver Island comprises 18 percent of BC's total population.
- There are an average of 34.3 people per sq km on Vancouver Island.

## Vancouver Island's Measurements

- **Total Area:** 32,261 sq km
- **Coastline length:** 3,440km
- **Distance north to south:** 451km

Sizable nations of aboriginal peoples had long established territories around the shores of Vancouver Island, and the "industry of [white] man with villages, mansions, cottages and other buildings" didn't come until many years after Captain Vancouver's return to England. The Colony of Vancouver Island was established in 1849, when the entire island, a total of 32,261 sq km, was leased to the Hudson's Bay Company for seven shillings a year. To try to colonize the island, the company was permitted to sell land and mineral rights to prospective settlers.

From its precarious beginning in 1843 with just 50 non-native souls at Fort Victoria (not to mention 1,000 or more aboriginal peoples camped around the fort to take advantage of trade opportunities, and thousands more in communities stretching northwards) Vancouver Island today has become the home of more than half a million relative newcomers.

The island stretches 451km from the BC capital of Victoria to Cape Scott, and has an average width of 80 to 100km. Overall, there are fewer than 16 people per sq km. Long Island, New York, nine times smaller than Vancouver Island, has a population density 135 times as high. But the entire northern half of Vancouver Island is inhabited by less than three percent of the island's total population – 97 percent live between Campbell River and Victoria, well over half live in and around Victoria.

Today's Vancouver Islanders are well aware that their home is like few other places in the world. More and more people are becoming environmentally conscious, striving to settle backwoods controversies. Community leaders are finding funds to dramatically alter the images of their towns, taking advantage of their picturesque seaside locations by putting their much-needed industries away from city centres. From Victoria to Port Hardy, new walkways, fishing piers, foot bridges, marinas, lawns, and flower gardens are replacing tank farms, mills, and other industrial eyesores that once cluttered downtown waterfronts. With care, Captain Vancouver's prediction may continue to hold true, that this island is indeed "the most lovely country that can be imagined."

# INFORMATION

**Tourism Association of Vancouver Island:** Write 302-45 Bastion Square, Victoria, BC, V8W 1J1. Call 382-3551; Fax: 382-3523 for info about Vancouver Island and the Gulf Islands. Addresses and phone numbers of local infocentres are in the *Log* with write-ups on each community.

# TRANSPORTATION

Getting to and around Vancouver Island is simple. The island is well served by ferries, airlines, buses, a railway, rental vehicles, and taxis. Paved highways lead to all major population centres, and much of the outback is accessible by logging roads, most of which are open to the public. Infocentres can provide info on major airlines and ferry operators as well as on small airlines and boat companies offering scheduled or charter services. They can also help with water taxis, bicycle and moped rentals, city bus routes and schedules.

## *Airlines*

Victoria International is the island's largest airport. Many Gulf Island and west-coast points are served by small airlines with scheduled and charter flights. Usually, travel agents can provide the most up-to-date information on Vancouver Island flights.

- **Air Canada:** 1-800-663-3721.
- **Canadian Airlines International:** 382-6111. Port Hardy, Campbell River, Nanaimo.
- **Air BC:** 1-800-663-3721. Serves Victoria Harbour and Victoria International Airport, Seattle-Tacoma International Airport, Nanaimo, Comox, Campbell River, Port Hardy. Several flights daily between Vancouver Island and mainland. Flights to Powell River, across Georgia Strait from Comox.
- **Horizon Air:** 1-800-547-9308. Connects Victoria International Airport with major international flights at Seattle-Tacoma International Airport.
- **Harbour Air:** 1-800-665-0212. Vancouver, Victoria, Gulf Islands, Duncan.
- **Kenmore Air:** 1-800-543-9595. Victoria Harbour-Seattle Harbour, north island fish camps.
- **Coval Air:** 287-8371. Vancouver, Campbell River, Discovery Islands.
- **Helijet Airways:** 382-6222. Based at Ogden Point near Victoria Harbour. Between downtown Victoria and downtown Vancouver or Vancouver International Airport. Also charters.
- **Orca Air:** 956-3339. Alert Bay, Port Hardy, Port McNeill.
- **Pacific Coastal Airlines:** Vancouver, Port Hardy, Qualicum, Texada Island.
- **Vancouver Island Air:** 683-5551 or 287-2433. Vancouver, Campbell River and northern coast.
- **Air Nootka:** 283-2255. Central and north coast.
- **Airspeed Aviation:** 655-4300. Victoria-Abbotsford.
- **Boxer Aviation:** 1-800-661-5599. Nanaimo-Vancouver.
- **Island Hopper:** 753-2020. Sunshine Coast-Nanaimo-Vancouver.
- **Awood Air Ltd:** 656-5521. Victoria-Vancouver airports.
- **Connectair:** 245-2256 or 383-8887. Vancouver-Nanaimo-Tofino-Victoria.
- **Wilderness Airline Ltd:** 1-800-665-9453. Campbell River, Vancouver, mainland coast, and Interior.

## *BC Ferries*

BC Ferries is a government-owned vehicle and passenger fleet with 40 ships serving 42 ports of call on the BC coast. It is one of the world's largest and most modern ferry fleets, carrying more than 20 million passengers a year, sailing 24 routes year-round. The fleet's first super-ferry, built 1993, seats 2,000 passengers and has room for 470 vehicles. The *Spirit of British Columbia,* on the Swartz Bay-Tsawwassen run, offers what the older ships have, but it's bigger, and has more: restaurant, cafeteria, snack bar, two video arcades, study and work cubicles with computer hookups, complete wheelchair accessibility, and a bridge "bristling" with high-tech gear. Its sister, *Spirit of Vancouver Island,* is right behind. Beam me up Scotty.

Call Victoria at 386-3431 or Vancouver at 669-1211 7am-10pm daily for general information on any route or schedule, or for reservations, taken only for mainland-Gulf Islands, the Inside Passage or Queen Charlotte Islands routes. For 24-hour recorded schedule information on Vancouver Island-mainland sailings, call 656-0757 in Victoria, 277-0277 in Vancouver, or 753-6626 in Nanaimo. Or write: BC Ferry Corporation, 1112 Fort St, Victoria, BC, V8V 4V2.

### Vancouver to Victoria

BC Ferries sail from Tsawwassen, on the mainland 30km south of Vancouver, to Swartz Bay, 32km north of Victoria, on Vancouver Island. Hourly sailings June-Sept 7am-10pm. (In summer there are approximately four extra sailings a day, including a 5:30am sailing from Swartz Bay). Other seasons, every two hours on the odd hour from 7am to 9pm, sometimes sailing during hourly peak times and holidays. The 44km trip is one hour and 35 minutes. Reservations not taken.

Bus services link Tsawwassen, Horseshoe Bay, and Swartz Bay ferry terminals to Vancouver and Victoria. There are pickup and dropoff locations en route, and tickets can be purchased on ferry. There are also regularly scheduled city buses to and from the ferry terminals, but the service between Victoria and Swartz Bay is particularly circuitous and time consuming. See *Bus Lines* below.

### Vancouver to Nanaimo

Vancouver Island's second major BC Ferry terminal is at Nanaimo (Departure Bay), where ships arrive from Tsawwassen as well as Horseshoe Bay in West Vancouver. From Horseshoe Bay, the trip is 50km, one hour and 35 minutes. The year-round schedule offers sailings every two hours on the odd hour from 7am to 9pm. From late June to early September extra sailings take the schedule round the clock Fridays through Mondays only, with 50 per cent savings on the 1am and 3am sailings. On Tuesdays, there are extra 1am, 3am, 5am, and 9pm summer sailings. On Wednesdays, an extra 7am and 9pm sailing; and Thursdays, extra 7am, 9pm, and 11pm summer sailings. Subject to change.

The Mid-Island Express from Tsawwassen offers eight round trips daily from 5:30am to 11pm. The trip is 60km, two hours.

Reservations are not available on either Vancouver-Nanaimo route.

### Gulf Islands and Points North

BC Ferries from both Tsawwassen and Swartz Bay also serve the southern Gulf Islands – Salt Spring, the Penders, Galiano, Mayne, and Saturna. Reservations are not taken for Gulf Island sailings from Swartz Bay, or for inter-island travel, but vehicle reservations are recommended for sailings from Tsawwassen to the islands, and back.

Between Victoria and Nanaimo, ferries cross Saanich Inlet from **Mill Bay** to **Brentwood Bay**, from **Crofton** to **Salt Spring Island**, and from **Chemainus** to **Kuper** and **Thetis islands**. Downtown Nanaimo is terminus for ferries to **Gabriola Island**. South of Courtenay, ferries run from **Buckley Bay** to **Denman Island** and from Denman to **Hornby Island**. Regular daily runs are made between **Comox** and **Powell River** and from Powell River to **Texada Island**. Ferries from **Campbell River**, 44km north of Comox, serve **Quadra Island**, and ferries run from **Quadra** to **Cortez Island**.

On northern Vancouver Island, BC Ferries run from **Port McNeill** to **Alert Bay**, on Cormorant Island, and **Sointula**, on Malcolm Island. **Bear Cove**, near **Port Hardy**, is the southern terminus for BC Ferries' "liner," *Queen of the North.* The ship, equipped for longer cruises, makes a 491km journey through the scenic Inside Passage to **Prince Rupert**, BC's most northerly coastal city. Late May through September it's a 15hour, one-

*On board a BC Ferries vessel.*

way day-cruise. The ship leaves Bear Cove one day, Prince Rupert the next. October to April there is one sailing weekly; from early May there are two sailings weekly. Reservations for passengers and vehicles should be made well in advance. Cabins are available. Travellers who need overnight accommodation at Port Hardy should book rooms when making ferry reservations. Travel counsellors on northern run. (See *North by Northwest* region, p. 207, for *Alaska Marine Highway* ferry linking Prince Rupert to Alaska).

Reservations are required on ferries from **Prince Rupert** to the **Queen Charlotte Islands** (148km, eight-hour trip) site of the new **South Moresby Gwaii Haanas National Marine Park Reserve**.

### Other Ferry Services

■ **Victoria to Seattle:** New passenger-vehicle service, daily May 1 - Sept 30. The refitted *Queen of Burnaby*, 190 vehicles, 900 passengers, leaves Victoria's Ogden Point 7:30am; leaves Seattle's Pier 48 at 1pm. Call Discover British Columbia at 1-800-663-6000 for up-to-date information. Final schedule and rates still pending.

■ **Black Ball Transport Inc:** 386-2202 in Victoria, 206-457-4491 in Port Angeles, Washington. The MV *Coho* runs each day year-round between **Port Angeles,** Washington, and **Victoria Harbour**. During summer the ship sails from Victoria four times a day from 6:30am. Return trips from Port Angeles begin at 8:20am. One hour and 35 minutes. No reservations taken. Fewer sailings during off-season.

■ **Victoria Rapid Transit Inc:** 361-9144 in BC; (206)452-8088 or 1-800-633-1589 in Washington. Victoria Express offers one-hour crossing to walk-on passengers travelling between **Victoria Harbour** and **Port Angeles**. Two sailings daily each way in spring and fall; four from late June to early Sept.

■ **Washington State Ferries:** In BC call 381-1551; in Washington 1-800-54-FERRY; outside Washington state, 206-464-6400. Ferries run from **Anacortes**, Washington, through San Juan Islands to **Sidney**, on the Saanich Peninsula 5km south of BC Ferry terminal at Swartz Bay. In summer, two sailings a day. First one from Anacortes leaves 8am, second leaves 2pm; first one from Sidney, 12:05, second leaves 6pm. In winter one daily sailing from each side. Takes about three hours. Vehicle reservations recommended in summer.

■ **Clipper Navigation Ltd:** 382-8100 in Victoria; 206-448-5000 in Seattle, or 1-800-888-2535. Fleet of three jet-propelled catamarans run year-round, daily service between **Victoria Harbour** and **Seattle's Pier 69**. Four daily sailings in summer, leaving Seattle at 7:45am, 8:45am, 9:30 am and 3:15pm; leaving Victoria 11:30am, 3:30pm, 5:45pm, and 7pm. Other seasons, one sailing, leaving Seattle at 7:15am, leaving Victoria 6pm. Two and a half to three hours. Wise to make reservations at least 24 hours in advance.

■ **Gray Line Cruises:** Toll-free 1-800-443-4552. 355 Harris Avenue, Suite 104, Bellingham, Washington, USA, 98225. New passenger-only service **Bellingham** to **Victoria**, once daily May-Oct, departing 9am to arrive in Victoria at noon; departing Victoria 4pm to arrive in Bellingham 7pm. Winter weekend schedule is likely.

■ **Nootka Sound Service Ltd:** 283-2325 or 283-2515. *Uchuck III* provides year-round freight and passenger service for coastal communities in Nootka Sound. Departs from **Gold River**. Sails to **Tahsis** and back on Tues. To **Kyuquot** Thurs and back to Gold River on Fri. On Wed in July and Aug only, sails to **Friendly Cove** and back.

■ **Alberni Marine Transportation Company:** Box 188, Port Alberni, BC, V9Y 7M7. 723-8313 or toll-free April-Sept, 1-800-663-7192. Based in Port Alberni, the MV *Lady Rose*, a 31m passenger and cargo ship, serves communities of Barkley Sound. Year-round, links **Port Alberni** to **Bamfield** via **Kildonan** and waypoints; sails Tues, Thurs, Sat only. June 1- Sept 25: also sails Mon, Wed, Fri to **Ucluelet** and **Broken Group Islands.** July 1-Labour Day, sails Fri to Bamfield and Kildonan, sails Sun to Bamfield and Broken Group. Canoe and Kayak rentals available.

### Bus Lines

■ **Pacific Coach Lines:** 1-800-661-1725. Between Victoria and Vancouver, leaving city bus terminals 75 minutes before each BC Ferry sailing.

*San Josef Bay, Cape Scott Provincial Park, northern Vancouver Island.*

■ **Island Coach Lines:** 385-4411. City-to-city service from Victoria to Port Hardy, several trips a day. Reservations not taken. Connects in Port Alberni with Orient Stage Lines, serving west-coast villages of Ucluelet and Tofino near Long Beach. Infocentres can help arrange bus and van charters.
■ **Maverick Coachlines:** 662-8051. Vancouver-Nanaimo.
■ **Gray Line of Seattle:** 206-626-6090. Seattle-Sidney.

## Railway

■ **Esquimalt and Nanaimo Railway:** 383-4324 in Victoria, 1-800-561-8630 outside Victoria. For a behind-the-scenes look at southern Vancouver Island, make a reservation on the E&N Railway, which has been running between Victoria and Courtenay since before the turn of the century. Now operated by VIA Rail Canada, a new Victoria station opened in 1985 downtown next to the Johnson St Bridge, with parking available nearby. A passenger dayliner leaves Victoria each day at 8:15am and makes up to 19 stops by the time it reaches Courtenay at 12:50pm. It returns to Victoria at 5:45pm. It's a fascinating trip that crosses deep canyons and passes waterfalls, salmon rivers, beaches, ghost towns, and historic sites.

Schedule subject to change.

*Fisgard Light, Victoria.*

## Car and RV Rentals

Highway travellers can rent cars from several agencies with offices at airports and downtown locations in island cities. Also RVs from some island companies.

## Vancouver Island Highway Project

Over 450km of "island highway" connect the unexpected and incongruous. Most of Vancouver Island's cities, towns, and villages are along this long east-coast road; most of the others are linked to it, either by logging roads or paved arteries that flow from the west, between island mountains.

The Vancouver Island Highway Project, announced in 1988, acknowledges recent dramatic increases in traffic, and the need for a safer transportation corridor through communities and mountain ranges and along ocean and lakeshores. The highway was recently described as "an overworked blood vessel burdened by a flow it can no longer handle." There are no fixed dates for completion of the five sub-projects:

■ Improvements to Pat Bay Hwy (Hwy 17–Swartz Bay to Victoria) – BC Ferries terminal expansion and McKenzie Ave interchange (complete);
■ Improvements to Trans-Canada Hwy (Hwy 1) Victoria-Goldstream Park;
■ Improvements to Parksville-Nanaimo route (Hwy 19);
■ Construction of Nanaimo Parkway, a four-lane expressway to hug western edge of Nanaimo; the current 21km section of Hwy 1 *through* Nanaimo has 19 stop lights, and is a major bottleneck creating hazards. As many as 50,000 vehicles a day travel this road. The new expressway will have five lights, coordinated so that "you should be able to blow through town without hitting a red light" as long as you stick to the 80km-h speed limit;
■ Construction of Inland Island Hwy to bypass coastal communities from Parksville to Campbell River. All access to the 100km four-lane route will be via interchanges (*i.e.* no lights). Many travellers, will of course, prefer to stick to the old, meandering route (sections of Island Hwy underway).

It is hoped planned changes will save time – an hour or more – and lives. For more information on the project, call 953-4949, and, please, drive carefully.

## City Travel

Taxis are plentiful. City bus services are available in Greater Victoria and Saanich Peninsula, Nanaimo,Campbell River, Comox-Courtenay-Cumberland, and Port Alberni. A new service links Cowichan Valley communities. Infocentres have bus information.

# VANCOUVER ISLAND EVENTS

### Alert Bay
- **Sports Weekend:** Mid-June.
- **Sea Festival:** Mid-Aug.

### Campbell River
- **Daiwa Fishing Derby:** Late May-Sept.
- **Mining Sports Competition:** Early July.
- **Rip Roaring Raft Race:** Mid-July.
- **Loggers' Sports:** Early Aug.
- **Summer Festival/Logger's Sports:** Early Aug.

### Chemainus
- **Fun Daze:** Early July.
- **Chemainus Ceilidh:** Mid-July. Scottish celebration.
- **Festival of Murals:** New murals painted mid-July to mid-Aug.

### Colwood
- **Luxton Rodeo:** Mid-May.
- **Gllangcolme Days:** June
- **Luxton Fall Fair:** Mid-Sept.

### Comox Valley
- **Courtenay Youth Music Camp:** Early July-early Aug. Indoor and outdoor concerts.
- **Filberg Festival:** Early Aug.
- **CFB Comox Air Show:** Early Aug.
- **Fall Fair:** Mid-Sept.

### Coombs
- **Coombs Country Opera:** Third Sat monthly. Fiddles, guitars, mandolins, accordions, cakes and cookies are swung into action.
- **Bikers' Swap Meet:** Early May. They come to exchange parts.
- **Coombs Country Bluegrass Festivals:** Late May, early Aug.
- **Coombs Rodeo:** Late June. Cowboys from all over BC.
- **Old Time Fiddlers Championships:** Early July.

### Cowichan Bay
- **Boat Festival:** Early June. At Maritime Centre. Classic boats, the Fast-and-Furious Boat Building Contest (build a boat and race it within four hours), boat-building house for children, folk singers, dancing.

### Cumberland
- **Empire Days:** Victoria Day weekend.
- **Miners' Memorial Day:** Late June.

### Duncan
- **Regional Heritage Days:** Mid-May.
- **Cowichan Indian Band Canoe Races:** May.
- **Summer Festival:** Mid-July.
- **Island's Folk Festival:** Mid-July.
- **Cowichan Exhibition:** Early Sept.
- **Christmas Chaos:** Nov.

### Esquimalt
- **Buccaneer Days:** Late May.
- **CFB Esquimalt Armed Forces Open House:** Late May.

### Galiano Island
- **Artist Guild Summer Sale:** Mid-July.
- **Lions Club Fiesta:** BC Day weekend.
- **Blackberry Festival:** Thanksgiving Sat.
- **Galiano Weavers Exhibit and Sale:** July and Nov.

### Gold River
- **Loggers' Sports:** Late June.

### Jordan River
- **Surf Slalom Social:** Late April. Windsurfers' gathering.

### Ladysmith
- **Dogwood Days:** Early Aug.
- **Fall Fair:** Mid-Sept.

### Lake Cowichan Area
- **Heritage Days:** May.
- **Lake Days:** June.
- **Honeymoon Bay Summer Festival:** July.
- **Drag Boat Races:** Aug.
- **Youbou Regatta:** Aug.

### Mayne Island
- **Summer Mania Fair:** July.
- **Springwater Lodge Salmon Derby:** July.
- **Mayne Island Fall Fair:** Aug.
- **Lions' Salmon Bake:** Early Sept.

### Metchosin
- **Metchosin International Summer School of the Arts:** Late June-early July. Lester B Pearson College Campus, at Pedder Bay.

### Mill Bay
- **Country Music Jamboree:** Late May, early June.
- **Malahat Band Canoe Races:** June.
- **Fishing Derby:** Early Aug.

### Nanaimo
- **Empire Days:** Mid-May.
- **Heritage Days:** Mid-June.
- **Nanaimo Marine Festival:** Early July. Culminating in famous Bathtub Race between Nanaimo and Vancouver's Kitsilano Beach.
- **Nanaimo Festival:** May-July. Theatrical performances based on area's history.
- **Salmon Festival:** Early Aug.

*Bathtub race to Vancouver, Nanaimo Marine Festival.*

- **Vancouver Island Exhibition:** Mid-Aug.
- **Roaring Twenties Dixieland Jazz Affair and Malahat Challenge:** Early Sept. Two-day celebration ending with antique car parade from Nanaimo to Victoria.

### Parksville

- **Brant Festival:** Mid-April. Organized by the Mid-Island Wildlife Watch Society, offers goose viewing stations, birding competition, nature talks by international experts, wildlife art, carving, photography, stories, children's activities.
- **BC Open Sandcastle Competition:** Mid-late July. Attracts 40,000 people.
- **World Croquet Championship:** Mid-Aug.

### Pender Islands

- **Annual Fall Fair:** Late Aug.

### Port Alberni

- **Golden Oldies Car Show and Mud Bog:** April or May.
- **Forestry Week:** Mid-May.
- **Salmon Festival:** Labour Day weekend.
- **Fall Fair:** Weekend after Labour Day.
- **Loggers' Sports:** Early Sept.

### Port Hardy

- **Filomi Days:** Mid-Aug. (Fishing, Logging, Mining Days.)
- **Regional Fall Fair:** Early Sept.

### Port McNeill

- **Port McNeill Daze:** Mid-May.
- **North Island Loggers' Sports:** Early July.

### Salt Spring Island

- **Sea Capers:** Mid-June.
- **Festival of Performing Arts:** July.
- **Farmers Institute Fall Fair:** Mid-Sept.
- **Guild Christmas Show and Sale:** Mid-Nov. Jewelers, painters, potters, weavers, woodworkers.
- **Christmas Ship:** Early Dec.

### Saturna Island

- **Canada Day Lamb Bake:** Held every July 1 weekend since 1949 on a farm below Mt Warburton Pike. Most celebrated annual event in the Gulf Islands.

### Sayward-Kelsey Bay

- **Loggers' Sports:** Early July.
- **Oscar Daze:** Early Aug.
- **Salmon Derby:** Labour Day weekend.

*Totem pole in Thunderbird Park, Victoria.*

### Sidney and Saanich Peninsula

- **Sidney Days and Jazz Festival:** Late June-early July.
- **Saanich Fall Fair:** Early Sept. The oldest agricultural fair west of the Great Lakes. Livestock, sheep shearing, show jumping, crafts, produce, home baking, fiddle competition, kids' rides. It's all here, from little piggies and giant pumpkins, to the best baron of beef anywhere. At Saanichton Fair Grounds.

### Sointula (Malcolm Island)

- **Winter Festival:** Late Nov. Local artists and musicians.

### Sooke

- **Sooke Region Museum Open House and Salmon BBQ:** Late June.
- **All Sooke Day and Annual Festival of History:** Third Sat in July. Loggers sports on Sat. Festival through to next weekend – fishing derby, heritage events, and pioneer fashion shows, tea parties, excursions.
- **Fine Arts Festival:** Early Aug. Sooke Arena, adjacent museum. One of BC's largest juried art shows. Week-long annual event that's got everybody hopping.

### Tahsis

- **The Great Walk:** Early June. 62km. One-day hike to Tahsis from Gold River.

### Telegraph Cove

- **Boardwalk Craft Fair:** Early Aug.

### Tofino

- **Whale Festival:** Mid-March to mid-April.Celebrating annual migration of some 20,000 Pacific grey whales.

### Ucluelet

- **Whale Festival:** Mid-March to mid-April.
- **Salmon Derbies:** July and Aug.
- **Pacific Rim Summer Festival:** Mid-late July.
- **Ukee Days:** Late July.

### Victoria

- **TerrifVic Dixieland Jazz Party:** Late April.
- **Victoria Days and Parade:** May Day.
- **Swiftsure Sailing Race:** Late May.
- **Oak Bay Tea Party:** Early June.
- **Jazz Fest International:** Late June-early July.
- **Victoria Folkfest:** Late June-early July.
- **Canada Day Celebrations:** July 1.
- **Victoria International Festival:** July and Aug.
- **First People's Festival:** Early Aug.
- **Sun Fest:** Mid-Aug.
- **Classic Boat Festival:** Early Sept.
- **Fringe Festival:** Late Sept.
- **British Fortnight:** Mid-Oct-early Nov.
- **First Night:** New Year's Eve.

### Zeballos

- **Fall Fair:** Sept. Firemen display 1947 La France fire truck.

*BC Parliament Buildings, above the Inner Harbour, Victoria.*

# Vancouver Island Routes and Highlights

## TRAVELLER'S LOGS



## HIGHLIGHTS



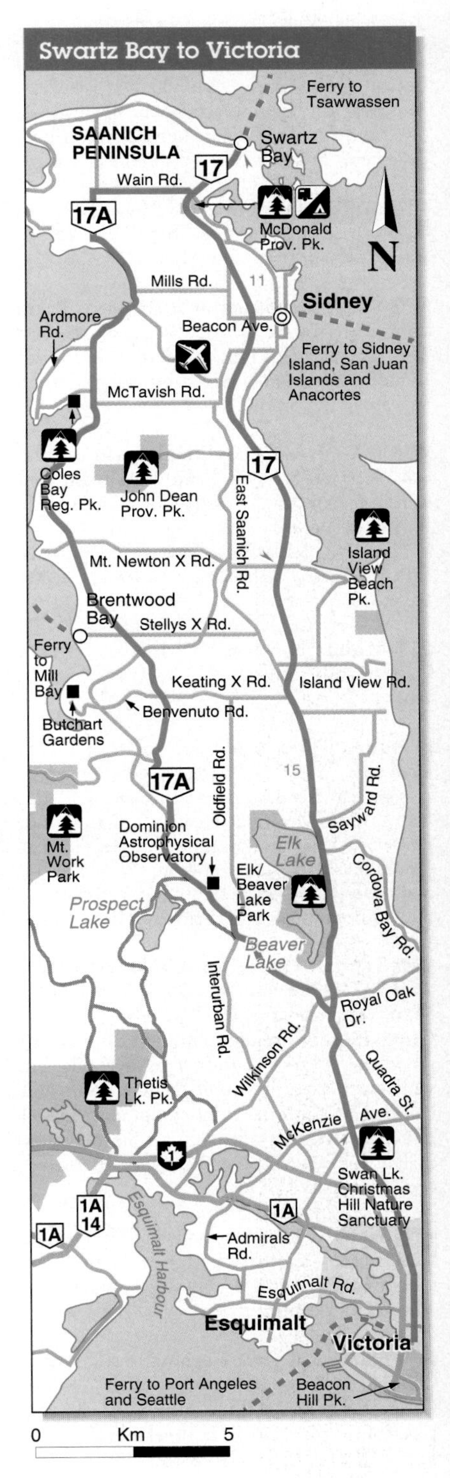


## Swartz Bay to Victoria

### PATRICIA BAY HIGHWAY (Highway 17)

For travellers arriving on Vancouver Island at BC Ferries' Swartz Bay terminal this is the most direct route to Victoria. Swartz Bay is the province's second largest and busiest ferry terminal after Tsawwassen, the world's largest in size and number of vehicles transported. Last year, over 7 million passengers walked, bussed, or drove through the Swartz Bay terminal on their way to or from the mainland and Gulf Islands. To comfortably accommodate more and more people, a $36-million upgrading – improved access to the terminal, parking, holding lounges, washrooms, and food outlets – was initiated in 1992.

Hwy 17 from the ferry terminal is an increasingly busy route, though the charm of this four-lane 80km-h path down the Saanich Peninsula remains. It leads through rolling farmland and past glimpses of Haro Strait and occasionally even Washington State's Mt Baker, shimmering to the east.

If you're not in a hurry, a quieter, even more scenic alternate to Hwy 17 is Hwy 17A, the old Pat Bay Hwy, skirting the western shores of **Saanich Peninsula**. This road meanders through pastoral countryside where wild deer often roam the same farmyards as sheep. Flowers, vegetables, eggs, and other produce are sold at roadside stands. Known as West Saanich Rd, Hwy 17A is a route to **Patricia Bay, Brentwood Bay, Butchart Gardens,** and the **Dominion Astrophysical Observatory**. *Log* covers Hwy 17 first, then Hwy 17A. Also see **gateway map**, *p. 47*.

### *Highway 17*

**McDonald Park-Wain Roads:** Second traffic light after ferry terminal. Turn west (right) on Wain Rd to get to Hwy 17A. Turn east 2km to get to McDonald Provincial Park and the backdoor route to Sidney.

**McDonald Provincial Park:** 20ha; 30 campsites. 387-4363. Good overnighter for campers arriving on a late ferry.

**Sidney:** (Pop. 10,082). With a high ratio of retirees, the "downtown" of the Saanich Peninsula. A pleasant place to shop or stroll on the wharf. There are restaurants, hotels, marinas, diving facilities, and the new Port Sidney development, with breakwater, marina, specialty shops, pub, waterfront park, and promenade. Washington State Ferries terminal for San Juan Islands and Anacortes is at 2499 Ocean Ave. Follow signs; see *Transportation*, p.32.

**Sidney Information:** Two infocentres are run by the Saanich Peninsula Chamber of Commerce, Box 2014, Sidney, BC, V8L 3S3. 656-3616. Main infocentre is on Hwy 17 halfway between BC Ferries terminal and Sidney. Year-round: 656-0525. Second infocentre is in Sidney on 1st St near Washington State Ferries terminal. This infocentre is open when ferries arrive and depart.

■ **Sidney Marine Mammal and Historical Museum:** 2538 Beacon Ave, near Sidney wharf. 656-1322. Daily in summer. Winter hours variable, please call. Pioneer and Coast Salish artifacts and photos; exhibits on the ecology of whales, sea lions, seals, and sea otters that make their home in the area.

**Sidney Spit Provincial Marine Park:** 177ha; 27 campsites. 478-

7411. On Sidney Island, 3km east of Sidney. Foot-passenger ferry from marina at end of Beacon Ave in Sidney. Mid-May to late Sept. Beautiful sandy beaches, lagoon, open meadows, and forests. Eagles, herons, waterfowl, large herds of fallow deer. A pleasant day trip.

**McTavish Rd:** West off Hwy 17, 7.5km south of Swartz Bay. Route to International Airport and Hwy 17A.

**Victoria International Airport:** 7.5km south of Swartz Bay, head west on McTavish Rd. Then 2km to Vancouver Island's main airport served by major airlines. (It's about 3.5km on McTavish to Hwy 17A.)

**John Dean Provincial Park:** 155ha. West off Hwy 17A onto McTavish, then north on East Saanich Rd about 2km to Dean Park Rd. West to park. Views of Saanich Peninsula, Gulf Islands, Cascade Mountains. Hiking trails. Climb to summit of Mt Newton. Day use.

**Mount Newton X Rd:** About 11km south of Swartz Bay. West for 5km to Hwy 17A.

**Island View Rd:** 14km south of Swartz Bay. West to Butchart Gardens (see *below*). East for 3km past farm land to Island View Beach Regional Park (25.5ha). Long, sandy beach, upland meadows, dunes, views of the Gulf Islands, and sometimes even the BC mainland. Good birdwatching, too. Righteous nudists occasionaly sun themselves here.

**Saanich Historical Artifacts Society:** 7321 Lochside Rd. 652-5522. Daily. Mornings in winter, all day early June-Sept. Group tours by arrangement. East off Hwy 17 on Island View Rd, follow signs. 12ha site with small lake, forest trails, nature pond, and working artifacts: farming equipment, model railroad, sawmill, planer mill. At Summer Fair in late June everything that works is turned on. Wagon rides, food, fun.

**Sayward Rd:** 18km south of Swartz Bay. East to Victoria's Marine Scenic Dr, Cordova Bay, and Mt Douglas Park (see *Victoria* for details).

**Elk/Beaver Lake Regional Park:** About 100m beyond Sayward Rd. 411ha. Greater Victoria's most popular park with two lakes joined by a narrow channel and extensive network of hiking and bridle trails. Four beaches, swimming, canoeing, rowing, waterskiing, windsurfing, 15km walking and bridle trails. Check for summer programs. The most heavily fished lakes on Vancouver Island.

**Royal Oak Dr:** 22km south of Swartz Bay. Exit leads to Broadmead and Royal Oak shopping area and Hwy 17A.

**McKenzie Ave:** 26km south of Swartz Bay. Vancouver Island's largest interchange. Traffic volume has increased beyond signal-controlled intersection's ability to get cars through. Completion date for lifting Pat Bay Hwy over McKenzie Ave and tying up loose ends: 1994. Downtown Victoria starts here. West for about 2km leads to Hwy 1 (Island Hwy). East to Swan Lake and University of Victoria.

**Swan Lake-Christmas Hill Nature Sanctuary:** 46ha. Access from McKenzie Ave, then Rainbow Rd. 479-0211. Year-round, nature house and programs for nature study. Floating boardwalk, trails, ponds, bird blinds. Excellent family day trip.

**University of Victoria:** 4.5km east of Hwy 17 via McKenzie Ave. 162ha campus for over 14,000 students. Individual or group tours by arrangement: 721-7645 or 721-7211. One of BC's four universities. Centre of activity with numerous public events; check newspapers. Pleasant grounds with chapel, walking/jogging trails, flower gardens – springtime rhododendron gardens worthwhile stroll.

**Victoria:** (Greater Victoria pop. 299,550). 6km south of McKenzie Ave. Encompasses southern knob of Vancouver Island and is home to more than half of island's residents. See *City of Sea and Gardens*, next page.

## Scenic Alternate Highway 17A (Swartz Bay to Victoria)

Hwy 17A, also known as West Saanich Rd, can be reached by turning west on Wain Rd at second traffic light south of Swartz Bay ferry terminal, and driving 2.5km to Hwy 17A. It is 24km from junction of Hwy 17A and Wain Rd to Royal Oak Dr, just north of Victoria, where Hwy 17A joins Hwy 17.

**Patricia Bay:** 1km south of Wain Rd on Hwy 17A. Gravel and sand beach with warm summer swimming. Wintering grounds for sea lions and waterfowl. Year-round for harbour seals, river otters. Holy Trinity Anglican Church, built 1885, overlooks bay. Federal Institute of Ocean Sciences on south side, offering tours by appointment only, Mon and Wed: 363-6518. Geographical centre seismographs monitor Juan de Fuca fault line.

**Mills Rd:** East off Hwy 17A, 2km south of Wain Rd. 3kmto Sidney and Hwy 17.

**Coles Bay Regional Park:** 4ha. West off Hwy 17A on Ardmore Rd, 3.5km south of Wain Rd. (Ardmore Rd is a horseshoe which intersects Hwy 17A at two points. Take the most southerly turn onto Ardmore). Twisty creekside trails for wandering, waterfowl, warm swimming in sea.

**McTavish Rd:** East off Hwy 17A, 6.5km south of Wain Rd. 3km to Victoria International Airport turnoff and Hwy 17.

**John Dean Provincial Park:** 155ha. East off Hwy 17A onto McTavish, then north on East Saanich Rd 2km to Dean Park Rd. West to park. See info column one.

**Mt Newton X Rd:** East off Hwy 17A, 10.5km south of Wain Rd. About 800m to St Stephen's Church, built in 1862, oldest church in BC still on original site. About 5km to **Hwy 17**.

**Brentwood Bay:** (Pop. 3,200). 12.5km south of Wain Rd. Part of Central Saanich municipality. The original part of this community is at the bottom of Verdier Ave, just before the ferry dock: it's still known as Moodyville to old-timers. Here's a bucolic seaside village, complete with weathered wharf, old inn-style pub, wee shops and pleasing cottages – summer retreats turned into year-round homes. In spite of all this, there is, it seems, a reason why at least some Moodyville folks are in fact, moody. "We're getting over it," one says. "There's not much we can do about that...that thing." Their new neighbour. Port Royale, it's called, a giant cream-coloured megalith, a 128-unit California-style condo complex terracing the shores overlooking the bay. "And not a tree in it." The subject of controversy, then criticism, and when it was all done, ridicule. One resident summed it up: "A horror to boaters entering the bay, but the people living in it have great views."

**Brentwood-Mill Bay Ferry:** 13.5km south of Wain Rd turn west on Verdier Ave in Brentwood Bay. Small car and passenger ferry crosses Saanich Inlet, by-passing Victoria. Hwy 1 is near terminal on Mill Bay side of inlet. Takes 25 minutes and runs approximately every hour and 10 minutes from either side, morning until early evening. 386-3431.

**Keating X Rd and Benvenuto Ave:** 15.5km south of Wain Rd. East for 3km to Hwy 17. West for 2km to Butchart Gardens.

**Butchart Gardens:** East off Hwy 17A at Keating X Rd. 800 Benvenuto Rd, Brentwood Bay. 652-5256. Open daily. What was a limestone quarry, became, in 1904, gardens of delight, drawing three-quarters of a million visitors a year. The 20ha gardens overlooking Tod Inlet offer up native flora and exotic shrubs, trees, and flowers and entertainment year-round. There are the Butchart Gardeners, who sing outdoors, Mon-Sat evenings, June 1-Sept 30; "Night Illuminations," subtly coloured lights on display June 15-Sept 15; fireworks set to music in July and Aug (come early to avoid disappointing lineups); Christmas lights and carollers, early Dec-early Jan. Restaurants and coffee bars.

**Butterfly World:** At Benvenuto Rd. and Hwy 17A, just beyond turnoff to Butchart Gardens. 652-7811. Open daily year-round. Folklore says it's good luck to have a butterfly land on you. At Butterfly World, with 1,500-2,000 butterflies of 120-

150 species from all over the planet, the odds are far better than the lottery. Many of these exotic, colourful insects represent rare breeds endangered in their own natural environments. These butterflies are all from breeding farms around the world, some of which are helping to rebuild natural populations. Second location in **Coombs**, see p.68.

**Dominion Astrophysical Observatory:** On Little Saanich Mountain, east side of Hwy 17A (5071 W Saanich Rd), 21km south of Wain Rd. Open daily May-Aug. Mon-Fri in winter. Also Sat nights early April-late Oct. 363-0001. A stargazer's delight, visited every clear night by astronomers from across Canada and around the world. Has what was once the world's largest telescope; 183cm and 41cm telescopes.

**Royal Oak Dr:** East off Hwy 17A, 24km south of Wain Rd. Short distance to Hwy 17. West onto Wilkinson Rd, leads about 5km to Hwy 1.

**Victoria:** (Greater Victoria pop. 299,550). See *Victoria, City of Sea and Gardens*, below. Hwy 1, the Trans-Canada, which leaves Vancouver Island at Nanaimo, begins in Victoria (see p.50). Hwy 14 runs from Colwood, a metropolitan Victoria municipality, to Port Renfrew on the island's southwest coast (see p.43).

# Victoria

## CITY OF SEA AND GARDENS

Victorians are a fortunate lot, for they live in one of the nation's most idyllic settings. Bounded by ocean on three sides, Victoria is a city of the sea. Its magnetic appeal draws people from around the world and many who settle become as attached as barnacles on a rock.

The city lies on the extreme southern tip of Vancouver Island, where the Canadian-American border has been stretched below the 49th parallel to keep all of the island in Canada. Not far from Victoria's harbour, Race Rocks lighthouse, the most southerly point in western Canada, is only 8km from the international boundary. Washington State's shimmering Olympic Mountains, 20km across Juan de Fuca Strait, form a dramatic backdrop to Victoria. On clear days the steel-blue slopes and wintry peaks seem as if they're standing in the city's backyard.

Victoria's mild climate and seaside location have been its most important assets since its beginnings in 1843 as a Hudson's Bay Company fort. In selecting the site, Sir James Douglas, an HBC chief factor, described it as "a perfect Eden." Initially, the fort was named "Camosun," approximating the Coast Salish name for the harbour, describing the rushing tide waters entering the Gorge, beyond the Inner Harbour. At this time, First Nations people had a permanent, fortified settlement at the north end of Cadboro Bay, seasonal settlements at the Inner Harbour and Esquimalt Harbour, and dozens of permanent and seasonal sites on adjacent islands and along the Saanich Peninsula. There is also evidence of an ancient village site at Beacon Hill Park. With the establishment of Douglas's fort, and its occupation by a mere 50 souls, thousands of aboriginal peoples from nations up and down BC's coast converged, seeking opportunities to trade and work. They set up a major encampment were the Parliament Buildings are now, and another one across the harbour, at what became the Songhees Indian Reserve.

*Empress Hotel and Victoria waterfront.*

As gold seekers and merchants traded along the western edge of North America in the late 1800s and early 1900s, they drastically shifted the population balance in favour of non-aboriginal peoples. Victoria became the busiest seaport north of San Francisco with nearly a thousand ships a year sailing between Victoria and the Orient, California, Australia, New Zealand, and Panama.

Today, Victoria remains a busy seaport with a Canadian Coast Guard station and regular visits by cruise ships, military ships, tall ships, and freighters. Ferries, tour boats, and jet-propelled catamarans are based in Victoria Harbour along with a sizable fleet of fishboats, houseboats, sailboats, and cruisers. Floatplanes and helicopters make some 25,000 takeoffs and landings a year.

On the streets above the harbour, summer tourists, cameras dangling, brochures in hand, crowd into double-decker buses and horse-drawn carriages for tours of the city. Pedal-powered kabuki cabs weave through the traffic, people pose beside a kilted bagpiper playing on a corner. The MV *Coho*, the *Victoria Clipper*, and *Victoria Express* drop new throngs of travellers from Port Angeles, and catamarans carry still more from Seattle.

Recent development has stepped up the tempo and brought a "big city" feel to Victoria. It is no longer the retirement capital of Canada, a place on the southern tip of Vancouver Island where Prairie farmers come to live with their parents: Victoria, which for years had the country's highest population of senior citizens, now has fallen behind Halifax and other Canadian communities as a retirement centre.

While the bustle of downtown Victoria is most noticeable with the annual torrent of tourists – over three million a year – the new growth throughout Greater Victoria is obvious year-round. Farms on the once pastoral Saanich Peninsula are rapidly becoming new residential and commercial subdivisions. The rural western communities of Colwood, View Royal, and Metchosin are now incorporated municipalities.

Victoria's population is nearly 300,000, an increase of more than 140,000 since the early '60s. The population is expected to reach 400,000 by the year 2010. Major expansions of the BC Ferries terminal and the Trans-Canada and Patricia Bay highways – the city's main commuter routes – are underway to relieve bumper-to-bumper rush-hour traffic, something Victorians once believed was only a mainland misfortune.

The new development is most noticeable in the downtown core where some buildings that speak eloquently of Victoria's past are being brought back to life. The city's largest hotel, the Empress, recently underwent a $45-million facelift. The landmark, built in 1908, has been impeccably restored to reflect its original opulence, yet it has managed to modernize at the same time.

Behind the Empress Hotel, the new Victoria Conference Centre, built at a cost of $22 million, is a 1,500-seat complex which takes advantage of the grace notes all around it: the Empress, the BC Parliament Buildings, the Crystal Garden, Thunderbird Park.

A few blocks from the conference centre, the new Eaton Centre is a $100-million, 150-store complex. Built to look old, the centre is a four-story, brick-faced structure with the facade of some heritage buildings that were demolished.

Across Victoria Harbour from the Empress, the old Songhees Indian land has recently been transformed from an industrial eyesore into upscale condominiums, with over 1,500 housing units, and the 250-room Ocean Pointe resort-hotel with conference and spa facilities.

The development includes the portion of the waterfront walkway from the Songhees land (it was sold to the BC government in 1910) to neighbouring West Bay. Currently, West Bay is a light industrial area, but that could change. A housing project for seniors has recently sprung up and the city would like to see more medium-density housing there.

Development on Songhees land and in West Bay is adding a new dimension to an area that has been considered "on the wrong side of the (Johnson Street) bridge" for years. But now, a 5km seaside promenade joins the two sides of the harbour (see *Windy Fringes*, p. 42, for details).

Esquimalt and West Bay are linked to downtown Victoria by the Johnson St Bridge, one of two remaining bascule lift bridges in Canada. Opened in 1924, its 635kg counterweights pivot each span like a massive trap door.

On the upstream side of the bridge is Victoria's intricate Gorge waterway, a long, meandering fjord which flows into Victoria Harbour. So strong are the tides at certain times that kayakers run them for white-water paddling practice. Kinsmen Gorge Park and the Gorge-side promenade are favourite spots for herring fishing, particularly for children, in late winter and early spring.

A short distance from the Johnson St Bridge, on Fisgard St, is Chinatown. Small but significant, Victoria's Asian quarter is the oldest in Canada.

The 1994 Commonwealth Games have also contributed to Victoria's emergence as a modern international host. The $22-million Saanich Commonwealth Place, just off the Pat Bay Hwy at Royal Oak, provides an aquatic venue for both community and world-class swimmers and divers. Its facilities include a 51m competition-class pool, a diving and synchronized swimmers' area, wave machines, shallow pool, and fitness rooms. The University of Victoria's Centennial Stadium has been expanded, and at the Juan de Fuca Recreation Centre, there's a new concrete oval velodrome for cyclists and international-scale lawnbowl greens.

Despite its growth, Victoria has managed to retain an Old-World charm that distinguishes it from other cities. Certainly on Vancouver Island, where the history and present-day economy are based on forestry and other resource industries, Victoria's gentility would seem an incongruity. However, while resource industries employ less than four percent of Victoria's work force, service industries employ nearly 40 percent. With Victoria being BC's capital and numerous federal workers employed at CFB Esquimalt and other federal institutions, more than 17 percent of Victorians are public servants. Fifteen percent are involved in trade businesses, mainly because of tourism and the high number of retired people.

The city was named in honour of Queen Victoria, who ruled Great Britain and Ireland from 1837 to 1901 when her empire was establishing roots on Vancouver Island. While other island towns are eager to display their industrial pasts, Victoria still flaunts its British heritage.

Victoria is perceived as having one major flaw: it dumps its raw sewage (though screened) into Juan de Fuca Strait. This has created an international controversy, angering US communities across the strait. Although some experts maintain that the sewage is immediately dissolved by the strait's strong currents, mounting pressure and tourist convention boycotts may force Victoria to opt for sewage treatment quicker than it now plans.

**Victoria Travel Infocentre:** 812 Wharf St, Victoria, BC, V8W 1T3. 382-2127. On the harbour front. Daily. A "one-stop shopping" centre for tourists. Licensed to carry out some travel agency functions: staff helps book hotel and B&B accommodation, tours and charters, restaurant meals, transportation, and entertainment. Up to nine languages are spoken here.

## City Fare

Although Victoria's climate and scenery may entice people outdoors, it is also a place for indoors lovers. Besides its parks and path-

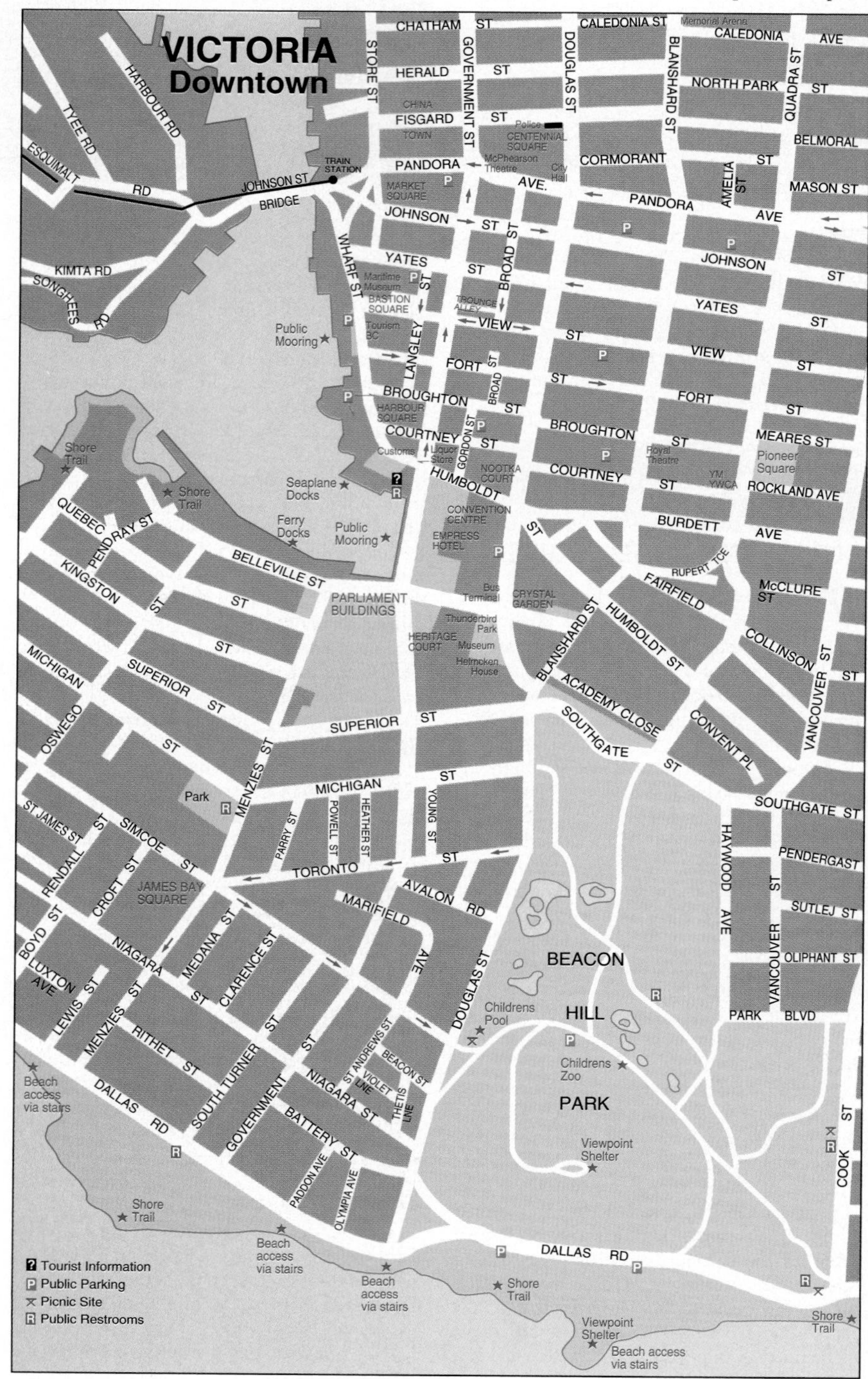

ways there are neighbourhood pubs, many decorated in pioneering styles, some serving their own home brews. Entertainment is provided in some pubs and lounges. Unlimited types of cuisine are served in the city's restaurants, cafés, and takeouts. Victoria has its own symphony and opera company as well as several theatre groups. Art shows, films, lectures, plays, concerts, and other performances are held throughout the year at theatres and galleries. The McPherson Playhouse, adjacent City Hall, is one of the most exquisite Edwardian-type performance venues in Canada. The Belfry Theatre company, at the heart of the old Fernwood district, performs in what was the Emmanuel Baptist Church, built in 1892.

Most events are advertised in the *Times-Colonist*, Victoria's daily newspaper, or in other local publications. *Monday Magazine*, a Victoria weekly, and *The Martlet*, University of Victoria newspaper, carry extensive calendars of arts events. Other events calendars available at the infocentre.

## Architectural Wonders

■ **BC Parliament Buildings:** On Belleville St above Victoria Harbour, 387-3046. Daily June-Sept; tours every 20 minutes. Weekdays in winter; tours hourly. Public galleries open when legislature in session. Buildings were constructed for $923,000 and opened in 1897, in time for the diamond jubilee of Queen Victoria. Gilded statue of Captain George Vancouver, first European to circumnavigate this vast island, stands atop the highest copper dome.

■ **Empress Hotel:** The grand old Empress, now totally refurbished, has watched over the harbour since 1908. The classic design and high teas, and shops at this Canadian Pacific Hotel are a show of Victoria's "Englishness."

■ **Crystal Garden:** 713 Douglas St, 381-1213. Daily. Glass-roofed Crystal Garden opened 1925. Originally a social centre with ballroom and British Empire's largest saltwater swimming pool, it was closed in 1971 because of soaring maintenance costs. Renovated and reopened in 1980, again as a social centre, with tea room, ballroom, and luxuriant tropical gardens with exotic plants, miniature monkeys, fish, macaws, parrots, flamingoes, but no swimming.

■ **Victoria Conference Centre:** 720 Douglas St, 361-1000. Behind the Empress Hotel and across from Crystal Garden, grand-scale modern-day architecture has recently joined that of past. Opened in 1989, it can host up to 1,500 delegates in the largest of its 15 meeting rooms. Lecture theatre seats 400. Totem pole and fountains in plaza and foyer.

■ **Ogden Point Breakwater:** Ship watchers often take binoculars here to eastern entrance of Victoria Harbour to view marine traffic. The breakwater, with a navigational light at the end, stretches 750m out to sea, providing partial protection for the harbour. Built of 18t blocks of granite, it was completed in 1917, at a cost of $1.8 million, nearly twice as much as BC Legislative Buildings. Its ledges and concrete surface are a favourite spot for fishermen and joggers.

■ **Craigdarroch Castle:** 1050 Joan Cres, 592-5323. Daily. Castle built shortly before turn of the century for Robert Dunsmuir, James Dunsmuir's father, who constructed Vancouver Island's Esquimalt and Nanaimo Railway. The castle's conspicuous stone towers rise from a hilltop in Victoria's prestigious Rockland neighbourhood, near Government House. Granites, marbles, and sandstone of the highest quality were used for the exterior. Inside, every piece of wood and stone was meticulously tooled. Intricate panelling adorns walls and ceiling of the main hall, follows the main staircase 87 steps into a dancing hall and main tower. Dunsmuir died before the castle was finished, but his widow remained there until her death in 1908. It was later used as a hospital for soldiers, a college, school board offices, and music conservatory. Today Craigdarroch is a museum being restored by a non-profit society.

■ **Christ Church Cathedral:** Quadra and Courtenay streets, 383-2714. Self-guided tour brochures available at front of church. Guided tours by arrangement. Built 1929, Christ Church Cathedral is one of few remaining Canadian churches with real bells. One pillar was named Robin Pillar after construction was delayed because a robin had built a nest on it. Inside, the choir screen and massive organ, with 3,000 pipes, are from Westminster Abbey. Pulpit is made from a 500-year-old oak tree.

## Museums and Galleries

■ **Royal BC Museum:** 675 Belleville St, 387-3014. Daily. One of Canada's finest museums, renowned for its displays of First Nations artifacts. Also a pioneer town, sawmill, fish cannery, coal mine, train station, and theatre. You can board Captain George Vancouver's ship, the *Discovery*, saunter through woods or along seashore, or take an undersea journey in a submarine. Excellent bookstore and giftshop.

■ **Maritime Museum of BC:** 28 Bastion Sq, 385-4222. Daily. Housed in city's first provincial courthouse, impressive turreted structure built in Bastion Square, 1889. Nautical artifacts from Victoria's early maritime history.

■ **Art Gallery of Greater Victoria:** 1040 Moss St, just off Fort St, 384-4101. Daily. In the past has offered walking tours that included gallery, Craigdarroch Castle, and Government House. Has only entire Shinto shrine outside Japan. Gallery occupies Spencer Mansion, built 1890. Free Thurs, 5-9pm.

■ **Carr House:** 207 Government St, 387-4697. Afternoons, year-round. Italianate-style home of artist Emily Carr. Furnished rooms and exhibit about artist.

■ **Emily Carr Gallery:** 1107 Wharf St, 384-3130. Victoria Day-Labour Day: Tues-Sun. Labour Day-Victoria Day: Tues-Sat. Paintings by Victoria's best-known artist, who died in 1945, are exhibited with works of her contemporaries. Shows change regularly.

■ **Maltwood Art Museum and Gallery:** University Centre, University of Victoria, 721-8298. Mon-Fri, plus Sun. Collection of the late sculptor, Katherine Maltwood, was donated to University of Victoria in 1964. Pieces from collection, comprised of decorative arts, paintings, furniture, and other items, are often incorporated into gallery's changing exhibits.

■ **Point Ellice House:** 2616 Pleasant St, 387-4697. Mid-June to Sept: Thurs-Mon. Early June and Sept: Sun only. Built as private home in 1861, now contains collection of Victoriana. Special events in summer.

■ **Craigflower Farm and School House:** 110 Island Hwy, 387-4697. Mid-June to Sept: Thurs to Mon. Early June and Sept: Sun only. Built in 1856 on one of Victoria's first farms. On same site is one of western Canada's oldest schoolhouses. Both now open to public. Portage Inlet here, nearly 9km from the head of Victoria Harbour, is a familiar sight to people commuting to Victoria on the Trans-Canada Hwy. Special events, summer, harvest time, and other times.

■ **Helmcken House:** Behind Thunderbird Park next to Royal BC Museum, 387-4697. Mid-June to Sept: Thurs to Mon. Early June and Sept: Sunday only. Built 1852, BC's oldest standing home. Special Christmas events.

## Squares and Alleys

■ **Bastion Square:** The heart of Victoria's Old Town and site of original Fort Victoria, where former saloons, hotels, bordellos, and warehouses have become restaurants, offices, and art galleries.

■ **Market Square:** Near the harbour, at foot of Johnson St. At turn of the century this busy section of town offered everything a body could want, and still does. Pre-1900 architecture has been restored to original elegance. Two-story balustraded gallery encircles a landscaped amphitheatre. Specialty shops, restaurants, entertainment.

■ **Chinatown and Fan Tan Alley:** British heritage may be the basis of Victoria's gentility, but other significant cultures have been preserved. During the Victorian era about 17,000 of the Queen's loyal subjects immigrated to BC. But more than 14,000 Chinese, who had an uncanny knack for finding gold in supposedly exhausted mines, arrived during the same period. Prohibited by law from preempting Crown land, many Chinese congregated in Victoria in the late 1800s.

Today a centre of commerce and culture for many Chinese Canadians, Victoria's Chinatown is the oldest on the west coast of North America. Around the turn of the century, production of opium in Chinatown was one of BC's largest industries. It's believed more than a dozen major opium dealers had thriving businesses based in Victoria, just blocks from the northwest coast's largest red-light district. Fan Tan Alley's nooks and crannies were once occupied by gambling houses offering mah jong, fan-tan, dominoes, and the numbers game to the men in black "pyjamas."

The entrance to today's Chinatown, at Government and Fisgard streets, was marked conspicuously in 1981 by the Gate of Harmonious Interest, with two hand-carved stone lions from Suchow, China, Victoria's "twin" city. Restaurants and shops sell food, art, herbs, and other items from China.

The Canadian College for Chinese Studies offers long and short-term courses in traditional Chinese medicine (including acupuncture),

Mandarin Chinese, calligraphy, brush painting, Chinese and Japanese culture, and martial arts. 853-859 Cormorant St, Victoria, BC, V8W 1R2, 385-6622.

■ **Centennial Square:** Douglas and Pandora streets. Here is Victoria's City Hall. Built 1897. One of first major downtown buildings to be refurbished in an effort to preserve city's architectural heritage. 385-5711 for tours by arrangement.

■ **Antique Row:** Up from waterfront, more Olde England is visible along this stretch of Fort St, where old Tudor-style buildings house several antique stores.

■ **Oak Bay:** More English than England. To arrive in this municipality is to step "Behind the Tweed Curtain" where tea houses are rife, and gentlefolk slip into the Oak Bay Beach Hotel's little "Snug" for a quiet drink. In prohibition days, amaretto and apricot brandy, called "Snug Tea", were concealed in brown betty puddings. There's a real tea party here, too, a big annual event, early June, on the sandy shores of Willows Beach.

■ **Uplands Estates:** Beyond Willows Beach the Marine Scenic Dr (see below) carries on past posh homes and gardens of Uplands Estates. Many of these homes look toward Chatham and Discovery islands, named for Captain Vancouver's ships. Uplands was originally site of Hudson's Bay Company's sheep farm, which supplied early colonists with foodstuffs.

## *Gardens and Parks*

With such a multitude of historic sites and a high population of retired people, Victoria is sometimes mistakenly viewed as a salty home for contented laggards and remittance men. But the city is anything but stodgy. Anyone arriving at Victoria Harbour on the sunny days of spring and summer is enveloped in the city's vivacity. Thousands of flowers on the harbour's Causeway spell "Welcome to Victoria". Bells ring in the Netherlands Carillon Tower, in front of the Royal BC Museum, and street performers add to the ambience. Up from the harbour, fiddlers, folksingers, accordionists, and classical ensembles "busk" on downtown streets. Known as the "City of Gardens", an annual average of 2,200 hours of sunshine help the flowers and blossoms bloom before any other city in Canada.

■ **Hanging Baskets:** From spring to fall, Victoria's streets are colourfully embellished by more than 900 hanging baskets, each with 25 flowering plants, that hang from antique-style lamps.

■ **Beacon Hill Park:** Each spring hundreds of thousands of daffodils and blue camas blanket the slopes of Beacon Hill, site of a 74ha city park with great ocean views. These flowers grow in addition to 30,000 flowers planted in the park twice a year. The park, with its streams and duck ponds, peacocks, aviary, shrubs, oak trees and firs, playgrounds, paths, flower gardens, and lovers' lane, is a quiet getaway in the midst of downtown Victoria. Rare in a city park, much of Beacon Hill is left wild (tended, but wild), and this is precisely what is most refreshing.

■ **Butchart Gardens:** Brentwood Bay. See *Swartz Bay to Victoria*, p.38.

■ **Thunderbird Park:** Corner of Belleville and Douglas streets. A long house, totems and other works of the northwest coast's native culture are on outdoor display. Haida, Tsimshian, Nuu-chah-nulth, Salish, Kwakwaka'wakw, and Bella Coola people are represented, and carvers can often be observed at work.

■ **Government House:** 1401 Rockland Ave, 387-2080. Grounds open daily. Meticulously maintained lawns and flower beds are a delight for flower lovers. The lordly mansion is home of BC's lieutenant-governor and is often used to accommodate visiting royalty.

■ **Horticultural Centre of the Pacific:** On Beaver Lake Rd, west of West Saanich Rd, 479-6162. Daily dawn to dusk. A 44.5ha gardeners' haven, where flowers are blooming every month.

■ **University of Victoria:** 14 parklike hectares within campus have jogging trails, and in spring, a blazing glory of rhododendrons. Duck ponds, and nearby, an English skylark nesting field. See *Swartz Bay to Victoria*, p.38.

■ **Ross Bay Cemetery:** 1495 Fairfield Rd, near start of Marine Scenic Dr, just beyond Clover Point. Some 27,000 graves on 11ha site. This is final resting place of such notable British Columbians as Robert Dunsmuir, Emily Carr, Sir James Douglas, and Sir Matthew Baillie Begbie, BC's first magistrate, known as "the Hanging Judge." Because little burial space is left, this cemetery is becoming more and more an historic park, invaded by strollers, joggers, artists, tourists, and scholars. A cemetery for the living, one might say. Old Cemeteries Society: Box 40115, 27-910 Government St, Victoria, BC, V8W 3N5, 384-0045, offers tours of Ross Bay and other city cemeteries in spring, winter, fall, and just Ross Bay in summer.

■ **Mount Douglas Park:** Summit of Mt Douglas provides beautiful views over city. Beaches below forests of fir and cedar are a favourite family picnicking place. Marine Scenic Dr continues through park, beyond Cordova Bay toward Hwy 17 on Saanich Peninsula.

■ **Saxe Point Park:** At south end of Fraser St, in Esquimalt. Sea breezes, waves, views of the Olympic Mountains, walking trails.

## *Windy Fringes*

The main similarity between Victoria and other island centres is the variety of outdoors opportunities. The attractions, both man-made and natural, in and around the city provide activities for cyclists, hikers, sightseers, canoeists and kayakers, sailors and boaters, joggers, naturalists, photographers, anglers, and general outdoors enthusiasts.

■ **Harbour Walkway and Victoria Harbour Ferries:** A close-up perspective of Victoria's raggedy shores via footpath and wee ferries. It's 10km or so from West Bay in Esquimalt to Ross Bay beyond downtown Victoria; most of the route is boardwalk and pathway. The first 2km stretch from West Bay Marina, called Westsongway, passes the new Songhees hotel-condo site, ending up at the Johnson St Bridge. The next 3km offers a slight detour around some of Victoria's oldest architecture, then connects with the Inner Harbour walkway, or another detour up onto Belleville St, and more walkway to Fisherman's Wharf. The next 6km skirts by the Canadian Coast Guard, Ogden Point, cruise ships, the breakwater, Dallas Rd, Beacon Hill Park, hang-gliders, windsurfers, sea gulls, Olympic Mt views, Clover Point.

Victoria Harbour Ferries connect points along the first 5km, picking-up and dropping off at West Bay Marina (near Spinnaker's Pub – home brew, halibut and chips), Songhees (Ocean Pointe Resort is here), Inner Harbour (the Empress for tea), Coast Harbourside, Fisherman's Wharf (Barb's fish and chips). And they scoot up the Gorge, stopping at Point Ellice House.

■ **Mile Zero and Marine Scenic Dr:** At the foot of Douglas St on the waterfront at Dallas Rd. Start of the Trans-Canada Hwy. Also start of Marine Scenic Dr that follows waterfront for about 30km to south end of Saanich Peninsula. A relaxing drive or bicycle ride with constant views of sea and Olympic Mountains.

■ **Victoria Beaches:** The beaches along Marine Scenic Dr are pleasant places to bask in summer sun or cool off with a dip in the chilly sea. Popular sunbathing beaches are Gonzales Bay, Shoal Bay, Willows Beach, Cadboro Bay, Mt Douglas Beach, and Cordova Bay. On the other side of Victoria: sandy shores at Esquimalt Lagoon, Witty's Lagoon, and Weirs Beach. But summer swimmers beware: BC's capital city, in spite of its recent rapid growth, continues to dump raw sewage into the sea – waters are tested and warnings posted when fecal coliform counts become dangerously high for swimming.

Victoria is hit by an average of eight winter gales a year, and these same balmy sunbathing beaches become particularly invigorating for beach walkers in a pitiless winter downpour and howling wind.

■ **Capital Regional District Parks:** Protecting and making accessible the most magical spots, offering nature walks, summer programs, nature houses. Parks are listed in *Logs*. For more info: Capital Regional District Parks, 490 Atkins Ave, Victoria, BC, V9B 2Z8. 478-3344 or 474-PARK.

■ **Victoria's Golf Courses:** There are 12 in Greater Victoria, both public and semi-private. Visitors are welcome at the semi-private clubs, though reservations should be made. Courses are situated in some of city's most scenic locations: ask at infocentre.

■ **Strategic Esquimalt:** Only 4km west of Victoria Harbour entrance is Esquimalt Harbour, home of Canada's Pacific naval fleet. Originally the west-coast base for the British Royal Navy (since 1865), Canadian Forces Base here today is a large centre with dockyards, moorings, and administrative quarters. Esquimalt was incorporated as a municipality in 1912. An older section of Greater Victoria, Esquimalt has several heritage buildings and numerous beaches with excellent views of Victoria Harbour and Juan de Fuca Strait. Much of Esquimalt's intriguing military history is depicted at the CFB Esquimalt Naval and Military Museum, 363-4395. Built in 1891 as an annex to the Royal Naval Hospital, the museum is inside the CFB Esquimalt gates, and open weekdays 10am-2pm.

■ **Whale-Watching Tours:** Ask at infocentre about excursions in search of killer whales, porpoises, sea lions, seals, and marine birds in waters around Victoria.

■ **Sea-Monster Spotting:** Cadborosaurus is said to have a horselike head and dragonlike tail, and bears a resemblance to the west coast native people's *Huyitliik*, "who moves by wiggling back and forth." Scientists believe in him...her. The best evidence so far is a photo of a half-digested infant serpent found in the stomach of a whale at a Queen Charlotte Islands whaling station in 1937. Statistics over the last century average one (reported) sighting a year. A relatively high proportion of these have been made in waters in and around Cadboro Bay.

### Victoria Attractions

■ **Anne Hathaway's Cottage:** 429 Lampson St, 388-4353. Daily tours. Outside downtown Victoria, in Esquimalt, Olde England Inn and Anne Hathaway's Cottage are part of a re-created 16th-century English village.

■ **Miniature World:** 649 Humboldt St, 385-9731. Daily. Displays in miniature, with figurines hand-carved by Canadian artists, depicting historic events, nursery rhymes, industry. A must for model-train and toy-soldier buffs.

■ **Royal London Wax Museum:** 470 Belleville St, 388-4461. Daily. Queen Victoria and Princess Di are among more than 200 wax figures.

■ **Undersea Gardens:** 490 Belleville St, 382-5717. Daily. Next to wax museum below harbour's Causeway. Descend beneath the sea for a look at native marine life.

## Victoria to Port Renfrew

### SOOKE ROAD (Highway 14)

Highway 14, or Sooke Road, is also known locally as the West Coast Road. It begins at Colwood Corners, on the outskirts of Victoria, and runs 95km to the village of Port Renfrew. To reach the start of Hwy 14, head north on Hwy 1 from Victoria and take the Hwy 1A underpass.

Hwy 14 leads to destinations along the southwestern side of Vancouver Island. The seashore here is exposed to weather systems that sweep down Juan de Fuca Strait, giving it a more rugged appearance than the other side of Victoria. The highway itself reflects that: it can be narrow, and sharp corners often creep up under thick west-coast fog banks. An added danger is the temptation, while taking corners at highway speeds, to scan the shimmering horizon for freighters, pods of killer whales, or whatever other adventures might be out there.

**Galloping Goose Regional Trail:** One of Canada's first "rail-to-trail" conversions, still under development. 47km long, but only 30m wide. A linear park on abandoned Canadian National Railway line. It begins on Atkins Ave, about 100m after Hwy 1A underpass when heading to Colwood. Turn right off Hwy 1A and watch for signs. Info (on this and other regional parks) from parks office at 490 Atkins Ave, Victoria, BC, V9B 2Z8, 478-3344 or 474-7275 (recorded info). Built for hikers, horse riders, and cyclists, it runs through communities of **View Royal, Colwood, Langford, Metchosin** and **Sooke**, all the way to abandoned **Leechtown**. It offers woods, creeks and ocean views. Trail, trestles and bridges currently upgraded for about 37km from Atkins Ave to Sooke Potholes Provincial Park. Can be hiked beyond Roche Cove. Trail is named after the historic gas-powered rail bus that carried passengers on the line to Leechtown.

**Fort Rodd Hill and Fisgard Light:** 42.5ha. 603 Fort Rodd Hill Rd, 363-4662. Daily 10am-5:30pm. Turn-off to Fort Rodd Hill 400m before Colwood Corners. Deer, arbutus, Douglas fir forests, and manicured lawns adorn this historic site at western entrance to Esquimalt Harbour, once a strategic defence position. Fisgard Light was the first on BC coast. Built in 1860, still operational. Military artifacts and modern exhibits. No pets.

**Colwood Corners:** Beginning of *Victoria to Port Renfrew* route. Set your trip gauge now. North leads to Hwy 1A and Hwy 1; west, to Hwy 14.

**Colwood:** (Pop. 13,468). 18km west of Victoria city centre. Incorporated 1985, the city of Colwood is one of BC's newest municipalities. Originally one of four large farms established outside Fort Victoria by Puget's Sound Agricultural Company. The 243ha farm, partially cleared in the 1850s, was named after a residence of EE Langford, who operated the farm.

**Colwood Information:** Infocentre, Juan de Fuca Chamber of Commerce, 697 Goldstream Ave, Victoria, BC, V9B 2X2, 478-1130 or 478-3242. Chamber of Commerce office and infocentre at corner of Hwy 1A (Goldstream Ave) and Millstream Rd in Langford, 2km north of Colwood Corners. Next door to Goldstream Region Museum. Open till 7pm in summer.

**Royal Roads Military College:** Sooke Rd, .5km west of Colwood Corners. 363-4660. Grounds open daily 10am - 4pm. Royal Roads Military College occupies Hatley Park, an elaborate estate built in 1908 by Robert Dunsmuir, who also built Craigdarroch Castle in Victoria. Centrepiece of property is stately Hatley Castle. Italian, Japanese, and rose gardens. College buidings are not open to the public

**Metchosin Rd:** South turn off Hwy 14, 2km west of Colwood Corners. Alternate route to Sooke offering a string of superb nature-viewing spots.

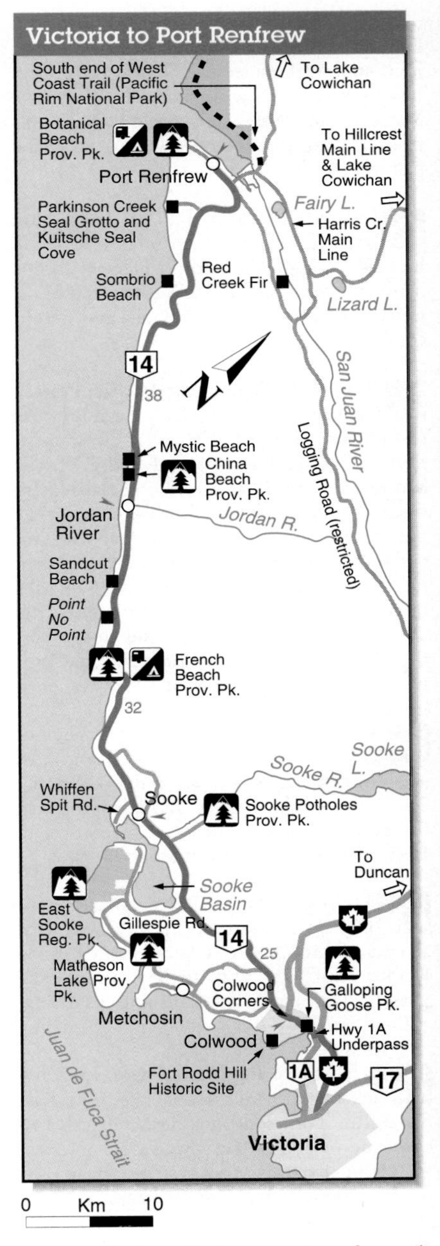


## SIDE TRIP

### to Metchosin and East Sooke

**Albert Head Lagoon Park:** 6.9ha. On Metchosin Rd turn south at Far Hill Rd (just past gravel pit), right at Lower Park Dr. Wildlife sanctuary, cobble beach for picnicking and sunbathing. Views of Albert Head, Strait of Juan de Fuca and Victoria skyline. Lagoon north of beach is home to an abundant wildlife population, including elegant swans.

**Witty's Lagoon Regional Park:** Parking 7km from turnoff at Hwy 14. 56.5ha. Guided walks, map at parking lot. 474-2454

or 474-7275. Birdwatcher's paradise. Luxuriant forests of Douglas fir and sword fern, and creeks surround Sitting Lady Falls. Long sandy beach with rocky shore leads to Tower Point. Seals and great blue herons make regular appearances. Marked trails and picnic grounds.

**Devonian Regional Park:** 13ha. 5km beyond Witty's Lagoon on William Head Rd. 478-3344. Nature sanctuary tucked between Metchosin farms. Walking and bridle trails, birdwatching, picnicking, and beachcombing.

**Pearson College of the Pacific:** Pearson College Dr. Take William Head Rd from end of Metchosin Rd. 478-5591. On shore of idyllic Pedder Bay. One of eight United World Colleges. Provides 200 scholarships to students from around the world who complete the equivalent of grade 12 and first-year university. Tours by arrangement Oct-April. Hosts many sea-sonal programs, including the mid-summer Metchosin International Summer School for the Arts, and co-sponsors the summer Rediscovery International program for indigenous teenagers.

**Metchosin Schoolhouse:** Corner of Metchosin and Happy Valley roads. Turn west at end of Metchosin Rd. 474-3167. Sat-Sun afternoons, April-Oct. First school in BC after province joined Confederation in 1871. Opened 1872, closed for good 1949.

**Matheson Lake Provincial Park:** 162ha. Turn west onto Happy Valley Rd at end of Metchosin Rd, then south onto Rocky Point Rd. 5km to Matheson Lake turnoff. Trail circles lake. Fishing, canoeing, swimming.

**East Sooke Regional Park:** 1,422ha. Just beyond Matheson Lake, take East Sooke Rd. Turn south on Becher Bay Rd or continue to end of East Sooke Rd to park. 478-3344. Extensive trail system can be confusing without maps: stop at Regional Parks' office (see *Galloping Goose Regional Trail* above) for maps. If planning long hike, allow for ample daylight hours. Do not leave any valuables in your car.

A major hiking and outdoors destination, for both the day-tripper and experienced adventurer. Especially invigorating in howling winter gales (check marine weather by calling 656-2714). Beautiful old forests of western red cedar and hemlock, Douglas fir, stately sitka spruce, stunted shore pine, and twisted arbutus. Bald eagles watch from forest's edge while pelagic cormorants and other divers fish along the rocky shores. River otters and mink scurry between driftwood logs and big sea lions are commonly seen swimming offshore Sept-May. Patient nature lovers are occasionally rewarded with a glimpse of willowy mist shooting from the blowholes of passing killer whales. Trails here vary from simple seaside strolls to rugged routes for the hale and hearty. Most challenging is the 10km Coast Trail, a six- or seven-hour trek along entire southern shoreline of the park. Inland trails to Mt Maguire (272m) and Babbington Hill (228m) lead to sweeping views of Juan de Fuca Strait and Washington's Olympic Mountains. Open fields and small beaches, many with offshore isthmuses and islets, make excellent picnic sites. Spin-casting for salmon is particularly good near kelp beds off Creyke Point and Beechey Head, at park's eastern end. On the northeast side, Anderson Cove is a tranquil backwater. Canoeists and kayakers can launch from a trail for an afternoon paddle around the sheltered waters of Sooke Basin and Sooke River estuary.

## Return to Highway 14

**Gillespie Rd:** 16km west of Colwood, just beyond 17 Mile House Pub. Road connects East Sooke Rd and Hwy 14. From here Hwy 14 skirts Sooke Basin and harbour.

**Roche Cove Park:** 117ha. South off Gillespie Rd, 3km. Ancient cedar forest, ocean views, trails.

**Sooke Potholes Provincial Park:** 7ha. 28km from Colwood. Turn north at Sooke River Rd. Nearly 5km to park. Cool, clear swimming holes. Often packed on hot summer days. Salmon spawning in autumn.

**Sooke Region Museum and Art Gallery:** 23km from Colwood, Sooke side of Sooke River Bridge on Hwy 14. 642-6351. Houses infocentre. An interesting look at pioneer life: actors invite guests into Moss Cottage and entertain them as if they were visiting a working family at turn of the century. Collection includes logging and fishing artifacts, Coast Salish objects, and a reconstruction of Sheringham Point Lighthouse. Afternoon teas and salmon barbecues. The art gallery features the work of a local artist each month, and annually hosts one of BC's largest juried art shows attracting hundreds of artists and thousands of art lovers. Closed winter Mondays.

**Sooke:** (Pop. 9,000). 24.5km west of Colwood. Bustling community overlooking the sheltered waters of Sooke Harbour, western Canada's southernmost harbour. In summer of 1864, this was a daily drop-off point for as many as 100 men who came to work some 40km of gold diggings on the Sooke and Leech rivers, 16km upstream from the sea. In the gold-rush frenzy, politicians predicted the area could employ 4,000 men. But within a year, after $100,000 worth of gold was taken, the rush was over. Sooke now is a logging and fishing community, famous for the logging events at its annual All Sooke Day and equally renowned for its excellent year-round salmon fishing. Infocentre has info on marinas, boat rentals, fishing charters.

Sooke Harbour is protected from choppy seas of Juan de Fuca Strait by a narrow strip of land known as **Whiffin Spit**. From the spit, the harbour stretches nearly 5km along the shores of downtown Sooke before opening onto Sooke Basin, a sheltered backwater twice the size of the harbour. Excellent paddling territory. Commercial fishermen mooring at government wharf in Sooke Harbour often sell fresh seafood from their boats.

Gourmets who want to sample local seafood and other produce can settle into a seaside seat at the Sooke Harbour House, a hotel and restaurant on Whiffin Spit Rd given top ratings in international gourmet magazines. Only BC cuisine – sea urchins, scallops, shrimp, geoducks, whelks and periwinkles, moon snails, flying squid, a variety of fish, and two dozen types of crab – are served here. Most meats – grass-fed lamb, suckling pig, rabbit, veal – are bought from nearby farms. Herbs and vegetables are grown on the restaurant grounds.

Sooke is an explorer's haven with dozens of activities organized through Edward Milne Community School. There are boat tours to sea caves and sea-lion haulouts, heritage tours by land and sea, lectures on astronomy, modern and natural history. Cruises aboard a classic yacht and helicopter trips to mountaintops, ancient forests, and remote beaches have been offered through the school. There has even been a big-band concert at Whiffin Spit, where the National Reserve Band from Halifax played on a barge moored in the harbour. For information call Edward Milne Community School, 642-6371, or check with infocentre.

**Sooke Information:** Travel Infocentre operates from Sooke Region Museum, Box 774, 2070 Phillips Rd, Sooke, BC, V0S 1N0. 642-6351.

**Whiffin Spit Park:** Short drive down Whiffin Spit Rd, 27km west of Colwood, on outside of town heading toward Port Renfrew, to 1,200m spit with Juan de Fuca Strait on one side, Sooke Harbour on other. The sand and gravel spit, a local landmark, was split by violent winter storms in 1983 and '84, prohibiting people from walking the entire spit at high tides. In 1989 the Sooke Community Association coordinated repairs, and now beachcombers once again can walk its full length. Sooke Harbour House within spitting distance.

**West Coast Beaches:** Between Sooke and Port Renfrew there are trails to several enchanting undeveloped beaches – **Gordons, Sandcut, Mystic, Sombrio** – on the shores of Juan de Fuca Strait. Many of these wash up enticing treasures, particularly after a storm. Beachcombing is not allowed in provincial or national parks. Use perseverance in searching for trailheads, sometimes signs are missing.

**French Beach Provincial Park:** 59ha; 69 campsites. 46km west of Colwood. 387-4363. Wooded trail to beach. Good views across Juan de Fuca Strait to Olympic Mountains. Hiking, spin-casting, wildlife, birdwatching.

**Point No Point:** 49km west of French Beach. Tearoom and cottages. Trails along shore and over headland with twisted trees battered by furious storms. Named for

*Beaver Lake Regional Park, near Victoria.*

confusion it caused early hydrographers who saw a distinct headland from one viewpoint, but no point at all from another. Don't miss the point of Point No Point, a 400m jutting land and rock mass breaking up ferocious waves. Grey whales delight visitors in spring and autumn; orcas pass by in summer.

**Sandcut Beach:** 52.5km west of Colwood, sign-posted trail to lovely beach. Walk up Sandcut Creek, which cascades onto beach. Delicious potholes.

**Jordan River:** (Pop. 284). 57km west of Colwood. A small logging community and home of the Jordan River Surf Club, where heavy surf pounds the shore off the river's mouth. A national magazine described these beaches as the "pumping hypothermic heart of Canadian surfing." Travel info is provided by infocentre at Sooke; or ask locally.

**China Beach Provincial Park:** 61ha. 61km west of Colwood. Waterfall, tide pools, sandy beach. Trail in leads through forest of giant Douglas firs, hemlocks, and western red cedars. May see grey whales offshore in spring and autumn.

**Mystic Beach:** About 62km west of Colwood. Steep trail to beach with waterfall dropping to shore. About 20 minutes' walk in, more coming back: no high heels on this trail. Mystic takes on new meaning here, as clearcuts gape beneath layers of eerie fog.

**Sombrio Beach:** About 80km west of Colwood. Site of an unsightly clearcut, which was once the last unlogged old-growth forest within a reasonable day-trip of BC's capital city. The hillside was logged despite widespread public objection, leaving only a small fringe of trees along the beach. About 10 minutes' hike in and may be very muddy. Visitors are rewarded with a long, sweeping surf-battered shore and picturesque creek flowing across one end and sea caves at other. Several elaborate squatters' shanties are built with materials from the great lumberyard of the sea. This is a very popular surfing spot.

**Parkinson Creek Seal Grotto and Kuitsche Seal Cove:** Site of proposed 42ha parkland to protect two unique seal colonies. To Parkinson Creek Grotto, a summer seal haven: turn south on unmarked gravel logging road 90km west of Colwood, just before long hill into Port Renfrew. 4km road is accessible to four-wheel-drive vehicles and hikers only. Past road's end, follow 400m rough pathway to waterfront. Grotto is a 3,000-sq-m natural cavern in seaside cliff connected to the open sea by wide chasm and underwater tunnel. The grotto's two waterfalls and four caves are retreat for west coast seals in the birthing season, May-Sept. Good viewing of seals and pups basking in the summer sun at caves' internal beaches, haulout ledges and beaches' expansive rocks. In winter, seals congregate at the Kuitsche Seal Cove, a 6km hike east along the waterfront from the grotto. A small U-shaped cove enclosing a reef is communal home to seals in winter. Cove's steep treed bluff and surrounding trails allow even more viewing than at the grotto.

Both areas are home to up to 75 seals per season, and the area is also prime viewing territory for orcas, bears, eagles. Grey whales feed at nearby kelp beds. Sooke resident volunteers, who built trails and natural viewing blinds, have been lobbying to preserve the seals' seasonal home as an ecological reserve. 642-6371 or 642-5371.

**Red Creek Fir:** About 94.5km west of Colwood. Sign-posted 12km gravel road to trail leading to Canada's biggest Douglas fir, when you combine tree's height with diameter. 73m to its broken top, it has spent over 900 years filling out to its current 4m diameter. The sole survivor of a well-worked industrial forest, it stands alone amidst slash burns and salmonberry.

**Port Renfrew:** (Pop. 158). At end of Hwy 14, 95km west of Colwood. Port Renfrew is in a scenic setting at the mouth of the San Juan River on Port San Juan. This small community serves many purposes. It's the southeast end of Pacific Rim National Park's famous **West Coast Trail**, a 77km tramp along the rugged southwest coast of Vancouver Island. It's also the starting point of logging roads to **Cowichan Lake**. This area is quintessential west coast – wet weather, lush forests, and outdoor adventure on all sides. The entire area is heavily used by hikers, beachcombers, paddlers, anglers, and hunters.

In 1988 the village's only general store burned down, but it has been replaced by Port Renfrew Cash and Carry.

**Port Renfrew Information:** Provided by the Travel Infocentre at Sooke or at West Coast Trail information centre (see below).

**Pacific Rim National Park:** In 1992, a reservation-registration system was implemented to reduce impact of traffic on the West Coast Trail. Each day the West Coast Trail is open, (May 1-Sept 30), 52 hikers are allowed into the trail; 26 from the northern terminus (Pachena Bay) and 26 from the southern terminus (Port Renfrew). Reservations are taken beginning March 1 for the upcoming hiking season only. For reservations, 728-1282.

A park information centre (647-5434) for hikers starting out from the southern end of the West Coast Trail is located at Deering Rd, 2km west of the entrance to Port Renfrew. Pre- and post-trip accommodation and transportation information available here.

**Botanical Beach Provincial Park:** 350ha. 4km beyond Port Renfrew. Follow Hwy 14 to its end. Sign indicates left turn on extremely rough 3.5km gravel road to Botanical Beach. Right turn to old Port Renfrew Hotel and government wharf. Botanical Beach, at the entrance to Juan de Fuca Strait, is one of southwest Vancouver Island's most intriguing beaches. Natural amphitheatre for would-be thespians; deep, clear tide pools, some teeming with marine life, others empty. Odd formations carved in sandstone from tidal erosion. Good viewpoint for Pacific grey whales, especially during spring migration.

Professor Josephine Tilden, University of

Minnesota, arrived here by native canoe in 1901. She and her students operated a marine biological station for about five years, but their efforts were inhibited by the lack of a road. The marine life here has been studied extensively by several universities. If you're travelling to Botanical Beach to see the intertidal life, it's pointless to go at high tide: check local newspaper under "Tofino Tides" for a day when there are good low tides during daylight hours.

**Deering Road:** 97km west of Colwood Corners. Turn north off Hwy 14 to begin 54.5km logging road to Lake Cowichan.

## SIDE TRIP

### to Lake Cowichan

**Logging Roads:** At junction just past wooden bridge. Signs posted. Turn east on Harris Creek Mainline to Lake Cowichan. Groves of second-growth Douglas fir and hemlock along winding, partially paved logging road. Outdoor options abound along rugged route. Swimming, fishing, camping, canoeing; hiking, mountain cycling on rough trails. See map, p.57.

**Fairy Lake:** 5.5km from Port Renfrew. Follow road past head of Port San Juan, crossing bridges over San Juan River, and turn east to campsite. 749-6805. 32ha lake is backwater off San Juan River. 36 camping sites accessible by gravel road. Tables, toilets and fire rings present. Excellent fishing, canoeing and picnicking on sandy beaches. Jointly maintained by users and local logging company.

**Lizard Lake:** On east side of road, about 16.5km from Port Renfrew, near site where Harris Creek runs into San Juan river. 749-6805. 8ha marshy lake with nine camping units. Campsite is vehicle accessible by gravel road. Tables, toilets, fire rings. Swimming, canoeing, birdwatching. Jointly maintained by users and logging company.

**Harris Creek Trail:** 18km from Port Renfrew, near start of rougher, unpaved road. Trail not posted. Following a 400m treacherous descent, courageous hikers are rewarded with refreshing pools of Harris Creek. In fall, the waters here are full of spring salmon, coho, and steelhead.

**Hillcrest Mainline:** About 32km from Port Renfrew. Continue northeast to Mesachie and Cowichan lakes on Hillcrest Mainline. Gravel roads are shared with logging trucks here. Use extra caution during weekdays, and drive with headlights on. Road winds above steep canyons and offers pleasing views, except where recent clearcutting has left richly forested mountaintops with stark bald spots. Harris Creek Mainline continues northwest on logging road to Gordon Bay Provincial Park.

**Mesachie Lake:** End of 54.5km logging road. Small town of Mesachie Lake just east of turnoff. Lake Cowichan, 7km east of turnoff. West to Honeymoon Bay, 5km, and Gordon Bay Provincial Park, 7km from turnoff. See *Lake Cowichan to Bamfield*, p.57.

# The Gulf Islands

The idyllic Gulf Islands lie in the rain shadow of the Vancouver Island Mountains, protected from moisture-laden storms that blow from the open Pacific. Rainfall here, in Georgia Strait, is about one-third as high as on Vancouver Island's west coast. There are some 200 Gulf Islands, but most are small, uninhabited, and without ferry access. Off the north end of the Saanich Peninsula, however, the larger islands are home to more than 11,400 permanent residents, about one-quarter of them retired. While some workers commute daily to Vancouver Island, trade among tourists and retired people still supports much of the islands' burgeoning economies.

The people who live here come from widely varied backgrounds, bringing an interesting, and often controversial, mixture of ideas, vocations, avocations. There are farmers and fishermen, bankers and lawyers, sculptors, authors, shipwrights, realtors, contractors, painters, and poets. These islands are one of those rare places where you choose your own lifestyle, set your own pace. More and more people are discovering this; in fact, the islands' population increased by 27 percent in the last decade.

While the lifestyle may appeal to some, it's the mild climate and inviting landscapes that attract the traveller. You can drive through valleys of pastoral farmland surrounded by forested mountains. From peaks of 700m you can watch ferries weave their ways through island channels. There are sweeping scenes of woods and water, gravel and shell beaches, cottages clustered around quiet coves, sheep, old farmhouses.

Seaside resorts and bed-and-breakfast homes make the Gulf Islands an appealing destination any time of year. Infocentres carry detailed listings of places to stay and some private cottage owners offer their cabins to tourists through newspaper ads. Although provincial campgrounds are limited, some of the nicest camping spots in southern BC are on the Gulf Islands.

The intricate network of waterways among the islands and islets are usually sheltered enough for canoes, kayaks, and other small boats. A rowboat or car-topper gets a lot of use on any Gulf Island. Hiking boots, gumboots, daypacks, and binoculars also come in handy.

The populated islands in southern Georgia Strait – **Salt Spring**, the **Penders, Galiano, Mayne**, and **Saturna** – can be reached by vehicle and passenger ferries from Tsawwassen, on the mainland, and from Swartz Bay, on Vancouver Island. Reservations are taken only for vehicles travelling from Tsawwassen, and sailing schedules vary with seasons and destinations. You can call BC Ferries 7am-10pm daily for vehicle reservations and info on any route or schedule. In Victoria: 386-3431; in Vancouver: 669-1211. Kayakers or canoeists can carry their boats aboard a ferry as hand luggage and some use the ferries to avoid wide crossings between major islands. The hundreds of cyclists who tour the Gulf Islands each year pay a fare for their bicycles.

These major islands have ample services to support their populations gas stations, stores, restaurants. Other Gulf Islands, reached from ferry terminals along the eastern side of Vancouver Island, are covered in the *Log*.

Populations in the Gulf Islands suddenly explode during summer. Many accommodations are booked several months in advance: people who don't book ahead, particularly in summer and on holiday weekends, may find themselves marooned with nowhere to stay. Provincial campgrounds operate on a first-come-first-served basis, so it's wise to head directly from the ferry to a campsite and leave the exploring until later. Fire is a major hazard on all islands and is prohibited in many areas: extreme caution should be exercised with cigarettes and campfires. Water is often in short supply during summer and should be used sparingly. Not everyone here is on holiday: though highways appear as meandering country roads, they are main thoroughfares for locals going about their daily business. Cyclists should ride only in single file and refrain from stopping on tight curves and hillcrests. All beaches are publicly owned, but the privacy of adjacent landowners deserves respect.

## Salt Spring Island

Salt Spring, with more than 180 sq km and 7,500 residents, is the largest and most populated Gulf Island. It was also the first of the islands to be settled, in 1857. And it is the only one with salt springs, 14 briney pools, ranging in size from 1m to 25m in diameter, situated somewhere at the island's north end. The Cowichan native people knew the island's assets better, their name for it was *Chu-an*, "facing the sea."

Because of its proximity to Victoria, Salt Spring has the highest number of commuters and the most frequent sailings – the last five years has seen a tripling of traffic to the island. Ferries to Vancouver Island run from Fulford Harbour to Swartz Bay and from Vesuvius to Crofton. Ferries to the mainland at Tsawwassen run from Long Harbour. There is Harbour Air Service from Vancouver (see *Transportation*, p.77), but island transit services are limited. The Salt Spring Bus Company operates Mon-Fri. There are taxis (537-9712) and car rentals.

The island is not only the largest, but the most diverse, with the highest peaks in the Gulf Islands and a dozen lakes. St Mary Lake, the largest, has some of BC's finest fishing for smallmouth bass, rainbow and cutthroat trout. Stowell, Weston, Blackburn and Cusheon lakes also provide excellent trout fishing.

Many of the attractions can be seen in a whirlwind two-hour, 60km drive, but thorough exploration of Salt Spring could take weeks. Visitors often complain that they didn't realize the island was so large. They leave inadequate time to see much, then go home disappointed. It is almost pointless to allow less than a full day for a trip to Salt Spring.

The island has resorts, hotels, B&B establishments, campgrounds; plus enough arts and crafts galleries and shops to serve a large population. Salt Spring is noted for its community of artists and craftspeople, and often their best work is found only on the island.

**Salt Spring Island Information:** Infocentre, Salt Spring Island Chamber of Commerce, Box 111, Ganges, BC, V0S 1E0. 537-5252. On Lower Ganges Rd in village of Ganges. Year-round. Maps of the island are available here.

The *Log* describes some of the sights you'd see if you landed at Fulford Harbour and explored the main routes.

**Fulford Harbour:** A tiny ferry dock settlement full of island spirit. There are a few cabins perched on the hillside, a grocery store/gas station, post office, Mexican restaurant, ice cream, pottery, curios, and a pub. It's the sort of place you don't mind hanging around, should you miss the ferry back to Swartz Bay. Unless it's the *last* ferry of the day. Make sure to check the schedule.

**St Paul's Church:** Tiny Catholic church overlooking Fulford Harbour. It's a heart-warming sight to travellers approaching the island on the ferry. The church was built between 1880 and 1883. Some building materials used were ferried from Vancouver Island's Cowichan Bay to Burgoyne Bay on Salt Spring, then hauled by oxen-drawn stoneboat (a land-going barge) to the Fulford site.

**Beaver Point Rd and Fulford-Ganges Rd:** Immediately out of Fulford Harbour, the sharp right is Beaver Point Rd. The Fulford-Ganges Rd follows the gentle contour of the harbour – look for geese and swans that winter here – before cutting northwest into Salt Spring's heart.

The *Log* first follows Beaver Point Rd, then returns, tracing the route into Ganges.

**Stowell Lake:** A small trout-fishing and swimming hole on Beaver Point Rd, about 1km from Fulford ferry terminal.

**Weston Lake:** 2km beyond Stowell Lake, Weston is known for its trophy sized trout. Swimming.

**Beaver Point Provincial Park:** 16ha. On Beaver Point Rd. This little park is site of the second-oldest school still standing in BC. It closed in 1951, after educating island youngsters for 66 years.

**Ruckle Provincial Park:** 486ha; 70 mostly walk-in campsites, at end of Beaver Point Rd. 387-4363 or 653-4209. The largest provincial park in the Gulf Islands. A working sheep farm. The original Ruckle home, erected in 1870s, stands near park entrance. Two other homes built around 1908

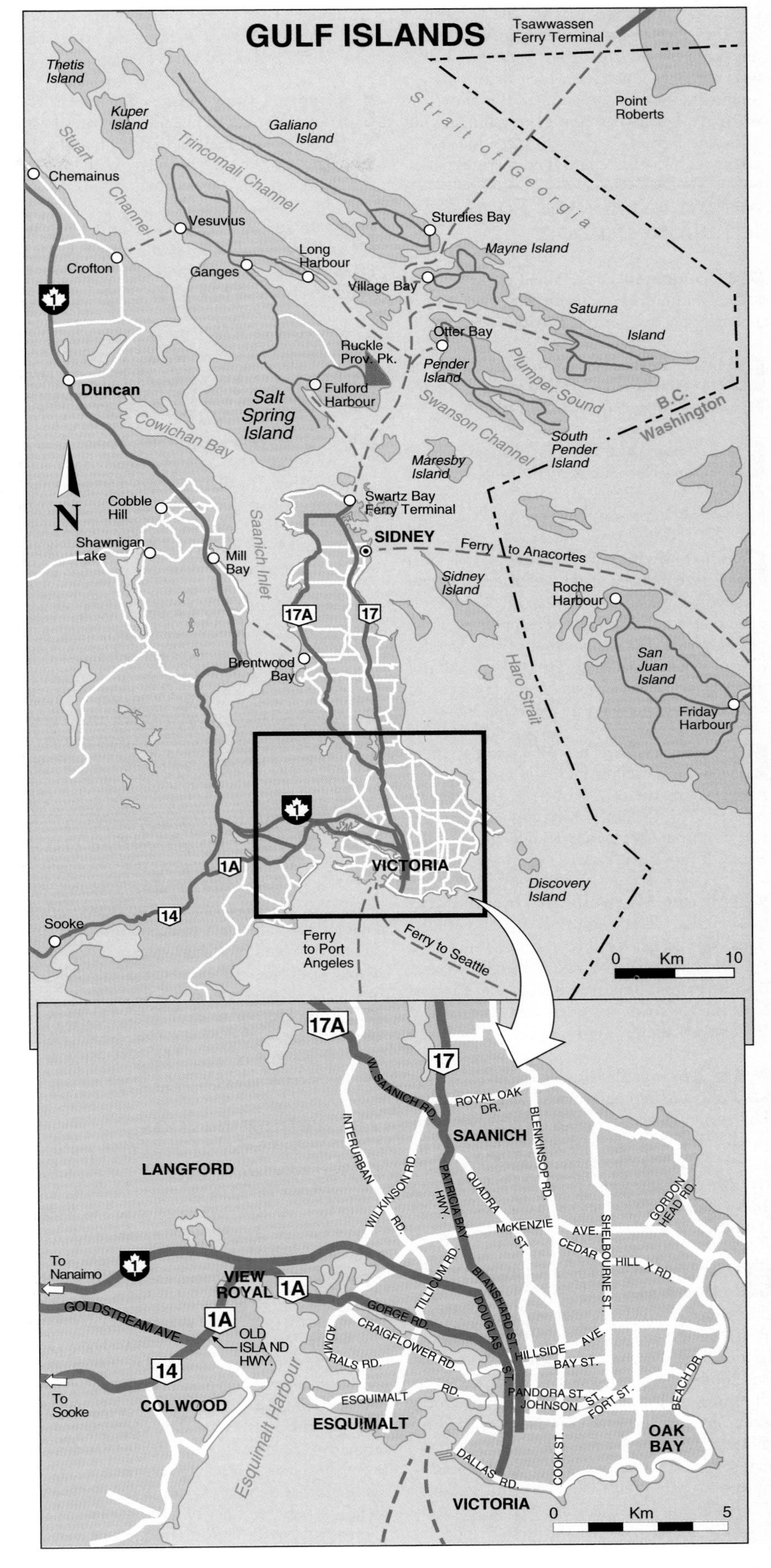

still house members of the Ruckle family. Another farmhouse was built in 1940s, but not occupied until park was established. It is now park headquarters. Much of the park is open, grassy field above a rocky shoreline where BC Ferries pass as they travel in and out of Swartz Bay. It's a pleasant place to walk or just sit and watch the birds and marine traffic.

## Return via Beaver Point Rd to Fulford Harbour

**Drummond Park:** Small park, at head of Fulford Harbour on west side. Site of a petroglyph: a sandstone carving of a seal.

**Bruce Peak:** 698m. On left side as you travel toward Ganges from Fulford Harbour. Highest point in Gulf Islands.

**Cusheon Lake Rd:** Less than 9km from Fulford Harbour ferry terminal. A short distance down the road, Cusheon Lake is a pleasant place for an August plunge.

**Cusheon Creek Hatchery:** Just past Cusheon Lake at corner of Stewart and Cusheon Lake roads. 537-2232. Volunteers operate hatchery in tidy cedar building. Their philosophy is that water safe for fish is safe for people, too. Teaching area where school groups and other visitors can learn how to analyze water and examine fish eggs.

**Cranberry Rd:** Turn off Fulford-Ganges Rd 2km beyond Cusheon Lake Rd. About 7km up this winding dirt road is Baynes Peak (595m), third highest peak on the Islands. Within the 197ha Mount Maxwell Provincial Park.

**Mount Maxwell Provincial Park:** 199ha. Take Cranberry Rd and follow signs. Too rough for RVs and low-slung cars. Breathtaking views of Fulford Harbour and islands beyond, Burgoyne Bay, Maple Bay and Sansum Narrows, between Salt Spring and Vancouver Island. Hiking trails.

**Mouat Provincial Park:** 23ha; 15-site campground at foot of Ganges Hill in the village of Ganges. 387-4363. This small park is a wooded getaway amid the activity of Salt Spring's major commercial centre. Mouats immigrated from Scotland in 1880s. The family is still a going concern on the island.

**Ganges:** (Pop. 1,133). A bustling seaside village, largest in the Gulf Islands, belies the belief that the Gulf Islands are sleepy hideaways on the western edge of Canadian civilization. It's a commercial centre with major development ongoing. There are banks and shopping malls, supermarkets, liquor store, galleries, restaurants, laundromats, public showers, pharmacies, real estate offices, marinas, service stations, and anything else needed by more than 7,500 islanders and visitors. There's an outdoor "Saturday Market", featuring fresh island produce and local artistry, at Centennial Park in the village centre. A new 2km seaside walkway at the park brings harbour bustle and ocean views closer yet.

**Upper-Lower Ganges Rd:** Both lead northwest out of Ganges, linking up with roads to Vesuvius Bay and Long Harbour, for ferries to Crofton on Vancouver Island, or the mainland.

**Salt Spring Island Golf and Country Club:** 9-hole course on Lower Ganges Rd, a short distance beyond Ganges. Open to public every day.

**Vesuvius Bay Rd:** Just beyond golf course. Northwest to Vesuvius Bay; southwest connects Upper Ganges Rd with Long Harbour Rd and ferries to mainland.

**St Mary Lake:** Totalling about 200ha. At junction of the Ganges roads and Vesuvius Bay Rd. This is Salt Spring's main resort area. Excellent trout and smallmouth bass fishing. Unfortunately there's only a small clearing at the roadside for public swimming and boat launching.

**Vesuvius Bay:** At the end of Vesuvius Bay Rd. A handful of unassuming, seaward bent homes, a restaurant, store, motel, and pub featuring local brews and enchanted views of Stuart Channel and Crofton, on Vancouver Island. BC Ferries sail there from here. In 1857, home of island's first settlers – nine American Blacks with newly purchased freedom.

**Sunset Dr:** Leads from Vesuvius to "the north end", the pointy end of Salt Spring, eventually joining up with North End Rd, North Beach Rd, Walker's Hook Rd, Stark Rd, and reconnecting with the Upper Ganges Rd. This is a pleasant tour offering rolling farmland, grazing sheep, and sea views across Trincomali Channel to Galiano Island.

**Long Harbour:** Southeast from Vesuvius Rd and Upper-Lower Ganges Rds junction. At the end of Long Harbour Rd. Site of BC Ferry terminal for sailings to mainland.

## The Pender Islands

North and South Pender Islands, joined by a bridge, encompass 34 sq km, and are inhabited by about 1,300 permanent residents.

Before the turn of the century the Pender Islands were linked by a wide land neck known as the Indian Portage. The islands were separated in 1903, when a canal was dredged, then rejoined by a highway bridge in 1955. About 90 percent of the Penders' residents live on North Pender, mainly around Magic Lake. The islanders have conspicuously marked many of their public beach accesses and there are several quiet coves and bays to enjoy. Many of these places are sheltered, and a small boat opens lots of areas for exploration. Terminal for ferries from both sides of Georgia Strait is at Otter Bay, on North Pender. The *Log* here describes some of the sights you'd find travelling from Otter Bay.

**Pender Islands Information:** No official infocentre but stores and businesses offer maps and advice to travellers. For bicycle tours, call 629-6592.

**Pender Island Golf and Country Club:** A 9-hole course on Otter Bay Rd between ferry terminal and Port Washington. Open to public.

**Port Washington:** On shores of Grimmer Bay, this is a small community with a government wharf.

**Hope Bay:** Another charming community with a government wharf. Trail rides to viewpoints and bird-watching areas. 629-6298.

**Driftwood Centre:** At intersection of Bedwell Harbour and Razor Point roads. The main commercial centre and infocentre for the two islands. Nearby is Browning Harbour with a marina, pub, camping, and accommodation.

**Prior Centennial Provincial Park:** 16ha. 17-site campground. Off Canal Rd. 387-4363. A nicely wooded provincial park, only public campground on the Penders that can be reached by vehicle. Hamilton and Medicine beaches within walking distance.

**Magic Lake:** Down Schooner Way, beyond Prior Centennial Park. Here is a major subdivision which, in the late 1960s and early 1970s, sparked a bitter controversy over development on the Gulf Islands. The debate led to the formation of the Islands Trust, a group of elected representatives who govern the Gulf Islands in much the same manner as a municipal council. Thieves Bay, near the end of Schooner Way, is the location of a private marina.

**Mortimer Spit:** A sandy shore near the bridge between the two islands with sheltered waters, good swimming beaches.

**Bedwell Harbour:** At the end of Spalding Rd. A full-service destination resort and marina. In summer there is a Canadian Customs Port of Entry here for air and sea craft. Also tours to Coast Salish archaeology site at North Pender side of canal. From the harbour a path leads short distance to Egeria Rock. Cliff face is carved with inscription "HMS EGERIA 1904". This British surveying vessel was stationed in Esquimalt, near Victoria.

**Church of the Good Shepherd:** On Gowlland Point Rd, short walk from Bedwell Harbour resort. Rustic, wooden Anglican church built 1938 by Pender Island pioneers. A pleasant place to contemplate. Sunday services.

**Beaumont Provincial Marine Park:** 34ha. 11 campsites. North side of Bedwell Harbour, water access only.

387-4363. One of the most popular marine parks in the Gulf Islands. Can be reached by rowboat from Bedwell Harbour Resort. Trail from the park leads to top of Mt Norman, at 260m, highest peak on the Penders.

## Galiano Island

Galiano is a long, narrow island on the outer edge of the southern Gulf Islands. It's the second largest of these islands, encompassing 57 sq km, with a population of about 800. The driest of the Gulf Islands, it has less than 60cm of rainfall a year. It's an attractive island with secluded beaches, sheltered harbours, and a relaxed pace that seems satisfactory to both locals and visitors. Ferries from both the BC mainland and Vancouver Island arrive on Galiano at Sturdies Bay.

Arts and crafts galleries, B&Bs, lodges, cottages, small resorts, seaside restaurants, bakery, pub, massage therapist, trail rides, kayaking tours, bike rentals and tours, fishing, sailing. The *Log* here describes sights you'd see travelling from Sturdies Bay toward Porlier Pass, at the northwest end of the island.

**Galiano Island Information:** Infocentre, Box 73, Galiano Island, BC, V0N 1P0. 539-2233. On Sturdies Rd near ferry terminal. Open weekends May-June, Sept-Thanksgiving. Daily July-Aug.

**Sturdies Bay:** At eastern end of Galiano Island. This is downtown Galiano, with a lodge, ferry terminal, infocentre, and stores.

**Bellhouse Provincial Park:** On south side of Sturdies Bay at Burrill Point. This rocky, moss-covered peninsula overlooking Active Pass, is the busiest waterway in the Gulf Islands. Spin-casting from shore for salmon, picnicking.

**Galiano Bluffs Park:** About 120m above Active Pass, this local park provides spectacular views of eagles, seabirds, sea lions (spring and fall migrants), seals, and other marine life in Active Pass, between Galiano and Mayne islands. Some of largest ships in BC Ferry fleet run alongside the bottom of the bluffs.

**Galiano Golf and Country Club:** A 9-hole course on Ellis Rd, off Porlier Pass Dr. Open to public.

**Montague Harbour Provincial Marine Park:** 87ha. 18 campsites. 8km from ferry terminal. 387-4363. The most popular provincial park in the Gulf Islands, there are two campgrounds here, one for boaters and bicyclists, one for vehicles. Shell beaches, warm summer swimming, and hiking trails are particularly attractive to families.

**Retreat Cove:** Turnoff 12km along Porlier Pass Dr from Sturdies Bay. Tiny cove with government wharf.

**Spanish Hills:** Officially North Galiano, a one-store stop for sushi, burgers, and groceries. About 25km from Sturdies Bay on Porlier Pass Dr.

**Race Point Lighthouse:** At the northwest end of Galiano Island, overlooking the turbulent waters of Porlier Pass. **Dionisio Provincial Park** (Coon Bay) here, has limited facilities. Open fires are not permitted.

## Mayne Island

A total of 21 sq km, this island has about 550 permanent residents.

Mayne Island, with its BC Ferry terminal at **Village Bay**, has several late 1800s to 1930s buildings to intrigue the history buff. **Miners Bay**, the island's commerce centre, is a pleasant seaside village overlooking Active Pass. When gold was discovered on the Fraser River in 1858, Miners Bay was inundated with fortune seekers travelling between Vancouver Island and the mainland. The bay is precisely halfway between Vancouver Island and the mouth of the Fraser, and was a convenient overnight stop for miners planning to row across Georgia Strait. That is comparatively recent history – middens excavated near Active Pass suggest at least 5,000 years of aboriginal occupation.

There are no provincial parks on Mayne Island, but nice beaches and sea views at **Village Bay, Miners Bay, Bennett Bay, Horton Bay,** and **Piggott Bay**. Sport fishermen often set up bases on Mayne Island to fish the waters in and around Active Pass, which provide some of the Gulf Islands' hottest salmon fishing.

**Mayne Island Information:** Stop at any business for information. Or write to Mayne Island Community Chamber of Commerce, Mayne Island, BC, V0N 2J0.

**Mayne Island Museum:** Opposite the community centre, off Fernhill Rd. Daily in summer. A small museum in a building

*Ganges Harbour, Salt Spring Island.*

which was built in 1896 as the Plumper Pass Lockup. It houses a variety of local artifacts depicting the island's history from the turn of the century.

**St Mary Magdalene Church:** Overlooking Miners Bay with a cemetery adjoining. Built in 1898, the church stands in a beautiful setting of arbutus and fir trees.

**Active Pass Light Station:** This station, on Georgina Point, is a familiar sight to people travelling aboard BC Ferries between Swartz Bay and Tsawwassen. Built in 1885.

**Dinner Bay Community Park:** Follow signs. Barbecue, washrooms. Great view.

**Mount Parke Regional Park:** Ask an islander for directions. Hiking trails and spectacular views from 255m peak.

**Centennial Well:** On Horton Bay Rd is the statue of a bearded angel watching over a well built as 1967 Canadian centennial project. The water is cold and clean.

### *Saturna Island*

Although Saturna Island, with a total of 31 sq km, is larger than Mayne Island, its population is only 250.

There are a few B&Bs and cottages available for accommodation. No public campgrounds. It is largely used by day trippers and bicyclists, but check ferry schedules as service is not as frequent as to other islands. A government wharf next to BC Ferry terminal at **Lyall Harbour** is a good launching point for canoeists or kayakers who want to explore the bays and channels between Boot Cove and Winter Cove.

**Saturna Island Information:** Infocentres in other areas can provide accommodation listings for Saturna, with telephone numbers to call for information. People at the island's two stores and at the Lighthouse Pub are always willing to offer information.

**Mount Warburton Pike:** At 490m the highest point on Saturna Island. Reached by a winding gravel road passing a 131ha ecological reserve, set aside to preserve a typical west-coast forest. Tremendous views from the peak. Named after local pioneer, sportsman and adventurer, Warburton Pike, author of *The Barren Grounds of Northern Canada.*

**Winter Cove Provincial Marine Park:** 91ha. At end of Winter Cove Rd. This provincial park, established in 1979, is a scenic stretch of beach and rocky shore with small marshes and forests above the tide line. It offers trails, picnic tables and other amenities, but no campground.

**East Point:** Site of lighthouse built in 1888, which looks towards the Canada-US border from most easterly point in Gulf Islands. Views of US Coast Guard Station on Patos Island and Mt Constitution on Orcas Island, and of the San Juan Islands.

East Point is a naturalist's paradise with strange formations in sandstone shores, seals, sea lions, and an endless array of seabirds – harlequin ducks, loons, cormorants, sandpipers, herons, and more. It is known as one of the best places in the Gulf Islands to see killer whales in summer. Much of the marine life here is attracted by strong tides that curl around the point, forming back eddies where small fish congregate. Birds and salmon feed on the fish and larger animals prey on the salmon. There's excellent spin-casting for salmon here. A trail leads to the beach that can be walked at high tide. Be careful not to trespass onto private land.

# Victoria to Nanaimo

## TRANS-CANADA HIGHWAY (Highway 1)

This, the westernmost stretch of the Trans-Canada Highway, begins at Mile Zero on Dallas Rd in Victoria, at the edge of Beacon Hill Park. (In downtown Victoria Hwy 1 is Douglas St.) This is the most direct route to the city of Nanaimo, 112km up Vancouver Island's east coast. The southern portion of the route passes through old forests to spectacular viewpoints overlooking the sea and islands. Traffic is growing heavier, especially in summer, though recent highway upgrading is taking the pressure off a few bottlenecks (see *Vancouver Island Highway Project,* p.33).

Farther north, in the Cowichan and Chemainus valleys, scenery gives way to old bastions of the forest industry, and visitors are invited into the work-a-day world of the present and past. There are museums, working boom boats, log dumps, sawmills, a pulp mill, even a "demonstration" forest. Here, too, First Nations people are welcoming visitors to experience the landscape as they know it.

The Trans-Canada Hwy leaves Vancouver Island at Nanaimo where BC Ferries sail to Horseshoe Bay near Vancouver, on the mainland. The *Log* begins in downtown Victoria on Douglas St (Hwy 1).

**Cloverdale Rd:** 2km beyond Victoria City Hall (Pandora St, downtown Victoria). Route to Hwy 17 for Victoria International Airport and BC Ferries at Swartz Bay. Continue on Douglas St (Hwy 1) for this *Log.*

**McKenzie Ave:** 3km beyond Cloverdale Rd. Busy Route to Hwy 17 and the University of Victoria.

**Portage Inlet Rest Area:** Just beyond McKenzie Ave. Overlooking shallow inlet. Boat launch.

**Helmcken Rd:** 2km beyond McKenzie Ave. Victoria General Hospital near Hwy 1. Route to highways 17A and 17.

**Hwy 1A:** 500m beyond Helmcken Rd. Underpass to highways 1A and 14.

**Thetis Lake Park:** 656ha. 11.5km from city centre. A popular swimming spot with sandy beaches and high cliffs. Consists of two lakes, and canoeists can squeeze through a culvert where the lakes are joined. Good trout and bass fishing, ideal paddling with forested shoreline, islands, and no powerboats. Forested trails around lakes.

**Millstream Rd:** 13km beyond Victoria city centre. Leads to bedroom community of Langford.

**All Fun Waterslide Park:** Turn north at Millstream Rd. June-early Sept. 474-3184. Some 10 slides, white-water river run, bumper boats, go-carts, driving range, mini-golf. 100-site RV park year-round: 474-4546.

**Lone Tree Hill Park:** 31ha. North at Millstream Rd. 7.5km on Millstream Rd to park. In the Highlands, overlooking Finlayson Arm. A "heritage tree" at summit: bonsai-like Douglas fir. Bald eagles, red-tailed hawks, turkey vultures.

**Mill Hill Park:** South on Millstream Rd to Atkins Ave. Left 1km to park. Mill Hill summit provides sweeping views of Esquimalt Harbour. Hiking trails through forest and wildflowers, wetlands.

**Goldstream Information:** Infocentre, Juan de Fuca Chamber of Commerce. 17km beyond Victoria city centre. Late May-Sept. Info on Victoria and the western communities.

**Goldstream Provincial Park:** 335ha; 150 campsites, sani-station. Turnoff to campground 18km from city centre; turnoff to day-use area 20km from city centre. 387-4363. Virgin forests of Douglas fir and 600-year-old western red cedar. Ferns, mushrooms, wildflowers, flowering dogwood trees, and others. Trails along river on both sides of Trans-Canada Hwy. Hikes to high viewpoints and waterfalls. Visitor centre and salt marsh area near estuary. Old mine shafts from late 1800s when miners took small amounts of gold. Thousands come to watch salmon spawn here in the fall.

**Malahat Drive:** 16km drive over Malahat Mountain begins at Goldstream Park. Originally a livestock track, sliced through rugged terrain in 1861. Upgraded to wagon-road standards in 1884; became a paved road, over a slightly different route, in 1911. It has undergone repeated upgradings. Spectacular drive.

**Shawnigan Lake South Cutoff:** West off Hwy 1, 28km north of Victoria. This road follows east shore of lake and rejoins Hwy 1 at Mill Bay. (Also a cutoff directly to north end of the lake, see *below.*)

## SIDE TRIP
### to Shawnigan Lake

Shawnigan Lake is a popular summer recreation and cottage area.

**Shawnigan Lake:** 7km drive through forest to lake. Well-established summer vacation area with old cottages and new houses along the lakeshores. Lake is 8km long and about 1km wide. Offers waterskiing, canoeing, swimming, fishing.

**Memory Island Provincial Park:** 1ha. Beautiful island with small beaches near south end of lake. The island was purchased by families who lost sons in World War Two, and presented to the province as a park in their memory. Boat access only.

**West Shawnigan Lake Provincial Park:** 6ha. On northwest side. Take West Shawnigan Lake Rd at intersection about 6km from Hwy 1. Swimming, boating, family picnics. Safe children's beach.

### *Return to Highway 1*

**Spectacle Lake Provincial Park:** 65ha. About 1km north of Shawnigan Lake south turnoff, turn west from Hwy 1. Good trout fishing. Trail around lake.

**Malahat Summit:** 31km north of Victoria. At 352m. Excellent views of lower Saanich Inlet, eastern Vancouver Island's only inlet, stretching 24km from Goldstream Park to Satellite Channel. Access for northbound traffic only.

**Arbutus:** 32km north of Victoria. Try out solar-panelled composting toilets.

**Gulf Islands Viewpoint:** 33km north of Victoria. A very worthwhile stop. Spectacular views across Saanich Inlet to Saanich Peninsula and southern Gulf Islands. Volcanic peak of Washington State's Mt Baker (3,285m) shimmers in background.

**Bamberton:** 36km north of Victoria. Over the next 20 years this former 630ha industrial site and cement factory, presently zoned for forestry and heavy industrial use, may become what some land developers promise will be "BC's first sustainable community". The plan, quite controversial, is to squeeze 12,000 people (three times Duncan's population), 4,900 homes, an 18-hole golf course, offices and commercial space, onto these western shores of Saanich Inlet. Adjacent Malahat Indian Band claims property.

**Bamberton Provincial Park:** 28ha. 50 campsites. 37km north of Victoria, east at bottom of Malahat Dr on Mill Bay Rd. Park entrance 1km. 387-4363. Oceanfront park with sandy swimming beach on Saanich Inlet. Good salmon fishing in inlet. There is a public boat launch farther along Mill Bay Rd at the end of Handy Rd.

**Brentwood-Mill Bay Ferry:** Just beyond Bamberton Park entrance on Mill Bay Rd is turnoff to ferry terminal. Car and passenger ferry across Saanich Inlet to Brentwood Bay, near Butchart Gardens. Sailings every hour and 10 minutes from early morning to early evening. 386-3431.

**Mill Bay:** (Pop. 953). 42km north of Victoria. It's worth a short detour off the highway to explore quiet waterfront streets and Gulf Island views. Nearby Satellite Channel good spot to see seals clamouring on floats and docks. Community is expanding, with service stations, shopping centre, marina, and liquor store. Also government wharf, public boat ramp, swimming.

**Mill Bay Information:** Infocentre, South Cowichan Chamber of Commerce, Frayne Centre, RR 1, Mill Bay, BC, V0R 2P0. 743-3566. On Hwy 1 at Shawnigan Lake-Mill Bay Rd. Daily year-round.

**Shawnigan Lake-Mill Bay Rd:** North end of Mill Bay. This is the north entrance to the community of Shawnigan Lake. 5km to lake and village.

**Shawnigan Lake:** (Pop. 1,020). Public beach on Renfrew Rd across from Mason's Store (turn right at village).

■ **Shawnigan Lake Museum:** In old firehall on four-corner stop in village, open afternoons July and Aug.

■ **Auld Kirk Gallery:** Exhibits work of artists attracted to area. 743-4811.

■ **Merridale Cider:** Along Shawnigan-Mill Bay Rd, turn right at Cameron-Taggert Rd, then right onto Merridale. 743-4293. Year-round tours and sales, Mon-Sat.

Beyond Mill Bay on Hwy 1, the scenery begins to reflect the distance between Victoria's sophistication and "up-island" realities. Highwayside businesses advertise their wares: second-hand goods, antiques, used cars, wood and wood stoves, taxidermy.

**Arbutus Ridge:** 44km beyond Victoria on Hwy 1. Another instant utopia: 676 homes planned, at least half already completed on 300-acre development by Canadian Retirement Corporation of Richmond, BC. 18-hole golf course open to public. Less charitably, "Arthritis Ridge."

**Cobble Hill-Cowichan Bay Roads:** 45.5km north of Victoria; 7km north of Shawnigan Lake-Mill Bay Rd on Hwy 1. West to **Cobble Hill** (village and area pop. 3,000) and **Shawnigan Lake. Quarry Regional Wilderness Park** offers 2-3km hike up Cobble Hill Mt, through mature forest and views over Shawnigan Lake, Gulf Islands, Saanich Peninsula, Cowichan Bay. Road east (Cowichan Bay Rd) leads to Cowichan Bay. Continues beyond bay, reconnecting with Hwy 1.

**Cowichan Rest Area:** East side of Hwy 1 at Cobble Hill-Cowichan Bay roads.

**Victoria to Nanaimo**

## SIDE TRIP
### to Cowichan Bay

**Cowichan Bay:** (Pop. 1,083). At Cowichan River estuary. Sport fishing and forestry village with hotels, pub, restaurants, marinas, charters, fish market. A salty, charming, weathered ambience. Major log dump and sawmill at head of bay. Boom boats operating. Road just north of village leads to Cowichan Indian Reserve (see *Native Heritage Centre*, under *Duncan*).

■ **Wooden Boat Society and Cowichan Maritime Centre:** Village centre. 746-4955.

Write Box 787, Duncan, BC, V9L 3Y1. Society, dedicated to preserving traditional skills, offers courses in small boat-building. Centre's maritime memorabilia shows area's development. Hands-on exhibits. New ecology station has aquarium exhibits of different BC marine habitats, and unusual mini-aquariums with microscopes for eyeball-to-eyeball encounters with little critters like hermit crabs, fan worms, and starfish. Daily in summer; otherwise Sat-Sun afternoons. Local artists in summer.

■ **Cowichan Bay Lawn Tennis Club:** Beyond village near head of bay at intersection of Cowichan Bay and Tzouhalem roads. Second oldest tennis club in British Commonwealth, after Wimbledon. Now a BC Heritage Site. Annual Grass-court Championships since 1887, one week, late June, early Aug. Lawn courts a rare pleasure. Open to public. 746-7282.

## *Return to Highway 1*

**Dougan Lake:** About 51km north of Victoria. Excellent trout fishing.

**Cowichan Station Rd:** 53km north of Victoria. Leads to Cowichan Station and **Bright Angel Provincial Park** on Koksilah River. Lovely cycling territory.

**Whippletree Junction:** 54km north of Victoria; 7km south of Duncan. Open daily. Recreated turn-of-the-century village with 14 restored buildings from Duncan's old Chinatown and elsewhere. Specialty, craft shops.

**Cowichan Golf and Country Club:** 56km north of Victoria. 18-hole, fullfacility course with enchanted views of Mt Tzuhalem. 746-5333.

**Cowichan Bay Rd:** 57km north of Victoria. Northerly turnoff (east) to Cowichan Bay.

**Old Farm Market:** Just beyond Cowichan Bay Rd. People come all the way from Victoria for fresh veggie-and-fruit market bargains.

**Cowichan River:** At southern edge of city of Duncan, 2.5km north of Cowichan Bay Rd. Silver Bridge spans the Cowichan River, Vancouver Island's most popular recreation fishing stream. Rubber rafting and inner tubing, canoeing, kayaking, fishing, swimming, hiking. From its headwaters at Cowichan Lake, the river winds 47km through canyons and forests, past Duncan, then through native reserve and pastoral farmland at its estuary on Cowichan Bay. The river is known for rainbow and steelhead trout and sizable salmon runs. One of only two BC river systems with brown trout, a trophy species introduced to the Cowichan and Qualicum rivers in the 1930s. A particularly accessible river, thanks to the **Cowichan River Footpath**, a 19km anglers' trail that leads to the most popular holes.

**Duncan:** (Pop. 4,301). 62km north of Victoria. A whistle stop at William Duncan's farm in the 1880s, today the main centre for the Cowichan Valley's 50,000 residents. The valley is home of the Cowichan natives, BC's largest band with about 2,200 people. They are known for their fine sweaters, toques, mitts, and other knitted garments. Their heritage is found throughout Duncan, calling itself the "City of Totems." 41 poles have been erected since 1985: some line the highway intersecting the city, most are located in the downtown area, linked by a trail of yellow footprints. A guidebook, available from the Chamber of Commerce for a small price, tells of the carvers, the traditional poles and the non-traditional, such as "Transition," depicting three killer whales and a seal, and the "Rick Hansen Man-in-Motion Pole," featuring the celebrated wheelchair athlete supporting the earth.

Duncan is also home of nationally acclaimed artist EJ Hughes. In 1949, Group of Seven artist Lawren Harris said he was "as distinctive and visionary a painter of the West Coast as Emily Carr." His oil landscapes are realistic, colourful renderings of local beaches, inlets, log booms, ferries gliding into Salt Spring Island's Fulford Harbour, views of Shawnigan Lake. Despite, or maybe because of his national reputation, his work is not easy to find on the west coast. Try the University of Victoria, Victoria Art Gallery, the Vancouver Art Gallery.

To appreciate browse-worthy Duncan, turn west off Hwy 1 thoroughfare.

**Duncan Information:** Infocentre, Duncan-Cowichan Chamber of Commerce, 381 Trans-Canada Hwy, Duncan, BC, V9L 3R5. 746-INFO (4636). On Hwy 1 at centre of town. Year-round Mon-Sat. Also Sun, June-Aug.

■ **Native Heritage Centre:** 200 Cowichan Way, Duncan, BC, V9L 4T8. 746-8119. West turn immediately after crossing Cowichan River on Silver Bridge. Large collection of native arts and crafts and books, Cowichan hand-knit sweaters, multi-media presentation, carving shed, children's program with knitting, weaving and beadwork, restaurant offering native foods. Feast and Legends program in summer. Open daily, year-round.

■ **Cowichan Valley Museum:** 120 Canada Ave, Via Rail or "Duncan" Station. Year round. May-Sept: Mon-Sat (sometimes Sundays too), 11-4. Winter: Thurs and Fri 11-4, Sat 10-1. Call 746-6612 or write Cowichan Historical Society, Box 1014, Duncan, BC, V9L 3Y2. Domestic artifacts, tools, and medical equipment displayed in period room settings. Also photo and archival collection.

■ **Cowichan and Chemainus Valleys Ecomuseum Society:** 160 Jubilee St, Duncan, BC, V9L 3X8. Downtown. 746-1611. Ecomuseum itself is without walls taking in the two valleys' 1,000 sq km. Only one of its type in Canada. Shows legacy of forest industry that developed area. Residents are actively involved in showing visitors their heritage, and the value and beauty of the region. Fascinating information on area sites. Natural history also available here. Daily, April-Oct: woods and mill tours. July and Aug: join in on Skutz Falls walking tours.

■ **Fun Pacific:** 2591 Beverley St, off Hwy 1 at north end of town. 746-4441. Driving range, mini-golf, go-carts.

■ **World's Largest Hockey Stick:** North end of town, near community centre on Hwy 1. It is 63m high; formerly at Expo 86.

## SIDE TRIP

### to Maple Bay

Turn east on the Trunk Rd in Duncan centre.

**Quamichan Lake:** Follow Trunk Rd to Tzouhalem Rd and take turnoff (left) to Maple Bay Rd. A few metres to Indian Rd leading to **Art Mann Park** on lake. Marshy shoreline and island with otters and abundant waterfowl. Especially good birdwatching during fall migrations and spring nesting. Good trout fishing. Launching from shore at park.

**Maple Bay:** (Pop. 1,098). 6km from start of Maple Bay Rd. Seaside community overlooking bay and Sansum Narrows, between Vancouver Island and Salt Spring Island. Municipal park beach, government wharf, marinas, charters, restaurants, shops, pubs. Kayaking, windsurfing, diving. Idyllic.

**Genoa Bay:** Sheltered cove off Cowichan Bay about 8km south of Maple Bay. Take Genoa Bay Rd off Maple Bay Rd and drive to end. Marina, restaurant. Hiking on Mt Tzouhalem.

## *Return to Highway 1*

**Somenos Lake:** Nearly 64km north of Victoria, just north of Duncan. East side of highway. 48ha nesting and wintering habitat, owned by Nature Trust of BC, for some two dozen waterfowl and several upland bird species. Good viewing from highway pullout, or take short trail, about 50m north of pullout to nesting project managed by Ducks Unlimited Canada. Good summer viewing for nesting birds, thousands of wintering waterfowl.

**BC Forest Museum:** 65km north of Victoria. Daily early May-late Sept. 746-1251. On more than 40ha near Somenos Lake. Portrays history of BC's forest industry through indoor and outdoor exhibits. Working sawmill and restored planer mill on the site provide lumber for the museum. Blacksmith's shop, pit saw, and activities such as shake splitting, log sawing, bucking, and paper making. Most intriguing feature is a narrow-gauge steam locomotive that travels through a farmstead, logging camp, and forest, and over the Somenos Lake trestle.

**Hwy 18:** Off Hwy 1, 67km north of Victoria. West 28km to Lake Cowichan. East onto Herd Rd to Maple Bay. See *Lake Cowichan* to *Bamfield*, p. 56.

**Crofton:** (Pop. 1,820). Turn east off Hwy 1, 74km north of Victoria. Overlooking Osborne Bay. One of BC's first instant towns, built in 1902 as a smelter site for copper from Mr Croft's mine on nearby Mt Sicker. Smelter closed in 1908. Since 1957, Crofton has been a pulp-mill town. There are pubs, motels, restaurants, RV park, fishing, swimming at Crofton Beach or Osborne Bay Regional Park. Half-hour hike to Maple Mountain Municipal Park. Ask at infocentre.

**Crofton Information:** Infocentre, Crofton Museum and Community Centre, Box 128, Crofton, BC, V0R 1R0. 246-2456 or 246-4231. Next to BC Ferry terminal at foot of Joan St.

**Salt Spring Island Ferry:** At foot of Joan St in Crofton. Car and passenger ferries to Salt Spring's **Vesuvius Bay** leave Crofton regularly from morning until early evening. 386-3431. For details on Salt Spring Island see *Gulf Islands*, p.46.

■ **Crofton (School) Museum:** Next to ferry terminal. Summer. Features Mt Sicker copper mining and refining industry in Crofton.

■ **Fletcher Challenge Pulp Mill Tours:** 246-6100.

Follow sign-posted back roads from Crofton to the small town of Chemainus, or continue on Hwy 1 for 15km, to Chemainus turnoff.

**Chemainus:** (Pop. 3,900). On Stuart Channel, 2km east off Hwy 1, 78km north of Victoria. Canada's largest permanent outdoor art gallery. Known as "The Little Town That Did," Chemainus, in the municipality of North Cowichan, faced economic uncertainty in the early 1980s after the town's sawmill shut down. But an ambitious revitalization program was launched, centred on the work of talented artists who painted murals depicting the area's history on downtown walls. Now as many as 250,000 visitors a year come to see the 32 larger-than-life murals. The town is becoming a major Canadian art centre. A new sawmill has opened, and Chemainus is now a two-industry town.

**Chemainus Information:** Infocentre, Chemainus and District Chamber of Commerce, Box 575, Chemainus, BC, V0R 1K0. 246-3944. In a red caboose in town centre on Chemainus Rd beside Heritage Square. Daily June-Aug. The Arts and Business Council of Chemainus is open year-round across the street from the historic waterwheel: 246-4701. In summer, a Mural Information Kiosk is open in the heart of Chemainus, next to the first mural, *Steam Donkey at Work.*

■ **Chemainus Theatre:** Corner of Chemainus Rd and Victoria St, downtown. In the building with the dome. Reservations: 246-9820 or 1-800-565-7738. New dinner theatre offers "high cuisine buffet," matinees and evening presentations of popular classics.

■ **Chemainus Valley Museum:** In Waterwheel Park. 246-2445.

**Thetis and Kuper Islands Ferry:** A small car and passenger ferry runs from downtown Chemainus to these two islands. Kuper Island (pop. 271) is native reserve and private land. Thetis Island (pop. 235) is an interesting place for a drive or bicycle ride. Its shores are often explored by paddlers. Summer sea is warm for swimming.

*Wall mural in Chemainus, east coast of Vancouver Island.*

**Mt Breton Golf Club:** On Henry Rd and Hwy 1 (Chemainus turnoff). Box 187, Chemainus, BC, V0R 1K0. 246-9322. 18 holes in a pretty setting.

**Ladysmith:** (Pop. 4,875). 87km north of Victoria. Overlooking its deepwater harbour, Ladysmith is the true Vancouver Island location of the 49th Parallel. This Canada-US boundary was extended south of Victoria to keep all of the island in Canada. Originally named Oyster Harbour for abundant oyster beds in area. Renamed by BC coal-mining magnate James Dunsmuir at time of Boer War, for Ladysmith, South Africa. Streets are named after Boer War generals: Kitchener, BadenPowell, Roberts, French. Town was home for coal miners. Many of the original buildings were brought by rail from Extension Mines near Nanaimo.

Ladysmith bears a slight resemblance to early San Francisco, with its old houses built on steep slopes above the sea.

Local economy turned from mining to forestry in the 1930s. Tourism is increasingly important. Downtown core and heritage buildings have been spruced up. Boat launch.

**Ladysmith Information:** Infocentre, Ladysmith Festival of Lights, Box 98, Ladysmith, BC, V0R 2E0. 245-2218. Look for infocentre sign on Hwy 1. Daily, June-Sept.

■ **Black Nugget Museum:** 12 Gatacre St, half a block off Hwy 1. June-Aug. 245-4846. In a partially restored hotel built in 1881. Native artifacts, period garments, furniture, household goods.

■ **Transfer Beach:** 5ha. Local park on Ladysmith Harbour. Warm summer swimming, picnicking. Horseshoe pitch, shelters, wooded waterfront walkway leading to heritage harbour site, and award-winning Kinsmen Kidland Adventure Playground. RV park.

■ **Ladysmith Arboretum:** On Hwy 1 just beyond Transfer Beach. Open daylight hours. Over 25 species of trees planted in 1947-48. Also "living fossil" tree of unknown species, grown from ancient seeds.

■ **Main Street Ladysmith:** Stroll by the restored heritage buildings on 1st Ave, also art gallery, gift shops, antiques and collectibles. Walking-tour map available.

**Stzuminus Park and Campground:** 90km north of Victoria. 245-7832. Former provincial park was returned to Chemainus natives as part of land claim. *Stzuminus* is native spelling of Chemainus. Visitors are welcome to visit day-use area: swim in Ladysmith Harbour's warm waters; view first-growth Douglas fir, stroll on nature trails. Overnight camping.

**Ivy Green Pullout:** 91km north of Victoria. Fresh mountain water.

**Cedar Rd (south access):** 93km north of Victoria, leads to Nanaimo bedroom community of Cedar, and along a more scenic route, via Yellow Point Rd, to Yellow Point.

## SIDE TRIP
### to Cedar and Yellow Point

The Cedar Rd-Yellow Point Rd junction is 3km east of Hwy 1. From here the road meanders westward and seaward past small farms and peaceful residences, about 8km to Yellow Point, the Yellow Point Lodge, peaceful sea and Gulf Island views, gravel beaches and sandstone shores.

**Roberts Memorial Provincial Park:** 14ha. About 3km beyond Yellow Point. Quiet spot on ocean. Picnicking, swimming, fishing.

**Quennell Lake:** About 4km beyond Roberts Memorial Park. Interesting 121ha canoeing lake with a number of long arms and narrow channels. Noted for its smallmouth bass and trout fishing.

**Hemer Provincial Park:** 93ha. On Holden Lake. Follow signs from Yellow Point Rd. Lovely walk through forest along lakeshore. Easy hiking, horseback riding, fishing, and canoeing.

From here, Yellow Point Rd continues northeast, eventually rejoining Cedar Rd.

**Brother Twelve:** Take Cedar Rd to Harmac Junction, near the Millway Store. Turn left onto Holden-Corso Rd. Follow it into the Cedar District, to Barnes Rd, then Fawcett Rd and Murdoch Rd.

He is long gone, but some of the houses here – now privately owned and renovated – are vestiges of the Twelfth Brother of an occult brotherhood, The Great White Lodge, said to guide the evolution of the human race. A series of remarkable visions led Brother Twelve, a middle-aged English sea captain named Edward Arthur Wilson, to this picturesque knob of land, Cedar-by-the-Sea, in the late 1920s. Here, sounding "the first trumpet blast of the New Age," the prophet shared his visions and accumulated vast sums of money from his thousands of followers. He also sought, and failed to gain world power by influencing the US presidency. The House of Mystery is on a cliff above the boat ramp at the foot of Nelson Rd. Little remains of another settlement on nearby **Valdes Island**.

Ultimately, Brother Twelve moved his utopia 2km across Stuart Channel, to **De Courcy Island**, only accessible by private boat. At the lagoon on the island's south end, now **Pirate's Cove Provincial Marine Park,** he established headquarters, hoarded gold in mason jars, and drove his followers to the point of revolt in the construction of his bastion against Armageddon. Brother Twelve, and his "bizarre" companion, Madame Zee, disappeared with some $400,000 in bank notes and gold. There's some evidence he died in Switzerland, shortly thereafter. There's some evidence he didn't. For more, read *Brother Twelve: The Incredible Story of Canada's False Prophet*, by John Oliphant.

From here Cedar Rd continues north and rejoins Hwy 1 about 11km north of Cedar Rd's south access.

The *Log* proceeds from the south access.

### Return to Highway 1

**Nanaimo (Cassidy) Airport:** Entrance road off Hwy 1, 2km north of Cedar Rd's south access. 95km north of Victoria. Scheduled and charter flights.

**Nanaimo River Bridge:** 97km beyond Victoria. A major recreational fishing stream, Nanaimo River runs more than 60km from its headwaters, west of Green Mountain, through a series of lakes to Nanaimo Harbour.

**Nanaimo Community Hatchery:** Turn onto Beck Rd (at Cassidy Inn), 97.5km beyond Victoria. Write Nanaimo River Salmonid Enhancement Program, 271 Pine St, Nanaimo, BC, V9R 2B7. 245-7780. Follow signs to hatchery: chinook, coho, chum. Open year-round.

**Cassidy Rest Area:** At turnoff to hatchery. Information board.

**The Bungy Zone and Nanaimo Lakes:** About 98.5km beyond Victoria, at Nanaimo Lakes Rd. Your chance to plunge 50m with just an elastic bungy cord tied to your ankles. Box 399, Station B, Nanaimo, BC, V9R 5L3. 753-5867.

Farther on, the Nanaimo River leads to the Nanaimo Lakes for wilderness camping, fishing, and chances to see elk, deer, black bears, maybe even the endangered Vancouver Island marmot. Paved road quickly becomes logging road: visitors must check in at the Fletcher Challenge security gate, about 22km from Hwy 1. Be well informed about road conditions before you head in: this is a route for "responsible" travellers. Contact Fletcher Challenge, 754-3032, and pick up their *Nanaimo Lakes Road Guide.*

**Fiddler's Green Golf Centre:** 100km beyond Victoria. 1601 Thatcher Rd, Nanaimo, BC, V9R 5X9. 754-1325. Offers nine holes.

**Cedar Rd (north access):** 105km beyond Victoria. Another route to the Yellow Point area. Described above.

*The Bastion in Nanaimo, east coast of Vancouver Island.*

**Petroglyph Provincial Park:** 2ha. About 106.5km north of Victoria. Trails to native rock carvings believed to be more than 10,000 years old. Represent humans, birds, wolves, lizards, sea monsters, and supernatural creatures. There are many petroglyphs around Nanaimo. Check with Nanaimo's museum.

**Nanaimo:** (Pop. 60,129). City centre is 3km beyond Petroglyph Park; about 110km north of Victoria. Hwy 19, known as the Island Hwy, begins on the north side of the Pearson Bridge, just past Comox Rd. Hwy 1, the Trans-Canada, crosses the bridge and continues to the east, leaving Vancouver Island at Departure Bay ferry terminal.

Nanaimo, or *Snenymo*, was long ago the meeting site of five separate Coast Salish bands who called themselves "great and mighty people." Later, Nanaimo became a coal mining town, with its first mine opening in 1852. The city was incorporated in 1874, making it BC's third oldest. Mining flourished here until the greater demand for oil in early 1930s spelled the demise of the coal industry.

Today the port of Nanaimo, with six deep-sea docks and a major ferry terminal, is the island's largest export centre, and the second fastest growing community in BC after Kelowna. Known as the "Harbour City," it is a hub of activity with freighters and fishboats, tugs and barges, yachts and floatplanes coming and going in the harbour.

The city is in the midst of major beautification projects: foundries, mills, and other heavy industries that once dominated the downtown waterfront, though still vital to the city's economy, are finding new locations away from downtown in places established specifically for industrial use. Seafront walkways, gardens, lawns, golf courses, and beaches are taking up the space they occupied.

People now can stroll along Nanaimo's waterfront past a new seaplane terminal and the Bastion, the city's most notable landmark, toward Departure Bay. A footbridge – the Lion's Great Bridge – built by the local Lion's Club across the Millstone River, links the walkway to the Queen Elizabeth Promenade. Recent waterfront enhancements emphasize the city's picturesque setting, with the harbour surrounded by wooded islands, the distant peaks of the Coast Mountains rising over Georgia Strait, and at night, the lights of Vancouver.

This city is known for its parks – about two dozen totalling 1,100ha. Visiting them could stretch a stay in Nanaimo to several days. Brochure available at infocentre.

Nanaimo is also known for its abundance of shopping centres. The multitude of shops is good news for consumers who can take advantage of the stiff competition.

Nanaimo's road system can be confusing. There are streets radiating from the old town centre like spokes of a wheel, there are culdesacs, and there are long windy roads leading to heaven knows where. Then there is the highway itself, interrupted by construction projects, mall entrances, driveways, and 19, count them, stop lights. Plans are in the wind for the Nanaimo Parkway, a four-lane expressway with only five lights, coordinated so that through traffic, cruising along the northern edge of the city at 80km-h, will not have to stop. Praise be...

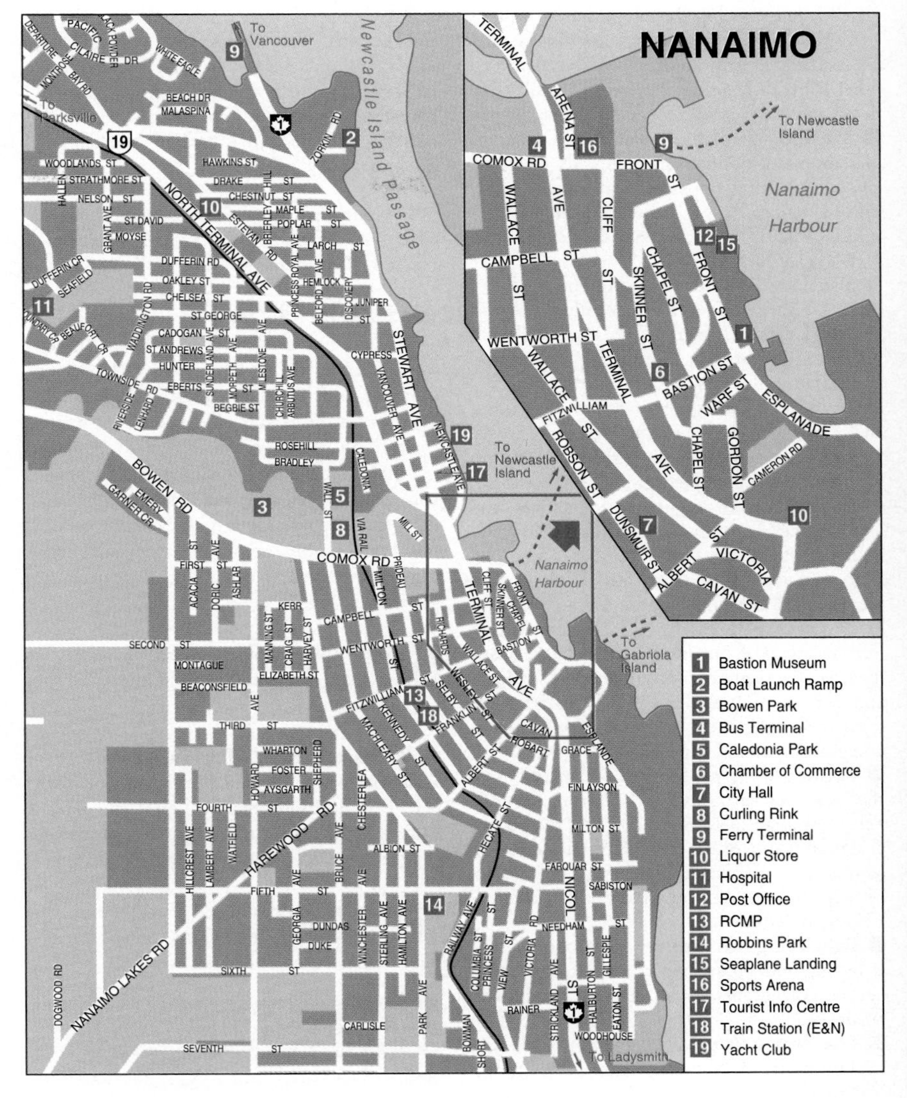


**Nanaimo Information:** Infocentre, Nanaimo Tourist and Convention Bureau, 266 Bryden St, Nanaimo, BC, V9S 1A8. Toll-free 1-800-663-7337 from BC or AB, or 754-8474. Located just beyond the Pearson Bridge at corner of Hwy 19 and Bryden St.

**Departure Bay Ferry Terminal:** At the end of the Trans-Canada Hwy on the north side of city. This is a major terminal for BC Ferries linking Vancouver Island with the Lower Mainland. Ferries from Nanaimo dock at Horseshoe Bay, in West Vancouver.

■ **Nanaimo Centennial Museum:** Adjacent to Piper Park at 100 Cameron St. 753-1821. Daily May-Sept. Rest of year: Tues-Sat. Displays depict human and natural history of Nanaimo area. Coast Salish diorama showing life prior to arrival of settlers. A coal mine, pioneer town, Chinese gallery, reconstructed miner's cottage in Piper's Park.

■ **The Bastion:** Corner of Bastion and Front streets. 754-1631 in summer, 754-8474 in winter. Daily July l-Sept 1. Housed in part of the original Hudson's Bay Fort, the Bastion's collection focuses on the period 1850-1880. Includes insignia, handguns, photographs. Archives of military records, property deeds, and personal documents. Site of Noon Gun ceremony. Each day during summer Bastion guardsmen, dressed in colourful naval uniforms of the 1850s, are led to the Bastion by a piper. Under the orders of an officer a cannon is elaborately cleaned, loaded, and fired over the harbour, a salute to visiting ships and people.

■ **Historic Buildings:** Include the Nanaimo Courthouse, completed 1896; the Palace Hotel, 1889; and Central Drugs, 1900-style pharmacy opened in 1985 (in the 1911 vintage Dakin Building). Adding to the scenic improvements downtown are old-fashioned lamp standards, brick sidewalks, cobblestone streets. Infocentre has guidebook.

■ **Swyalana Lagoon Park:** On downtown waterfront. Site of Canada's first man-made tidal lagoon. Once an abandoned strip of waterfront, lagoon now is a favourite swimming hole and picnic ground. From a bridge across the mouth of the lagoon, people can watch water running through a series of pools and spillways. It's a constant flow that aerates the water for sea cucumbers, starfish, and other subtidal creatures stocked by local scuba divers.

■ **Morrell Wildlife Sanctuary:** Corner of Nanaimo Lakes and Dogwood roads. 111.5ha. 11.5km walking trails and self-guided interpretive walks. Beaver habitats, ponds, rocky knolls. Pacific coast forests, displays, films. 753-5811.

■ **Seaplane Terminal:** Along the walkway toward Fishermen's Wharf. Locally known as the Lighthouse Bistro, this new building resembles a Victorian lighthouse, with a pub and restaurant overlooking the harbour.

■ **Malaspina College:** 900 5th St, Nanaimo, BC, V9R 5S5. A 67ha campus on the lower slopes of Mt Benson with views over Nanaimo Harbour and across Georgia Strait. It features a 276-seat theatre for live performances, the Tamagawa Gardens, an arboretum and the Museum of Natural History. 753-3245.

■ **Nanaimo Art Gallery and Exhibition Centre:** At Malaspina College. 755-8790.

■ **Departure Bay:** Next to Departure Bay ferry terminal. A major recreational area, heavily used by sunbathers, windsurfers, sailors, and swimmers. Includes a public market with fresh meats, produce, bakery goods, seafoods, and gourmet items. Open daily.

■ **Pacific Biological Station:** On Hammond Bay Rd, 2km around the bay from the BC Ferry terminal. Established in 1908, this federal station is one of the largest fisheries research laboratories in Canada, providing information to help manage and enhance Pacific fisheries. Visitors welcome.

■ **Sightseeing Adventures:** At harbour, several fishing and sightseeing charters to see seals, herons, cormorants, eagles, sea lions, and killer whales.

■ **The Bungy Zone:** 35 Nanaimo River Rd. 13 km south of Nanaimo. Box 399, Stn A, Nanaimo, BC, V9R 5L3. Daily, year-round. North America's first Bungy bridge: people leap, lemminglike, with giant rubber bands attached to their ankles, from specially designed 43m bridge over Nanaimo River.

■ **Vancouver Island Military Museum:** 5km north of Nanaimo centre, at Rutherford Village Mall. 255-4750 Rutherford Rd, Nanaimo, BC, V9T 4K6, 756-2554. Open Mon-Sat.

**Newcastle Island Provincial Marine Park:** 336ha. 18 tent sites. Reached by private boat or foot-passenger ferry that leaves from Swyalana Lagoon. Ferry runs several times a day early May-mid-Oct. Weekends rest of year and by request. 753-5141. Canoes, kayaks, and small cartop boats can be launched from ferry wharf or from Brechin Marina, site of a public ramp near Departure Bay ferry terminal (turn toward water on road just before terminal). For overnight parking check with infocentre. Beautiful island in Nanaimo Harbour with steep sandstone cliffs and gravel beaches. Caves and caverns, forests, native middens. Formerly a coal-mine site and luxury resort.

Pavilion, built in 1931, has been restored and is being used again for dances, theatre productions, and other events. Also, displays of natural and cultural history. Interpretation programs in summer. Hiking, swimming, playground, picnicking, paddling, waterskiing, fishing. Snacks and rentals of recreational equipment at Pavilion.

**Gabriola Island Ferry:** Car and passenger ferry leaves from downtown Nanaimo several times daily.

### Gabriola Island

This pretty island totals 50 sq km and has a population of 2,513. Provincial parks at opposite ends of island. Degnen Bay, on the southeast side, is site of island's best-known petroglyph. There are many petroglyphs on Gabriola. Island is also known for the eagles and seabirds that roost and nest on high bluffs. Nature tours operate out of Nanaimo. Pubs, restaurants, shops, accommodation, dive shop, marinas, service stations, golf course, art galleries.

**Drumbeg Provincial Park:** 20ha. On island's eastern end. Swimming, fishing, beachcombing.

**Gabriola Sands Provincial Park:** 6ha, with its Twin Beaches, is on northwest end. Beautiful sand beaches. Near this park is Malaspina Point, site of unusual sandstone galleries caused by frost wedging. Picnicking.

**Sandwell Provincial Park:** 12ha. On northeast tip of island. Sandy beach, lightly forested upland. Day use.

## Lake Cowichan to Bamfield

### (Highway 18)

Truly a side road to adventure: the start of long, unpaved roads cutting right across southern Vancouver Island, from the gentle shores of the east coast to the wave-battered west coast. From cities and retirement communities to logging and fishing villages like Cowichan Bay, Youbou, Bamfield. To ancient forests, like Carmanah, now protected, and others, being logged. From the land of the Coast Salish peoples to where the Nuu-Chah-Nulth live. Please remember that logging roads are the domain of logging trucks: obey signs, turn on your headlights, stay well to the right, keep your eyes on the road no matter how distracting the scenery, and make sure you have a spare tire and the skills to put it on.

**Hwy 18:** Off Hwy 1, 67km north of Victoria, just north of Duncan. See *Victoria to Nanaimo*, p.52, for exact point of departure.

**Mount Prevost:** 1.5km west of Hwy 1, turn north onto Somenos Rd, then drive slightly more than 1km and turn left onto Mt Prevost Rd. About 8km on rough road to parking lot below 786m summit. Great views of Cowichan and Chemainus valleys, and cairn honouring World War Two veterans.

**Cowichan Valley Demonstration Forest:** All along Hwy 18 as far as Lake Cowichan, and around Cowichan Lake's shore. Trail network includes short nature walk perfect for families. Inquire at the BC Forest Museum, or call 746-1251. Signs explain how forest is managed to maintain aesthetic and provide an outdoor classroom of forest management practices.

**Skutz Falls:** South off Hwy 18 about 20km west of Hwy 1. Camping area on bank of Cowichan River. Fish ladders, swimming, fishing, and hiking on Cowichan River Footpath.

**Lake Cowichan:** (Pop. 2,241). 28km west of Hwy 1. On one of Vancouver Island's largest lakes, 32km long by 3km wide. Excellent trout fishing, waterskiing, boating. Private and public campsites. 75km drive around lake.

**Lake Cowichan Information:** Infocentre, Cowichan Lake District Chamber of Commerce, Box 824, Lake Cowichan, BC, V0R 2G0. 749-3788. At entrance to village. Daily mid-June-Labour Day.

■ **Kaatza Station Museum:** 125 South Shore Rd. 749-6142. June-Aug: Wed-Mon. Sept-May: Tues-Sun. In former railway station. Features logging and history. Children can ride a railway pump car. Excellent diorama. Short nature walks on Beaver Creek where beavers are working and herons browsing. Fletcher Challenge Lake Cowichan tours, Mon, Wed, Fri, Feb-Nov, explain forest practices, sights, history, native culture. 749-3244.

**North Shore Rd and South Shore Rd:** From Lake Cowichan village at the east end of Cowichan Lake, one road skirts the north shore, another, the south shore. They meet at the lake's west end, from whence a third logging road leads to **Nitinat Lake, Carmanah Provincial Park,** and **Bamfield**. Below, we follow the North Shore Rd first, then the South Shore Rd. Finally, we continue along that third road toward Nitinat Lake.

### North Shore Route

As you enter the village of Lake Cowichan on Hwy 18, the road skirting Cowichan Lake's north shore leads to community of Youbou.

**Youbou:** Lakeside community 15km west of Lake Cowichan on north shore of Cowichan Lake. Pub, restaurants, marina, stores, accommodation. Last chance for gas before 108km logging road to Bamfield.

From here, it's 23km to junction with South Shore Rd. Pleasant campsites.

## South Shore Route

Start from southwestern end of village of Lake Cowichan.

**Mesachie Lake:** 7km beyond Lake Cowichan. This small community is home of Cowichan Lake BC Forest Research Station, and turning point for 54.5km logging road to Port Renfrew. Open during non-operating hours. Check at Mesachie Lake store. Good fishing at Lizard Lake, 39km from Mesachie Lake. Fishing and camping at Fairy Lake, 49km from Mesachie Lake. See also *Victoria to Port Renfrew*, p.46.

**Honeymoon Bay:** Small lakefront community on South Shore Rd, 12km from Lake Cowichan. Post office, stores, service station, camping, boat rentals.

**Gordon Bay Provincial Park:** 49ha. 130 campsites, sani-station. 14km beyond Lake Cowichan. 749-3415 or 387-4363. One of the most popular family camping parks on southern Vancouver Island with safe sandy beaches, warm swimming. Often full in summer.

**Honeymoon Bay Wildflower Ecological Reserve:** 15km beyond Lake Cowichan. On flood plain of Sutton Creek. Vancouver Island's largest known concentration of pink easter lilies (*erythronium revolutum)*, on display late April. This 7.5ha ecological reserve protects the lilies and two dozen other wildflower species, including wild bleeding heart, smooth wood violet, wild ginger, and white trillium. Area named because local settlers and farmers, Henry and Edith March, spent their honeymoon here.

**Caycuse:** 26km beyond Lake Cowichan. Pretty campsite. The surrounding mountains are now lush with second-growth timber, and quiet. But the nearby community of Caycuse was, until recently, the thriving centre of a succession of logging companies that logged these very hills. It is believed to be the longest operating logging camp in Canada, some say in North America. Layoffs and relocations have left Caycuse practically idle for the first time since 1927. There are hopes Caycuse will be preserved as a heritage site. Ask about it at the **Cowichan and Chemainus Valleys Ecomuseum Society**, 160 Jubilee St, Duncan.

**To Nitinat Lake, Carmanah Provincial Park, Bamfield:** At west end of Cowichan Lake, where North and South Shore roads meet. 25km west of wildflower reserve. Heather Campground is nearby.

**To Nitinat Lake, Carmanah Valley, Bamfield:** 19km from end of Cowichan Lake. Well sign-posted. Bridge across Nitinat River on right leads 65km to Bamfield. Left turn leads nearly 10km to campsite on wind-blown shores of Nitinat Lake.

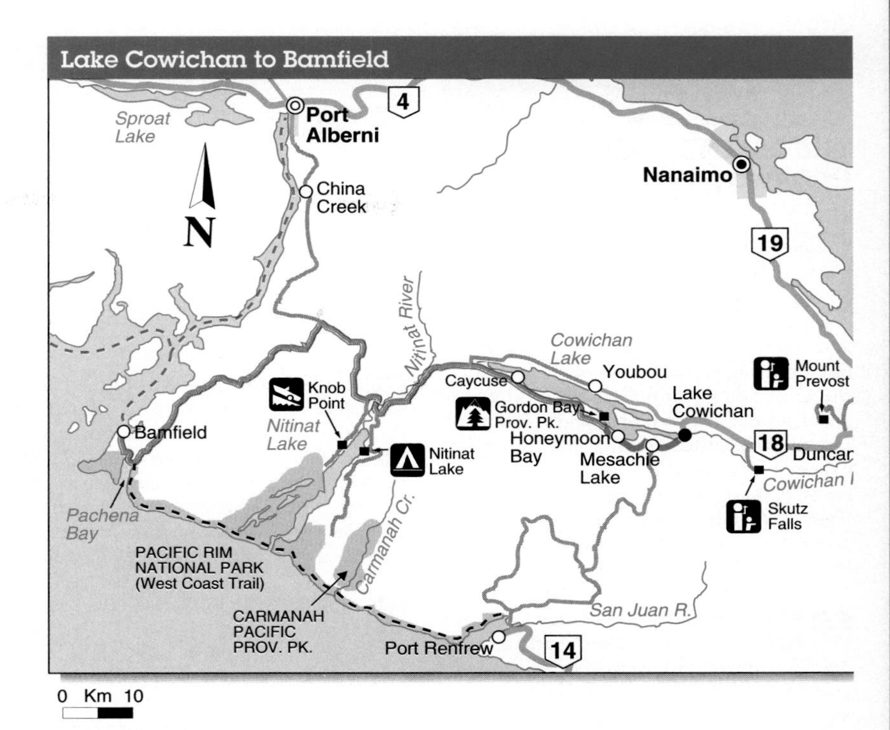


## To Nitinat Lake and Carmanah Park

**Nitinat Lake:** Major base for windsurfers. Nearby Nitinat Wilderness Estates' private RV development has store, windsurfing rentals. Restaurant and more facilities planned. Nitinat Lake is actually something of a tidal inlet, connected to the Pacific Ocean by Nitinat Narrows. This 24km lake smells like the sea, and has tides, "confused sea" conditions, and a pioneering population of sea anemones, jellyfish, and starfish. It is renowned for its constant thermal winds (15-20 knots), providing what windsurfing publications consider to be the best windsurfing conditions in North America. Nitinat Windsurfing Triathlon, Sail-Ride-Run (late July) and Windsurfing Summer Final (late Aug). Private RV and forest service campground at north end of lake.

**Carmanah Pacific Provincial Park:** About 45km beyond Nitinat Lake campground. This extraordinary ancient forest has been recently at heart of industry-vs-environment controversy. As you approach Carmanah, you drive through a vast, dispiriting clearcut. Steep one-hour hiking trail from road to pristine waters of Carmanah Creek. Streamside trails through groves of sitka spruce, some of them believed to be among world's tallest. More than 230 of these spruce stand over 70m high, with trunks 3-4m in diameter. Many are 85m tall, and one, the Carmanah Giant, is 95m – thought to be the tallest tree in Canada, and the largest sitka spruce in the world. There's no public access to lower part of park surrounding Carmanah Giant – these trails are extremely steep, muddy, and dangerous. Wilderness camping only, at upper section, to avoid the danger of flooding and protect the fragile environment. No access from here to the West Coast Trail. Remember, hikers must be prepared for a wilderness park, not a Sunday stroll. Watch for flash floods, as weather systems approaching Vancouver Island are funnelled into the valley. 728-3234 or 647-5434 for trail conditions.

**Nitinat Triangle:** Turn south at junction 2km beyond Nitinat River bridge. About 10km to Knob Point, launching point for paddle down northwest shore of Nitinat Lake to start of Hobiton-Tsusiat watershed. It is a rough, back-breaking 17km canoe route through Nitinat Triangle, part of Pacific Rim National Park.

## To West Coast Trail and Bamfield

**West Coast Trail and Pachena Bay:** Start of the famous West Coast Trail is 105km by logging road from Youbou, 83km from west end of Cowichan Lake. Road open to public at all times except during extreme fire hazards. Write Pacific Rim National Park, Box 280, Ucluelet, BC, V0R 3A0. 726-7721. Camping here in park on long, surf-battered sandy shores, or at adjacent native reserve. Trail, for serious hikers, takes five to seven days and follows 77km of Canada's most spectacular shoreline, along beaches and through virgin forests to Port Renfrew. Be prepared for adverse weather, particularly rain. Reservations are now required: see *Ucluelet ot Tofino*, p.70, and *Activities Outdoors*, p.19.

**Bamfield:** (Pop. 256). 3km beyond Pachena Bay turnoff, or 108km from Youbou. For details on Bamfield see *Parksville to Ucluelet Junction*, p.70.

# Nanaimo to Campbell River

## THE ISLAND HIGHWAY (Highway 19)

Highway 19, the Island Hwy, begins at Nanaimo and runs a total of 391km north to Bear Cove, near Port Hardy. In the 152km between the cities of Nanaimo and Campbell River, it's two lanes for the most part, skirting much of the island's gentle east coast, offering pleasing views of Georgia Strait, the Gulf Islands and Coast Mountains of mainland BC. Between the "larger" communities of Parksville, Qualicum, Courtenay, Comox, and Campbell River are smaller pockets of civilization: pretty spots – Oyster Bay, Fanny Bay, Union Bay – ferry docks, hotels and restaurants with recurring names: Sea Breezes, Sea Views, Bay Views.

**Long and Divers Lakes:** At Jingle Pot Rd, 5km from Nanaimo city centre, turn west to Divers Lake, east to Long Lake. Trout and smallmouth bass. Rest area off Hwy 19 just beyond Jingle Pot Rd.

**Brannen Lake:** Continue on Jingle Pot Rd and Biggs Rd. Nearly 110ha. Cutthroat and rainbow trout up to 2.5kg.

**Lantzville:** (Pop. 408). 10km north of Nanaimo, east off Hwy 19. Picturesque seaside community. As many as 400 sea lions winter some years off the Lantzville waterfront on Ada Islands. Nature cruises from Schooner Cove, 8km to east. Road through Lantzville returns to Hwy 19, 5km from the southern turnoff.

**Nanoose Bay:** Hwy 19 skirts edge of harbour just north of Lantzville. Site of the Canadian Forces Maritime Experimental and Test Ranges. Good clam digging if no paralytic shellfish ban in effect.

**Nanoose Bay Rest Area:** 18km north of Nanaimo, west side of Hwy 19, looking over Nanoose Bay. Two outhouses for people, and for doggies, a hydrant with a fence.

**Hwy 4 Bypass to Port Alberni:** 26km north of Nanaimo. Bypasses Parksville. For Port Alberni, see *Parksville to Ucluelet Junction*, p.68.

**Brant Goose Feeding Area:** Just beyond bypass, Parksville-Qualicum Beach is located on the Pacific Flyway for migratory waterfowl. As many as 20,000 of the elegant black-fronted mallard-sized Brant geese stop to rest and feed at local coastal waters each spring, en route from their winter home in Baja, California and Mexico to summer breeding grounds in Alaska. Parksville-Qualicum Beach's annual three-day Brant Festival, mid-April, organized by the Mid-Island Wildlife Watch Society, offers goose viewing stations, birding competition, nature talks, wildlife art, carving, photography, stories, children's activities. 248-4117.

**Rathtrevor Beach Provincial Park:** 347ha. 174 campsites, sanistation. 248-3931 or 755-2483. On southern outskirts of Parksville, 29km north of Nanaimo. More than 2km of sandy shore, 4km of hiking trails, nature house, amphitheatre, summer interpretive programs. One of the most popular family camping spots on Vancouver Island. May be full some summer weekends.

**Englishman River (The Orange) Bridge:** Just beyond Rathtrevor Provincial Park; crosses Englishman River. The river's estuary was saved in 1992 when the Nature Trust of BC emptied its bank account to help other conservation groups buy an 87ha parcel of land destined to become a 900-site trailer park. The cost: $2.7 million.

**Parksville:** (Pop. 7,306). On Hwy 19, 35km north of Nanaimo. Well-established resort community where hundreds of hectares of open sand are exposed at low tides. Ebbing tides leave large shallow pools in the sand, perfect digging spots for young castle builders. Steamy veils of vapour rise from the beach as the summer sun beats down on the sand. Water coming in over hot sand warms to comfortable swimming temperatures.

Much of the highway through Parksville is fronted by unappealing strip development. No lack of pizzas and hamburgers here. The resorts vary from rustic, turn-of-the-century cottages to luxury hotels with full convention facilities. There's an almost continuous string of resorts and tourist facilities between Parksville and Qualicum Beach.

Community was named after Nelson Park, first settler and postmaster.

**Parksville Information:** Infocentre, Parksville and District Chamber of Commerce, Box 99, Parksville, BC, V9P 2G3. 248-3613. On Hwy 19 at south entrance to town. Year-round: Mon-Fri. Also weekends June-Sept.

■ **Craig Heritage Park Museum:** Hwy 19 at Craig Park, about 3km south of town. Daily, mid-May-Labour Day. 248-6966. Small collection of local pioneer and native artifacts. Newspaper and photograph archives. Restored 1942 fire hall with 1946 fire truck.

■ **Parksville Community Park:** 6.5ha. Turn off Hwy 19 in town at Beachside Dr, first road north of Corfield Rd. Access to huge, open beach. Swimming, clamming, trails, sports field, playground and picnic area, children's waterpark.

■ **Canadian Coast Guard Search and Rescue Station:** End of Beachside Dr beyond Parksville Community Park. 248-2724. One hovercraft serving area north of Comox, south to Nanaimo, including Powell River and Sechelt on the mainland. Tours and presentations by arrangement.

■ **St Anne's Anglican Church:** 4km north of Parksville, turn left on Wembley Rd, then left on Church Rd. 248-3114. Built 1894, one of island's oldest churches.

■ **Morningstar Golf Course:** 525 Lowry's Rd. 248-8161. 18 holes.

■ **Paradise Seaside Resort:** 375 W Island Hwy. 248-6612. Two 18-hole mini-golf courses, amusement centre, the Old Woman's Shoe (where kids have birthday parties) and other distractions from sun and sand. Daily, late March to mid-Oct.

**Highway 4:** Downtown Parksville. 47km to Port Alberni. Route to Bamfield, Pacific Rim National Park, Ucluelet, and Tofino. See *Parksville to Ucluelet Junction*, p.68.

**French Creek:** About 40km north of Nanaimo, east on Lee Rd. Marina, campgrounds, cabins, motels, local park, fishing charters. Seafood sold from commercial fishboats. Good fall fishing from beach at mouth of creek.

**Lasqueti Island:** East off Hwy 19 at Lee Rd. Foot-passenger ferry only. Ferry has three sailings every day except Tues in summer; no Tues or Wed off-season. Carries 60 passengers for 45-minute, 17km cruise halfway across Georgia Strait. Kayaks, canoes, and bicycles can be carried aboard ferry.

### *Lasqueti Island*

This 68-sq km island is largely undeveloped, supporting a population of about 300. A small number of gravel roads, popular among mountain bicyclists who take the ferry to False Bay and ride 15km to Squitty Bay Provincial Park, at the island's eastern end.

Lasqueti's many sheltered coves and bays, offshore reefs, islets, and islands make it fascinating paddling territory. Eagles, turkey vultures, seabirds, river otters, seals, sea lions, and whales are commonly seen. False Bay is "downtown" Lasqueti Island with a general store, marina, and limited accommodation. For information on Lasqueti Island and ferry schedules check at the ferry terminal at French Creek, or at the Parksville Infocentre. French Creek Marina and Store, 248-8912 is helpful.

**Qualicum Airport:** About 44km north of Nanaimo, west off Hwy 19. Scheduled and charter flights.

**Qualicum Beach:** (Pop. 4,418). 47km north of Nanaimo on Hwy 19. Retirement and tourist community known largely for good golfing, salmon fishing, and beachcombing. Enlightened waterfront policies make for easy access to sweeping sandy beaches. The small village is less than 1km inland from the beach with restaurants, specialty shops, groceries, and galleries. One of Vancouver Island's most pleasant and salubrious communities.

Hwy 4A is a scenic alternate route from Qualicum Beach to Hwy 4.

**Qualicum Beach Information:** Infocentre, Qualicum Beach Chamber of Commerce, Box 103, Qualicum Beach, BC, V0R 2T0. 752-9532. Marked by a totem pole on Hwy 19. Year-round: Mon-Sat. Daily April-Sept.

■ **The Old School House Gallery and Art Centre:** 122 Fern W Rd. Box 1791, Qualicum Beach, BC, V0R 2T0. 752-6133. Daily, July-mid-Sept. Rest of year: Mon-Sat. Non-profit cultural centre. Artists painters, printmakers, weavers, carvers, jewellers, photographers, crafts makers at work. Each studio offers classes. Also public gallery featuring local, regional, and national artists. Workshops, demonstrations, special events.
■ **Eaglecrest Golf Club:** 2.5km south of Qualicum Beach on Island Hwy. 752-6311. Offers 18 holes.
■ **Qualicum Beach Memorial Golf Club:** Crescent Rd, 752-6312. Has nine holes.

**Little Qualicum River:** Mouth of river near Hwy 19, 51km north of Nanaimo. Good fishing for steelhead, rainbow, and cutthroat trout.

**Spider Lake Provincial Park:** 65ha. 61km north of Nanaimo, west on Horne Lake Rd. 8km by gravel road off Hwy 19. Long arms and grassy islets. Excellent smallmouth bass fishing. Large but harmless water snakes. Hiking trails, swimming, fishing, picnicking.

**Horne Lake Caves Provincial Park:** 29ha. 61km north of Nanaimo, west off Hwy 19 at Horne Lake Rd. 15km to park at lake's western end. Road follows north shore. Two caves open year-round for self-guided tours; three cave tours available in summer and on a more limited basis in winter. Take a spare flashlight and common sense. Most delicate caves are gated but tours, extremely worthwhile, and stressing conservation, may be available. Check with the Qualicum Beach Infocentre or call BC Parks: 248-3931 or 755-2483. Horne Lake, headwaters of Qualicum River, is 8km long by 1.5km wide. Good year-round fishing for kokanee, cutthroat and rainbow trout. Caves named after Hudson's Bay Company explorer Adam Grant Horne.

**Big Qualicum River Fisheries Project:** West at sign just north of Big Qualicum River Bridge, just beyond parks' turnoff. More than 100,000 salmon return each year to hatchery, which produces millions of fish. Educational displays and self-guiding paths. Daily, dawn to dusk, year-round. 757-8412.

**Bowser:** (Pop. 130). 66km north of Nanaimo on Hwy 19. Overlooking Georgia Strait. The Bowser Hotel made history in the 1930s by having a dog that served beer to patrons. The community is named for William John Bowser, BC Premier, 1915-16.

**Deep Bay:** 70km north of Nanaimo, take Gainsburg Rd. Pleasant fishing-resort area and excellent wharf. Everything to warm a fisherman's heart.

**Rosewall Creek Provincial Park:** 63ha. West off Hwy 19 about 76km north of Nanaimo. Pleasant fishing.

**Cougar Smith Rd:** 82km north of Nanaimo. Named after "Cougar" Cecil Smith, professional cougar hunter, who shot more than 1,000 cougars between 1890 and 1940 when a bounty was offered by the provincial government.

**Fanny Bay:** (Pop. 110). 83km north of Nanaimo on Hwy 19. Tiny seaside community on shores of Baynes Sound. Site of landmark Fanny Bay Inn, known to Vancouver Islanders as the FBI. The name, Fanny Bay, arose from Captain GH Richards' surveys in 1860s. Fanny is an unknown person, enshrined nevertheless for posterity.

**Brico:** Near Fanny Bay Inn. Once a cable-laying ship. Was hauled ashore and made into a restaurant.

**Denman and Hornby Islands:** Terminal at Buckley Bay, 86km north of Nanaimo. Car and passenger ferries run several times daily to Denman Island, and from Denman to Hornby Island. Schedule information: 335-0323. A drive across Denman is necessary to reach Hornby Island terminal.

## *Denman Island*

This 50-sq km island (19km long, 6km wide) has about 800 year-round residents. There are 48km of public road, about half of that paved. Beautiful sandstone and gravel shores. Oysters, rock crabs, clams. Eagles and seabirds. Black-tailed deer. Good salmon fishing, particularly off south end. Trout fishing in Chickadee and Graham lakes. Limited accommodation and only one small provincial campground. Call ahead or go straight there. Cycle rentals, public art gallery.

This lush, fertile, low-lying paradise has its concerns: in the last decade the island's small population has doubled, and is expected to double again by the end of the decade. Some 97 percent of Denman has now been subdivided, or is available for development, and 25 percent of that is owned by forest companies for potential logging.

**Hornby-Denman Tourist Association:** c/o Sea Breeze Lodge, Hornby Island, BC, V0R 1Z0. 335-2321. Denman Island General Store and Café: visitor and accommodation information, food, liquor, fishing licences. 335-2293.

**Fillongley Provincial Park:** 23ha. 10 campsites. 248-3931 or 755-2483. On Lambert Channel, facing Hornby Island. Small but pleasant park with creek for children, forest, grassy fields, and expansive gravel and shell beach. Can walk for several kilometres on beach.

**Sandy Island Provincial Marine Park:** 33ha. 8 campsites. Water access only. Group of beautiful wooded islands off sandy north end of Denman. Easily reached by small boat. Launching ramp next to ferry terminal on Denman. Accessible by foot from Denman Island at extremely low tides, swimming, fishing.

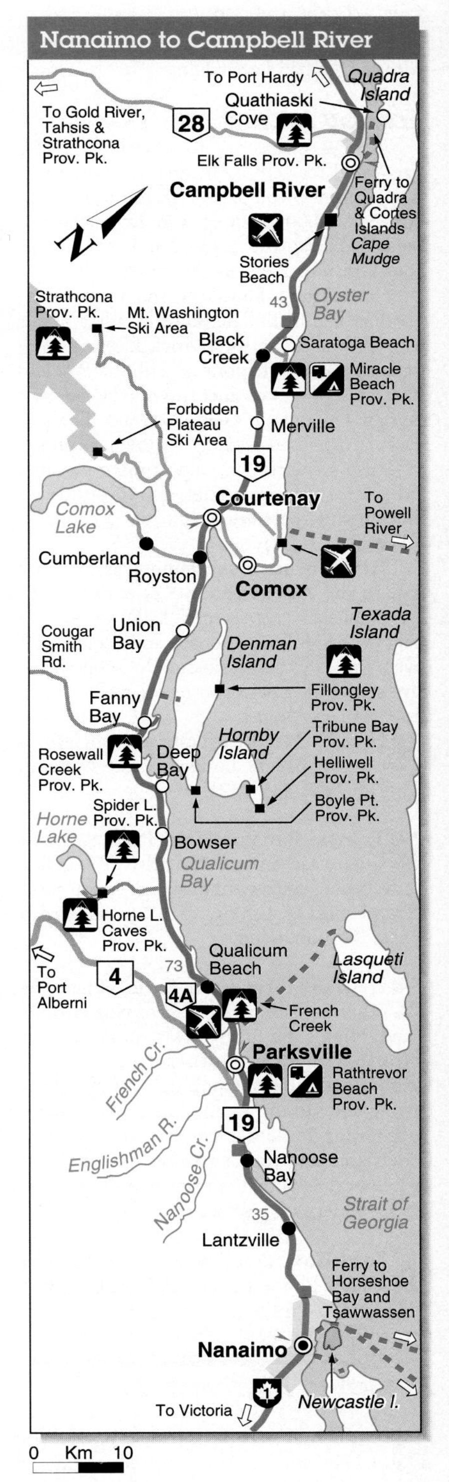


**Boyle Point Provincial Park:** 125ha. Southern tip of Denman, beyond to Hornby Island ferry terminal. Dramatic ocean views from steep escarpment over boulder-strewn beach. Scattered old-growth Douglas fir mingle with second-growth forests. Hiking.

**Denman Seniors and Museum Society Activity Centre:** 1111 Northwest Rd, in Seniors Community Hall. Daily July-Aug. 335-2979. Local natural and human history, shells, fossils, butterflies, northwest-coast native artifacts, European settlement items, work of Denman Lace Club.

### Hornby Island

This 30-sq km island has about 1,000 year-round residents. And many, many more in the summer – on one 1990 summer day, an estimated 10,000 visitors were savouring this wee isle. Ferries run across Lambert Channel from Gravelly Bay, on Denman, to Shingle Spit, on Hornby. Hornby is more mountainous than Denman. The powerful force of the sea has beaten the softer rock faces, leaving dramatic cave formations at Tribune Bay and other sites. Some consider this one of the most appealing islands in Georgia Strait. The primary industry here is crafts – weaving, pottery, art – also some fishing, and farming of cattle and sheep. No provincial campgrounds on Hornby, but there are a number of commercial ones.

Hornby is becoming famous as the only place in the world where the primitive, deep-sea, sixgill shark moves into shallow waters (as shallow as 15m), occasionally interfacing with divers. So far, these fearsome-looking sharks have shown themselves to be relatively docile. See *Ford Cove, below.*

**Hornby-Denman Tourist Association:** c/o Sea Breeze Lodge, Hornby Island, BC, V0R 1Z0. 335-2321.

**Tribune Bay Provincial Park:** 95ha. At southeast end of Hornby. Beautiful sandy beach. Safe swimming for small children, picnicking, fishing. Only excuse needed to visit Hornby Island.

**Helliwell Provincial Park:** 69ha. The other only excuse needed to visit Hornby Island. High cliffs, grassy fields, and forests on St John Point, at southeast entrance to Tribune Bay. Beachcombing, hiking, spin-casting for salmon from shore. Particularly invigorating in winter storms. Park includes underwater area running from St John Point to Lambert Channel – primitive deep-water sharks, underwater caves, shipwreck sites.

**Ford Cove:** Southwest end of Hornby Island. Phone Ed Lip of Hornby Island Diving, 335-2609, for diving information, reservations.

### Return to Highway 19

**Union Bay:** (Pop. 615). 91.5km north of Nanaimo on Hwy 19. Once a major shipping area for coal from mines at nearby Cumberland. Boat launching here for 4km cruise to Sandy Island Provincial Park, off north end of Denman Island. Ice cream, pub. Looking east and slightly north, across the Strait of Georgia: views of **Texada Island**, and beyond to **Powell River** with its steamy pulp and paper mill (see p.100).

**Cumberland Rd:** 102km north of Nanaimo. West for 6km to Cumberland and beyond to outdoor recreation areas.

*Craft fair, Cortez Island.*

## SIDE TRIP
### to Cumberland

**Cumberland:** (Pop. 2,200). 6km west of Hwy 19 on Cumberland Rd. Founded in 1888, by coal baron Robert Dunsmuir, and named after the famous English coal-mining district, Cumberland. Here was the heart of a rich coal field that ran along Vancouver Island's east coast. British, Italian, Chinese, and Japanese immigrants, living in segregated neighbourhoods, made this a colourful place in its heyday. The population then was five times greater than now. There were bars and brothels, gambling houses, fortune tellers, and two 400-seat theatres where touring Chinese singers and acrobats performed. But greed and indifference to safety on the part of the Dunsmuir barons and subsequent mine owners made this a dangerous place to be. In all, 295 miners lost their lives here. Ultimately, wage and safety cuts here and at other mines ignited the bitter Vancouver Island coal miners' strike in 1912. WJ Bowser, acting premier at the time, sent in 1,000 soldiers to "keep the peace" – *i.e.* the mines running. Four years later, more unrest followed the slaying, just outside Cumberland, of Ginger Goodwin, popular labour leader, pacifist, and "troublemaker" as far as the authorities were concerned. Goodwin had been taking refuge here from a conscription order.

Mine production fell in the late 1920s, the last mine closed in 1966, but much remains of Cumberland's past: piles of slag and sheets of rusted corrugated iron scattered around derelict buildings; remnants of Bonanza Number Four, which in 1912 produced some 2,540 tonnes of coal a day; a downtown mural portrays the community's Chinese heritage. Several buildings – survivors of 1932-33 fires – have been refurbished; one houses an art gallery and several craft stores.

For more, read *Ginger: The Life and Death of Albert Goodwin,* by Susan Mayse, Harbour Publishing, BC, 1990.

**Cumberland Information:** Infocentre, Cumberland Chamber of Commerce, Box 74, Cumberland, BC, V0R 1S0. 336-8313. On the main street at 2755 Dunsmuir Ave. Mon-Fri year-round. Daily July-Aug.

■ **Cumberland Cultural Centre and Museum:** Corner of First St and Dunsmuir Ave. Daily. 336-2445. The Cultural Centre, with its historic facades, is new, and the museum has expanded into it, making room for more of the community's dramatic history –

including poignant photographs of Japanese community developed from a large collection of glass plate negatives rescued from neglect.

■ **Japanese Cemetery, Chinese Cemetery, Ginger Goodwin's Burial Site:** On Cumberland Rd, east of the village.

**Comox Lake:** 50-site campground on south side of lake with trails and lake access 5km west of Cumberland on Comox Lake Rd. North and west sides of lake can also be reached by roads from Cumberland. Major recreation area. Lake is 14.5km long by 1.5km wide. Part of Puntledge River system. Excellent year-round fishing for kokanee, Dolly Varden char, big cutthroat, rainbow trout. Boaters beware of high winds and submerged stumps from raising of lake level.

**Lakes Chain:** Two small lakes –Willemar and Forbush – reached by logging road from Comox Lake. Wilderness camping, excellent canoeing. Lakes joined by easy-flowing stretch of Puntledge River. Rough trail into Strathcona Park through old-growth forest from upper end of Forbush Lake. Lots of black bears; wolves may howl at night.

## Return to Highway 19

**Royston:** (Pop. 1,219). 102km north of Nanaimo, east off Hwy 19. Oceanfront community near the mouth of Comox Harbour.

**Courtenay-Comox:** (Pop. 19,905). 107km north of Nanaimo. The Comox Valley cities of Courtenay and Comox are among the few places where you really can ski in the morning and play golf in the afternoon. They sit comfortably in the rain shadow of the Vancouver Island mountains, surrounded by incredible mountain views and pastoral farmland. Ski areas at Forbidden Plateau and Mt Washington are known for both downhill and cross-country skiing, as well as summer hiking and mountain climbing.

Salmon fishing is good in surrounding waters, notably at **Kye Bay, Bates Beach** and off north end of **Denman Island.**

An area near Courtenay on the bank of the Puntledge River was designated a provincial heritage site after fossilized remains of a dinosaur were discovered in 1988. The remains, believed to be 80 million years old, were those of an elasmosaur, a long-necked swimming reptile which could have weighed 4t and measured 14m long. The find was the first significant fossil discovery in BC west of the Rockies.

Comox is site of a large Canadian Forces Base specializing in air-sea rescue and long-range maritime patrol. **Filberg Lodge**, on Comox Ave, was private residence of Robert J Filberg, president of Comox Logging Company. The house was built of local materials in English arts and crafts style. A native petroglyph was built into the fireplace. At **Mack Laing Nature Park**, at the end of Comox Ave, is Shakesides, which was private residence of naturalist Mack Laing (1883-1982). Pleasant walks on waterfront and in fir and cedar forest.

**Courtenay-Comox Information:** Infocentre, Comox Valley Chamber of Commerce, 2040 Cliffe Ave, Courtenay, BC, V9N 2L3. 334-3234. Marked by black steam engine at the south entrance to Courtenay on Hwy 19. Serves Courtenay and Comox. Daily year-round.

■ **Courtenay and District Museum and Archives:** 360 Cliffe Ave. Daily in summer. Sept-April: Tues-Sat. 334-3611. Housed in Native Son's Hall, historic log building. Features native artifacts, logging and farming equipment, fossils, local Chinese and Japanese culture, an unusual doll collection, archives of local and regional history.

■ **Puntledge River and Hatchery:** Important river for chum, pink, coho, and chinook salmon as well as steelhead trout. 338-7444. Year-round. Reached from south entrance to Courtenay by taking Lake Trail Rd, turning right at Powerhouse Rd and following signs.

■ **Forbidden Plateau:** On Mount Becher's lower slopes, west of Courtenay, in Strathcona Provincial Park. 334-4428 or 338-1919. A 25-minute drive. Can see ski runs from Courtenay. Vertical drop of 366m. Lift up to 1,100m level. Double chairlift, three T-bars, one handle tow; 24 runs and extensive cross-country tracks for intermediate and experienced skiers. Day lodge with cafeteria, lounge, and other facilities. Accommodation in Courtenay, and RV parking on mountain. Equipment rentals, ski school. Chairlift also open late June to early Sept to take visitors into alpine terrain. Summer campground beside lodge. Lodge used for many summer activities. Alpine lakes offer good fishing in late summer, early fall.

■ **Mt Washington Ski Area:** 31km west of Courtenay. Follow signs from town. Mt Washington's 1,590m peak looms above the ski area. Spectacular views of surrounding mountains, forests, and glimpses of sea. Vertical drop is 488m. Two triple and two double lifts, a new quad-chair, more than 20 runs, most above 1,200m level. Full-service day lodge open evenings for dinners and entertainment. There's a ski school, equipment, and facilities for children. Many of the 200 private chalets and condominiums in Mt Washington's village can be rented by skiers. Full-service RV park in the village. Nordic skiing is also extensive: 30km of track-set trails, and accessibility of nearby Strathcona Provincial Park. More than $1 million recently spent expanding lodge, washrooms, food and beverage areas, retail shops, children's and barbecue areas. New trail markers. Write to Mt Washington, Box 3069, Courtenay, BC, V9N 5N3. 338-1386. Snow report 338-1515.

■ **Mt Washington in the Summer:** Alpine Café, camping, mountain biking and rentals, tours, hiking. Chairlifts: weekends from late June; daily late July-early Sept; weekends to mid-Sept. Contact above.

■ **The Beaches:** At Kye Bay, 5km northeast of Comox, are long and sandy, ideal family picnic and swimming spots. Still a bit of a secret, though some families have been summering here for generations. Cottage resorts.

**Courtenay Airstrip:** Behind infocentre off Hwy 19.

**CFB Comox:** Airstrip at the base is used by commercial airlines for scheduled and charter flights. Take Ryan Rd off Hwy 19 from Courtenay bypass. Air Force Museum at entrance to CFB Comox is open year-round.

**Powell River Ferry:** Take Ryan Rd off Hwy 19 from the Courtenay bypass and follow signs. Car and passenger ferries run 27km, 75 minutes, four sailings daily to Powell River, on mainland north of Vancouver.

**Merville:** (Pop. 865). 121km north of Nanaimo. Cluster of stores and homes near Hwy 19. Named after location in France of Canadians' first field headquarters. This is where BC author Jack Hodgins grew up and collected his first impressions for such books as *Spit Delaney's Island* and *Barclay Family Theatre.*

**Black Creek:** (Pop. 1,950). 124km north of Nanaimo on Hwy 19. Primarily service centre for campers at Miracle Beach Provincial Park.

**Country Market:** 129km north of Nanaimo.

**Miracle Beach Provincial Park:** 135ha. 193 campsites. 248-3931 or 337-5121. East of Hwy 19, 131km north of Nanaimo, 24km north of Courtenay. One of Vancouver Island's most popular parks. Perfect family camping spot if you don't mind company. Long, safe sandy beach, wooded trails, amphitheatre, visitor centre, interpretive programs. Pleasant spot in Oct to fly-fish for coho from the beach at the mouth of Black Creek.

**Mitlenatch Island Provincial Park:** 155ha. 13km northeast of Miracle Beach at north end of Georgia Strait. Boat access only. Naturalists' paradise. Nesting glaucous-winged gulls, pelagic cormorants, pigeon guillemots. Spring and summer wildflowers. Check with Courtenay Infocentre or Miracle Beach Park for possibility of naturalist boat tours.

**Saratoga Beach:** 133km north of Nanaimo, east off Hwy 19. Sandy beach with golf course, commercial campground, marina, boat launch, and other facilities near mouth of Oyster River. Good fishing at Salmon Point.

**Stories Beach:** Sandy beach alongside Hwy 19 on the shores of Oyster Bay. Resorts, cabins.

**Rest Area:** 137km north of Nanaimo. Very dramatic views of the Coast Mountains across the strait.

**Campbell River Airport:** West on Erickson Rd, 146km north of Nanaimo. 5km to airport. Scheduled and charter flights.

**Rotary Beach Park:** Just beyond airport. Approaching Campbell River, much of the foreshore traced by the highway is actually seaside park – featuring sparkling views of Quadra Island and the First Nations village, Cape Mudge. In Johnstone Strait: seals and herons, and seagulls, and children, paddling logs to freedom.

**Campbell River:** (Pop. 21,175). 152km north of Nanaimo. Thousands of sports fishermen converge in Campbell River every year and catch literally hundreds of thousands of salmon. Some call it the Salmon Capital of the World. The city is home of the famous Tyee Club, for fishermen in rowboats who catch a salmon over 13.5kg under strict club rules. The Tyee Club record, set in 1968, is 32kg. Powerful tides off Campbell River, though hazardous, are an asset to anglers. Bait fish congregate in back eddies, attracting salmon and other marine life. These fish, of course, attract fishermen – it's estimated that 60 percent of Campbell River's visitors come to fish.

Some of those salmon are landed at Canada's first salt-water fishing pier, built in 1987, and measuring 180m long and 6.6m wide. It has been an overwhelming success, attracting thousands upon thousands of people. Like Nanaimo, Campbell River is in the midst of developing its downtown seafront with pleasent new walkways and open areas, viewpoints, cruise ship docks and marinas.

Campbell River is also well-known for excellent freshwater fishing. There are many lakes and rivers yielding rainbow and cutthroat trout, and steelhead.

Scuba diving is popular in Campbell River, especially during winter when ocean waters are particularly clear. Strong tides produce an abundance of colourful underwater scenery. Georgia and Johnstone straits, joined by Discovery Passage just north of Campbell River, are considered among the world's most fascinating diving areas.

From as early as the turn of the century, Campbell River has been known as a resort and sport-fishing centre, though the major industry is forestry. Mining is also important to the area economy. Campbell River today is well-prepared to accommodate its visitors with many hotels, motels, resorts, campgrounds, restaurants, and shopping facilities.

Hwys 19 and 28 on the north side of Campbell River lead to several interesting destinations, including salmon hatcheries, caves and Strathcona Provincial Park. See *Campbell River to Port Hardy*, next page.

**Campbell River Information:** Infocentre, Campbell River and District Chamber of Commerce, Box 400, Campbell River, BC, V9W 5B6. 287-4636. In museum building. At 1235 Shopper's Row in Tyee Plaza. Daily June-Sept. Rest of year: Mon-Sat.

■ **Campbell River Museum and Archives:** 1235 Shopper's Row in the Tyee Plaza. 287-3103. Daily in summer. Sept, April, May open Mon-Sat. Winter, Tues-Sat. Vancouver Island native cultures, European exploration and pioneer history. Contemporary native art and books on history and ethnology. Field trips to historic sites.

■ **Sequoia Springs Golf:** 700 Peterson Rd, Campbell River, BC, V9W 3H7. 287-4970. Offering 18 holes.

**Quadra and Cortes Islands:** Car and passenger BC Ferries make several sailings daily, 45-minute crossing from downtown Campbell River to Quathiaski Cove on Quadra Island. Ferries from Quadra at Heriot Bay run to Whaletown on Cortes Island. 286-1412.

## *Quadra Island*

This 276-sq km (full-facility) island has a population of 1,962. It has several sheltered harbours. Islands and islets dot its coast. Like Campbell River, it's a good fishing and diving area and also has many lakes. There are communities at Quathiaski Cove and Heriot Bay. No provincial campgrounds, but commercial campsites, lodges, fishing resorts, cottages, and other accommodation.

■ **Kwagiulth Museum:** Cape Mudge Village. Daily July-Sept. Sept-July: Tues-Sat. 285-3733. The building, inspired by the shape of a sea snail, houses part of a potlatch collection. Kwagiulth (Kwakwaka'wakw) artifacts, totem poles, and ceremonial regalia. More than 300 potlatch items were returned here, to their rightful owners, in early 1980s, after having been seized by the government in 1922 (potlatches were banned in Canada). Some potlatch participants of that time were jailed.

■ **Tsa-Kwa-Luten Lodge:** Follow signs from ferry dock. Guided fishing, Kwagiulth Feast and Dance. Box 460 Quathiaski Cove, BC, V0P 1N0. 285-2042.

**Petroglyphs:** Ancient stone drawings in small park across from Kwagiulth Museum. Others at Wa Wa Kie Beach and Francisco Point.

**Rebecca Spit Provincial Marine Park:** 177ha. Narrow 1.5km spit on east side of Drew Harbour. Boat launch, sand beaches, trails, picnicking, swimming, fishing.

**Octopus Islands Provincial Marine Park:** 109ha. Boat access only. Cluster of small islands on northeast side of Quadra Island.

## *Cortes Island*

This 125-sq km island has a population of 543. Lies at the entrance to Desolation Sound, one of BC's most celebrated cruising areas. Like Quadra Island, Cortes has an intricate shoreline with sheltered harbours, islets, coves. Squirrel Cove, on the east side, is a well-known anchorage with a small tidal waterfall. Gorge Harbour is a large sheltered cove entered through a narrow channel flanked by steep cliffs. Commercial accommodation and a provincial campground.

**Smelt Bay Provincial Park:** 16ha. 23 campsites. 248-3931 or 755-2483. At southwest end of island. Beachcombing, swimming, fishing, paddling, hiking. Known for thousands of spawning smelt here.

**Mansons Landing Provincial Marine Park:** 100ha. Short distance north of Smelt Bay on west side. Another sheltered cove. Hague Lake. Nice beaches, swimming, hiking, paddling.

**Von Donop Provincial Marine Park:** 1,277ha, includes 360ha of foreshore. At Von Donop Inlet. Wilderness camping. 935-6536. First Nations-BC Parks joint venture protects saltwater lagoons, tidal passes, and old-growth forest of *Hathayim*, as this place is known to local Klahoose nation.

# Campbell River to Port Hardy

## NORTH ISLAND HIGHWAY (Highway 19)

The North Island Highway is the main route to Port Hardy. Bear Cove, near Port Hardy, is terminal for BC Ferries sailing to Prince Rupert. Ferry travellers planning to stay overnight on the north island should book accommodation at the same time as making reservations for the ferry, to make sure they have somewhere to stay.

Before the opening of the North Island Hwy in 1979, when the area was accessed by logging roads, Campbell River was often mistakenly referred to as "the north island." Campbell River is, in fact, only halfway along the east coast of Vancouver Island a full 220km from it's northern end, 231km from its southern tip.

A few km from the outskirts of Campbell River, the population thins out considerably. Fewer than three percent of the island's residents live on the northern half. The highway narrows to two lanes and moves inland through the forest; the clusters of roadside motels, service stations, eateries, and shopping malls so noticeable in the south disappear.

The differences between north and south are profound. There's a frontier feeling on the north island: heavy machinery and logging trucks share the highways with hunters, anglers, campers, canoeists, and sightseers. Ponds and marshlands lie along the roadsides. Fireweed and other spring flowers grow in expansive clearcuts between mountains of replanted timber.

Up here are fishing-logging-milling-mining towns. In the past two decades, recognizing the need to grow beyond resource extraction, they have added tourism to their resumés. North island towns that depend on and take pride in chopping down the biggest trees and hooking the biggest fish share particular affinity for the Tallest, Widest, Longest, and Most Outrageous when advertising their attributes.

**Highway 28:** About 2km north of Campbell River city centre. West 92km to Gold River. Route to **Strathcona Provincial Park** and other attractions. Several wilderness campsites on lakes and streams between Campbell River and Buttle Lake.

## SIDE TRIP

### to Gold River and Tahsis

**Quinsam River Hatchery:** Take Hwy 28 and watch for hatchery sign on left. Winding road 2.5km to hatchery. Self-guided tours. Pink and chinook salmon in Sept, coho in Oct, steelhead in early March. Open daily year-round. 287-9564.

**Elk Falls Provincial Park:** 1,086ha. 122 campsites. 248-3931 or 337-5121. On Hwy 28 just over 1km west of Hwy 19. Confluence of Campbell and Quinsam rivers in park. Waterfalls, swimming, fishing, hiking. John Hart Dam nearby. Tours available.

**Elk Falls Rest Area:** 3km west of Campbell River.

**Strathcona Provincial Park:** 211,973ha. 161 campsites in two campgrounds plus wilderness camping. 248-3931 or 755-2483. Strathcona is the largest provincial park on Vancouver Island. Its easternmost point is only 13km from the sea at **Comox Harbour**, while its extreme southwest corner reaches tidewater at the head of **Herbert Inlet**, on the opposite side of Vancouver Island. The park is roughly triangular, extending about 65km south from the 50th parallel of latitude. Within its boundaries are Mt Golden Hinde, at 2,200m Vancouver Island's highest peak, and **Della Falls**, at 440m the highest waterfalls in Canada.

Established in 1911, it is the province's first park. With its challenging peaks, alpine meadows, and forests, Strathcona is a hiker's paradise. Its multitude of small lakes attract summer canoeists and anglers. Contact BC Parks (see BC *Introduction*) for a brochure and map of trails and facilities.

The main accesses to Strathcona are off Hwy 28 from Campbell River and at Forbidden Plateau outside Courtenay. Della Falls, described i n *Parksville to Ucluelet Junction*, p.70, can be reached by boat and backpack from Great Central Lake near Port Alberni.

■ **Strathcona Park Lodge and Outdoor Education Centre:** Box 2160, Campbell River, BC, V9W 5C9. 286-8206. On Upper Campbell Lake along Hwy 28, 38km west of Hwy 19. Well-known for its programs in wilderness skills. Outdoor summer camps, family excursions. For everyone. Provides accommodation and meals. Also the COLT (Canadian Outdoor Leadership Training) Centre, with 100-day intensive programs developing water and land-based outdoor skills, environmental awareness, and teaching ability in experiential education. For adults 19 and over. Call 286-2008 or 286-3122.

**Ralph River:** 76 campsites. Reached by driving 45km on Hwy 28 to a bridge between Upper Campbell and Buttle lakes. Don't cross bridge, but continue south along east shore of Buttle Lake for about 25km.

**Westmin Resources Mine:** 12km beyond Ralph River campground and around south end of Buttle Lake. Mainly copper and zinc. Tours: 287-9271.

**Big Den Rest Area:** About 1km beyond Westmin mine.

**Buttle Lake:** 85 campsites. Drive across bridge between Upper Campbell and Buttle lakes. Turn south after bridge and take short road to campsite.

**Gold River:** (Pop. 2,166). 89km west of Campbell River. A modern "instant town" in a frontier setting. It's nicely nestled in the Gold River Valley where the river, known for its excellent steelhead fishing, runs to the sea at the head of Muchalat Inlet. New 9-hole golf course, and aquatic and leisure centre. From here unpaved roads lead to Tahsis and back to Hwy 19 at Woss.

**Gold River Information:** Infocentre, Gold River Chamber of Commerce, Box 160, Gold River, BC, V0P 1G0. 283-2418 or (municipal office) 283-2202. At town centre in Village Square Plaza. Daily mid-June-mid-Sept. Rest of year: Mon-Fri.

**Nootka Sound Service:** MV *Uchuck III* departs from head of Muchalat Inlet, 12km south of Gold River town centre to sail intricate northwest coast. In BC, call 283-2515, 283-2325. Year-round freight and passenger service for westcoast communities in Nootka Sound Gold River, Yuquot (Friendly Cove), Tahsis, and Kyuquot. See *Transportation*, p.32. Ship is a converted US mine sweeper from 1943.

**Upana Caves:** About 17km west of Gold River. Take Head Bay Forest Rd west toward Tahsis. Turn at Branch H27 and stop at parking lot short distance up road. Access trail runs 150m to register entrance. Self-guided tours. About one hour through main caves. Several undeveloped caves in one group. 15 known entrances with passages totalling 450m. Caves vary from single rooms to several branching passages. Take reliable flashlight and rubber-soled boots. For supervised group tours contact SpeleoLec Tours, Box 897, Gold River, BC, V0P 1G0. 283-2691.

**Tlupana/Conuma Salmon Hatchery:** About midway between Gold River and Tahsis. Look for sign. Write Box 247, Tahsis, BC, V0P 1X0. Fish to see year round. Steelhead fishing in Conuma River when permitted.

**Tahsis:** (Pop. 1,053). 65km west of Gold River. Tahsis is a forestry community at the head of Tahsis Inlet. Also served by Air Nootka and the MV *Uchuck III*. Sheltered cruising, kayaking and canoeing, eagle watching, caving, fishing, hiking, tours of Canadian Pacific Forest Products modern sawmill. Marine facilities include marina, fuel dock, public floats, boat launch, charters and rentals. Tour bus in summer.

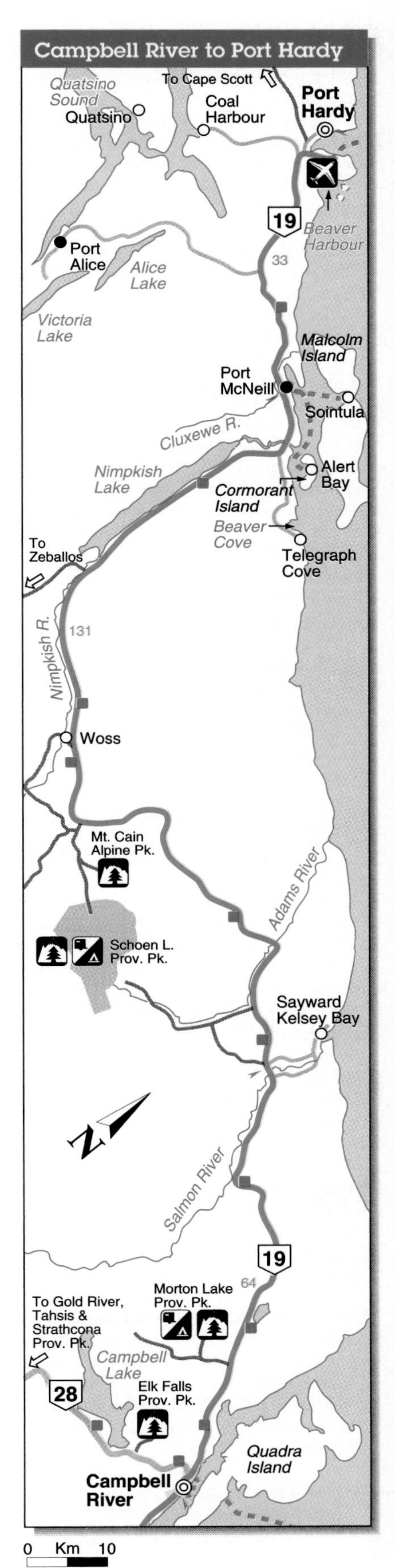

**Tahsis Information:** Infocentre, Box 278, Tahsis, BC, V0P 1X0. 934-6667. July-Aug. Local businesses can provide information other times.

**Nootka:** 8km down Tahsis Inlet from Tahsis. This is the traditional territory of the Mowachaht people. Captain James Cook landed in 1778 at Yuquot, or Friendly Cove, on southeast corner of Nootka Island. He is credited with being the first European to land on the coast of what later became BC. The British called the people who lived here "Nootka," though the people who live in the area today laugh, and say nootka was a warning to the sailors, "circle round," to avoid hitting the rocks. Trade between the Yuquot people and the British began immediately – sea otter and other furs for items not available here – and Nootka became an international trading centre. Today, just one native family lives here, though there's still a church and a few old buildings left from thriving times. One totem pole, built in 1925, remains. The MV *Uchuck III* carries visitors here in the summer.

## Return to Highway 19

**Elk Falls Mill:** Turn east off Hwy 19 on Elk Falls Mill Rd, 4km north of Campbell River. Fletcher Challenge Canada Ltd. (amalgamation of BC Forest Products and Crown Forest) pulp and paper mill. For tours: 287-9181.

**Seymour Narrows and Ripple Rock Rest Area:** Historic site about 11km north of Campbell River. A perilous pass where tides run up to 10 knots. The ominous twin peaks of Ripple Rock were once just below the surface near the channel's centre. This nautical nuisance is said to have caused two dozen major shipwrecks and claimed more than a hundred lives. It was blown out of the water in 1958 with one of the largest non-atomic blasts in history.

**Trail to Ripple Rock:** Watch for a hiker's sign about 6km north of historic site. Two trails to cliffs above Seymour Narrows. About three hours return.

**Morton Lake Provincial Park:** 67ha. 24 campsites. 248-3931 or 755-2483. West off Hwy 19 at Adams Resort Rd, 20km north of Campbell River. Fishing, windsurfing, hiking, swimming.

**Link and Pin Logging Museum:** About 30km north of Campbell River. Museum open daily June-late Sept. 287-9421. Boasts the island's best collection of logging tools: handsaws, stamp hammers, jiggers. Also a collection of antique oil lamps and old photos of north island coast.

**Roberts Lake and Rest Area:** 32km north of Campbell River, east side of Hwy 19. Kokanee, Dolly Varden char, cutthroat trout. One of dozens of excellent fishing lakes along logging roads on both sides of highway. Detailed maps can be purchased in Campbell River.

**McNair Lake:** 35.5km north of Campbell River. Hiking trail.

**Rock Bay Rd:** 37km north of Campbell River. East to unpaved 17km route to Rock Bay on Johnstone Strait. 4km farther to Chatham Point Lighthouse. Road passes McCreight Lake, another hot fishing spot.

**Big Tree Creek Rest Area:** About 47km north of Campbell River.

**Salmon Lookout:** 52km north of Campbell River.

**Darymple Creek:** 57km north of Campbell River. Hiking trail.

**Road to Sayward:** 64km north of Campbell River. East on paved road, 10km to village of Sayward and wharf at Kelsey Bay. Turn west to go short distance to infocentre.

Here is the southern boundary of the Regional District of Mount Waddington, which encompasses all of northern Vancouver Island and a portion of the mainland. Named for Mt Waddington, at head of Knight Inlet on the mainland, highest mountain totally within BC. Mt Waddington wasn't discovered until 1925, when its 4,016m peak was spotted from Vancouver Island.

## SIDE TRIP
### to Sayward-Kelsey Bay

**Sayward-Kelsey Bay Information:** White River Court Infocentre, RR 1, Site 11, Box 1, Comp 7, Sayward, BC, V0P 1R0. 282-3265. At Sayward Junction, turn west off Hwy 19, and proceed a few hundred metres until you reach service station and coffee bar.

**Valley of a Thousand Faces Gallery:** Between the infocentre and Sayward junction. 282-3303. The park with its Thousand Faces painted on tree slices was closed for a time, but it's open again, and Hetty Fredrickson may still show you around.

**Salmon River:** Reputed to hold largest steelhead on island, 74km river empties into Johnstone Strait at Kelsey Bay. Road to Sayward crosses river twice as river and road wind down the Salmon River valley. Private campgrounds along lower reaches.

**Hkusam Mountain:** El 1,671m. East side of Salmon Valley. Look closely for the steamy ring around its peak – locally it's known as an "Indian blanket." Natives called the mountain *Hiatsee Saklekum*: where the breath of the sea lion gathers at the blowhole. A marsh and small lake are said to be the cause of the mysterious fog.

**Cable Café:** About 1km beyond Sayward Junction after you cross the bridge. Café features 26t of logging cable welded to a steel frame. And a 6m-high steel totem, erected in honour of BC's loggers.

**Sayward-Kelsey Bay:** (Pop. 406). Service centre for the Salmon River valley area, which has about 1,200 inhabitants, mainly farmers and loggers. Division headquarters for MacMillan Bloedel forestry operation. First settled in early 1890s.

The wharf at Kelsey Bay was once the southern terminus of BC Ferries' Inside Passage sailing to Prince Rupert. Fishboats and charter boats tie up here. Boat launch.

## Return to Highway 19

**Keta Lake Rest Area:** 74km north of Campbell River.

**Adam River Bridge:** 83km north of Campbell River. Picnic site 2km south of bridge is pleasant place to inhale forest air. To the south, are the peaks of Mt Juliet (1,637m) and Mt Romeo (1,661m). These mountains are birthplace of the Adam and Eve rivers, whose courses come together near their estuary, above Johnstone Strait.

**Eve River Rest Area:** 93km north of Campbell River. Miles and miles of logging-scape: ironically beautiful.

**Logging Rd to Schoen Lake:** 93km north of Campbell River. The Nimpkish River system, with its headwaters at Mt Alston, about 32km south of this junction, is Vancouver Island's largest watershed. On its 145km journey to the sea, it is joined by the waters of major lakes such as Schoen, Vernon, Woss, and the Klaklakama Lakes.

## SIDE TRIP
### to Schoen Lake

Schoen Lake is considered by some to be one of the most scenic lakes on Vancouver Island.

**Schoen Lake Provincial Park:** 8,170ha. 10 campsites. 248-3931 or 755-2483. South off Hwy 19 and left a short distance from the highway. A stunning wilderness park encompassing mountains, streams, and woodlands. The 1,802m summit of Mt Schoen reflects off the waters of Schoen Lake, a narrow, 5km stretch of canoeing water. Several mountain trails follow water courses around the lake, one leading to Nisnak Meadows, where subalpine wildflowers bloom late spring and summer. Hikers occasionally cross the paths of black bears, beavers, wolves, cougars, black-tailed deer. Also Roosevelt elk, most often seen at twilight. A good time to drive with extra caution, though the straight road invites carefree speeds.

**Mt Cain Alpine Park:** Mt Cain – el 1,646m. On road to Schoen Lake, 16km from Hwy 19. Chains required in winter.

Write Mt Cain Alpine Park Society, Box 1225, Port McNeill, BC, V0N 2R0. Access road recently improved. Vertical drop 450m. Two T-bars, rope-tow. 16 downhill runs. 20km unmarked cross-country trails. Day lodge, rentals, lessons. Open winter weekends and school holidays. Hiking in summer. Wildflowers and blueberries. Fragile ecology features alpine and bog vegetation.

**Klaklakama Lakes:** On road to Schoen Lake about 7km south of Hwy 19. Two lovely, small campsites, one on each lake. Beautiful canoeing. Much like Schoen Lake.

### *Return to Highway 19*

**Hoomak Lake Rest Area:** About 125km north of Campbell River.

**Woss Junction:** 130km north of Campbell River. West off Hwy 19, about 2km to Woss.

**Woss:** (Pop. 469). Logging on the north island is not only big business, it's old business. Displayed at Woss, a Canadian Forest Products community, is an antique steam locomotive, once used to haul logs from bush. Popular five-hour tours in summer aboard logging railway run about 25km through Nimpkish Valley to dryland sort and 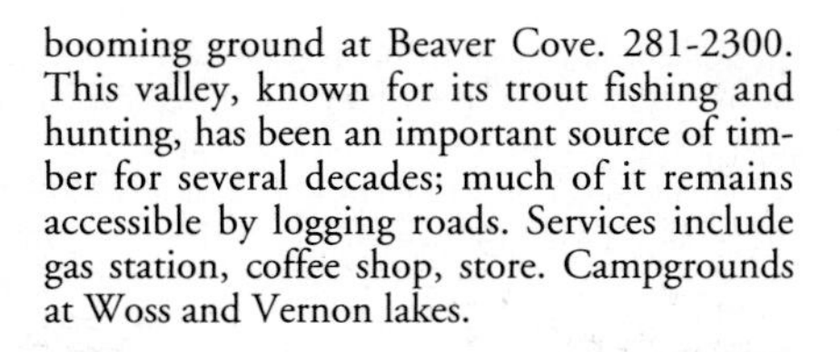 booming ground at Beaver Cove. 281-2300. This valley, known for its trout fishing and hunting, has been an important source of timber for several decades; much of it remains accessible by logging roads. Services include gas station, coffee shop, store. Campgrounds at Woss and Vernon lakes.

**Eagle's Nest Rest Area:** About 136km north of Campbell River. River view.

**Zeballos Rd:** 151km north of Campbell River, west off Hwy 19, 21km on unpaved road to Zeballos.

## SIDE TRIP
### to Zeballos

**Little Hustan Cave Regional Park:** Short distance on Zeballos Rd. Not suitable for oversize vehicles. Follow signs. Good caves for inexperienced cavers with sink holes, canyons, and a cathedral entrance. Large arches and swift-flowing river that disappears and reappears in rock formations.

**Zeballos:** (Pop. 220). At head of Zeballos Inlet. Pretty village beneath mountains with high cliffs and waterfalls. Once an important gold-mining town with a population over 1,500. Exploration for the mineral is ongoing, but mainstays are logging and fishing. Base for boat trips to the long inlets and waterways around Nootka Island. Though small, the village has campgrounds, a hotel, motel, and other accommodation. Excellent sport fishing.

**Fair Harbour:** 35km northwest of Zeballos by unpaved road. Launching point for kayakers and boaters exploring waters of Kyuquot Sound, including Brooks Peninsula and Checleset Bay. Brooks Peninsula is site of a new Provincial Wilderness Recreation Area, covering 28,780ha.

This is the home of Canada's only sea otters, endearing, whiskery-faced clowns that once thrived along the entire coast of North America. Today, about 800 remain in Canada, descendants of Alaskan otters transplanted in late 1960s and early 1970s. The luxurious fur of these marine mammals was not only the cause of their near demise, but one of the main reasons for early exploration of the BC coast. They were an extremely valuable commodity for merchant seamen eager to satisfy the fashion-conscious mandarins of China. Literally thousands were slaughtered by whites and native peoples well past the turn of the century. Vancouver Island's last sea otter was shot dead in 1929 at Kyuquot, near Fair Harbour. Since the transplants, they remain among that worrisome class of animals known as endangered species, but they appear to be re-establishing themselves at an annual growth rate of 12 percent. They are starting to disperse themselves up and down the coast, gourmandizing on red sea urchins.

### *Return to Highway 19*

**Nimpkish Lake:** Highway skirts most of the east side of this narrow, 22km-long lake. Legend tells us the Nimpkish people derived their name from a mythical and monstrous halibut that devoured canoes and caused a terrible tide rip near Alert Bay, off the mouth of the Nimpkish River. Early Aug, this is site of annual Nimpkish Speed Slalom Weekend for windsurfers. Picnic area. Gas station and store. There is good canoeing on nearby Anutz Lake.

**Forestry Tours:** North Island Forestry Centre, operated by five forest companies, near turnoff to Beaver Cove (next). 956-3844. Tours depart from various North Island locations, including Port Alberni, Port Hardy, Port McNeill and Woss, depending on day. Forestry, logging camp and boom, and fish hatchery tours, visits to old-growth forests, boat and steam-train rides. Advanced booking required.

**Beaver Cove Turnoff:** 187km north of Campbell River. Southeast for 13km to log-sorting grounds at Beaver Cove. Another 2km to Telegraph Cove. (Last 8km is logging road.) Fletcher Challenge at Beaver Cove (928-3023) offers woods tours of logging operations.

FRED FELLEMAN/IMAGE FINDERS

*Orca breaching in waters off Vancouver Island.*

## SIDE TRIP

### to Telegraph Cove

A good takeoff point for whale watching in Johnstone Strait.

**Telegraph Cove:** (Pop. 18). Telegraph Cove, on charming boardwalks, was built before World War One as northern terminus of a telegraph line strung from tree to tree along Vancouver Island's coast. Later this was a thriving sawmill community, now a major destination for lovers of coastal wilderness.

Campground just beyond Telegraph Cove. Boat launch, boat gas, post office, general store, fishing charters, daily cruises to view killer whales and explore North Island's native culture. About 20km down Johnstone Strait to now-famous Robson Bight. The bight is location of an ecological reserve established in 1982 to protect killer whale habitat. Every summer, pods of whales come here to rub on gravel beaches at the mouth of the Tsitika River. There are strict regulations for whale watchers, and people are asked not to enter the reserve area.

### *Return to Highway 19*

**Cheslakee (Nimpkish River) Salmon Hatchery:** Less than 2km beyond Beaver Cove Junction cross Nimpkish River Bridge and turn right. 956-4712.

**Port McNeill:** (Pop. 2,641). 194km north of Campbell River, east off Hwy 19 for 2km. Port McNeill, with a sheltered harbour and modern townsite, is home for many who work in surrounding forests. Also a launching point for sports fishermen who test their skills in the channels around many islands between Vancouver Island and the mainland, and in nearby lakes and rivers. Town was named for William Henry McNeill (1801-1875), a Boston-born Hudson's Bay Company factor who in 1849 helped establish Fort Rupert Coal Mines north of here.

*Whale jawbone at Coal Harbour, northern Vancouver Island.*

**Port McNeill Information:** Infocentre, Port McNeill Chamber of Commerce, Box 129, Port McNeill, BC, V0N 2R0. 956-3131. On the waterfront on Beach Dr, next to BC Ferries terminal. Daily early June-early Sept.

**Regional District of Mount Waddington Information:** 2044 McNeill Rd (across from high school). Drop in for maps of highways, logging roads and regional parks. For information by mail, contact infocentres in individual communities.

**Port McNeill Airstrip:** About 2km south of Port McNeill on sign-posted road. Charter flights, private aircraft.

**Alert Bay-Sointula:** Car and passenger ferries from Port McNeill run triangular route across Broughton Strait to Alert Bay, on Cormorant Island, and Sointula, on Malcolm Island. About nine sailings daily. 956-4533.

## SIDE TRIP

### to Alert Bay and Sointula

**Alert Bay:** (Pop. 628). On 6.5-sq km Cormorant Island. By ferry from Port McNeill. Alert Bay and Cormorant Island were named for British warships HMS *Alert* and HMS *Cormorant*, which surveyed coastal waters 1846-1861. Nimpkish River Band First Nations people moved here to live and work after the establishment of a salmon saltery and church mission in the 1870s. Nowhere is the mystical native heritage so vivid as at Alert Bay, now a half-native, half-non-native village. There's an inexplicable eeriness to the totems in the Nimpkish Band's burial ground (visitors please view from respectful distance) towering above the beach, as if demanding respect from passing sailors.

Fishing and tourism are mainstays. With only 18km of road, Alert Bay claims more taxis per km than anywhere in the world. Shops sell native art, fish bonkers, curios. Accommodation and campground on the island. Whale-watching tours, fishing charters. Boat launch, moorage, fuel, groceries.

**Alert Bay Information:** Infocentre, Village of Alert Bay, Box 28, Alert Bay, BC, V0N 1A0. 974-5213. On Fir St. Turn right after disembarking from ferry. Mon-Fri year-round. Daily June-Sept.

**Alert Bay Airstrip:** About 2km from village centre. Chartered flights.

■ **Alert Bay Art Gallery:** Shares infocentre complex. Local artists. Alert Bay street scenes in watercolour.

■ **Alert Bay Public Library and Museum:** 199 Fir St 974-5721. July-Aug: daily, afternoons. In winter: Mon, Wed, evenings; Fri, Sat afternoons. Kwakwaka'wakw and local artifacts. Photo and archival collection. Nearby St George's Anglican Chapel, built in 1925, is opened for visitors on request.

■ **U'mista Cultural Centre:** Front St. 974-5403. Early May-late Sept: daily. Oct-April: Mon-Fri. In modern building reminiscent of a Kwakwaka'wakw big house. Repatriated potlatch collection. Historic and contemporary Kwakwaka'wakw materials. Cultural activities.

■ **Gator Gardens:** Trails and boardwalks through an unusual ecological park. Old cedar snags, hemlock and pine trees draped with moss, ravens, eagles, migratory birds.

■ **World's Tallest Totem Pole:** Beside the Big House, 53m. Carved by six Alert Bay natives, it represents the history of the Kwakwaka'wakw people. 13 figures represent separate groups of BC native peoples.

**Sointula:** (Pop. 672). On 83-sq-km Malcolm Island. By ferry from Port McNeill and Alert Bay. A quaint fishing village which began as a Finnish cooperative community. Sointula, "A Place of Harmony," established in 1901 by leader-philosopher-playwright Matti Kurrika. The colonization company he founded collapsed in 1905, but some 100 Finns remained, as do their descendants. Listen for Finnish being spoken.

It's a wonderful place to wander and absorb the maritime atmosphere. Explore Malcolm Island by logging roads. Walk the beaches.

Look for exquisitely soft sea-green rugs, made from fishnet. Dockside art gallery. Traditional co-op general store (c. 1909). Accommodation and campgrounds. Whale-watching and fishing charters.

■ **Sointula Finnish Museum:** Left on First St immediately after disembarking from ferry. Next to tennis courts. Call 973-6353 and someone will come and show you through. No long distance charges from Port McNeill. Artifacts reflect fishing and farming roots of Finnish community.

### *Return to Highway 19*

**World's Largest Burl:** 1.5km north of Port McNeill turnoff. Burl from a 351-year-old spruce tree. Weighs more than 20t and measures 13.5m around. Was discovered by surveyors near the head of Benson River, 40km south of its current resting place.

**Misty Lake Rest Area:** About 211km north of Campbell River.

**Port Alice Rd:** About 214km north of Campbell River, west off Hwy 19 for 58km on paved road to Port Alice. Keep an eye on your *pick-i-nick* basket: black bears, at home along this road, often venture right into Port Alice.

## SIDE TRIP

### to Port Alice

**Beaver Lake:** Small shallow lake just off Hwy 19 on Port Alice Rd. Day-use swimming and picnic area. Cutthroat and Dolly Varden.

**Seven Hills Golf and Country Club:** On Port Alice Hwy, 1km from Hwy 19. A shot of civilization in the middle of an absolute wilderness. Nine holes, restaurant, great hazards. Hornsby steam tractor here was built in 1910 in England and used in Dawson City to haul coal. Later brought to Holberg

Inlet area to haul logs, but at 40t it got bogged down and was abandoned.

**Marble River Recreation Area:** About 30km off Hwy 19. Large treed campground. Boat launch. Fishing, canoeing, swimming, waterskiing, hiking trail. Headquarters for north island day trips.

**Link River Regional Campground:** 50km off Hwy 19. 30 campsites. Canoeing and fishing on river, waterskiing on Alice Lake.

**Port Alice:** (Pop. 1,371). At foot of mountains and at head of Neroutsos Inlet in Quatsino Sound. Bears a remarkable resemblance to the town of Port Annie described by Vancouver Island author, Jack Hodgins, in one of his best novels, *The Resurrection of Joseph Bourne.* This logging and pulp mill town was actually named after Alice Whalen. In the period after World War One, the Whalen family operated three pulp mills in the area. In 1965 Port Alice was incorporated as BC's first instant municipality. A new townsite was built to replace the original company town 4km up the inlet, near the pulp mill. Old town closed in 1967.

Full tourist facilities, including accommodation and campgrounds. Boat-launching for exploration and fishing in long inlets of Quatsino Sound. Good fishing and camping at nearby Alice and Victoria lakes.

**Port Alice Information:** Infocentre operates year-round out of Quatsino Chalet, Box 280, Port Alice, BC, V0N 2N0. On the main street at 1061 Marine Dr. Open Mon-Fri. 284-3318.

■ **Port Alice Golf and Country Club:** Off Port Alice Hwy, beyond Port Alice townsite and left of the pulp mill. So steep there's a periscope at the second tee. Nine holes, nine sand traps, four water hazards. 284-3213.

**Logging Rd to Mahatta River:** 75km from Port Alice to Side Bay and Klaskino Inlet on the open Pacific. Ribbon-marked trail off Restless Main to beach, and eight-hour serious hike to Lawn Point. No fresh water, no facilities, no signs. Plane wreckage on beach. Consult Western Forest Products maps or ask at Port Alice Infocentre.

## Return to Highway 19

**Port Hardy Airport:** About 225km north of Campbell River, east off Hwy 19, 2km to airport.

**Beaver Harbour:** Take airport turnoff. Marine recreation area near Fort Rupert, a Hudson's Bay post established in 1849. A crumbling chimney is the only remnant of the fort. Fort Rupert today is a Kwakwaka'wakw reserve. Several native carvers, including members of the well-known Hunt family, produce southern Kwakwaka'wakw art at The Copper Maker. Workshop and gift shop open to public. 949-8491. Beautiful sandy shore, and residential area at Stories Beach.

**Bear Cove:** About 1km beyond turnoff to airport road continues east to Bear Cove. 5km to BC Ferries terminal. Public boat launch 4km towards terminal. Straight on Hwy 19 for about 4km to Port Hardy.

**Rd to Coal Harbour:** West off Hwy 19, about 2km beyond airport turnoff, a few metres beyond Quatse River bridge. East is the scenic route to Port Hardy.

**Coal Harbour:** (Pop. 206). 14km south of Hwy 19 near mouth of Holberg Inlet. Enormous jawbone of a blue whale stands as a monument to village's past as a thriving whaling station (1947-67). Was also a base for Royal Canadian Air Force (1941-47). Café. Lots of marine traffic as well as a lovely view from wharf. Floatplanes for Quatsino and logging camps up the inlet.

**Quatsino:** (Pop. 91). Accessible from Coal Harbour by water taxi. Fishing for salmon, cod, red snapper. Beachcombing, hiking, berry picking. Historic Eagle Manor Retreat on six secluded hectares serves lunch if you call ahead. 949-7895. May see porpoises or whales.

**Port Hardy:** (Pop. 5,082). 230km north of Campbell River. Port Hardy, the north island's main centre, is among those island communities that have recently taken advantage of their scenic settings. A paved seaside path runs along the town's beach at the edge of Hardy Bay, a favourite gathering place for bald eagles, Canada geese, and other birds. There are also wooden signs, carved by a local artist, depicting fish and wildlife frequently seen by north islanders in their day-to-day travels.

Known by some as "King Coho Country," Port Hardy waters have often given up coho salmon in the 9kg range. Fishing for larger chinook salmon and other species is good year-round in local waters.

Campgrounds are plentiful in and around Port Hardy. But reservations for hotels and motels are absolutely necessary during summer. Call North Island Reservations and Information 949-7622.

Port Hardy is also a takeoff point for Brooks Peninsula Provincial Recreation Area – 28,780ha of wilderness facing the open Pacific Ocean. 248-3931.

**Port Hardy Information:** Infocentre, Port Hardy and District Chamber of Commerce, Box 249, Port Hardy, BC, V0N 2P0. 949-7622. On Market St near ocean. Daily early June-late Sept. Mon-Fri rest of year.

**Prince Rupert Ferry:** At Bear Cove. From Port Hardy junction take sign-posted route to BC Ferry terminal. For details on ferry, see *Transportation*, p.32.

■ **Port Hardy Museum and Archives:** 7110 Market St. 949-8143. Open afternoons Tues-Sat, longer hours in summer. Native history, discovery and exploration of coast, a settler's kitchen. Public programs in summer and workshops in winter.

■ **Quatse River Salmon Hatchery:** Write Northern Vancouver Island Enhancement Society, Box 1409, Port Hardy, BC, V0N 2P0. 949-9022. On Hardy Bay Rd, just off Hwy 19 and across from Pioneer Inn. Coho, chinook, and chum. Campground, picnic areas, nature trails along river, fishing.

**Rd to Cape Scott:** 60km unpaved road leads from Port Hardy to Holberg, Winter Harbour, hiking.

## SIDE TRIP

### to Cape Scott

Those who want to see the extreme northwest tip of Vancouver Island, the largest North American Island in the Pacific, must don backpacks and boots and hike the historic Cape Scott trail.

**Georgie Lake Campground:** 6km along road to Cape Scott sign indicates access road leading another 6km to lake. Lakeside trail, great canoeing, spectacular sunsets.

**Holberg:** 42km west of Port Hardy at the head of Holberg Inlet. Groceries and fuel. Once known as world's largest floating logging camp. Café, pub.

**Winter Harbour:** (Pop. 54). 20km south of Holberg at mouth of Quatsino Sound. Shelter for fishermen from the open waters of the Pacific. Houses along the waterfront joined by boardwalk. Trail leads to rainforest hiking. Campground. Fishing, logging, fish farming are mainstays. Store, marina.

■ **Kwaksistah Regional Park and Campground:** On road into Winter Harbour. 12 campsites.

■ **Botel Trail:** At end of road, past store. 20-minute hike to the next bay.

**Cape Scott Provincial Park:** 15,054ha. Small campground on San Josef River at trail head and wilderness camping. 248-3931 or 755-2483. For experienced and well-equipped hikers. 40-minute hike to sandy beaches of San Josef Bay for hikers unwilling to walk the longer, historic Cape Scott Trail (at least eight hours). Rugged wilderness, covering 64km of extraordinary coastline with 23km of sandy beaches. A network of trails, laboriously carved through the tangled bush by enterprising Danish colonists at the turn of the century, has been rescued from encroaching rain forests, re-opening the tortuous 27.5km route to the cape. A few manmade relics, the odd tumbledown cabin and rows of weather-beaten driftwood fences remain as testimony to efforts defeated when the government broke its promise to provide the settlers with road access to markets.

The Cape Scott Sand Neck is a peculiar bridge of sand that actually joins the cape to the mainland of Vancouver Island. This is the only place where both sides of Vancouver Island can be seen at once. Beyond the sand neck you can climb a wooden plank road to a lighthouse, high above the sea. From here the view is staggering.

## Parksville to Ucluelet Junction

### HIGHWAY 4

Highway 4 to the Pacific Rim begins at Parksville and runs through Port Alberni to the west-coast villages of Ucluelet and Tofino 140km away. As the highway leaves east-coast Vancouver Island seascapes, it cuts westward through mountains and dark evergreen forests, into the heart of Vancouver Island. Beyond Cameron Lake, it winds between towering 800-year-old Douglas firs of Cathedral Grove, in MacMillan Provincial Park.

Northbound travellers on Hwy 19 can bypass Parksville and reach Hwy 4 by turning west 30km north of Nanaimo. The bypass route is well-marked. Southbound travellers on Hwy 19 can take Hwy 4A to Hwy 4 from Qualicum Beach.

The 42km stretch of Hwy 4 between Ucluelet and Tofino, which includes Long Beach, is under *Ucluelet to Tofino*, p.71.

**Emerald Forest Bird Gardens:** 1420 Island Hwy. 248-7282. 4.5km west of Parksville. 260 tropical birds – parrots, macaws, canaries – offer up a splash of... colour and a lot of noise. Birds in re-created natural habitats flatter their visitors by perching on hands, arms, even heads. Daily, year-round.

**Englishman River Falls Provincial Park:** 97ha. 105 campsites. 248-3931 or 755-2483. South turn 5km west of Parksville. 9km to park. Take your snorkel and air mattress. Great swimming. Scenic waterfalls and gorge, lush forest, hiking trails, naturalist programs in summer. Steelhead, rainbow, and cutthroat trout.

**Coombs:** (Pop. 840). Just over 9km west of Parksville. There's much more to Coombs than those goats eating the sod roof of the Old Country Market. After the turn of the century, Coombs was part of the Salvation Army's immigration program that brought nearly a quarter of a million poor English and Welsh to Canada. Several families settled here, under the Salvation Army's Ensign Crego. The community was named after Thomas Coombs, the army's commissioner in Canada. Today's Coombs is an eclectic collection of folk who like freedom and simple country living. In some ways a throwback to the 1960s.

The bustling Old Country Market offers fresh produce and many other treasures. The Coombs Emporium and Frontier Town has 33 craft oriented shops, mini-golf, trail rides. It's nose-to-nose tourists in summer. Visit Coombs General Store (serving the community's every need since 1910), the Frontiersman Pub, and the bakery.

**Butterfly World:** 1km west of Coombs. 248-7026. Open daily. Hundreds of live, "free-flying" butterflies from all over the world. And everything you always wanted to know about the personal lives – courtship, egg laying, caterpillar rearing – of butterflies. Second location on West Saanich Rd, near Victoria. See *Swartz Bay to Victoria*, p.38.

**Hwy 4A:** North off Hwy 4, 4.5km west of Coombs Bridge. Known as Hilliers Cutoff. 6km to Qualicum Beach. See *Nanaimo to Campbell River*, p.58.

**Little Qualicum Fish Hatchery:** 2.5km beyond Hwy 4A Junction, turn onto Melrose Rd and follow signs. Best times to visit are Oct-Nov and Feb-June. More than four million chinooks reared. Open 8-4. 752-3231.

**Little Qualicum Falls Provincial Park:** 445ha. 91 campsites. 248-3931 or 752-6305. North off Hwy 4, 4.5km west of Hwy 4A. Beautiful falls and forests. Includes the entire southern shore of Cameron Lake, which feeds Little Qualicum River. Hiking, swimming, snorkelling, paddling, fishing, summer naturalist programs. Only BC river besides the Cowichan, to have brown trout. Fish in the dark with big, fuzzy flies.

**Cameron Lake Picnic Site:** At outlet of lake, 4km west of Little Qualicum Park turnoff. Part of Little Qualicum Park. Cameron Lake, 12km long by 1km wide, can become dangerously choppy with little warning. Boaters: keep an eye on winds. Fishing, swimming, windsurfing. Folklore says its bottomless.

*Preparing for a kayak trip, Tofino, west coast of Vancouver Island.*

Parksville to Ucluelet Junction

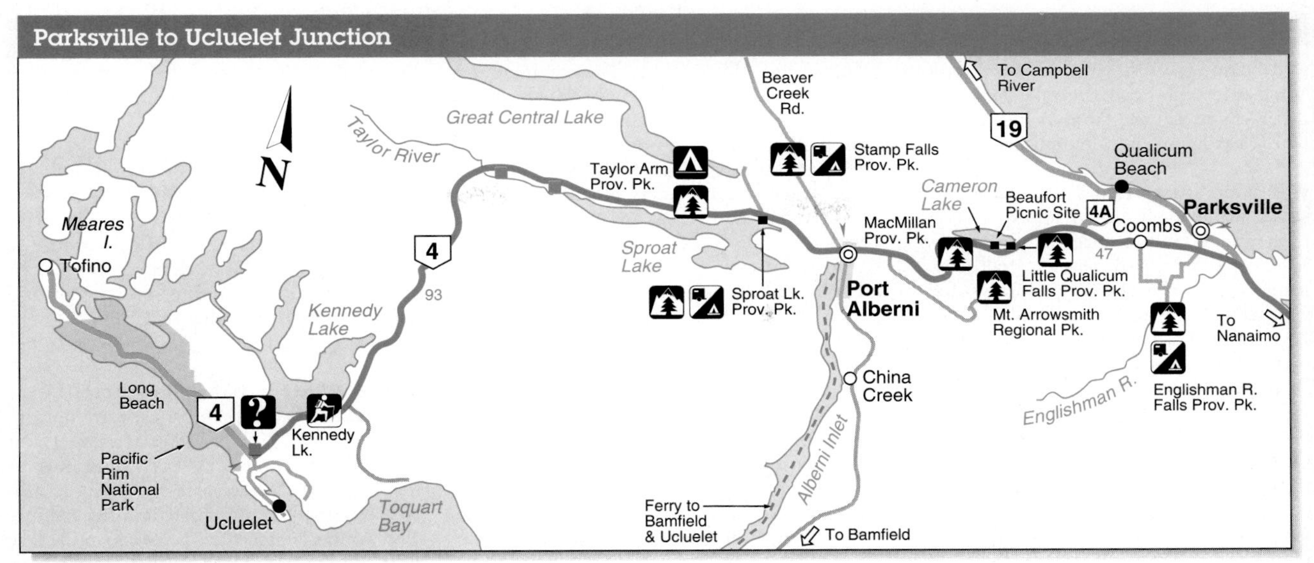


**Angel Rock:** About 2km beyond picnic site. Striking rock juts out over highway. Where young Port Albernians sometimes advertise their love for one another in spray paint.

**Beaufort Picnic Site:** Nearly 3km west of Cameron Lake Picnic Site. Part of the same park.

**MacMillan Provincial Park (Cathedral Grove):** 136ha. End of Cameron Lake, 31km west of Parksville. Includes lakeshore. Site of Cathedral Grove. Some of the largest remaining Douglas fir trees on the island, many up to 800 years old. Trail through forest. Park donated by Harvey Reginald MacMillan, first provincial chief forester for BC (1909-13), he Later headed HR MacMillan Export Company (now multinational MacMillan Bloedel). Picnicking, fishing, hiking.

**The Hump:** About 36km west of Parksville, engine test begins. Highway leads 2km to Port Alberni Summit, el 375m.

**Mount Arrowsmith Regional Park:** 925ha. South off Hwy 4, 41km west of Parksville. Another 27km to facilities. Scenic skiing and hiking. Vertical drop of 183m. Two T-bars, one rope tow, day lodge. Ski facilities open weekends and holidays during season. Downhill and cross-country, snowshoeing, rock and ice climbing. Summer hiking, wildflowers, fishing. Great views from Mt Arrowsmith (1,817m) and Mt Cokely (1,616m). Very wise to carry chains.

**Port Alberni Access:** 42.5km west of Parksville. Southwest to south Port Alberni, west to continuation of Hwy 4. Infocentre, see below, located here.

**Port Alberni:** (Pop. 18,403). On Hwy 4, 47km west of Parksville. At the head of Vancouver Island's longest inlet. This is a saltwater town a full 40km from the coast. The inlet rivals the fjords of Norway with wooded peaks up to 1,300m and dozens of streams running down the mountains. In spite of its distance from the open seas, the city received considerable *tsunami* damage in 1964 when seas rose nearly 3m above high water. Some people looked out windows to see their cars floating by.

From its early days as a copper, gold, and silver mining town, Port Alberni has been largely regarded as an industrial centre. Now with the forest industry in increasing peril here, the town's heavy industry is becoming part of its tourist industry. Visitors take tours of still active logging areas, sawmills, and pulp mills; people strolling on government docks buy fresh seafood from the fishboats; many displays in the local museum focus on industries of the Alberni Valley. During provincial Forestry Week in May, trucks and heavy equipment are brought in from the bush, polished and paraded through downtown streets.

The Alberni Harbour Quay is in south Port Alberni at the foot of Argyle St. It's home port for the *Lady Rose*, a 31m passenger and cargo ship serving the communities of Barkley Sound. It's also a place for people, with stores and restaurants, an infocentre, charterboat outlets, and picnic grounds. On summer weekends, *Two Spot*, an old steam engine once used to haul lumber, takes passengers along the waterfront.

The town is well-known for its salmon fishing: one of the island's two "Salmon Capitals of the World" (Campbell River is the other). The city is well-equipped to deal with sport fishermen. There are marinas, accommodation, tackle and outdoors shops, charters and boat rentals.

Art galleries display native crafts, oil and watercolours, jewelry.

**Port Alberni Information:** Infocentre, Alberni Valley Chamber of Commerce, RR 2, Site 215 C10, Port Alberni, BC, V9Y 7L6. 724-6535. At 2533 Redford St. Well-posted building near entrance to town. Mon-Fri year-round. Daily late spring to early fall.

**Alberni Marine Transportation Company:** Operators of the *Lady Rose* serving communities of Barkley Sound Bamfield, Ucluelet, Kildonan, Broken Islands. Based at Alberni Harbour Quay. 10-hour cruises between Port Alberni and Ucluelet, through the Broken Islands, during summer. See *Transportation*, p. 32, for schedule. Ask about canoe and kayak rentals here. The *Lady Rose* was built in 1937 in Glasgow, Scotland. During World War Two she carried army personnel, mail, and food for 7,000 servicemen.

**Port Alberni Airport:** About 12km west of city centre on Hwy 4 turn right onto Coleman Rd. Scheduled and charter flights. Another airport is across Somass River Bridge on Hwy 4 about 3km west of city centre. First road on left after crossing bridge. Floatplanes and grass strip.

■ **Alberni Valley Museum:** Echo Recreation Centre, 4255 Wallace St. 723-2181. Daily. Innovative community museum with operating waterwheel electrical generator, visitor-operated steam engine and other working displays. Major collection of western Vancouver Island artifacts.

■ **Dry Creek Municipal Park and Campground:** 60 tent/vehicle campsites, sanistation. Hookups, showers. On Napier St, but ask at infocentre for directions. In a forest beside a lovely creek that often dries in summer. Pleasant trails, walking distance to Harbour Quay, close to downtown, marina.

## SIDE TRIP
### to Bamfield and the West Coast Trail

Port Alberni is starting point of a 102km unpaved road to the village of Bamfield, and the start of the famous West Coast Trail. To find the beginning of the Bamfield Rd, take the south Port Alberni turnoff as you enter town from the Parksville side and follow signs carefully.

**China Creek:** About 14km south of Port Alberni on Alberni Inlet. Site of marina and campground with boat launch. Windsurfers who come to take advantage of the inlet's strong and steady winds use it as a base. Heavily used by salmon fishermen.

**West Coast Trail:** 77km beach and forest hike along the infamous "Graveyard of the Pacific." Once a telegraph and lifesaving route for shipwrecked mariners, trail now is a long, soul-stirring tramp amid some of Canada's most magnificent scenery. A part of Pacific Rim National Park, the northwest end of the trail is at Pachena Bay, 3km from Bamfield. Summer travel infocentre. Five to seven days for hikers who must be well-prepared for all the rain, dampness, and exhaustion the west coast is capable of throwing at them. Due to over-use of the trail (9,000 hikers annually), a quota of 52 hikers per day has been instituted. A Back-country Park Use Permit is now required for all overnight use of the trail. The trail is open May 1-Sept 30, and reservations can only be made beginning in March of the year in which the hike will take place. Reservations are by telephone only: 728-1282. For more information on registration, waiting lists, safety, maps, tide tables, sanitation, references, equipment, and accommodation: Pacific Rim National Park, Box 280, Ucluelet, BC, V0R 3A0. 726-7721. Also see *Activities Outdoors*, p.19.

**Bamfield:** (Pop. 256). By unpaved road 102km south of Port Alberni or 108km west of Youbou on Cowichan Lake (see *Lake Cowichan to Bamfield*, p.56). Or come via the *Lady Rose* from Port Alberni.

Salmon fishing is one of the main reasons why the population of Bamfield, on southeast side of Barkley Sound, jumps to more than 2,000 in summer. Sport fishermen use Bamfield as a base to fish the waters of Barkley Sound and Alberni Inlet. The community is also inundated each year by hundreds of hikers, canoeists, scuba divers, kayakers. Despite its small size, the community is well-equipped with general stores, accommodation, charters, boat rentals, liquor outlets, other services.

The village itself is an enchanting place with a seaside boardwalk along one side and trails to pretty beaches. Only one side of Bamfield Inlet is accessible by road, so the inlet is the village's highway. You can lean against a rail on the boardwalk and watch a steady stream of boats flowing past the shops and houses that overlook the inlet.

About 12km west of Bamfield, in the centre of Barkley Sound, are the Broken Group Islands. A part of Pacific Rim National Park, these 100-odd islands and islets lure canoeists, kayakers, cruisers, and sailors from around the coast. These mariners commonly run across killer whales and grey whales, porpoises, seals, sea lions, river otters, basking sharks, nesting cormorants, and bald eagles.

**Bamfield Information:** Bamfield Chamber of Commerce, Box 5, Bamfield, BC, V0R 1B0. Brochures available at infocentre, stores, restaurants, and businesses.

■ **Bamfield Marine Station:** Near mouth of Bamfield Inlet, accessible by road. Write Bamfield Marine Station, Bamfield, BC, V0R 1B0. 728-3301. Was trans-Pacific cable station at turn of century. In 1969 became marine biological research station for the five western Canadian universities. Lobby area, with scientific and historical displays, and video tape of station activities, is open year-round. Guided tours: May-Aug, Sat-Sun 1-3.

### Return to Port Alberni and Highway 4

DALE SANDERS

*Crimson anemone hosts an orange decorator crab.*

**Highway 4 to Pacific Rim:** As you enter Port Alberni from Parksville, drive into downtown. At Somass River turn north toward Pacific Rim Park. Well-posted. Known locally as the Pacific Rim Hwy.

**Stamp Falls Provincial Park:** 236ha. 22 campsites. 248-3931 or 755-2483. About 400m after turning toward Pacific Rim Park is the start of a 12km road to Stamp Falls Park. Cool, clear waters ideal for snorkeling and swimming. Pretty falls and fishway to help spawning sockeye, coho, and chinook salmon.

**Sproat Lake Provincial Park:** 39ha. 59 campsites, sani-station. 248-3931 or 723-2952. On Hwy 4, 10km beyond turnoff to Stamp Falls. Busy in summer. Nice beaches and lots of boating territory. Petroglyphs, hiking, swimming, fishing. The world's largest water bombers, in the lake near the park, are used to fight forest fires. Measuring 36.5m long with a wingspan of 61m, each Martin Mars Bomber can carry 27t of water. Park named for the energetic Gilbert Malcolm Sproat (1834-1913), sawmill manager, Agent General in London, Indian Reserve Commissioner, and Gold Commissioner.

**Great Central Lake:** Its access is at opposite side of Hwy 4 from Sproat Lake Park turnoff.

## SIDE TRIP
### to Great Central Lake

Large lake, 34km by 2km. Good fishing. Boat and backpack route to Della Falls.

**Robertson Creek Fish Hatchery:** Near outlet of Great Central Lake about 7km northwest of Hwy 4. One of main causes of tremendous sportfishing success in Alberni Inlet and Barkley Sound. Built in 1959 to introduce pink salmon to the Stamp-Somass river system, primary spawning grounds for Alberni Inlet salmon. Expanded in 1980 to produce millions of smolts annually – nine million chinook, 1.5 million coho, 250,000 steelhead. See adult coho and chinook Sept-Nov, spawning steelhead in Feb, juvenile coho and steelhead year-round, chinook fry April-May. 724-6521.

**Della Falls:** At 440m, Canada's highest waterfalls, the world's sixth highest. In Strathcona Provincial Park. Reached by boating to head of Great Central Lake and hiking historic Drinkwater Creek trail for 16km. The falls, surrounded by some of the island's highest peaks, tumble in three cascades to valley of Drinkwater Creek. Boat launching and charters at Ark Resort, near Robertson Creek Hatchery. Scenic flights from local airlines.

### Return to Highway 4

Hwy 4 ascends gradually as it skirts the shore of Sproat Lake. Beyond the end of the lake it follows Taylor River for about 7km before crossing it. From here, road climbs over Sutton Pass in the Mackenzie Range. It then turns south and follows Kennedy River as it meanders through the Mackenzie Range to Kennedy Lake and its final destination, Tofino Inlet.

**Taylor Arm Provincial Park:** 79ha. About 5km beyond Sproat Lake Park. Forested park with hiking trails, fishing, swimming. Undeveloped campsites.

**Sproat Lake Rest Area:** 33km beyond Port Alberni.

**Taylor River Rest Area:** 37km beyond Port Alberni.

**Road to Toquart Bay:** 81km west of Port Alberni. As Hwy 4 skirts Kennedy Lake, watch for a logging road running parallel to highway, opposite lake. Rough 16km road to hard-packed sandy beach. Boat launching. Good base for fishing and paddling excursions into Barkley Sound. Expect lots of company.

**Kennedy Lake:** Picnic spot about 83km west of Port Alberni. Not only Vancouver Island's largest lake at 69 sq km, but also one of its nastiest. Although it can be a good fishing and boating lake, it is also hemmed in by steep mountains and subject to sudden, strong winds.

**Ucluelet - Tofino - Port Alberni Junction:** 140km west of Parksville. Southeast for 8km to Ucluelet. Northwest for 34km to Tofino. Long Beach, in Pacific Rim National Park, is between this junction and Tofino. See *Ucluelet to Tofino (Long Beach).*

## Ucluelet to Tofino: Long Beach

### PACIFIC RIM HIGHWAY (Highway 4)

The 41.5km stretch of Hwy 4 between Ucluelet and Tofino provides road access to the Long Beach section of Pacific Rim National Park. There are plenty of signs indicating where to find information, or where to camp, hike, or stroll on the beach. For the 800,000 visitors a year, there are several hotels, motels, resorts, and campgrounds outside the park boundaries. Tourism is a year-round industry here and reservations for accommodation are highly recommended.

**Ucluelet:** (Pop. 1,595). On Ucluth Peninsula, 8km southeast of the Ucluelet-Tofino-Port Alberni Junction. Ucluelet is a tourist, fishing, and logging village about a third of the way up Ucluelet Inlet from Barkley Sound. It's a base for both commercial and sport fishermen, and for operators of nature and whale-watching cruises.

The town – with a multitude of shops, restaurants and accommodation – has most amenities needed by tourists. There are galleries and specialty shops that exhibit and sell the work of local artists, both native and non-native.

The village's name comes from the native Nuu-chah-nulth word for "people of the sheltered bay." A safe landing place for canoes.

**Ucluelet Information:** Infocentre, Ucluelet Chamber of Commerce, Box 428, Ucluelet, BC, V0R 3A0. 726-4641 or 726-7289. Two infocentres. One in village centre at Davidson Plaza. Daily in summer. Rest of year: Tues-Sat. Another infocentre at Ucluelet-Tofino-Port Alberni Junction. Daily July-Aug. Weekends late May-Sept.

■ **Canadian Princess:** Downtown. An historic west-coast steamship (built 1932) which has become a floating hotel. A former Canadian Hydrographic Service vessel, now the mother ship for launches venturing into nearby waters for fishing and nature trips.

■ **Amphitrite Point:** On southern tip of Ucluth Peninsula. Canadian Coast Guard provides marine communications and vessel traffic services here. Dozens of ships within the system's coverage area are notified of one another's whereabouts. Marine advisories and notices to ships are broadcast regularly from the centre.

Amphitrite Point Lighthouse, established in 1905, has a commanding view over the open Pacific and Barkley Sound. Stroll around on concrete paths. Lovely sunsets.

**Ucluelet - Tofino - Port Alberni Junction:** 8km from Ucluelet. Northeast to Port Alberni, northwest to Long Beach and Tofino.

**Pacific Rim National Park:** Boundary for the Long Beach unit of the park is 1km toward Tofino from junction. This section of the park encompasses 8,100ha. The entire park, including the West Coast Trail and Broken Group Islands and 22,300ha of ocean, is 51,300ha.

Before the advent of Pacific Rim Park, there was no place on the west coast of Canada where large tracts of land and sea, representative of this magnificent area's natural features, were preserved forever as a national park. Through painstaking negotiations, land acquisitions, and timber rights trades, the forests of the park have been saved.

Long Beach, a long-standing secret among Vancouver Islanders, was accessible by a meandering dirt track from Port Alberni. (It was referred to as "Long Bay" by the first settlers who arrived just after the turn of the century. Many of the bays and beaches – Grice, Chesterman, MacKenzie – are named after them). The paving of Hwy 4 in the early 1970s brought a never-ending stream of tourists: though some islanders share their secret with reluctance, there has been no effort to stem the flow. In spite of the growing number of visitors, there are still lots of out-of-the way places, quiet coves, and deserted beaches not far from the more crowded, easily accessible areas.

More than half of the 30km of shoreline at Long Beach is sand: you can hike the beaches and headlands for 19km from Schooner Cove to Half Moon Bay. There are parking lots and wheelchair ramps within easy reach of the main beaches. Hiking trails lead to other beaches and enchanting forests throughout the Long Beach area. The Canadian Parks Service has produced several publications about Pacific Rim Park, including a brochure on hiking trails. Available at park's infocentre.

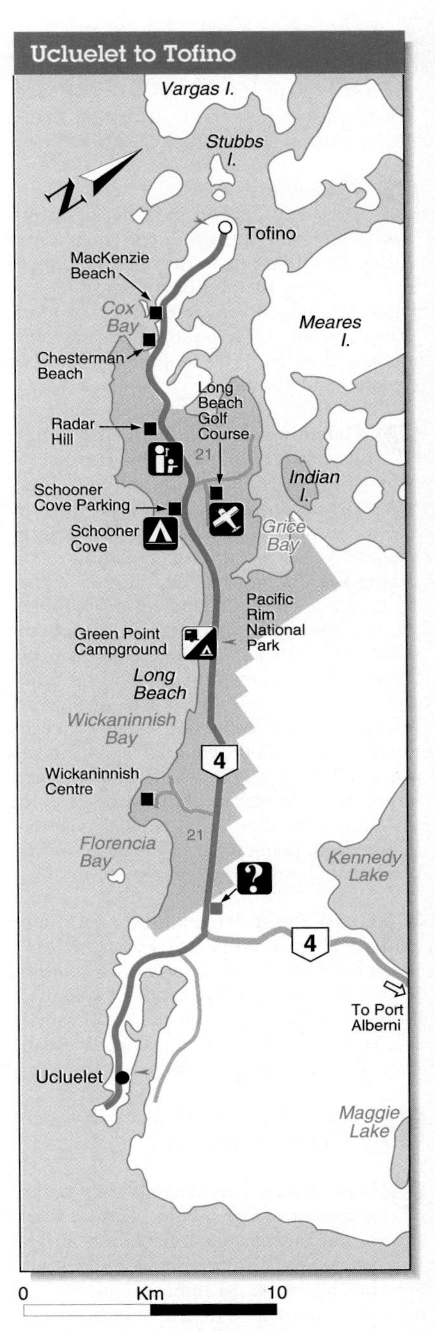


**Pacific Rim Park Information Centre:** 3km northwest of Ucluelet-Tofino-Port Alberni junction. Info on all sections of the park as well as on tourist facilities and attractions outside park boundaries.

**Long Beach Rd:** Southwest of Hwy 4, 2km northwest of infocentre. To Florencia and Wickaninnish bays.

**Florencia Bay:** South off Long Beach Rd 1.5km from Hwy 4. 1km to parking and trail. Also known as Wreck Beach. Inhabited by squatters in driftwood shacks before creation of the park. Lovely 5km beach.

**Wickaninnish Centre:** At end of Long Beach Rd, beyond park headquarters. Two observation decks with telescopes. Open during day late spring to early fall. To provide understanding of the north Pacific Ocean. Films, exhibits, murals, restaurant, and more. Wickaninnish, a Clayoquot chief, was often mentioned in late 1700 accounts by maritime explorers and fur traders.

**Wickaninnish Bay:** More long sandy, surf-battered shore. From late Feb to May you can look out to sea and catch glimpses of willowy mist shooting high above the waves. It's coming from Pacific grey whales on their northward migration to the Bering Sea. As many as 20,000 pass within sight of Vancouver Island on a 10,000km journey from Baja California and Mexico, the longest migration of any mammal on earth. Some whales remain as year-round residents, and may be seen by keen observers. Infocentres have details on whale-watching tours: some 15,000 people a year are taken out to mingle with the whales. Some experts fear for both the welfare of the whales, and the watchers (the danger, it seems, is spinal injuries from pounding over the waves in rubber dinghies).

**Green Point:** 94 campsites. Southwest off Hwy 4, 8km northwest of Long Beach Rd. Often long lineups during summer. High above beach where soothing sounds of the surf will lull you to sleep. Lots of activity at Green Point Theatre in evenings, usually early enough for sleepy children.

**Tofino Airport:** 4km northwest of Green Point campground.

**Long Beach:** Southwest off Hwy 4, 4km northwest of Green Point. Surfers, windsurfers, and kayakers test their skills here. The long, sandy beach is a favourite for hikers, joggers, beachcombers. In summer you can kick off your shoes and walk the beach with the pounding surf slurping up the shores, swirling around your bare feet. It's particularly invigorating in winter, when furious storms lash the headlands, shaking the trees and spattering salt spray on your face. Bundle up in warm, wet-weather gear and listen to the surf as you brave the elements. Sedentary types can put their feet up in a seaside cottage and watch the activity through big picture windows while sipping something warm.

**Schooner Cove:** 2km northwest of Long Beach parking lot. Walk-in campsites. A 15-minute walk leads to beach where up to 80 tents are allowed on the sand.

**Grice Bay:** North off Hwy 4, less than 1km north of Schooner Cove. Boat launch 2km from highway. Large shallow bay near Tofino Inlet. Important wintering area for thousands of birds.

**Long Beach Golf Course:** At junction of Hwy 4 and Grice Bay Rd. Nine holes, coffee shop. 725-3332

**Radar Hill:** Southwest turn off Hwy 4, about 3.5km northwest of Schooner Cove. 1.5km to the 96m summit. Spectacular views. Take your binoculars. Exciting in strong winds. Was site of World War Two radar station.

**Chesterman Beach:** Southwest off Hwy 4, 5km northwest of Radar Hill turnoff. 2km beach outside the park with a delightful islet that can be reached at low tides. Don't get marooned.

**MacKenzie Beach:** Southwest off Hwy 4, 2.5km northwest of Chesterman Beach turnoff. Sandy beach nearly 1km long. Accommodation and campground.

**Tofino:** (Pop. 1,103). At end of Hwy 4, 34km northwest of Ucluelet-Tofino-Port Alberni Junction. At the tip of Esowista Peninsula, a 16km land neck near the entrance to Clayoquot Sound.

Tofino is a pretty fishing village surrounded by impressive islands forested by impressive trees. It takes its name from Tofino Inlet, named by the Spaniards in 1792, for the hydrographer Vincent Tofino de San Miguel. But this is traditional territory of the Nuu-chah-nulth Nation of First Peoples, long known to newcomers as Nootka, or West-coast people. There are five Nuu-chah-nulth communities in this area. The Tla-o-qui-aht community lives mainly at Opitsat, on Meares Island, and at Esowista, just south of Tofino.

Tofino is a rapidly growing supply centre for tourists visiting Pacific Rim National Park and for about 700 people who live on secluded shores and islands in Clayoquot Sound. It's also a gateway to markets where fishermen and oyster farmers sell their wares – salmon, cod, halibut, prawns, crabs, and other seafoods. One of Tofino's government wharves is known locally as the "crab dock" and is used by crab fishermen to store traps and tie up their boats. If you happen to be there when a crab fisherman arrives, you could buy some fresh from the traps.

With the recent influx of tourists to Tofino, local residents are learning to fight vigorously to protect their scenic, and fragile, environment. In demonstrations and court battles, they have challenged the big logging companies that seem determined to clearcut the magnificent surroundings that make this corner of the world so special. Tofino and its environs is one of the hottest of the environmental hot spots in Canada today.

**Tofino Information:** Infocentre, Tofino-Long Beach Chamber of Commerce, Box 476, Tofino, BC, V0R 2Z0. 725-3414. On Campbell St, main road into town. Open daily July-Aug. Weekends May-June, Sept.

■ **West Coast Maritime Museum/Whale Centre:** In town centre. 725-3163. Daily, March-Oct. Maritime and trade history. Artifacts from sunken ships, Nuu-chah-nulth people, and sea life. Also whale exhibits and marine excursions.

■ **Eagle Aerie Gallery:** 350 Campbell St. Lounghouse-style gallery designed by Tsimshian eagle clan artist Roy Vickers. Offers shelther from the rain and warmth for the spirit. Vickers paintings, mixing elements of traditional native art with colourful graphic images, fetch a high price worldwide. *A Meeting of Chiefs* was presented to Queen Elizabeth in 1987.

■ **House of Himwista:** 346 Campbell St. First Nations art: prints, jewelry, carvings.

■ **Clayoquot Sound:** Stretching 65km southeast from Hesquiat Peninsula to just beyond Kennedy Lake. With temperate, old-growth rain forests vanishing at an alarming pace, this 3,000 sq km of forest and sea surrounding Tofino holds worldwide significance and attention. In 1993, the government's decsion to let logging companies take two-thirds of the sound's old trees sparked Canada's largest civil disobedience action ever. By summer's end, thousands had visited the Peace Camp pitched in a clearcut just east of the Tofino-Ucluelet junction, and over 800 people had been arrested in daily attempts to stop logging trucks from getting though.

■ **Island Views:** West to east, Stubbs and Arnet (or Tibbs) islands. The community of Clayoquot, on Stubbs Island, was settled by Europeans in 1850s, before Tofino was established. Arnet Island was home of eccentric young Englishman Fred Tibbs. In a 36m fir tree he built a seat so he could enjoy both his gramophone and the view.

■ **Meares Island:** At 8,600ha it's smaller than Nantucket, larger than Hong Kong or Bermuda. Dominates the intricate waterways around Tofino. Stands of centuries-old cedar and hemlock, the subject of bitter controversy between forest companies and environmentalists. Site of Nuu-chah-nulth village Opitsat. Local charter-boat operators offer tours of island's ancient forests: see them while you can.

■ **Vargas Island:** 5km by boat from Crab Dock in Tofino to vast sandy beaches, whale watching and private inn. Accommodation, camping, day trips, swimming, exploring. Vargas Island Inn: 725-3309.

**Hot Springs Cove:** In 39ha Maquinna Provincial Park. Site of Vancouver Island's only known hot springs, 37km northwest of Tofino. Boats and float planes available in Tofino. The springs look much like a typical west-coast creek, but the steaming water is 50 degrees C at its source and it cools as it flows over a waterfall and through a series of pools to the sea. Unforgettable day trip from Long Beach area. Bathing suits here are optional.

*Cape Beale lighthouse at the entrance to Barkley Sound, west coast of Vancouver Island.*

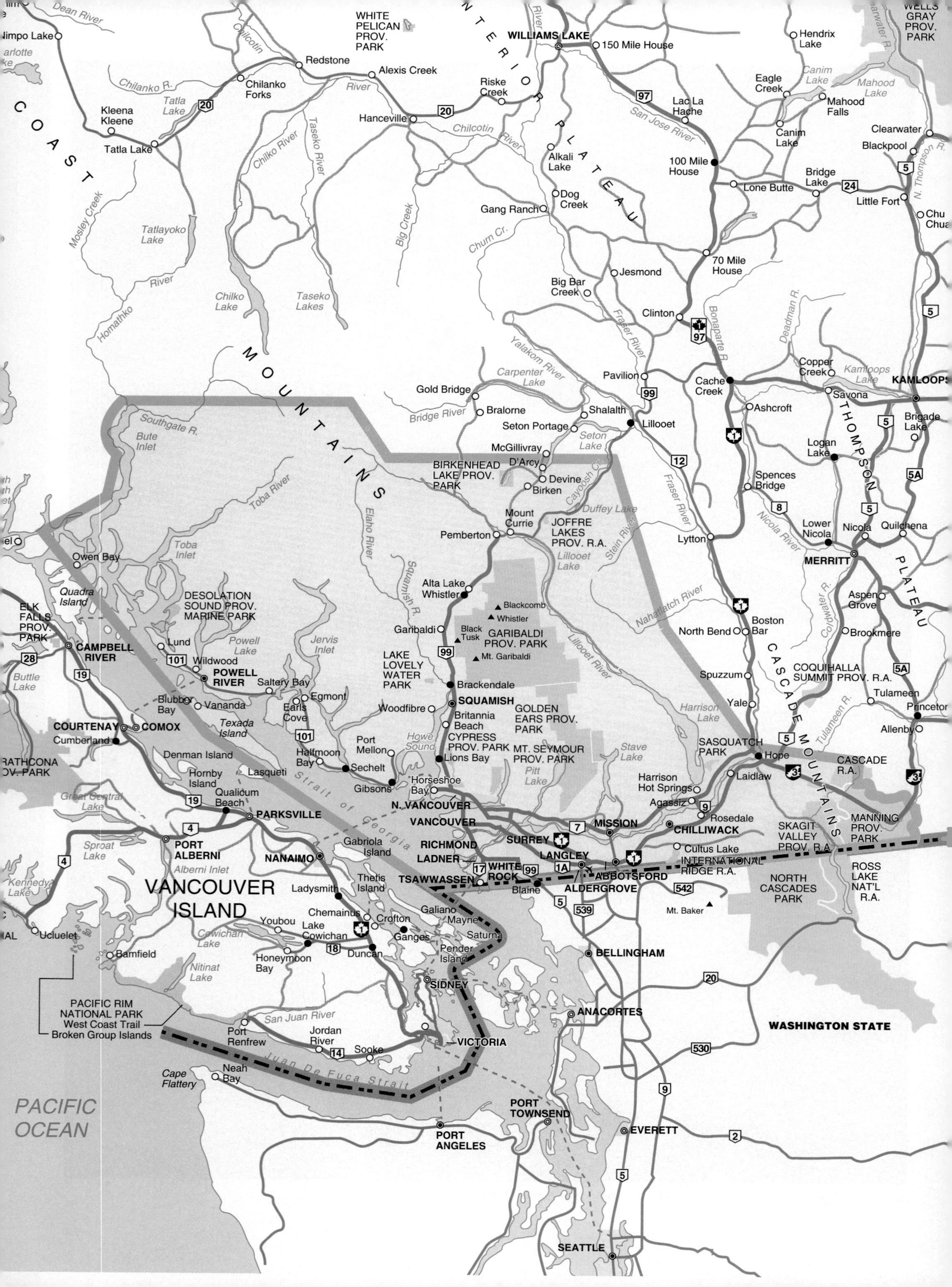

Dean River
Nimpo Lake
WHITE PELICAN PROV. PARK
INTERIOR PLATEAU
WILLIAMS LAKE
150 Mile House
Hendrix Lake
WELLS GRAY PROV. PARK
Chilcotin
Redstone
Alexis Creek
Chilanko R.
Chilanko Forks
River
Riske Creek
Eagle Creek
Canim Lake
Mahood Lake
Mahood Falls
COAST
Tatla Lake
Kleena Kleene
20
Hanceville
97
Lac La Hache
San Jose River
Canim Lake
Clearwater
Blackpool
Chilcotin River
Chilko River
Taseko River
Alkali Lake
100 Mile House
Bridge Lake
24
Lone Butte
Little Fort
N. Thompson R.
5
Dog Creek
Gang Ranch
Mosley Creek
Tatlayoko Lake
Big Creek
Churn Cr.
70 Mile House
Jesmond
River
Chilko Lake
Taseko Lakes
Big Bar Creek
Homathko
Clinton
Bonaparte R.
Deadman R.
Fraser River
MOUNTAINS
Yalakom River
Carpenter Lake
Pavilion
Copper Creek
Kamloops Lake
Cache Creek
KAMLOOPS
Gold Bridge
99
Savona
Ashcroft
Bralorne
Bridge River
Shalalth
Lillooet
Brigade Lake
THOMPSON
Southgate R.
Bute Inlet
Seton Portage
Seton Lake
McGillivray
Logan Lake
D'Arcy
12
BIRKENHEAD LAKE PROV. PARK
Devine
Birken
Cayoosh Cr.
Spences Bridge
5A
Toba River
Duffey Lake
Fraser River
8
Mount Currie
Pemberton
JOFFRE LAKES PROV. R.A.
Stein River
Lytton
Lower Nicola
Nicola
Quilchena
Nicola River
MERRITT
Toba Inlet
Elaho River
Lillooet Lake
PLATEAU
Owen Bay
Squamish R.
Alta Lake
Whistler
Nahatlatch River
Quadra Island
DESOLATION SOUND PROV. MARINE PARK
Blackcomb
Whistler
Coldwater R.
Aspen Grove
ELK FALLS PROV. PARK
Garibaldi
Black Tusk
GARIBALDI PROV. PARK
North Bend
Boston Bar
Brookmere
CAMPBELL RIVER
Lund
Powell Lake
Jervis Inlet
LAKE LOVELY WATER PARK
Mt. Garibaldi
CASCADE
COQUIHALLA SUMMIT PROV. R.A.
28
101
Wildwood
Lillooet River
19
Buttle Lake
POWELL RIVER
Saltery Bay
Brackendale
Spuzzum
Tulameen
Blubber Bay
Vananda
Egmont
SQUAMISH
Woodfibre
Earls Cove
Britannia Beach
GOLDEN EARS PROV. PARK
Harrison Lake
Yale
Tulameen R.
Princeton
COURTENAY
COMOX
Texada Island
Cumberland
101
Howe Sound
CYPRESS PROV. PARK
Allenby
Port Mellon
SASQUATCH PARK
MOUNTAINS
Halfmoon Bay
Sechelt
Lions Bay
MT. SEYMOUR PROV. PARK
Stave Lake
Hope
CASCADE R.A.
STRATHCONA PROV. PARK
Denman Island
Hornby Island
Lasqueti
Gibsons
Pitt Lake
Laidlaw
3
Qualicum Beach
Strait of Georgia
Horseshoe Bay
Harrison Hot Springs
Great Central Lake
19
N. VANCOUVER
Agassiz
9
PARKSVILLE
VANCOUVER
7
MISSION
Rosedale
MANNING PROV. PARK
4
SURREY
CHILLIWACK
SKAGIT VALLEY PROV. R.A.
Sproat Lake
PORT ALBERNI
Gabriola Island
RICHMOND
LANGLEY
Cultus Lake
Alberni Inlet
NANAIMO
LADNER
17
WHITE ROCK
99
1A
ABBOTSFORD
INTERNATIONAL RIDGE R.A.
ROSS LAKE NAT'L R.A.
Kennedy Lake
VANCOUVER ISLAND
Ladysmith
Thetis Island
TSAWWASSEN
Blaine
ALDERGROVE
542
NORTH CASCADES PARK
Chemainus
Crofton
Galiano
Mayne
Mt. Baker
5
539
Ucluelet
Youbou
Lake Cowichan
Saturna
Cowichan Lake
18
Ganges
Duncan
Pender Island
Bamfield
BELLINGHAM
Honeymoon Bay
Nitinat Lake
SIDNEY
20
PACIFIC RIM NATIONAL PARK
West Coast Trail
Broken Group Islands
San Juan River
ANACORTES
Port Renfrew
Jordan River
WASHINGTON STATE
14
Sooke
VICTORIA
530
Juan De Fuca Strait
Cape Flattery
Neah Bay
9
PACIFIC OCEAN
PORT TOWNSEND
EVERETT
2
PORT ANGELES
5
SEATTLE

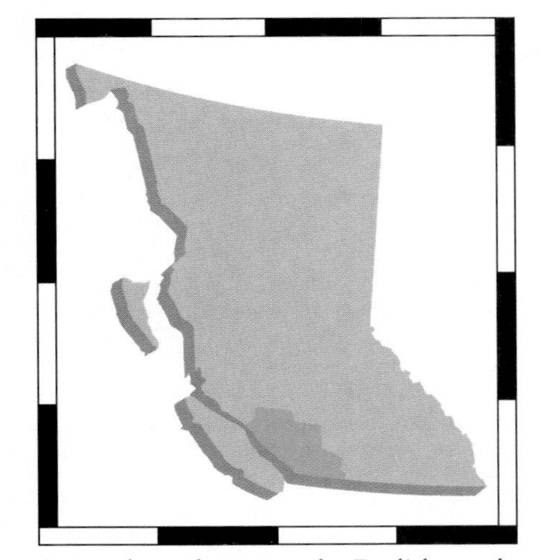

# Southwestern BC

## *Cities in the Wild*

In the early 1790s, the English naval commander, Captain George Vancouver, in his sloop of war, the *Discovery*, along with the armed tender, *Chatham*, searched inlets up and down the northwest coast, looking for a water route into the interior of the continent. The coastline, with all its indentations, is over 27,000km long, and the captain covered many thousands of these, surveying carefully as he went. Particularly, he was trying to find out if the interior could be reached by "arms of the sea, or by the mouths of large rivers."

The answer in the end was neither, but Captain Vancouver was not to know that, and he continued his attempts to penetrate the vastness of the land along the fingers of the tapering saltwater inlets.

In some ways, Southwestern BC has remained unchanged over the centuries. The narrow lowland in the southwest corner – now called Greater Vancouver – has the most intense population concentration in the province, and has obviously undergone cataclysmic change since the days of the first explorers. But the balance of the region is still vast and trackless. A look at the map, and the story is told: much of it is blank, no roads, no rail lines. Most of this region – which is the size of Vancouver Island – is still wilderness, inaccessible except by helicopter or boat, or logging road. The historic corridor may be the broad Fraser River valley, but the region also takes in hundreds of kilometres of deeply indented coastline north past Desolation Sound to Bute Inlet; as well as wild mountainous country from Bute Inlet east almost to Lillooet on the fringes of the Cariboo. The eastern boundary cuts through the Stein River valley, curving southeast to include part of the new Coquihalla Hwy, and Manning Provincial Park on the US border.

The south perimeter is a long, roadless stretch neighbouring another country, a segment of the world's longest undefended border. Manning Provincial Park and the Skagit Valley Recreation Area, snug against the 49th parallel that separates Canada and the US, offer alpine meadows, waterfalls, untouched forests, and abundant wildlife, very different from the smoothly rolling Fraser Valley.

All this is scarcely more than two hours' drive from downtown Vancouver. One can travel from the silver bridges of a river and seaside metropolis to roadless wilderness, all within the space of a pleasant excursion, a morning away from the once elusive river's mouth. In fact, north of Vancouver, and connected only by ferry, are the laid-back, salty-dog communities of the Sunshine Coast,

*Vancouver's West End.*

populated partly by intrepid commuters who have found a way to keep the natural life. And a mere 60km northeast into the mountains, standing sentinel to the town of Squamish, is the Stawamus Chief, a 652m granite monolith offering ultimate challenges to the mountain climber. Beckoning north along Howe Sound is Garibaldi Provincial Park, and the fabulous resort town of Whistler perched wondrously between the twin peaks of Whistler and Blackcomb.

However, the historic part, the soft belly of the region, has always been the fertile valley of the Fraser River that eluded the discoverers for so long. And the giant river mouth where salt and fresh waters mingle in the bays and inlets.

The history of Southwestern BC is intimately bound to one of the world's most formidable rivers, yet ironically the great river was exceedingly hard to find. Obscured by "stinking fogges," Spanish and British sailing ships roamed the coast for more than a decade without discovering it. Captain James Cook, accompanied by Vancouver, voyaged halfway up the west coast of Vancouver Island to Nootka Sound in 1778, and he, too, missed the Fraser.

At last, in 1791, the mouth of the Fraser was found, by a pilot in the Spanish Navy, Jose Maria Narvaez, who was surveying the Strait of Georgia in his tiny ship, the *Santa Saturnina*. The next year he was followed by two more Spaniards, Galiano and Valdes, who filled in more details of the coastal topography. The Spaniards left a legacy of lyrical place names: Malaspina Strait, Toba Inlet, and the islands of Texada, Lasqueti, Redonda, Hernando, Sonora. The English were less romantic: Vancouver's False Creek got its name during one of the many thwarted attempts to find the Fraser's mouth. It was just another salt-water inlet, not the creek they wanted (though it became the site, 200 years later, of Expo 86).

Meanwhile, oblivious to man, the great river was continuing its sweeping push down to the Pacific Ocean from headwaters high in the Canadian Rockies near Tête Jaune Cache. The Fraser cuts an unnavigable swath north-south through the centre of the province, virtually on a rampage, undammed, untamed, for hundreds of kilometres, through the boiling canyon at Hells Gate, south to Lady Franklin Rock at Yale (where later upriver boat traffic was brought to a halt).

Once out of the canyon and on to the delta, the river quietens down and broadens to an immense width. At Hope, 142km from Vancouver, it finds a passageway through the Coast Mountains and starts its home stretch, travelling smoothly across the Fraser lowlands to the sea. At its estuary, which begins in New Westminster, the Fraser splits into north and south arms that hug the community of Richmond.

So the entrance to the province, the gateway, was almost impossible to find from the ocean, and virtually unnavigable for the traveller coming overland. It is no wonder this west coast remained isolated for so very long.

Explorer Simon Fraser, the 1,370km river's eventual namesake, was the first white man to travel the Fraser River to its mouth — in an incredible expedition in 1808. He did not like the river: he found it remorseless, it tested his endurance beyond heroic limits.

"I have never seen anything equal to this country," he wrote, "for I cannot find words to describe our situation at times. We had to pass where no human being should venture."

Fraser found the river mouth, but for nearly the whole of his 35-day downriver journey from Prince George, he believed himself to be travelling the Columbia River. His disappointment was bitter and profound on July 2, 1808, when he reached the mouth of the Fraser and realized it was the wrong river, and a perverse, intractable one at that.

Fifty years later, in the spring of 1858, some 20,000 determined prospectors (many from California where the gold rush of 1849 had petered out) swarmed across the Strait of Georgia from the little Hudson's Bay Company stockade of Fort Victoria, and up the Fraser River in search of gold. By the fall of 1858, an estimated 30,000 miners were prospecting on the lower Fraser.

Within a dozen years, the gold rush had subsided, leaving many a near ghost town in its wake. But the prominence of the region was assured when Canada's Prime Minister John A Macdonald promised BC a railway to the coast – down through the Fraser Canyon. It was that promise which led BC, in 1871, to enter Confederation rather than join the Union of States to the south. So the land was finally penetrated, but not by boat on salt or fresh waters: it was the Iron Horse that finally made history.

In 1885 the Canadian Pacific Railway was completed, linking Canada at last from coast to coast. The first cross-country train arrived in Port Moody on July 4, 1886, and the following year, the rails were extended the 20km into Vancouver. Southwestern BC was finally able to get on with the task of establishing its farms, towns, industry and commerce.

There was one major setback, however. On June 13, 1886, just two months after Vancouver was incorporated as a city, a western squall caught the flames from clearing fires at the west end of town. In 20 minutes, some 1,000 buildings, with hundreds of others that were underway, burned to the ground. Three thousand people were left homeless. With the resilience of true pioneers, Vancouverites rebuilt their city, living for months in tents and makeshift quarters.

Southwestern BC continues to grow and develop as the heart of the province, yet wilderness is never far from the average back-

*Robson Square, in downtown Vancouver.*

*Canada Place and downtown Vancouver.*

yard, and history is never far from the present day. In his book, *The Fraser*, Bruce Hutchison notes that "unlike other great rivers, it has produced no songs, no myths, not even a special type of riverman," and he speculates that the river is "too violent, hurried and solitary." However, the human significance of the Fraser reverberates within its fertile valley, and a thousand and one tales are told in the histories of the cities, towns, and villages that have grown up along its banks.

## INFORMATION

**Southwestern BC Tourism Association:** #204 -1755 W Broadway, Vancouver, BC, V6J 4S5. 739-9011. Fax 739-0153. Addresses and telephone numbers of local infocentres are given in the *Logs* with the write-ups on each community.

## TRANSPORTATION

Transportation corridors and facilities in Southwestern BC are extensive, and infocentres can provide valuable information on all types of transportation, including boat charters, water taxis, and canoe, kayak, bicycle, and moped rentals. Free Vancouver city bus schedules and specially priced bus tickets are available at the Vancouver Travel Infocentre, Plaza Level, 200 Burrard St Vancouver, BC, V6C 3L6. 683-2000. Day Pass gives unlimited rides on buses, SkyTrain and SeaBus.

### By Road

Highways and roads in the region are in excellent or good condition. However, there are certain areas where caution is advised. On the Sechelt Peninsula, Hwy 101 narrows at Secret Cove just beyond Sechelt. It's advisable to drive slowly and use pullouts to let faster traffic pass. Hwy 99, known as the Squamish Hwy, can also be a challenge at night, or in rain or snow.

### Airlines

Over nine million passengers each year pass through Vancouver International Airport, off Hwy 99 in Richmond, a 25-minute drive from downtown Vancouver. In addition to domestic and international carriers operating out of this airport, floatplanes depart daily from Vancouver Harbour to Victoria and other destinations.

■ **Air BC:** 688-5515. Flights to many points in the province. Several departures daily between Vancouver Island and the Mainland, including flights from Powell River across the Georgia Strait to Comox.

■ **Air Canada:** 688-5515.

■ **Airspeed Aviation:** 852-9245. Half-hour flights between Abbotsford and Victoria.

■ **Awood Air Ltd:** 273-3521. Vancouver-Nanaimo airports.

■ **Baxter Aviation:** 1-800-661-5599. Vancouver-Nanaimo, harbour to harbour.

■ **Canadian Airlines International:** 279-6611.

■ **Connectair:** 244-8071. Connecting flights between Vancouver, Nanaimo, Tofino and Victoria.

■ **Coval Air:** 681-0311. From Vancouver, over 170 coastal destinations including Campbell River, Minstrel Island, Qualicum, Stuart Island, Sullivan Bay.

■ **Harbour Air:** 688-1277. Flights to Duncan and southern Gulf Islands – Salt Spring, Pender, Saturna, Galiano, Mayne, Thetis. From Vancouver's Coal Harbour Rd, two blocks west of Canada Place.

■ **Helijet Airways:** 273-1414. Regular flights from Vancouver International Airport and Vancouver Harbour to Whistler. Downtown Vancouver to downtown Victoria, harbour to harbour, several times daily.

■ **Pacific Coastal Airlines:** 273-8666 or 1-800-663-2872. Flights to Bella Bella, Powell River and Port Hardy from Vancouver International Airport's south terminal.

■ **Shuswap Air:** 1-800-663-4074. Vancouver to Salmon Arm. Salmon Arm to Kelowna on alternate days.

■ **Island Hopper:** 753-2020. From Coal Harbour's Tradewinds Barge in downtown Vancouver to Nanaimo Harbour and Sechelt Peninsula.

■ **Vancouver Island Air:** 287-2433. Scheduled floatplane service from Vancouver's downtown Harbour to Campbell River, and to many points on northern Vancouver Island and mainland coast.

■ **Wilderness Airline Ltd**: 276-2635. Vancouver to Anahim Lake, Bella Coola, Campbell River, Dean River, Kimsquit.

### Ferries

■ **BC Ferries:** a government-owned vehicle and passenger fleet with 42 ships serving 42 ports of call on the BC coast. One of the world's largest and most modern ferry fleets, carrying more than 20 million passengers a year, sailing 24 routes year-round.

Call Vancouver at 669-1211, or Victoria at 386-3431, 7am-10pm daily for general information on any route or schedule, or for reservations, which are taken only for Mainland-Gulf Islands, the Inside Passage or Queen Charlotte Islands routes. For 24-hour recorded schedule information on Mainland-to-Vancouver Island sailings, call 277-0277 in Vancouver, 656-0757 in Victoria, or 753-6626 in Nanaimo. Or write: BC Ferry Corporation, 1112 Fort St, Victoria, BC, V8V 4V2.

#### Vancouver to Victoria

BC Ferries sail from Tsawwassen, on the mainland 30km south of Vancouver, to Swartz Bay, 32km north of Victoria, on Vancouver Island. Hourly sailings June-Sept:

7am-10pm. Other seasons, every two hours on the odd hour from 7am-9pm, sometimes hourly sailings during peak times and holidays. Every summer, there are approximately four extra sailings a day, including a 5:30am sailing out of Swartz Bay (Vancouver Island). The 44km trip is one hour and 35 minutes. Reservations not taken. (To reach Tsawwassen direct when driving east on Hwy 1 – that is, bypassing Vancouver – take Hwy 10 south through Langley and east 49km to Hwy 17 at Ladner.)

All ships carry cars, campers and RVs, trucks, and buses. Vessels have elevators and special facilities for disabled travellers.

Bus services link Tsawwassen, Horseshoe Bay and Swartz Bay ferry terminals to Vancouver and Victoria. There are pickup and dropoff locations en route and tickets can be purchased on the ferry. There are also regularly scheduled city buses to and from the ferry terminals. See *Bus Lines.*

### Vancouver and Horseshoe Bay to Nanaimo

BC Ferries from both Tsawwassen, south of Vancouver, and Horseshoe Bay in West Vancouver serve Nanaimo (Departure Bay), Vancouver Island's second major ferry terminal. From Horseshoe Bay, the trip is 50km, one hour and 35 minutes. The year-round schedule offers sailings every two hours on the odd hour from 7am to 9pm. From late June to early Sept extra sailings take the schedule round the clock Fridays through Mondays only, with 50 percent savings on the 1am and 3am sailings. On Tuesdays, there are an extra 1am, 3am, 5am, and 9pm summer sailings. On Wednesdays, an extra 7am and 9pm sailing; and Thursdays, extra 7am, 9pm, and 11pm summer sailings.

The Mid-Island Express from Tsawwassen offers eight round trips daily from 5:30am to 11pm. The trip is 60km, two hours.

Reservations are not available on either Vancouver-Nanaimo route.

### Ferries to Gulf Islands and Sunshine Coast

Ferries from both Tsawwassen and Swartz Bay also serve the southern Gulf Islands – Salt Spring, the Penders, Galiano, Mayne, and Saturna. Vehicle reservations are recommended for sailings from Tsawwassen to the islands and return. Please note that reservations are not taken for Gulf Island sailings from Swartz Bay, or for inter-island travel.

Ferries from Horseshoe Bay to Langdale on the Sunshine Coast (40-minute trip) depart eight times daily. In summer, one extra sailing on Sundays and holiday Mondays. In winter, one extra sailing on long weekends. Ten sailings daily from Powell River to Blubber Bay on Texada Island (35 minutes) – only nine on dangerous-cargo Wednesdays. Five daily sailings in summer (four in winter) from Powell River to Little River, Comox, on Vancouver Island, a 75-minute trip.

## Bus Lines

■ **Cascade Bus Lines:** Call 662-7953. Covers Southwestern BC as far east as Harrison Hot Springs.

■ **Greyhound Lines:** 662-3222. In Canada: 1-800-661-8747. Province-wide.

■ **Maverick Coach Lines:** Call 255-1171. To the Sunshine Coast and Pemberton via Whistler and Blackcomb. Vancouver to Nanaimo via BC Ferries.

■ **Pacific Coach Lines:** Call 662-8074. Vancouver to Victoria via BC Ferries with a connecting shuttle service from Vancouver International Airport. Connecting service for Tsawwassen and Swartz Bay terminals for Gulf Island foot passengers. Connecting service with Mid-Island Express in Tsawwassen.

■ **Perimeter Transportation:** Call 273-9023; 261-2299; 1-800-663-4265. Airport Express bus service connects Vancouver International Airport with major downtown hotels and Vancouver bus depot. Travel time 35 to 45 minutes. Also ski-season service from Vancouver International Airport to Whistler Village.

## Railways

■ **BC Rail:** Call 984-5246; 631-3500. Departs 7:30am daily from North Vancouver's BC Rail station. Along Howe Sound, through coastal forests and mountains, badlands, and rangelands. Daily service to Prince George late June-mid-Sept. Rest of year on Wed, Fri and Sun. The train reaches Lillooet (Mile Zero of Cariboo Wagon Road that carried gold rushers north), at about 1:05pm. Can be a one-day excursion, with lunch in Lillooet and back to Vancouver for a late dinner. Train divides at Lillooet: one Budd car returns to Vancouver, the other completes the 745km excursion (with stops along the way) to Prince George. Among BC Rail's many stops is Whistler, where there is free shuttle bus service to and from Whistler Village throughout ski season. Reservations required for points beyond Lillooet.

■ **VIA Rail:** Toll-free 1-800-561-8630. New first-class transcontinental service on board *The Canadian*: routed from Vancouver through Jasper to Edmonton, and points east to Toronto. These trains, refurbished for vacationers with dining cars, sleeping accommodations and showers, are reminiscent of the golden days of passenger rail service in Canada. The two-and-a-half day trip originates from Vancouver at 9:00pm, to allow daylight travel though the Rocky Mountains.

■ **Rocky Mountain Railtours:** Great Canadian Rail Tour Company, Suite 104-340 Brooksbank Ave, Vancouver, BC. V7J 2C1. 1-800-665-7245. Sublimely, through the Rockies. Vancouver to Jasper, Vancouver to Banff, optional to Calgary. Travels only in daylight. Passengers going east or west spend the night in Kamloops. Continental breakfast, lunch, hotel included. May-early Oct.

■ **Royal Hudson Steam Train:** 688-7246. Six-and-a-half-hour boat-train excursion combines voyage from Vancouver Harbour to Squamish, at the head of Howe Sound, aboard *MV Britannia* with return trip on the Royal Hudson steam train to North Vancouver's BC Rail station. Mid-May-Sept. Advance bookings recommended for weekends.

## Car and RV Rentals

Consult the Yellow Pages of Vancouver phone book for complete listings of car and RV rentals. Infocentres can also assist.

*Parade through Vancouver's Chinatown.*

## *City Travel*

■ **BC Transit:** 261-5100. Bus service for Vancouver, Burnaby, New Westminster, Richmond, North Vancouver, Coquitlam, Port Coquitlam, Maple Ridge, Pitt Meadows, Langley, White Rock, Surrey, Delta, South Delta (Ladner), BC Ferries terminal at Tsawwassen and Vancouver International Airport. Many buses provide wheelchair-and scooter-accessible service. Infocentres carry BC Transit info and schedules, as well as special rate tickets.

■ **SkyTrain:** 261-5100. Introduced 1986. Vancouver's light rapid transit system is North America's longest, completely automated, driverless rapid transit system. Designed to carry 100,000 people a day, at speeds up to 80km an hour. Cars have specially designated wheelchair areas and all stations, except Granville Station, have elevators. SkyTrain links 17 stations along the 24.5km route from downtown Vancouver's Waterfront Station to Scott Rd Station, at King George Hwy in Surrey. Trip includes a 1.5km haul beneath the city of Vancouver, and generous above-ground views of coastal mountains.

■ **SeaBus:** 261-5100. Two 400-passenger catamaran ferries, the *Burrard Beaver* and the *Burrard Otter,* link downtown Vancouver to the North Shore. The trip across Burrard Inlet takes about 12 minutes and carries an average of 16,000 passengers on summer weekdays. SeaBus has become a major tourist attraction – offering a sweeping view of the North Shore mountains, Stanley Park and the city skyline. Buses connect with SeaBus sailings near the SeaBus terminal at Waterfront. Bicycles permitted during off-peak weekday runs, and all day weekends and holidays. SeaBus is wheelchair- and scooter-accessible.

■ **West Vancouver Transit System:** 985-7777. BC Transit bus, SkyTrain, and SeaBus transfers can be used on the West Vancouver Transit System. Blue Buses serve West Vancouver, including British Properties, Horseshoe Bay, and Lions Bay.

■ **handyDART:** For bookings call 264-5000, local 5101. Lift-equipped vans carry disabled passengers unable to use public transit. Regular commuting and occasional trips may be booked, at least 24 hours in advance, and up to seven days in advance. Accommodates wheelchairs and scooters.

■ **Langley Greyhound Bus Depot:** 534-4737. For points beyond Langley terminus of BC Transit.

■ **Link Bus Service:** Provides connecting service from main BC Transit routes to rural areas of Maple Ridge (Haney) and Pitt Meadows. Call BC Transit, above.

■ **Taxis:** Consult Yellow Pages. Luxury limousine service available.

*Reflection of the Marine Building, Vancouver.*

# SOUTHWESTERN BC EVENTS

### Abbotsford/Clearbrook/ Matsqui

- **Abbotsford International Band Festival:** Late April. 859-4891. More than 80 bands.
- **Sheep and Wool Fair:** Early May. Matsqui Agricultural Fairgrounds in Clearbrook.
- **Abbotsford Berry Festival:** Early July.
- **Agrifair:** Late July-Aug. Central Fraser Valley Exhibition Grounds. 852-6674.
- **Heritage Festival:** First week in Aug. Kariton House Cultural Centre, Matsqui. Arts, crafts, history. Live performances. 852-9358.
- **Abbotsford International Airshow:** 2nd weekend Aug. Abbotsford Airport. Mt Lehman Rd 3km south of Hwy 1. 852-8511. North America's leading airshow, attracting 300,000 people. Major three-day event, latest in aircraft technology, daredevil aerobatics.

### Agassiz

- **Fall Fair and Corn Festival:** Mid-Sept.

### Aldergrove

- **Bradner Flower Show:** Mid-April. In Matsqui Municipality, but just east of Aldergrove (north of Hwy 1 on Bradner Rd). 400 varieties of bulbs on display.
- **Festival Days:** Mid-June. Fireworks, outhouse races.

### Brackendale

- **Bald Eagle Count:** Jan. BC Wildlife event.

### Burnaby

- **Burnaby's Birthday Party:** Sept. Burnaby Village Museum.

### Chilliwack

- **Krafty Raft Race:** July. Cultus Lake.
- **Chilliwack Exhibition:** Aug.
- **Chilliwack Country Music Festival:** Aug.
- **Chilliwack Antique Threshing Bee:** Aug.
- **Bluegrass Festival:** Sept.

### Coquitlam

- **Festival du Bois (Festival of the Woods):** Early March. In Maillardville, part of downtown Coquitlam. BC's only French-Canadian festival.
- **Coquitlam Festival:** Events all summer: Teddy Bear picnic, model marine boat show, fishing derby.

### Delta

- **Delta Pioneer Days:** May.
- **Fraser River Festival:** June. Deas Island Regional Park.

### Fort Langley

- **May Day Celebrations:** May Pole dancing, parade.
- **JR Country:** Music! Mid-July.
- **Fur Brigade Days:** Early Aug.
- **Fort Langley Country Fair and Equestrian Grand Prix:** Mid-Aug.
- **Festival of the Performing Arts:** Aug.

### Gambier Island

- **Arts and Crafts Fair:** Aug. 10-min. passenger ferry ride from Gibsons.

### Gibsons (Sunshine Coast)

- **Sea Cavalcade:** Mid-July. Swimming race from Keats Island to Gibsons, water parade.

### Halfmoon Bay (Sunshine Coast)

- **Halfmoon Bay Country Fair:** July. Kids' fishing derby, car rally, crafts.

### Harrison Hot Springs

- **Harrison Festival of the Arts:** July. 796-3664. Concentrates on arts and cultures of the Third World, especially African and Latin American performers. Off-beat and exotic.
- **Sand Sculpture Classic:** Early Sept. 796-3425. On the beach at Harrison Lake, largest sand sculptures ever produced, up to 4.5m.

### Hope

- **Ducks Amuck Easter Race:** Easter Sunday.
- **Brigade Days:** Weekend after Labour Day.
- **Lights of Hope:** All Dec.

### Ladner

- **Snow Bird Festival:** Nov. Reifel Bird Sanctuary.

### Lund (Sunshine Coast)

- **Lund Days:** Early Aug.

### Maple Ridge

- **Mountain Festival Parade:** Early May.
- **Ridge-Meadows Fair:** Late July. It's been happening since 1905.
- **Whonnock Days:** 3rd Sunday in Sept.

### Mission

- **Annual Mission Indian Friendship Centre Powwow:** 2nd weekend July. 826-1281. Going nearly 20 years. Native dancers from all over North America. Buffalo burgers, salmon bake.
- **Folk Music Festival:** July.
- **Pioneer Week Celebrations:** Late July.

### Mount Currie

- **Lillooet Lake Rodeo:** Long weekends in May and Sept. Held by Lil'wat Band of the Stl'atl'imx nation.
- **"Voices for the Wilderness" Festival:** Now called "The Earth Voice Festival," and moved to Seabird Island. See below.

### New Westminster

- **New Westminster Jazz Festival:** March.
- **Hyack Festival:** 522-6894. Week-long festival starting Victoria Day weekend. History of New Westminster celebrated. Highlight is ancient and honourable Hyack Anvil Battery which fires a deafening "21-gun" salute to the Queen each Victoria Day, using anvils instead of cannons. Longest running annual event of its kind in the Commonwealth.
- **Finnish and Portuguese Festivals:** June.
- **Fraser Fest:** July. Westminster Quay. Boat show, working boat sailpast, tug demonstrations.

### North Vancouver

- **Lions Parade and North Van Folkfest:** End of June.
- **Edgemont Bavarian Festival:** Sept.

### Pemberton

- **Canada Day Celebrations:** Parades, parties, loggers' sports, canoe races.

### Pitt Meadows

- **Pitt Meadows Day:** June.
- **Pitt Meadows Blueberry Festival:** Aug.

### Port Coquitlam

- **Greek Days:** Late July.

### Port Moody

- **Golden Spike Day Fest:** Canada Day.

### Powell River

- **Kathaumixw International Choral Festival:** July. Biannual: 1994, 1996. 483-3346.
- **Sea Fair:** Mid-July. Loggers' sports and Sidewinder Rodeo.
- **Bathtub Races:** Aug. The only fresh-water sanctioned bathtub race in BC.
- **Blackberry Festival:** Late Aug.
- **Sunshine Folkfest:** Labour Day Weekend.

*World Championship Sand Sculpture Competition at Harrison Hot Springs.*

## Richmond

- **South Arm Family Festival:** June.
- **Annual Workboat Parade:** July.
- **Steveston Salmon Festival:** July 1.
- **Multi-fest:** 2nd Sunday in Aug.
- **Fraser River Carol Ship:** Christmas carolling on the water.

## Roberts Creek (Sunshine Coast)

- **Creek Daze:** Aug. Talent show, craft fair, and the world-famous Mr Roberts Creek contest.

## Seabird Island

- **Indian Festival:** Late May. Salmon BBQ.
- **The Earth Voice Festival:** End of July. A continuation of "Voices for the Wilderness" begun by the First Nations Peoples of Mount Currie and Lytton to save the Stein Valley from logging. One of the largest open-air gatherings of its kind in North America.

## Sechelt (Sunshine Coast)

- **Sunshine Coast Arts and Crafts Fair:** Aug.
- **Festival of the Written Arts:** Mid-Aug. At Rockwood Centre, Cowrie St. 885-9631. Top Canadian authors, readings, workshops.
- **Rockwood Centre StoryTelling Festival:** First weekend Oct.

## Squamish

- **Inaugural Run of Royal Hudson Steam Train:** Victoria Day.
- **Squamish Days Logger's Sports:** First weekend Aug. At logger's sports grounds next to Mamquam River. World's largest logger's sports show.
- **Windsurfing Competitions:** Aug.
- **Squamish Open Air Regatta:** Aug.

## Surrey

- **Cloverdale Rodeo:** May. The Big One. Rated No. 1 in North America.
- **Surrey Fall Fair:** Mid-Sept.
- **Harness Racing:** Oct-April.

## Texada Island

- **Texada Sandcastle Contest:** Midsummer.

## Vancouver

- **Polar Bear Swim:** Jan 1. Jericho Beach.
- **Annual Ice Sculpting Competition:** Jan. Seymour Ski Country. 986-2267.
- **Vancouver International Marathon:** Early May.
- **Vancouver Children's Festival:** Mid-May. 687-7697. Vanier Park.
- **Canadian International Dragon Boat Festival:** June. A major Pacific Rim event, growing every year. More than 2,000 paddlers. 100,000 spectators line False Creek.
- **DuMaurier International Jazz Festival:** Last two weeks of June.
- **Gastown Grand Prix:** Late June. International bicycle race.
- **Italian Week:** July.
- **Sea Festival:** Mid-July.
- **Vancouver Folk Music Festival:** Mid-July.
- **Vancouver Comedy Festival:** End of July.
- **Vancouver Chamber Music Festival:** Late July, early Aug.
- **Benson & Hedges Symphony of Fire:** Late July-Aug. English Bay. Fireworks set to music.
- **International Triathlon:** Aug.
- **Powell Street Festival:** First week Aug. A Japanese festival. Oppenheimer Park.
- **Pacific National Exhibition:** Last two weeks of Aug to Labour Day. 253-2311.
- **Vancouver Fringe Festival:** Mid-Sept.
- **Terry Fox Run:** Sept.
- **Vancouver International Film Festival:** Oct.
- **Vancouver International Writers' Festival:** Late Oct. On Granville Island.
- **Hadassah Bazaar:** Early Nov.
- **Christmas Carol Cruises:** Dec.
- **Festival of Lights:** Early Dec.
- **Vancouver Children's Winter Fest:** Christmas holidays.
- **First Night:** Dec 31. Festival of Arts, downtown. Over 70,000 people attend. First Nights also in Richmond and Burnaby.

## West Vancouver

- **Coho Festival:** Weekend after Labour Day.
- **Community Day:** First Sat, June. At the Rec Centre in the 2000 Block Marine Drive.
- **Sail Out to Horseshoe Bay:** Father's Day. Horseshoe Bay's Family Festival.

## Whistler

- **Great Snow Earth Water Race:** May.
- **Country and Blues Festival:** Late July.
- **Classical Music Festival and Mile-High Symphony Orchestra:** Aug. Highlight is Vancouver Symphony Orchestra performing atop Whistler Mountain. Getting the cellos and tubas up there, and retuning the orchestra, is quite some business.
- **Smirnoff Challenger Men's Professional Tennis Tournament:** Sept.
- **Octoberfest:** Early Oct.

## White Rock

- **May Fair:** May. Midway, crafts.
- **Tour de White Rock Cycle Race:** Late June.
- **Crescent Beach Triathlon:** Aug.
- **Sea Festival:** First weekend Aug. Torchlight parade, duck race, bathtub race.

*Lions Gate Bridge over First Narrows to Vancouver's North Shore.*

# Southwestern BC Routes and Highlights

## TRAVELLER'S LOGS



## HIGHLIGHTS



*"In earlier times, this Fraser River resembled an enormous dish that stored up food for all mankind; for the Indians flocked here from every quarter to catch the fish that abounded in its waters."*

– Storyteller, Fraser River Katzie tribe, 1936

## The Gateway Cities

Vancouver and its sister cities and municipalities enjoy a sumptuous setting spread across the estuary of the Fraser River, and they offer bounteous food for body and soul, just as the river itself has done for millennia. Now, as long ago, the river is a natural magnet for travellers, and a lifeline for settlers.

For thousands of years the Coast Salish peoples occupied the shores of the Fraser. Two tribal divisions lived around present-day Vancouver in more than 100 village sites, including Musqueam, Locarno Beach, Squamish, Kitsilano, the mouth of the Capilano River, Stanley Park. Today, totem poles in Stanley Park and at the University of British Columbia's Museum of Anthropology commemorate BC's First People and their culture.

Where these aboriginal communities long ago dotted the Fraser's shores, nearly a dozen communities now border the port of Vancouver. The Greater Vancouver Regional District (GVRD), with a total population of 1.5 million, encompasses the cities of Vancouver, New Westminster, North Vancouver, Richmond, Surrey, Port Coquitlam, White Rock, Langley, and Port Moody; the districts of Burnaby, Coquitlam, Delta, North Vancouver (a city and a district), Langley (city and district), West Vancouver; villages of Anmore, Belcarra, and Lions Bay; and three electoral areas (University Endowment Lands, Ioco, and Bowen Island).

An intense population core, it embraces half of BC's residents. Industry vies with residential and agricultural demands for coveted land. Over 100,000 people work in shipping and related industries.

Vancouver and its suburban communities form a gateway into the province, welcoming thousands of travellers a year. They come on jets from Europe and the Orient, on liners, yachts, and skiffs from up and down the coast, and in automobiles from everywhere. Greater Vancouver is a gateway, but also a destination in itself. Endless pleasurable days could be spent in "downtown British Columbia." For this reason, and also because of their size and location, **Vancouver, The North Shore (North Vancouver and West Vancouver), Burnaby, New Westminster, Surrey**, and **Richmond** have each been given a section in the pages following. Other Gateway cities and municipalities will be found along the appropriate routes.

Transportation corridors are clearly marked on the Gateway map (p.84), and followed in detail in the appropriate *Log.*

## Vancouver

### YOUNG AND SPLASHY

*"What a great sleepiness lies on Vancouver as compared with an American town."*

– Rudyard Kipling, 1900

**Vancouver:** (Pop. 471,844). A city bounded by water on three sides. To the north, Burrard Inlet separates Vancouver from North and West Vancouver. The inlet is spanned by two major bridges, the Lions Gate Bridge at First Narrows, and the Second Narrows Bridge, 9km inland. The Strait of Georgia (Pacific Ocean) is Vancouver's western boundary. To the south, the north arm of the Fraser River separates Vancouver from its southern satellite communities. Five major bridges span this torrent: Oak St, Knight St, Pattullo, Alex Fraser, and Port Mann.

**Vancouver Travel Infocentre:** Plaza level, Waterfront Centre, 200 Burrard St, Vancouver, BC, V6C 3L6. 683-2000. Reservations: 683-2772. From US: 1-800-888-8835. Open daily, May-early Sept. Mon-Sat rest of year. One-stop shopping for touring needs, catering to some 120,000 inquiries annually. At Reservation Area, travellers can book sightseeing tours, boat cruises, and accommodation. Highly recommended (and sold at the infocentre): the BC Transit DayPass ($4 adults; $2 children 5-13 and seniors; under 5 free). DayPass allows unlimited rides on buses, SkyTrain and SeaBus on day of purchase.

**Vancouver International Airport:** On Sea Island in Richmond south of Vancouver. From Vancouver, cross Arthur Laing Bridge at the foot of Granville St; or off Hwy 99 at Bridgeport Rd and Sea Island Way to Sea Island Bridge. Opened 1968. Nine million passengers pass through annually. All major carriers represented. For flight info and reservations, call individual airline companies or travel agencies.

Kipling visited the sawmill shantytown at the turn of the century, and at the time, his comments were probably apt. America, just 40km to the south, was a bustling, busy country; Vancouver was just beginning.

However, in less than a hundred years, the city of Vancouver has come of age, sprawling across the estuary of a giant river, ebullient, vital, invigorating. Today Vancouver is sophisticated and splashy, host to Expo 86, western focus of the world's second largest country. New theme adopted by the tourism office is "Spectacular by Nature." Vancouver is also clean and relatively safe, important words this late 20th century.

Today Vancouver would leave Kipling breathless. Yet no doubt he would notice a laid-back west-coast feeling to the city, marking it out from large North American cities. Perhaps it's the ocean salt in the air, or the slowing of the pulse at sea levels. Maybe it's just the constant lapping of water at Vancouver's edges that gives the city its "Bank Holiday" feeling. Vancouver is a city of and for the water. The Coast Mountains' sharp peaks are reflected in the city's mirrored skyscrapers – but it's the water that has dictated Vancouver's design, and its activities. On a peninsula between the Burrard Inlet and the Fraser River, the city breathes with the ebb and flow of tides on nearly every side.

Vancouver's port facilities export millions of tonnes annually. From the days of its first cargo export in 1864 (pickets to Australia) to today, the port of Vancouver – with 25 specialized terminals handling everything from coal and petroleum to forest products and minerals – has continuously increased its influence. Its sheltered location is a favourable one, in the lee of Vancouver Island, and about

midpoint on North America's west coast. Giant freighters in English Bay, waiting for berthing, are daily testimony to the port's industry. More than 3,000 foreign ships, representing the trade of 90 nations, enter the harbour each year.

With its exceptional locale and climate, Vancouver makes the most of its year-round attractions. In the spring, 60,000 plum and cherry trees are in bloom. In summer, fleets of windsurfers – their canvasses a riot of colour – dart between grain freighters anchored in the bay. For office workers to enjoy on their lunch breaks, there are nearly a dozen city beaches, including Wreck Beach, where bathing suits are optional. In the fall, the beauty of the 10km seawall walk around Stanley Park is heightened by the gold of autumn leaves. And come December, the Skyride on Grouse Mountain is a silver thread in the distance.

A phenomenon of recent years, arts, entertainment, sports and recreation, dining, and shopping have exploded in a rich variety that reflects the city's love for the flamboyant and innovative. There's even an **Arts Hotline** (684-ARTS). Indeed the arts scene is lively, with a public art gallery housed in a heritage courthouse, an opera company, several dozen theatres, and ballet and dance companies. Almost a city in itself is the **University of**

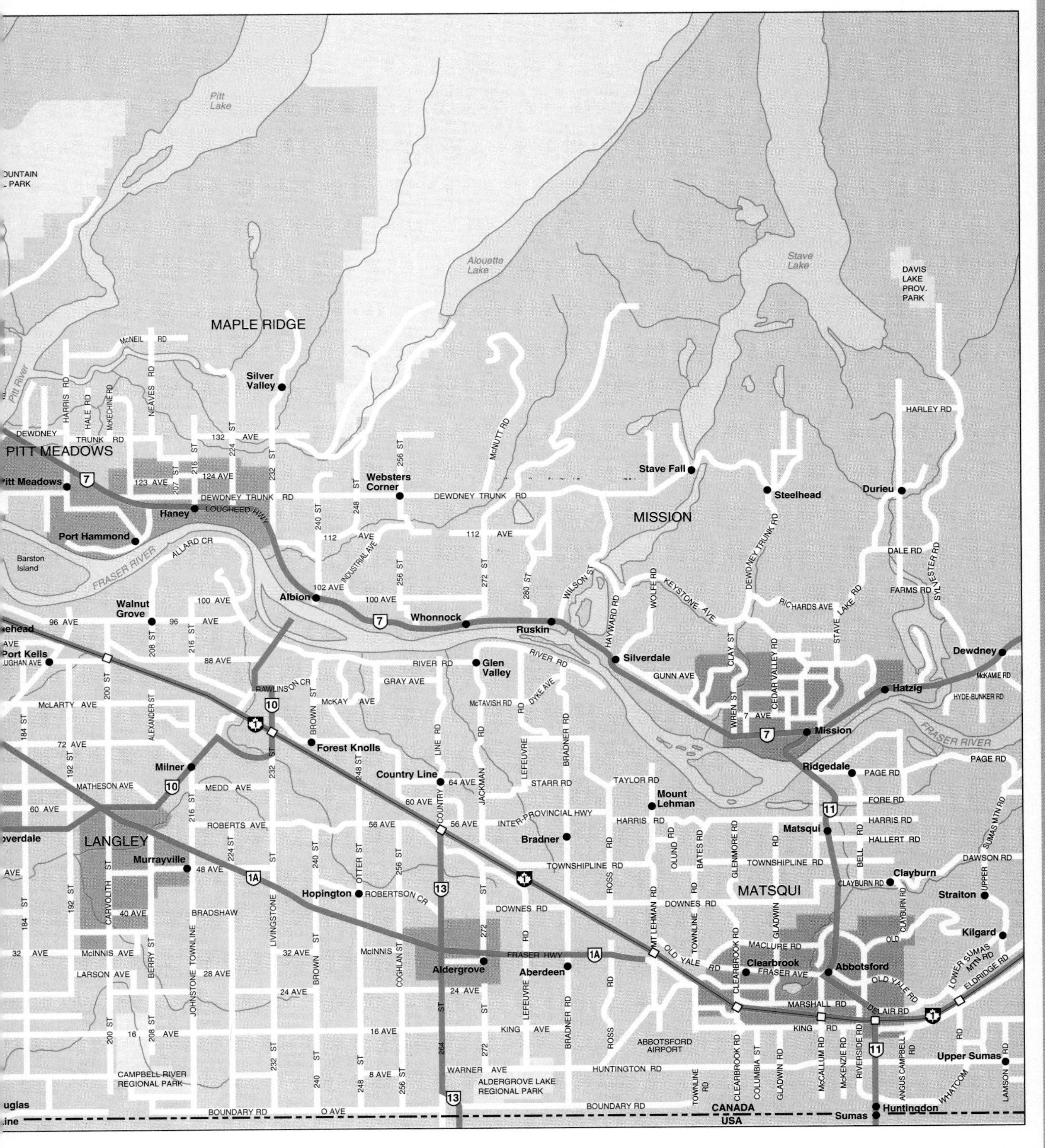

**British Columbia (UBC)**, a major international university with its own museums, theatres, art gallery, Botanical and Nitobe gardens, music, restaurants, English teas, and – this being Beautiful Vancouver – wonderful trails on the beach.

Multicultural differences are celebrated. Authentic pockets of Europe and the Far East are open for everyone to explore. Robson Street, a continental shopping thoroughfare, has been affectionately called "Robsonstrasse" for decades. Vancouver's Chinatown is the second largest in North America (after San Francisco's).

To everyone's delight, dining out in Vancouver is an ongoing feast with more than 4,000 restaurants, representing the cuisine of more than 25 nationalities. From Chinatown's Sunday morning *dim sum*, to French cooking and Japanese sushi bars in Gastown, eating well in Vancouver is an international affair.

Eating well can also begin with any one of the fresh produce markets proliferating in the city. The largest and most colourful is on **Granville Island** under the Granville St Bridge, a short hop by car or public transit from the downtown shopping core.

Indoors or outdoors, Vancouver is no longer the raggle-taggle town of Kipling's day. Born on the banks of the Burrard Inlet, it has grown into a complex and fascinating city.

## Museums, Galleries, and Attractions

Rain or shine, Vancouver is a family-oriented city with a wealth of activities to enjoy. Easy to get to by car or local transit, the following attractions are highly recommended.

■ **University of British Columbia:** In Point Grey, on a stunning site jutting out into the Strait of Georgia. Famous for its **Museum of Anthropology, Botanical Garden**, and **Nitobe Memorial Garden** (see below), as well as the **MY Williams Geological Museum**, plus an art gallery of its own, theatres, an observatory, aquatic centre, sports facilities. There is even a **HOTLINE** Tues-Wed afternoons (822-5858), in case your plants are acting up. UBC is cultural home to 34,000 students a year, and a major resource and inspiration to 70,000 others a year who visit the campus for non-credit courses, events, lectures.

■ **UBC Museum of Anthropology:** 6393 NW Marine Dr, UBC campus. 822-3825. Daily (Sept-June: closed Mon). Commemorates centennial (1971) of BC's entry into Confederation. Designed by BC architect Arthur Erickson, the award-winning glass-and-concrete building shares its site with a simulated Haida village. Front doors carved by 'Ksan native craftsmen. Works of art include Haida artist Bill Reid's yellow cedar sculpture, "The Raven." Research collections are visible in unique storage system. Walk outdoors among contemporary totem poles and mortuary poles. There's a new three-gallery wing, also an Erickson design, housing a permanent display of European ceramics. Inclusion of European art marks a threshold: "We should be anthropologizing everyone or no one," states Director Michael Ames.

■ **Vancouver Museum:** 1100 Chestnut St, south end of Burrard Bridge. Recording: 736-7736; or 736-4431. May-Sept: daily. Oct-April: Tues-Sun. Tues free for seniors. Canada's largest civic museum. Permanent and visiting exhibits of history and art of Canada's native people, history of Vancouver, decorative arts. 19th century period rooms. Haida masks.

■ **HR MacMillan Planetarium:** 1100 Chestnut St (Vanier Park). Recording: 736-4431; or 736-3656. July-Aug: daily. Sept-June: closed Mon. Journey through galaxies with Star Theatre, plus programs from laser/rock concerts to family and children's matinees.

■ **Gordon Southam Observatory:** 1100 Chestnut St. 738-2855. Fri-Sun, weather permitting. A Zeiss 15cm refractor telescope in a 9m dome. 50-seat lecture room.

■ **The Maritime Museum:** 1905 Ogden St. Five-minute walk from Vancouver Museum at foot of Cypress St. 737-2211. 10-5 daily. Vancouver's marine history. The *St Roch*, an historic RCMP vessel housed within the museum, is a National Historic Site. Visiting ships moor behind museum at Heritage Harbour.

■ **The Canadian Craft Museum:** 639 Hornby St. 687-8266. Open daily. Formerly the Cartwright Gallery, became "The Canadian Craft Museum" in 1990, reflecting its national stature. Backed by a 99-year lease of the new three-level museum building at Cathedral Place in heart of downtown. The first national cultural facility dedicated to craft. Historical and contemporary exhibits, collections, education programs, workshops, travelling exhibitions.

■ **The Vancouver Aquarium:** In Stanley Park. Recording: 682-1118. Or 685-3364. Daily. More than 8,000 species of aquatic life. A new Arctic exhibit with the beloved beluga whales (the "marshmallows of the sea"). Orcas or killer whales in $10-million outdoor pool. Amazon jungle gallery.

■ **CN IMAX Theatre:** 201-999 Canada Place. 682-4629. Daily. Specially designed theatre with IMAX technology. Screen is five stories high; film frame is the largest in motion picture history, 10 times larger than conventional 35mm frame. Viewers feel as if they are "in" the film as the camera travels through space or across the Grand Canyon.

■ **Science World:** Near Main St SkyTrain Station, in geodesic dome at east end of False Creek. 268-6363. A $50-million project in former Expo Centre. Dynamic interactive science exhibits and events, live performances. Bytes Cafeteria, gift shop. Also houses **Omnimax Theatre,** world's largest domed screen, 10 tonnes of sound equipment. Separate admission. 268-6363.

■ **BC Place Stadium:** 777 Pacific Blvd S. Events Info Line 661-7373. Stadium 669-2300. World's largest air-supported domed stadium. 760m in circumference, 60m high. First covered stadium in Canada, home to BC Lions football team. The 60,000-seat facility, covering 10ha, is used for sports, concerts, trade shows. Called the "Giant Pincushion."

■ **Harbour Centre Observation Deck:** Across from Waterfront SkyTrain Station and SeaBus, at 555 W Hastings St. 689-0421. Glass skylift elevators carry visitors 167m to a

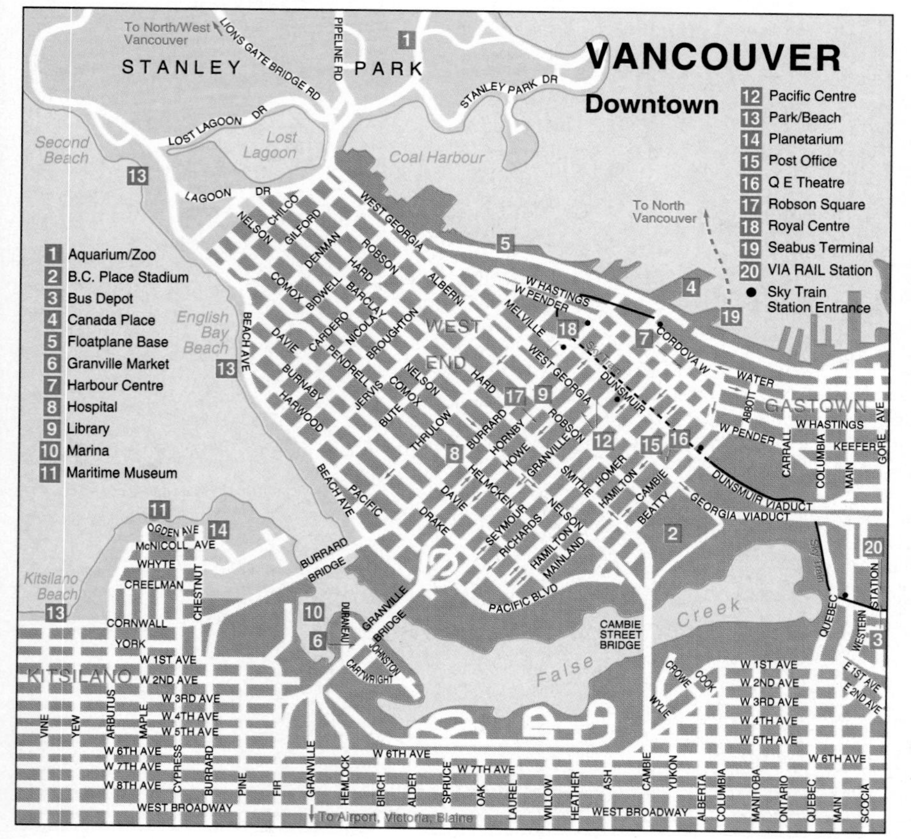

*Queen Elizabeth Park, Vancouver.*

360 degree view of Vancouver. Multimedia show, 8:30-10pm.

■ **PNE (Pacific National Exhibition) Grounds:** On Hastings between Renfrew and Cassiar. 253-2311. Site of the Big Exhibition (2nd largest in Canada, 7th in North America) mid-Aug-Labour Day. Big name entertainment, demolition derby, livestock, timber shows, midway. Also home of the **Racetrack** and **Playland.**

■ **The Track:** McGill and Renfrew. 254-1631. Thoroughbred racetrack, clubhouse, grandstand. Mid-April-mid-Oct.

■ **Playland:** Exhibition Park. 255-5161. Canada's largest wooden roller coaster. 40 major rides, street entertainment, magic shows. Weekends, holidays spring and fall, daily in summer. (Becomes midway for PNE.)

■ **BC Sports Hall of Fame:** 669-2300. BC Place.

## Parks and Gardens

Vancouver is called "just one big garden." Parks surround it, and almost every yard abounds with foliage and colour.

■ **Stanley Park:** Foot of W Georgia St. On a 405ha peninsula between English Bay and Burrard Inlet. One of North America's largest and most impressive city parks. Dedicated "to the use and enjoyment of people of all colours, creeds and customs for all time" by Lord Stanley, governor general of Canada 1888-1893. The **Stanley Park Public Zoo**, the **Children's Zoo**, **Miniature Railway**, and **Vancouver Aquarium** are located off West Georgia St entrance.

■ **The Stanley Park Seawall:** Along 10km of park perimeter. The dream of Park Commissioner MS Logan who, in 1916, began seeking federal grants to extend existing seawalls. He envisioned a seawall walk devoid of automobiles, passing under shady trees beside sandy beaches and rocky foreshores, with magnificent views of harbour, mountains, and forest. On July 22, 1971, the last granite blocks were put in place. The seawall today is everything Logan dreamed of, even more appreciated now that Vancouver is a major metropolis. Used as a walkway and bicycle route. (Bicycle rental across from park entrance.)

■ **Stanley Park Scenic Dr:** Begins and ends at W Georgia St. Circles perimeter of park. Brockton Point offers panorama of Burrard Inlet and North Shore Mountains. Road continues to Prospect Point. Siwash Rock can't be seen from road, but footpaths lead to seawall and famous landmark. Ferguson Point has view of Third Beach, the Point Grey Peninsula, and Vancouver Island. Road continues past Second Beach and Lost Lagoon. Good parking within walking distance of most attractions.

■ **UBC Botanical Garden and Nitobe Memorial Garden:** Both botanical gardens are on the university campus, but Nitobe Memorial Garden is separated from the Main Garden (information below).

The **UBC Botanical Garden** is at 6804 SW Marine Dr (corner of 16th Ave and SW Marine Dr). 822-4208. Open daily all year. Canada's oldest botanical garden, and not a show garden, but a 29ha living museum of plants from around the world. Over 10,000 species in eight separate gardens: Alpine, BC Native, Contemporary, Evolutionary, Physick (16th century herb garden), Food, Asian, and Winter. Over 400 rhododendrons in the Asian Garden, plus giant snow lilies from the Himalayas, and kiwi fruit (Chinese gooseberries) growing naturally like ivy up a Douglas fir. The Physick Garden is laid out around a sun dial; collection even includes belladonna. Shop-in-the-Garden, 822-4804.

The **Nitobe Memorial Garden** is near Gate Four on NW Marine Dr. 822-6038. Daily year-round. An authentic 1ha Japanese stroll and tea garden created in 1960 by Dr Kannosuke Mori. A serene place, giving a sense of seasonal change and harmony.

■ **Queen Elizabeth Park and Bloedel Floral Conservatory:** 33rd Ave and Cambie St. 872-5513. Daily. Former site of two stone quarries, now a 53ha park. Little Mountain, city's highest point, stands 152m above sea level. Displays of every major native species of tree and shrub, several foreign specimens, all in as native a habitat as possible. Bloedel Conservatory, illuminated at night, is a triodetic dome (made of 1,490 plexiglass bubbles) with 500 species and plant varieties. The **Civic Arboretum**, Canada's first, is a unique combination of park and botanical garden.

■ **VanDusen Botanical Gardens:** 37th Ave and Oak St. 266-7194. Daily. 22ha. A gorgeous garden with notable fuchsias, roses, hanging baskets, heathers. Oriental displays, international flora and fauna. Many rarities, Elizabethan hedge maze, topiaries, children's garden.

■ **Dr Sun Yat-Sen Classical Chinese Garden:** 578 Carrall St (in Chinatown). 689-7133. Daily. First authentic classical Chinese garden built outside China. A $5-million Ming Dynasty replica, built by artisans from Suzhou, a Chinese city famous for its gardens. Every pebble has been placed with painstaking awareness of harmony.

## Places and Plazas, Streets and Alleys

Vancouver's shopping areas are a mix of retail stores with art galleries and studios, restaurants and cafes. People-watching and window-shopping.

■ **Granville Island:** South side of False Creek, beneath Granville St Bridge. Access via W 4th Ave. Decaying warehouses and boat sheds transformed into shopping, residential, entertainment complexes. Giant indoor market open daily except Mon. Galleries, studios, two theatres, a brewery, hotel, restaurants, tennis courts, children's water play area, walkway along False Creek. Can also be reached by water bus from Beach Ave dock behind Vancouver Aquatic Centre.

■ **False Creek:** The meandering salt-water inlet that snakes its way into the heart of downtown Vancouver. "False" because it was not the elusive mouth of the Fraser that explorers had hoped for. False Creek was scene of decay and toxic waters for decades, an eyesore impossible to avoid, for thousands of motorists crossed it daily via either the Burrard, Granville St, or Cambie St bridges. Since chosen as site of Expo 86, False Creek has been given miraculous new life, and now people are surmising it may become the new heart of downtown Vancouver. First the water's edge was reclaimed for Expo. That area has now become **Plaza of Nations**, with room enough for over 100,000 celebrators to cheer on the dragon boats in the mammoth June festival. Another Expo legacy: **Science World (and Omnimax Theatre)**. Nearby is **BC Place Stadium.**

Renewal now extends back into north, south, and finally the east shores, with the opening in 1992 of **Citygate**, a major residential project. The whole area has become an award-winning urban redevelopment project, a blend of residential housing, marinas, parks, and restaurants, linked by a seawall promenade. Vancouver Parks is completing a marine park greenbelt from Vanier Park, at the Planetarium, all the way around False Creek to Wainborne Park at the foot of Richards St, near the north footings of the Granville St Bridge. And every inch of this greenbelt is waterfront. Moreover, now that industries have been forced to relocate, and sewage, chemicals, and heavy metals are no longer being dumped into the creek, this once toxic sea has become clean enough and clear enough to swim in. Proof came in the summer of 1992, when a thousand swimmers dove into the waters for the first leg of a triathlon.

■ **Robson St:** Blend of old and new. From Vancouver Art Gallery in a 19th-century historic courthouse, to modern gallerias where high-end fashion is sold. Robson St, between Howe and Broughton streets, was, at one time, mainly German, earning it the nickname of Robsonstrasse. Today, it's known for chic clothing, accessory, specialty shops.

■ **Robson Square:** Robson St between Hornby and Howe streets. Heart of downtown Vancouver. Parades, marches, speeches, New Year's Eve celebrations all take place here. Some BC government offices. Covered skating rink. Robson Square Media Centre hosts events from lectures to films and premieres.

■ **Granville and Georgia Streets:** Centre of commercial ventures. Six blocks of the Granville St Mall are closed to traffic, except buses and taxis, during the day. Major department stores and malls. **SeaBus Terminal** to North Vancouver is located at bottom (north end) of Granville St.

■ **Pacific Centre:** Downtown. 700 W Georgia St. Three levels, two major department stores.

■ **Chinatown:** Between Carrall St and Gore Ave. North America's second largest Chinese Community. Fresh fruits, vegetables, jade, ivory, bamboo, rattan, brassware, silk, brocade, and ginseng. Phone booths with pagoda-style roofs; street names in English and Chinese; sidewalk corners inlaid with street names in polished brass. Features "World's Thinnest Office Building," see "Architectural Points of Interest," below.

■ **Punjabi Market:** Main St between 49th and 51st. A social, religious, commercial, and cultural centre for BC's 80,000 south Asians from India, Pakistan, Fiji, East Africa, and Sri Lanka. Over 20 percent of shopping clientele are non-Asian, coming to enjoy the music, food, and fashions of ancient cultures. Over 105 businesses flourish.

■ **Gastown:** Carrall, Powell, Water, and Alexander streets meet at Maple Tree Square to form Gastown. Named after "Gassy Jack" Deighton, pioneering tavern keeper whose statue stands in Maple Tree Square. As the city grew, it moved westward and changed its name to Vancouver; Gastown became Old Vancouver, and slid into decline. In 1971, it was designated a heritage area, and renewal began. Now a fertile mix of old and new, with the vigour and excitement of one of the world's largest seaports just two blocks away. Water St is noted for period gaslights, cobblestones, storefronts. Two-tonne 1887 Gastown Steam Clock, at corner of Cambie and Water, is world's first. Operates on steam generated from heating system in nearby buildings. Whistles every 15 minutes, emits bursts of steam on the hour.

■ **Commercial Dr:** Between Broadway Ave and Hastings St. Locals call this part of town "The Drive." Coffee bars, Italian restaurants, Santa Barbara Market. New Mercato Mall at 1st and Commercial.

■ **Downtown Waterfront and Waterfront Centre:** Downtown shore of Burrard Inlet, including **Canada Place** (see below) and the restored **CPR Station**, have undergone dramatic and invigorating changes. New buildings, hotels, shopping corridors and centres, green spaces, waterfalls. Waterfront Hotel, part of **Waterfront Centre**, is one of the new buildings. **CPR Station** is **SeaBus** and **SkyTrain** terminal.

■ **Tour of the Port:** Vanterm public viewing area at Vanterm Container Terminal, 1300 Stewart St. 666-6129. From an overhead walkway, watch longshoremen in the loading, unloading, transporting processes. From an observation deck on 4th floor of terminal's administration building, entire terminal is seen: container cranes, straddle carriers, and lift trucks. Unrestricted view of Burrard Inlet from Vancouver wharves on the west to Seaboard Lumber Terminal on the east.

■ **South Granville:** Granville St between 4th Ave and 16th Ave. Largely shopping, with upscale fashion stores, galleries, delis.

## The Best of the Beaches

■ **Vancouver Beaches:** They curve 16km along English Bay from Wreck Beach (the city's unofficial nude beach) to First Narrows beach. There are 11 in all: Wreck Beach, Locarno, Jericho, Point Grey, Kitsilano, Sunset, Second, Third, and Ambleside, Spanish Banks, and English Bay. It's possible at low tide, if you're athletic, to walk from Kitsilano Beach along the shoreline to Wreck Beach. From June to Sept, the outdoor pool at "Kits" Beach is available for use.

■ **Kitsilano Showboat:** A tradition since 1935. Open-air amphitheatre on Kitsilano Beach offering unique no-cost outdoor beachside entertainment. Mid-June -Aug. Evenings. Mon, Wed, Fri.

## Architectural Points of Interest

Vancouver is a modern city, just 100 years old. A comparison of old and new architecture – from the mansions of Shaughnessy to high rises of the West End – puts history into perspective.

■ **The Law Courts:** 800 Smythe St between Hornby and Howe. 660-2847. Mon-Fri.

*English Bay, in Vancouver.*

Designed by city's own Arthur Erickson. Concrete building is enclosed by glass from 4th to 7th floors. Covers a city block.

■ **Canada Place:** 999 Canada Place on Burrard Inlet, at foot of Howe St. 775-8687. Open daily. Built as Canada Pavilion for Expo 86. Five teflon-coated "sails" create a nautical feel. Promenade is three city blocks long, excellent views of the port. Cruise ship terminal, **Vancouver Trade and Convention Centre** (641-1987), restaurants, ballrooms, exhibition halls, shops, hotel, **CN IMAX Theatre**.

■ **Sinclair Centre:** Between Granville and Howe, Hastings and Cordova. 666-4483. A commercial centre. Four restored buildings cover entire city block, linked together by a two-level glass roofed Heritage Court and Galleria. Heritage buildings (1910-37) include Old Post Office, RV Winch Building, Customs Examining Warehouse, Federal Building.

■ **Dominion Building:** 207 W Hastings St. 13-storey 1908 building was called the most modern office building in Canada and the tallest building in the British Empire.

■ **"World's Thinnest Office Building":** At corner of Pender and Carral streets in Chinatown. A structure 1.8m wide and two stories tall. Won the *Ripley's Believe It or Not* designation first, as "world's thinnest," then achieved a Guinness World Record as "shallowest commercial building in the world," becoming the first and only building in Canada in *The Guinness Book of World Records*. Without really even trying, the Sam Kee Thin Building ("Slender on Pender," "Thin Wins") is becoming a tourist destination.

■ **The West End:** This is the highest density housing in Canada. There are still a few samples of the original wood-frame homes (see **Barclay Square** below). But high and low rises, shops, movie houses, restaurants, cafés, supermarkets now predominate. Stroll along Denman St from English Bay and enjoy some of the best ice cream in the city.

■ **Barclay Heritage Square:** West End, bounded by Barclay, Nicola, Haro and Broughton streets. Unique parksite developed by Vancouver Board of Parks and Recreation. Includes nine historic West End houses, 1890-1908, in original settings with period landscaping and gardens. Six have been rehabilitated for family accommodation, creating a unique link with the past. Centrepieces are Barclay Manor, a venue for senior citizens' events, and the Roedde family's house, now **Roedde House Museum**, Vancouver's first "house" museum. Roedde House is open for public viewing, and may be rented for small receptions. 684-7040.

■ **Shaughnessy:** Above W 16th Ave and Granville St. Here are the imposing homes of Vancouver's elite. In 1907, Canadian Pacific Railway began to transform this former tract of forest into premier residential land when the West End began losing its exclusive character. Note the curving streets, generous lots, *porte cochères* for carriages.

■ **New Vancouver Library:** Between Robson and Georgia. To be completed in 1995. The largest capital expense in the city's history, an estimated $100-million project. Winning design by team of Moshe Safdie and Downs/Archambault includes four-storey oval coliseum style library, with 21-storey federal tower curving around one corner.

### Arts and Culture

Vancouver offers a bevy of entertainment, from Broadway shows and international entertainers to a fringe theatre festival (every Sept). More than a dozen theatres showcase plays, concerts, and dance; nearly 60 galleries feature everything from Inuit to avant-garde. Call the **Arts Hotline**, 684-ARTS.

■ **The Orpheum Theatre:** 884 Granville St at Smythe. 665-3050; 280-4444 for tickets. Vancouver's oldest, most dignified concert hall. Home of Vancouver Symphony Orchestra. Refurbished to its original splendour. One-thousand-bulb crystal chandeliers, original Wurlitzer organ.

■ **The Queen Elizabeth Playhouse and Theatre:** 600 Hamilton St (at Georgia). Call 665-3050 for info, 280-4444 for tickets. Opera, ballet, live theatre, music.

■ **The Vancouver Art Gallery:** 750 Hornby St, Robson Square. 682-5621 or 682-4668. Daily (free 5-9 Thurs). In city's former courthouse, built 1911. Architect Francis Rattenbury also designed Empress Hotel and Legislative Buildings in Victoria. Permanent collection includes works of Victoria's Emily Carr.

■ **Complete Arts and Entertainment Listings:** Consult city's two daily newspapers, *The Province*, a morning tabloid, and *The Vancouver Sun*. *The Georgia Straight* is a free weekly tabloid with extensive entertainment listings.

# The North Shore

## NORTH VANCOUVER AND WEST VANCOUVER: MOUNTAIN PLAYGROUND

Vancouver's North Shore ("So much more," they say, and it's true) is home to 135,000 people in three municipalities: the City of North Vancouver, District of North Vancouver, and District of West Vancouver. While not merging identities, they merge as a geographic and recreational destination. In the North Shore Mountains, the twin peaks of the Lions preside over the lands below, reminding everyone that there's year-round recreation up top: Cypress Bowl, Grouse Mountain, Mt Seymour. Grouse is even served by public transportation. South is Burrard Inlet, creating an exciting waterfront: industry, shoreline parks, marine life, shopping, wining and dining. Don't miss Lonsdale Quay Market.

### North Vancouver

**North Vancouver:** (Pop.38,436). This city lies 8km north of downtown Vancouver, on the north shore of Burrard Inlet, east of Lions Gate Bridge on Marine Dr and Hwy 1/99. The District Municipality of North Vancouver (pop. 75,157) surrounds the city borders except for the waterfront, from Capilano River (and West Vancouver) to the west and Indian Arm to the east.

Originally site of Squamish Indian village Homulcheson. Named Moodyville by lumber entrepreneur Sewell "Sue" Prescott Moody around 1867. He also declared this a dry town – which may have been a factor in the establishment of a ferry service across inlet to saloons and hotels of Brighton and Gastown. District incorporated in 1891, became a city in 1907. North Vancouver's waterfront was one of the first developed on the Lower Mainland and remains one of Greater Vancouver's most active port areas. Early sawmills, including the first built by Philip Hicks in early 1860s, have given way to shipbuilding and rail-oriented activities. Long ago Lonsdale Ave was a log-skid for clearing the forests; now it's the main shopping street, and there's also the **Lonsdale Quay Market** with over 80 shops and restaurants.

North Vancouver overlooks Burrard Inlet and is backed by the Coast Mountain range, some of Lower Mainland's finest scenery with an array of natural attractions from alpine wilderness and ski terrain to spectacular canyons and rivers.

**North Vancouver Information:** Infocentre, 131 East 2nd St, North Vancouver, BC, V7L 1C2. 987-4488. Weekdays 9-5 year-round. Two info booths operate daily in summer, one at junction of Capilano Rd and Marine Dr, other at Lonsdale Quay.

■ **North Shore Museum and Archives:** 333 Chesterfield Ave. 987-5618. Wed-Sun: 12-5pm. Domestic exhibits, logging, shipbuilding, farming, small businesses, and Coast Salish artifacts. Photograph gallery. Gift shop.

■ **Presentation House:** 333 Chesterfield Ave. 986-1351. Wed-Sun. 12-5pm. Photographic exhibits, historic and contemporary.

■ **Lonsdale Quay Market:** At foot of Lonsdale Ave. 985-6261. Take the SeaBus direct from Waterfront Station in Vancouver. Lots of excitement under one big roof, plus an observation tower to take in the view.

■ **Park and Tilford Gardens:** Adjacent Tilford Shopping Centre at Cotton Rd and Brooksbank Ave. 984-8200. Wheelchair accessible. Free. Gardens include: Rose, Oriental, Colonade, Greenhouse, Native, Display.

■ **Maplewood Farm:** 405 Seymour River Pl. 929-5610. Tues-Sun, holiday Mondays. 2ha farm with domestic animals and birds. Children's petting areas: "Goathill" and "Rabbitat."

■ **Capilano Suspension Bridge and Park:** 3735 Capilano Rd. 985-7474. Daily. Park opened 1899. Longest suspension bridge in the world. First bridge, made of wood and hemp, was called the "Laughing Bridge" by native peoples. Current bridge, in place since 1956, is built of wire rope with wood decking and stretches 137m across the canyon and 70m above the river. 6ha park with a 60m waterfall, ponds, river, and walking trails.

■ **Cleveland Dam:** North on Capilano Rd to Nancy Greene Way. In northern section of

Capilano Canyon Park. Built 1954. Dam created Capilano Lake, which supplies much of Vancouver's drinking water. Hiking trails and picnicking sites.

■ **Capilano River Regional Park:** Accessible from Capilano Hatchery turnoff or Cleveland Dam parking lot. 432-6350. Extensive trails, kayaking, picnicking. 7km Capilano Pacific trail leads from Cleveland Dam to Ambleside Park.

■ **Capilano Salmon Hatchery:** 4500 Capilano Park Rd. 666-1790. Daily. Established in 1977 by federal and provincial governments. BC's first "fish farm". Walk-through exhibits of salmon in various stages of development. Working models and diagrams showing salmon's life cycle.

■ **Grouse Mountain and Skyride:** 6400 Nancy Greene Way, north along Capilano Lake. 984-0661. Snow Phone: 986-6262. Take Skyride to top of Grouse Mountain for panoramic view of city's skyline and harbour, and Georgia Strait. Skyride takes eight minutes, rises from 290m to 1,250m above sea level. Daily, year-round. At the top, well-known Grouse Nest Restaurant. Reservations: 986-6378 (Skyride ticket included). At the Theatre in the Sky, see 30-min multimedia film, "Our Spirit Soars." Free. The earliest developed ski area around, and quite a Vancouver institution. About a dozen ski runs, many visible from downtown Vancouver. Night skiing can be gorgeous, and the twinkling lights up the mountain are a part of Vancouver's nightlife. In summer: hang-gliding.

■ **Lynn Headwaters Regional Park:** 4,685ha. 432-6350. From Second Narrows Bridge or Lions Gate Bridge, take Hwy 1 to Lynn Valley Rd in North Vancouver. Follow Lynn Valley Rd to park entrance. Rugged mountain wilderness at city's edge. 20km of developed forest trails. Panoramic vistas.

■ **Lynn Canyon Park and Ecological Centre:** 3663 Park Rd. 987-5922. Daily Feb-Nov, Sundays rest of year. 120ha. A natural park surrounding a deep gorge cut into the mountains by Lynn Creek. The suspension bridge is 68m long, hovers a thrilling 82m above the waters. **Ecological Centre**, built in the shape of a dogwood, features displays showing interdependence of plants, animals, man.

■ **Seymour Demonstration Forest and Seymour River Fish Hatchery:** 5,600ha. Call 432-6286. North on Lillooet Rd, past Capilano College, through cemetery and along gravel road to forest entrance. 40km of roads and trails. Cycling on weekends. Canoeing, kayaking, fishing.

■ **Mt Seymour Provincial Park:** 3,508ha. 929-1291. On Mt Seymour Rd off Mt Seymour Parkway, eastern area of North Vancouver. The park is named after Frederick Seymour, BC's governor from 1864 to 1869. Mt Seymour is the closest provincial park to Vancouver. It offers mountaineering, challenging hikes, and day trips through terrain that reaches height of 1,508m at Mt Bishop. Four main trails cut through the park. Visit Goldie and Mystery lakes. Drive the Mt Seymour Parkway for spectacular views.

■ **Seymour Ski Country:** In Mt Seymour Provincial Park. Contact: 1700 Indian River Rd, North Vancouver, BC, V7G 1L3. 986-2261 or Snow Phone: 879-3999. Mystery Peak chairlift climbs 1,200m. Skiing and snowshoeing through the park's forests offer every level of difficulty. Four double chairlifts and two rope tows for alpine skiers. Ski rentals. Ski school. Night skiing. Bakery.

■ **Cates Park:** 24ha. 986-9141. On the Dollarton Hwy at Roche Point, jutting out into eastern reaches of Burrard Inlet. On shores of Indian Arm, park is a popular summer picnic spot. Swimming, boat-launch facilities, two play areas. A 15m Indian war canoe, built in 1921 by Chief Henry Peter George, is on display.

■ **Deep Cove:** 8.5km east of Dollarton Hwy Interchange. Part of District Municipality of North Vancouver.

With homes clinging to the hills above and Coombe Park and Jug Island across the water, Deep Cove offers some of the most beautiful scenery in the Lower Mainland. A charming pocket cove on the west shore of Indian Arm (northern extension of Burrard Inlet). Boats are moored offshore or at the marina; there's scuba diving, swimming, water skiing, picnicking.

**Deep Cove Information:** North Vancouver Infocentre, 131 East 2nd St, North Vancouver, BC, V7L 1C2. 987-4488. Open weekdays 9-5 year-round.

## West Vancouver

**West Vancouver:** (Pop. 38,783). Just west of Lions Gate Bridge, on Marine Dr. Incorporates four villages spread out loosely along the north shore of Burrard Inlet, from Ambleside, to Dundarave, then Caulfield, and Horseshoe Bay. Marine Dr and Taylor Way intersection near the Lions Gate Bridge is, in a sense, downtown West Vancouver. The Park Royal Shopping Centre covers both sides of Marine Dr west of Taylor Way.

West Vancouver is one of Canada's most picturesque residential communities. It lies along the lower slope of 1,324m Hollyburn Mountain between the Capilano River valley and Horseshoe Bay, bordered by Burrard Inlet to the south and Howe Sound to the west.

*Office buildings and high rises of Burnaby's Metrotown.*

West Vancouver has close to 2,500ha of park and recreation land, and boasts the highest per capita income in Canada. The British Properties, a 1,600ha area, sprawling halfway up Hollyburn Mountain, contains some of Vancouver's most expensive and stately homes. The shoreline is dotted with parks, many kilometres of seawalls and walks, and marina facilities at Fisherman's Cove and Horseshoe Bay.

**West Vancouver Information:** Infocentre, 1563 Marine Drive, West Vancouver, BC, V7V 1H9. 987-4488. Weekdays in winter, daily in summer.

■ **Ambleside Park:** 922-1211. Off Marine Dr between Capilano River and Keith Rd. On Burrard Inlet across the water from Stanley Park. Seawalks and beaches.

■ **Lighthouse Park:** 922-1211. 12km south of Horseshoe Bay. South of Hwy 1/99 via Caulfield Dr. Turn southwest to park. Semi-wilderness retreat on the mouth of Burrard Inlet. East from the park, across English Bay, is a view of Stanley Park and downtown Vancouver. West is Bowen Island. Hiking trails through rain forest to Atkinson Lighthouse. No camping.

■ **Cypress Provincial Park:** 2,849ha. Year-round. Funline: 926-6007. 12km north of Cypress Bowl Rd and Hwy 1/99 junction. Cypress Mountain is part of the North Shore mountain chain overlooking Vancouver. Mountain meadows, lakes, forests. Vistas of 1,646m Lions Mountain, Howe Sound, Gulf Islands. Hiking trails. Alpine ski area, two chairlifts, double rope tow, eight varied downhill runs, 16 ski touring trails. A snowshoe and winter-hiking trail connects parking lot with Hollyburn Lodge. Ski school and ski rentals. Snowmobiling. Restaurant and licensed sundeck.

■ **Whytecliffe Park:** Off Marine Dr in Horseshoe Bay. Trails, picnics. Departure point for diving excursions.

## Burnaby

### ROOM WITH A VIEW

**Burnaby:** (Pop.158,858). 10km east of Vancouver city centre. Main entrances into Burnaby from Hwy 1 are Sprott St, Grandview Hwy, Willingdon Ave, Cariboo Interchange.

The municipality of Burnaby is bordered by Burrard Inlet to the north, and the north arm of the Fraser River to the south. It is named for Robert Burnaby (1828-1878), British colonist, merchant, and businessman. The trees of Central Park, a 90ha area on the western edge of the municipality, were first thinned out in 1863 by the Royal Engineers looking for masts for the British Navy's sailing ships.

Incorporated in 1892, Burnaby today is the most heavily populated district in Greater Vancouver. It carries a mixture of commercial and industrial development, second only to Vancouver as a centre of employment.

**Burnaby Information:** Infocentre, 6525 Sprott St, Burnaby, BC, V6B 3B8. 421-0084. Daily in summer, weekdays winter.

■ **Simon Fraser University:** Atop Burnaby Mountain, on Gaglardi Way 6km beyond the junction of Hwy 1 and Cariboo Rd. 291-4323. Established 1965, and notable for its striking architecture by Arthur Erickson and Geoffrey Massey. Museum of Archaeology and Ethnology, open daily, features traditional Northwest Coast Indian art, domestic utensils, tools. SFU and **Burnaby Centennial Park,** also on the mountain, offer spectacular views of Burrard Inlet, Burnaby, and Vancouver. Wheelchair accessible. Group tours.

■ **Deer Lake, Century Park, and Deer Lake Park:** Deer Lake is a small lake in the heart of Burnaby (south of much larger Burnaby Lake), offering two quite different park experiences.

On north shore is **Century Park**, a formal area including **Century Garden, Burnaby Art Gallery, James Cowan Theatre, Burnaby Arts Centre, and Burnaby Village Museum** (more below). Century Park is accessed from Gilpin St on the west; or from Canada Way to Sperling Ave to Deer Lake Ave.

**Deer Lake Park**, accessed from Sperling Ave, offers fishing, swimming, boating, jogging, picnicking, and casual strolling. Lake is home to a variety of waterfowl. Wonderful views on a clear day: immediate scenes of the lake, distant glimpses of Vancouver's towered structures, Burnaby Mountain, and North Shore peaks.

■ **Burnaby Art Gallery:** 6344 Deer Lake Ave. 291-9441. Tues-Sun. In graceful Ceperly Mansion overlooking Deer Lake Park.

■ **Burnaby Village Museum:** 6501 Deer Lake Ave. 293-6501. Daily March-Oct. Open-air historical village. Over 30 buildings and outdoor displays depicting life in Lower Mainland from 1890 to 1925. Guides often wear traditional dress.

■ **Burnaby Lake Regional Park:** A 300ha nature park in the centre of the municipality, between the Lougheed and Trans-Canada highways. Over 200 species of birds nest in this urban park, from hummingbirds to bald eagles; shore animals include coyotes, muskrat, and mink. The trail system offers hikes within a setting ranging from cool, shady forest to open marshland. About 5km of trails along lake's north side. Lake vistas provide opportunities for quiet contemplation, to watch a rower, or study a great blue heron along the shore.

Much of the park has been designated a wildlife sanctuary. Nevertheless, Burnaby Lake is in serious trouble, and could be nothing but a bog in 30 years. Two attractive but lethal plants are threatening its existence: lovely white water lilies, and tall purple loosestrife. The latter, called the "Beautiful Killer," is becoming a disaster plant across Canada. All other plants are crowded out, so the marsh creatures lose their shelter and food. In badly infested lakes, it becomes impossible to fish, or even find the water. Studies are being done on Burnaby Lake at the moment.

■ **The Burnaby Lake Nature House:** 4519 Piper Ave. On north side of Burnaby Lake at foot of Piper Ave off Winston St. Mid-May-Aug: 420-3031. Weekdays year-round: 432-6322. Daily May-Aug. July-Aug: programs for children. Hikes with staff naturalists. Lakes, bugs, and plant life are themes for walks. Canoe programs.

■ **Central Park:** On east boundary of Burnaby, on Boundary Rd between Kingsway and Imperial. 294-7450. SkyTrain to Patterson Station. Large urban park with exceptional children's playground, pitch and putt golf course, trails, stadium.

■ **Metrotown Centre:** Kingsway, between Boundary Rd and Royal Oak. A massive commercial, residential, and entertainment complex, next to SkyTrain Metrotown Station. Eaton Centre Metrotown has more than 175 shops and services, three major department stores. Linked to SkyTrain with a covered passerelle.

## New Westminster

### ROYAL CITY

**New Westminster:** (Pop. 43,585). 12km southeast of downtown Vancouver, on the estuary of the Fraser River, upstream from delta islands of Lulu and Annacis.

Throughout the 1860s, New Westminster was a Fraser River boom town populated by thousands of gold prospectors. Known as the "Royal City," it was founded in early 1859 by Colonel Moodie of the Royal Engineers, and named by Queen Victoria that same summer. A year later, in July 1860, New Westminster became the first incorporated municipality west of the Great Lakes, and, until 1866, capital city of the mainland colony of BC.

About that time, in 1863, Walter B Cheadle, an early tourist, described the city: "New Westminster stands on rising ground above the river, amidst the densest forest, which has cost fortunes to clear away, averaging $3 a stump.... It is finely placed and will be a pretty place in time."

From 1866 to 1868, New Westminster continued as capital city, now of the joint mainland BC and Vancouver Island colony. But by the late 1860s, the gold rush had ended and the city's population and importance as a commercial centre had declined, at least for the time being. In 1868, title of capital city was transferred to Victoria.

Today, New Westminster is a bustling city in the heart of the Lower Mainland, a large fresh-water port, and an important supplement to the port of Vancouver. Cities and municipalities now surround it on all sides. The city used to be known for its **Pattullo Bridge**, not so affectionately called the "Pay-Toll-O Bridge" for its unpopular toll, long since removed. Now "New West" is known for its historic architecture, parks, and innovative development, particularly on the waterfront, with its glittering, bright blue two-storey public market. Columbia St, the main road, was dusty and unused right through the

1970s. Expo year, 1986, marked the opening of the **SkyTrain**, a light rapid transit system that linked New Westminster easily with Vancouver, and things started to change. There was an invasion of visitors during Expo, and a swelling of population once New West became a viable commuter city for Vancouver workers. Businesses started pulling up their socks, renovating, remodelling. New businesses moved in. New heritage-look structures appeared. No longer a mishmash of decaying buildings, New Westminster in some ways resembles San Francisco, with its hilliness, its waterfront and bridges, even its gold-rush history.

New Westminster's three **SkyTrain** stations are at: 8th St just north of Westminster Quay; 22nd St at 8th Ave; and the Columbia St terminus. Continuous departures for downtown Vancouver; 27 minutes. A bridge has been built parallel to the Pattullo, and SkyTrain now extends south into Surrey, to the Scott Rd Station at King George Hwy.

? **New Westminster Information:** Two Infocentres, one at 333 Brunette Ave, New Westminster, BC, V3L 3E7. 521-7781. Weekdays in winter, daily in summer. The other at New Westminster Quay. 526-1905.

■ **Westminster Quay and Public Market:** The heart of New Westminster's waterfront redevelopment. Open daily. Shops, dining, entertainment. Walkway along Fraser River. The Inn at Westminster Quay is well worth a look, excitingly designed on pillars reaching out over the river.

■ **Fraser River Connection:** 525-4465, or 525-5944. Tickets at Chamber of Commerce (333 Brunette Ave) or Westminster Quay. River cruises aboard *The Native*, a 27m replica of a paddle-wheeler. Mon-Wed: three-hour cruise to Poplar and Douglas islands. Thurs-Sun: all-day, 57km return trip from the Royal City to Fort Langley and back. Board at the Inn on the Quay. Riverside views of Whalley, Coquitlam, Pitt Meadows, Surrey, Port Hammond, Haney. Narrated, and billed as a "Trip through History." One-way trips available. Fully licensed, luncheon, snackbar. Also dinner cruises. Paddle-wheeler holds up to 100 people.

■ **Irving House and Museum:** 302 Royal Ave. 521-7656. May-mid-Sept: Daily except Mon. Mid-Sept-April: weekend afternoons. Wed-Sun: tours by appointment. Original residence of Captain William Irving, "King of the River," completed in 1864.

■ **New Westminster Museum:** 302 Royal Ave. 521-7656. May-Aug: Daily except Mon. Oct-April: weekend afternoons. Near Irving House. Artifacts and displays of local history including an 1876 Dufferin Coach.

■ **Regimental Museum:** The Armoury, 530 Queen's Ave. 526-5116. Mon-Fri: 11-3. Collection of military artifacts related to New Westminster dating back to 1863.

■ **SS *Samson V* Maritime Museum:** Waterfront, between public market and the Inn. 522-6894. Sat, Sun, and holiday afternoons. Extended hours in summer. SS *Samson V* was the last sternwheeler to operate on the Fraser River. Built in 1937, she operated until 1980.

■ **Canadian Lacrosse Hall of Fame:** Centennial Centre, 65 E 6th Ave. 526-2751. Daily on request. Lacrosse is Canada's national sport.

■ **Queen's Park:** 1st St and 3rd Ave. Nice wooded areas. Also in park is **New Westminster Arts Centre** and **Vagabond Playhouse**. Plus Rainbow Playland with colourful spray pool, petting farm, adventure playground. Open May long weekend to Aug.

■ **Canada Games Pool:** 6th Ave and McBride Blvd. 526-4281. Daily. Olympic size. 65m warm pool with rope swing, trolley ride, tubes, mats, indoor waterslide. Fitness centre, sauna, whirlpool.

# Surrey

## BLENDING OF WORLDS

**Surrey:** (Pop. 245,173). Surrey sits nicely between a curve of the Fraser River to the north, and Boundary Bay and the Canada-US Border to the south. Surrey only recently became a city. Previously, was BC's largest municipality, covering 203 sq km, and, in terms of population, was one of the fastest growing ones. Surrey still has a laid-back country feel. It has a rich natural environment – some areas, such as Mud Bay, are ecologically important; there are uncrowded beaches like Crescent to play on; and the famous Cloverdale Rodeo – rated No. 1 in North America.

James Kennedy was the first British subject to take up land in the area. He preempted it at a price of one dollar an acre in 1861. Surrey incorporated in 1879 when there were fewer than 1,000 residents over approximately 200 sq km. The first city hall, completed 1881, is now part of the Centennial Museum.

The big push to develop the area came in 1891 when the first railway, the New Westminster Southern, passed through. Surrey's growth has closely followed the development of the rail system.

Surrey incorporates five townships, little pockets of development that grew. They include **Whalley**, in the northwest corner, which holds the key to much of the area's history; **Guildford**, newest of the townships and the current business centre; **South Surrey**, also known as Sunnyside, which includes Crescent Beach, a hot spot for sun worshippers, and is more like a summer resort; **Newton**, started as a stop along the old interurban rail line; and **Cloverdale**, home of the Surrey Fall Fair and Cloverdale Rodeo.

Today Surrey blends residential and commercial use, greenbelts, farmlands, and industrial lands. The **SkyTrain** now extends south into Surrey at Scott Rd Station (Scott Rd and King George Hwy in north Surrey). Two more stations are planned: 102 Ave and 108 Ave, both near King George.

? **Surrey Information:** One infocentre is at 15105A-105th Ave, Surrey, BC, V3R 7G9 (in Guildford). 581-7130. Year-round.

■ **Surrey Museum and Archives:** 6050-176th St (in Cloverdale). 574-5744. Weekday afternoons. The story of Surrey's pioneers is told through farm implements, furniture, other household items. Early native artifacts. Housed in the oldest remaining log cabin in Surrey.

■ **Canadian Museum of Flight and Transportation:** 13527 Crescent Rd (in South Surrey). 6.5ha park setting. 535-1115. Daily April-late Oct. Restored World War Two and early Canadian aircraft. 38 craft from 1920s to present in outside display.

■ **Surrey Arts Centre and Bear Creek Park:** Art in the Park, at 13750-88th Ave (between King George Hwy and 140th, in Guildford). 596-7461. Daily except Mon. Arts complex with gallery, theatre, classrooms. Park offers excellent picnic and play facilities for all ages.

■ **Historic Stewart Farmhouse and Hooser Weaving Centre:** 13723 Crescent Rd (South Surrey), in **Elgin Heritage Park** on the waterfront. 574-5744. Victoria-style farmhouse built in 1894 by the Stewart family, who lived in the home and farmed the land for six decades. The Peace Arch Weavers and Spinners Guild operates Hooser Weaving Centre in the farmhouse. Displays of spinning and weaving beginning June.

■ **Cloverdale Fairgrounds and the Cloverdale Rodeo:** 6050-176th St at 60th Ave in Cloverdale. 576-9461. Harness Racing, Oct-April. Home of the Cloverdale Rodeo, May long weekend. The Stetson Bowl seats close to 7,000. Usually over 500 entries. "More cowboys and cowgirls than any other rodeo in Canada," it's claimed. Steer wrestling, wild-horse racing, ladies' barrel racing, wild-cow milking. Pancake breakfasts, midway, saloon, the works.

■ **Tynehead Regional Park:** 100ha. 530-4983. Enter at the Tynehead Hatchery, 16585-96 Ave. Visit the salmon hatchery, look for wildlife, or hike trails through second growth forests and rolling meadows. The park has been carefully redeveloped over past two years.

■ **Semiahmoo Fish and Game Club Hatchery:** 1284-184th St in South Surrey, near US border. 535-8366. Coho, steelhead, cutthroat, chinook. Year-round.

■ **Redwood Park Arboretum:** 20th Ave and 176 St near US Border. A strange and moving story behind the planting of this arboretum. The land was given to twins Peter and David Brown by their father on their 21st birthdays in 1893. Both had become deaf in their teens after bouts with scarlet fever. They systematically began replanting where logging had stripped the hilltop. Over the years, the "Tree Twins" collected seeds and seedlings from all over the world for their arboretum. They also grew solitary, living apart from the world in a two-story tree house. The park is now owned by Surrey.

■ **Newton Wave Pool:** 13730-72nd Ave. Call 594-SURF. Open daily. A 38m pool with two 60m waterslides, hydro pool, steam room, children's pool, lounge, and concessions.

■ **Softball BC Complex (Softball City):** 24th Ave and 148th St in South Surrey. 531-3220. A state-of-the-art complex, with four baseball diamonds, making Surrey the Softball Capital of Canada.

■ **Crescent Beach and Blackie Spit:** One of the most popular beaches around, and Blackie Spit is *the* sunning spot. Also check out Ocean Park Rd running south from Crescent Beach; it fronts a rockier beach, interesting for its marine life.

■ **Serpentine Fen Bird Sanctuary:** King George Hwy near 48th Ave in South Surrey. A natural area for walking, birdwatching. Skate on the dykes in winter.

■ **Surrey Public Market:** 64th and King George Hwy. 596-8899. Everything under one skylit roof.

■ **Guildford Mall:** At 104th Ave and 152nd St. 585-1565. One of BC's largest malls. Two shopping complexes joined by overhead walkways. Over 230 shops, plus a free ride on an antique Merry-Go-Round. In the Guildford Town Centre.

■ **Rainforest Reptile Refuge:** 16th Ave and 176 St. 538-1711. Devoted to exotic reptiles and amphibians.

# Richmond

## HOME OF VANCOUVER INTERNATIONAL AIRPORT

**Richmond:** (Pop. 126,624). Sits immediately north of George Massey Tunnel. The city of Richmond is actually an "island city," consisting of a number of islands between the north and south arms of the Fraser River as it flows into the Gulf of Georgia. Biggest is Lulu Island, where lies the main part of Richmond. Just north is Sea Island, location of the Vancouver International Airport. Small islands are Mitchell, Twigg, and Deadman.

The city is accessible by the Arthur Laing, Oak St, or Knight St bridges to the north, Hwy 91 to the east, or the George Massey Tunnel (Hwy 99) to the south. Exit Hwy 99 at Steveston Hwy for the Village of Steveston, or at Bridgeport Rd for the airport.

Richmond was named by an Australian farming family, the McRoberts, who settled here in the early 1860s. They nostalgically named the area after a place in Australia.

Once known as the Garden City, Richmond is one of BC's oldest communities. Added to its earlier industries of farming, fishing, and waterborne trade is a balance of major commercial, recreational, and residential developments. There are over 2,200 hotel rooms and a modern 250-unit RV park and campground here, making Richmond BC's third largest accommodation base.

There are many pleasures, many of them natural – buying fish on the old Steveston docks, sandbar fishing, or enjoying the unique trail system on the dykes. No. 3 road is for shopping: over 800 stores in a 1.5km radius.

**Richmond Information:** Two year-round infocentres. 203-8171 Park Rd, Richmond, BC, V6Y 1S9. Weekdays year-round. Other on east side of Hwy 99, just beyond George Massey Tunnel. Daily in summer, weekdays in winter. Summer only: infocentre on the Landing at Steveston Village. Same phone for all: 278-9333.

**Vancouver International Airport:** On Sea Island. Accessed from the north by the Arthur Laing Bridge at foot of Granville St; or off Hwy 99 at Bridgeport Rd and Sea Island Way to Sea Island Bridge. Within Richmond, can also be accessed over Dinsmore Bridge north of Westminster Hwy on Gilbert Rd. Opened in 1968. Nine million passengers pass through annually. All major carriers are represented. For flight info and reservations, call individual airline companies or travel agencies.

■ **Richmond Art Gallery:** 7671 Minoru Gate, in **Richmond Arts Centre**. 231-6440. Daily. Local, Canadian, international.

■ **Richmond Museum and Archives:** Adjacent to Richmond Art Gallery. 231-6440. Daily. Richmond's history. Turn-of-the-century living room, wedding dresses and veil from late 1800s. Lace-making display.

■ **Minoru Park Complex:** Borders Gilbert Rd and Granville Ave. 276-4107. Downtown delight. Pierrefonds Gardens, Minoru Lake, Historic Minoru Chapel, an all-weather track, aquatic centre, tennis courts, ice arenas.

■ **Richmond Nature Park and Nature House:** 11851 Westminster Hwy (at corner of No. 5 Rd). 273-7015. Daily. Over 80ha of unique preserved bog environment. Four trails, longest over 1.6km long. Nature house with displays of birds, snakes, frogs, salamanders, and working beehive. Nature games for children. Pond in park.

■ **Bridgepoint Harbour Market:** 8811 River Rd (in north Richmond, facing Sea Island). 273-8500. Public boardwalk, pier, shops, marina, family restaurant and pub.

■ **London Farm:** 6511 Dyke Rd on south arm of the Fraser River, near Steveston. 271-5220. Former London family farmhouse, restored to the period 1880 to 1914. Tours, picnics.

■ **Steveston Community Centre:** Southwest corner of Richmond. 8km off Hwy 99 along Steveston Hwy. Call 277-6812. Steveston is a designated "heritage village." Rustic buildings, old net lofts and sheds that attract artists and photographers. Crafts, antiques, museums, galleries, restaurants. Wharf where you can buy fresh salmon, tuna, sole, halibut, shrimp, prawns, and crab directly from fishboats. The Gulf of Georgia Cannery, built 1894, was one of largest canneries on the lower Fraser waterfront, referred to as "the monster cannery at Steveston." The last cannery intact on the Fraser River, as late as 1979 its premises were still being used for herring reduction.

The historic 3ha Britannia Shipyard complex – which includes the cannery, Japanese boatworks, bunkhouse, and boardwalks – is being developed by the city of Richmond as a park and year-round exhibition. For info, call Richmond's Parks and Leisure Services, 276-4107.

■ **Steveston Museum:** 3811 Moncton St. 271-6868. Daily. On main street in village of Steveston. Displays of local fishing industry and early settlement.

■ **Chinese Buddhist Temple:** 9160 Steveston Hwy. 274-2822. Open daily. Outstanding example of Chinese palatial architecture, bonsai garden, Buddhist museum, exhibits, ceremonies in progress.

*Steveston Landing, Village of Steveston, in Richmond.*

■ **Sikh Temple:** 18691 Westminster Hwy. Called Nanak-sar, this striking sky-blue onion-topped temple rises from farmlands like a blue vision of the Taj Mahal.

■ **Fantasy Garden World:** 10800 No.5 Rd, at Steveston Hwy. 277-7777. Daily. 5ha. Formal rose garden, Biblical garden, fuchsia garden, windmill, carillon bell tower, aviaries, miniature train. Christmas light show with over 75,000 lights. Sunday brunch in Glass Conservatory. Banquets.

■ **Iona Beach Regional Park:** 60ha at the tip of a finger of Sea Island jutting northwest out into Georgia Strait. Just north of the airport. Extensive tidal flats.

This newly created regional park will protect breeding habitat of many local birds, as well as foreshore areas of the delta that are vital to migratory birds. A bravo to the Greater Vancouver Regional District for this important addition to the regional parks system.

# US Border to Horseshoe Bay

## NORTH-SOUTH CORRIDOR (Highways 99 and 99/1)

The route from the Canada/US border to Horseshoe Bay passes through the most populated region of BC, taking in the city of Vancouver itself. It is well served with accommodation and amenities of every kind.

At the same time, the criss-crossing of freeways and highways can make passage through the city limits and environs bewildering. This section is designed to assist the traveller in getting into or through Vancouver, or to White Rock, Delta, West Vancouver, and so on. It is not intended as a trip in itself. Follow the route map provided here or, for an overview, see the *Gateway* map, pp.84-85.

Hwy 99, four lanes, leaves the Canada/US border and continues through Delta and Richmond into Vancouver. It crosses the Oak St Bridge over the Fraser River, jogs west along 70th Ave to Granville St (Hwy 99), continuing through downtown Vancouver. After passing through 404ha Stanley Park, Hwy 99 crosses the Lions Gate Bridge, with its spectacular view of Burrard Inlet.

Route continues as Hwy 1/99 to Horseshoe Bay on Howe Sound. From here, travellers can go north on Hwy 99 (the Squamish Hwy) to Squamish, Whistler, Pemberton, and over the mountains into the Cariboo; or take a BC Ferry to Vancouver Island, Bowen Island, or the Sunshine Coast. The distance from Peace Arch Provincial Park at the border, to Horseshoe Bay is 71km.

**Peace Arch Provincial Park:** 10ha. 463-3132. At Canada/US border. Commemorates the lasting peace between Canada and US. Dedicated in Sept, 1921. The park, declared "international territory," straddles both sides of the border and is jointly maintained by BC and Washington State. Visitors from either side of the border may enjoy the park without passing through customs. Formal gardens, rockeries, group picnic sites.

**Campbell River Rd (8th Ave):** West 2.5km to White Rock.

**White Rock:** (Pop. 16,314). On Boundary Bay, 5km beyond border on Hwy 99. Bordered on the south by the US, north and east by District of Surrey, west by Semiahmoo Bay.

The community is named for the 40t white rock deposited on the beach, limed white by the guano of thousands of roosting seabirds. A Semiahmoo Indian legend says the Sea God's son threw it across Strait of Georgia from Cowichan Bay, and then with his Cowichan princess, followed it here to begin a new life and a new tribe. The Peace Arch is visible from White Rock's pier.

White Rock is picture-perfect, with more than 4.5km of beachfront and a warm, dry climate. More sunshine in White Rock than anywhere else on the Lower Mainland. Industrial and residential activity burgeoned at turn of the century with the establishment of the Great Northern Railway along the city's waterfront. By 1937, area was a summer seaside resort with population of more than 1,000. Incorporated as a city in 1957 when it separated from Surrey.

**White Rock Information:** Infocentre, White Rock and South Surrey Chamber of Commerce, 1554 Foster St, White Rock, BC, V4B 3X8. 536-6844. Weekdays in winter, daily in summer.

■ **White Rock Museum and Archives at Station Centre:** 14970 Marine Dr. 531-5253. Daily in summer. In restored 1913 Great Northern Railway station.

■ **White Rock Pier:** Near Station Centre. A well-known local structure extending 469m out into Semiahmoo Bay. The original pier was built on this site in 1913-14. Open for walking and sightseeing.Wheelchair accessible.

**Sunnyside Rd (24th Ave) and Crescent Beach:** 5.5km beyond border. West 10km to Crescent Park, and popular Crescent Beach and Blackie Spit. See *Surrey*, p.92.

**Nicomekl River:** Crosses under Hwy 99, 9km beyond border. 25km long. The river flows through the bottomland of Surrey into Mud Bay. Part of a historic portage route. Cutthroats, jacks, and coho.

**King George Hwy (Hwy 99A) Interchange:** An important interchange, 10km north of Canada/US border.

Exit north for Trans-Canada Hwy 1 (Via Hwy 10); or for access into Surrey; or through Surrey, north to New Westminster (note that new Hwy 91, coming up to the west, is a better connection with New Westminster).

■ **For Connection with Trans-Canada Hwy and Points E ast:** Take east exit (to Hwy 10) off King George Hwy 4km north of interchange with Hwy 99. Hwy 10 travels east 20km to join the Trans-Canada Hwy northeast of Langley.

■ King George Hwy crosses north-south through the city of **Surrey**. It travels 16km north from the interchange with Hwy 99, then over the Pattullo Bridge to **New Westminster**. For details, see *New Westminster*, p.91, and *Surrey*, p.92.

**Serpentine River:** 2.5km beyond Nicomekl River. Flows through Surrey into Mud Bay. A narrow stream, 32km long. Cutthroat, Dolly Varden, rainbow, coho, and steelhead.

**Hwy 91 (Annacis Island Hwy):** 8km northwest of King George Hwy Interchange. A new highway. Exit north to **New Westminster**, over Annacis Island and the Alex Fraser Bridge.

**Hwy 10 (Ladner Trunk Rd):** 4km west of Hwy 91 (22km north of US Border). Exit east, 26km to Langley; about 10km farther to Hwy 1 (Trans-Canada). Exit west to **Ladner** and the **District Municipality of Delta**. (Western portion only of Hwy 10 is called Ladner Trunk Rd). Details on Langley in *Vancouver to Hope – South Bank*, p.106.

## SIDE TRIP

## to North Delta and Ladner

**Municipality of Delta:** (Pop. 88,978). On Hwy 10, 8km west of junction with Hwy 99 (30km beyond border). Known as "Tunnel Town," for George Massey Tunnel that goes under the Fraser River via Deas Island.

Early occupants of the area were the Tsawwassen Band and other Coast Salish Indians. European settlers began moving into the area in late 1860s. By 1868 the first farmland claims were filed. Thomas and William Ladner filed for land next to the Chillukthan Slough. Municipality of Delta incorporated in 1879.

Delta's 336 sq km are bounded by Fraser River, Surrey, Strait of Georgia, and the Canada/US border at Boundary Bay. The tip of the peninsula drops below 49th parallel, so there is a small part of America at **Point Roberts**, south of Boundary Bay.

Most of Delta is low-lying farmland. In the centre lies **Burns Bog**, ecologically very interesting, but of uncertain fate as yet. Delta has three urban communities: **North Delta** (bordering Surrey), **Tsawwassen** (to the south), and the **village of Ladner**. Industry is concentrated in three distinct areas: Tilbury Island, Annacis Island, and the Roberts Bank deep-sea superport. Considerably marine-related, Ladner is a supply base for commercial fishing boats, which makes for interesting shopping.

**Delta Information:** Infocentre, 6201-60th Ave, Delta, BC, V4K 4E2. 946-4232. Daily summer, weekdays in winter.

■ **Delta Museum and Archives:** 4858 Delta St. 946-9322 or 946-6262. Daily except Mon. Three floors in 1912 heritage building. Local historic displays include period rooms and Coast Salish artifacts.

■ **Village of Ladner:** A riverport community older than Vancouver. Fish for sale at the government wharf, riverfront walks, seafood restaurants.

■ **Reifel Bird Sanctuary:** At 5191 Robertson Rd, on northern tip of Westham Island, 10km west of Ladner. 946-6980. Daily. One of North America's major waterfowl habitats. More than 230 species of birds from plentiful Canada geese to the uncommon black-crowned night herons, and extremely rare Temminck's stints. Gatehouse, gift shop, parking, picnicking.

**Tsawwassen Ferry Terminal:** To reach the terminal from Ladner, return east on Hwy 10 (Ladner Trunk Rd) to Hwy 17; terminal is about 12km south. (Ferries to Victoria, Nanaimo, Gulf Islands.)

*Return to Highway 99*

**Hwy 17 (Ladner Interchange):** 8km beyond junction of Hwys 99 and 10 (30km from US border). Exit southwest, 14km to Tsawwassen Ferry Terminal. Exit northeast to 60th Ave, and Deas Island Regional Park.

## SIDE TRIP

### to Tsawwassen, Tsawwassen Ferry Terminal, and Vancouver Island

**Tsawwassen:** A part of the Municipality of Delta (for info, see Delta, above). Name may have come from a aboriginal word meaning "facing the sea," because indeed it does. Beautiful beaches, super windsurfing off the spit to the ferry.

**Tsawwassen Ferry Terminal:** On Hwy 17, 14km southwest of junction with Hwy 99. BC Ferries run from Vancouver (Tsawwassen) to Victoria (Swartz Bay) on Vancouver Island. Also, to Nanaimo on Vancouver Island, and to other Gulf Islands. Sailing time to Swartz Bay is 95 minutes (then a 30-minute drive to Victoria). Sailing distance is 38.5km. Many BC Ferries can carry 300 automobiles, 1,350 passengers. For info on ferry sailings: 277-0277.

**Splashdown Park:** On Hwy 17, near BC Ferry Terminal. May-Sept. 943-2251. 3ha, 11 waterslides, hot tub.

**Boundary Bay Regional Park:** 30ha. 432-6350. South on Hwy 17 towards ferry, then left at 56th St, left (east) at 12th Ave. Road winds through farmland and residential areas to Centennial Beach parking lot. 1.6km sandy beach, mud flats, dikes, sand dunes, salt marshes, lagoon. Excellent bird-watching.

*Return to Highway 99*

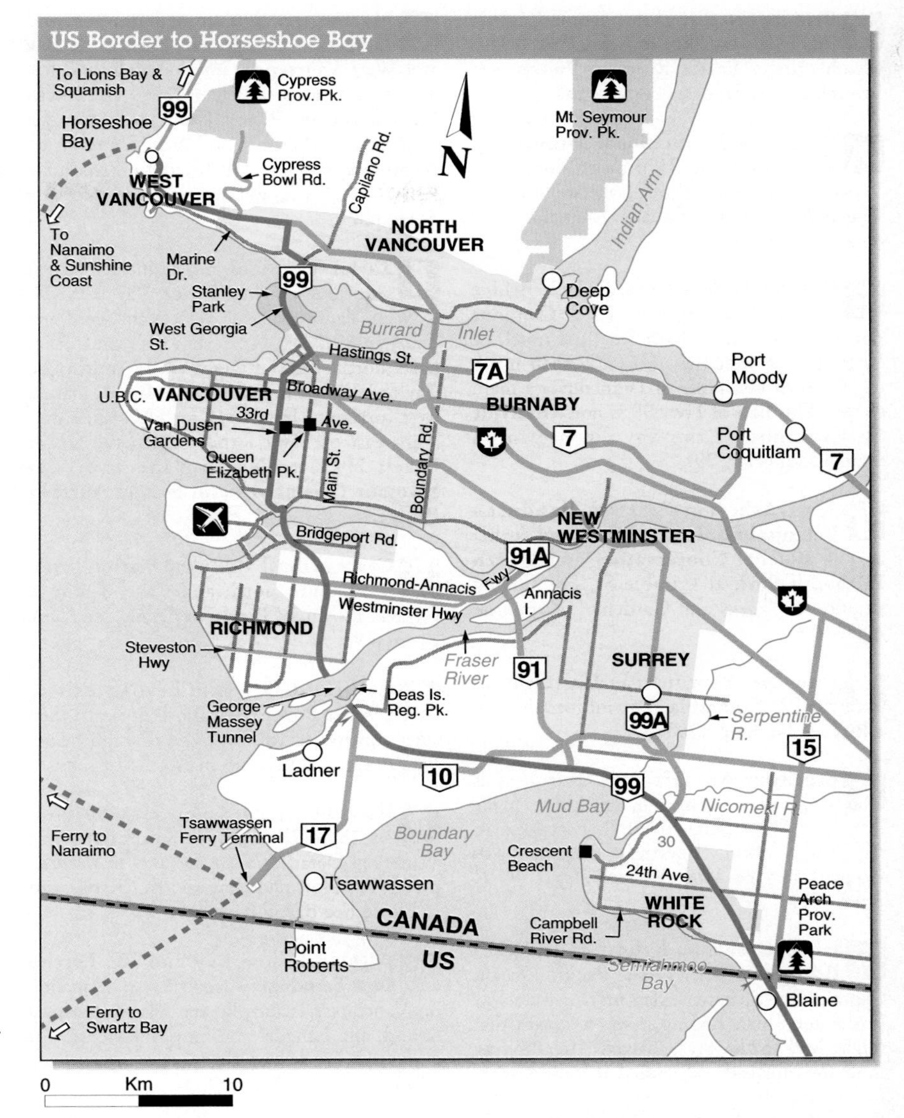


**Deas Island Regional Park:** 70ha. 432-6350. Exit northeast at Hwy 17 (Ladner Interchange). Follow 62B St (River Rd) 4km to park. Inverholme Schoolhouse, a heritage school from 1909, acts as infocentre. May-Sept. Burrvilla, 1905 Queen Anne style home, is decorated with antiques and period furnishings which are for sale. Fraser River viewing tower. Nature trails to west of island. Sand dunes, marshes, and view of vehicles disappearing into George Massey Tunnel. Parking, picnics, shelters and facilities, many accessible to disabled.

**Fraser River:** For history, see *Introduction, Southwestern BC*, p.76.

**George Massey Tunnel:** 2km beyond the junction of Hwys 99 and 17. 1.6km long, completed 1959, passes under the Fraser River linking Delta to Richmond. Still called the Deas Island Tunnel by diehards.

**Steveston Hwy Interchange:** 1km beyond the George Massey Tunnel. First exit to Richmond and Village of Steveston.

**Richmond:** (Pop. 126,624). Township of Richmond consists of a number of islands, the main one being **Lulu Island**, cradled between north and south arms of the Fraser River. The **Vancouver International Airport** is on Sea Island, north of Lulu. For more info on Richmond and Village of Steveston, which is part of it, see *Richmond*, p.93.

**Richmond East/West Freeway (Hwy 91):** 5km beyond the Steveston Hwy Interchange. Exit east, 16km to Annacis Island, where highway divides. Then, either go north on Hwy 91A to New Westminster via the magnificent new **Alex Fraser Bridge**; or turn south on Hwy 91 10km to North Delta. **Note:** To access **Knight St** and **Knight St Bridge** into Vancouver (an alternate route), turn east Hwy 91, then north on Knight St.

This is a new highway, the first freeway-to-freeway exchange in BC, and part of the new Annacis System which uses **Annacis Island** in the Fraser River as focus of a $444 million connecting corridor system. (The Alex Fraser Bridge is included in the cost.)

**Bridgeport Rd:** 1km beyond Cambie Rd. Exit west 2km to Sea Island Bridge which crosses Fraser River to **Vancouver International Airport**. Follow signs.

**Vancouver International Airport:** On Sea Island, in Richmond, south of Vancouver. Opened 1968. Nine million passengers pass through annually. All major carriers are represented.

**Oak St Bridge:** Cross Oak St Bridge over north arm of Fraser River. Continue north on Oak St to Park Rd (just north of 64th St). Jog west (left) on Park, then north (right) onto Granville St (Vancouver's main street). This part of Hwy 99 is now **Granville St.** Continue all the way downtown on Granville St (Hwy 99).

**33rd Ave:** Turn east to **Vandusen Botanical Garden** at Oak St, and farther east to **Bloedel Conservatory and Queen Elizabeth Park** at Cambie St. For further details, see "Parks and Gardens," *Vancouver*, p.87.

**16th Ave:** West (left) to **University of British Columbia.** For information on UBC, see *Vancouver*, p.86.

**Broadway Ave (Hwy 7):** (Broadway is 9th, if you're counting, and it does make it easier.) West (left) to UBC. East 9km to Burnaby; 9km beyond Burnaby to Coquitlam. See *Vancouver to Hope, North Bank*, p.110.

**False Creek and the Granville St Bridge:** An inlet of the Pacific Ocean. Captain GH Richards sailed up this waterway in the late 1850s hoping it was a stream that might lead to the Fraser River. After finding mud flats instead, he named it False Creek. Granville St Bridge arcs over popular **Granville Island** and its **Public Market**.

**Granville and Georgia Streets:** Main intersection of downtown Vancouver. Highway turns north (left) at Georgia St.

**Stanley Park:** At foot of W Georgia St. For details on this magnificent natural park, see *Vancouver*, p.87.

**Lions Gate Bridge (First Narrows):** First Narrows waterway flows past Stanley Park, under the Lions Gate Bridge into Burrard Inlet. Completed in 1938, bridge was named for the twin-peaked Lions Mountains that overlook Vancouver. The Lions Gate was built by the Guinness family (British brewers) to link the North Shore's British Properties with Vancouver. Became toll-free in 1955 when BC government paid $6 million for it.

**Burrard Inlet:** Focus of Vancouver's early development. Century-old port bustles with supertankers and freighters from around the world. Inlet extends 24km west to Port Moody, and north along Indian Arm, 23km, past Deep Cove to the Wigwam Inn.

**Marine Dr:** Exit immediately beyond Lions Gate Bridge. For **Horseshoe Bay** and **West Vancouver**, travel straight and follow the off ramp to Taylor Way. For **North Vancouver** and **Deep Cove**, turn east on Marine Dr. For info on West Vancouver, North Vancouver, Mt Seymour Provincial Park, Cates Park, and Deep Cove, see *North Shore*, p.89.

**Taylor Way:** Crosses Marine Dr at first set of traffic lights. Taylor Way is basically West Vancouver (for West Van, see *North Shore*, p.89). For Horseshoe Bay and other parts north, travel straight ahead (north) on Taylor Way. At junction with Hwy 1, make a west turn onto Hwy 99/1 for Horseshoe Bay. Turn east on Hwy 1 (here called the Upper Levels Hwy) to **North Vancouver**, **Mt Seymour Provincial Park**, **Second Narrows Bridge**.

**Cypress Bowl Rd:** 6km west of Taylor Way. Turn north and travel 12km to Cypress Provincial Park. For details, see *North Shore*, p.91.

**Caulfield Dr:** 5km beyond exit to Cypress Provincial Park. Exit north then turn south and follow signs to Lighthouse Park in Caulfield.Details in *North Shore*, p.91.

**Hwy 99:** At this point, Hwy 99 turns north to Lions Bay, Squamish, and Whistler. Details: *Horseshoe Bay to Lillooet*, p.105. For Horseshoe Bay and BC Ferries, exit to Horseshoe Bay, follow signs.

**Horseshoe Bay and BC Ferries Terminal:** Departures to Nanaimo on Vancouver Island, Bowen Island in Howe Sound, and Langdale on Sunshine Coast. For Bowen Island and Sunshine Coast, see *Horseshoe Bay to Lund*, p.96.

**Whytecliffe Park:** Off Marine Dr in Horseshoe Bay. Trails, picnics. Departure point for diving excursions.

## Horseshoe Bay to Lund

### THE SUNSHINE COAST (Highway 101)

The Sunshine Coast, though on the mainland and north of Vancouver, is islandlike in its existence, depending largely on car-carrying ferries for its connection to the rest of the world. A main segment, Sechelt Peninsula, is just barely a peninsula. It's also a benchland barricaded from the rest of the mainland by the forbidding Coast Mountains. Much of the peninsula is covered by second-growth western red cedar and Douglas fir. Winters are mild and wet and summers are sunnier and drier than many other coastal areas.

The Sunshine Coast may be close in distance to cosmopolitan action, but to reach its southernmost part means a 45-minute ferry ride across Howe Sound from Horseshoe Bay. To reach Powell River and Lund – the northernmost terminal for Hwy 101 and the farthest you can go by conventional means – another ferry ride takes 50 minutes, from Earls Cove to Saltery Bay. Other ferries link the Sunshine Coast with Vancouver Island and with the offshore islands of Texada and Savary.

The coastline offers some of the world's best scuba diving, with underwater seascapes that rival the tropics for colour and variety. The 2,400 hours of yearly sun make the maze of inlets, channels, and straits even more attractive. With all its nooks and crannies and its reflective lifestyle, the Sechelt Peninsula boasts a thriving artistic community. Painters, writers, craftspeople, and musicians are as rife as yachtsmen and retired salts.

As you disembark from the ferry at Langdale on Sechelt Peninsula, the two-lane Hwy 101 wanders through Gibsons, a delightful coast town made famous by the long-running and now-cancelled CBC television series, *The Beachcombers*. Beyond Sechelt the highway becomes winding.

Excellent views of Strait of Georgia from the town of Sechelt and other points on the highway. Elsewhere, for good water views, locals recommend detours down one of the peninsula's many side roads. Some argue that this 165km drive, together with the scenic ferry rides, is the prettiest in the province. Though not as tourist-oriented and as quaint as the Sechelt Peninsula, Powell River, near the end of this sinuous drive, is worth the effort of taking the second ferry. Some would say that this mill town, enclosed by ocean and wilderness lakes and clearcut-pocketed forest, is one of BC's best-kept secrets.

Infocentres provide hourly updated information on availability of provincial park and private campsites. Book into a campsite as early in the day as possible. Provincial parks are on a first-come, first-serve basis, most are full by 2:30, especially those on the more accessible Sechelt Peninsula. And be prepared for long ferry lineups and waits, particularly in summer and especially on weekends.

**Horseshoe Bay:** (Pop. 1,037). Junction of Hwys 1 and 99. Terminal for BC Ferries to **Langdale** on Sunshine Coast, Departure Bay in **Nanaimo** on Vancouver Island, and **Snug Cove** on Bowen Island. BC Ferries information, call 277-0277.

Huge *Queen of Cowichan* (370 cars, 1,500 passengers) normally sails route across Howe Sound between Horseshoe Bay and Langdale. The ferry passes between Bowen and Gambier islands in its 15.5km, 35-minute trips. A ferry just built in 1991 and boosting high-tech steering gear makes the short hop to **Bowen Island**. Called the *Queen of Capilano* (85 cars). See also below, **Saltery Bay**. For description of Horseshoe Bay, a picturesque village, see *Horseshoe Bay to Lillooet,* p.102.

## SIDE TRIP

### to Bowen Island

Ferry from Horseshoe Bay arrives at Snug Cove on Bowen Island, a 20-minute 5km ride. A "bedroom community," many Bowen residents commute daily to Vancouver. Named after James Bowen (1751-1835), a British Navy rear-admiral.

Bowen Island was once Vancouver's Coney Island, a resort where residents escaped on weekends to dance, picnic, and play. But it's still an excellent place for a refreshing day trip, and without the merry crowds that were once brought in by the Union Steamship Company until 1950.

It's a short walk from the ferry (if you don't take your car) to the island's pubs, restaurants, and shops. The old Union Steamship Company Store (1924), has been turned into a library and post office. A walk down a tree-lined road brings you to a freshwater lagoon and Deep Bay.

■ **Crippen Regional Park:** 260ha. 432-6350. 2km walk to Killarney Lake and 4km loop trail through flooded forest and marsh rich with bird life. Signs at Union Steamship Company Store point to park's entrance. See coho, maybe cutthroat, in Terminal Creek Fishway.

### Return to Highway 101

**Langdale:** (Pop. 137). On Howe Sound, opposite Horseshoe Bay. Named after Robinson Henry Langdale (1835-1908), a European who settled here in 1892. Jumping-off point for touring the Sechelt Peninsula. **Earls Cove**, the next ferry landing at peninsula's other end, is 81km away on Hwy 101. For ferry info call 886-2242.

**Port Mellon Rd:** Northeast (right) out of Langdale leads 10km to tiny communities of Hillside and Port Mellon, popular destinations for boating excursions. Port Mellon has a state-of-the-art pulp mill founded by Captain HA Mellon in 1908 and upgraded to the tune of $1 billion in recent years. Signs lead to Sunshine Coast Salmonid Enhancement Society Hatchery.

**Soames Hill Hiking Trail:** 3.5km beyond Langdale Ferry Terminal on upper highway (North Rd). Turn left on Chamberlain and left on Bridgeman. It's a 20-minute climb to the top, using steps, handrails, and cedar walkways. Great view from 243m of Keats Island, Gibsons Harbour, Strait of Georgia, Barfleur Pass. On a clear day, see Vancouver Island 30km away.

**Gibsons:** (Pop. 3,138). Veer left westwards from Langdale Ferry Terminal on Hwy 101 (Marine Dr) to downtown Gibsons, 4km away and running past the tiny settlements of **Hopkins Landing** and **Granthams Landing**. Go straight ahead on upper highway (North Rd), which skirts fringes of town and rejoins lower highway.

Named for George Gibson who settled in 1886. When he and his two sons were trying to sail a sloop to Oyster Bay on Vancouver Island, a southeaster blew them off course and into Howe Sound. Anchored in the lee of **Keats Island**, they beheld the headland that they would make their home. Originally called "Gibson's Landing." In 1947 locals persuaded post office to drop the "Landing," but the name persists on some tourist brochures as "Gibsons Landing."

Built on a hillside overlooking Shoal Channel and Howe Sound. Upper Marine Dr leads to shopping area; Lower Marine Dr to waterfront, the tourist precinct, and a cluster of interesting shops along Gower Pt Rd. **Molly's Reach Cafe**, the set of CBC Television series until 1991, *The Beachcombers,* an internationally popular weekly sit-com about a log-salvaging company. Molly's Reach is slated to become a real cafe. Take a stroll along the seawalk, just down from Molly's Reach.

Port Mellon Pulp Mill is area's major employer, but that doesn't take away from fact that Gibsons is a bona fide fishing village and is now a booming bedroom community to the metropolitan bedlam of Vancouver. Rapid development here and elsewhere on the Sechelt Peninsula for urban refugees and retirees may alter the bucolic lifestyle that has made the Sunshine Coast so attractive in the first place. A privately run commuter ferry is in the cards to help handle increasing demand.

**Gibsons Information:** Infocentre, Box 1190, Gibsons, BC, V0N 1V0. Call 886-2325. Follow signs off Hwy 101 to Lower Marine Dr and Gower Point Rd (kitty-corner from Molly's Reach Cafe). Weekdays in winter, daily in summer. This infocentre features a burial plot for George Gibson and family members, a somewhat haunting touch that was done as part of a 1985 downtown revitalization scheme. You will definitely feel the pull of history as you pose your travelling companions at the tombstones, a step away from the infocentre's doorstep.

■ **Gibsons Seawalk:** From Government Wharf to Gibsons Marina in Lower Gibsons. 10-minute walk. Lit at night. Completed in 1986.

■ **Gower Pt Rd and Ocean Beach Esplanade:** If you take Gower Pt Rd west and north out of downtown, you'll be treated to an incomparable drive that turns away from Howe Sound to face the Strait of Georgia. You may also decide to lose yourself in a labyrinth of residential streets called the Bluff. **Chaster Provincial Park** at Gower Pt has picnic tables. Captain George Vancouver stopped here in 1792.

■ **Elphinstone Pioneer Museum:** 716 Winn Rd, downtown Gibsons. Call 886-8232. Daily May-Sept, or on request. Focus is on Sunshine Coast. Bedford Shell Collection is one of largest in Canada. Also Coast Salish Indian life and pioneer displays.

**Roberts Creek:** (Pop. 2,236). 9km beyond Langdale off Hwy 101 along scenic **Lower Roberts Creek Rd** that eventually loops back to highway. A 6km drive takes you to the library and General Store with its in-the-know bulletin board. On Strait of Georgia. Named for Thomas Roberts who settled here in 1889. Natural beauty and quiet surroundings. Known for its bed-and-breakfast facilities.

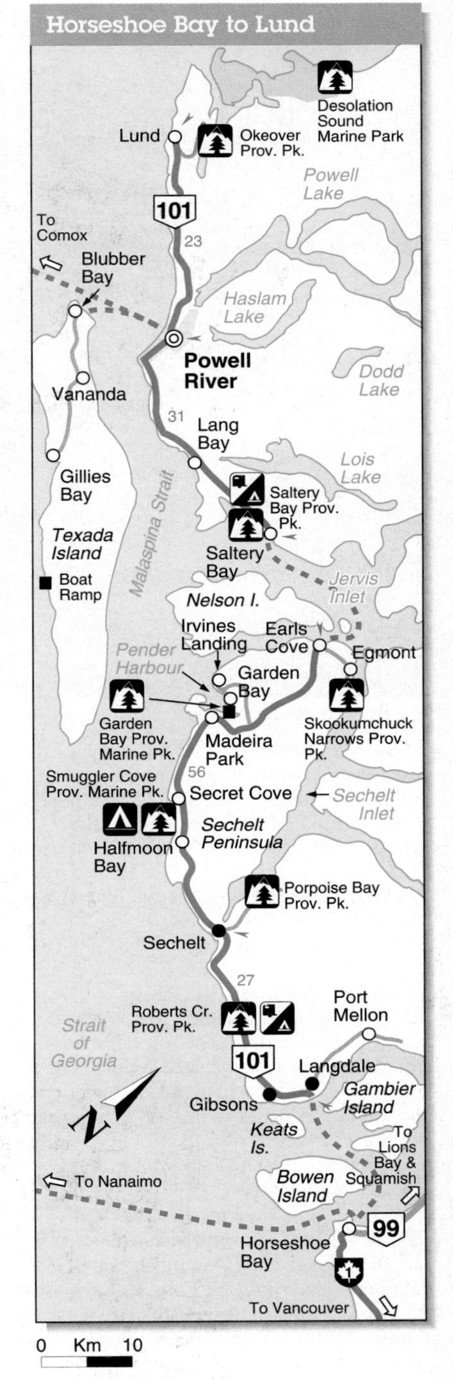


**Roberts Creek Information:** Gibsons Travel Infocentre.

■ **Cliff Gilker Regional Park:** 65ha. Nature trails, two creeks (Clack and Roberts), cedar bridges, waterfalls (Leisure and Shadow), picnic site, toilets. Along Hwy 101 just before Roberts Creek Road, 16km from Langdale.

*Seaside village of Lund, north end of the Sunshine Coast*

■ **Sunshine Coast Golf & Country Club:** Next to Gilker Park. 9-hole course that offers 18-hole experience with alternate tee boxes. Tough, loaded with water hazards and sand traps. 885-9212.

**Roberts Creek Provincial Park:** 40ha; 24 campsites. 885-9019 or 898-3678. 18km from Langdale off Hwy 101. A separate day-use section is found 1.5km southeast on Beach Road, or, if you're driving west, off Hwy 101 at Flume Rd, 17km from Langdale. Water is chilly, but people swim here. At low tide, this beach picnic area is good spot to find sea stars, mussels, and oysters. Flume Rd marks course of a long-gone 6km flume on which were floated cedar blocks from inland forests to booming grounds at Roberts Creek mouth.

**Davis Bay:** 22km from Langdale. Hwy 101 swings along Georgia Strait. This beautiful sandy beach is one of the most accessible and beautiful in the region. Resort atmosphere. Davis Bay pier good for fishing. Take a walk to **Mission Point** at Chapman Creek's mouth. Watch for sea lions and harbour seals. Leaving Davis Bay, you drive up a hill before entering Sechelt.

**Sechelt:** (Pop. 6,123). 27km beyond Langdale on Hwy 101. An intriguing, lovely location. Town sits on narrow sandbar, barely a kilometre in width. Strait of Georgia to south, Sechelt Inlet to north. This land bridge prevents Sechelt Peninsula from being an island.

This isthmus village is base for the Sechelt People, whose influence on this coast is pervasive. What you first see as you enter Sechelt is an imposing cultural centre – the House of hewhiwus (House of Chiefs), completed in 1991 and containing offices of Sechelt Indian Government District, the South Campus of Capilano Community College, a museum, 280-seat Raven's Cry Theatre, gift shop, and the local infocentre. Behind the centre and facing Trail Bay in neat rows are homes of the local Sechelt. Decimated in the last century by smallpox, the Sechelt Nation is now thriving and achieved self-government in 1988. Sechelt means "a place of shelter from the sea."

Check out downtown's **Snickett Park** and **Pebble Beach** for relaxing and swimming. The Boulevard provides a bracing waterfront walk. Ask the locals or the infocentre on how to get **Kinnikinnick Park**. It's hard to find, but worth the effort.

The coastline around Sechelt is accessible for scuba diving, cruising, and salmon fishing.

Sechelt plays host to two distinctive events: the **Rockwood Centre Storytelling Festival**, first weekend in Oct, and the **Festival of Written Arts**, mid-Aug.

**Sechelt Information:** Infocentre, Box 360, Sechelt, BC, V0N 3A0. Call 885-3100. In Sechelt Indian Cultural Centre. Weekdays in winter, daily in summer.

■ **Sunshine Coast Arts Centre:** Junction of Trail and Medusa roads. 885-5412. Wed-Sun. Undergoing expansion, the centre is a driving force behind all the arts in the region.

■ **Rockwood Lodge Gardens:** Built in 1936 at top of Cowrie St. Year-round. Free to wander among rhododendrons, fuchsias, roses. Home of the Festival of the Written Arts. 885-2522.

**Inland Sea:** Sechelt town sits at the southern tip of an oceanic waterway with 480km of mountain-sheltered coastline. The main inlet is **Sechelt**, branches of which are Salmon and Narrows inlets. At its far end is foreboding **Skookumchuck Narrows**, see below. Except for a few small settlements, the Inland Sea is much the same as it was when gouged out by a wall of ice 10,000 years ago. Eight marine parks are found along the Inland Sea, plus some private marinas and resorts. See *Sechelt Inlets Provincial Marine Recreational Area* next page.

■ **HMCS *Chaudière*:** This 118m Canadian warship, a decommissioned destroyer escort, requires some effort to visit. You have to dive 35 metres below Sechelt Inlet off Kunechin Point, 6km north of Sechelt. The gutted ship was scuttled December, 1992 in an ambitious project by the Artificial Reef Society of BC. It thudded into the seabed on a tilt, canting over hard on its port side, the twin barrels of the forward gun jammed into the mud. The idea is that the ship will become a reef that encourages marine growth and attracts both fish and divers.

**East Porpoise Bay Rd:** Travels northeast (right) out of Sechelt to Porpoise Bay Provincial Park 4km beyond town. Signs also lead to **Sechelt Hatchery** operated by the Sechelt Indian Government District. Call 885-5562.

**Porpoise Bay Provincial Park:** 61ha. 84 campsites. Also features six cycle-in campsites and a group campground for 100 that can be reserved. Sani-station. 885-9019 or 898-3678. Turn northeast at Sechelt, follow road 4km to park. Swimmers enjoy the wide, sandy beach at this park on Sechelt Inlet's east side. Sunbathing and canoeing; fishing in inlet and various rivers and creeks for salmon, coho, and cod. In fall, **Angus Creek** features a chum salmon run. Park also provides access to Sechelt Inlets Marine Recreation Area for canoeists and car-toppers. Get there early in day to get a campsite in summer. Wheelchair accessible.

**Sechelt Inlets Provincial Marine Recreation Area:** 155ha. 20 wilderness/walk-in campsites. 885-9019. No vehicle access. Largely undeveloped. Eight sites on sheltered waters east of Sechelt Peninsula. Fishing for salmon and cod.

**Redrooffs Rd:** Off Hwy 101 at **Sargeant Bay**, just beyond Sechelt's western outskirts, 34km from Langdale. This alternate route into **Halfmoon Bay** follows Strait of Georgia coastline. Twisty, narrow, hilly, windy. RV drivers, proceed with caution.

**Sargeant Bay Provincial Park:** 57ha. Day use. Mostly undeveloped. Just west of Sechelt, off Hwy 101. Opened in 1991. Fresh-water marsh for birdwatching. Sandy beach for walking and sunbathing. Abundant intertidal life. Fish ladder for spawning salmon. Fragile habitat. Keep dogs leashed.

**Halfmoon Bay Lookout:** 13km beyond Sechelt on Hwy 101, overlooking Halfmoon Bay, **Welcome Pass**, **Malaspina Strait**, and **Thormanby Islands**. Strait named for Captain Alexandro Malaspina, Spaniard who explored the Pacific Coast from 1789-1794. These are now popular yachting waters.

**Halfmoon Bay:** (Pop. 260). A large scoop of a bay protected from open sea by South Thormanby Island. Public wharf, general store, liquor store, post office, low-tide public boat launch. Halfmoon Bay has five regional parks. One is **Coopers Green Regional Park,** on Fisherman Rd, off Redrooffs Rd; picnic area, boat launch. Another, **Redrooffs Trail & Pier,** off Redrooffs Rd, has nature trail, picnic area, and beach walk.

**Smuggler Cove Provincial Marine Park:** 182ha. 5 wilderness/walk-in campsites. 885-9019. 14km beyond Sechelt. Follow Brooks Rd off Hwy 101. Hike in 1km or paddle from Brooks Cove through Welcome Passage. Small, all-weather, protected anchorage. Forested uplands, rocky headlands. Fishing, swimming, hiking. **Frenchman's Cove**, a shallow inlet at park's southeast corner, may be entered by boat from Halfmoon Bay.

**Secret Cove:** (Pop. 3). 16.5km beyond Sechelt. Private marine park with year-round fishing for red snapper, salmon, coho, flounder, cod. Three marinas service hundreds of private boaters.

The landscape becomes more rugged as you head northwards to Pender Harbour away from the shelfland between Gibsons and Sechelt. Hwy 101 winds, climbs, and dips at the base of the **Caren Range**. Spectacular views of ocean and small islands unfold as you enter the Pender Harbour area. Roads curve around gemlike lakes as they dead-end in magical coves and resort enclaves.

**Pender Harbour:** A beautiful, deep harbour, about halfway between Vancouver and Princess Louisa Inlet (as a boat travels). It incorporates communities of **Madeira Park**, to south, **Irvines Landing** at the mouth of the harbour on north side, and **Garden Bay**. Although Madeira Park and Garden Bay have their own post offices, residents here are more likely to consider themselves simply Pender Harbourites – very closely connected by water.

This is a prime sports-fishing area, with a dozen resorts and marinas, cabins and campgrounds, moorage, diving facilities. Also, a 9-hole golf course.

Population is still somewhat scarce here, but foreign investment is beginning to pour in, and it remains to be seen how long this splendid labyrinth of delights can escape the pressure of development moving up the peninsula.

**Madeira Park Rd:** Just past Paq Lake, 29km beyond Sechelt and 59km from Langdale. Turn off Hwy 101 to reach Madeira Park business section.

**Madeira Park:** (Pop. 669). Rural district. 29km beyond Sechelt and 59km from Langdale. Named by Joseph Gonsalos, who settled here in early 1900s from the Madeira Islands, Portugal. Pender Harbour's largest community, with grocery stores, a post office, pharmacy, bank, liquor store, beauty shop, bingo hall. Just beyond the business section is lovely **Welbourn Cove**. A marina, picnic area, boat launch and cultural centre (library, art gallery and music school).

**Madeira Park Information:** Pender Harbour and Egmont Infocentre, Box 265, Madeira Park, BC, V0N 2H0. 883-2561. Seasonal.

**Road to Garden Bay, Garden Bay Provincial Marine Park, and Irvines Landing:** 5.5km beyond Madeira Park. Turn west. Both Garden Bay and Irvines Landing are 8km away. Irvines Landing Rd splits off westwards from Garden Bay Rd as latter veers southwards along **Garden Bay Lake**.

**Garden Bay Provincial Marine Park:** 163ha. Fronted by 200m of shoreline on Garden Bay. Includes 471m Mt Daniel, known by Sechelt Indians as *Swiss Cham*, of great ceremonial significance. Long ago the eastern peak was site of puberty rites of Sechelt Indian maidens. Western peak offers view of lakes, inlets and islands. Summit and native cemetery on waterfront are protected archeological sites. Open anchorage. Dinghy float. Little development.

**Mt Daniel Hiking Trail:** Take Garden Bay Rd from Hwy 101 to first road on left past Oyster Bay Rd (trail not well marked).

**Katherine Lake Regional Park:** This park is on the smallest of the four superb lakes in and around Irvines Landing and Garden Bay. An ideal base from which to hop around the Pender Harbour area. Sandy beach and swimming area. Picnic tables. Showers. Camping on high ground.

**Garden Bay:** (Pop. 216). Another spellbinding locale. Shouldn't be missed, especially if you are a hopeless romantic. Hotels, resorts, marinas, restaurants, even a drive-in deli, a totem pole. Gorgeous views up Pender Harbour.

Back on Hwy 101, you take the last leg of your journey up the lower Sunshine Coast, heading 16km for **Earls Cove** and another wondrous ferry ride, or one last side trip to **Egmont** and the trail head to legendary **Skookumchuck Narrows**.

**Irvines Landing:** (Pop. 57). Irvines Landing Rd climbs up from Garden Bay Lake past Mixal and Hotel lakes and down into the landing at the entrance to Pender Harbour. Consists of marina, pub, boat launch, and cold beer and wine store. Picturesque view of harbour. Named after Charles Irving, who started a trading post on this site around 1865. Steve Danes, a Latvian seaman, bought the landing in 1898. With his father-in-law, Joseph Gonsalas of Madeira Island, Danes built the Irvines Landing Hotel and Store. After being a fish-processing centre, the landing has become a popular anchorage and vacation spot.

■ **Pender Hill Hiking Trail:** Offers a spectacular view of Pender Harbour and surrounding waters. Trail start marked by a turquoise telephone pole, 60m east of Lee Rd.

**Sakinaw and Ruby Lakes:** Sakinaw Lake Rd is 14km from Madeira Park. Hwy 101 begins to skirt Ruby Lake just beyond. These bigger peninsula lakes draw paddlers and anglers. 1.3km portage between the lakes. Sudden winds can make Sakinaw dangerous.

## SIDE TRIP

## to Egmont and Skookumchuck Narrows

**Egmont Rd:** Just south of Earls Cove, turn east 16km beyond Madeira Park on Hwy 101. About 5km, skirting northern tips of North and Waugh Lakes.

**Egmont:** (Pop. 119). Village on Secret Bay offers moorage and supplies as last stop for yachters heading up **Prince of Whales Reach** for incomparable **Princess Louisa Inlet**, see below. It is also the trail head for **Skookumchuck Narrows**, see below. As you drive into Egmont you will see 1,982m Mt Churchill that overlooks Prince of Whales Reach in the wild beyond.

**Skookumchuck Narrows Provincial Park:** 35ha. 885-9019. Northeast tip of Sechelt Peninsula overlooking narrows. 4km trail leads from parking lot at Egmont to Roland Pt.

Skookumchuck is Chinook jargon meaning "turbulent waters" or "rapid torrent." As the tides move through the narrows, they form rapids that boil and bubble with an audible roar. In spring, rapids can attain 12-14 knots.

Trail network leads to Roland and Narrows points, prime viewing areas for the phenomenon. Explanatory signs. Picnicking and day use. After the 45-minute hike over a reasonable trail, try to time your arrival there with peak tidal flows.

## Return to Highway 101 and Earls Cove

**Earls Cove:** Board BC Ferries from Earls Cove to **Saltery Bay** on north shore of **Jervis Inlet**. The 50-minute ferry ride is a wonderfully scenic respite before you can continue up Hwy 101. The ferry heads northwards up **Agamemnon Channel** before rounding the northern tip of sparsely populated **Nelson Island** into Jervis Inlet and southwards to Saltery Bay. Rugged Coast Mountains rise over trackless wilderness. The *Queen of Chilliwack*, a Norwegian vessel bought and converted by BC Ferries, was recently put on this run, replacing a new high-tech ferry called the *Queen of Capilano* that didn't catch on with the locals because it was too plastic in decor and often breaking down. The older and bigger *Chilliwack* (115 cars) has caught the fancy of both locals and crew members because it has real wood and brass, has a homey feel to it, and is reliable. The highly manoeuvrable *Capilano* (85 cars), its technical problems resolved, has been relegated to the short run between Horseshoe Bay and Bowen Island. For BC Ferries information call 669-1211.

**Jervis Inlet:** Cuts inland 74km from Malaspina Strait, leads to Hotham Sound, Sechelt Inlet, Prince of Wales Reach, Princess Royal Reach, and Queens Reach. Named by Captain George Vancouver after Rear-Admiral Sir John Jervis. Steep mountainous shores and deep water (over 200m).

**Princess Louisa Inlet:** Off Queens Reach and what at first looks like a large stream is **Malibu Rapids**, a 6km passage that leads to this small fabled inlet hidden in the recesses of the Coast Mountains. Sailors throttle through this dangerous entrance at the right tidal moments to enjoy this peerless natural paradise. At the inlet's head is a marine park, a tremendous 1,524m cliff, and spectacular 37m **Chatterbox Falls**, a roar within a vast wild silence. Mountain goats travel the cliff.

**Saltery Bay:** (Pop. 90). Terminal for ferry to and from Earls Cove (see above). 487-9333. Limited anchorage for small craft. Booming ground. From here Hwy 101 winds westward along Jervis Inlet and Malaspina Strait becoming Marine Ave as it turns north into Powell River's downtown 30km away.

**Saltery Bay Provincial Park:** 69ha. 42 campsites, sani-station. 485-4178. North Shore of Jervis Inlet, 1km beyond Saltery Bay ferry terminal. This is a rare, underused provincial park, and some say it has the most beautiful waterfront in the parks system. A 3m bronze mermaid was recently placed under 20m of water here, symbolic of just one of several great scuba-diving spots along this coast. A ramp for handicapped divers and swimmers descends into the water. Swimming, boat launch, hiking, fishing. Two beach front areas on north shore of Jervis Inlet. Mounds of seashells on the beach reveal that this was originally a native Indian fishing ground. Killer whales and sea lions can sometimes be seen.

**Lois River:** 11.5km from Saltery Bay. Flows from 1,414ha Lois Lake, which was created by a hydro dam, into Malaspina Strait. Fish for rainbow, kokanee, and Dolly Varden.

**Lang Bay:** (Pop. 264). 12km beyond Saltery Bay. Small community on Malaspina Strait. Country farmers raise Scottish Highland cattle, sheep, turkeys. Their homes look over the sea. There's a "good mile" of lovely sand; public beach access at north end of this protected bay. Safe swimming. Horseback riding. Eagle photography – the birds swoop down the creek in fall when it's chock-full of spawning chinook. Canoeing: access to first portage of Lois Lake, one of the Powell Lakes chain. (For more details see *Powell Forest Canoe Route* below.) Private campground.

**Westview Ferry Terminal:** Just as you enter Powell River's downtown in its Westview neighbourhood, 31km from Saltery Bay, turn left (or west) to Wharf or Courtenay streets. 485-2943. From here, ferries travel to **Comox** (Little River) on **Vancouver Island** and **Blubber Bay** on **Texada Island**. The *Queen of Sidney*, one of the first two vessels built by BC Ferries, holds 135 cars and 700 passengers and takes 75 minutes to travel the 27km across the Strait of Georgia to Comox. Contrary to the highly busy ferry runs from the Vancouver area to Victoria and Nanaimo on Vancouver Island, this ferry is usually only partly full and makes for a comfortable and scenic trip. Four sailings a day, the last one leaving at 8:45pm. The *North Island Princess* ferry to Texada Island carries 49 cars, 175 passengers. 35 minutes, 7km, 10 daily sailings.

## SIDE TRIP
### to Texada Island

The largest island on the lower coast's inside waters, Texada is 43km long and roughly 8km wide and home to 1,200 people, many of whom commute to Powell River to work. Part of the Regional District of Powell River. First charted in 1792 by Spanish explorers Cayento Valdés and Dionisio Alcala Galiano. Island's two main settlements are at Gillies Bay and Vananda.

Texada has a long history and used to be an industrial hotbed. Mining for iron began in the early 1880s and made Vananda a going concern with saloons, hotels, stores, a jail, newspaper, and even an opera house. The island has the richest limestone deposits in the Pacific Northwest and they play an important role in the island's economy. Barges ship out limestone from Blubber Bay.

Good place for hiking, beachcombing, camping, and for scuba-diving in clear waters. Vananda has a hotel and Gillies Bay a motel, a general store with liquor outlet, and an art gallery. Boat launches and moorage.

A ridge of rugged mountains runs island's length, reaching highest elevations in the undeveloped southern end.

"Flower rocks," unique to the island, look as if they have white flowers embedded in them. Used for making jewelry.

Take your vehicle with you on the ferry. No public transportation on Texada.

**Texada Island Information:** Contact Powell River Infocentre. See below.

**Shelter Point Regional Park:** 40 campsites. Sani-station. Boat launch. 483-3231. On Texada's west coast, just past Gillies Bay, 19km from Blubber Bay. Year-round. Newly developed trails.

## Return to Highway 101

**Powell River:** (Pop. 12,991). 31km beyond Saltery Bay. A recent issue of *Beautiful British Columbia Magazine* called the Powell River area BC's best-kept secret, largely because of its encircling environment of ocean, lakes, and wilderness, but also because of the pleasantness of the city itself.

Powell River was built up around the massive MacMillan Bloedel pulp-and-paper mill after it began operations in 1910. The original neighbourhood, called the Townsite, spread up from the waterfront mill. The 30 commercial buildings and 400 Victoria-style homes make the Townsite a historic set, possibly the most complete in the province. It will give you the nostalgic feeling of being in a time warp. A preservation program is being considered for this evocative precinct. Do take a tour.

Powell River has three other neighbourhoods, all distinctive from each other. Westview, the section you encounter entering Powell River from Saltery Bay, is the main residential and shopping area. Cranberry, which lies farther back from the waterfront than the other neighbourhoods, feels like a separate small town: friendly corner stores, a bird and wildlife sanctuary on Cranberry Lake, and large residential lots. On the other side of the river as you head up Hwy 101 for Lund and the end of the road, you skirt Wildwood, both upscale and pastoral.

Powell River is famous outside Canada for its international choral festival known as Kathaumixw, a Coast Salish word for a gathering of different peoples. The biennial event draws choirs from all over the globe. Nicknamed "River City" by the locals, this mill town is also noted for its own musical and dancing talents. Its Boys Choir and its Youth Choir have received international acclaim. Its School of Dance is a source of talent for the prestigious Royal Winnipeg Ballet.

Powell River residents are sensitive to people with disabilities. Streets and buildings have been made easier to use, a wheelchair trail has been put around a nearby wilderness lake.

Powell River bills itself "The Dive Capital of Canada," with its clear waters and diverse sealife (including uncommonly large octopuses and wolf eels). 20 major dive sites nearby, including Octopus City and The Hulks, a ring of old ships forming a breakwater near the mill.

Year-round salmon fishing. Several marinas. Close to 30 lakes within easy reach of the city, many have fishing for cutthroat trout.

**Powell River Information:** Infocentre, 6807 Wharf St, Powell River, BC, V8A 1T9. 485-4701. Just up from BC Ferry terminal. Weekdays in winter, daily in summer. Inquire about walking tours here.

■ **Valentine Mountain Viewpoint:** End of Crown St. Panoramic view of Strait of Malaspina from 182m lookout. Reached by 20-minute hike along trail, and rock stairway. Bald eagles year-round. In late fall, dozens of eagles are attracted by salmon spawning.

■ **Willingdon Beach Park:** A municipal 70-site campground on Powell River's waterfront, just a few minutes from downtown on Hwy 101.

■ **Powell Forest Canoe Route:** Begins at Lois Lake, 20km southeast of Powell River. Portages and streams connect 12 lakes over 80km. Suitable for children and adults who are experienced in the outdoors, route has canoe resting racks, 20 campsites, picnic spots.

■ **Inland Lake Site and Trail System:** The BC Forest Service encircled Inland Lake with a 13km wheelchair-accessible trail, complete with special cabins and wharves. Camping, fishing, boating. Open April 15-Oct 15. Follow Cranberry St to Haslam, which becomes Inland Lake Rd.

■ **Powell River Historic Museum:** Hwy 101 across from Willingdon Beach. 485-2222. Third largest photo archives in BC. Artifacts and displays of area's history include notorious "Billy Goat" Smith's cabin. Smith (d. 1958) was reputed to have been involved in Chicago murder of architect Stanford White at turn of century.

■ **MacMillan Bloedel Pulp and Paper Mill:** One of the biggest such complexes in the world. It created Powell River. Tours in summer. 483-3722.

**Powell River and Lake:** On Hwy 101, as you leave the Townsite for Lund, you cross Wildwood bridge over the second shortest river in world, only about 500m in length flowing from Powell Lake. Powell River Dam crosses the river, making water available to the mill. Just past the bridge is the turnoff right to **Powell Place**, a marina complex with pub and restaurant, built on the site of an old shingle mill. Charter houseboats here to tour Powell Lake, which recedes 50km into mountainous wilderness. Recent discoveries of trapped saltwater 120m below surface suggest Powell Lake was once an inlet until just after the last ice age.

You are now on the last leg of Hwy 101 as you head to Lund, midway on the west side of Malaspina Peninsula. Landings on the peninsula are jumping-off points to **Savary Island** and **Copeland Islands Marine Park**, off the peninsula's western shores, **Desolation Sound** and **Desolation Sound Marine Park**, off its northern tip, and **Okeover Inlet**, which runs along its eastern shores. This is another paradise for yachtsmen, kayakers, fishermen, and beachcombers.

**Sliammon:** (Pop. 650). 3km beyond Powell River. This is the Sliammon Indian Band's village. Road to village is just past bridge over Sliammon Creek, flows from Sliammon Lake to Malaspina Strait. Here the band operates Sliammon Hatchery. Year-round fishing for kokanee and cutthroat. Best salmon fishing end of Sept. Offshore is Harwood Island, owned by the band.

**Dinner Rock Park:** 16.5km northwest of Powell River. Turn west down dirt road. A small, rustic forestry campsite with minimal facilities on Malaspina Strait.

**Okeover Arm Provincial Park:** 4ha. 5 campsites. 898-3678. 17.5km northwest of Powell River, turn east onto paved Malaspina Rd, travel 5km. Park is on east side of the Malaspina Peninsula on Okeover Inlet. Canoeing, kayaking, searching out marine life. Walk through lightly forested upland. Fishing. Nearby floats indicate oyster farms.

**Lund:** (Pop. 204). 23km beyond Powell River at northern end of Hwy 101. Swedish brothers Frederick and Charles Thulin, who settled here 1889, named site after a city in Sweden. The renovated Lund Hotel, its pub now a watering hole for loggers and tourists, was built by the Thulins in 1895. When logging was main industry of this isolated settlement, it was supplied by steamboat. Ocean laps under the deck of a charming coffeehouse. Salmon sports fishing starts right off Lund breakwater. Marina and public floats. Seafood shop. Post office. Store. Water taxi to **Savary Island** (see below). Boat charters. In summertime, this quiet seaside village often becomes a bedlam of vacationers, mainly coming and going from Savary, fishing waters, and nearby marine parks.

**Lund Information:** Powell River Infocentre, 6807 Wharf St, Powell River, BC, V8A 1T9. 485-4701. Open weekdays in winter, daily in summer.

**Savary Island:** 6km offshore from Lund. Less than 50 people live year-round on this pearl of an island, which looks like it floated up from the South Seas. Unlike most Gulf Islands, Savary runs east-west and is really a 8km-long clay ridge covered in sand. Two centuries ago, explorer George Vancouver observed Savary, with its white-sand beaches, as having "beauty such as we have seldom enjoyed." Good oystering. Great swimming in clear, warm waters. North shore has vast sandy beaches. South shore, facing strait winds, has big rollers and attracts surfers. An oddity is biggest arbutus tree in BC, on north shore, a walk across the narrow island. Only public access is via 12-minute water-taxi ride (483-9749) from Lund. Bed and breakfast facilities. No campsites. Many Lower Mainlanders have summer cabins on island and voted against having electricity. Public wharf and floats at **Keefer Bay**.

**Copeland Islands Provincial Marine Park:** 437ha. Mossy, undeveloped. Also known as "Ragged Islands." An easy day trip for kayakers paddling northward from Lund. Thulin Passage, separating islands from BC mainland, is 137m wide, just enough for boom-toting tugs to squeeze through.

*Anchored at Mouat Bay, Texada Island.*

**Desolation Sound:** Joins Lewis Channel between Cortes and West Redonda islands and joins Hombray Channel along East Redonda Island. So misnamed by Captain George Vancouver in 1792. Wrote the captain in his log: "Our residence here was truly forlorn; an awful silence pervaded the gloomy forests. . .the steep rocky shores prevented the use of the seine, and not a fish at the bottom could be tempted to take the hook." Tell that to the thousands of boaters who come here to play and fish in the summer.

**Desolation Sound Provincial Marine Park:** 8,256ha. 898-3678. BC's largest marine park, and it's a beauty. On north shore of **Gifford Peninsula**. No road access. More than 60km of shoreline, several offshore islands, a gradually rising upland which contains a number of lakes, waterways, and waterfalls. Unwin Lake, a l73ha body of fresh water, is park's largest.

Set back to the north and east, Coast Mountains soar to more than 2,400m. Warm waters surrounding park teem with sea life. Ideal for swimming and scuba-diving. Several safe anchorages: **Prideaux Haven**, **Tenedos Bay**, and **Grace Harbour**.

## Horseshoe Bay to Lillooet

### SQUAMISH HIGHWAY and DUFFEY LAKE ROAD (Highway 99)

The Squamish Hwy (Hwy 99) from Horseshoe Bay to Pemberton (135km) follows dramatic Howe Sound to Squamish, continuing north to Whistler Resort, and the town of Pemberton. (It's an even 100km from Horseshoe Bay to Whistler.)

The next portion of this highway, from Pemberton to Lillooet (about 100km), has only recently become an extension of Hwy 99, with the paving of Duffey Lake Rd (84.5km) through the Cayoosh Range (the Duffey Lake Rd section starts on p.105).

Also called the "Sea to Sky Highway," the Squamish Hwy is a spectacular drive, though not exactly a relaxing one. In the stretch between Horseshoe Bay and Squamish, the highway is often cut out of the cliff, following the scenic shoreline of Howe Sound from on high, and there is the occasional switchback. For the first 20km, there is a sign almost every kilometre warning: "ROCKFALL HAZARD AREA NO STOPPING." Extreme caution is advised, especially at night or during heavy rains. As a local said, "The road is beautiful. But in the mountains, you drive with care and respect." Watch the signs, take it easy, and don't push it: the two-lane highway widens at regular intervals to allow passing.

There are alternatives to motor travel on this route. BC Rail runs its refurbished passenger service from the North Vancouver station with stops at Whistler Creek (near Whistler Resort) and Pemberton en route north. (For details on the railway, see *Introduction*, p.78 ) The Royal Hudson steam train and MV *Britannia* also offer an unusual six-and-a-half hour train-steamship outing. Call 688-7246.

**Horseshoe Bay:** (Pop. 1,037). 20km northwest of Vancouver on Hwys 99 and 1. This is the terminus for BC Ferries travelling to Departure Bay (Nanaimo) on Vancouver Island; the Sechelt Peninsula (Langdale); and Bowen Island.

Horseshoe Bay lies at the entrance to Howe Sound. The first Europeans, Spaniards under Commander Jose Narvaez, landed here in 1791. One year later, British Captain George Vancouver explored the area, describing Howe Sound as "a solemn inland sea, studded with beautiful forest-clad islands, covered with towering trees whose branches at high tide are lapped by clear waters teeming with fish."

Today's Horseshoe Bay is a charming recreational and bedroom community for Vancouver. Its small village offers shopping, tourist facilities, and a marina with boat rentals.

**Horseshoe Bay Information:** North Vancouver Infocentre, 131 East 2nd St, North Vancouver, BC, V7L 1C2. 987-4488. Daily in summer, weekdays off-season.

**Viewpoint:** On Hwy 99, 2km beyond Horseshoe Bay. Watch the ferries make their way through Howe Sound from Vancouver Island, Sunshine Coast, and Bowen Island. Plus pleasure craft of every size and description.

**Viewpoint:** 6km beyond Horseshoe Bay. Views of Howe Sound, Queen Charlotte Channel, and nearby Gambier, Bowen, and Anvil islands.

**Lions Bay:** (Pop. 1,328). 11km beyond Horseshoe Bay on Hwy 99. A quiet residential area overlooking Howe Sound. To the north is 1,646m Lions Mountain.

**Lions Bay Information:** Lions Bay Municipal Hall, Box 141, Lions Bay, BC, V0N 2E0. 921-9333 or 921-9811. Open Mon, Tues, Thurs.

**Porteau Cove Provincial Park:** 50ha; 44 campsites, 14 walk-in. 898-3678. 22km north of Horseshoe Bay, on east shore of Howe Sound between Lions Bay and Britannia Beach. Developed park, picnic areas. Great for scuba-diving, windsurfing, snorkeling, swimming, fishing. Boat-launch facilities. Park is set between the Coast Mountains and Howe Sound islands, and the cove itself is a snug haven at park's south end. Two entrances 1.5km apart.

**Britannia Beach:** (Est. pop. 299). 33km beyond Horseshoe Bay on Hwy 99. From 1930 to 1935, Britannia Beach was the British Empire's largest producer of copper. Over its 70 years of operation, the Britannia mine produced some 600 million kg of copper, employing more than 60,000 people. Permanently closed in 1974, it operates now as BC Museum of Mining.

■ **BC Museum of Mining:** In Brittania Beach. 896-2233, or 688-8735 toll-free from Vancouver. May-early Sept: Wed-Sun. Mon-Tues: open for booked tours only. In Sept, weekends only, closed rest of year. Recently declared a National Historic Site. Guided underground tours on electric trains. Over 365m of continuous displays. Operational mining equipment including slushers, muckers, and drills. Gravity-fed concentrator building, one of the last standing in the world. At its peak, building processed over 6.4 million kg of ore daily. In museum building, view "Britannia, the Story of a BC Mine," with its hundreds of photos and artifacts.

**Murrin Provincial Park:** 24ha. 3km beyond Britannia Beach, straddling Hwy 99, and featuring pretty Petgill Lake. Donated by BC Electric; named after company president who served from 1929-1946. Swimming, fishing, sunbathing, walking trails, picnics. Steep, almost vertical, cliffs suitable for novice and intermediate rock climbers.

**Shannon Falls Provincial Park:** 28ha. 898-3678. East off Hwy 99, 7km beyond Britannia Beach. Picnicking, hiking. Splendid views of 335m Shannon Falls right from your car. Six times the elevation of Niagara, well worth pulling over for. Viewing platform at base of falls.

**The Stawamus Chief:** Just north of Shannon Falls, east of highway. One of the most spectacular sights in the province, rising up almost from the highway, is the awesome sheer face of the 652m Stawamus Chief, pinnacle of a rock climber's dreams. Supposedly the second largest piece of granite in the world (Gibraltar is first), the towering monolith offers some 180 routes, some a challenge for the novice or intermediate, others strictly for top-ranking climbers from around the world.

**Squamish:** (Pop. 11,709). 11km beyond Britannia Beach. Squamish is at head of Howe Sound, overlooked by 2,678m Mt Garibaldi and the Stawamus Chief. European settlers arrived in the area in 1888. By 1891, store and post office had been established, and logging of giant cedar and fir trees was underway. Giant logs are dumped and boomed (gathered together) for towing into Howe Sound.

Squamish means "Mother of the Wind," and the Squamish River area is becoming known throughout North America as premier windsurfing territory. The winds are truly a phenomenon. Situated at the head of the sound in a narrow corridor, Squamish is surrounded by massive, sheer rock faces which heat up between 10am and 5pm, creating a geothermal effect. These geothermals are intensified further by steam from a pulp mill. Some spots are suitable for beginners, or you can go right up to world championship levels in some particularly "squamishy" spots.

As well, Squamish is a rock climber's heaven, not just for the Chief, but for the more varied, and sunnier, Smoke Bluffs that overlook the town.

Diving, horseback riding, glacier-landing tours, hiking, and llama backpacking are also on the menu; and the golf course gets rave reviews.

**Squamish Information:** Infocentre, 37950 Cleveland Ave, Squamish, BC, V0N 3G0. 892-9244. Daily in summer, weekdays in winter.

■ **Squamish Valley Museum:** Downtown Squamish on 2nd Ave. Daily, Wed-Sun. In a heritage home, displays artifacts pertaining to the varied history of the Squamish Valley.

■ **Glacier Tours:** Departing from Squamish Municipal Airport. 898-9016. Varied departure times, May-Nov. Ski planes leave the airport three times daily, flying passengers over some of the largest glaciers and icecaps in North America. The icecaps of the Tantalus Range can be up to 457m thick and several kilometres long.

■ **Sta-wa-mus Native Cultural Centre:** About 1km south of Squamish on Hwy 99. 892-5166. Sta-wa-mus band has carvings and jewelry to view.

■ **Squamish Valley Golf and Country Club:** Just north of town off Hwy 99. 898-9521. 18 holes. A prestigious course. Also has curling, squash.

**Garibaldi Highlands:** 5km north of Squamish. A new community.

**Garibaldi Highlands Information:** Daily July and Aug. Write Squamish Infocentre, Box 1009, Squamish, BC, V0N 3G0. 892-9244.

**Viewpoint:** About 6km north of Squamish. Nesting grounds of the bald eagle, and the BC Wildlife Branch yearly bald eagle count. Jan-Feb may bring as many as 2,500 eagles here. Great photo opportunities.

**Squamish River:** Joins with Cheakamus River 8km beyond Squamish. The two rivers then flow south into Howe Sound. Excellent windsurfing.

**Brackendale:** (Est. pop. 1,100). 10km beyond Squamish. A quietly active, arts-minded residential community. Winter home of the bald eagle, and year-round venue for the never-to-be-underestimated BAG (Brackendale Art Gallery) Society. Only in Brackendale can you hire a llama to pack your gear on a hike to view eagles.

**Tenderfoot Hatchery:** Just outside Brackendale turn onto Cheekye Rd. Travel 5km, cross bridge, turn right on Paradise Rd, then right on Midway for 3km. 898-3657. Chinook, coho, and steelhead. Year-round.

**Lake Lovely Water Provincial Recreation Area:** 1,300ha. West side of Squamish River across from Brackendale. Trail access only to this pocket wilderness.

**Alice Lake Provincial Park:** 397ha; 88 campsites. 898-3678. 13km beyond Squamish. Dominated by towering Coast Mountains, and surrounded by dense forests and grassy areas. Picnicking, birdwatching, swimming, canoeing. Fish for small cutthroat and rainbow. Excellent cross-country ski trails.

**Viewpoint:** West side of Hwy 99, 25km beyond Squamish. Views of Cheakamus River. Winter fishing for steelhead; summer, spring salmon; fall, coho and Dolly Varden.

**Garibaldi Provincial Park:** 194,904ha. 196 wilderness/ walk-in campsites. 898-3678. Signs on Hwy 99 between Squamish and Whistler indicate trails for access the park. Developed trail systems provide primary entry into the five most popular areas: Diamond Head, Black Tusk/Garibaldi Lake, Cheakamus Lake, Singing Pass, and Wedgemount Lake. Park offers azure-blue lakes, including Garibaldi, Corrie, and Helm; and the Coast Mountain Range including 2,678m Garibaldi Mountain and 2,438m Mt Sir Richard; glaciers, alpine tarns, cascading streams, and rivers, including Tawasus and Iceworm creeks and the Cheakamus and Pitt rivers. Meadows filled with alpine flowers. Many of park's features were formed by volcanic action.

Diamond Head area, often with 5m of snow, is popular with experienced Nordic skiers. Overnight accommodation at Elfin Shelter. The skiing at Diamond Head is challenging and exhilarating.

**Taylor Campground Trail:** Turn off 31km beyond Squamish on east side of Hwy 99. Trail, 4.5km long, follows Rubble Creek to Garibaldi Lake, major campsite in Garibaldi Provincial Park.

**Daisy Lake:** Off Hwy 99, some 31km beyond Squamish. Small lake formed by dam on the Cheakamus River. Fish for rainbow, Dolly Varden, and kokanee. Boat launching.

**Brandywine Falls Provincial Park:** 148ha; 15 campsites. 898-3678. Off Hwy 99, some 37km beyond Squamish. Picnicking, swimming, fishing, hiking trails, and views of the falls, Daisy Lake and mountains of Garibaldi Provincial Park (2,316m Black Tusk). The 66m falls are smooth, wide, and impressive, and less than a 10-minute walk from highway.

**Function Junction:** 49km beyond Squamish, west side of Hwy 99. Funky name for an industrial park and mall.

**Whistler Museum and Archives:** Across highway from Function Junction. 932-2019. Interesting small museum featuring Whistler and Rainbow Lodge nostalgia, early logging tools and ski equipment.

**Cheakamus Lake:** In Garibaldi Provincial Park. Enter by Cheakamus

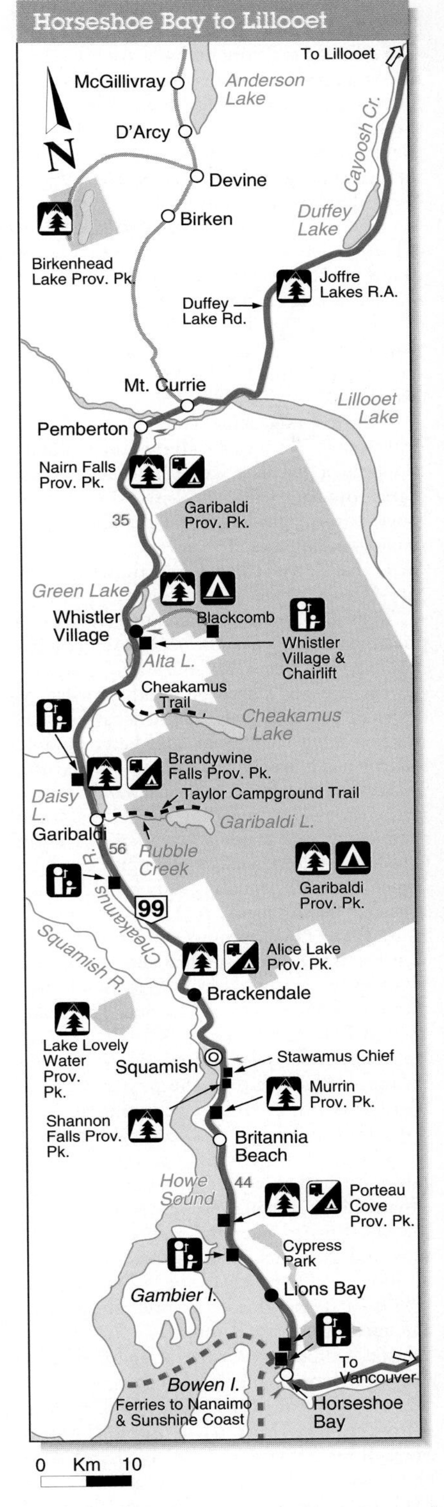


Trail entrance off Hwy 99, 49km beyond Squamish. Road leads from Hwy 99 to trailhead, an easy 3km hike to spectacular Cheakamus Lake. Fish for rainbow and Dolly Varden.

**Whistler Resort:** (Pop. 4,459). 56km beyond Squamish in the Coast Mountains. Whistler is a fabulous, four-seasons world-destination resort community cradled by two magnificent mountains, Whistler (2,182m), and Blackcomb (2,287m). Chairlifts for each rise up from the village – a three-minute stroll from accommodation (the Express gondola for Whistler, the Wizard, and the Solar Coaster high-speed quad lifts for Blackcomb). Five pretty lakes are strung through the valley, beads on a necklace: Alpha, Nita, Alta, Lost, and Green.

The resort – which takes 4,000 people to operate – has been rated "The Best Overall Resort in North America" by *Snow Country Magazine*, and is considered one of the top five ski resorts in the world. Indeed, for two years running, Japanese readers of *Blue Ski Guide* have named Whistler their No.1 ski destination.

Centre of everything, and unique in North America, is **Whistler Village,** an intimate European-style village with cobbled streets and plazas, outdoor cafes and bistros, walkways, movie theatre, underground parking, shops, restaurants, lounges, a variety of accommodation, and daily street entertainment from May-Oct.

Whistler Resort is not so much a place as a phenomenon. Now BC's fastest growing municipality, just a bit more than a decade ago the site was a garbage dump prowled by bears. In the early '70s, Whistler's ski value was becoming recognized, and hasty random building of weekend cabins was going unchecked. The foresight of a few wise people in the early '70s, including Al Raine, former head coach of Canada's National Ski Team (and husband of Canada's Olympic champion Nancy Greene) brought a quick halt to this scattered development. In 1975, the government froze development, and established Whistler as the province's first and only Resort Municipality. Firm controls were established, and a long-range plan carved out. The resort opened Dec 1980. Now Whistler Village North has been started: the existing village will be doubled in size over the next few years, Whistler North eventually becoming an integral part of the valley. All according to plan.

Whistler Village itself is so new, it has a gauzy unreality, an unbelievable quality, enhanced by a knockout palette of pastel colours brushed over the architecture: pale aqua and green metal roofs, rose pink trim, turquoise walls, peach facing. Even the new (1989) Chateau Whistler is apricot-beige with blue-green turrets and tops. The 3,250-sq-m Whistler Conference Centre is landmarked by an eye-catching tentlike roof in aquamarine.

Everyone tries for a bit of history with Whistler, but there isn't much. There's Marvellous Myrtle and her husband Alex Philip, who trekked up the Pemberton Trail in 1911, took a buckboard to Brackendale, and a packhorse beyond. They bought land on the shores of Alta Lake and there, with romance in their hearts that was to last a lifetime, they built their Rainbow Lodge, and named the places (River of Golden Dreams, for one). The fishing lodge ran until 1948, always to capacity, especially after the PGE Railway came through from Squamish in 1915. Myrtle's 1920s photograph appears everywhere: she graces a beached canoe, with her catch before her, a row of 12 freshly caught silvery trout. But Myrtle and Alex have little to do with Whistler as we know it today.

Whistler is said to be named for the whistling of the little hoary marmot, its mascot. But it could also be the whistling of the winds through "Singing Pass" between the mountains. The real history of Whistler seems to be geological – the development of the mountains and the glaciers over millennia.

**Whistler Area Information:** Infocentre, Box 181, Whistler, BC, V0N 1B0. 932-5528. At junction of Hwy 99 and Lake Placid Rd, at Whistler Creek gondola base. In summer, extra drop-in infocentres at Village Square and Village Gate. Daily. Information also from the **Whistler Resort Association**, Box 1400, Whistler, BC, V0N 1B0. 932-3928. For accommodation reservations: 932-4222; (Vancouver) 685-3650; or toll free (US and Canada, except BC): 1-800-944-7853.

Whistler Activity and Information Centre: 932-2394.

## Whistler in Summer

Whistler Resort features an amazing variety of summer activities for all ages and interests. It's pricey if you want it to be, but you can also pick and choose where to stay, what to do. The five picturesque lakes offer six lakeside parks, most with beaches. A scenic 15km valley trail connects all the parks at Whistler Village. Mostly paved, the trail is ideal for strolling, jogging, or biking. There's also, of course, picnicking, swimming, windsurfing, canoeing, fishing, boating.

Both Whistler and Blackcomb mountains operate their lifts year-round. Views, guided naturalists' tours, restaurants. Blackcomb offers summer skiing, the only mountain in North America to do so (on Horstman Glacier). Other summer activities: golfing, horseback riding, white-water rafting, jet-boating (new), kayaking, guided tours on foot, bicycle, bus, or plane, heli-hiking, hot air ballooning (tethered and untethered), paragliding, llama treks, roller blading, hayrides.

## Whistler in Winter

For winter, both mountains offer exceptional downhill skiing, with a combined total of over 200 runs and 27 lifts. Whistler Mountain is official ski area in the Lower Mainland for the Canadian National Ski Team. It has North America's second longest lift-serviced vertical at 1,530m. Blackcomb is called "The Mile-High Mountain," with the longest lift-serviced vertical (1609m) and longest uninterrupted fall-line skiing in North America. Also cross-country skiing, heli-skiing, snowmobiling, sleighrides.

For current snow conditions on either mountain, call (in Vancouver) 685-1007. Local number for Whistler: 932-4191. Blackcomb: 932-4211.

■ **Gondolas and Chairlift Rides:** Whistler Village. For Whistler Mountain: 932-3434. Blackcomb: 932-3141. Summer hiking, skiing and exploring; winter ski access to the mountains.

■ **Chateau Whistler Resort:** Billed as a "castle in the mountains," the $50-million, 12-storey, 343-room edifice is the largest resort hotel to be built in Canada since the turn of the century. The grandeur of yesteryear is

*Whistler Resort village in the Coast Mountains.*

translated through early Canadian pine *armoires*, Mennonite hooked rugs and quilts, aboriginal twig furniture, and friendly folk art from decoys and rocking horses to birdhouses. Even if you're camping, check out the Great Hall and the Mallard Bar. Call 938-8000.

■ **The Whistler Golf Course:** A richly scenic 18-hole course designed by Arnold Palmer. Next to Whistler Village. Call 932-4544. A second is in the works, **The Chateau Whistler Golf Course**, designed by Robert Trent Jones II. On the hillside of Blackcomb, the strenuous course will include rock faces, canyons, and waterfalls. Golf carts will be mandatory.

■ **Trail Riding:** Scenic guided trail rides. Call 932-6623.

**Nairn Falls Provincial Park:** 171ha. 88 campsites. 898-3678. 28km beyond Whistler. 60m Nairn Falls tumble into Green River. Hiking. Rainbow and Dolly Varden.

**Pemberton:** (Pop. 502; about 700 in area). 35km beyond Whistler on Hwy 99. A farming village lying flat in a startling steep-walled alpine setting, Pemberton is proud to call itself "the disease free capital of the world for seed potatoes." Surrounding mountains hide delightful, relatively unknown, hot springs. A host of other outdoor activities: golf, hiking, fishing, llama treks, horseback riding, river rafting, jet boating (to Nairn Falls or Skookumchuk Village). Contact Adventure Centre, 894-5200.

A well-maintained road, paved then gravel, goes northwest to Pemberton Meadows, continuing either northwest to Meager Creek Hot Springs, or northeast through to Gold Bridge. Road is paved for only about 23km. Just before pavement ends, road forks. Take right onto Lillooet Forest Rd (north side of Lillooet River). A few kilometres farther, there's a junction: continue on for the hot springs; or turn right (northeast) over Hurley Pass to hook up with Bridge River Rd along Carpenter Lake. See "Side Trip on Bridge River Rd," *Cariboo-Chilcotin, Lillooet Road*, p.195.

**Pemberton Information:** Infocentre in town centre at junction of Hwy 99 and Portage Rd. Daily July-Aug. Or Pemberton Chamber of Commerce, Box 370, Pemberton, BC, V0N 2L0. 894-6175.

■ **Pemberton Museum:** 7424 Prospects St, Pemberton Village. Daily July-Aug, or by appointment. Main buildings focus on two cultures. Settler's house contains Fraser River gold-rush exhibits. Two other houses on site originally belonged to native peoples in local Mount Currie and D'Arcy communities near Pemberton.

■ **Meager Creek Hot Springs:** 75km northwest of Pemberton on part paved/part gravel road through Pemberton Meadows. See directions above. Three communal pools, camping.

■ **Skookumchuck Hot Springs:** 77km south on the Lillooet River, on the original Cariboo Wagon Rd. One of the springs, **The St Agnes Well,** was named in the 1860s by Judge Matthew Baillie Begbie. Natural and undeveloped. The hot spring and the cold spring intermingle under a cedar A-frame, where taps let bathers adjust the temperatures. On private land, springs are taken care of by users.

**Road to D'Arcy:** This is part of the old Douglas Trail, the original (and arduous) route to the 1858 Cariboo Gold Rush. Douglas Trail was actually a series of portages between four big lakes (Harrison, Lillooet, Anderson, and Seton) from the upper Fraser Valley to Lillooet. This section, which follows the Birkenhead River for about its first 15km, was the trail between Lillooet and Anderson lakes. Abandoned when the Cariboo Road over the Fraser Canyon was completed in 1863. BC Rail trackage between North Vancouver and Lillooet also follows this route, which goes over Pemberton Pass.

## SIDE TRIP
### to D'Arcy

This recently paved road opens up rugged mountain scenery to recreation and tourism. It winds 38km to D'Arcy at the southwestern end of dazzling Anderson Lake. From Mount Currie, turn north, following Birkenhead River. Two Forest Service campsites are found along the first 10km.

**Birken:** (Pop. 109). 23km from Mount Currie. Just over Pemberton Pass, on Gates Lake. Settlement for logging, farming, and tourism. Camping and cabins at resort across from Gates Lake.

**Devine:** (Pop. 35). 29km from Mount Currie. Former sawmill site. Handful of residents remain.

**Birkenhead Lake Provincial Park:** 99 campsites. Turn northwest at Devine. Good gravel road, 18km to park facilities. In snow-topped Coast Mountains, remote 6km-long Birkenhead Lake provides fishing for kokanee, rainbow trout, Dolly Varden, whitefish. Extensive forests are home to moose, deer, black bear, marten, bobcat, beaver. Mountain goats appear in spring.

**D'Arcy:** (Pop. 60). A largely native community with a great view of an imposing lake. Two private lakeside campgrounds. To go farther up the lake one encounters a challenging 4x4 road, not for faint of heart. It goes up and down mountain to Seton Portage, between Anderson and Seton lakes, and then on to Bridge River Rd into Lillooet. See also *Cariboo-Chilcotin, Lillooet Rd*, p.195.

■ **Gates Creek (Salmon) Project:** At D'Arcy. See sockeye salmon adults mid-Aug to mid-Sept. Displays and film explain life cycle.

### *Return to Mount Currie and Highway 99*

**Mount Currie:** (Pop. 1400). 6km east of Pemberton on Hwy 99. Village is the base of the Mount Currie Indian Reserve, the Lil'wat group of the Stl'atl'imx nation. The village, which sits under a mountain of like name, is noted for its rodeo, held twice a year, on long weekends in May and Sept. Mount Currie was named after a Scot, John Currie, who took up ranching in the area with his Lillooet native wife in 1885 after failing to strike it rich in the California and Cariboo gold rushes.

Mount Currie has been growing lately, and a new site, called Xitolacw, including a school and community centre, has sprung up southeast of the old village near Lillooet Lake. Near the start of the Duffey Lake Rd, take a north turn uphill for 4km.

**Start of Duffey Lake Rd (Extension of Hwy 99):** The Duffey Lake Rd officially begins about 9km past Mount Currie, on the northwestern shore of Lillooet Lake, where the Birkenhead River outflows (and where the pavement begins).

Until recently, this dramatic 84.5km route through the Cayoosh Range to the Cariboo was strictly 4x4 fare. Today, $22.5 million later, the Duffey Lake Rd is paved and widened, and, except for the 9km gravel and washboard stretch through the Mount Currie Reserve which has not yet got band approval, it's pavement all the way from Pemberton to Lillooet (100km total). The new road opens up the Pemberton area even more for recreation activities, and gives travellers and locals a direct and reliable route into the Cariboo.

It's an exciting route, traversing two climatic zones, from the Coast Mountains through to semi-arid ranchlands. This was originally a logging road, not a tourist route, so drive with utmost care and attention. One memorable stretch features a sequence of three double-backed switchbacks. The first half of the road traverses mountains, eventually tracking the south shore of narrow 6.5km-long Duffey Lake to its eastern point.

**Joffre Lakes Provincial Recreation Area:** About 10km from start of Duffey Lake Rd. 1,460ha. 898-3678. Features a trail connecting three turquoise lakes with the road. The first of eight Forest Service campsites is found here. The next is on Duffey Lake, most of the rest being sited on Cayoosh Creek other side of the divide.

**Halfway Mark:** 42km from start. Say goodbye to Duffey Lake. From here, road follows Cayoosh Creek down towards Lillooet. And it will be downhill much of the way: expect a 13 percent grade at some points, one of the steepest grades in BC. The road is very beautiful, with thimbleberries and all, but there are few pullouts, and there can be rocks on the road (lots of rocks).

**Seton Lake:** About 80km from start and 5km from Lillooet. With a whiff of sagebrush in the air, the road opens high on a vista of stunning green Seton Lake. Good picnic area, camping down on lakeshore.

**BC Hydro Dam:** 1km from Seton Lake (down an 11 percent grade). Left of highway. Dams Seton Creek.

**Seton Creek Spawning Channel:** Just beyond Hydro Dam, left of highway. Pink salmon return here to spawn in early Oct, every other year, in the odd years. Displays of life cycle of salmon.

**Lillooet:** (Pop.1,782). 84.5km northeast of start of Duffey Lake Rd. See *Cariboo-Chilcotin, Lillooet Rd*, p.194. From this point, go north on Hwy 99 (former Hwy 12) to Hwy 97 just north of Cache Creek; or south on old Hwy 12 to Lytton. See *Lillooet Rd*, p.194.

## Vancouver to Hope (South Bank)

### TRANS-CANADA HIGHWAY (Highway 1)

The Trans-Canada Hwy starts from Mile Zero in Victoria, travels north up island to Nanaimo, and crosses from there to the mainland at Horseshoe Bay. Eastbound travellers can pick up Hwy 1 at any spot that is convenient to them (the North Shore; or south across the Second Narrows Bridge into Vancouver or Burnaby; or at any points farther east). Follow the route map provided, and the Gateway map, p.84, which has even more details on web of intersections from Vancouver to just beyond Abbotsford.

The Trans-Canada Hwy between Vancouver and Hope is a direct and efficient route. It leads through Burnaby, skirts New Westminster, and bears east providing access to Langley, Aldergrove, Clearbrook, Abbotsford and Chilliwack before reaching Hope. It traverses BC's most heavily populated strip. More than half of all British Columbians live in Vancouver or the Fraser Valley, on or near this route. Yet it is attractive, leading not only through densely populated areas and zones of heavy industry, but also through rich agricultural country, with rolling farmlands and historic villages. And all the while, the mountains rise, blue and shadowy on the edges of the valley.

Via Hwy 1, the distance to Hope from downtown Vancouver at the south end of the Second Narrows Bridge (the junction of Hwys 1 and 7A) is 147km.

**Second Narrows Bridge:** On Hwy 1. Spans Burrard Inlet to link the North Shore with Vancouver and Burnaby. Burrard Inlet was the focus of early development, and today is the city's busy deep-water port. The inlet extends east, past the Reed Point Marina, to Port Moody, and north, beyond Deep Cove, to Wigwam Inn on Indian Arm. For details, see *North Shore*, p.90.

**PNE Grounds and Racetrack:** Just over the bridge, exit right (west) at Hastings St for Pacific National Exhibition Park. Details under *Vancouver*, p.87.

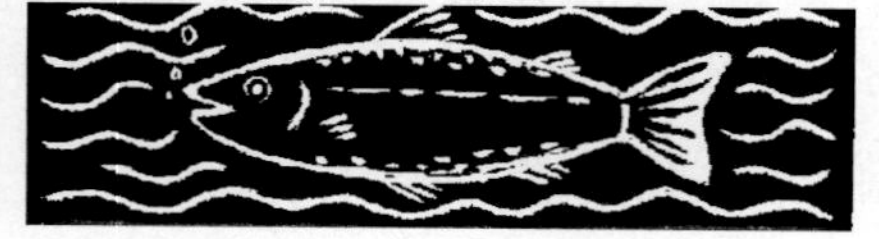

**Boundary Rd:** 3km beyond junction of Hwys l and 7A. Hwy 1 crosses Boundary Rd which marks the boundary between Vancouver and Burnaby. Exit here for Burnaby, and for further details, see *Burnaby*, p.91.

**Grandview Hwy:** Just past Boundary Rd junction, Grandview Hwy (an extension of 12th Ave) comes in from the west and dissolves into Hwy 1.

**Willingdon Ave:** Just over 1km beyond Grandview Hwy junction. Exit for Burnaby, or for connections with Hwys 1A/99A (south), or Hwys 7 and 7A (north).

**Burnaby:** (Pop. 158,858). 10km from Vancouver city centre. Vancouver's immediate eastern neighbour. Exit from Hwy 1 at Willingdon Ave, Sprott St, Cariboo Interchange. See *Burnaby*, p.91.

**Sprott St:** 3.5km beyond Willingdon Ave Interchange. Exit to Sprott St north, turn east to Burnaby Lake Regional Park. Exit at Sprott St south to Canada Way. Follow signs from junction of Sprott St and Canada Way to Deer Lake and park. For info on Burnaby Lake and Deer Lake, see p.91.

**Cariboo Rd Interchange:** 4km beyond Sprott St junction. Exit north, follow road to Gaglardi Way. Gaglardi Way leads 6km to **Simon Fraser University** and **Burnaby Centennial Park**, both on Burnaby Mountain. For info on SFU, see *Burnaby*, p.91.

**Brunette Ave Interchange:** Nearly 3km beyond Cariboo Rd. Exit south and drive 1km to New Westminster.

**New Westminster:** (Pop: 43,585) Turn south 1km beyond junction of Hwy 1 and Brunette Rd. See *New Westminster*, p.91.

**Lougheed Hwy (Hwy 7):** 4.5km beyond Brunette Rd Interchange. Exit north to Coquitlam. Follow signs to Hwy 7 (Lougheed Hwy) and travel 9km to Port Coquitlam. For info on **Coquitlam and Port Coquitlam**, see *Vancouver to Hope - North Bank*, p.110.

**Port Mann Bridge:** Crosses Fraser River 2km beyond Lougheed Hwy (Hwy 7) Interchange. Links Coquitlam with Surrey. Bridge is 2,094m long, 16.5m wide.

**Fraser River Delta and Estuary:** Pitt and Coquitlam rivers flow into the Fraser northwest of Port Mann Bridge. One of the most productive fish and wildlife areas of the world. As many as 300 million young salmon leave the estuary every year. More than one million migrating waterfowl stop here on their way between Siberia and South America.

**Surrey:** (Pop. 245,173). Immediately beyond the Port Mann Bridge on Hwy 1. Once BC's largest municipality in terms of area, covering 203 sq km. Now a new city. For details, see *Surrey*, p.92.

**152nd St (Johnston Rd):** 9km beyond the Lougheed Hwy Interchange. Exit south into the heart of Surrey and its five townships (Whalley, Sunnyside, Newton, Guildford, and Cloverdale); continue farther south to White Rock (22km south of Hwy 1). Details in *Surrey*, p.92; on White Rock, in *US Border to Horseshoe Bay*, p.94.

**Hwy 15 (176th St or Pacific Hwy):** 6km beyond l52nd St junction. Turn south, through Surrey (and township of Cloverdale), 21km to Douglas Border Crossing (Canada/US).

**Carvolth Rd (200th St):** 6km beyond Hwy l5 junction. Exit south 8km to city of Langley (first of two main exits off Hwy 1 to the city).

**Hwy 10:** 8km beyond Carvolth Rd junction. Exit south and drive 9km to **Langley**. From there it's 48km southwest to **Tsawwassen and BC Ferries terminal.** Exit north on Hwy 10, 1km to **Fort Langley**.

## SIDE TRIP

### to Fort Langley and Langley

**Fort Langley:** (Pop. 16,200). 2km beyond southern terminus of Albion Ferry. First European establishment in Fraser Valley, originally part of a network of trading posts established by Hudson's Bay Company.

The first fort site, built 1827, was 48km up from the mouth of the Fraser. It was abandoned so the fort could be closer to larger tracts of fertile land for farming. Second fort was 4km farther up the river. In late 1850s, Fort Langley became a starting-off point for the rush to the Fraser gold fields. Today, as well as being a gold-mine of history, Fort Langley is a thriving agricultural and residential area with tourist services.

**Fort Langley Information:** Infocentre, 23325 Mavis St, Langley, BC, V0X 1J0. 888-1477. Daily May-Sept. Weekdays in the winter.

**Albion Ferry:** 660-8770. Free. Daily every 15 minutes from 5am-1:30am across the Fraser, giving motorists a direct connection between Hwy 1 on the south shore, and Hwy 7 on the north. (See *Vancouver to Hope – North Bank*, p.111, for connecting points on north shore.)

■ **BC Farm Machinery and Agricultural Museum:** 9131 Kings St. Downtown Fort Langley. 888-2273. Daily, mid-March-early Sept. Collection of machinery from many areas of BC, notably Fraser Valley. Also, household furnishings, logging and fishing equipment.

■ **Langley Centennial Museum and National Exhibition Centre:** Corner of Mavis and King. 888-3922. Daily summers,

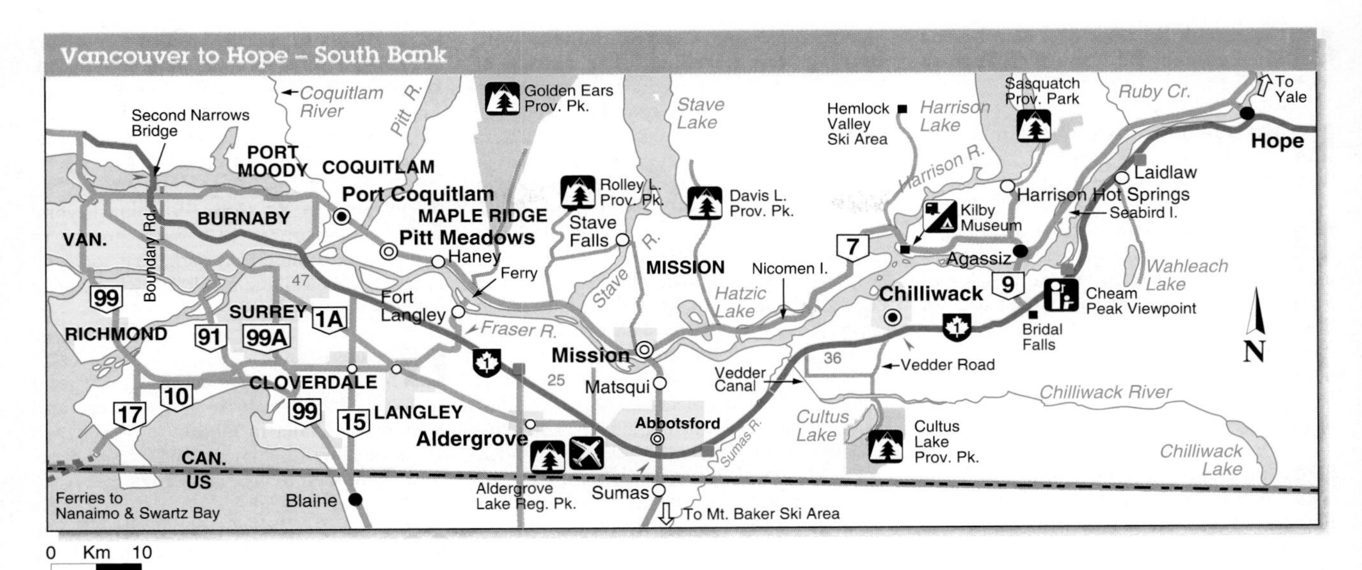


Tues-Sun off-season. Coast Salish Indian, 19th century pioneer. Recreated rooms include homesteader's kitchen, Victorian parlour, and Noel Booth General Store. Year-round exhibits and programs. An active museum!

■ **Fort Langley National Historic Park:** 23433 Mavis St, on banks of Fraser River across from McMillan Island. 888-4424. Daily. From the time of its construction in 1827 to its decline in 1880s, Fort Langley played a major role in the development of what is now the province of BC.

Through its gates passed the adventurers who opened up the mountainous Interior: traders travelling the Brigade Trail north in search of furs for "the Company," natives trading salmon and furs, and nearly 30,000 prospectors heading for the gold fields of the upper Fraser River.

It was in the "big house" at Fort Langley that BC was declared a crown colony in 1858. The fort functioned primarily as a provisioning and administrative centre for Hudson's Bay Company operations in the Pacific Northwest. Salmon processing and agriculture were vital. At its peak, the fort distributed one to two thousand barrels of salmon each year. Each barrel weighed up to 365kg.

Operations ceased at Fort Langley in 1886. The site deteriorated until 1923 when it was declared "of national historic interest," and marked with a commemorative plaque. In May 1955, the fort was established as a national historic park. Careful restoration work has been done on the palisades, buildings, furnishings to create a glimpse of Canada's pioneering past. Costumed staff demonstrate blacksmithing, barrel making, pioneer cooking.

■ **Fraser River Cruises:** Call 525-4465, or fax 525-5944 (New Westminster) for info on "The Fraser River Connection," an all-day, 57km return trip from the Royal City to Fort Langley and back, aboard a 27m paddlewheeler. Riverside views of Haney, Port Hammond, Surrey, Pitt Meadows, Coquitlam, and Whalley. Board at the Inn on the Quay, New Westminster. Boat docks at Bedford House Restaurant, 9272 Glover Rd, in Fort Langley with a layover time of one to two hours, depending on the river. Narrated, and billed as a "Trip through History," Thurs-Sun. One-way trips available.

**Langley:** (City and township pop. 66,040). At Carvolth Rd and Hwy 10, 9km south of Hwy 1. There are actually two Langleys – the district municipality, and the city in the middle of that. Each has its own mayor. The District Municipality of Langley stretches from Canada/US border north to the Fraser River. This is an important farming and residential region.

**Langley Information:** Infocentre, 20420 Fraser Hwy, Langley, BC, V3A 4G2. 530-6656. Weekdays.

■ **Derby Reach Regional Park:** 80ha. Camping. Near Fort Langley off 200 St. Edgewater Bar considered one of the finest fishing bars on the Fraser. Original site of Fort Langley and Derby town site.

■ **Campbell Valley Regional Park:** 535ha. 432-6350. From Hwy 1 eastbound take 200th St exit south for 14.5km. Turn Left on 8th Ave, look for park signs. Diverse natural habitats created by logging, farming, irrigation. 20km of walking trails, horseback riding, picnics. Visitor centre programs July-Aug. 534-4060. Turn-of-century Annand/Rowlatt Farm.

■ **Blair Wave Pool:** 22200 Fraser Hwy. 530-WAVE. Daily year-round. Wave machine makes bathers feel they're face to face with the Pacific. Volcano erupts, lights flash. Waterfall, fitness centre, sauna.

■ **Trio Bronze:** #105 - 20081 Industrial Ave, Langley, V3A 4K6. 534-1490. One of the few fine art casting foundries in BC.

## Return to Highway 1

**264th St (Hwy 13):** 7km beyond Hwy 10 junction. Exit south 4km to Hwy lA (Fraser Hwy), Aldergrove, and the Aldergrove/Lynden border crossing.

**Aldergrove:** (Pop. 9,600). 5km beyond junction of Hwys 1 and 13, on Hwy 1A. On south side of lower Fraser Valley, near Fraser River. Named for abundant second growth of alder trees. Famous for dairy, chicken, raspberry, and strawberry farms.

**Aldergrove Information:** Contact Langley Infocentre/ Chamber of Commerce, 20420 Fraser Hwy, Langley, BC, V3A 4G2. 530-6656. Weekdays.

■ **Vancouver Game Farm:** 5048-264th St. 856-6825. 48ha. Daily. From Aoudad to Zebra, more than 60 species from around the world, including giraffes, jaguars, hippos, and rhinos. Petting zoo for children.

■ **Aldergrove Lake Regional Park:** Junction of Hwy 13 and Huntingdon Rd. Enter on 8th Ave, 5km south of Aldergrove and 1.5km east of Hwy 13. On US border. Small, manmade lake surrounded by gently rolling terrain. Walking, equestrian trails. Excellent views of Mt Baker (3,285m) just south of the border in Washington State. North America's answer to Mt Fuji, picturesque Mt Baker is one of a chain of volcanoes in the Cascade Range that includes Mt St Helen's in Oregon, which erupted catastrophically in l980.

■ **Aldergrove/Lynden Border Crossing:** Alternate route from Fraser Valley and Hwy 1 to US. Duty Free Shop at border crossing for tourists leaving Canada.

**Mt Lehman Rd (Exit 83):** 10km east of Hwy 13 junction. South 3km to Abbotsford International Airport/Tradex Conference Centre.

**Abbotsford International Airport:** On Mt Lehman Rd, 3km south of Hwy 1. 855-1001. A regional airport. Contact individual airlines for info on arrivals and departures. Site of the **Abbotsford International Airshow**, biggest in North America attracting 300,000 people every Aug. 852-8511 (more info below). For **Tradex Conference Centre**: 850-1533.

**Clearbrook Rd (Exit 87):** 8km beyond Mt Lehman Rd. South 2.5km to Matsqui Recreation Centre.

**McCallum Rd (Exit 90):** 4km beyond Clearbrook Rd. South 4km to Abbotsford-Matsqui Travel Infocentre.

**Hwy 11/Sumas Way (Exit 92):** 2.5km beyond McCallum Rd. Exit (north) to enter Abbotsford. Mission, on north bank of Fraser River, is 11km beyond Abbotsford on Hwy 11. For details see *Vancouver to Hope – North Bank*, p.112. Hwy 11 exit south leads 4km to the Sumas (Canada/US) border crossing, and beyond to Mt Baker ski area in Washington State.

**Abbotsford/Matsqui:** (Pop: 86,928). 25km beyond Langley on Hwy 1. The Raspberry Capital of Canada, the districts of Abbotsford and Matsqui comprise about 36,900ha, bounded by the Fraser River to the north, and Canada/US border to the south. Original commercial areas in each district were Abbotsford itself, and Clearbrook (in Matsqui). However, continued commercial expansion has effectively joined the two areas. Although they belong to separate districts, with separate governing bodies, residents have come to think of the area as one community.

The communities received their names in very different ways. Abbotsford was named in 1899 after Harry Abbott, general superintendent of the Pacific Division of the CPR. Clearbrook was originally named Pinecrest after a nearby auto court. The name was made official in 1952, but locals complained about it so much that it was changed to Clearbrook. Matsqui comes from Coast Salish Indian word meaning "easy travelling." The districts of Matsqui and Abbotsford draw on a trade area of about 180,000 people, providing a centre of trade and industry for the fruit, livestock, and dairies of the surrounding Fraser Valley.

**Abbotsford/Matsqui Information:** Infocentre, 2462 McCallum Rd, Abbotsford, BC, V2S 3P9. 859-9651. Daily July-Aug, weekdays in winter.

■ **Abbotsford International Airshow ("The Flight Begins"):** On Mt Lehman Rd, 3km south of Hwy 1. 852-8511. Second weekend in Aug. Running for over 30 years and the undisputed king of North American airshows. Military and civilian precision aerobatic teams, historical and experimental aircraft, stunt flyers from around the world. The Snowbirds and others sign autographs. There are hot-air balloons, pancake breakfasts, kite-flying contests, paper planes, old-fashioned picnics, and socials. Everyone goes plane-crazy.

■ **Matsqui-Sumas-Abbotsford (MSA) Museum, Trethewey House, and Heritage Gallery:** 2313 Ware St. 853-0313. Main floor of Trethewey House is restored to 1920s period. Visual history of region's first residents, the Coast Salish Indians, and early pioneers.

■ **Mill Lake and Centennial Park:** Downtown Matsqui. Family outings. Canoeing, picnicking, walking and jogging trails.

■ **Fraser Valley Trout Hatchery:** 34345 Vye Rd. 852-5388. Visitor Centre: 852-5444. Daily in summer. View species of trout at various stages of growth in a living stream, with integrated computer systems. Guided tours.

■ **Matsqui Trail Regional Park:** 60ha. Off Riverside St on south shore of Fraser. 432-6350. 10km of Fraser River dikes for walking or cycling. Fishing for trout, salmon, sturgeon.

■ **Abbotsford/Sumas Border Crossing:** Alternate route from Fraser Valley and Hwy 1 to US and Hwy I-5. Duty Free Shop at border crossing for tourists leaving Canada.

**Whatcom Rd (Exit 95):** 6km beyond Sumas/Route 11. Exit north to Wonderland Amusement Park. Exit south on Lower Sumas Mountain Rd to reach camping facilities.

**Vedder Canal:** On Hwy 1, some 19km beyond Hwy 11 junction. Constructed in early 1920s to drain Sumas Lake and reclaim 13,355ha in Chilliwack Valley. In 1954, canal was used for rowing races associated with the Commonwealth Games.

**Vedder Rd:** 17km beyond Vedder Canal. Exit south, 13km to Cultus Lake Provincial Park. Exit north, 1km to Chilliwack.

**Chilliwack:** (Pop. 49,531). 1km north off Hwy 1 onto Yale Rd. Mild climate and fertile soil give it the accolade "Green Heart of British Columbia." But the name Chilliwack itself originates from language of local Halkomelem Indian tribe. Early spellings include Chillwayhook, Chil-whey-uk, Chilwayook, Silawack. The name likely means "backwater travelling." City is in the heart of the Upper Fraser Valley, a farming and dairy region. Area is well known for fishing in nearby lakes and rivers, including Chilliwack and Lindemen lakes, and Chilliwack and Vedder rivers. Also excellent riding trails.

*Farm in the Fraser Valley, Lower Mainland.*

**Chilliwack Information:** Infocentre, 44150 Luckakuck Way, Sardis, BC, V2R 1A9. 858-8121. Daily summer, Mon-Sat in winter.

**Chilliwack Airport:** Young Rd South. 792-3430. Small, busy airport on southern border of Chilliwack. One paved runway. Operates 24 hours a day and handles a variety of aircraft.

■ **Chilliwack Museum and Historical Society:** 45820 Spadina Ave. 795-5210. Daily except Sun. In Chilliwack's only National Historic Site, the old city hall. Artifacts explain history. China baskets, farm and medical equipment. Art gallery.

■ **Canadian Military Engineering Museum:** Canadian Forces Base Chilliwack, Vedder Crossing. 858-3311. Weekdays May-Sept. Sun in winter. Shows contribution of Canada's military engineers from 1608 when French engineers first arrived in Quebec. Period weapons, models, uniforms. Original 1860 log cabin built for Royal Engineers.

■ **Chilliwack Hatchery:** Off Chilliwack River Crossing at junction of Slesse Creek and Chilliwack River. 858-7227. Chum, coho, chinook, steelhead. Year-round.

**Chilliwack River Provincial Park:** 23ha. 10km along Vedder Rd, then 7km east on Chilliwack Lake Rd. Picnic, day-use area. Popular for fishing and paddling.

**Chilliwack Lake Provincial Park:** 162ha. 100 vehicle/tent campsites. 858-7161. 30km beyond Chilliwack River Park on Chilliwack Lake Rd. Offers all that's expected of a pretty lake. Fishing, swimming, boating. Hiking in area.

**Cultus Lake Provincial Park:** 656ha. 300 campsites, sani-station. 858-7161. Exit south on Vedder Rd, travel 13km to park. Cultus Lake was known as *Swee-ehl-chah* or *Tsowallie* by the local Coast Salish Indians. Cultus, a word derived from the Coast Salish *kul*, means "worthless" or "bad." A Slellucum or supernatural being in the form of a great bear was said to inhabit the lake area. This being was responsible for fierce storms on the lake, which became a taboo area, and, locals attest, is not without its mysteries even today. Nevertheless, park is one of the most popular in Southwestern BC.

Four separate campgrounds: Clear Creek, Delta Grove, Entrance Bay, Maple Bay. Picnicking, swimming, hiking and bridle trails, boat launch. Fishing for rainbow and cutthroat trout, Dolly Varden. July-Aug, park naturalists are on hand. Also, self-guiding interpretive trail.

**Cultus Lake Waterpark:** Follow signs. Waterslides, boating, golfing, fishing, hiking, horseback riding, camping. Weekends from Victoria Day in May, daily from second weekend in June until Labour Day weekend.

### Return to Highway 1 and Vedder Road Junction

**Hwy 9:** 16km beyond Vedder Rd junction. Exit south 3km to Bridal Veil Falls Provincial Park and other attractions.

**Bridal Veil Falls Provincial Park:** 32ha. 858-7161. 25m waterfall cascades down a rocky mountain face. A 15-minute stroll through a forest of cedar and fir leads to a viewpoint at base of the falls.

**Trans-Canada Waterslide:** Intersection of Hwys 1 and 9. 794-7455. Weekends late May-mid-June. Daily mid-June-Sept.

**Flintstones Bedrock City:** Intersection of Hwys 1 and 9. 794-7410. Early June-Sept. Rides, live stage show.

## SIDE TRIP

### to Minter Gardens, Agassiz, and Harrison Hot Springs

Take Hwy 9 north, past Minter Gardens turnoff, then over the Fraser River. 10km to Agassiz; 14km beyond Agassiz to Harrison Hot Springs. Details on Agassiz and Harrison, in *Vancouver to Hope – North Bank*, p.113.

**Minter Gardens:** 52892 Bunker Rd, near Hwy 9, just north of Hwy 1. 794-7191. Daily April-Oct. Eleven gardens on 11ha with spectacular views of Cheam Peak. Maze, aviaries, topiary animals, fragrance garden for the blind, colonial floral ladies, rose and fern gardens, Chinese garden with Penjing rock bonsai. Restaurant.

### Return to Highway 1

**Cheam Peak Viewpoint:** 8km beyond Hwy 9 junction. Looks toward 2,107m Cheam Peak and 2,357m Welch Peak.

**Rd to Wahleach Lake:** 5km beyond Cheam Peak Viewpoint. Take Laidlaw and Jones Lake Exit.

**Wahleach Lake:** On Wahleach Lake logging road 11km south of Hwy 1. 342ha lake is also known as Jones Lake. Fish for rainbow, kokanee, some cutthroat, May-Sept. A glacier-fed hydro reservoir, lake's water level fluctuates through summer months. Areas around the lake offer good examples of the effects of clearcut logging.

**Laidlaw Rd:** 20km beyond the junction of Hwys 1 and 9. Exit to Laidlaw.

**Laidlaw:** (Pop. 158). On Laidlaw Rd 20km beyond Hwy 9 junction. Farmer WF Laidlaw had insisted a Canadian Northern Railway station be named in his honour when the railroad laid tracks across his farm. Southeast: 2,076m Isolillock Peak.

■ **Remember When Doll Museum:** 869-5155. Large collection of antique dolls and toys. Free admission. Daily April-Oct.

**Hunter Creek Information Centre and Rest Area:** 25km beyond junction of Hwys 1 and 9. Hunter Creek flows north into Fraser River. Named after a storekeeper who acquired land in the area in 1889.

**Hope Business Route:** 9.5km beyond Laidlaw. Exit south for connection with Flood Hope Rd (old Hwy 1) to reach Skagit Valley Recreation Area. Or take Silverhope Creek exit, 5.5km east of Hope Business Route.

## SIDE TRIP

### to Skagit Valley Provincial Recreation Area

**Silver Lake Provincial Park:** 77ha. Primitive camping. On unpaved Silverhope Creek Rd, 6km south of Hwy 1. Fishing and hiking in area.

**Skagit Valley Provincial Recreation Area:** 32,570ha. 123 campsites in two campgrounds. 840-8836. Silverhope Creek Rd leads southeast 35km to recreation area entrance; 26km farther to Ross Lake.

An environmental success story from the 1970s. The beautiful wild Skagit River rises in Manning Park, runs south through its stunning forest valley, and then vanishes south of US border in a reservoir behind a hydro dam. The whole Skagit Valley on the Canadian side was nearly flooded, too, but for the efforts of a handful of early activists. Bravo!

Area is now jointly managed by Canada and the US through Skagit Valley Commission. Recreation area extends from Ross Lake on Canada/US border, north to Crowsnest Hwy, its east border running alongside Manning Park. Part of Ross Lake expands into park in early summer, receding back across border in spring. Within the recreation area, dense vegetation and rushing streams. Boisterous Skagit River cuts through the wide glaciated Skagit Valley, fringed with impressive mountain peaks, including Mt Brice, 2,163m; Shawatum Mountain, 2,158m; Silvertip Mountain, 2,250m; and Whitworth Peak, 2,294m. Campgrounds are: Ross Lake and Silvertip. No fee. Hiking, canoeing, swimming, boating, fishing, hunting, snowshoeing, cross-country skiing (no set tracks).

### Return to Highway 1

**Hwy 3 (the Crowsnest):** Goes 5km southeast to junction with Hwy 5 (Coquihalla Hwy). For info on the new Coquihalla Hwy north to Merritt (115km) and Kamloops (98km beyond Merritt), see *Hope to Kamloops*, p.174. Hwy 3 east leads 20km to Manning Provincial Park. See *Hope to Princeton*, p. 114.

**Hope:** (Pop. 3,147). At junction of Hwys 1 and 3, 38km beyond junction of Hwys 1 and 9. For details, see *Hope to Princeton*, p.114.

# Vancouver to Hope (North Bank)

## TRANS-CANADA HIGHWAY (Highway 7)

Highway 7, the Lougheed, is an older route connecting Vancouver and Hope, separated by a distance of 142.5km. This route follows the north shore of the Fraser River as it moves through the broad Fraser Valley, between imposing peaks of the Coast Mountains. It leads through residential areas, farming regions, and large undeveloped areas.

Since information about Greater Vancouver is provided separately, coverage will begin with the city of Port Moody, at the head of Burrard Inlet. Both Hwy 7A (the Barnet Hwy) and Hwy 7 (the Lougheed) lead there from downtown Vancouver. Follow the route map on p.111 or, for greater detail on the Coquitlam/Maple Ridge districts, see the two-page Gateway map, pp.84-85, which covers the area from Vancouver to Mission.

Vancouver's Hastings St becomes the Barnet Hwy as it begins to skirt the southern shores of Burrard Inlet. This scenic drive offers quite stunning views of the mountains layered down the inlet. The distance on this highway (7A) from Boundary Rd in Vancouver, to Port Moody is 14.5km. On Hwy 7, slightly to the south, it is 21km from downtown Vancouver to Port Moody. Hwy 7 offers access to Burnaby.

**Port Moody:** (Pop. 17,712). 14.5km east of downtown Vancouver on Hwy 7A, and 2km west of junction of Hwys 7 and 7A. Port Moody was named in 1860 for Colonel Richard Moody (1813-1887), commanding officer of the Royal Engineers stationed in BC between 1858 and 1863.

The city was the Canadian Pacific Railway's western terminus. The first train from Montreal arrived here on July 4, 1886. In 1887, the line was extended the extra 20km to Vancouver, and Port Moody's status as a trading centre diminished. It is now an important residential area.

**Port Moody Information:** Coquitlam Infocentre, Suite 135-3030 Lincoln Ave, Coquitlam, BC, V3B 6B4. 464-2333. In Lincoln Centre Mall. Open weekdays.

■ **Port Moody Station Museum:** 2734 Murray St, Willingdon Park. 939-1648. Weekdays. In a restored 1907 CPR station on site of original western terminus. Pioneer artifacts and railway memorabilia.

■ **Belcarra Regional Park:** 690ha. Just east of Port Moody, from Hwy 7A take Belcarra turnoff to Ioco Rd. Follow signs for 8km to White Pine Beach or continue 4km to Belcarra Picnic Area. 9km of ocean shoreline, three beaches, sandy coves, mud flats. Diving and boating. Inland there's hiking, swimming at Sasamat Lake.

**Hwys 7A and 7 (Lougheed Hwy):** Junction is 2km east of Port Moody. Hwy 7A ends here, continuing as Hwy 7.

**Coquitlam River:** Passing under Hwy 7, 1.5km beyond junction of Hwys 7 and 7A. A narrow, winding, 14km river flowing from Coquitlam Lake, through Coquitlam and Port Coquitlam, into the Fraser. 10km of shoreline with access from Coquitlam River Park (details below). Cutthroat and coho in the fall; steelhead in spring.

**Coquitlam:** (Pop. 84,021). On Hwy 7 at junction of 7 and 7A, 2km east of Port Moody. City of Coquitlam, and the District Municipality of Coquitlam, are named after a type of landlocked salmon. "Coquitlam" means "little red fish" in the Coast Salish language. District is bordered on the east by the Coquitlam River, and south by the Fraser River; it extends north over Port Coquitlam to include Burke Mountain and Minnekhada regional parks. A fast-growing municipality with residential, industrial, and commercial interests. For recreation: swimming, canoeing, hiking. Skiing at several parks and lakes, including Blue Mountain, Mundy, and Belcarra parks, Como and Buntzen lakes, and Burke Mountain.

**Coquitlam Information:** Infocentre, 135-3030 Lincoln Ave, Coquitlam, BC, V3B 6B4. 464-2333. Open weekdays in winter, daily in summer.

■ **Maillardville:** Oldest francophone settlement in the Lower Mainland was at Maillardville (today commonly pronounced "mallardville" as in duck), now part of Coquitlam. In 1909, Maillardville was settled by French-Canadians who had moved west to work in Fraser Valley mills. About six downtown blocks just north of Hwy 7, bordered by Burnet, Schoolhouse, Rochester and Blue Mountain streets, constitute the core of old Maillardville.

There's a Society of Maillardville, representing a dozen francophone associations with a combined membership of about 1,500; the *caisse populaire* with bilingual tellers; *foyer Maillard*, a bilingual seniors residence; Our Lady of Lourdes Church and Rectory, declared heritage; and Laval Square, at Laval just off Burnet. *On parle français.*

■ **Place des Arts:** 1120 Brunette Ave. 526-2891. Daily except Sun. Paintings, weaving, quilts, stone carvings, pottery.

■ **Coquitlam River Park:** Turn north off Hwy 7 at Shaughnessy St, 1km to riverside picnic site. Fish for coho and steelhead.

■ **Minnekhada Regional Park:** 17ha. 432-6350. From Lougheed Hwy, turn north on Coast Meridian Rd and travel 2.5km to Apel Dr. Head east to Victoria Dr. Follow Victoria Dr 3.5km to park entrance off Quarry Rd. Marsh with wildlife, rocky knolls overlooking Pitt River flood plain. 10km of trails from Quarry Rd to Minnekhada Marsh and wildlife management area. The Lodge, built in 1934 to resemble a Scottish hunting lodge, was made of cedar and true to the decade. Formerly owned by two of BC's lieutenant-governors.

**Port Coquitlam:** (Pop. 36,773). On Hwy 7, 2km east of Coquitlam. Coquitlam and Pitt rivers run along east and west borders of Port Coquitlam. Fishing on western side of the Coquitlam River is best late Aug-March. Steelhead, cutthroat trout, coho.

A major industrial and commercial area. Home to CP Rail marshalling yards and International Submarine Research Company.

**Port Coquitlam Information:** Coquitlam Infocentre, 135-3030 Lincoln Ave, Coquitlam, BC, V3B 6B4. 464-2333. Weekdays in winter, daily in summer.

**Pitt River and Pitt Lake:** Pitt River Bridge on Hwy 7 passes over river 9km east of Port Moody. Pitt River flows south from 7,700ha Pitt Lake, world's largest fresh water tidal lake. Lakeshore provides natural boat launch, offers fishing for steelhead trout and pink, coho, spring, and sockeye salmon. When boating on lake, stay within navigation markers as it is shallow at the south end. Cold water, logs, debris, and high winds make this a hazardous lake, especially for small craft.

Pitt River continues southwest past Hwy 7, 4.5km to Fraser River. 18km of fishable shoreline. Coho, Dolly Varden, cutthroat. Spring and fall fishing is best.

**Pitt Meadows:** (District pop. 11,147). 11km beyond Port Moody. Incorporated in 1914, this district is on north bank of the Fraser between Port Coquitlam and Maple Ridge. Forestry and agriculture play a major role. Dairy, cranberry, blueberry farms. It's also horse country.

**Pitt Meadows Information:** Contact Chamber of Commerce, Box 273, Pitt Meadows, BC, V3Y 2E6. 465-7820.

**Pitt Meadows Airport:** From downtown Pitt Meadows, Harris Rd leads south 3km to airport. This 278ha airport is one of the few opened by BC Ministry of Transportation solely for use by small planes. Facilities include three paved runways, float-plane dock on north side of the Fraser River, and control tower.

■ **Pitt Meadows Historical Museum:** 12484 Harris Rd. Sat afternoons. Heritage house with photos, paintings, and history of local Coast Salish Indians.

**Laity St:** 5km beyond Harris Rd. Exit to Maple Ridge.

**Maple Ridge:** (Pop. 48,422). In Fraser Valley, 15km beyond Port Moody on Hwy 7. First known as Port Haney, after Thomas Haney, who settled in 1876. The old town of Haney played an important role as a riverside community. First exploration by Europeans of this area took place between 1837 and 1858, when settlers cleared the heavily forested areas to make way for dairy and fruit farms. With the development of railway and highway systems, and decline in the use of river steamers, importance of the town as a trading centre dwindled. Today: sawmills, fruit-processing plants, dairy, cranberry and blueberry farms. Horse Capital of BC: more than 160km of trails through gorgeous riding country. Riding trail brochure available at infocentre.

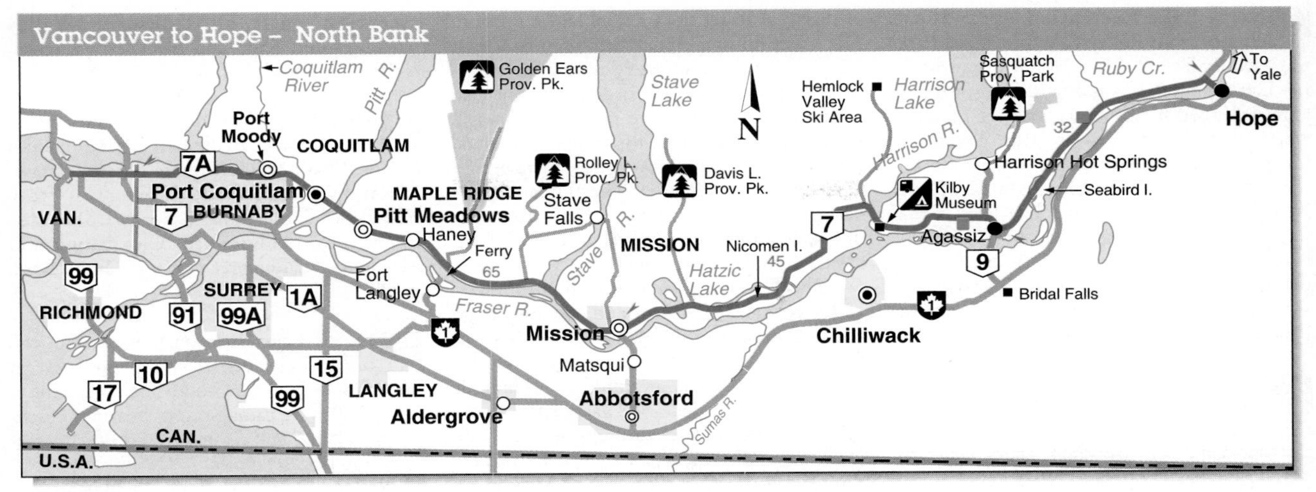


**Maple Ridge Information:** Maple Ridge Infocentre, 22238 Lougheed Hwy, Maple Ridge, BC, V2X 2T2. 463-2202. Daily June-Aug. Weekdays Sept-May.

■ **Haney House:** 11612-224th St. 463-1377. Wed-Sun afternoons. Daily except Mon-Tues in summer. Groups and afternoon teas by arrangement. Built in 1878 for the Haney family, wood-frame house is located in an attractive garden near the Fraser River. It remained Haney family residence until 1979 when it was restored with three generations of family furnishings.

■ **St John the Divine Anglican Church:** Laity St and River Rd. Daily. The oldest church in BC, built 1859. Was moved here in 1882 from a site 3km upstream.

■ **"The Beast":** Don't miss the town clock outside the Municipal Hall and Police Station. Atop the clock tower is a controversial metal horse – something out of the *Wizard of Oz* – that rears up every hour on the hour. Designed by municipal employee Don Brayford to be a symbol of horse country, its cost was a sore point, but The Beast is proving a wonderment.

■ **Maple Ridge Art Gallery:** 11995 Haney Place. 467-5855. June-Sept: daily except Mon. Sept-June: Thurs-Sun.

■ **Maple Ridge Museum:** 22535 River Rd. 463-5311. May-Aug: daily except Mon-Tues. Sept-April: Wed and Sun. A 1907 home overlooking historic Port Haney on the Fraser River. Pioneer artifacts, photo archives, and a railway diorama created by the Dewdney-Alouette Railway Society.

■ **Kanaka Creek Regional Park:** 200ha. 432-6350. From 224th St turn right onto Dewdney Trunk Rd, then south onto 256th St. Park protects 12km of a natural stream corridor in Maple Ridge Municipality. Creek begins in headwaters of Blue Mountain, travels through mature second-growth forests, sandstone canyons, meadows and marshes, before joining the Fraser River. Home to native salmon, trout, and the one-tailed frog. Waterfalls, wetlands, and wildlife. Walking, canoeing, riding. Note: equestrian trail requires riders to ford Kanaka Creek, hazardous during high-water conditions.

■ **Kanaka Creek/Bell-Irving Hatchery:** 1km south of Dewdney Trunk Rd on 256th St, sign at entrance. 462-8643. Year-round. Tours 2-3pm daily. Cliff Falls downstream.

**232nd St:** Eastern edge of Maple Ridge, turn north, 8km to **Malcolm Knapp Research Forest**; or north 5km to Fern Crescent which leads east 6km to **Golden Ears Provincial Park**.

## SIDE TRIP
### to Research Forest and Golden Ears

**Malcolm Knapp Research Forest:** On 232nd St 8km north of Hwy 7. 463-8148. Daily. This 5,157ha forest was established in 1949 as a facility for forestry demonstration and instruction. Managed by UBC Faculty of Forestry. Walking and hiking trails. No dogs or bikes.

**Golden Ears Provincial Park:** 55,594ha. 343 campsites in two large campgrounds; over 150 picnic tables. 463-3513. A massive park north of Hwy 7 on Fern Cres. North on 232nd St; 5 km to Fern Cres; east 6 km on Fern Cres. Once part of Garibaldi Provincial Park, establishment of Golden Ears Provincial Park in 1964 recognized the mountain barrier, including the 2,583m Mamquam Mountain, dividing the two parks. Named after its famous twin peaks.

The 1,055ha Alouette Lake, a 16km lake within the park, was once a traditional native fishing area. Natives trapped fish in weirs (series of woven enclosures). Swimming, windsurfing, waterskiing, canoeing, boating, hiking, exploring, climbing, and fishing for cutthroat and Dollies.

Through the 1920s until 1931, when a disastrous fire swept through the valley, the forested slopes above Alouette Lake were site of BC's largest railway logging operation. The Abernathy and Lougheed Logging Company laid more than 135km of railway lines to take out the harvested fir, hemlock, red cedar, and balsam trees. These abandoned railway grades make up part of the 42km of bridle trails and 80km of hiking trails in the park. Hiking trails vary in difficulty, from **Centennial Trail** (2.5-hour, a good introduction); to a strenuous 7-hour hike to Golden Ears Mountain at an elevation of over 1,700m. Check information boards at parking lots for lists of activities.

### Return to Highway 7

**240th St:** Exit south .5km to the Albion Ferry.

**Albion Ferry:** Crosses Fraser River to **Fort Langley** and **Fort Langley National Historic Park**. Ferry is free, and runs every 15 min. 5am-1:30am daily. Trip is 5 minutes. Two ferries, 23 cars each. 660-8770. Ferry is a part of the provincial highway system and enables motorists to make a direct connection between Hwys 7 and 1. For information on Fort Langley, see *Vancouver to Hope – South Bank*, p.106.

**272nd St:** 6.5km east of 240th St. To Rolley Lake Provincial Park.

## SIDE TRIP
### to Rolley and Stave Lakes

**Rolley Lake Provincial Park:** 115ha. 64 campsites. 463-3513. Turn north on 28th St (it becomes Wilson St), then east on Dewdney Trunk Rd to Bell St. Bell St leads 4.5km to park. The 20ha Rolley Lake was named after James and Fanny Rolley who homesteaded here in 1888. In the early 1900s, lake was used as a holding pond for shingle bolts destined for the Sholtze mill at Ruskin. A wooden flume sped the bolts 5km downhill to the mill. In 1930s, park area supported a small Japanese-Canadian hand-logging operation typical of many that existed throughout the province. Today: walking around the lakeshore, picnicking, swimming, canoeing. Visitor programs. Rainbow, cutthroat, Dolly Varden, and brown bullhead fishing best in spring and fall. No powerboats.

**Stave Lake Recreation Area:** 50ha. Return from Rolley Lake Provincial Park to Dewdney Trunk Rd and follow it northeast for 5km to Stave Lake and falls. Hudson's Bay Company had a cooperage at Fort Langley where BC's first barrels were made. The wood for the staves for these barrels was hewed on the banks of this river, thus its name, Stave River, and the lake's, too. The lake is the result of a dam built across Stave River. Trails, beach, boat launch, swimming, fishing for cutthroat, Dolly Varden, and rainbow. Stave Falls Dam and Powerhouse was location of recent Paramount film, *We're No Angels.*

**Hayward Lake Reservoir Recreation Area:** South of Stave Falls Dam. Many trails, swimming, canoeing, picnicking.

## Return to Highway 7

**Crescent Island:** 12km east of Maple Ridge, what you see to the south is a 3km sliver of an island, undeveloped, at Stave River mouth.

**Storyland Trails**: 4km past Crescent Island (8km west of Mission). 826-6480. 400 story characters, from Humpty Dumpty to Old Woman-in-a-Shoe.

**Mission:** (Pop. 26,202). On Hwy 7, 26km east of Maple Ridge and 50km east of Port Moody. Named for a Roman Catholic Mission, built in 1861 atop a hill overlooking the river. The dream of an Oblate priest, Father Fouquet, who came from France in that year to set up a school and a mission. The "Westminster Abbey Seminary of Christ the King" was a monastery retreat for members of the Benedictine order. Mission also ministered to local native peoples and was a popular stopping place for trappers, settlers, and other river travellers. Today, there are 30 life members in the order. They live a self-sufficient lifestyle, and include in their daily routine welcoming guests who want to spend a few days in meditation and in peace.

The District of Mission, incorporated 1892, covers 233 sq km and includes large portions of agricultural land. Also known as the Shake and Shingle Capital of the World. Fraser River sandbars are fun for rockhounds in search of agates, jade, and garnets.

**Mission Information:** Infocentre, Box 3340, Mission, BC, V2V 4J5. 826-6914. Tourist info booth is 3km east of Mission on Hwy 7, at St Mary's Park. Weekdays in winter, daily in summer.

■ **Museum and Archives of Mission:** 33201 Second Ave. 826-1011. Mon-Fri: 10-4. Sat-Sun: 2-4. In old Bank of Commerce, a 1907 two-storey prefab building. Historical artifacts, native hunting technology.

■ **Westminster Abbey:** North off Hwy 7 on Dewdney Trunk Rd. Visiting hours 1:30-4pm. 28 years in the making, the Abbey was completed in 1982. Dome rises 18m above the altar, has 64 stained glass windows.

■ **Fraser River Heritage Regional Park:** 16.5ha. Off Hwy 7 on Stave Lake St, right on 5th Ave. Ruins of St Mary's Mission and Indian Residential School. **Norma Kenney House**, two-storey log building, is park's reception centre, also houses the Valley Treasures Gift Shop and Blackberry Kitchen, serving light meals. 826-0277.

**Hwy 11:** In Mission. Turn south across the Mission Bridge to Matsqui Trail Regional Park on south shore of Fraser; travel 12km to Abbotsford; 5km south from Abbotsford to the Sumas (Canada/US) border. For info on Abbotsford, Clearbrook and Matsqui, see *Vancouver to Hope – South Bank*, p.108.

**Hatzic Lake Recreation Area:** 8km east of Mission. Turn north on Shook Ave. A horseshoe-shaped lake, south shore adjacent to Hwy 7. Private campground, boating, beaches, picnicking, and fishing for cutthroat, rainbow, and black crappies.

■ **Neilson Regional Park:** In Hatzic area, right off Draper onto McEwen; left onto East Edwards Rd. 2km of walking trails, picnic tables, cookhouse, beach, canoe launch.

**Cascade Falls Regional Park:** 9.5ha nature park. On Hwy 7, 2km east of Hatzic Lake, turn north on Sylvester Rd, right on Ridgeview Rd. Features a waterfall on Cascade Creek. Upper falls drop 25m to a large pool; series of smaller falls to valley floor.

**Davis Lake Provincial Park:** 192ha. On Sylvester Rd just north of Cascade Falls Regional Park, a total of 20km north of Hwy 7. Undeveloped. Fishing, swimming.

**Dewdney and Hawkins-Pickle Rd:** Small community of Dewdney is past the Sylvester Rd junction, 10km east of Mission, at start of the Nicomen Slough.

**Inch Hatchery:** North on Hawkins-Pickle Rd .5km past the dogleg; pavement leads left, hatchery is on gravel road to right. Write Box 61, 38620 Bell Rd, Dewdney, V0M 1H0. 826-0244. Chum, chinook, coho, trout, cutthroat; best times, spring, winter.

**Dewdney Nature Regional Park:** 7ha. Outside the dyke on east side of River Rd South. Good river fishing, boat launch.

**Nicomen Slough Bridge:** The other side of Dewdney (and 10km east of Mission). Highway crosses the slough onto **Nicomen Island.**

**Nicomen Island:** Highway traverses 15km-long Nicomen Island, one of a series of islands on the Fraser River between Mission and Agassiz. This island is one of the prime truck farming areas in the Fraser Valley. **Nicomen Slough**, north of the highway, runs parallel to the Fraser River, along the northern shores of Skumalasph and Nicomen islands. The slough offers 21km of fishable length with coho, steelhead, and cutthroat.

**Deroche Bridge:** Highway crosses the slough north to community of Deroche, 15km east of Dewdney.

*"Seadooing" in Alouette Lake, Golden Ears Provincial Park.*

**Harrison Mills and Morris Valley Rd:** 30km east of Dewdney. Turn north on Morris Valley Rd, 14km to Hemlock Valley Ski Area.

## SIDE TRIP

### to Hemlock Valley Ski Area and Salmon Hatchery

**Ski Area:** Turn north onto Morris Valley Rd. Follow road for 14km to ski area. 1-800-665-7080 or 797-4411. Open Dec-March. Longest night-skiing season in the Lower Mainland. Located in a natural snow bowl, Hemlock has 365m-vertical drop, one triple chair, two double chairs and one handle tow. Toboggans and snowmobiles for rent. A ski patrol, ski rentals, and repair shops round out the facilities.

**Chehalis Hatchery:** On Morris Valley Rd about 10km north of Hwy 7. 16250 Morris Valley Rd, Harrison Mills, BC, V0M 1L0. 796-2281. Chum, coho, chinook, steelhead. Something to see year-round.

**Chehalis Band Hatchery:** On Morris Valley Rd look for sign indicating Indian Reserve. Ask at Band Office for directions. Write Hatchery manager, Chehalis Indian Band, Chehalis Rd, RR1, Comp 66, Agassiz, BC, V0M 1A0. 796-9846. Chum salmon Oct-May.

**Weaver Creek Project:** On Morris Valley Rd take right fork about 300m from highway, signs lead 13km to spawning channel. Chum, sockeye, pink. Displays, literature, films.Great eagle-watching, too.

### Return to Highway 7

**Harrison Bay:** 2km beyond Morris Valley Rd on Hwy 7. Area is Sasquatch (or Bigfoot) Country, so keep a close eye on the tall timbers for BC's "abominable snowman." The Sasquatch, hairy giants twice the size of humans, supposedly came down from the hills in days of yore to abduct Indian maidens. The beasts sealed the maidens' eyes with pitch so that they couldn't see where they were being taken. If you do catch a glimpse of a Sasquatch in the tall timbers, contact the local authorities. However, you are more likely to see bald eagles, blue herons, or mallards, or catch a glimpse of a black bear or even a cougar.

**Harrison River:** Hwy 7 crosses the river, 33km beyond Mission. River feeds into Harrison Bay from Harrison Lake. One of the larger tributaries of the Fraser in the Fraser Valley. Fish for cutthroat and Dolly Varden, spring and fall.

**Kilby Provincial Historic Park:** 3ha; 38 campsites. 858-7161. On a promontory where the Harrison River meets the Fraser. 2km south of highway. Picnicking, swimming, fishing, boat launch.

**Kilby General Store Museum:** Adjacent Kilby Park. 7ha. Picnic facilities. Operated by BC Heritage Attractions and Kilby Museum Historical Society. 796-9576. July-Aug: daily, 10am-5pm. Reduced schedule May-June and early fall. School programs and bus tours can be booked year-round.

General stores played a crucial role in the province's history. At Kilby, visitors can poke around the general store which served the close-knit community of Harrison Mills in the 1920s and 1930s. In a single moment, step back 70 years. Thomas Kilby, and particularly his son Acton who took over in 1928, were pack rats. They saved everything, from the attic to the root cellar, every bill and order form. The old store is a museologist's dream come true. Long-forgotten brands and types of goods fill the shelves, with sundries hanging from the ceiling. A checkerboard sits by a pot bellied stove where local folk once socialized.

Kilby is on the cutting edge of museums. Innovative educational programs, including a period-complete store in the basement where schoolchildren can weigh out bulk foods, measure beans by the quart, crank the old phone, and press apples for cider. Event every weekend throughout summer.

**Hwy 9:** 14km beyond Harrison River. Turn north to Harrison Hot Springs and Sasquatch Provincial Park.

## SIDE TRIP

### to Sasquatch Provincial Park and Harrison Hot Springs

**Harrison Hot Springs:** (Pop. 655). On Hwy 9, just 6.5km beyond the junction of Hwys 7 and 9. The discovery of warm water in Harrison Lake came in 1859, when a pioneer, canoeing on the lake, overturned his boat. Instead of perishing in the cold waters, as he might have expected, the canoeist found the water warm and comfortable.

Harrison Hot Springs, known as the "Spa of Canada," is on the southern shores of Harrison Lake. Town is a health and vacation resort with two mineral springs and a sandy beach on the lakeshore. The source of the hot springs is two sulphur-potash outlets which emerge from mountains on the western shore of the lake. Temperatures from these two springs register 58 degrees C and 62 C.

Surrounding area is good for rockhounds. Lucky visitors may be able to pay for their trip with finds of jade, garnets, agates, fossils, and gold.

**Harrison Hot Springs Information:** Travel Infocentre, Box 255, Harrison Hot Springs, BC, V0M 1K0. 796-3425. Year-round.

■ **Harrison Public Hot Pool:** Corner of Harrison Hot Springs Rd and Esplanade Ave. Daily. Over 204,416 litres of hot spring water is piped from hot spring source, then cooled to a comfortable 39 degrees C.

■ **Harrison Lake:** North-south oriented lake over 70km long. Lake was part of late 1850s gold-rush route for miners travelling between the Fraser River and gold fields in the Cariboo. Today there is swimming, canoeing, and fishing for cutthroat, steelhead, and coho. Boat ramp. Rowboat and sailboat rentals and lessons available on lake. Boat tours of the lake sail three times daily from the Harrison Hotel during summer.

**Sasquatch Provincial Park:** 1,220ha; 177 campsites. 858-7161. 6.5km beyond Harrison Hot Springs on Rockwell Dr. Though the park is named for the legendary Bigfoot, most visitors report seeing the more plentiful deer, squirrels, and beaver. There are four lakes here, including the 112ha Hicks Lake; and forests surrounded by mountains, including the 1,524m Lookout Peak. Camping, canoeing, swimming, fishing, hiking. Lovely evergreen and deciduous forest.

■ **Green Point Picnic Area:** In Sasquatch Provincial Park, 8km north of Harrison Hot Springs on Rockwell Rd between Trout and Harrison lakes. The picnic area borders Harrison Lake. Boat launch.

### Return to Highway 7

**Agassiz:** (Pop. 4,000). At Hwy 9, 45km beyond Mission on Hwy 7. Community named after Captain Lewis N. Agassiz, formerly of the Royal Welsh Fusiliers. After working the Cariboo goldfields, he turned to farming in the Fraser Valley, establishing residence in 1867.

**Agassiz Information:** Contact Harrison Hot Springs Travel Infocentre, Box 255, Harrison Hot Springs, BC, V0K 1K0. 796-3425.

■ **Agassiz-Harrison Historical Museum:** 6947 Hwy 7, on the grounds of the Federal Research Station. 796-3545. Daily, May-early Sept. In a former CP Rail station, built 1893. Telegraph office and waiting room have been restored to original state.

**Fraser Delta:** Viewpoint and stop-of-interest plaque on Agassiz Mountain, 8km beyond Agassiz. Once through the mountains of BC's Interior, the Fraser River slows, dropping sediment gathered along its course. It has built a broad fertile delta 100km from here to the sea.

**Seabird Island:** On Fraser River between Agassiz and Ruby Creek. Island was named after the American paddle-wheeler, *Sea Bird*, which ran aground here in the summer of 1858. Now the site of the Earth Voice Festival, end of July, begun by the Mount Currie and Lytton Bands, to focus on environmental issues, first local (the Stein Valley), now global. One of the largest open-air gatherings of its kind in North America.

**Maria Slough:** On eastern outskirts of Agassiz, next to Seabird Island. Fish for cutthroat and rainbow trout in the spring, coho in the fall.

**Johnsons Slough Rest Area:** About 16km beyond Agassiz.

**Ruby Creek:** Flows under Hwy 7, 20km beyond Agassiz. Named for the rubies and garnets found here. (Would-be rockhounds should note that they are not gem quality, and are of little monetary value.) Fish for coho, cutthroat, and steelhead along the creek's 4km of fishable shoreline.

**Hwy 1:** 32km beyond Agassiz. Turn north 22km to Yale. See *Hope to Cache Creek*, p.163. Or turn south over the Fraser Bridge 3km to Hope and the junction of Hwys 1 and 3. See *Hope to Princeton*, below.

## Hope to Princeton

### MANNING PROVINCIAL PARK (Crowsnest Highway, Highway 3)

Hope is the western terminus of the trans-provincial Hwy 3, "The Crowsnest." This portion of the Crowsnest winds its way east and south through lakes-and-mountains country, and through the 71,400ha Manning Provincial Park, before cutting north to Princeton. Hope to Princeton is 136km.

People still talk of "driving the Hope-Princeton" as if it were something of a feat, and though the highway is a good one, there's no doubt this is not an easy stretch. There are dramatic turns and switches, some when you least expect them. So take it easy, heed the signs, and don't expect to make time. There are lots of passing lanes.

The origin of the name Crowsnest here is something of a mystery, though it may have come from the Crow Indians, a tribe of the Sioux who migrated west from the Missouri River area in 1700s, to settle in the Rockies near today's BC/Alberta border. On the other hand, the highway may be named after the flocks of crows that habitually nest along the route.

**Hwys 3 and 1:** North on Hwy 1 leads 32km to Yale. For details on Yale, see *Hope to Cache Creek*, p.164.

**Hope:** (Pop. 3,147). 53km beyond Chilliwack on Hwy 1. At junction of Hwys 1 and 3. Hope sits at the entrance to the Fraser River Canyon, nestled in a mountain-ringed valley. In 1848-49, Henry Newsham Peers, of the Hudson's Bay Company, established a fort here to build an all-British route between Fort Kamloops, in the Thompson River region, and Fort Langley, on the Fraser River.

In 1863, Walter B Cheadle, an early tourist, observed as he travelled down- river: "We passed Hope, a town of 30 or 40 houses, size of Yale. It is most beautifully situated in a large flat with a magnificent amphitheatre of mountains behind. Prettiest site I have seen in the Colony."

It's still pretty today, and has attracted Hollywood location scouts (Hope was used as Rambo's birthplace in *First Blood*). Hope boasts one and only one set of traffic lights (near the park which centres the town). Only 15 minutes away on Kawkawa Lake Rd are the Othello-Quintette Tunnels (see below), one of the engineering feats of the world. Hope's economy is based on forestry, construction, and service industries. Many nearby lakes, including Kawkawa, Lake of the Woods, Silver, and Ross, are warm, clear, and inviting, with boating, swimming, fishing, picnicking. Greenwood Island in the Fraser River is a heron sanctuary. Croft Island just behind it attracts gold panners. And local mountains – Mt Ogilvie, Mt Hope, Thacker Mountain, and Holy Cross Mountain – lure hikers and picnickers.

**Hope Information:** Infocentre, 919 Water St, Hope, BC, V0X 1L0. 869-2021. Open weekdays, year-round.

■ **Hope Museum:** 919 Water St. 869-7322. Daily May-early Sept. Restored gold concentrator, a ball mill originating from a gold mill in the Coquihalla River Valley, local pioneer and native artifacts.

■ **Christ Church:** Downtown Hope. Anglican church, built in 1859. One of BC's oldest churches.

■ **Memorial Park:** Downtown Hope. Recently completed bandstand in the park offers varied musical entertainment throughout summer. Famous trees in the park have developed root rot. Local chainsaw carver Pete Ryan is gradually carving the stumps into animal forms. First came an eagle sitting on a stump; next a black bear and her cubs. A triumph of art over nature.

■ **Japanese Gardens:** Next to Memorial Park. Recently completed with meticulous care, gardens are dedicated to Japanese-Canadians who were placed in Tashme internment camp during the second World War. (Tashme is 24km from Hope on Hwy 3.)

■ **Centennial Park:** Along Fraser River. **Mountain Sign Post** points out surrounding peaks, and gives names and elevations.

■ **"H-Tree":** Near intersection of Hudson's Bay St and Fifth Ave. Two saplings were entwined back in the early days; now they create an "H" for "Hope."

■ **Fort Hope Cairn:** Hwy 1 and Wallace St. Commemorates establishment of Fort Hope by the Hudson's Bay Company in 1849.

■ **Sucker Creek/Kawkawa Creek Salmon Enhancement Site:** Left on Kawkawa Lake Rd. Take boardwalk to see spawning pink, chum, coho, and sockeye salmon (in autumn).

**Kawkawa Lake Provincial Park:** 7ha. 5km beyond Hope on Kawkawa Lake Rd. Can be reached from Hwy 3, but it's trickier. Easiest access is from town: take Wallace St (the main drag) east to 6th Ave; turn right at the bowling alley; then left at the ball park (which is Kawkawa Lake Rd), and follow signs. Shallow waters, not glacial fed, make this warm lake perfect for swimming and boating. Fish for kokanee, rainbow trout, cutthroat trout, and squawfish.

**Coquihalla Canyon Provincial Recreation Area and Othello-Quintette Tunnels:** 150 ha. East l0km beyond Kawkawa Lake Provincial Park. Take Kawkawa Lake Rd to turnoff for Othello Rd. Follow Othello Rd to Tunnels Rd. Signs mark route to park. This is where first Rambo movie, *First Blood*, was filmed with Sylvester Stallone. Spectacular scenery in gorge has also brought Hollywood here to film *Fire with Fire*, *Shoot to Kill*, and *National Dream*.

Truly a "Don't Miss" is a stroll through the famous Kettle Valley Railway's Othello-Quintette Tunnels. Construction began in 1910 on this railway that was to connect the Kootenay region with the coast. 61km of track were routed through the Coquihalla Valley from the Coquihalla Summit to junction of the Canadian Pacific Railway mainline situated across the Fraser River from Hope. Construction was laborious: one particular mile, built in 1914, cost $300,000 to complete. Greatest challenge was the Coquihalla Gorge, where Coquihalla River cut a 91m-deep channel in solid granite.

Chief engineer Andrew McCulloch surveyed the canyon from the vantage point of a wicker basket hanging over the gorge, and decided that he didn't need to bypass the canyon. Instead, he built right through the gorge, tunnelling through five different rock faces in a series of short tunnels. He named tunnels and stations after his daughters and characters from Shakespeare's plays. The Kettle Valley Railway opened in 1916. After a checkered history of service, and much legend and song, the line was officially closed in 1961. Flashlights are a good idea.

### Return to Hope and Highway 3

**Coquihalla Hwy (Hwy 5):** From Hope, northeast 115km to Merritt. For details, see *Hope to Kamloops*, p.174.

**Nicolum River Provincial Park:** 24ha. Nine campsites. 840-8836. 7km beyond Hope on north side of Hwy 3. Camping, picnicking, fishing for cutthroat, coho, and squawfish on shores of the clear, cool Nicolum River. The 2,286m Tulameen Mountain and 2,438m Mt Outram overlook the park, cutting off the summer's afternoon sun. Evenings are cool.

**Hope Slide Viewpoint and Rest Area:** 18km beyond Hope. One of BC's most devastating slides took place here in January, 1965. 46 million cubic metres of earth, rock, and snow – the entire side of a 1,983m-high and 1km-wide mountain – bore down into the valley at a speed in excess of 160km-h. Four people were killed, two were never found. It took 21 days to build a temporary road through the disaster.

**Manning Provincial Park:** 65,884ha. 353 campsites in four campgrounds. 840-8836. Also Manning Park Lodge, cabins, chalets: 840-8822. Manning Park, in the Cascade Mountain Range, was established in 1941. Hwy 3 bisects the park: it is 57km from the West Gate to the East Gate.

**Park Headquarters are at exact midpoint between Hope and Princeton, 68km from each town.**

Within the park are forested mountains, deep valleys, alpine meadows, azure-blue lakes. Manning Park is enjoyed year-round.

Four campgrounds include: **Hampton** with 98 campsites, 4km east of park headquarters on Hwy 3; **Mule Deer**, 49 campsites, 8.5km east of Park Headquarters on Hwy 3; **Coldspring**, 63 campsites, 2km west of headquarters on Hwy 3; and **Lightning Lake/Spruce Bay**, 143 campsites, 6km south of headquarters on Gibson Pass Rd. Wilderness campgrounds are located at Monument 78/Pacific Crest, Frosty Creek, Poland Lake, Mowich, Buckhorn, Kicking Horse, Nicomen Lake, and the south end of Strike Lake.

In the summer, a good paved road leads 9km to the Cascade Lookout for views of valley and surrounding peaks. Gravel road leads 6km to Blackwall Peak subalpine meadows, Alpine Naturalist Hut, and Paintbrush and Heather trails. Horseback riding, concession, canoe rentals. In winter, slopes and trails of Gibson Pass Ski Area here challenge skiers of all abilities. Two chairlifts, a T-bar, and poma lift. At least 150km of cross-country trails. Winter camping in tents and RVs at several locations in park.

**Manning Provincial Park West Gate:** 26km beyond Hope. Watch for the wood carving of a hoary marmot that marks park entrance. The marmot is a delightful park resident, and signs throughout the park note the best hoary marmot watching spots. In summer, these quite large rodents (up to 9kg) like sunning themselves on the rocks at Blackwall Peak. They have a piercing whistle.

**Rhododendron Flats:** 33km from Hope. One of the few places in BC where wild rhododendrons grow in their natural state. The red blossoms of this flowering evergreen are at their best early to mid-June. 2km walking trail.

**Cascade Provincial Recreation Area:** 16,680ha. 840-8836. Adjacent northern boundary of Manning Provincial Park. Access on foot or horseback along sections of three heritage trails, the Dewdney (1860), the Whatcom (1858), and the Hope Pass (1861). These trails are silent reminders of earlier attempts to cross the inhospitable Cascade Mountains. Wilderness camping at Paradise Valley.

■ **Dewdney and Whatcom Trails:** Access at the **Skagit Bluffs** and **Snass Creek**, 3km east of Rhododendron Flats. Parking for your car, hitching post for your horse. Bridle and hiking paths along Snass Creek's old Dewdney Trail, which leads to turnoff to Whatcom Trail.

■ **Hope Pass Trail:** Access at **Skaist River**, 6km from Snass Creek, 44km east of Hope. Park at **Cayuse Flats**, south side of Hwy 3. (Cayuse Flats is 24km west of park headquarters.)

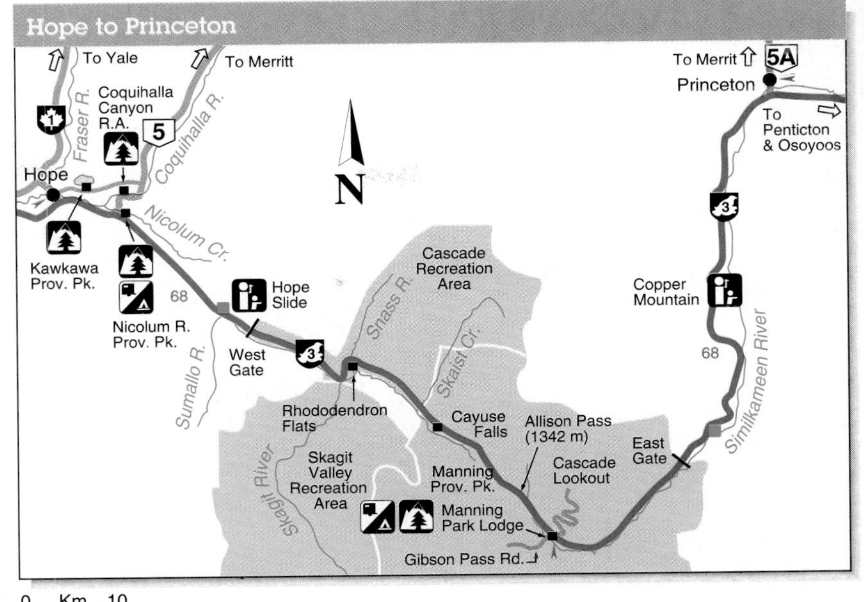


**Skagit River:** East of Rhododendron Flats. Hwy 3 follows river for about 20km into Manning Park, sometimes going over it (there are two short bridges). Coming from Ross Lake south across the Canada/US border, the Skagit cuts north through the **Skagit Valley Recreation Area** on Manning Park's western boundary. A provincial wilderness walk-in campsite is located along the Skagit River. Major part of Skagit Valley Recreation Area is accessed from Silverhope Creek Rd *west* of Hope: see *Vancouver to Hope – South Bank*, p.109.

**Allison Pass:** 58km east of Hope (10km from park headquarters). 1,341m. Named after John Fall Allison, an early Princeton rancher.

**Manning Park Resort:** At 67km east of Hope (9km east of Allison Pass), "the Lodge" is almost halfway between Hope and Princeton on Hwy 3, and a natural stopping-place. 840-8822. Gibson Pass Rd leads out just behind the Lodge to the ski area.

**Manning Park Corral:** Just behind the resort, .5km up the road to Lightning Lakes. Hourly, day, and multi-day rides, also pony rides, wagon rides. 840-8844.

**Park Headquarters and Visitor Centre, Cascade Lookout:** 1km east of the lodge, equidistant from Hope and Princeton (68km either way). Open daily in summer, it has displays of area's natural and human history. Naturalists answer questions and conduct morning and afternoon walks in July and Aug. The valley walk reveals everyday things in nature often missed. Alpine meadows walk leads through mountain slopes, carpeted with flowers. Each summer evening, park naturalists give talks or slide shows at Amphitheatre on Gibson Pass Rd south of the Lodge. Check at Visitor Centre or information boards for details.

**Manning Provincial Park East Gate:** 15km beyond Park Headquarters. Large wood carving of a black bear stands at this entrance. Black bears are a chief resident, occasionally seen near park's campgrounds. Park bears are wild animals and should never be approached, offered food, or tormented.

**Copper Creek Rest Area:** 7km beyond the East Gate.

**Copper Mountain Viewpoint:** 35km beyond East Gate. The mountain lies on the opposite side of the Similkameen River gorge. Until 1957, was site of one of North America's largest copper mines. Between 1920 and 1957, mine produced over 2,718 million kg of copper and thousands of grams of gold and silver.

**Princeton:** (Pop. 2,796). At junction of Similkameen and Tulameen rivers, 136km beyond Hope. For details on Princeton, see *Princeton to Rock Creek*, p.121. Hwy 3 (the Crowsnest) continues east beyond Princeton through Osoyoos and Crowsnest Pass into Alberta. From Princeton, Hwy 5A leads north to Merritt, through some of North America's finest rainbow trout country. See *Princeton to Kamloops*, p.182.

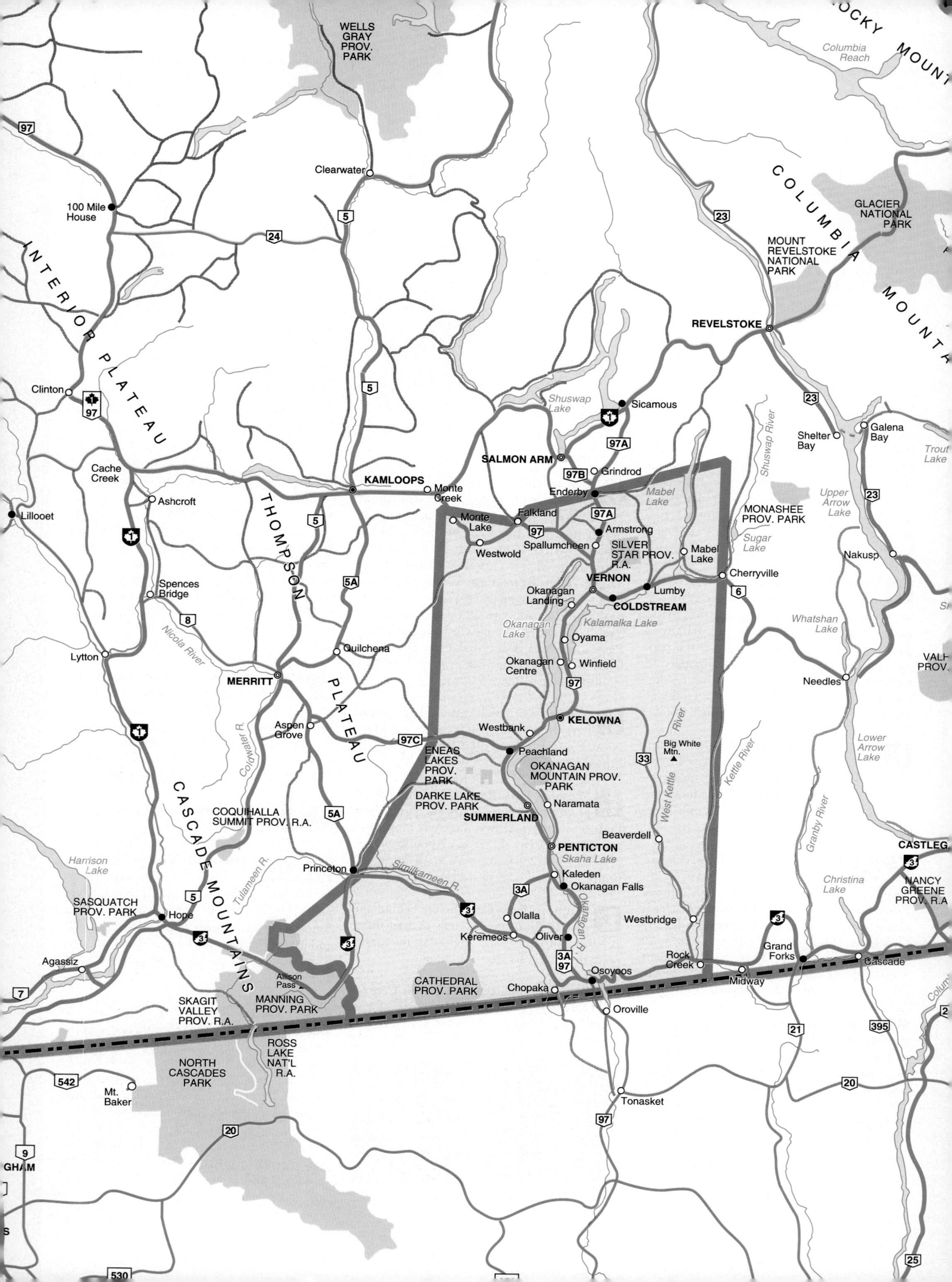

WELLS GRAY PROV. PARK
ROCKY MOUNT
Columbia Reach
Clearwater
100 Mile House
INTERIOR PLATEAU
COLUMBIA MOUNTA
GLACIER NATIONAL PARK
MOUNT REVELSTOKE NATIONAL PARK
REVELSTOKE
Clinton
Shuswap Lake
Sicamous
SALMON ARM
Grindrod
Enderby
Mabel Lake
Cache Creek
KAMLOOPS
Monte Creek
Ashcroft
Lillooet
THOMPSON PLATEAU
Monte Lake
Falkland
Armstrong
Westwold
Spallumcheen
SILVER STAR PROV. R.A.
VERNON
Lumby
Cherryville
Okanagan Landing
COLDSTREAM
Spences Bridge
Nicola River
Okanagan Lake
Kalamalka Lake
Oyama
Quilchena
Okanagan Centre
Winfield
Lytton
MERRITT
KELOWNA
Westbank
Aspen Grove
Peachland
ENEAS LAKES PROV. PARK
OKANAGAN MOUNTAIN PROV. PARK
Big White Mtn.
DARKE LAKE PROV. PARK
SUMMERLAND
Naramata
COQUIHALLA SUMMIT PROV. R.A.
CASCADE MOUNTAINS
Coldwater R.
Harrison Lake
Tulameen R.
Princeton
Similkameen R.
PENTICTON
Skaha Lake
Kaleden
Okanagan Falls
Beaverdell
West Kettle
Kettle River
SASQUATCH PROV. PARK
Hope
Olalla
Keremeos
Oliver
Okanagan R.
Westbridge
Agassiz
Allison Pass
MANNING PROV. PARK
CATHEDRAL PROV. PARK
Chopaka
Osoyoos
Rock Creek
Midway
Grand Forks
Cascade
SKAGIT VALLEY PROV. R.A.
Oroville
ROSS LAKE NAT'L R.A.
NORTH CASCADES PARK
Mt. Baker
Tonasket
Shuswap River
Shelter Bay
Galena Bay
Trout Lake
Upper Arrow Lake
MONASHEE PROV. PARK
Sugar Lake
Nakusp
Whatshan Lake
Needles
Lower Arrow Lake
Granby River
Christina Lake
CASTLEG
NANCY GREENE PROV. R.A.
97
5
24
23
1
97A
97B
97C
8
5A
33
3A
3
6
7
542
20
9
21
395
25
530

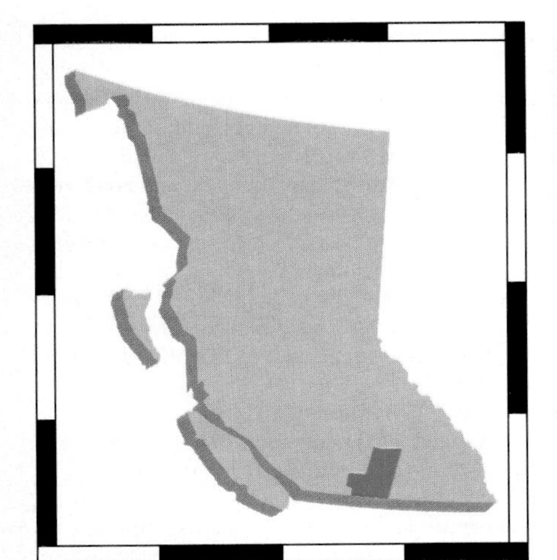

# Okanagan – Similkameen

## *It's Dry, Wet, Hot, and Cold*

With dirty corduroy trousers, scuffed riding boots, and the long black skirts of his religious gown pinned up at the waist, Father Charles Marie Pandosy would have cut a dramatic, if not ungodly figure as he rode through the Okanagan-Similkameen on horseback in 1859.

It is said that he arrived at L'Anse au Sable (Sandy Cove) on Okanagan Lake with little more than his breviary, a blanket, a piece of bacon, and the conviction that he had found an hospitable place to establish a mission. "It is in a great valley near the middle of Great Okanagan Lake," he wrote of the flood plains just south of present-day Kelowna, and "the cultivable land is immense."

Pandosy was not the first "civilized intruder" into the largely uncharted and little-known Interior region of BC. The fur trade had climaxed a decade before. Now villages, with churches and schools, were rising fast between the Rocky Mountains and the Pacific Ocean to accommodate those who had settled in its wake. Gold prospects in the southern Interior were attracting fortune-seekers from the Fraser Canyon and Cariboo.

Yet, while prospectors fleeced the Interior creeks and streams, the Oblate priest bent forward to tap the real mother-lode: arable land. Within a year or two of breaking ground at Okanagan Mission, Pandosy was able to introduce apple trees into the Okanagan. These produced a deep-red apple like the Delicious, and a fruitful legacy that remains a mainstay of the region.

A long, five-and-a-half month growing season, abundant reserves of standing water and running streams that could be harnessed for irrigation, and relatively mild winters, all worked together to foster the first orchards. By the turn of the century, more than a million fruit trees were planted and the Okanagan-Similkameen became known as the best fruit-cultivating environment north of the 49th parallel.

The Okanagan-Similkameen is the sunshine hot spot of BC, with a regional average of almost 150 days a year when the average daily maximum temperature is 18 degrees C. Hot, sunny days in the land of long summers are typically followed by refreshingly cool evenings. Overall, it has one of the mildest, driest climates in Canada, with average annual precipitation a meagre 25cm.

Comparable to Germany's Rhine Valley, the climate is as hospitable to grape vines as fruit trees. The first commercial vineyard was established here in 1926. There are 22 wineries in the region, drawing from more than 1,200ha of vineyards, all located within a triangle between the towns of Osoyoos, Winfield, and Keremeos. A summer wine-tasting tour through the Okanagan-Similkameen reveals why BC wines are winning awards internationally.

The western boundary of the Okanagan-Similkameen lies in the rain shadow of the Cascade Mountains, just west of Princeton. Its southern border extends east to the Monashee Mountains; the northern border runs through

*Sailing on Okanagan Lake, near Penticton.*

rolling hills and fertile valleys to the High Country region.

The Okanagan-Similkameen is small in relation to the province as a whole – occupying only about three percent of BC's total area – yet contains the Interior's largest concentration of people. About eight percent of the provincial total inhabit the region's three major cities: Kelowna, Penticton, and Vernon. And popularity is growing: *Chatelaine* Magazine cites both Kelowna and Penticton among the 10 best places to live in Canada.

The southern section, around Osoyoos, Oliver, and Penticton, is unlike any other place in the province. This incredibly arid landscape is located at the northern tip of the Great Basin Desert of Oregon and Nevada, and supports such subtropical flora and fauna as cactus and sagebrush, rattlesnakes and painted turtles.

The Central Okanagan, from Penticton to Vernon along the sandy shores of Okanagan Lake, is the Hawaii of Canada. Names suggest something warm and exotic: Naramata, Summerland, Peachland, Kelowna, and the stretch north to "the lake of many colours" – Kalamalka – through Winfield and Oyama to Vernon. Known locally as the Lake Country, it is also the region's fruitbelt and the heart of its wine industry.

Okanagan Lake, which covers 352 sq km, is the largest vestige of the glaciers of 10,000 years past. All of 128km long, it is 2- to-5km wide, and, in places, at least 550m deep: said to be a perfect environment for the legendary Ogopogo, which over the years has been spotted by credible witnesses. Native peoples called the monster *N'ha-a'ith*, and perhaps have recorded its existence in pictographs. Some speculate that this lake monster, which supposedly lives in the depths of the "bottomless" lake, was hatched from a dinosaur egg released by movement in the earth's crust.

A 1990 video recording of something unusual moving on the surface of the lake created headlines across the nation. The recording was enough to persuade the provincial government to put Ogopogo under the Wildlife Act as protected fauna. Experts examining the tape later on pretty much agreed that the creature looked and moved suspiciously like an ordinary beaver.

Whatever it was, the taped evidence created a lot of excitement in scientific circles. Even if it were a beaver, that does not discount hundreds of sightings of some other monster by varied witnesses since the earliest days on Okanagan Lake.

North Okanagan is dairy country. From Vernon through Armstrong and Enderby to the Shuswap Lake district, the valleys are surrounded by green, rolling hills. Clay soils foster the hardier vegetable, hay, and alfalfa crops typical of range country. And Armstrong is home of Armstrong cheese, one of BC's most famous exports.

Three major ski resorts offer a full range of downhill and cross-country terrain: Apex Alpine, a 30-minute drive from Penticton; Big White Mountain, east of Kelowna; and Silver Star, about 30 minutes east of Vernon. There are also the smaller, more intimate hills, like

*Cherries in the Okanagan Valley.*

Mt Baldy, near Osoyoos, and Snowpatch, near Princeton.

Ghost towns are another attraction. Granite City, west of Princeton, in 1885 was the fourth largest city and "the biggest, gaudiest mining camp in the province." But perhaps the best-kept secret about the region is its exceptional diversity of wildlife, from mountain goats, California big horn sheep, and a dense population of white-tailed deer, to myriad bird species, from rare rock and canyon wrens, to migrant waterfowl.

Diverse and plentiful as the wildlife may be, though, sun is what makes the Okanagan-Similkameen one of the province's most popular vacation destinations. While many visitors appreciate the flora and fauna, the vineyards and the wine tasting, the orchards with their perpetually open fruit stands, and the more than 30 golf courses, most are drawn to the clear, clean air, brilliant blue waters, and clean sandy beaches of Lake Country. It's only when you get here that you find there's so much more.

## Information

**Okanagan-Similkameen Tourism Association:** #104-515 Highway 97 South, Kelowna, BC, V1Z 3J2, or call 769-5959. Fax: 861-7493.

Addresses and phone numbers of local infocentres are in the *Logs* with write-ups on each community.

## Transportation

Moving around Okanagan-Similkameen is as much recreation as destination oriented. Travel infocentres in each district have information on everything from two-wheeler and watercraft rentals to hang-gliding clubs, hot-air balloons, and riding stables.

### By Road

Okanagan travel is primarily a driving proposition. The region's main routes, Hwys 3, 97, and 97C, are predominantly four lanes, in excellent condition, with solid paved shoulders, regular passing lanes, and good visibility. Paved secondary roads such as Hwys 33 and 6 pose no problem for vehicles from bicycles to motor homes. Back roads are accessible to four-wheel-drive vehicles. Speed limits average between 80 and 90km-h; Hwy 97C, the Coquihalla Connector, has limits as high as 110km-h.

The Crowsnest Hwy (Hwy 3) enters the Okanagan-Similkameen from the eastern boundary of Manning Provincial Park. The Hwy 3A cutoff at Keremeos is a popular shortcut to Penticton. It is also possible to enter the region from the north after travelling the Coquihalla Hwy to Merritt, taking Hwy 97C and joining Hwy 97 between Peachland and Westbank.

Farther east, Hwy 3 climbs nearly 900m in the 32km between Osoyoos and the 1,233m summit of Anarchist Mountain. Highway grades reach 9 percent, and average between 6 and 7 percent. Steep for a long ascent.

Hwy 33 north from Rock Creek to Kelowna is a paved, but relatively untravelled, secondary road through open range country and ghost towns. Hwy 6 enters the Okanagan at Cherryville and ends at Vernon, intersecting Hwy 97. This scenic secondary paved road is most travelled by local farm vehicles and travellers coming from the Kootenays.

### Bus Lines

■ **Greyhound Canada:** Call Vancouver 662-3222, or specific cities: Penticton 493-4101; Kelowna 860-3835; Vernon 545-0527. The only daily motor coach service in this region. Non-stop express buses run three times daily between Kelowna and Vancouver, and offer juice, coffee, movies. Buses depart three times daily for Calgary.

■ **City Buses:** BC Transit offers public transportation in Penticton, Kelowna, and Vernon.

### Taxis, Car and RV Rentals

Taxis can be hired by the kilometre for out-of-town trips. Travel infocentres can advise. Auto rental agencies are located at airports and city centres in Penticton and Kelowna.

### Railways

■ **VIA Rail:** Toll-free 1-800-561- 8630. Transcontinental service from Vancouver stops at Kamloops (*High Country*) en route to Jasper.

■ **Rocky Mountain Rail Tours:** Greyhound buses link to Okanagan-Similkameen.

### Airlines

Kelowna Airport is BC's busiest after Vancouver and Victoria. Major carriers also serve Penticton. Two airlines serve Kelowna and Penticton with direct scheduled flights to Vancouver and Calgary. Smaller airline and helicopter companies also serve licensed airstrips in Vernon, Oliver, and Princeton.

Check local yellow pages for information about light aircraft and helicopter charters. Summer flight schedules for all airlines are in effect May through Sept.

■ **Canadian Airlines International:** Toll free 1-800-663-3502 or Kelowna 763-6620. Daily flights from Kelowna to and from Calgary and Vancouver. Regular connecting flights to Canadian, American, and international destinations.

Canadian Airlines offers winter ski tours to Big White and Silver Star out of Kelowna. Packages include air fare, bus transportation, and on-mountain accommodation, lift tickets.

■ **Canadian Regional Airlines:** Canadian Airlines' commuter partner, serves Penticton and Kelowna. Contact Canadian Airlines.

■ **Air BC:** 1-800-663-3721 or Kelowna 861-8441, Penticton 492-2165. Several flights daily directly to Vancouver; three to Calgary. Air BC is Air Canada's Okanagan connector airline. Although all Air BC flights are listed in Air Canada's timetable, the independently operated company books its own reservations.

### Water Aerodromes

Three Okanagan-Similkameen communities have seaplane facilities. The licensed Penticton water aerodrome is located adjacent to Skaha Lake beach, at the south end of the Penticton airport. At Winfield, north of Kelowna, Wood Lake Marina operates a licensed dock facility. In the Vernon area there is an unlicensed seaplane landing on the northeast arm of Okanagan Lake; there is also a licensed facility at Swan Lake. For more information, call local airport managers listed in the local phone book.

## OKANAGAN-SIMILKAMEEN EVENTS

### BLOSSOM TIMES

**Apricots**: Mid-late April.
**Cherries**: Mid-April to mid-May.
**Peaches**: Mid-April to early May.
**Prunes**: Late April to early May.
**Pears**: Late April to early May.
**Apples**: Early-late May 1.
**Grapes**: Mid-late June.

### FRUIT RIPENS

**Cherries**: Mid-June to mid-July.
**Apricots**: Early July to mid-Aug.
**Peaches**: Late July to mid-Sept.
**Prunes**: Mid-Aug to mid-Sept.
**Pears**: From mid-Aug.
**Apples**: From late July.
**Grapes**: From mid-Aug.

■ **Okanagan Wine Festival:** Throughout Oanagan Valley. Late-Sept. Ask at infocentres.

### Armstrong

■ **Interior Provincial Exhibition:** 4-day agricultural fair. Early Sept.
■ **Annual Balloon Rendezvous:** Mid-Oct.

### Beaverdell

■ **High Water Days:** Early June.

### Bridesville

■ **Horse Show:** Late Aug.

### Hedley

■ **Hedley Heritage Fair:** June.
■ **Hedley Blast:** Star-studded country music festival. Some 20,000 attended last year. Early July.

### Kelowna

■ **Snowfest:** Parade of lights, bonfire, fishing derby, bed races. Mid-Jan.
■ **Ski-to-Sea Race:** Skiing, mountain biking, running, 10-speed biking, and then canoeing. Begins at Big White ski hill, ends in Okanagan Lake. March.
■ **Knox Mountain Hill Climb:** Motorized madness in specially built cars. May long weekend.
■ **Black Mountain Rodeo:** May long weekend.
■ **Mardi Gras:** Early Aug.
■ **Kelowna Apple Triathlon:** 1.5km swim, 40km bike, 10km run. Late summer.

### Keremeos

■ **Chopka Rodeo:** Real working cowboys .
■ **Similkameen Powwow:** Native peoples from BC and Washington State meet for dancing and drumming. May long weekend.
■ **Keremeos Rodeo:** Parade, professional cowboys, ornery critters. May long weekend.

### Lumby

■ **Lumby Snofest:** Lions' Snoarama, dances, human dogsled race, snogolf, Tacky Tourist contest, ski hill triathlon. Jan.
■ **Lumby Days:** Ping Pong Ball Drop, amateur logging show, and a Chicken-Flying Contest. May.

### Oliver

■ **Fairview Days:** Commemorates mining heritage. Mid-June.

### Osoyoos

■ **Cherry Fiesta:** Canada Day long weekend.
■ **Kobau Star Gazing Party:** Aug.

### Peachland

■ **Peachland Fall Fair:** Labour Day Weekend.

### Penticton

■ **Mid-Winter Breakout:** Dance, tricycle races, ice-carving competitions, polar bear dip. Feb.
■ **Peach Festival:** Raft race on Okanagan River Channel, picnics, parade, dances. Late July.
■ **Square Dance Jamboree:** Thousands of dancers. 2nd week Aug.
■ **Iron Man Canada:** International qualifier for Hawaii triathlon. Gruelling trials in swimming, running, biking. Late Aug.

### Princeton

■ **World Snooshing Championships:** Teams of four, on 2.5m two-by-fours, in a contest of good humour and endurance. Jan.
■ **Princeton Racing Days:** Canada Day Long weekend.
■ **Princeton Rodeo and Fall Fair:** Mid-Sept.

### Summerland

■ **Action Festival:** Festivities and Mud Bog truck race. June, 1st weekend.
■ **Summerland Rodeo:** July, 2nd weekend.
■ **Festival of Lights:** Christmas celebration, lights, carollers, and merriment to match town's tudor theme. Late Nov.

### Tulameen

■ **Tulameen Daze:** Early Aug.

### Vernon

■ **Winter Carnival:** Ice sculptures, sleigh rides, stock car ice-racing derby, polar bear swim, coronation of Silverstar Queen. Early Feb.
■ **Cowboy Poetry Roundup and Trappings Show:** A weekend of pickin and singin, poetry and art, and cowboy culture. O'Keefe Ranch. Late May.
■ **Bella Vista Triathlon:** Bike-run-swim. Early Aug.
■ **Oldtime Fiddler's Contest:** Early Aug.

*Arrow-leaf balsam-root in profusion near Vaseux Lake in the Okanagan.*

# Okanagan-Similkameen Routes and Highlights

## TRAVELLER'S LOGS



## HIGHLIGHTS



## Princeton to Rock Creek

### CROWSNEST HIGHWAY (Highway 3)

Highway 3, the Crowsnest, traverses some 159km of the Okanagan-Similkameen, west to east. For much of that journey the gently winding highway follows the green Similkameen River. From Princeton, in the foothills of the Cascade Mountains, the river takes Hwy 3 through sun-browned hills, almost to the border near Osoyoos. Here, the Similkameen departs, making its way south into Washington State, while Hwy 3 continues east just north of the border. This route also follows the path of history. In the 1880s, miners scoured the Similkameen River and its creeks for gold, and many settlements in Boundary Country – to the east beyond Osoyoos – were gold-rush boom towns.

Keep an eye out along the highway for traces of the Vancouver, Victoria and Eastern Railway (VV&E), a subsidiary of the Great Northern, which ran from the US border through Keremeos and Hedley to Princeton.

**Princeton:** (Pop. 2,796). 135km east of Hope, el 640m. At confluence of Tulameen and Similkameen rivers. For downtown turn north off Hwy 3 onto Vermilion St or Bridge St. Downtown has recently had a facelift, with refurbished store fronts, repaved streets, new lamps, plants and trees.

"A lake a day as long as you stay", they say – at least 30 good trout lakes (especially Otter, Thynne, Allison, Osprey, and Tepee) within an 80km radius. Secluded sandy beaches along the Tulameen and Similkameen rivers.

Princeton Golf Course, 3km east of town on Hwy 3, is a sporty nine holes set in contrasting landscape of green and sagebrush dry hills. In winter: the family ski hill, Snowpatch, offering three tows, is 10 minutes from downtown, west on Tulameen Ave, north on Snowpatch Rd.

Princeton and district is ripe with mining lore: the old mining towns of Tulameen (pop. 117), Coalmont (pop. 82), Granite City, Blakeburn, and Allenby are nearby. Also a recreational gold-panning reserve. Contact Government Agent (see *below*) for maps and instructions. You can also go rockhounding, and searching for native pictographs.

Princeton received its name in 1860 to honour the Prince of Wales' visit to eastern Canada that year. Before then, the community was known variously as Vermilion Forks and Red Earth Forks, because red ochre, (*yak-tulameen*), was found 3km upstream on the Tulameen. The prized red earth was used for face painting.

An unusual RV campsite called Castle Rock at northeast outskirts of town features massive ruins of an old cement plant and power-generating station. RVs camp on a bench overlooking Allison Creek. Princeton today is a trade and distribution centre for an area that depends on forestry and mining.

**Princeton Information:** Infocentre on Hwy 3 at eastern outskirts of town. Year-round. Write: Princeton and District Chamber of Commerce, Box 540, Princeton, BC, V0X 1W0. 295-3103.

**Princeton Airport:** 2.5km beyond Princeton on Hwy 5A. 492-3001. Operated by Transport Canada.

■ **Princeton and District Pioneer Museum and Archives:** 167 Vermilion Ave. 295-7588. Daily, July and Aug. Pioneer furnishings, clothing, mining exhibits, Welby Stage Coach, farm equipment, fossils and minerals, art. Interior Salish, and Chinese artifacts (Chinese played a major role in early development of mining and railway construction industries).

■ **Princeton Municipal Campground:** 2km east of town on Hwy 3, on south the shore of the Similkameen.

**Hwy 5A:** Three blocks beyond Vermilion St. Continue half a block, then turn right. 89.5km to Merrit, see *High Country*, p.182, for details of route. Less than 1km from Princeton is turnoff to **Old Hedley Rd** (see *side trip* below). Also, follow signs **for Back road to Summerland** (Hwy 40). This 90km paved and gravel road traces part of old Kettle Valley Railway through scenery, lakes, fishing. See *Penticton to Kelowna*, p.128. For details on KVR, see *US Border to Penticton*, p.127.

## SIDE TRIP

### Along Dewdney Trail

The paved **Old Hedley Rd**, a leisurely and historic route, parallels Hwy 3 east. It follows the Similkameen River's north shore and the Dewdney Trail, completed in 1865 to connect the Kootenay region gold fields to BC's coast. After 27km the Old Hedley Rd rejoins Hwy 3 at the Stirling Creek Bridge, 7km west of Hedley. Some 22km along, watch on road's north side for faded shadows of ancient animal symbols and hieroglyphics about eye level on rock bluff. Pictographs are not marked, and there are no pullouts. Ask at Princeton Museum for directions.

### *Return to Highway 3*

**Bromley Rock Provincial Park:** 149ha; 17 campsites. 21km east of Princeton. 494-0321. South side of Similkameen River. Park named for large rock bluff. Below it, one gem of a swimming hole.

**Stemwinder Rest Area:** 31.5km east of Princeton.

**Stemwinder Provincial Park:** 4ha; 23 campsites. 33km beyond Princeton. 494-0321. Similkameen runs fast here: strong swimmers only. Early native settlement: pit-house depressions. Look out for poison ivy on riverbank.

**Nickel Plate and Mascot Mines:** 35km east of Princeton on Hwy 3. Remains of cable tramway and a jumble of wooden ruins (Mascot's bunkhouses) perched 1,200m on a Lookout Mountain cliff. From 1904 to 1955, $47 million in gold was taken from this mountain.

**Hedley:** (Pop. 402). 40km beyond Princeton. In 1898 gold miners struck it lucky at nearby Nickel Plate (a mine and a town). So much gold, copper, and silver poured out of the mine that a stamp mill was built, and an aerial tramway 3km long, then the longest in the world, was installed to feed it with ore. Mascot mine also became a bonanza. Hedley sprang up in the valley. Area population was more than 5,000. At least six hotels gave Hedley an air of prosperity. There were saloons, dancing girls, and fashionable stores selling European lace, China tea, and mink coats. Town's name is for Robert Hedley, who managed a smelter in Nelson.

Starting in 1909, the VV&E Railway stopped at Hedley, shipping ore and carrying passengers, but during a lean spell caused by World War One, the track was torn up and much of the right-of-way was taken over by what is now Hwy 3. For centuries before, this was undisturbed native Indian country. Native people called it *Sna-za-ist*, the "Place of the Striped Rock". There was a village near here called Chuchuawa where people bartered red jasper used for arrowheads.

Today, visitors can still try panning for gold in the Similkameen River, or in nearby 20 Mile Creek. Probably better luck with rainbow trout.

With its surrounding (or overhanging) dramatic landscape, and its own beckoning charm, Hedley is worth a stop and a stroll. **Woodley Park**, right downtown behind the 1903 **Grace United Church**, has picnic tables. Sit and soak up the little town's atmosphere.

Every July, the "Hedley Blast", a weekend-long star-studded country music festival, is held in a nearby farmer's field. An estimated 20,000 attended last year.

**Hedley Information:** No infocentre, but Nickel Plate Restaurant can help. Or write Hedley Heritage, Arts and Crafts Society, Box 218, Hedley, BC, V0X 1K0.

■ **Heritage House:** Modern cultural centre devoted to Hedley's heritage and arts and crafts. Displays of social and mining history. Artifacts outside include ore car and section of flume. "What's capturing people's imagination, though, is our small garden of drought-resistant plants," says Helen Moore, of the Hedley Heritage, Arts and Crafts Society. Such as prickley pear and succulents. She adds that visitors from as far away as Europe are finding Hedley, some of them on genealogical quests, putting down remarks in the guest book to this effect: "I came to see where my grandfather worked."

**Gold Operation:** Outskirts of Hedley, both sides of highway, Candorado Mines Ltd heap-leaching operation, to recover gold from old stamp-mill tailings.

**Hedley Cemetery:** North off Hwy 3. Pioneers buried here include Harry Durnford Barnes, who wrote up Hedley's history until 1948 and recorded that the town was named after Robert Rist Hedley, manager of the Hall Smelter in Nelson.

**Corkscrew Rd:** Leaves Hwy 3, 4km east of Hedley. Living up to its name, road is rough and steep, only suited to toughest vehicles. 13km to remains of Mascot mine. Old Nickel Plate mine reopened as an open-pit gold mine. Get permission before walking through Nickel Plate townsite to Mascot's remains. Also wise to ask in Princeton or Keremeos for details on this (rugged) road.

**The Hubcap Ranch:** 9km east of Hedley. 12,000 hubcaps.

**American Railway Rest Area:** 62km east of Princeton. A welcoming little rest area, pungent sage to the left, the swirling Similkameen to the right.

**Cathedral Provincial Park:** 33,272ha; 65 campsites. Turn south off Hwy 3, 63km beyond Princeton, or 5km west of Keremeos. **Ashnola River Rd** (gravel) leads 21km past small ranches to Cathedral Lakes Resort base camp. From here, two choices. First one: drive 1km to parking lot, and hike uphill (within park, 32km of wilderness hiking trails, including part of Centennial Trail to Manning Provincial Park). Second choice: reserve ground transportation with Cathedral Lakes Resort for 4X4 taxi up Jeep Rd. Fully equipped lodge also has cabins. For park info: 499-5848.

Besides the tranquil turquoise Cathedral Lakes, the park offers immense peaks, and bizarre mountain forms like Devil's Woodpile, Stone City, Macabre Tower, and Grimface Mountain. Wildlife includes mountain goats, California bighorn sheep, mule deer, squirrels, pika, golden eagles, hawks. Rainbow, cutthroat trout in lakes and creeks.

**Red Bridge:** On Ashnola River Rd just off Hwy 3. This covered wooden bridge, three spans across the Similkameen, was built about 1907 by Great Northern Railway for its VV&E spur to Princeton. Deep pools below bridge are a delight for swimming.

**Keremeos:** (Pop. 933). 66km east of Princeton. An irresistible stop. Keremeos sits on a bench where valley of Keremeos Creek joins Similkameen River. All around, the mountains (Apex to north, Snowy south, Kobau to east) rising 1,800m to 2,400m.

Village itself, with wood-fronted buildings dating from early 1900s, emits aura of the Old West. Fur trader Alexander Ross was the first white man to show up, in 1813, at what was an ancient native village site. Started out as Hudson's Bay Company trading post in 1860, became a ranching centre; from the 1930s, also developed into a fruit-growing hub.

The village's present site wasn't its first. It had been located twice elsewhere before settling down. Initially it sprang up on what was known as Coleman's Hay Field up on the bench about a kilometre northwest of the present village. Then, following the water supply, it was moved farther west up the banks of the Similkameen River. When the Keremeos Hotel was built in 1906 (later to burn down) on the present-day site, the village was dismantled again and reconstructed around the hotel.

The name Keremeos – from *Keremeyeus*, a Simulkameen Salish word – is moot point. Perhaps it's from a native word meaning flat land cut by water. *The Canadian Encyclopedia* says "wind channel in the mountain." Another favourite, "valley of the winds."

A long growing season first established fruit growing here by 1910. With perhaps 30 individual stands, this town may be "Fruit Stand Capital of Canada." Tender spring asparagus; then cherries, apricots, peaches; finally autumn apples and grapes.

**Keremeos Information:** Infocentre, Box 452, Keremeos, V0X 1N0. 499-5225. In Memorial Park town centre, on Hwy 3.

■ **South Similkameen Museum:** 6th Ave and 6th St. 9-5, May-Oct. In former Provincial Police office and jail. Exhibits include police uniforms, pioneer artifacts.

■ **The Grist Mill and Tea Room:** Upper Bench Rd, 2.5km from museum. May-mid-Oct. Beside Keremeos Creek. Orchard setting. Built 1877. Now restored, only operating water-powered grist mill in BC.

■ **Similkameen Valley Museum:** Main St, 2nd floor of Lower Similkameen Band Office. 499-5528 for hours. Indian tools, dance costumes, photo exhibit.

■ **St Laszlo Vinyards Ltd:** 499-2856. Daily, year-round. Tours and tasting.

**Hwy 3A:** Just east of town centre. North 50km to Penticton. Also, south access to Apex Alpine Ski Resort.

## SIDE TRIP
### on Highway 3A

**Keremeos Columns Provincial Park:** 20ha; no development. North on Hwy 3A for 4km. East at cemetery. Pavement ends; from here, route is on private property: get permission from residents. Hot, steep 8km hike; take water canteens. 30m-high, 100m-wide columnar basalt cliffs formed by volcanic activity 30 million years ago.

**Olalla:** (Pop. 341). 6km from Hwy 3. Diner, grocery store. Local art in Ken Christmas Art Gallery.

**Green Mountain Rd:** 13.5km. Turn northwest on gravel for Apex Alpine Ski Resort, Apex Mountain Provincial Recreation Area, and Nickel Plate Provincial Park. See *US Border to Penticton*, p.126.

**Yellow Lake Rest Area:** 17km. Turn south. Car-top launch. Ice fishing.

**Another Yellow Lake Rest Area:** Other end of 2km Yellow Lake.

**Twin Lakes Rd:** 20.5 km from Hwy 3. Details on White Lake Valley in *US Border to Penticton*, p.125.

**Marron Valley:** Hwy 3A cuts through southern tip of Penticton Indian Reserve 3km beyond White Lake Rd and fringes it again at just before Hwy 97 junction.

**Hwy 97:** 31.5km beyond Keremeos. Details in *US Border to Penticton*, p.124.

### *Return to Highway 3 after Keremeos*

**Cawston:** (Pop. 843). On Hwy 3, 5km south of Keremeos. Named for first homesteader, KL Cawston, whose home was

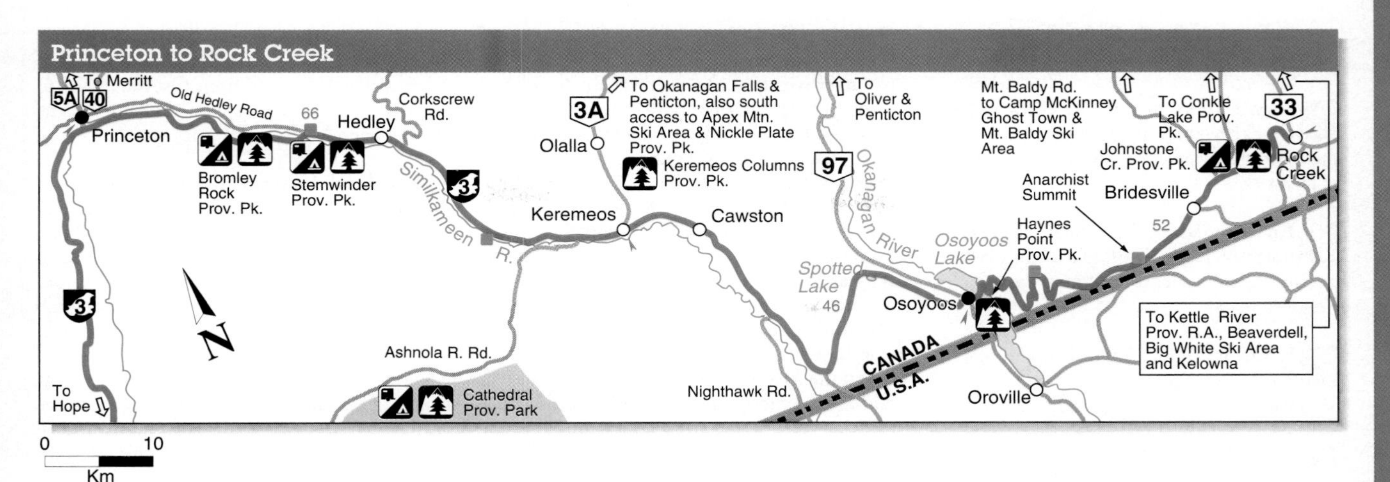


Hudson's Bay Company post. "Best Delicious apples in the world."

■ **Siesta Cactus:** Daly Drive. Daily. 400 varieties of cacti; also cacti for sale.

**Night Hawk Rd:** At beginning of Richter Pass, 24km beyond Keremeos. Leads 10km to border crossing at **Chopaka** and **Night Hawk** native communities. Chopaka, on Canadian side, has historic buildings, early church.

**Richter Pass Summit:** (El 2,234m). 33km beyond Keremeos. Local pioneer was Francis Richter (1837-1910), Bohemian immigrant from 1860, and Hudson's Bay Company employee. Later a big rancher in area.

**Spotted Lake:** 38km beyond Keremeos along Richter Pass, 8km before Osoyoos. Two lakes, first one Spotted Lake. Sometimes spots (called salt plates) not easily identifiable. The 12ha lake's spots are due to deposit of Epsom salts rising to surface. Native people used lake to soak away pain of arthritis and rheumatism. They called it *Klilok* or "Medicine Lake", and believed its waters – mainly Epsom and Glauber's salts with small amounts of baking soda, washing soda, salt, and calcium sulphate – also had healing power on the spirit. A soak brought both youth and wisdom. Warring enemies met in peace here to soothe battle wounds. Lake is on private property.

**Viewpoint:** 41km beyond Keremeos. All of a sudden, Osoyoos, below.

**Hwy 97:** 46km beyond Keremeos. North leads 20km to Oliver and beyond (to Penticton, Kelowna, Vernon).

**Osoyoos:** (Pop. 3,403). At junction of Hwys 3 and 97. For details see *US Border to Penticton*, p.124.

**Banana Farm:** Only one in Canada. Produce sold at Fernandes market on Hwy 3, 1km east of Hwy 97 junction. See *Osoyoos*, p.124.

**Osoyoos Viewpoint:** 11km east of town. Full panoramic view of Osoyoos Lake and the spit cutting it in two.

**Wagon Wheel Ranch:** 28.5km east of Osoyoos. 446-2466. Daily 10-4, evenings by reservation. Trout pond and fallow deer farm.

**Anarchist Summit:** (El 1,233m). 32km east of Osoyoos. Named for settler Richard Sidley who held some "anarchist" views. Still the odd anarchist around. Switchbacks are among province's most memorable. Climb is rewarded with rest area, views of Osoyoos's oasis and surrounding desert. Has been described as "one steep sucker."

**Bridesville:** (Pop. 66). 37km east of Osoyoos. David McBride held water rights to creek from which Great Northern Railway water tanks were supplied. Every third year or so, there's a store or a café. Horse Show and Western Games in August.

**Mount Baldy Rd:** 39km east of Osoyoos, north at **Rock Creek Canyon Bridge** to cross over Rock Creek. An impressive gorge.

## SIDE TRIP
### to Mt Baldy

**Camp Mckinney:** Ghost town 11.5km northwest of Hwy 3 on Mt Baldy Rd. Midst turn-of-the-century ruins, modern-day prospectors are still looking for the mother lode. Between 1887 and 1903, the Cariboo mine here yielded more than 80,000 ounces of gold, making it one of BC's richest pioneer mines. Buried treasure is said to be in the area still, in the form of two large gold bars taken from a mine official at gunpoint. Use caution in the area, don't venture beyond fenced areas. Wise to stop in at Osoyoos Infocentre.

**Mount Baldy Ski Area:** 7km beyond Camp McKinney. Also accessible from Oliver (details in *US Border to Penticton*, p.125).

Continue to Oliver (34.5km along Camp McKinney Rd). Or return with *Log* to Hwy 3 east.

### Return to Highway 3

**Conkle Lake Provincial Park:** 587ha; 26 campsites. 44km east of Osoyoos, north on Johnstone Creek West Rd. Park is 26km north of Hwy 3 junction. 825-4421. Road is extremely rough, not suitable for trailers. But once you get there – a nice spot for a quiet vacation.

**Johnstone Creek Provincial Park:** 38ha; 16 campsites. 44.5km east of Osoyoos on Hwy 3. 825-4421. Waterfall on Johnstone Creek.

**Hwy 33 North:** 51.5km beyond Osoyoos, virtually in Rock Creek. North to Westbridge, Beaverdell, Carmi, Kettle River Provincial Recreation Area, Big White, and Kelowna.

## SIDE TRIP
### along Highway 33

**Kettle River Provincial Recreation Area:** 179ha; 49 campsites. 6.5km north of Rock Creek and Hwy 3 junction. 825-4421. Park has abandoned Kettle Valley Railway right-of-way in its boundaries. Swimming, canoeing (caution advised), fishing. Cross-country skiing.

**Westbridge:** (Pop. 80). 13.5km north of Rock Creek. Farming community at confluence of Kettle and West Kettle rivers. Post office established in 1900, and bridge across West Kettle River – thus the name. Last gas until Beaverdell.

**Beaverdell:** (Pop. 280). 47.5km north of Rock Creek. Beaver dams still common. Beaverdell Hotel, established 1904, exhibits area artifacts and boasts BC's longest continuously operating pub.

**Carmi:** (Pop. 44). 56km north of Rock Creek. Mainly abandoned since 1940s, three decades after short heyday. No amenities or facilities.

**Road to Big White Ski Area:** 96km north of Rock Creek. Turn east, continue for 22km to resort. See *Penticton to Kelowna*, p.131.

**Kelowna:** (Pop. 75,950). At end of Hwy 33, 133km northwest of Hwy 3 junction. See *Penticton to Kelowna*, p.129.

### Return to Highway 3

**Rock Creek:** (Pop. 550). 52km east of Osoyoos. Details in *Kootenay Country*, p.141.

Hwy 3 (the Crowsnest) continues east, through *Kootenay Country*. Next major centres are Castlegar (173km) and Trail (175km).

# US Border to Penticton

## HIGHWAY 97

Hwy 97 originates at the Canada/US border, 4km south of Osoyoos. The 64km highway north from Osoyoos to Penticton is heavily used by rural traffic: fruit trucks and tractors are as common as fruit stands on the two-lane road. It mostly follows the Okanagan River linking the Okanagan Valley's major lakes. Hwy 97 takes you first through near desert along Osoyoos Lake and beyond for startling contrasts between brown tones, stark burnt hills, irrigated strips of green, and the blues of Osoyoos, Vaseux, and Skaha lakes. It's the sort of drive that energizes the senses.

**Haynes Point Provincial Park:** 38ha; 41 campsites. 2km north of border, 2km south of town on Osoyoos Lake. 494-0321. 5ha of this park is a distinctive sand spit reaching three-quarters across soupy-warm Osoyoos Lake. Wade chest-high across the remaining quarter. This was an original shortcut for horses being herded from pioneer Haynes Ranch. Look for Canada's tiniest bird, the Calliope hummingbird, plus yellow-bellied marmots, pygmy horned toads, painted turtles. Some say this is the most popular park in all of Canada. All campsites are beachfront, and locals have named them all. Most treasured is the "Corner Suite." Boat launching, wheelchair access.

**Hwys 3 and 97:** 4km north of border. Main St in Osoyoos is Crowsnest Hwy 3, going west over Richter Pass, 36km to Keremeos, and beyond to the Similkameen Valley and Princeton; east leads 46km to Rock Creek, and beyond to Greenwood and Grand Forks. See *Princeton to Rock Creek*, p.141.

**Osoyoos:** (Pop. 3,403). 4km north of border. Town's name translates roughly to "narrowing of the waters" or "sand bar across" which accurately describes Osoyoos's location, on both sides of a narrowing of the lake, where a neck of land and a bridge joins main part of town with East Osoyoos. A farming and tourism centre. Easy access to the "pocket desert" (see *below*) from Inkaneep campsite off 45th St. (This lakeside campsite is another delight).

Still undergoing renovation, downtown Osoyoos is somewhat reminiscent of Spain. The townspeople decided, in 1974, to capitalize on the Mediterranean-type climate and terrain by decorating the town with white stucco, red tile, decorative brick and wrought iron, creating the "Spanish Capital of Canada."

When it comes to fruit, Osoyoos has everything (even bananas). Starting with cherries (mid-June); then apricots, early peaches, plums, late peaches; apples and grapes in fall. Mid-April is blossom time.

Osoyoos has been oddly pockmarked by glacial activity. There are a number of round, steep-sided holes, called kettles, formed by blocks of ice caught against some obstacle. See *A Short History and Description of Osoyoos*, by long-time resident Dorothy Fraser. Some potholes or kettles are big enough to fish in.

Osoyoos is a leader in creative use of sewage. On West Bench, the greens of the 18-hole golf course and the Desert Park Racetrack are sprinkled with "reclaimed water", an almost-drinkable effluent. In 1964, residents voted to stop putting effluent in lake, and opted for sewage lagoons on West Bench. In 1980, the treated effluent was put to work. Golfers don't notice anything peculiar, though no one is allowed on brilliant green fairways until two hours after sprinkling.

Other unusual features: an operational windmill, built in 1974 by a local Dutch couple (tours). A recent mural on the old packinghouse. And Canada's only banana farm, see *Princeton to Rock Creek*, p.124.

**Osoyoos Information:** Infocentre at Hwy 3 and 97 junction, under a giant Canadian flag. Box 227, Osoyoos, BC, V0H 1V0. 495-7142.

■ **Osoyoos Museum:** Community park; Box 791, Osoyoos, BC, V0H 1V0. Open daily, June-Sept. Bird specimens, Okanagan native artifacts, Inkaneep children's art, history of irrigation, exhibit on BC Provincial Police, established in 1858 during gold rush. Original 1891 log schoolhouse.

■ **Osoyoos Art Gallery:** 8711-76th Ave. 495-2800.

■ **A Touch of Holland:** 1km east of bridge on Hwy 3. 495-7318. Store and bakery open daily, year-round; tours daily, April-Oct. Replica of Dutch windmill built 1816. Grain grinding, bread from stoneground flour.

■ **Banana Farm:** Produce sold at Fernandes market on Hwy 3, 1km east of the Hwy 97 junction.

■ **Wild Rapids Water Slide:** East Lakeshore Dr. 495-2621. Daily, July-Aug.

**Osoyoos Indian Reserve:** (Pop. 516). Osoyoos or Inkaneep band of Okanagan Indian tribe, of Interior Salish linguistic group. Hwy 97 follows eastern boundary of reserve, which extends from Osoyoos Lake to 4km below Vaseux Lake. Inkaneep means "bottom end."

**Federal Ecological Reserve (Pocket Desert):** 100ha. Approaching Oliver, at 7.5km north of Osoyoos, turn east onto Road 22. Travel 1.5km, passing abandoned farm buildings. This is access into a preserved section of the Okanagan Valley's "pocket desert". One of the most unusual geographical regions in Canada. This is the northern tip of the American Great Basin Desert, which extends south to Mexico. Since 1921, irrigation has transformed arid land into productive orchards and vineyards. This ecological reserve is trying to save a bit of the remaining desert from man's efforts. A variety of rare, even unique, plant and animal species are here. There is a burrowing owl re-establishment program. Also turkey vultures, Great Basin spadefoot toads, timid northern Pacific rattlesnake. Bats, mice, lizards, amphibians. Black-headed grosbeak, American redstart, northern oriole, Lewis' woodpeckers, chukar partridge. Antelope bush, sage, rabbitbrush, prickly pear cactus.

**Oliver:** (Pop. 3,743). 20km north of Osoyoos. Established under a land grant in 1921 by BC Premier "Honest" John Oliver as a settlement for veterans from First World War. They built a dam north of town on Okanagan River, and an irrigation canal still in use today (called "The Ditch"). The old Canadian Pacific Railway station, built in 1923, has been restored as a centre for the Arts Council and Chamber of Commerce. The Okanagan River dike offers 18km of hiking and biking. Oliver is the first stop on any Okanagan wine tour, where two of region's four wineries represent BC in Canadian embassies.

World's largest cherry pie, baked here in 1990, was recognized by the *Guiness Book of World Records*. The pie, weighing 17,106kg, was cooked over 6.5 hours within a pit 1.2m deep and 11m in diameter. The townspeople ate it all up.

**Oliver Information:** Infocentre located in the CPR station at 35205-93rd St. First left after traffic light. Box 460, Oliver, BC, V0H 1T0. 498-6321.

**Oliver Airport:** East of Hwy 97 as you enter town. On Airport Rd. 498-8971.

■ **Oliver Heritage Society Museum:** 9728-356 Ave. 498-4027. Open 9-4, Mon-Sat. Exhibits include desert's flora and fauna, early mining artifacts, and the jail from Fairview, the original gold mining settlement in the area (see *below*).

■ **Wine Tours:** A full day to visit Brights, Divino, Gehringer, Okanagan, the four local vintners. Tours, wine tasting May to Sept. Brights and Okanagan open year-round. Ask at infocentre.

■ **Okanagan Valley International Peace Park:** 498-4781. 1km of paved trail along Okanagan River, 20km of prepared road bed, from McAlpine Bridge to Road 22. Ask locally.

■ **Okanagan-Similkameen Cooperative Growers' Association:** East 9th St. 498-3491. Summer tours of Oliver's packinghouse (operating since 1923); also tour of "test" orchard.

**7th St and Hwy 97:** Turn west at stop light onto 7th St; becomes Oliver-Cawston Rd leaving town.

## SIDE TRIP
### to Ghost Town

**Fairview:** 4.5km southwest of Oliver on the steep Fairview Rd. Just a marker now to indicate site of former gold town. Named Fairview for commanding view of Osoyoos Lake below. Up to 500 persons lived here in 1890s: gold was high grade but not plentiful.

**Fairview-White Lake Rd:** North at Fairview for **Willowbrook**, 6.5km. A scenic drive passing the Surprise (Wild Boar) Ranch and an exotic bird aviary.

**Green Lake Rd to Okanagan Falls:** At Willowbrook turn northeast for Okanagan Falls, 13km. Or continue straight on Fairview-White Lake Rd for 7km north to **White Lake Valley** and **Dominion Radio Astrophysical Observatory**, and Hwy 97 junction 8km beyond there. See *Side Trip to White Lake Valley*, below.

### *Return to Highway 97 at Oliver*

**Park Dr (79th St) and Hwy 97:** East on 79th St. Cross bridge over Okanagan River, continue past arena, then right onto 362 Ave which becomes **Camp McKinney Rd. Mt Baldy** is 34.5km southeast. South through Camp McKinney to Hwy 3, 11.5km.

**Mount Baldy Ski Area:** Directions as above. 12 runs over 550m vertical drop accessed by two T-bars. Box 250, Oliver, BC, V0H 1T0. 498-2262.

**Tugulnuit Lake Rd:** 6km north of Oliver on Hwy 97. Leads to Inkaneep Provincial Park and Tugulnuit Lake.

**Inkaneep Provincial Park:** 21ha; 7 campsites. West off Tugulnuit Lake Rd onto Campsite Rd for short distance. 494-0321. Wildlife and bird sightings, canoeing, fishing.

**Tugulnuit Lake:** Return to Tugulnuit Lake Rd and continue south for 2.5km. Spring-fed lake. Can also access from Oliver, turn right on 79th St, left on Harrison Way (370 Ave) to public beach.

**Vaseux Lake:** 14.5km north of Oliver on Hwy 97. Federal wildlife and migratory bird sanctuary. Shallow, weedy lake – 4km long and 1km wide – bordered by sandy beaches. One of Canada's foremost birding areas. Resting point for virtually all birds migrating through here in spring and autumn. Among birds rare or unknown in other parts of Canada are the canyon wren, white-throated swift, and white-headed woodpecker. No powerboats. McIntyre Bluff, named after one of 1862 Overlanders, rises southwest of lake. Vaseux in French means muddy. Fishing for bass.

**Vaseux Wildlife Centre:** 14.5km north of Oliver. Year-round, operated by Vaseux Nature Trust. Write RR 1, Site 6, Comp-26, Okanagan Falls, BC, V0H 1R0. Trails, bird watching blinds, opportunities to see BC's largest herd of California bighorn sheep, and unique flora and fauna of Osoyoos desert biotic zone.

**Vaseux Lake Provincial Park:** 6ha; 14 campsites. 15km north of Oliver. 494-0321. Adjacent Canadian Wildlife Service sanctuary; bird and mammal sightings. Surrounding cliffs are part of California bighorn sheep spring and winter range. Beavers, bats, rattlesnakes. Good canoeing, ice fishing.

**Okanagan Falls:** (Pop. 1,700). 20km north of Oliver, "OK Falls" to locals. Native legend recalls that waters here fell "with the voice of thunder and spray as white as wild cherry blossoms." The twin falls have been reduced to rapids by water management facilities. Good sandy beaches on southern end of Skaha Lake. Tourist and orchard centre.

After running along east side of Vaseux Lake, Hwy 97 cuts through Okanagan Falls before heading up west side of Skaha Lake.

■ **Bassett House Museum:** South end of Okanagan Falls on Hwy 97. A 1909 T Eaton Co catalogue home featuring restored residence of the pioneer Bassett family. Open May-Sept.

■ **Memorial Rose Garden:** On Hwy 97, in front of library and fire hall. Blooming May-Oct.

■ **Wine Tours:** Wild Goose Vinyards and LeCompte Winery.

**Skaha Lake:** Called Dog Lake, but Skaha is prettier Shuswap native name for same thing. Lake is a beautiful deep blue. Name refers to a hard winter when hungry Hudson's Bay Company traders were reduced to eating dogs. Lake stretches from OK Falls (formerly Dog Town) to Penticton, 20km. Skaha originally part of larger Okanagan Lake until silt deposits created the delta on which Penticton now sits.

**Lakeside Rd:** Paved 16km secondary highway circling east side of Skaha Lake past Skaha Lake Marina into outskirts of Penticton. Lakeside alternative to Hwy 97.

**Christie Memorial Provincial Park:** 3ha; day use. At Okanagan Falls town. 200m beach on Skaha Lake. Good swimming.

**Okanagan Falls Provincial Park:** 2ha; 22 campsites. Just past Christie Memorial Park in OK Falls. Turn off south.

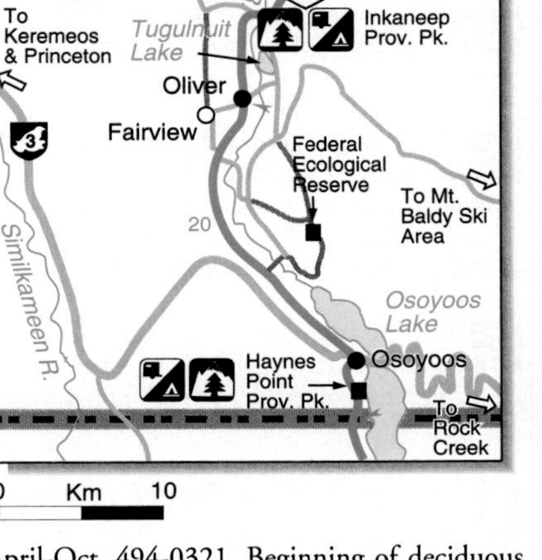


April-Oct. 494-0321. Beginning of deciduous trees above Okanagan River. Large bat population: 14 species found in Okanagan. Wheelchair access.

**White Lake Rd:** 5km north of Okanagan Falls at Kaleden junction. Turn southwest off Hwy 97 to begin 28.5km loop (includes the 11km stretch of Hwy 3A).

## SIDE TRIP
### to White Lake Valley

An interesting and idyllic back-road circle tour within the vee of converging Hwys 97 and 3A. Could take an hour, or you could dawdle a whole day away in this hidden valley.

About 7km down road, before observatory, is first of two golf courses: St Andrew's By-The-Lake, nine holes, par 36.

**Dominion Radio Astrophysical Observatory:** A startling futuristic contrast to White Lake Valley. Guided tours Sunday afternoons July-Aug. Self-guided tours year-round. Call ahead: 493-2277. Visitor centre explains use of radio telescopes for gathering astronomical data. On property is pond-sized White Lake, a haunt for ornithologists. Sandhill cranes, loggerhead shrikes, long-billed curlews, Brewer's sparrows, sage thrashers.

White Lake Ranch, just beyond observatory, is noted for its prize Aberdeen Angus cattle, which are auctioned off Labour Day weekend.

Just before junction to busy Hwy 3A is Twin Lakes Golf and Country Club, a pretty 18 holes.

To complete side trip, return to Hwy 97 at Kaleden junction by turning northeast on Hwy 3A through Marron Valley. By turning southwest on Hwy 3A, you head to Hwy 3 junction at Keremeos. From the Kaleden junction, it's 2km to the pleasant suburban community of Kaleden.

## Return to Highway 97

**Hwy 3A:** 500m beyond White Lake Rd. See *above.*

**Kaleden:** (Pop. 1,118). 7km north of Okanagan Falls on west shore of Skaha Lake. Town's name is a combination of the Greek word *Kalos*, meaning beautiful, and Eden, paradise. Name was picked in a contest in 1909.

**Okanagan Game Farm:** 9km from Okanagan Falls, Box 100, Penticton, BC, V2A 6J9. Daily, year-round. 497-5405. Home to 500 creatures, 125 species: everything from ankoli to zebras, llamas to lions.

**Stop of Interest:** 11km from Okanagan Falls. Viewpoint over Skaha Lake. Picnic table. Sign tells of Salish natives and first white settler, Tom Ellis. More in *Penticton* below.

**Channel Parkway Bypass:** 15km from Okanagan Falls. Turn west at light to skirt City of Penticton. Bypass runs 8km adjacent to Okanagan River on west side of town. Turn off on Green Mountain Rd to Apex ski resort 3km north.

## SIDE TRIP
### to Apex Mountain

**Apex Mountain Provincial Recreation Area:** 575ha. 32km southwest of Penticton on Green Mountain Rd. No park facilities. 494-0321. Views of Manning and Cathedral provincial parks from the 2,000m-plus summits of Mt Riordan, Beaconsfield Mountain, and Apex Mountain.

**Apex Alpine Ski Resort:** Sunniest of Okanagan ski areas, with on-mountain accommodation and RV sites. 36 runs over 600m vertical drop. 12km of groomed, track-set cross-country ski trails. Write 275 Rosetown Ave, Penticton, BC, V2A 3J3. 493-3200. Toll-free BC/Wash/AB: 1-800-663-1900 and 292-8222.

**Nickel Plate Provincial Park:** 105ha; wilderness camping. 494-0321. Park is situated 15km west through Apex resort. Wilderness, sandy beaches on Nickel Plate Lake. Big glacial boulders scattered on north shore. 39km of cross-country trails.

## Return to Highway 97

Return to Hwy 97 at Channel Parkway Bypass, enter Penticton, or head north along Okanagan Lake for Kelowna.

**Penticton:** (Pop. 27,258). 20km north of Okanagan Falls; 60km north of border crossing at Osoyoos. On 3.5km-wide delta between Skaha and Okanagan lakes, Penticton boasts a warm and dry climate. Region's second largest urban centre, and major tourist destination, geared mainly to family vacations. Name is Interior Salish native word meaning "place to live forever."

First settler, Tom Ellis, arrived 1865. In 1877, when the Okanagan tribe was moved to a reserve, he preempted their land east of the Okanagan River, which he soon expanded to 16,000ha on his way to becoming a cattle baron. It was not until Southern Okanagan Land Company purchased the "Ellis Estate" in 1905 that the settlement could begin to grow.

By 1909 when the town was incorporated, a guide to the Okanagan attested to the "perfect system of ditching and fluming...the extensive planting of fruit trees and their equally prolific growth." According to this guide, the new city was thriving. "Touches of ancient and modern British Columbian life (combining the backwoodsman, the prospector and the old 'Prairie Schooner' with the fruit-grower, the steamboatman, and the carriage) are real object lessons in progression." Today Penticton is the key packing, processing, and shipping centre for extensive soft-fruit and apple-growing operations in the southern Okanagan. Some 1,012ha of orchards lie within city limits. During April and May, when its thousands of fruit trees are in full bloom, the city is stunningly beautiful, and awash with fragrance.

Wildlife experts claim that, within city limits, anyone who cares to look can find every species of bird, mammal, and reptile living in the Okanagan-Similkameen. There are plenty of golfing opportunities here, too. (See *below*).

**Penticton Information:** Infocentre at Jubilee Pavilion, 185 Lakeshore Dr, Penticton, BC, V2A 1B7. 492-4103. Extra summer infocentre on Hwy 97, 5km south of Penticton.

■ **Penticton (RN Atkinson) Museum and Archives:** Library and museum complex. 785 Main St. 492-6025 for info or group tours. Mon-Sat, 10-5. Open to 8:30 Tues/Thurs. Interior Salish and pioneer artifacts, natural history, military memorabilia.

■ **SS *Sicamous*:** Beached since 1951 on Okanagan Lake off Lakeshore Dr near exit to Kelowna. 72m sternwheeler plied lake between Vernon and Penticton 1914-1935. Under restoration. Tours in summer. Off-season call 492-6025. SS *Naramata*, historic CPR tug is still afloat and being restored.

■ **Rose Gardens:** Next to SS Sicamous. Hundreds of varieties.

■ **Art Gallery of the South Okanagan:** 11 Ellis St. 493-2928. Tues-Fri, also Sat-Sun afternoons. Lectures, workshops, special events, exhibits.

■ **Bill Barlee's Museum of the Old West:** 954 W Eckhardt Ave. 492-5116. Historical items from all over BC, focusing on mining and ghost towns.

■ **Leir House:** 220 Manor Park Ave. 492-7997. Home of Penticton and District Community Arts Council and a venue for local artists. One of the city's finest historical buildings, built 1927.

■ **Penticton Trade and Convention Centre:** 273 Power St, Penticton, BC, V2A 7K9. 492-6893. Recently expanded: 4,320 seats. Walking distance to 1,200 motel and hotel rooms. Two blocks from lake.

■ **Okanagan River Channel:** 7km man-made channel – a straightening of the Okanagan River – flows from Okanagan to Skaha Lake. Locals love rafting the channel, especially on hot days. Perfection is to sunbathe and swim in the morning at Okanagan Beach, then float down the channel to cap the day at Skaha Beach. Jaycees and Jaycettes have recently spent $800,000 beautifying channel's banks with landscaping, jogging/biking paths. Up to 30,000 people daily float by on summer long weekends; just a few thousand on regular days. Dinghies and tire tubes can be rented at river's head; also transportation back.

■ **Golf Courses:** Penticton Golf and Country Club, 18 holes, W Eckhardt Ave, 492-8727. Pine Hills, nine holes, 1.5km north of city on Hwy 97, 492-5731. Pleasant Valley, nine holes, 2.5km east of Main Street on Penticton Ave, 492-6988.

*O'Keefe Historic Ranch, north of Vernon.*

■ **Wonderful Waterworld Ltd:** 225 Yorkton Ave. 493-8121. Open Victoria Day-Labour Day. 12 water slides, hot bath, RV park.

**Naramata Rd:** Leads from northeast Penticton up east side of Okanagan Lake for 14km. A pretty drive: beautiful rural homes and lakeside vistas. Look for signs to Hillside Cellars and Lang Vineyards. Lang was BC's first farmgate winery, Hillside was the second. See *Penticton to Kelowna* map, p.129.

# SIDE TRIP

## to Naramata

**Naramata:** (Pop. 1,069). 16km north of Penticton on east side of Okanagan Lake. Naramata, with its hauntingly poetic name, was originally founded in 1907 as "East Summerland," but this led to confusion. Village's founder, John Moore Robinson, who established the other Summerland (1902) and also Peachland (1897), finally renamed it. At a seance, he heard the name *Nar-ra-mat-tah* spoken by deceased Sioux Indian chief "Big Moose." The disembodied chief said this was the name of his beloved wife and meant "Smile of Manitou." Robinson was so taken that he adopted the name. Thank you, Mr Robinson. And Big Moose.

Naramata lives up to its name. Pleasing to the eye, it was backdrop to acclaimed movie, *My American Cousin.* It also draws artists, writers.

■ **Naramata Museum:** At 3rd and Ritchie. Open by request. Community history. Ask about Rock Ovens Park. Ovens likely built by Italian railway workers in early 1900s; view of Okanagan Lake.

The road continues north out of Naramata, becoming loose gravel, eventually petering out near borders to **Okanagan Mountain Wilderness Park**, below. This route also provides access to old **Kettle Valley Railway bed**, also below.

**Okanagan Mountain Provincial Park:** 10,542ha; walk-in campsites. Boat or hike in only. East side of Okanagan Lake, opposite Peachland. Access to park boundaries on secondary roads from both Naramata (south) and Kelowna (north). Facilities include horse-loading ramps and 24km of hiking trails. Desertlike wilderness. Rattlesnakes.

**Kettle Valley Railway Bed:** Ask at Kelowna or Penticton infocentres for "unofficial" maps to points of interest along the Naramata-Summerland portion of KVR. The story of this daring Coast-to-Kootenay railway brings Interior BC landscape to life. After 5 years of adventurous construction, service began in 1916, and ended, in stages, 1959 to 1972. The reasons why, and more on KVR and its "engineer extraordinaire", Andrew McCulloch, are under *Hope to Kamloops*, p.174. For more depth, find and read *McCulloch's Wonder*, by Barrie Sanford.

The tracks are torn up, but the bed remains, leading the way to spectacular Okanagan vistas, magnificent trestle bridges crossing deep canyons, tunnels through mountainsides. Plans are in the works for a linear railway park. Meantime, there are no signs or facilities to speak of. Here are directions to set you on your way from Naramata, but do check with those infocentres. From Naramata Rd, turn right onto Smethurst Rd and follow it up the hill until you cross the railbed. Just past here, you can park, and begin your explorations.

From Kelowna, access to the KVR bed requires a city map. Find June Springs Rd and follow it to Little White Forestry Rd – rough, but *usually* passable by *most* vehicles. Drive 4km along Little White Forestry Rd, take first left, park. Here is the railbed; first trestle is 2km northeast. A second access point is via McCulloch Rd, past Gallagher's Canyon Golf Course. Turn right onto Myra Forest Service Rd and follow for 8km to informal parking. First trestles are to the west.

A third access point is via Kelowna's Mission area. Follow Chute Lake Rd. Turn left at Hedeman Rd. Turn right onto Gilliard Forest Service Rd and proceed for 8.5km (the *No Trespassing* sign beside the road applies to the property it sits on, not the road you'll be travelling). When you arrive at a major intersection, you've reached the KVR. From here, a right turn takes you 12km to the Chute Lake Resort; left leads 4km to tunnels and trestles.

For further interest, Back Road from Summerland to Princeton (Hwy 40) traces part of original KVR route (see *Penticton to Kelowna*, p.128, and *Princeton to Rock Creek*, p.121).

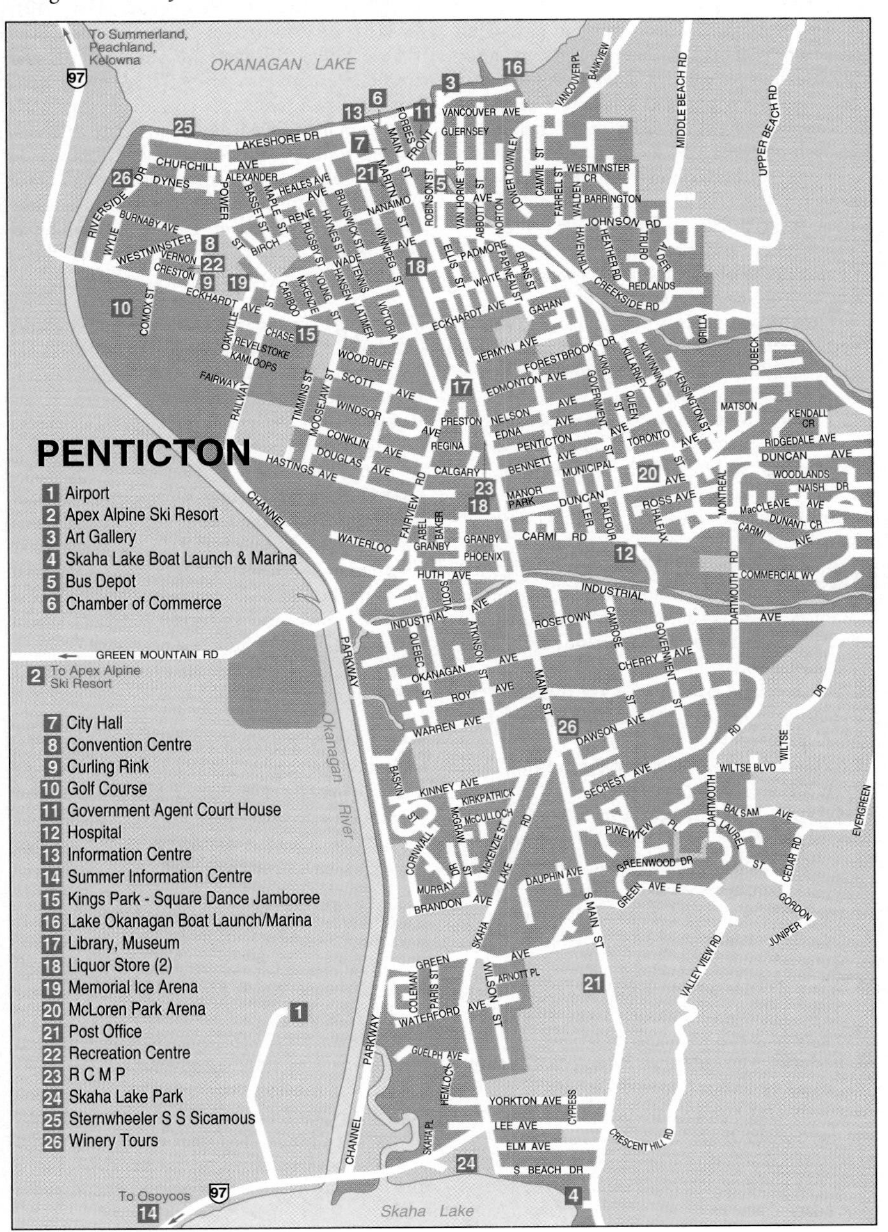


### Return to Penticton

From Penticton, travellers can go north on Hwy 97 to Summerland, Peachland, Kelowna, and beyond. See *Penticton to Kelowna*, following.

# Penticton to Kelowna

## HIGHWAY 97 NORTH

From Penticton, scenic Hwy 97 runs adjacent Okanagan Lake 60km to Kelowna, twisting through the heart of the Okanagan. With orchards lining the route, you drive, in spring, through a fairyland of blossoms; in summer and fall, past a continuing array of fruit stands. Vineyards line the scene, and both commercial and estate wineries offer tasting tours. Back-country parks on both sides of the lake provide a largely untouched wilderness alternative to the busy beach scene along the highway. And this is also Ogopogo Country. The deep 128km Okanagan Lake, carved out by ice-age glaciers, is said to be occupied by Ogopogo, an allegedly friendly prehistoric monster, claimed to have been seen at various times by credible witnesses and now protected under the BC Wildlife Act.

**Penticton:** (Pop. 27,258). 60km north of border at Osoyoos. See *US Border to Penticton*, p.126.

**Hoodoos:** Leaving Penticton on Hwy 97, look west for eerie hoodoo land formations high up on the benchland.

**Kickininee Provincial Park:** 49ha; no campsites. Three lakeside locations, from 8-10km north of Penticton. Day-use, beaches at Kickininee, Soorimpt, and Pyramid. Boat launch at Soorimpt.

**Sun-Oka Beach Provincial Park:** 15ha; no campsites. 10km north of Penticton. Lots of summer fun. Summerland Kinsmen Polar Bear Swim in Jan. Boat launch.

**Prairie Valley Rd:** 12km north of Penticton. To Darke Lake and Eneas Lakes provincial parks.

## SIDE TRIP

### to Provincial Parks

**Darke Lake Provincial Park:** 1,470ha; 5 campsites. 20km northwest on gravel road. 494-0321. In pine and fir forest, nice trout.

**Eneas Lakes Provincial Park:** 1,036ha; no development; limited access on rough road, 4km past Darke Lake Park. 494-0321. Wilderness camping, fishing, and hiking around all four Eneas lakes.

### *Return to Highway 97*

**Summerland:** (Pop. 9,253). 16km north of Penticton on Hwy 97. At head of three fertile valleys – Garnett (north), Prairie (centre), Peach (south) – the District Municipality of Summerland has been under cultivation since the turn of century. After he arrived in 1902, founding father John Moore Robinson advertised to prospective residents: "Heaven on earth with summer weather forever!" His brother, a Baptist minister, came up with the name from the Protestant "Summerland Hymn":

*Let us pass life's golden days*
*Till in gladness and in joy we stand,*
*At the portals of the gates*
*Where that gleaming city waits*
*of the heavenly Summerland.*

As he had done earlier in Peachland, Robinson subdivided Summerland, set up an irrigation system, and then lured long-suffering prairie farmers to paradise and fruit growing.

Robinson patter was echoed by the Board of Trade in 1909: "Summerland has some of the finest fruit soil on the planet. Its land and trees grow in value while you sleep. It has a clean moral record. The magistrate's gloves are white. It has a noble sheet of water for pleasuring."

And Robinson's vision came to pass as his irrigation systems created vivid greens along the sunbaked shores. By 1900, a million fruit trees had been planted and the Okanagan became one of the finest fruit belts north of the 49th parallel.

Today Summerland rivals Kelowna as a major fruit-processing centre in the Okanagan valley. It has a fruit-packing house run by BC Fruit Packers and Beavan's orchard cannery. It's also home of Summerland Sweets, specializing in fruit candies, syrups, and jams.

Downtown storefronts exhibit a Tudor theme, reflecting a restoration program that began in 1977. Note the wrought-iron flower carts outside front doors.

The area is geared for tourists. Lake beaches, two golf courses, one 18 holes. Mutts are even welcomed: Dog Beach, on Lakeshore Dr, has been set aside for man's best friend. The community has taken on a Tudor taste in recent years.

**Summerland Information:** Infocentre, Summerland Chamber of Commerce, 15600 Hwy 97 (at Thompson Rd), north end of town. Box 1075, Summerland, BC, V0H 1Z0. 494-2686.

- **Summerland Museum:** 9521 Wharton St. Afternoons year-round, extended tours July and Aug. 494-9395.
- **Summerland Art Gallery:** Above museum. Open summer weekdays 10-4.
- **Giants Head Park:** On Giants Head Mountain (el 832m), overlooking Summerland. Resembles a man's head. Five-minute walk to summit for views of Okanagan Valley. Summerland's coat of arms shows mountain encircled by sunflowers and motto: "A Giant in Stature."
- **Wine Tours:** Sumac Ridge Estate Winery, on Hwy 97 north out of town. 494-0451. Also 9-hole, par-3 golf course.
- **Federal Agricultural Research Station:** Just south of Trout Creek Bridge on Hwy 97. Methods and equipment developed here for production of more than 100 fruit and vegetable products for use around the world. 494-7711. Interpretive centre open, tours, weekday afternoons, July and Aug. Ornamental gardens open 8am-8:30pm, offer exotic flower beds, rose gardens, and giant weeping willow trees.
- **Trout Creek Canyon Trestle:** Visible from gardens at research station, above. 500m long and 72.5m high, one of the largest steel-girder bridges of its kind in North America. Great views – but too dangerous to walk on. An engineering feat of now-defunct Kettle Valley Railway.
- **Provincial Trout Hatchery:** 13405 South Lakeshore Dr. Daily. Two million rainbow and eastern brook trout raised annually and stocked in 250 lakes in surrounding mountains. 494-0491.
- **Beaven's Orchard Cannery Tour:** 7915 Hespler. 494-9111. On-site sales and tours. Call ahead.
- **Summerland Sweets:** Canyon View Rd. July-Aug: Mon-Fri. 494-0377. Manufacturers of fruit candy, syrups, jams, wine pulp.

**Back Road to Princeton (Hwy 40):** From downtown Summerland, take Prairie Valley Rd west. An adventurous, and scenic alternative to Hwy 97/3A route west; but not a shortcut, as you may hope. It's 90km, mostly paved, but very twisty in spots, tracing route of old Kettle Valley Railway – first visible at small community of Faulder (9.5km). Section from Faulder to Osprey Lake (50km) is rough gravel. Primitive camping at First Bridge (27km), Thirsk Dam (41.5km), and Chain Lake (about 60km).

**Okanagan Lake Provincial Park:** 80ha; 161 campsites. 494-0321. 13km north of Summerland. Sani-station. Boat ramp. International assortment of Russian olive, China elm, Norway maple, Lombardy poplar. Sandy beaches and views.

**Ogopogo's Home:** Viewpoint overlooking Rattlesnake Island and Squally Point on the east side of the lake. 6km past Okanagan Lake Park. Ogopogo is said to make his/her home in an underwater cave just off the point, and monster-watchers claim repeated sightings here. Good views of both Kelowna and Penticton, if Ogopogo doesn't show up.

**Antlers Beach Provincial Park:** 2ha; day use only. 1.5km past Ogopogo's Viewpoint. Both sides of Hwy 97. Good swimming one side; other has Deep Creek and a waterfall. There is a kokanee spawning run at Deep Creek from mid-Sept.

**Peachland:** (Pop. 3,459). 21km north of Summerland, halfway to Kelowna, Peachland faces Okanagan Lake with its back to abrupt rocky bluff. Manitoba newsman and entrepreneur John M Robinson founded townsite in 1897. Robinson (who founded Summerland in 1902, and Naramata in 1907) arrived for mining prospects that didn't pan out. But when he tasted the peaches at dessert at a settler's home, he forgot his mining losses and set about subdividing his benchland into 4ha lots, putting in irrigation and encouraging settlers.

Peachland boasts a new community centre with library. The Peachland Promenade offers a relaxing stroll along the lakeshore. Ponderosa Golf and Country Club, on Hwy 97, 18 holes, full dining. Hardy Falls offers a peaceful nature walk.

**Peachland Information:** Peachland Museum, 5890 Beach Ave, Peachland, BC, V0H 1X0. In summer call museum, 767-3441, or Municipal Office, 767-2647. 5806 Beach.

■ **Peachland Museum:** 5890 Beach Ave. Daily, July and Aug. 767-3441. In former Baptist church, an 8-sided 1910 wood structure. Photos of orchard development.

■ **Wine Tours: Chateau Ste Claire,** Trepanier Bench Rd, 767-3113. Daily tours April 1-Sept 30. **Hainle Vineyards Estate Winery,** also Trepanier Bench Rd. 767-2525. Recently opened. Specialty wines. Summer: Tues-Sun, 10-5. Nov-April: Thurs-Sun, 1-5.

**Princeton Ave:** At Peachland's only stoplight. West to Silver Lake Forestry Centre and Pennask Lake Provincial Park. Pavement peters out into gravel road.

## SIDE TRIP
### to Pennask Lake

**Silver Lake Forestry Centre:** 16km west of Peachland off Hwy 97. Well posted. Princeton Ave to fork in road. Take right fork, to Brenda Mine. Dawn to dusk, all year. 860-6410. Artifacts from logging, construction, harvesting, and fire fighting. BC Forestry Association.

**Pennask Lake Provincial Park:** 244ha; no developed campsites. 55km northwest of Peachland. As above, head west out of Peachland on Princeton Ave. At fork in road, turn left on rough gravel road. A slow, bumpy drive, but okay in summer with a two-wheel drive. Watch out for logging trucks. Picnicking, fishing, canoeing.

### *Return to Highway 97*

**Okanagan Connector (Hwy 97C):** At Drought Hill Interchange, just north of Peachland.

Terminus of major 108km extension of Coquihalla freeway from Merritt. Connector extends freeway from Lower Mainland into heart of the Okanagan Valley, averting circuitous and slower highway routes that dance by the northern and southern extremities of the valley. This straight and fast shortcut reduces six-hour-or-so trip to just four hours. The Coquihalla Hwy has had a major impact not only on Peachland but on the entire Okanagan Valley. For details of route, see *High Country*, p. 177.

**Westbank:** A Kelowna satellite, 10km north of Peachland on Hwy 97. Hwy 97 forks at Paynter's Market. Two lanes running northbound through Westbank are separated by a city block from two lanes southbound.

**Westbank Information:** Infocentre open late May-Sept. Box 571, Westbank, BC, V0H 2A0. 768-3378. At fork in Hwy 97 on northbound road (see *below*).

■ **Westbank Museum:** On southbound part of Hwy 97. June-Aug, Tues-Sat. 768-0110. Travelling north, go one block past fork in highway to Brown St traffic light. Turn left and left again on Hwy 97 southbound for museum and infocentre.

■ **Wine Tours:** Mission Hill Vineyards, Mission Hill Rd. 768-7611. Daily tours May-late fall. A small winery, Mission Hill is concentrating its energies on fine premium wines. Quail's Gate Vineyard Estate Winery, 3303 Boucherie: in an historic setting. 769-4451.

■ **Wild N' Wet:** Water slide, about 1km east of Westbank on Old Okanagan Hwy. 786-7600.

**Westside Rd:** 9km north of Westbank, at last light before floating bridge into Kelowna. North for Bear Creek Provincial Park, Lake Okanagan Resort, Fintry, and Vernon via west side of Okanagan Lake. The windy, paved road joins up with Hwy 97 beyond O'Keefe Historic Ranch and some 12km northwest of Vernon. Vernon is 55km from Kelowna's floating bridge via this route.

## SIDE TRIP
### *to Bear Creek Park and Fintry*

**Bear Creek Provincial Park:** 167ha. 80 campsites, sani-station. 8km north of Hwy 97 junction. 494-0321. A delightfully varied park. Some 10km of hiking and easy walking trails through lakeshore delta and uplands plateau. Creek, with waterfall, winds down a canyon to delta and lakeshore.

This is the spot where, a few years ago, salesman Ken Chaplin took controversial video footage of what he thought was Ogopogo. The international furor brought in experts from everywhere, but when the waters cleared, most biologists agreed that this particular monster was actually a beaver.

Full visitor program. Crimson waters mark the onset of kokanee spawning rituals in Bear Creek (officially Lambly Creek), mid-Sept. Boat launch, wheelchair access.

**Lake Okanagan Resort:** 17km from Hwy 97 junction. Accommodation includes condos, chalets, suites. Riding, tennis, par-3 golf, beach, marina, scuba diving. Casual or gourmet dining, lounge, pub, poolside bar. Year-round. 769-3511, or 1-800-663-3273 (BC and AB).

**Fintry:** (Pop. 24). Some 33km from Hwy 97 on Westside Rd. Charming, tiny settlement on Shorts Creek delta. Beach access.

### *Return to Highway 97*

**Kelowna Floating Bridge:** Bisects Okanagan Lake and continues as Hwy 97 through Kelowna. Built in 1958, opened by Princess Margaret, 640m pontoon structure was North America's first and largest floating bridge. Vast improvement over ferry service that dated from 1904 with the *Skookum*, and later (from 1927) the *Kelowna-Westbank*.

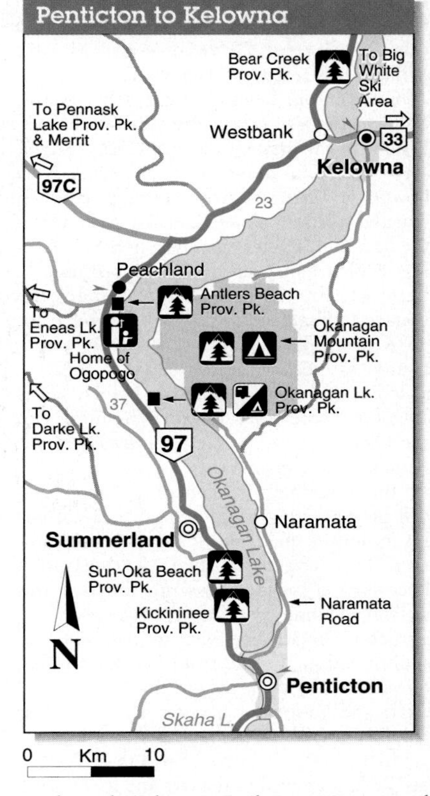


**Kelowna:** (Pop. 75,950; area pop. about 120,000). 60km north of Penticton, on east shore of Okanagan Lake, just over the Floating Bridge. Its first location was slightly inland, called *L'Anse au Sable* or Sandy Cove. In 1892 the townsite survey for incorporation shifted the settlement from Mission Creek out to Okanagan Lake, where supplies and people could be easily ferried by steamboat to points north and south. Thus Kelowna's eminently accessible siting.

Kelowna means grizzly bear. Okanagan natives were amused by one of the early settlers, a rough-hewn and bewhiskered blacksmith, August Gillard, apparently a huge man. They called him *Kim-ach-touch*, or "brown bear", and the name soon applied to both himself *and* his land. But the word was difficult for the white tongue to pronounce, and it gradually mutated into "Kelowna."

Soon after its incorporation in 1892, Kelowna boasted 11 sawmills, three fruit-packing plants and two canneries. Tobacco was an original crop (cigars the product), but the slump after World War One did that one in. This land was destined to yield sweeter things.

Kelowna has long been the Okanagan-Similkameen's largest urban centre, hub of its marketing and distribution activities, focal point of government services. (It is also home to two BC premiers, WAC Bennett – who founded the Social Credit Party in BC and was premier for 20 years – and his son William R Bennett, premier from 1975-86.)

But to folk beyond the peach curtain, Kelowna has always been the City of Summer. It's one of the prettiest of small cities – bright, airy, fresh – a lakeshore community with downtown lakefront parks and sandy beaches, situated midway along the eastern shores of the beautiful, mysterious, flickering and flashing, 128km long lake that has slipped itself in between the Interior Plateau and the Okanagan Highland.

Kelowna has always been a juicy, warm, sunny, sailing/swimming/surfing "regatta" style hotspot, a family summer holiday place. The stress here is on *summer*. Kelowna and the Okanagan as a whole have always meant "summer" to everyone else.

But something is happening. Kelowna is still pretty, sitting in its piece of heaven, but it's no longer small, and it's not just for summer. This long-established vacationland is becoming a rapidly growing tourism and retirement community, an attractive (some say gorgeous) small city with its own style of sophistication. People from afar are finding out about Kelowna, they're investing in real estate and businesses, moving here with their families to live by the lake year-round.

In the last six years, more than 20,000 people have moved to the city and its suburbs, increasing the area population to more than 120,000. Kelowna itself has grown by 38 percent. Of course this has brought an onslaught of development, road congestion, and enough growing pains to tax the talents of any municipal planner. "It's just like California," sighs one resident.

Partly responsible for this growth spurt was the completion in October 1990 of the Peachland Connector from the Coquihalla freeway. Greater Vancouver now lies within four hours of Kelowna. Some families are even commuting, working four days in Vancouver and returning to the Okanagan for three-day weekends.

Also responsible – isn't praise grand! – is a spate of national publicity extolling the valley's lifestyle, climate, and comparatively low real estate prices. In 1991, *Chatelaine* magazine named Kelowna one of Canada's 10 best places to live (Penticton topped the list the next year). People from metropolises like Vancouver and Toronto learned there were profits to be made in selling their high-priced homes and moving to the Okanagan where, almost as a bonus, life is so pleasant.

Kelowna is also surprisingly central these days. It is 454km from Vancouver, and 623km from Calgary, and Kelowna's airport – third busiest in BC – is less than an hour from either. And Kelowna is activity-oriented: there's access to all water sports, sailing, rowing, canoeing, houseboating, wind surfing, waterskiing, para-sailing. Indoor and outdoor racquet courts are located throughout the city. There's a good range of restaurants and nightclubs. For skiers, Big White resort is only 55km from Kelowna on Hwy 33, which follows the old Kettle Valley Railway grade.

Cultural life is lively. Theatre, music, arts, ballet, and crafts all come under the umbrella of the Kelowna and District Arts Council. The 900-seat Kelowna Community Theatre is home of Sunshine Theatre and the Okanagan Symphony, both offering special summer programs. Kelowna's newspaper is *The Daily Courier*.

**? Kelowna Information:** Infocentre at 544 Harvey Ave (Hwy 97), Kelowna, BC, V1Y 6C9. Call 1-800-663-4345 in BC or AB, 861-1515 in Kelowna.

■ **Kelowna Centennial Museum and National Exhibition Centre:** 470 Queensway. 763-2417. Variable hours, July-Aug; Sept-June, Tues-Sat. Interior Salish pit dwelling, 1861 trading post, Kelowna's first radio station.

■ **Kelowna Art Gallery:** 470 Queensway. 762-2226. Same hours as museum. International, national, and local art. Growing collection of BC art.

■ **City Park:** 14.5ha. Along 1km of lakeshore – from foot of floating bridge to large sculpture, *The Sail*, by Dow Reid at foot of Bernard Ave.

■ **Father Pandosy Mission:** Southeast of city centre at corner of Benvoulin and Casorso roads. Daily, April-Oct. Founded in 1859 by Oblate priest, Father Charles Pandosy, mission served both native Okanagan people and white settlers. Restored from original log buildings, the mission, chapel, and schoolhouse provide a vivid illustration of Okanagan Valley life a century ago. Declared an official heritage site in 1983 following discovery of Father Pandosy's grave in abandoned cemetery near his mission.

■ **BC Orchard Industry Museum:** 1304 Ellis St. 763-0433. Summer: Mon-Sat. Winter: Tues-Sat. This satellite of Kelowna Museum tells tale of BC's orchard industry. Exhibits deal with all aspects of orchards; also a re-created packing plant and "hands-on" area. Apple Fair in Oct.

■ **Wine Tours: Calona Wines**, 1125 Richter St, 762-9144. Daily tours, year-round. Okanagan's biggest and oldest (since 1932) winery. **St Hubertus Vineyards:** 5205 Lakeshore Rd, 764-7888. **Cedar Creek Estate Winery**, 5445 Lakeshore Rd, 764-8866. An estate winery in a picture-book setting.

■ **Okanagan Orchard Tours:** 2755 KLO Rd, East Kelowna. 762-8092 or 860-2462. One-hour tour of Canada's largest orchard and vineyard. Open May-Sept.

■ **Sun-Rype Products Plant Tours:** 1165 Ethel St. 470-6417. Weekdays, June-Sept. Fruit-processing plant makes commercial juices, pie fillings, apple sauce. Wear close-toed shoes.

■ **Lion's Park/Sutherland Hills Nature Walks:** Off Springfield and Benvoulin roads. Pastoral setting. Sept 15-Oct 15 is largest spawning run of local kokanee. Guided tours at this time.

■ **Kasugai Gardens:** Tucked behind Bennett Fountain, on Queen St. Japanese garden complete with boulder-ringed pond, waterfall, stone garden. Kasugai, in Japan, is Kelowna's sister city.

■ **Guisachan Heritage Park:** 1060 Cameron Ave. Part of one of Kelowna's earliest ranches, pre-empted by John McDougall in 1861; then home of Lord Aberdeen, Governor General of Canada, 1893-1898. Perennial gardens with plants all labelled. Restaurant.

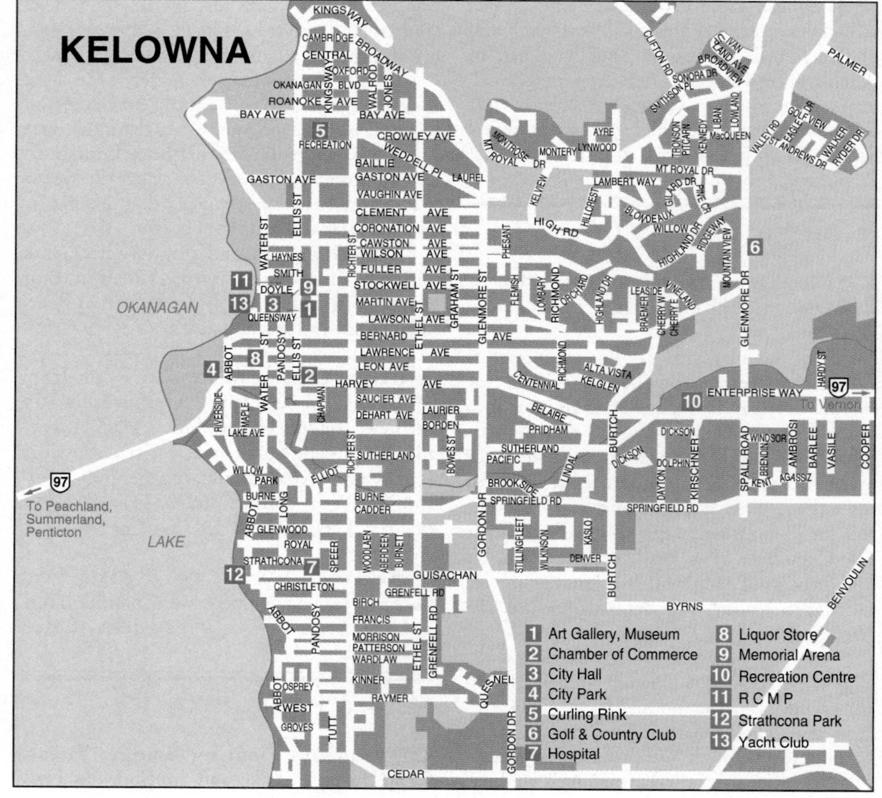

■ **Bertram Creek Regional Park:** End of Lakeshore Rd. Beaches, picnics.
■ **Knox Mountain Nature Park:** North end of Ellis St. Hiking and picnicking. At foot of Knox Mountain is a diving park called **Paul's Tomb**, where a 522kg, 7m-long model of Ogopogo lurking 8m below the surface, awaits adventure-seeking divers.
■ **Honey Farm Vacation Tours:** 2910 Glenmore Rd. 762-8156. May-Sept; call ahead for tours anytime. Honey tasting, bird-watching, canoe trips.
■ **Okanagan Butterfly World:** 1190 Stevens Rd. 769-4408. Daily April-Oct, 10-4. Tropical butterflies flying free in the gardens; all stages of life cycle displayed.
■ **Wild Waters, Flintstone's Bedrock City, Scandia:** Water slide and amusement parks on Hwy 97, about 10km north of floating bridge.
■ **Old MacDonald's Farm:** Hwy 97 South at Westbank. 768-5167. Petting zoo and amusements. Daily May-early Sept.
■ **Pioneer Country Market and Museum:** Benvoulin Rd, daily. 762-2544. Where Onion King John Casorso produced record-breaking crop in 1909. Grape-vine baskets, wonderful jellies.

**Hwy 33 to Big White:** Turn off Hwy 97 6.5km after it crosses Kelowna's floating bridge and after it goes through downtown as Harvey Ave.

## SIDE TRIP
### to Big White

**Big White Rd:** 33km along Hwy 33 (Black Mountain Rd). Turn east 24km for ski resort.

**Big White Ski Resort:** 20km to lower-chair. El 2,317m, highest resort in BC. Long season with more than 550cm of light, dry snow. 52 runs on vertical drop of 625m. More than 25km of cross-country trails. Write: Box 2039, Stn R, Kelowna, BC, V1X 4K5. Toll-free from BC or AB, 1-800-663-2772, or 765-3101.

### Return to Highway 97

Hwy 97 now proceeds on the east side of Okanagan Lake northwards through Vernon to access Trans-Canada Hwy (1) at three locations: Sicamous, Salmon Arm, and Monte Creek. See *Kelowna to Sicamous*, next, or *Index*.

## Kelowna to Sicamous

### HIGHWAYS 97 and 97A

The 47km of Hwy 97 between Kelowna and Vernon slices between Okanagan Lake on the west, and a glacial lakes chain – Ellison (or Duck), Wood, Kalamalka, and Swan lakes – on the east. All dazzlers. Beyond Vernon, the highway travels north 75km between the rolling hills of the Thompson Plateau in the west, and Monashee Mountains in the east. Dairy, vegetable, hay, and alfalfa farms begin to dominate the landscape.

**Kelowna:** (Pop. 75,950). At the junction of Hwys 97 and 33. 60km north of Penticton, 47km south of Vernon. See *Penticton to Kelowna*, p.129.

**Kelowna Airport:** 8km beyond Hwy 33 junction in Kelowna, east of highway.

**Duck Lake Pullout:** 4km beyond the airport.

**Hiram Walker and Sons Ltd Distillery:** Between northern outskirts of Kelowna and Winfield, 5km north of airport on Jim Bailey Rd. Take Beaver Lake Rd, east off Hwy 97 for less than 1km; turn south onto Jim Bailey. Tours May-Aug. Phone ahead: 766-2431 or 763-4922. No children under 12; no open-toed shoes.

**Winfield:** Small community on northern edge of Kelowna, 6km north of airport.
■ **Gray Monk Cellars Estate Winery:** West off Hwy 97 in Winfield at Berry Rd (second set of lights), 4km to Camp Rd. Well-signed. 10-5, tours every hour on the hour from 11-4, mid-May through Oct. Winter hours vary. Call ahead: 766-3168.
■ **Okanagan Bicycle Tours:** 763-9993. Tours to Kettle Valley Railway beds.

**Okanagan Centre Rd:** 3km north of Winfield at south end of Wood Lake.

**Okanagan Centre:** (Pop. 360). On Okanagan Centre Rd about 3km west of Hwy 97. Situated magnificently on hillsides overlooking Okanagan Lake. Perfect orchard and vineyard country.

**Wood Lake:** Between Okanagan Centre and Oyama, Hwy 97 hugs this lake named for pioneer Thomas Wood. This distinctly rectangular lake, 6.5km-by-1.5km, offers good fishing for Kokanee and rainbow trout.

**Oyama:** (Pop. 1,332). 6.5km north of Okanagan Centre Rd on land bridge between Wood and Kalamalka lakes. Just east of Hwy 97. An orchard and fruit-packing community named after Prince Iwao Oyama (1842-1916), a Japanese field marshall.

**Kalamalka Lake Viewpoint:** 8km beyond Oyama. Fabulous view of "Lake of a Thousand Colours." When illusive (and legendary) "Kalooey" bears of Kalamalka swish their tails in the waters, they leave behind brilliant pools of emerald green. The lake is actually named after the colourful and amorous Indian Chief Kalamalka who lived at the lake's head.

Panoramic view takes in Coldstream Valley and mountains stretching forever eastward. At Kalamalka Lake's north end is a golden sandy shore.

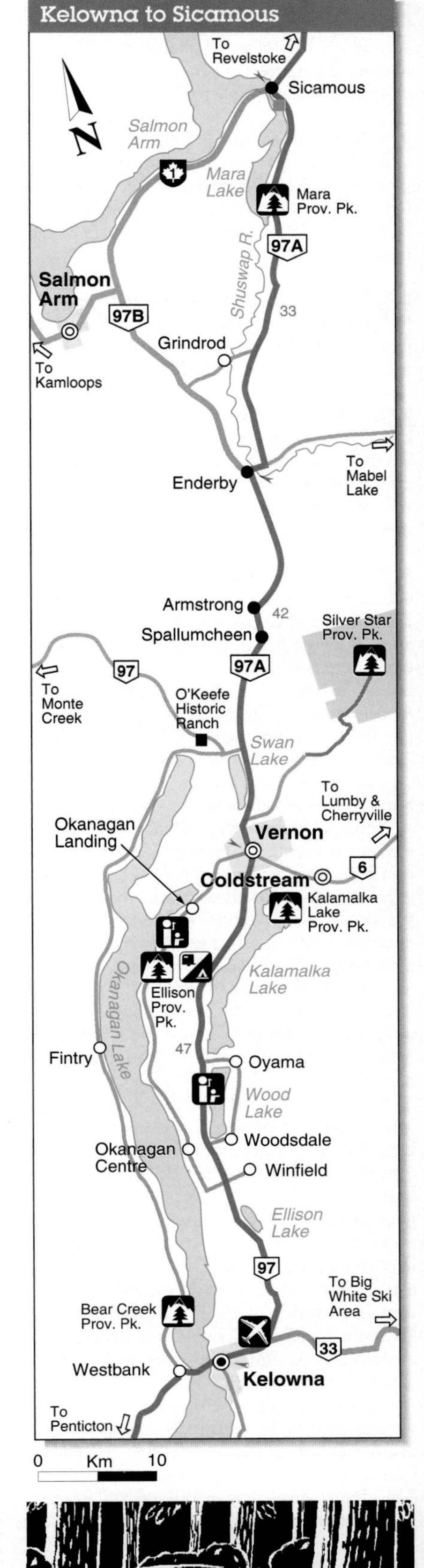

**College Way:** 1km past viewpoint. Turn east, follow Kickwillie Loop to Westkal Rd, which becomes Kalamalka Rd. Leads to **Kalamalka Lake Provincial Park**. A kickwillie is an ancient-style native pit-house.

**Kalamalka Lake Provincial Park:** 978ha; day use, no camping. Follow signs. 494-0321. Nesting and feeding habitat for a wide variety of birds. Brilliant show of wildflowers. Wheelchair access. Beware of rattlesnakes!

**Predator Ridge Golf Resort:** 9km north of Oyama, take Bailey Rd exit to Commanage Rd. Follow Commanage Rd past the Vernon Fish and Game Club. 542-3436.

**Kekuli Bay Provincial Park:** 57ha, day use, no camping. One of the best boat launches on Kalamalka Lake. 3km beyond Bailey Rd, take Kalamalka Lakeview Dr, then Highridge Rd. 3km to park. Very busy mid-summer weekends.

**Vernon:** (Pop. 23,514). 10km north of Kekuli Bay turnoff; 47km north of Kelowna on Hwy 97. Picturesque Vernon sits at confluence of four valleys – Priest, Pleasant, Coldstream, and Mission. Pleasant Valley is the main one, stretching north through Armstrong and Enderby to the houseboat capital of Canada at Sicamous, a distance of about 75km. Vernon is also bounded by three spectacular lakes – Okanagan, Kalamalka, and Swan – with endless sandy beaches.

Incorporated in 1892, Vernon is the oldest city in the province's Interior. The city's location is the key to its history. Lakes here provided more than transportation, they allowed the large-scale irrigation which, when introduced in 1908, transformed the region into an agricultural Shangri-la.

The city was named in 1887 for George Forbes Vernon, Chief Commissioner of Lands and Works. Natives had called this area *Hun-cul-deep moose-chin* or "jumping-over place."

In the 1860s, about the time Forbes Vernon and his brother Charles were getting established, Cornelius O'Keefe was driving cattle from Oregon to the Cariboo to provide beef for gold-seeking miners. Finding bunchgrass at the head of Okanagan Lake "higher than a horse's belly," he paused to wonder why he was driving cattle when he could raise cattle right where he was. Natural meadows were ideal cattle and sheep pasturage. By 1867 O'Keefe had preempted land, brought in breeding stock, and set to work to become a formidable cattle baron.

The region's first commercial orchards were planted by Lord Aberdeen in 1891. The Scottish emigre and future governor general of Canada (1863-1898), with the eccentric Lady Aberdeen, bought 5,367ha from Forbes Vernon and renamed it Coldstream Ranch. At the time a thriving ranch with some 2,000 head of cattle, 80 horses, plus poultry and hogs, Coldstream was to become for many years one of the largest producers of fruit in the British Empire.

In 1917 alone (more than a quarter of a century after Lord and Lady Aberdeen had left the North Okanagan behind) some 800 boxcars of apples and 200 of miscellaneous fruit, valued at $1 million, were shipped. Vernon today is on the northern edge of the Lake District fruit belt, with a climate both cooler and wetter than that of the area to the south. This limits growing to hardier types of apples, prunes and plums, as well as hay and alfalfa.

Fishing is especially good around Vernon, where more than 100 lakes are within an hour's drive of the city. Walking tours in the area include sawmills in Lumby and Okanagan Brewery. Some of the many local artists are happy to receive visitors who join walking tours organized by the Chamber of Commerce.

**Vernon Information:** Travel Infocentre at 6326 Hwy 97 N, Box 520, Vernon, BC, V1T 6M4. 542-1415. Year-round. One extra seasonal infocentre open May-Sept.

■ **Greater Vernon Museum and Archives:** Civic Centre Complex, 3009-32nd Ave. Mon-Sat. 542-3142. History of area, plus district archives and research facility.

■ **Vernon Public Art Gallery:** Above museum and archives in Civic Centre. Mon-Sat. 545-3173. Exhibits.

■ **Polson Park:** 25th and 132 streets. Japanese gardens are worth seeing.

■ **Atlantis Waterslides:** 5km north of Vernon off Hwy 97. 549-4121. Slides, hot tub, RV parking, mini-golf. June-Aug.

■ **O'Keefe Historic Ranch:** 12km north of Vernon on Hwy 97. See *Monte Creek to Cherryville*, p.134.

■ **Walking Tours:** Maps available from Chamber of Commerce or infocentre.

■ **Okanagan Spring Brewery Tour:** 2801-27A Ave. 542-2337. Brewing Fridays. Call ahead.

**Hwy 6 East:** In Vernon, at 25th Ave, 3km north of College Way junction. Leads 50km east to Cherryville. See *Monte Creek to Cherryville*, below. Heading west Hwy 6 (25th Ave), also called Okanagan Landing Rd, leads short distance to Okanagan Landing and Ellison Provincial Park.

**Okanagan Landing:** (Pop. 1,406). South of Vernon, on Okanagan Lake. Follow 25th Ave about 6km west out of Vernon. Becomes Okanagan Landing Rd.

Okanagan Landing was northern terminus for rail barges and lake steamers until 1936 when roads and rails ended things. Here Captain TD Shorts launched area's first steamer in 1886. SS *Sicamous* steamed in here from her last voyage.

■ **Paddlewheel Park:** Commemorating days of steamers and paddle-wheels on Okanagan Lake. SS *Naramata* on display.

**Ellison Provincial Park:** 200ha; 54 campsites. 10km southwest of Okanagan Landing along Okanagan landing Rd; east shore of Okanagan Lake. 494-0321. Small boat launch 2km north of park entrance: Full facility 8km north. Six archaeological sites; visitor programs.

■ **Underwater Dive Area:** Snorkelling, scuba diving. Equipment rentals: 549-2040.

**Silver Star Rd:** 2.5km north of Hwy 6 junction in downtown Vernon. Turn east to hot springs and ski area.

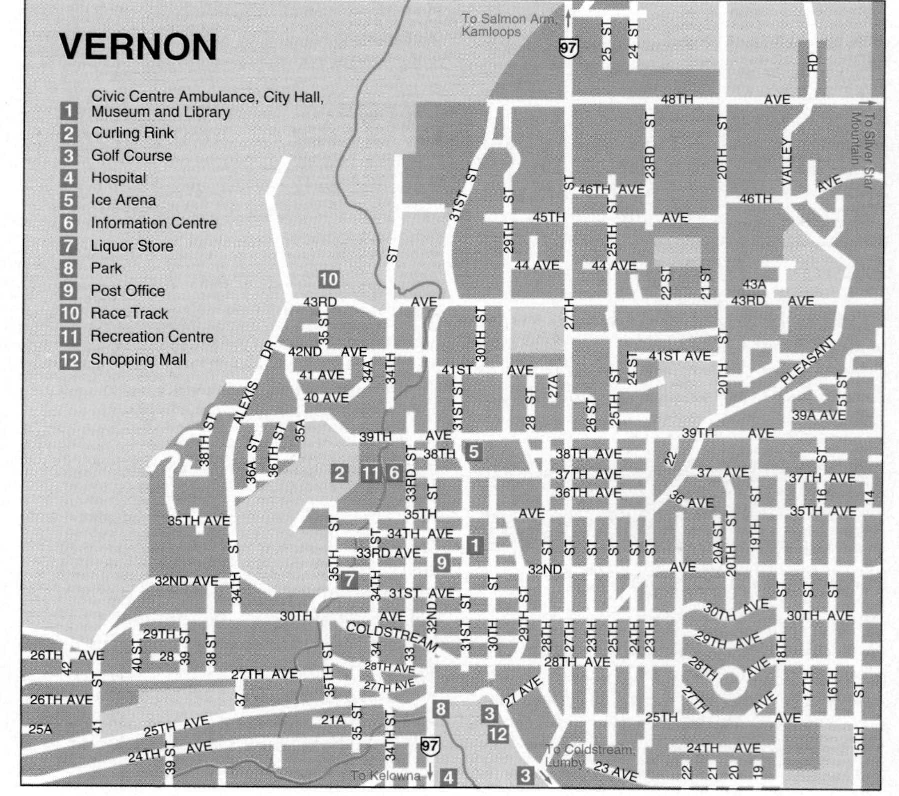

## SIDE TRIP
### to Skiing at Silver Star

**Silver Star Ski Resort:** On Silver Star Rd, 17.5km east of Hwy 97. Write Box 7000, Vernon, BC, V1T 8X5. 542-0224. Toll-free (in western Canada) 1-800-663-4431 for reservations year-round. Most northerly ski area in region (some call this "a poor man's Whistler"), with 55 runs on 485m vertical drop. North America's longest detachable quad chairlift travels 3km. Full resort facilities with accommodation, restaurants, outdoor hot tubs. Night skiing. 8km of groomed cross-country trails which connect to vaster network of trails in recreation area cited below.

In summer, resort features Silver Star, a turn-of-century mining town. Chairlift carries sightseers up 300m for views from summit of Silver Star Mountain, mountain biking and hiking in alpine meadows.

**Silver Star Provincial Park:** 8,714ha. 2km beyond Silver Star Ski Resort on Silver Star Rd. Day use only. Sovereign Lake area offers about 80km of cross-country ski trails; 25km of snowmobile trails.

### Return to Highway 97

**Swan Lake:** Hwy 97 follows lake for 3km beginning 2.5km north of Silver Star Rd junction. Summer infocentre. A fishing and boating lake only (no beach). Public boat launch halfway down east shore.

**Hwy 97 and 97A:** "Swan Lake Junction" is 4km north of Swan Lake, 9km north of Vernon. Hwy 97 turns west for Trans-Canada Hwy 1 and Kamloops via Monte Creek. See *Monte Creek to Cherryville*, following. This *Log* follows Hwy 97A towards Sicamous.

### Highway 97A

**Okanagan Bobslide:** About 500m north of Swan Lake Junction. "Endless lift" system operates Olympic-style bobslides on 720m of stainless steel track. Also go carts, gold panning. Daily March-Oct. 542-0104 or 524-2997.

**Spallumcheen:** (Pop. 4,719). 4km north of Swan Lake Junction. Spanning the breadth of Spallumcheen Valley surrounding Armstrong: more than 26,000ha of prime mixed agricultural land. Scenic drives, good hiking, snowmobiling.

**Spallumcheen Information:** Infocentre on Smith Dr in Armstrong. Write Box 118, Armstrong, BC, V0E 1B0. 546-8616, off-season 546-8155.

**Armstrong:** (Pop. 3,200) On Hwy 97A, 7km north of Swan Lake Junction. Geographic and commercial centre of beautiful Spallumcheen Valley, rich agricultural area. Named for EC Heaton Armstrong, head of London bank that floated bonds for the Shuswap and Okanagan Railway in 1892. Today known for its cheese, and for Caravan Theatre, Canada's only itinerant band of professional thespians.

**Armstrong Information:** Infocentre on Smith Dr. Write Box 118, Armstrong, BC, V0E 1B0. June-Sept. 546-8616. Off-season 546-8155.

■ **Armstrong-Spallumcheen Museum, Archives and Art Gallery:** Railway Ave. Thurs-Mon, June-Sept. Weekends in winter. 546-8318. Area history exhibits feature railway, agriculture, turn-of-the-century lifestyle.

■ **Armstrong Cheese Factory:** Two blocks north of museum on Pleasant Valley Rd. Viewing window affords good view of factory activity, plus video and slide display. Cheese-making days are Sat-Mon-Thurs, depending on milk supply. 546-3084.

■ **The Olde School House:** 546-9593. Mainland BC's oldest school house. Now serves lunches and afternoon teas. Fresh strawberries and fruits in season with Devonshire cream.

■ **Canoga Carriages:** 546-3824. A cance to view the building and restoration of horse-drawn carriages.

**Enderby:** (Pop. 2,128). 13km north of Armstrong. At 610m, Enderby Cliffs on the east shore of the Shuswap River dominate townsite. Rock face picks up surprising colour, especially at sunset. Shallow, slow Shuswap River running from Enderby to Mara Lake is popular route for kayakers and houseboat vacationers. Local dairy ranchers ship their milk products south to Armstrong for cheese processing.

**Enderby Information:** Infocentre on Railway Ave. Write Box 1000, Enderby, BC, V0E 1V0. 838-6727.

■ **Enderby and District Museum:** 901 George St, Hwy 97, City Hall complex. 838-7099. Mon-Sat. Area history; local art in April.

**Road to Mabel Lake:** North end of Mabel Lake can be reached by 35km road east out of Enderby. Lake also accessed from south on Hwy 6. See *Monte Creek to Cherryville*, following.

**Hwy 97B:** Hwy 97A forks 6km north of Enderby. Hwy 97B travels northwest 15km to Trans-Canada Hwy junction and Salmon Arm. Hwy 97A continues north, to Sicamous.

**Grindrod:** (Pop. 421). 4km north of Hwys 97A and 97B junction on the Shuswap River. Named for first inspector of telegraphs on Canadian Pacific Railway in BC.

**Mara Provincial Park:** 5ha; day use. On Mara Lake Rd, 13km beyond Grindrod on Hwy 97A, east side of Mara Lake. Green forest and lush cattle pasture herald changing climate at top of Okanagan region. Archaeological site, boat launch.

**Mara Lake Rest Area:** 7km beyond park. On lakeshore.

Hwy 97A continues 15km to Trans-Canada Hwy 1 junction at Sicamous – 230km north of the Canada-US border.

**Sicamous:** (Pop. 2,501). About 7km beyond Mara Lake rest area. On Hwy 1 at junction of Hwy 97A. For details see *High Country*, p.169.

*Hot-Air Balloon Rendezvous at Armstrong, in the Okanagan.*

## Monte Creek to Cherryville

### HIGHWAY 97 and HIGHWAY 6 (East)

This short 140km trip juxtaposes two distinct north Okanagan-Similkameen landscapes, the golden hills of ranchland, and the green country beyond. At the outset, Hwy 97 at Monte Creek borders on the High Country that encompasses Kamloops and the Thompson River valley. This is horse country, where ranching is the mainstay. Cattle ranches dominate the landscape between here and Vernon. The greener landscape on Hwy 6 east of Vernon supports forest and tree-fruit industries, petering out at the Monashee Mountain peaks that form the boundary between BC's Okanagan-Similkameen and Kootenay regions.

**Monte Creek:** (Pop. 65). At the junction of Hwys 1 and 97. 30km east of Kamloops, and 85km northwest of Vernon. Stop of interest near the railway station recalls the infamous "gentleman bandit," Bill Miner, who netted less than $15 in a 1906 Canadian Pacific Railway train hold-up. A feature film, *The Grey Fox*, tells his life story.

**Monte Creek Rest Area:** 2.5km beyond Monte Creek.

**Monte Lake:** (Pop. 68). 17km beyond Monte Creek, north end of lake. Farming community with accommodation, some services.

**Douglas Lake Rd:** Leads south, 26km beyond Monte Creek. Mostly unpaved road travels 80km through cattle country. Passes by **Douglas Lake Ranch** en route to **Quilchena** on **Nicola Lake**, Hwy 5A. For over 100 years, the Douglas Lake Cattle Company has operated its 200,000ha ranch, largest in Canada. See *High Country*, p.183.

**Westwold:** (Pop. 369). Small service centre about 1.5km beyond Douglas Lake Rd. First called Grande Prairie, changed to avoid confusion with Alberta town of the same name.

**Pinaus Lake:** 6km east of Westwold. 8km south on Pinaus Lake Rd. Rainbow trout. Ice fishing. Campground.

**Falkland:** (Pop. 361). 10km east of Pinaus Lake Rd at junction of Hwy 97 and Chase-Falkland Rd, leading to community of Chase on Hwy 1. Named for Colonel Falkland FGE Warren, a friend to settlers here.

**Silvernails Rd:** 1.5km east of Falkland. North off Hwy 97. 6km to start of lakes: **Bolean**, **Blair** (or Arthur), and **Spa**. Rainbow trout, ice fishing. Cabins and campground.

**Una Rest Area:** 10km beyond Silvernails Rd.

**Salmon River Rd:** 6km east of rest area. Turn north for picturesque 35km route along Salmon River to Hwy 1 at Salmon Arm.

**Westside Rd:** 13km beyond Salmon River Rd. Travels west shore of **Okanagan Lake**. See *Penticton to Kelowna*, p.129.

**O'Keefe Ranch and Interior Heritage Society:** On Hwy 97, about 1km beyond Westside Rd. Near northern tip of Okanagan Lake. Mid-May-Thanksgiving. 542-7868. One of first ranches in area, founded in 1867 by Cornelius O'Keefe. The 8,094ha ranch became a major cattle empire. Restored buildings include a Roman Catholic church, general store, post office, O'Keefe Mansion, and Cowboy Ranching Gallery (a museum with guns and saddles and other cowboy stuff).

**Swan Lake Bird Sanctuary:** About 4km east of O'Keefe Ranch (just west of Hwy 97A junction). Swampland at north end of lake is protected area for feathered folk. Undeveloped, but fine birding. White geese, swans, herons.

**Hwy 97A:** At Swan Lake – locally "Swan Lake Junction." This *Log* follows Hwy 97 south to Vernon, then Hwy 6 from there. Hwy 97A leads due north from here, to **Armstrong** and **Sicamous**. See *Kelowna to Sicamous*, p.133.

### Highway 97 to Vernon

**Vernon:** (Pop. 23,514). 9km south of Hwys 97 and 97A junction. Details, p.132.

**Hwy 6:** In downtown Vernon. Leads east 51km to **Cherryville**, and beyond to **Nakusp**.

### East on Highway 6

**Kalamalka Lake Provincial Park:** 978ha; day use, no camping. 1km east of Hwy 97 junction, turn south off Kalamalka Rd onto Postil Dr, then right onto Kidston Rd. Follow park signs. 494-0321. Nesting and feeding habitat for a wide variety of birds. Brilliant show of wildflowers. Wheelchair access. Beware of rattlesnakes!

**Coldstream:** (District Municipality – Pop. 7,999). About 7km east of Vernon on Hwy 6. The Vernon brothers, Forbes and Charles, first ranched here before selling to Lord and Lady Aberdeen during the 1890s. Still one of the biggest ranches, producing beef and tree fruit. Ranch not open to public.

Coldstream was home of naturalist, Anglican priest, and schoolteacher, Reverend Austin Mackie (1879-1965). One of his pupils died from a rattlesnake bite in the 1920s, so he waged serious war against the rattlesnake population, killing thousands, bringing them near extinction in some places. He gave names such as Vatican Den to the serpents' lairs.

**Lumby:** (Pop. 1,265). 17km east of Coldstream, on Hwy 6. A beautiful location at junction of three valleys: the Trinity, Creighton, and Coldstream. Gateway to the **Monashee Mountains** and region's lumber

*Grapes on the vine, Okanagan Valley.*

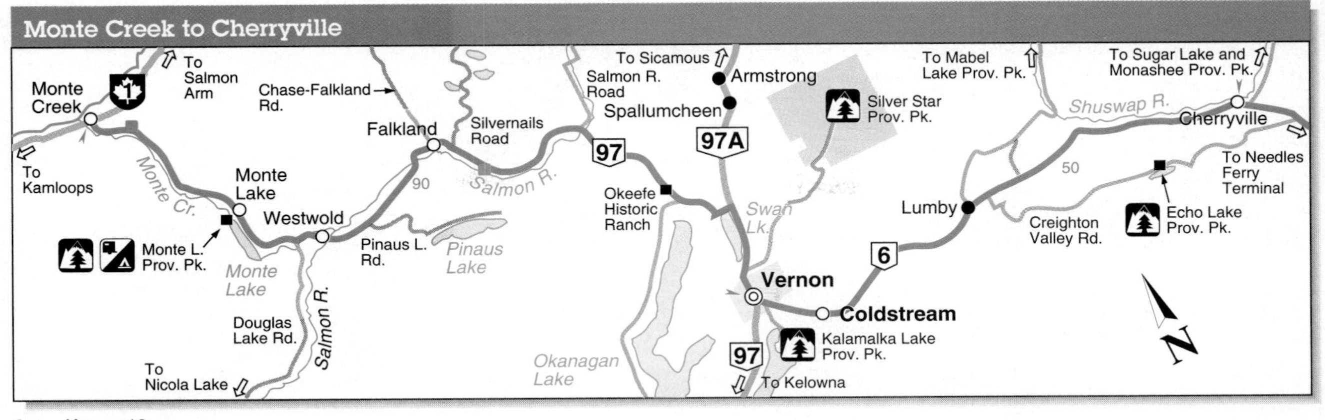


centre – in an area of lakes, streams, and hills. Extensive dairy and beef cattle industry, and natural setting for fishing, trail riding, hiking, and cross-country skiing. Several sawmills and pole plants in Lumby. Potters, weavers, and other artisans have gravitated here.

**Lumby Information:** Infocentre on Hwy 6. Write Box 534, Lumby, BC, V0E 2G0. Fax: 547-2300. July-Aug.

**Mabel Lake Provincial Park:** 182ha; 81 campsites. On gravel road to Mabel Lake that exits north from Lumby. 35km to park. 2,100m developed beach with boat launch. 494-0321. A steep, glacier-etched valley. Shuswap Highlands rise to merge with Monashee Mountains to the east. Western view provides a contrast with dry, ponderosa pine and Douglas fir forests of the Thompson Plateau. Rainbow fishing.

**Creighton Valley Rd:** 4km east of Lumby. Goes south to Echo Lake Provincial Park.

**Echo Lake Provincial Park:** 154ha. 4km east of Lumby on Hwy 6, Creighton Valley Rd leads 20km to park. For organized group camping only, reservations through parks' district office. 494-0321. For Echo Lake Resort: 547-6434.

**Cherryville:** (Pop. 500). On Hwy 6, some 22km east of Lumby. From 1876-1890, Cherryville was a placer gold camp in a narrow draw along banks of south fork of Cherry (now Monashee) Creek. In its heyday, it was home to about 100 miners seeking gold and silver-lead.

**Monashee Provincial Park:** 7,513ha; 12 campsites. Northeast out of Cherryville on Sugar Lake Rd to Spectrum Creek. Parking lot at creek. No further road access. 494-0321. Fishing. Details on Sugar Lake and Monashee Provincial Park in *Kootenay Country*, p.150.

Hwy 6 continues 84km to Needles Ferry on west side of Lower Arrow Lake in *Kootenay Country*. See *Cherryville to Nelson*, p.150, for details of this route.

*California bighorn sheep, Vaseux Lake.*

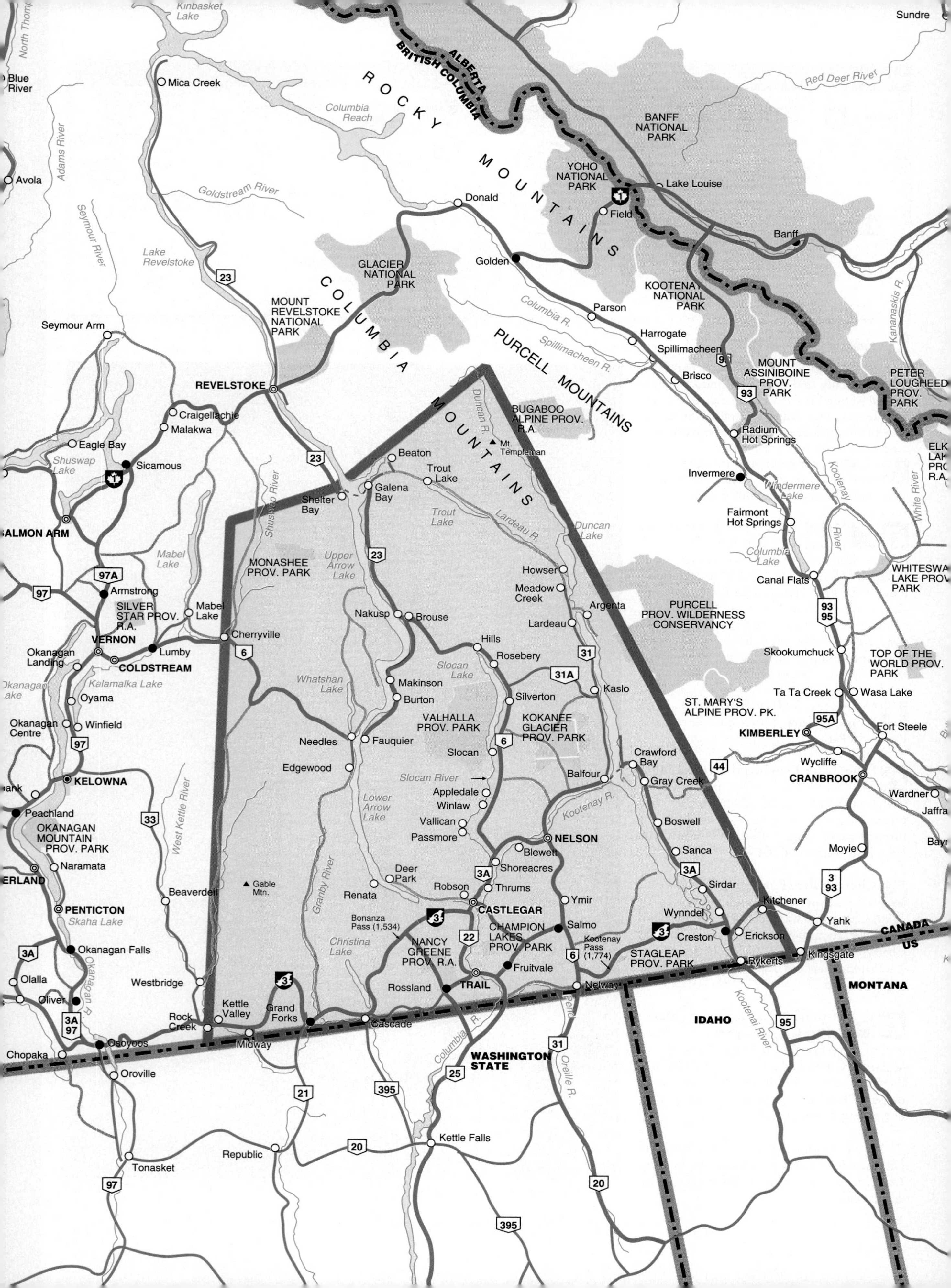
ROCKY MOUNTAINS
COLUMBIA MOUNTAINS
PURCELL MOUNTAINS
ALBERTA
BRITISH COLUMBIA
BANFF NATIONAL PARK
YOHO NATIONAL PARK
GLACIER NATIONAL PARK
MOUNT REVELSTOKE NATIONAL PARK
KOOTENAY NATIONAL PARK
MOUNT ASSINIBOINE PROV. PARK
PETER LOUGHEED PROV. PARK
BUGABOO ALPINE PROV. R.A.
PURCELL PROV. WILDERNESS CONSERVANCY
MONASHEE PROV. PARK
SILVER STAR PROV. R.A.
VALHALLA PROV. PARK
KOKANEE GLACIER PROV. PARK
TOP OF THE WORLD PROV. PARK
ST. MARY'S ALPINE PROV. PK.
WHITESWAN LAKE PROV. PARK
OKANAGAN MOUNTAIN PROV. PARK
NANCY GREENE PROV. R.A.
CHAMPION LAKES PROV. PARK
STAGLEAP PROV. PARK
Kinbasket Lake
Mica Creek
Blue River
Avola
Columbia Reach
Goldstream River
Lake Revelstoke
Adams River
Seymour River
Red Deer River
Sundre
Lake Louise
Field
Banff
Donald
Golden
Parson
Harrogate
Spillimacheen
Spillimacheen R.
Columbia R.
Brisco
Radium Hot Springs
Invermere
Windermere Lake
Fairmont Hot Springs
Columbia Lake
Canal Flats
Skookumchuck
Ta Ta Creek
Wasa Lake
Kimberley
Fort Steele
Wycliffe
Cranbrook
Wardner
Moyie
Yahk
Kingsgate
Kitchener
Erickson
Rykerts
Creston
Wynndel
Sirdar
Boswell
Sanca
Gray Creek
Crawford Bay
Kootenay R.
Kootenay River
White River
Kananaskis R.
Seymour Arm
Revelstoke
Craigellachie
Malakwa
Eagle Bay
Shuswap Lake
Sicamous
Salmon Arm
Mabel Lake
Armstrong
Vernon
Coldstream
Lumby
Cherryville
Okanagan Landing
Kalamalka Lake
Oyama
Okanagan Lake
Okanagan Centre
Winfield
Kelowna
Peachland
Naramata
Penticton
Skaha Lake
Okanagan Falls
Okanagan R.
Olalla
Oliver
Osoyoos
Chopaka
Oroville
Tonasket
Westbridge
Beaverdell
West Kettle River
Rock Creek
Kettle Valley
Midway
Grand Forks
Cascade
Gable Mtn.
Shuswap River
Mt. Templeman
Duncan R.
Duncan Lake
Beaton
Trout Lake
Galena Bay
Shelter Bay
Lardeau R.
Upper Arrow Lake
Howser
Meadow Creek
Argenta
Lardeau
Nakusp
Brouse
Hills
Rosebery
Slocan Lake
Kaslo
Whatshan Lake
Makinson
Burton
Silverton
Needles
Fauquier
Slocan
Edgewood
Slocan River
Appledale
Winlaw
Vallican
Passmore
Lower Arrow Lake
Balfour
Nelson
Blewett
Shoreacres
Thrums
Robson
Castlegar
Deer Park
Renata
Granby River
Ymir
Bonanza Pass (1,534)
Christina Lake
Salmo
Kootenay Pass (1,774)
Fruitvale
Rossland
Trail
Nelway
Pend Oreille R.
WASHINGTON STATE
IDAHO
MONTANA
Kootenai River
CANADA
US
Republic
Kettle Falls
1
3
3A
6
20
21
22
23
25
31
31A
33
44
93
95
95A
97
97A
395

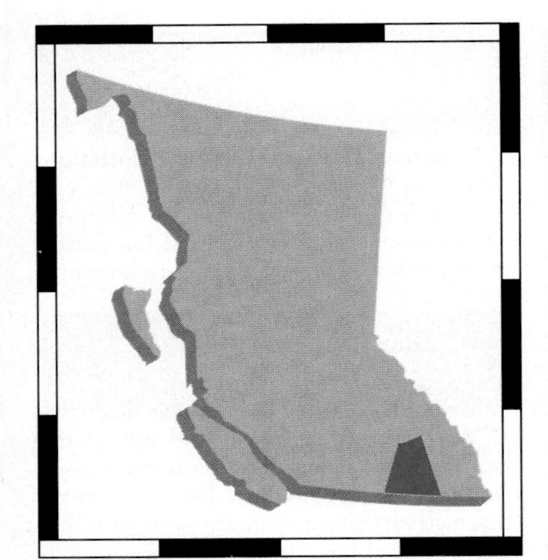

# Kootenay Country

## *No Frenzy Here Anymore*

> *"What is it about the Kootenays that appeals so much to strangers; why do they, like me, feel so at home here? Few people can say. Perhaps it's the land itself: it's so old, and yet parts of it are so young. There are some who say it speaks to people on an unconscious level. I can't tell you – the things that happen in these mountains."*
>
> – Wayne Choquette, Archaeologist, 1988

The Lower Kootenay natives have been living in this region that bears their name since before many of the landscape's features were creatd. They navigated the changing whims of rivers, and weathered "little" ice ages, such as the most recent, which receded only 200 years ago. But they cannot remember a time when they were not protected by the mountains.

European and Asian settlers have only been here 100 years. They have come from landscapes as various as their nationalities. But already they too feel as though these valleys (some where the mid-winter sun is barely seen) have always been their home. The peaks, once considered obstacles, are now their guardians.

The Purcells form the easternmost of three parallel rocky walls that separate Kootenay Country from the rest of Canada.

The next chain, the Selkirks, is an implosion of ranges within ranges. The Selkirks themselves form the backbone of the larger Columbia system extending 580km north from the 49th parallel. Its vertebrae are the subranges: the lofty Goat, incorporating Kokanee Glacier Provincial Park and the 3,045m Mt Cooper; the Kokanee; the Nelson, towering above Kootenay Lake; the soft, forested Bonnington; and the rugged Valhalla, named for the Vikings' palace in heaven.

The third range, the Monashees, is tame by comparison. In its southern subranges "moderately pointed" summits below 2,200m prevail.

In Kootenay Country, the mountains determine everything. Even the sudden, expansive Creston Flats are considered only in relation to the summits one has to overcome to get there.

People live in small pockets of land separated by rocky mountains, the rivers, and six major elongated lakes – Kootenay, Arrow reservoir (formerly Upper Arrow and Lower Arrow lakes), Slocan, Trout, Duncan, and Christina. They depend on winding highways and the unceasing labours of free ferries to keep them in touch with each other.

People's dreams and ideals have changed considerably since the Kootenay region's cities sprang up during the copper, gold, and silver booms of the 1890s. In those days, Greenwood's population was over 3,000. Fifteen hotels were squeezed into the Boundary Creek valley. Today, its population is 725, and three motels and a few campgrounds are plenty.

We can only imagine the frenzy that reigned here in the Kootenays just before the turn of the century. Thousands of immigrants, single-minded in their lust for silvery galena and copper, inadvertently almost, built the foundations – the cities and transportation networks – for the entire region today. They literally blasted their way through barriers previously considered impenetrable. It took just the right combination of forces: TNT, steam trains, sternwheelers, and a still unsatisfied appetite for gold and silver.

In 1881, this region was practically unknown. In 1882, a group of American prospectors found galena on the east shores of Kootenay Lake, and staked a claim. The claim became a camp, the camp, the town of Riondel. During the next 10 years claims/camps/towns burst into existence

*Selkirk Mountains in the Kootenays.*

*Creston Flats, "The Valley of the Swans," south of Kootenay Lake.*

throughout the region. The Toad Mountain discoveries in 1886 gave rise to the city of Nelson. There was Rossland in 1890. Slocan and Kaslo in 1891. In 1895, Sandon was cabins, rocks, and stumps. By 1897 more than one hundred new buildings, many adorned with bay windows, elaborate cornices, and velvet drapes, crowded into this deep and rugged gulch at the head of Carpenter Creek.

By 1897, the West Kootenays were producing almost all of Canada's silver and lode gold, and all of its lead. By World War One, all of the British Empire's copper was coming from the region's southwest corner, known as Boundary Country.

It's a lot quieter here now. The mining flickered, and nearly died out (not quite entirely: there's always someone looking for "gold in them thar hills"), leaving a residue of people, settlements, and ghost towns in a vast and wonderful landscape. The world's largest zinc and lead smelting complex is situated in Trail, but most of its ores come from mines outside the region. Construction of major hydroelectric projects, starting with the Hugh Keenleyside Dam on the Columbia River in 1969, followed by the Kootenay Canal on the Kootenay River, and the Seven Mile Dam on the Columbia south of Trail, has also been a source of employment.

But the extraction of resources is not a priority for many of the region's residents who only want to earn enough to be able to live here – in relative peace and solitude. There seems to be an inordinately high number of artisans, painters, writers, and other individualists, working in backwoods publishing houses, galleries, and museums, in some of the strangest, and most beautiful, parts of the Kootenay region.

Today most people talk about the age, not the value of the rocks here. Some of the world's oldest – 1.6 billion years old, midst the youngest, are found in the Purcells and Selkirks. And they speak passionately about the wealth of wilderness and natural wonders that are better protected if they are shared, rather than hoarded.

When it comes right down to it, Kootenay Country inhabitants are proud, almost amazed, at their mining history. (Many of them were miners; a few of them still are.) Hundreds of heritage buildings in Nelson (once BC's third largest city, now about 24th), and other communities, have been preserved with care. Locals, and visitors, have become prospectors for played-out mines, measuring and sometimes trying to slow the decay of ghost towns like Sandon, Zincton, Camborne, Ferguson.

Indeed, there is a good deal of respect here for the miners who managed to break down the mountain barriers, opening the way for those who came later, wanting to make the mysterious valleys their home.

## Information

**Kootenay Country Tourist Association:** Write 610 Railway St, Nelson, BC. V1L 1H4. 352-6033. Fax: 352-1656. Addresses and telephone numbers of local infocentres are in *Log* with write-ups on each community.

## Transportation

Getting into, around, and out of the Kootenay Country region is much easier than it was in the old days. There is an excellent highways system complete with six inland ferries – all of them free – as well as reasonable airlines and bus service.

Infocentres can help with boat, canoe, kayak, bicycle, and moped rentals.

### By Road

Most travellers arrive by road. One of BC's most intricate highway systems links major centres and most smaller communities, not to mention several ghost towns. There are no freeways here yet — nothing wider than two lanes and occasionally just one lane fits between lake and mountain. Much is accessible by logging roads, most of which are open to the public.

The Crowsnest Hwy 3 skirting the US border is the major "all-Canadian" route entering from the east and west. The Kootenay Region is an easy seven or eight hour drive from either Vancouver or Calgary. (It is 529km from Creston to Calgary, for example.)

Travellers from the US (via Washington and Idaho) have the following seven entrance points to choose from: Midway, Carson/Grand Forks, Cascade/Christina Lake, Paterson/Rossland, Waneta/Trail, Nelway/Salmo, and Rykerts. Border crossings are open between 8am and midnight, except Midway and Waneta/Trail (9am-5pm). The nearest 24-hour border crossing is Kingsgate situated at the eastern corner of the Rocky Mountain region.

### Bus Lines

■ **Greyhound Bus Lines:** Call Vancouver 662-3222 or specific cities. Offer limited service into the region. Daily service begins from Vancouver, entering Kootenay Country via Hwy 3. Coaches stop at waypoints between Castlegar and Nelson, then follow Highway 6 over the Salmo Skyway and on to Creston before making their way into Alberta. A separate line serves Trail and Rossland.

■ **Spokane-Trail Vanlines:** 368-8400. Offers a Mon-Fri link between Trail and Spokane, Washington.

■ **Empire Bus Lines:** 509-624-4116. Connecting Creston with Coeur d'Alene, Idaho, and Spokane, Washington.

### Inland Ferries

The provincial transportation and highways ministry operates a small fleet of inland ferries to complete the highway system where there are no bridges. These ferries are free, carry passengers and vehicles. Schedules should be used only as a guideline since operating times can change on short notice.

### Kootenay Lake

■ **Balfour to Kootenay Bay** (Hwy 3A): Call Nelson 354-6521. From Balfour hourly 6am-midnight. From Kootenay Bay hourly 7am-1am. 45 minutes. MV *Balfour*: 38 cars, 150 passengers. MV *Anscomb*: 42 cars, 136 passengers. Additional sailings in summer.

### Arrow Lakes

■ **Shelter Bay to Galena Bay** (Hwy 23): Call Revelstoke 837-7646, or New Denver 358-2212. From Galena Bay hourly 5:30am-10:30pm; plus 12:30am. From Shelter Bay hourly 5:10am-10pm; plus midnight. 30 minutes. MV *Galena*: 40 cars, 200 passengers.

■ **Needles to Fauquier** (Hwy 6): Call New Denver 358-2212, or Vernon 549-5440. From Fauquier every half hour 6am-10pm. From Needles every half hour 6:15am-9:45pm. On call 10pm-6am. 28 cars, 200 passengers.

### Columbia River

■ **Arrow Park** (25.5km south of Nakusp): Ondemand between 5am-12:05pm; and 3:15pm-10:35pm. Five minutes. Cable ferry: eight vehicles, 20 passengers. Service may advance two hours in fire season.

### Kootenay River

■ **Harrop/Procter area to Longbeach** (24km east of Nelson): Crosses the West Arm. On demand 24 hours. Five minutes. Cable ferry: 10 vehicles, 55 passengers.

■ **Glade to Thrums:** 22.5km west of Nelson. On demand 5am-2:30am. Three minutes. Cable ferry: eight cars, 115 passengers.

## Airlines

The only air terminal for the Kootenay region is at Castlegar. Two airlines offer daily service to Vancouver, Calgary, and Edmonton. Daily flights, Castlegar to Penticton.

■ **Time Air:** Toll free 1-800-665-1177.

■ **Air BC:** Toll free 1-800-663-3721.

## Railways

There is no rail passage directly into the Kootenay region.

■ **VIA Rail:** Toll free 1-800-561-8630. Transcontinental service stops at Salmon Arm and Revelstoke a few hours' drive north of Nakusp. No direct bus from either to Nakusp.

## Car and RV Rentals

Cars can be rented at the Castlegar airport and downtown locations in most cities. RV rentals are in Penticton, Vernon, and Salmon Arm. Call infocentres.

# KOOTENAY COUNTRY EVENTS

### Balfour

■ **Fishing Derby:** Thanksgiving weekend.

### Boswell

■ **Fish Derby:** Mid-June.

■ **East Shore Craft Faire:** Aug long weekend.

### Castlegar

■ **West Kootenay Trade Fair:** April.

■ **Sunfest:** Early June.

### Christina Lake

■ **Sandcastle Contest:** Early Aug.

■ **Baseball Tourney:** End of Aug.

### Crawford Bay

■ **Fall Fair:** Labour Day weekend. Held since 1910.

### Creston

■ **Blossom Festival:** Victoria Day weekend. Chuckwagon and chariot races, demolition derby, fiddlers, parade, midway, and more.

■ **Fall Fair:** Sept.

### Grand Forks

■ **Grand Forks International Baseball Tournament:** Teams from as far away as Japan. Five days through Labour Day weekend.

■ **Grand Forks Fall Fair & BSHA (Boundary Stock Horse Assoc) Horse Show and Rodeo:** Early Sept.

### Gray Creek

■ **Gray Creek Sailing Regatta:** Labour Day weekend.

### Greenwood

■ **Founders Day Celebration:** Mid-July. Family picnic.

### Kaslo

■ **Kaslo May Days:** May Day Weekend, celebrated here for 90 years. Loggers' sports, gymkhana, parade, May Queen coronation, children's events.

■ **Kaslo Jazz Festival:** First weekend Aug.

■ **Kaslo-on-the-Lake Summer School of the Arts:** Three-week program in Aug. Call Langham Cultural Centre 353-2661, or write Box 1000, Kaslo, BC, V0G 1M0.

■ **Kaslo Beachcomber Derby:** Nov.

### Nakusp

■ **Nakusp Fishing Derby:** June.

■ **Minto Days:** Local fun. Late June.

■ **Nakusp Slo-Pitch Tournament:** End of July.

■ **Nakusp Fall Fair:** Sept.

### Nelson

■ **Sno' Fest:** Early Feb. All kinds of races: kegs, waiters, outhouses. Snowshoe obstacle course.

■ **Mid-summer Curling Bonspiel:** Early July.

■ **Kootenay Summer School of the Arts:** Two weeks beginning mid-July. 352-2402. Running for nearly 40 years.

■ **Slo-Pitch Tournament:** End of July.

■ **Cyswogn' Fun Triathlon:** Aug.

### Rock Creek

■ **Rock Creek and Boundary Fall Fair:** Mid-Sept. Cutting horses, bale slinging, cow chip bingo. The real thing.

### Rossland

■ **Winter Carnival:** End of Jan. Luge and bobsled races, snowmobile race, bigolfathon (snow golf), saloon, play-money casino.

■ **Rubberhead Classic Mountain Bike Race and Festival:** Mid-Sept. Two-day event, parade and pasta feed.

■ **Golden City Days and Fall Fair:** Early Sept. Cancans, saloons, dancing waiters. Plus everything a country fair should offer — competitions in veggie growing, jam making, baking, and brewing.

### Slocan Valley

■ **New Denver May Days:** Mid-May.

■ **Silverton Days:** July 1.

■ **Slocan City Logging Show:** Early July.

### Trail

■ **Square Dance Jamboree:** April.

■ **Silver City Days:** Mid-May. Italian sidewalk cafe, grape stomp, spaghetti-eating contest, midway, jet-boat river racing.

■ **Silver Pom Pom Bonspiel:** Nov.

*Cow parsnip thriving in Kootenay Country.*

# Kootenay Country Routes and Highlights

## TRAVELLER'S LOGS



## HIGHLIGHTS



## Rock Creek to Castlegar

### CROWSNEST HIGHWAY (Highway 3)

Highway 3, or the Crowsnest Hwy, is the main route into Kootenay Country. The first 96km, from Rock Creek to Christina Lake, taking in Kettle River and Boundary Creek valleys, is "Boundary Country", buffer zone between the fertile Okanagan-Similkameen, and the rocky peaks of the Kootenays. Name comes from Boundary Creek, flowing into the Kettle River at the border just south of Midway. Towns here are survivors of the gold and copper rushes that began in the 1860s.

From Christina Lake, the highway climbs 74km, through Bonanza Pass, and a wilderness of cedar and hemlock forests to Castlegar.

**Rock Creek:** (Pop. 142). 52km east of Osoyoos on Hwy 3. In 1857, Charlie Dietz started the first rush here, for gold. 5,000 people came, but the mother lode was never found. Copper was, though, and architectural reminders of 1890s copper mining boom line the highway.

■ **Rock Creek Hotel:** Built in 1893, still operating the Gold Pan Restaurant, pub, and general store.

**Kettle Valley:** Small community just off Hwy 3, 7.5km beyond Rock Creek. A handful of ranchers, one of BC's oldest golf courses, a little church. The church was actually built in Riverside, a once-upon-a-time mining town 1km east of Rock Creek. First service held in 1912. In 1923 Howard Pannell, carpenter and newspaper editor, accepted an offer of $600 to roll the church, on logs, to Kettle Valley. But he failed to earn the $100 bonus by completing the task in 100 days or less.

**Sawmill:** 15km beyond Rock Creek, 3km east of Midway. Complex operated by Pope and Talbot, major employer.

**Kettle Valley Railway Station:** 3km beyond sawmill, on outskirts of Midway. The 90-something-year-old station was terminus of Kettle Valley Railway, which crossed the mountains to Hope. Now a restored railway museum. Completed in 1916, the KVR formed a long-called-for southern Canadian railroad from Alberta to the Pacific. Known as "McCulloch's Wonder," after CPR engineer who pushed the railway through with single-minded determination, naming stations after his daughters and characters in Shakespeare's plays. One of the greatest engineering feats in railway history. By 1959, after avalanches, mud slides, and declining traffic, "McCulloch's Wonder" was shut down. For information about western end of railway, see entry on *Coquihalla Canyon Provincial Recreation Area*, near Hope, p.114.

**Midway:** (Pop. 611). Less than 1km past the KVR Station, 19km east of Rock Creek and 56km west of Grand Forks. Halfway point between Rockies and Pacific. Also midway on old Dewdney Trail that went west-east from Hope to Wild Horse Creek, near Fort Steele. Also midway for freight wagons en route from Marcus, Washington, to Fairview near Oliver. They changed horses at Eholt's ranch. Terminus of Kettle Valley line.

Was first farmland, then smelter site, now sawmill town with a penchant for its railway and mining history. It is certainly a town of museums (it has three), and historic railway stations (there are two). Midway has had an airstrip since 1936, unpaved, and right in the town; no commercial flights.

**Midway Information:** Located in Kettle Valley Railway Station. Write Box 149, Midway, BC, V0H 1M0. 449-2614. Mid-May to mid-Sept. Off-season, call Midway Village Office, 449-2222.

■ **Riverfront Municipal Campground:** 12 formal campsites, lots of flat space; sani-station. Three blocks off Hwy 3, in Midway. Canoeing, swimming, on river.

■ **Kettle River Museum:** A new museum next to the old CPR Railway Station, which also houses its own museum. 449-2222 or 449-2614(fax in winter). Daily July and Aug. Other times, other hours. Kettle River history, plus 1895 schoolhouse, 1939 caboose, and bleakly nostalgic trapper/ prospector's cabin. 1895 Mining Recording Office Courthouse has displays on BC police forces. Informal tours May-Sept. Contact infocentre or (off-season) museum.

■ **Entwined Trees:** Adjacent the new Medical Clinic. When boundary between Canada and US was established in 1846, near today's Midway, it separated Okanagan native bands who used to converge here to fish and pick berries. Some say the two sapling pines were entwined by the natives to symbolize their spiritual unity.

■ **Kettle River Railway Bed:** If not for erosion and washed-out bridges you could drive it all the way to Penticton. Ask anyone in town where to walk it.

■ **Great Northern Railway:** Drive 2km down "Dump Road" and walk old rail bed to first tunnel. Built in 1906, connection to US.

**Rd to America:** Road through village leads south to border crossing of Midway and a link road via Ferry and Curlew, Washington, to US Hwy 21.

**Boundary Creek:** Meets Hwy 3 at border. Road follows creek north 16km through Greenwood.

**Boundary Falls:** At Boundary Creek Bridge, 7.5km beyond Midway on Hwy 3. Undeveloped. Was a smuggling depot, power generation site, and water source for hydraulic mining nearby.

**Boundary Creek Provincial Park:** 2ha; 18 campsites. 1km beyond falls on Hwy 3, just north of border. 825-4421. Camping under cottonwood trees on banks of Boundary Creek. Remnants of stack and slag heap from old BC Copper Company smelter can be seen. Before World War One, was North America's largest copper processor. Served some 20 copper and gold mines in the surrounding hills 1901 - 1919.

**Greenwood Smelter Site/Lotzkar Park:** 3.5km beyond Boundary Falls, just outside Greenwood city limits. Smelter stack stands 55m high; plaque gives mining history. Industrial "ruins" on smelter site have now been developed into a park, with hiking trails, picnic area.

**Greenwood:** (Pop. 725). 16km beyond Midway, at junction of Boundary and Twin creeks. Canada's smallest city, though at the turn of century, Greenwood was on its way to becoming one of the west's major centres. In 1895, an optimistic merchant, Robert Wood, surveyed a 3.2km townsite and named it Greenwood. Incorporated in 1897 early in the mining boom, Greenwood had 3,000 residents, three banks, 16 hotels, 15 general stores. In its heyday this was a wild town with boisterous pianos and night-long gambling parties patronized by such regulars are Pie-Biter Smith, Two-Fingered Jack, and Dirty George. It was the service centre for dozens of mines, including the rich Mother Lode Mine. With the collapse of the mining boom after World War One, Greenwood became a ghost town. In early 1940s over 1,000 Japanese Canadians were sent from the coast, to be interned in Greenwood's empty buildings. Many stayed on.

Under the heritage revitalization program, 20 turn-of-the century buildings have been restored; noteworthy, the Courthouse, Post Office, and McArthur Centre. At infocentre, pick up maps of "Outdoor Trails around Historic Greenwood."

Greenwood's City Park offers free camping facilities.

**Greenwood Information:** Infocentre, Greenwood Museum, Copper St (Hwy 3). 445-6355.

■ **Greenwood Museum:** Copper St (Hwy 3). 445-6355. Daily mid-June to mid-Sept. Old mining days, people and their stories of grief and joy, and the Japanese community which began with the internment camps in 1942. This is a small museum, but it speaks from the heart.

■ **Sacred Heart Catholic Church:** Southeast corner of Wood and Church streets. Built in 1900, still used.

■ **Parish House:** Daily. Built 1906, contains collection of furnishings, vestments, and nine reed organs.

■ **Courthouse:** One block from museum. Built 1905. Wood, with stained-glass windows representing original provinces of Canada. Tours from museum mid-May to mid-Sept.

**Jewel Lake Provincial Park:** 49ha. 1km beyond Greenwood, unpaved road off Hwy 3 leads 10km to 3km lake. Fly-casting for rainbow trout in summer, ice fishing and cross-country skiing in winter. In 1913, a record-keeping 17kg rainbow trout was caught in this lake. Facilities include Jewel Lake Resort, open year round. Trails to remnants of Spotted Horse Mine, Jewel Lake Mine, and ghost town of Eholt.

**Wilgress Lake:** Small lake 16km beyond Greenwood. Rest area and picnic site, boat launching ramp.

**Phoenix Ski Hill:** Turn right 20km beyond Greenwood, follow signs for 13km on gravel road. 442-2813. Fall-line skiing with 244m vertical drop. Runs named after old copper-mine claims. Day lodge with cafeteria, T-bar, beginners' tow, cross-country trails, rentals shop (rent cross-country skis in Greenwood), and ski school. Same road leads to Phoenix Mine site and signs of recent open-pit mining.

**Doukhobor Homesteads:** Along Hwy 3, en route to Grand Forks, simple two-storey brick houses clustered with barns and workshops are vestiges of the "spirit wrestlers" or Doukhobors. They took refuge in Saskatchewan in late 1800s fleeing persecution in Russia for their unorthodox religious beliefs; came here in 1908.

In the 1920s there were about 90 Doukhobor communes in BC, each with about 60 people. They made their own bedding, clothing, and tools, farmed, followed rules based on the *Bible*. System began to break down after death of leader, Peter Verigin, in 1924, and under pressures of the Depression (more information in Castlegar section, following).

Not to be confused with main Doukhobor community are the Freedomites, or Sons of Freedom. This radical sect has become well-known for sensational demonstrations (nude parades, fires, and hunger strikes) against what it considers the adoption of impure or materialistic values.

About 5,000 Doukhobor descendants are in and around Castlegar, many speaking Russian, and they are still pacifists. Communal homesteads have been abandoned as they have integrate into mainstream BC.

**Viewpoint:** On Hwy 3, 13km beyond turnoff to Phoenix Ski Hill. View of Grand Forks and Granby River valley. Also called the Sunshine Valley, beautiful, broad and inviting, with rich, fertile soil.

**Hwy 41:** 2km beyond viewpoint. 1km to junction for Carson/ Danville border.

**Grand Forks:** (Pop. 3,610). 5km beyond Hwy 41 junction, 40km beyond Greenwood. An attractive valley town (the "Sunshine Valley" it's called) with tree-lined streets, named for its location near convergence of Kettle and Granby rivers.

Fastest growing town in the Kootenays, a good 10 percent a year for last few years. Population may be close to 5,000 by press time. Hundreds of interesting home-based businesses.

Community owes its existence to the copper mines of Phoenix. The Granby Smelter was built between 1898-1900; at that time was largest copper smelter in British Empire. Smelter closed in 1919. Glistening ebony slag now being used as an abrasive in sandblasting.

Numbers of locals here trace origins to the Doukhobors; Russian is taught in schools.

Check phone book for names like Abetkoff. Famous for ethnic foods: look for voreniki, pyrahi, galooptsi, and borscht on the menus.

Town is presided over by wedge-shaped Observation Mountain to the north, and Rattlesnake Mountain to the east (aptly named, they say). There is a municipal airport within city limits; paved; no commercial flights.

**Grand Forks Information:** 7362-5th St, Grand Forks, BC, V0H 1H0. Off Hwy 3, next to Boundary Museum. 442-2833.

■ **Farmers Market:** Great activity all day Tues and Fri. Behind Courthouse on 5th St.

■ **Grand Forks Municipal Park:** 28 sites with hook-up, unlimited tenting. End of 5th St, by Kettle River. Playground. 442-2833.

■ **Mountain View Doukhobor Museum:** North off Hwy 3 (Central Ave) onto 19th St, then follow Hardy Mountain Rd for 5km. Open most days June to Oct. 442-8855. In 1912 Doukhobor communal farmhouse. Curator Peter Gritchen shows how his parents and grandparents lived. Beyond, along Hardy Mountain Rd, more Doukhobor architecture.

■ **Grand Forks Milling Cooperative:** Off Hwy 3, just west of city. Mill was built in 1915 to supply flour for Grand Forks' Doukhobor community. Pride of the Valley Flour still made without additives, from locally grown wheat when possible. Jack Makortoff, 442-8801, or John Faminoff, 442-3257, for tours.

■ **Boundary Museum:** Hwy 3 and 5th St. Open year-round (weekdays in winter). 442-3737. For area's rich cultural history.

■ **North Fork Scenic Drive:** Loops 30km along Granby River. Infocentre has maps.

■ **Downtown Tour:** Soak up mountain-city ambience midst revitalized turn-of-century architecture.

■ **Grand Forks Art Gallery:** 7340-5th St, year-round. 442-2211. Continuous exhibitions in four galleries.

**Highway 395:** 18km east of Grand Forks. Leads southeast 4km to border crossing at Cascade; another 144km to Spokane, Washington.

**Christina Lake:** (Area pop. 1,100). 21km beyond Grand Forks. Lakeside community swells to 6,000 in summer when travellers converge on "the warmest lake in BC." (There are three "warmest" lakes in BC: Osoyoos and Wasa also make the claim. Truth is, they're all warm). 19km long and just 55m deep, July water temperature averages 23 degrees C.

Reservations recommended at the eight commercial campgrounds. Back-to-basics camping is available on the north end of the lake, at Forest Service recreation sites accessible only by boat, and at Texas Creek Provincial Park, 15km beyond community centre, 6km off Hwy 3.

**Christina Lake Tourist Association:** At Hwy 3. 447-6109.

**Christina Lake Provincial Park:** 6ha at southern tip of Christina Lake. Has everything: sand and shade, change rooms,

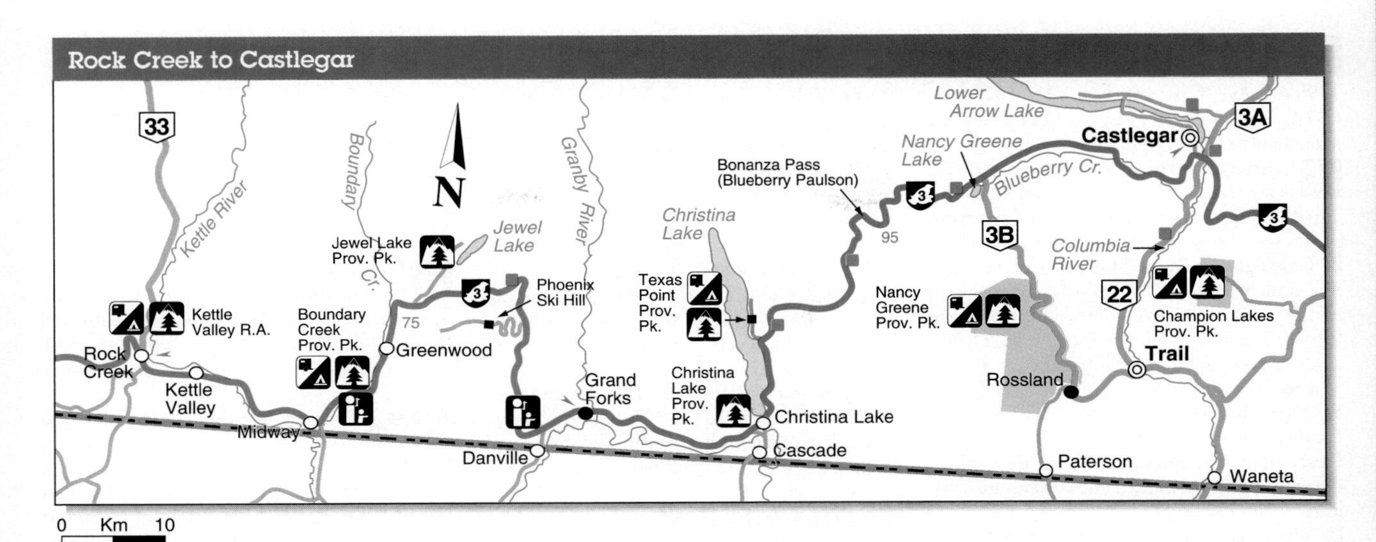


swimming, windsurfing, waterskiing, boat launch, fishing.

**Texas Creek Provincial Park:** 112ha; about 32 informal campsites. 825-4421. Lakefront sites on east side of Christina Lake, north of the community. Beautiful sandy beach. Picnicking, swimming, fishing.

**Cascade Gorge:** South on Hwy 395. 300m beyond turnoff, water boils through series of small falls and kettles.

**Christina Lake Golf and Country Club:** 18 holes set among pines. On Hwy 395, 3km south of community. 447-9313.

From Christina Lake Hwy 3 climbs through forests of cedar, hemlock, fir, birch, and some pine.

**Rest Area:** 11km beyond Christina Lake. South side of highway.

**Paulson Bridge:** 13.5km beyond rest area. Sits 90m over McRae Creek.

**Walker Creek Rest Area:** 4.5km beyond Paulson Bridge. Footbridges over creek.

**Bonanza Pass:** 6km beyond rest area. Known locally as the "Blueberry Paulson Summit," 1,535m.

**Rd to Ski Trails:** Signs indicate right turn 6km beyond Bonanza pass. Cross-country skiing.

**Nancy Greene Provincial Park:** 198ha; 12 campsites. On Hwy 3, 4.5km beyond road to ski trails. 825-4421. Subalpine lake named for local hero, Nancy Greene of Rossland, who won alpine skiing gold medal for Canada in 1968 Olympics. In all, some 45km of trails up and around the lake, including a self-guiding nature trail circling the lake. Great cross-country skiing and hiking. Rainbow trout.

**Hwy 3B:** Just beyond the park, 47km from Christina Lake. South to Nancy Greene Recreation Area; 28km to Rossland, 38km to Trail.

## SIDE TRIP

### to Recreation Area

**Nancy Greene Recreation Area:** 8,085ha. Back-country camping. 825-4421 for information and maps. Extends south on 3B from Nancy Greene Provincial Park 25km to Rossland city limits. Excellent hiking and wildlife spotting in Rossland Range. Old Glory Mountain, the area's highest at 2,400m, offers views from Forest Service lookout. Huckleberry picking in late summer.

**Red Mountain Ski Area:** On Red Mountain Rd, 25km from Hwy 3/3B junction, 3km north of Rossland Museum on Hwy 3B. Contact Red Mountain, Box 670, Rossland, BC, V0G 1Y0. 362-7700 or toll-free 1-800-663-0105. For snow report 362-5500. First Canadian Downhill Championships were held on Red Mountain in 1897, and western Canada's first chairlift was installed in 1947. Red and Granite mountains, constituting Red Mountain Ski area, have produced more Canadian National Ski Team members (including 1968 Olympic gold medal winner Nancy Greene) than any other ski area.

Facilities include Granite's 854m vertical drop, a 7.5km intermediate run, a world-class downhill course, the "powderfields," and over 50km of machine-groomed cross-country ski trails, plus more off the beaten track. Lodge, ski school, and rental shop.

**Rossland:** (Pop. 3,557). 28km south of Hwy 3 on 3B. See *Five-Town Loop*, p.147.

### *Return to Highway 3*

**Castlegar:** (Pop. 6,579). 27km beyond Hwy 3B junction. 170km from Rock Creek. Dramatically situated on a strip of benchland on west bank of Columbia River, opposite its junction with Kootenay River. Crossroad of the Kootenays, Castlegar is also at junction of several highways, Hwy 3 from the west, Hwy 22 coming north from Trail, and Hwy 3A heading north, to Nelson.

Kootenay River flows down from the northeast, and pours into the Columbia River, forming a giant Y. The newest section of Castlegar sits on west bank of the Columbia, directly opposite the incoming Kootenay. This area began as residential site for Cominco employees at Trail. Meanwhile, Hwy 3, with its bridge across the Columbia River, has drawn development southeast of town. As a result, over the years, Castlegar has somewhat crept down the road towards Trail, becoming a city shaped like a dumbbell with two rivers in its centre.

The flatlands on Columbia's east bank, and between the two rivers, were first occupied in 1908 by the Doukhobors, a pacifist group of Russian emigrants. There were at least 24 villages, constituting the settlement named Ooticshenia or Ootischeniye, the Valley of Consolation, reflecting the difficulties that finally brought these refugees here. Six villages were located at Brilliant; others at Raspberry, Robson, Glade, Shoreacres. They all had names in Russian, which meant things like Blessed, Meadowland, The Beautiful, and The Cross. The Doukhobors planted orchards and gardens, built sawmills, pipe works, jam factories. The settlement was one of the more successful communal enterprises attained in North America. After almost 40 years, community met an involuntary end (see *Verigin's Tomb*, below).

Much of this area is now occupied by Castlegar Airport, golf course, and Hwys 3 and 3A. But some vestiges of this community that thrived under the motto "Toil and a Peaceful Life" have survived. See note on Doukhobor Homesteads (previous page).

In 1988 the Castlegar and District Heritage Society revived the old rail station as a museum, moving it closer to heart of downtown, and restoring its interior. Station now centrepiece of a revitalization program. Modern infrastructure includes 25m swimming pool, hot pool, steam room, and gym.

**Castlegar Information:** Chamber of Commerce and Travel Infocentre, 1995-6th Ave, Castlegar, BC, V1N 4B7. 365-6313. Located off Hwy 3, near Hwy 22 Interchange. Year-round. Follow signs.

**Castlegar Airport:** On Airport Rd, off Hwy 3A, 6.5km beyond city centre. Thrilling landings: wing tips of incoming planes seem almost to touch mountain peaks.

■ **Castlegar Railway Station:** Corner 13th Ave and 3rd St. Daily May-Sept. Check in winter. 365-6440. The unofficial town centre for half a century, built in 1902, rebuilt 1907 after a fire. Declared heritage and now restored as a museum.

■ **Doukhobor Museum:** Across from Castlegar Airport. April 1-Sept 30. 365-6622. Descendants of Doukhobors guide visitors through replica of early 1900s communal village.

■ **West Kootenay National Exhibition Centre:** Adjacent Doukhobor Museum. 365-3337. Tues-Sun. Local and travelling exhibits of historical, scientific, ethnological, and artistic interest.

■ **Zuckerberg Island Heritage Park:** Near downtown. Turn right at RCMP station on corner of 9th St, and proceed to 7th Ave. Call Castlegar City Hall 365-7227 or Zuckerberg Island 365-5511 for information. This 2ha part-time island (sometimes it's a peninsula), born of two rivers, offers a microcosm of the area's history. Thousands of years ago, the Lakes Salish built their winter pit houses here; and in 1811, intrepid explorer and map-maker David Thompson sailed past. A century later, in 1931, Alexander Feodorovitch Zuckerberg arrived to teach area's Doukhobor children, settling on this island. His "castle" was an onion-domed Russian Orthodox Chapel House that he built himself of mitered logs, with ornate windows, a square rear tower, and carved masks. Bought by the city in 1981, has been restored from neglect suffered since the gentle Russian's death in 1961. Reached by a 145m pedestrian suspension bridge (90m span).

■ **Hugh Keenleyside Dam:** 8km upstream from town centre via Columbia Ave. Informal tours on request. 365-5299. Completed in 1965, the 50m-high earthfill and concrete structure controls a 3,650,000ha drainage area, and holds back the Arrow reservoir (part of the Columbia River system) extending 232km north to Revelstoke.

Several communities were affected by the new lake. Fauquier, Burton, and Edgewood were reestablished on higher ground. Others like Needles, now only a ferry dock, were abandoned.

The dam has one of western Canada's few navigation locks, 15m wide inside, and 88m long between gates. It lifts river traffic, including pleasure craft, some 23m to new lake levels. The waterway is also a "logging highway" for tugs and log booms headed for the sawmill and pulp mill downstream.

■ **Arrow Lakes Waterway:** The long and narrow (1-to-2km-wide) Arrow Reservoir stretches from Hugh Keenleyside Dam north to Revelstoke and 230km south, to Grand Coulee Dam, in Washington State. That's over 400km of fishing for kokanee, Gerrard rainbow, Dolly Varden, ling cod, walleye pike, sturgeon. It also means wilderness, from the "flatlands" of Washington, to the cliffs and glaciers of the northern reaches. Sandy beaches, creeks, waterfalls. Plenty of places to pull the boat in for back-to-basics camping. Scottie's Marina is one of two in Castlegar that can provide boats (and houseboats), maps and charts, and all the advice you need.

Water level is controlled by the dam, and can fluctuate 20m from spring through to late summer. The levels can change as much as 30cm in one day.

■ **Castlegar Golf Club:** 18-hole championship course. 365-5006. High above Columbia valley with views of Columbia and Kootenay rivers, and wildlife.

### *Bridges into Past*

■ **Doukhobor Suspension Bridge:** In Brilliant, at bottom of Airport Hill. Can be seen from Hwy 3A. Hand-poured concrete suspension bridge built in early 1900s. Crosses Kootenay River to Ootischenia.

■ **Columbia River Bridge at Kinnaird:** Carries Hwy 3 across Columbia River. Was largest and longest span of its design in the world when built in 1950s. Received award of excellence in 1968 for creative use of concrete.

■ **Train Bridge:** Across Columbia River near former ferry crossing at Robson. Once swung parallel to the river to allow sternwheelers passage. Parts of the swing mechanism still visible.

■ **Zuckerberg Island Bridge:** At the end of 9th St in downtown Castlegar. This 91m, hand-built wooden suspension bridge was built in 1980, for pedestrians only.

■ **Brooklyn Bridge:** Also known as Renata Natural Bridge. 16km upriver from Hugh Keenleyside Dam, on Bulldog Mountain. Accessible only by boat. Trail leads up a bank to what is probably Canada's largest natural rock bridge. Ask at local marinas for directions. This erosion sculpture, 20m high and 43m long, spans a cascading brook among towering cliffs some 275m above the Lower Arrow Lake and site of early boom town of Brooklyn (now "just a field").

## SIDE TRIP

### Along Columbia's North Shore

Cross Brilliant Bridge, east off Hwy 3A, to Broadwater Rd. Note that a new bridge is in the works, crossing the Columbia at Raspberry.

**Verigin's Tomb:** On Broadwater Rd, 800m beyond Hwy 3A. Peter (Lordly) Verigin instituted many reforms in Doukhobor community. In 1924, he was killed by a bomb exploding in his railway coach.

**Pass Creek Regional Park:** 37 campsites. On Broadwater Rd, 2km beyond Hwy 3A. May-Sept. 365-3386. Swimming, hiking to Rosebud Lake, Tulip Creek Falls, Lions Head.

**Robson:** Residential area for Castlegar, 2km beyond park. Casual fruit ranching. Little evidence that this was once a busy rail and barge terminal for ore en route from Rockies to Trail.

**Hugh Keenleyside Dam:** About 1km beyond Robson. Road leads across dam, onto Arrow Lakes Dr, past Celgar pulp mill (tours available) and Westar sawmill on south bank of Columbia, back to Castlegar.

**Syringa Creek Provincial Park:** 226ha; 60 campsites, sani-station. 825-4421. A few km beyond Robson; 19km northwest of Castlegar, on Broadwater Rd. East side of Lower Arrow Lake at foot of Columbia Mountains' Norns Range. Archaeological site. Water sports, hiking, outdoor nature displays, interpretive programs. **Yellow Pine Trail** is a leisurely 45-minute self-guided walk. May see bighorn sheep, black bear, deer.

Broadwater Rd ends at Syringa Creek, but the unpaved and rustic Deer Park Rd carries on to a pretty area complete with waterfall known to locals as "Deer Park."

### *Return to Castlegar*

**Hwy 22:** South off Hwy 3, south of downtown Castlegar, Columbia Ave becomes Hwy 22, a two-laner winding south along the west bank of the Columbia River for 26km to Trail. On the way, passes small bedroom communities for Trail with utopian names like China Creek, Blueberry Creek, Genelle, Rivervale, and Oasis. Current too strong for swimming, but good fishing.

From here, Hwy 3 (the Crowsnest) leads southeast 39km to Salmo, and a further 83km to Creston. See *Castlegar to Kitchener*, p.148. Hwy 3A leads northeast 41km to Nelson. See *Five-Town Loop*, following.

# Five-Town Loop

## CASTLEGAR, NELSON, SALMO, TRAIL AND ROSSLAND (Highways 3A, 6, 3B)

The complete circle – Castlegar back to Castlegar – is 148km. Including the 10km on to Rossland, the loop covers 158km of highway, taking in the region's three largest cities (Castlegar, Nelson, and Trail), three of its most important rivers, and three of its highways. Please note that this circle route is not suggested as a trip in itself: this is simply a convenient way to package up the busiest part of the Kootenay region. Wherever you travel in the Kootenays, you will probably "do" some portion of this loop, which is cross-referenced to other *Logs*.

So read your map carefully, to catch all the curves, and welcome to the heart of Kootenay Country. Loop begins at Castlegar, at the junction of the Columbia and Kootenay rivers. It follows Hwy 3A, and the Kootenay River northeast, to Nelson. Then Hwy 6 leads quietly south through the forest along the Salmo River to Salmo. From Salmo, Hwy 3B moves west through Fruitvale and Montrose to Trail and Rossland. Hwy 22 north from Trail returns to Castlegar.

**Castlegar:** (Pop. 6,579). See *Rock Creek to Castlegar,* p.143.

**Hwy 3A and Broadwater Rd:** In Castlegar. Hwy 3 across Kinnaird Bridge leads to Kinnaird Interchange. Here, on east side of Columbia River, Hwy 3A leads 3km through Ootischenia to Brilliant, originally Doukhobor settlements, now districts of Castlegar. Highway then crosses Brilliant Bridge over Kootenay River. From here Hwy 3A leads northeast, 38km to Nelson, and Broadwater Rd leads 5.5km to Robson and beyond to Syringa Creek Provincial Park. See *Rock Creek to Castlegar,* p.144.

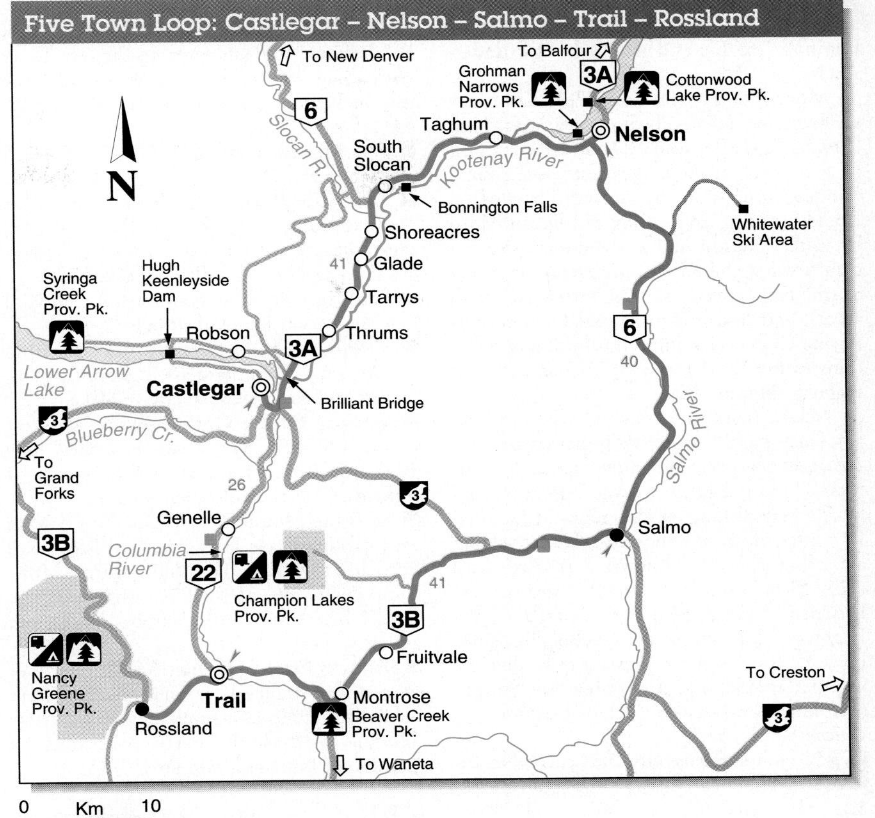


## Highway 3A to Nelson

**Brilliant Rest Area:** 6km beyond Castlegar at Kinnaird Bridge. View of Kootenay River and hydro dams.

**Thrums:** (Pop. 312). On Hwy 3A, 8km beyond bridge. Some services. Fresh veggies in season. Named after Scottish village in Sir James Barrie's *A Window in Thrums.*

**Tarrys:** (Area pop. 256). 5km beyond Thrums (13km from Castlegar).

**Ferry to Glade:** 3km beyond Tarrys (16km from Castlegar), a road leads south 2km to free cable ferry crossing Kootenay River to community of Glade (pop. 351). 5am-2:30am.

**Shoreacres:** (Pop. 349). 1.5km beyond Tarrys. Some services.

**Hwy 6:** 2.5km beyond Shoreacres, 20km beyond Castlegar. Leads north 127km through serene and silvery Slocan Valley to hot springs resort town of Nakusp. See *Cherryville to Nelson,* p.150. Hwy 6 east joins Hwy 3A as far as Nelson, then veers south to Salmo.

**South Slocan:** (Pop. 142). On Hwy 3A, 2km beyond Hwy 6 junction.

**Bonnington Falls:** 3km beyond junction. Series of low falls prevented navigation between vast Kootenay and Columbia river systems. Today there are four dams in about 5km: South Slocan, Lower Bonnington, Upper Bonnington, and Corra Linn (north of Bonnington Falls). All operated by West Kootenay Power Ltd.

BC Hydro also takes advantage of Bonnington Falls by operating the Kootenay Canal, which diverts water from Kootenay River just above the Corra Linn Dam. The canal carries water along Kootenay's east side to turbines near South Slocan Dam. BC's first hydroelectric plant was erected on Cottonwood Creek, just south of Nelson, in 1897.

Bonnington Falls was once a major fishing area for the Lakes or Kootenay First People, who caught thier salmon in baskets. This was probably a village site as long ago as 4,000 years.

**Taghum:** (Pop. 142). 11km beyond the falls, 14km beyond the junction. Here, Hwy 3A/6 crosses to south side of Kootenay River. Taghum means "six" in Chinook jargon (railway siding here was about six miles west of Nelson).

**Grohman Narrows Provincial Park:** 5.5km beyond Taghum, 19.5km beyond the junction, on south shore of Kootenay Lake's west arm. Narrows Island and an abandoned orchard. Picnic site, trails.

**Nelson:** (Pop. 8,760). 2km from Grohman Narrows Park; 41km northeast of Castlegar on Hwy 3A; 120km northwest of Creston. On the slopes of Selkirk Range, overlooking the West Arm of Kootenay Lake.

Surely the most civilized backwater in the province (if there are any backwaters left, in this day of faxes and modems). Nelson's steep streets, clear mountain skies, and turn-of-the-century architecture, nearly outshone even Steve Martin, who starred in the comedy *Roxanne* filmed here. Tourists still circle round the Fire Hall where so much of the story, about lovers of beauty, took place.

When BC's Gold Commissioner, Gilbert Malcolm Sproat, in 1887, selected the Toad Mountain silver-mine townsite that later became Nelson, he dreamed "that here, where nature was so bountiful, there might be, could we keep out newspapers and lawyers, the town of all towns for civilized habitation." A century later, Nelson is a town with a genuine atmosphere, a Streetcar named Desire (#23), and more artists and craftspeople per capita than any other city in Canada.

And also more heritage buildings. By the turn of the century, Nelson, by then BC's third largest community, was called the "Queen City." (Now there are 25 cities ahead of it, plus several very large "district municipalities.") Today some 350 of Nelson's homes, hotels, shops, and office buildings have heritage status. F M Rattenbury, famous architect of Victoria's Parliament Buildings and Empress Hotel, also designed Nelson's courthouse and city hall. Ornate and grandiose High-Victorian style of much of remaining architecture was an anomaly: introduced to Nelson by miners with *nouveau-riche* tastes, modified by conservative English settlers, and two or three decades behind the times even during construction.

In 1977, provincial Heritage Conservation Branch did a pilot study, concluding that Nelson's large inventory of fine old buildings was a resource that should be managed. It was suggested that Nelson had better get busy before it was too late. Restoration began in 1981, and residents watched with awe and pride as stucco and vinyl and metal panels were torn off downtown buildings, revealing luminous marble and rich red brick underneath.

More history: the first West Kootenay sternwheeler, able to "float on dew", was built here, in 1891. Between 1891 and 1957 a fleet of at least 11 of these "graceful white swans" (ranging from 40m - 61.5m) was operated on Kootenay Lake, connecting rail lines divided by water. Nelson had a speedboat (launch) club, rowing club, and horse racing on Baker St (the main street), plus 23 hotels (each with a bar), and four saloons. Local Dam Busters Diving Club (ask at infocentre) will give directions to history that has gone under, such as tugboat *Ymir*, in 1929.

Nelson is still the "town of all towns" on Kootenay Lake, with a daily newspaper, the *Nelson Daily News*, and ample niceties for visitors. There is endless hiking, climbing, and huckleberry picking on mountains in summer. In winter, downhill and cross-country skiing are 19km away at Whitewater Ski Area, and only 8km away on locals' mountain, Morning. Hwy 3A, the "North Shore Highway," leads north over Nelson Bridge to Hwy 31, to what some consider to be divinely inspired apres-ski, at Ainsworth Hot Springs (46.5km from Nelson). Details in *Balfour to Galena Bay*, p.152.

**Nelson Information:** Infocentre, Nelson and District Chamber of Commerce, 225 Hall St, Nelson, BC, V1L 5X4. Year-round. 352-3433.

**Norman Stibbs Airfield:** Off Lakeside Dr, 500m from city centre. Air strip, heliport, and floatplane base.

■ **City Tourist Park:** 40 campsites. Downtown, corner of High and Willow streets. Trailer hook-ups, showers. May-Oct. Reservations: City Hall, 502 Vernon St, Nelson, BC, V1L 4E8. 352-9031.

■ **Heritage Walking/Motoring Tour, and Tour of the Cemetery:** Maps at infocentre. A free tour of heritage buildings with a costumed guide available daily in summer. 352-3433.

■ **Artwalk:** 75 artists display their work in 12 gallery locations that change monthly. Maps at infocentre.

■ **Streetcar No. 23 Restored:** BC's only running historic streetcar. By infocentre. Nelson, in 1899, was probably the smallest city in the world to have its own streetcar. Derailments were frequent on the steep grades, however, and passengers occasionally were delivered through windows of Baker St shops. Not so today. The electric tram with the 11 picture windows runs safely the length of the city along the lakeshore. Only one loonie for a round-trip.

■ **Capitol Theatre Restored:** On Victoria St, 352-6363. One million dollars later: open again for live performances. In 1927, the Capitol introduced talkies to Nelson.

■ **Chamber of Mines Eastern BC Museum:** 215 Hall St. Year-round. 352-5242. Largest rock collection in BC, geologist guide available (arrange ahead), mining reference library, historic photos, maps.

■ **Nelson Museum:** Corner of Nelson Ave and Anderson St. Afternoons in summer, closed Sun in winter. 352-9813.

■ **Canadian International College (CIC):** For Japanese students learning English. Every year, about 200 students arrive, to spend one year in Nelson, one year in Vancouver. 352-5311.

■ **The Murals:** Four of them, on 300 block of Vernon St.

■ **Lakeside Park:** Off Nelson Ave, near Nelson Bridge. Lakeshore walkway, picnics, sandy beach, boat rentals, adventure playground, greenhouse, walkabout tree tour.

■ **Sculpture for the People:** Lakeside and Gyro parks, Chahko-Mika Mall.

■ **Viewpoint:** At Gyro Park, two blocks from downtown. Trails, gardens, children's pool, playground, great views of city and lake.

■ **Granite Pointe Golf Course:** On West Richards St. 352-5913. Newly expanded, hilly 18-hole course with stunning views of Kokanee Glacier and Kootenay Lake.

■ **Morning Mountain:** Off Granite Rd, 8km west of Nelson on Hwy 3A. Day skiing Sat, Sun, Mon, 9:30-3:30. Night skiing Mon-Thurs 6:30-9:30. 352-9969. Family-oriented. One T-bar, 150m vertical drop. Concession, rentals.

■ **Blalocks Estate:** On Hwy 3A 6km north of Nelson. Eye-stopper of a Tudor mansion built in the late 1930s as a summer cottage yet for Selwyn G Blalock, early president of Cominco. Now condominiums.

**Hwys 3A and 6:** West of downtown Nelson. East on Hwy 3A leads 34km to Balfour and free ferry to Crawford Bay. See *Balfour to Galena Bay*, p.152. Hwy 6 leads south 40km to Salmo.

## Highway 6 to Salmo

An impressive stretch of road that skirts the Selkirks, then cuts right through them.

**Cottonwood Lake Regional Park:** 8ha. 5km beyond Nelson on Hwy 6. Fishing (no motor boats) on 35ha lake. Hiking, cross-country skiing, roofed shelter.

**Nelson Nordic Touring Centre:** 5km beyond Nelson, groomed trails developed by Nelson Nordic Ski Club. Night skiing, parking, registration, shelters. Watch for highway signs. Nelson Infocentre has maps.

**Whitewater Ski Area:** 10km beyond Nelson, then left on Whitewater access road for another 10km. 354-4944. Snow report call 352-7669.

Whitewater also called "WH20," the Powder Formula. Recent *Ski Canada* magazine rated Whitewater as having best lift-serviced powder in Canada and the Pacific Northwest. In a natural snow bowl under spire of Mt Ymir. Averages over 13m of light, dry snow annually. 20 runs, two double chairs, one T-bar. Vertical drop 395m. Base lodge with cafeteria, lounge, retail and rental shop, ski school.

**Salmo:** (Pop.1,069). On the Salmo River 40km south of Nelson, at the junction of Hwys 3 and 6. See *Castlegar to Kitchener*, p.148.

## Highway 3 West to 3B

**Erie Lake Rest Area:** On Hwy 3, 5km west of Salmo. Small roadside lake. Bass and rainbows.

**Hwy 3 and 3B:** 11km west of Salmo. *Log* follows south on 3B to Trail and Rossland.

**Champion Lakes Provincial Park:** 1,425ha; 89 campsites, sani-station. 825-4421. West off Hwy 3B, 7.5km west of Hwy 3 junction. Chain of three lakes, connected by trails, in Bonnington Range, between Columbia River and Beaver Creek. Excellent hiking around first and second lakes. Good rainbow trout fishing. Squirrels, chipmunks, porcupines, black bears, deer, coyotes, pikas, beavers, and variety of birds. Adventure playground, amphitheatre for weekend interpretation programs, ramp for manually powered boats. Swimming, snowshoeing, cross-country skiing.

■ **Champion Lakes Golf Course:** On the Champion Lakes Rd, just off Hwy 3B. A new 9-hole course split by Marsh Creek, a natural water hazard, plus three ponds and 41 bunkers, to test the golfer. 367-7001.

**Beaver Valley Outdoor Recreation Area:** 4km west of Champion Lakes Rd. Situated on Marsh Creek, just off Hwy 3B (2.5km east of Fruitvale). Wheelchair accessi-

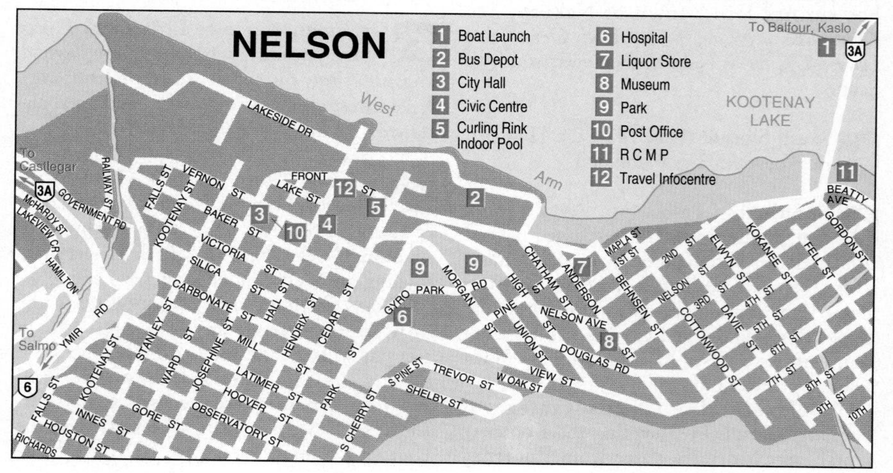

ble. Tenting, some hook-ups, showers, kitchen, hiking, cross-country skiing. Group picnics and socials. Call Beaver Valley Arena, 367-9319, or 367-9311.

**Amanda Ranch:** On the highway, near BV Recreation Area. 367-7705. Daily April-Sept. For the family: miniature horses and goats, potbelly pigs, horse rides, trail rides.

**Fruitvale:** (Pop. 2,062). On Hwy 3B, 2.5km west of BV Rec Area. Bedroom community for many of Trail's Cominco employees. Service centre, accommodation, restaurant, pubs. Only 5.5km separate Fruitvale and Montrose (with the small community of Beaver Valley in between), and all share the beautiful Beaver Valley itself, its amenities and attractions.

**Beaver Falls:** Small community about 2km west of Fruitvale. Main feature is Beaver Falls, said to be highest natural falls in Kootenay Region. A short walk along the railroad track. Ask locally.

**Montrose:** (Pop. 1,197). On Hwy 3B, 5.5km west of Fruitvale. Named by a Trail lawyer, A G Cameron, after his hometown in Scotland. Service centre, accommodation.

■ **Beaver Valley Pool:** Year-round indoor swimming pool. 367-7333.

**Waneta Junction (Hwy 22A):** 3.5km west of Montrose (34km west of Salmo, 7km east of Trail). Follows Columbia River south for 10.5km to border crossing at Waneta, BC.

## SIDE TRIP
### on Highway 22A

**Beaver Creek Provincial Park:** 44ha, 15 campsites. 825-4421. On Hwy 22A, 2km south of Waneta Junction. On Columbia River's east side. Two archaeological sites, fishing, boating, paddling.

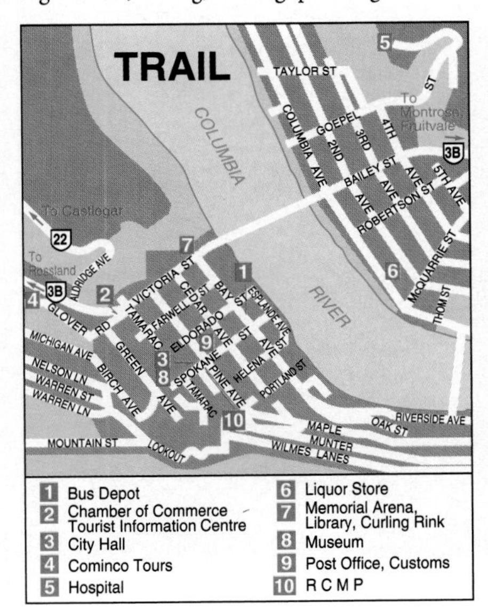


**Pend d'Oreille River Dams:** The Pend d'Oreille River flows in a northwesterly direction crossing the international boundary twice. It loops through BC for about 24km; at Waneta, joins the Columbia River, and flows back into the US.

■ **Waneta Electric Power Plant and Dam:** On the Pend d'Oreille River at its confluence with the Columbia, 10.5km south of Waneta Junction, adjacent the border crossing.

■ **Seven-Mile Dam and Generating Station:** 11km east off Hwy 22A, upstream from the Waneta power plant. Tourist building and viewpoint at top of rock cut above power house access road.

### *Return to Highway 3B*

**Trail:** (Pop.7,919). 7km west of Waneta Junction, on the west and east banks of the Columbia River. Trail is 18km north of border; 26km south of Castlegar, via Hwy 22. Or, it is 108km east of Grand Forks via Hwy 3B. (This *Log* is moving from east to west, an easier entry into Trail, but note that it can be more than exciting coming down into Trail from the west. Down and around on the switchbacks from Rossland to Trail, Hwy 3B descends more than 610m in a distance of only 11km. Check brakes first!)

Trail's beginnings were quiet. It was simply Trail Creek Landing, a cluster of small buildings in a bowl where the old Dewdney Trail forded the Columbia. By 1891, the community was slightly larger, serving as a landing for steamers taking gold, silver, and copper ore to American smelters from nearby booming Rossland.

Home of Consolidated Mining and Smelting of Canada Ltd, the city is often called "Cominco Ltd with Trail built around it." Trail took firm root as one of BC's key industrial cities. In 1895, American entrepreneur Augustus Heinze had established smelter here to reduce costs of shipping ore to US. Now Trail has more than 50 percent of region's manufacturing.

Today, though local mines are played out, Cominco's Trail unit operates world's largest zinc and lead smelting complex. More than 300,000t of zinc, and 135,000t of lead are extracted each year from ores shipped from around the world. Cominco employs more than 2,500 people here.

Commercial section is concentrated on a low terrace on river's west bank, with a retaining wall to protect from high waters. On the higher levels, Cominco's 120m-tall smokestacks are part of the scenery, along with the surrounding forested mountains, and wide and soupy Columbia River rushing under the Victoria St Bridge.

West Trail, with steep and narrow streets overlooking river, and terraced lots lush with vegetables and vineyards, is romantically compared with Italy. 30 percent of Trail's population is of Italian birth, or descendants of "old country" emigrants who began arriving in late 1800s to work the mines and smelters. Rossland Ave (Hwy 3B in west Trail) is the "gulch" where the first Italians settled, known as "Spaghetti Lane." The best Italian food in BC is said to be in Trail. Daily newspaper is the *Trail Daily Times.*

**Trail Information:** Infocentre, Trail Chamber of Commerce, 843 Rossland Ave, Trail, BC, V1R 4S8. Year-round. 368-3144. Summer Infocentre at Nancy Greene Provincial Park (shared by Rossland and Trail), at junction of hwys 3 and 3B. 362-7722.

■ **Cominco Tours:** Trail Chamber of Commerce, 368-3144. Call well ahead. Retired company employees show visitors (must be over 12 years old) where ores are melted and separated. They'll also describe the "greening of Trail" over past six decades as pollution-control has improved, waste products converted into fertilizer.

■ **Italian Community Archives:** In Cristoforo Columbo Lodge (est 1905), 584 Rossland Ave. Chamber of Commerce, 368-3144, to arrange visit. The only Italian archives in North America. Call well ahead.

■ **City of Trail Museum:** In Trail Memorial Centre (see below). Weekdays, June-Sept.

■ **Gyro Park:** In east Trail. A 3km long stretch of riverside park. Stroll, jog, cycle, swim, build sandcastles.

■ **Trail Memorial Centre:** 1051 Victoria St. Daily year-round. 368-6484. Sports Hall of Memories shows that Trail is also "The Home of Champions."

■ **Waneta Dam Tours:** Hydroelectric dam on confluence of Columbia and Pend d'Oreille rivers. Free guided tours. Chamber of Commerce, 368-3144. See *Side Trip on Hwy 22A*, above. Call well ahead.

■ **Rock Island:** In east Trail, off Hwy 3B, near Waneta Plaza. Small river island is easily accessible, good for fly, spinner, and bait fishing. Current too rapid for canoes and rowboats.

■ **Golfing:** Two courses, 18-hole Birchbank Championship Course, 6km north of Trail on Hwy 22; and Rossland's adventurous 9-hole mountain track (there's a rope tow from tee to green) 8km west of Trail, or 2km east of Rossland, on Hwy 3B. **Rossland Trail Country Club**, 693-2366, or 362-5045.

**Hwys 3B and 22:** In downtown Trail, on west bank of Columbia. Hwy 22 leads north, 26km to Castlegar (for details, see *Rock Creek to Castlegar*, p.144), thus completing this circle trip. Hwy 3B leads west 10km in an ascent to Rossland.

### *Highway 3B to Rossland*

**Warfield:** (Pop. 1,814). 6km west of Trail on Hwy 3B. Economic basis is Cominco plant.

**Rossland:** (Pop. 3,557). (El 1,040m). On Hwy 3B, 10km west of Trail. A mountaintop city in the Rossland Mountains, in the eroded crater of a long-extinct volcano. Long the "Home of Champions," with Olympic Champion skiers Nancy Greene and Kerrin Lee-Gartner. Now its unique geography has also made it the "Mountain Bike Capital of Canada."

From the intersection of Columbia Ave and Washington St look north and a little west to see **Red Mountain** (1,580m), and some of the remains of **Le Roi Gold Mine**, which excited investors around the world after its discovery by itinerant prospectors Moris and Bourgeois in 1890. Three million dollars came out of this mine in the ancient volcano crater, most famous of some 100 claims in the area. Between 1900 and 1916, Rossland, the "Golden City," with population of 7,000, produced 50 percent of BC's gold.

Since 1929, Rossland has depended on giant Cominco smelting operations at Trail, though recently there has been a small resurgence of mining for silver and gold. Nevertheless, Rossland is still mainly as a bedroom community for Trail.

**Rossland Information:** Infocentre in Rossland Historical Museum, Box 26, Rossland, BC, V0G 1Y0. At junction of hwys 3B and 22. Mid-May - mid-Sept. 362-7722. Also, infocentre shared with Trail at Nancy Greene Lake, at junction of Hwys 3 and 3B. Seasonal. 362-7722. Or **Rossland Chamber of Commerce:** 2185 Columbia Ave, Le Roi Mall, Rossland, BC, V0G 1Y0. 362-5666.

■ **Rossland Historical Museum:** At junction of Hwys 22 and 3B. Daily mid-May to mid-Oct. 362-7722. 2ha museum complex on site of the Black Bear Mine. Tells of geology, Salish Indians who camped here summers, gold rush, Cominco Ltd, and western Canada's famous skiers. Tearoom.

■ **Le Roi Gold Mine Tour:** On museum grounds. Daily mid-May to mid-Sept. 362-7722. The only hard-rock gold mine in Canada open to public. Main haulageway leads 267m into Red Mountain to intersection with Le Roi shaft, 100m below surface. A taste of the Rossland mines' 140km of drilled, blasted, and hand-mucked tunnels.

■ **Heritage Walking Tour:** By 1898 Rossland had five banks, seven newspapers, stock exchange, and 30 saloons doing business 24 hours a day. Today 30 surviving buildings in the commercial sector have been given heritage status. Infocentre has map.

■ **Rossland Miners Union Hall:** 1854 Columbia Ave. Daily June-Aug. 362-7328. First union hall in BC, built by Western Federation of Miners in 1897.

**Hwys 22 and 3B:** At Rossland. Hwy 3B leads north 3km to Red Mountain Ski Area, 28km north to junction with Hwy 3. Hwy 22 leads 11.5km to BC/Washington border crossing at Paterson. From Paterson it's another 16km to Northport. **King George VI Provincial Park** is just north of the border. 162ha; 12 campsites. 825-4421.

## Castlegar to Kitchener

### HIGHWAY 3

This is a route for mountain lovers and mountain climbers. It's 151km of mountains and trees, trees and mountains, an attractive blend of wilderness, wildlife (elk, moose, deer, bear, coyotes, even wolves), and well-spaced humanity. A high point is indeed a high point – 36.5km beyond Salmo is the Skyway, Canada's highest highway pass.

Hwy 3 from Castlegar runs southeast 28km to junction with Hwy 3B; then a farther 11km beyond to downtown Salmo, where Hwys 3 and 6 become one. At Burnt Flat Junction, about 15km south of Salmo, Hwy 6 continues south to the American border, and Hwy 3 runs east through Creston (137km from Castlegar); then a further 14.5km to Kitchener.

**Castlegar:** (Pop. 6,579). For details, see *Rock Creek to Castlegar*, p.143.

**Viewpoint:** Off Hwy 3, 5km east of Kinnaird Bridge in Castlegar. Peaceful view of the Kootenay River flowing into the Columbia. All the turbulence is beneath the surface. The **Mel DeAnna Nature Trail** (2.5km) around Champion Ponds begins at the viewpoint. Ponds were set aside as an environment study area for local schools to research pond life. West Kootenay Naturalist Club, led by the late Mel DeAnna, sponsored the project, named in his memory.

**Hwy 3B:** 27km southeast of Castlegar. Leads southwest 27km to Trail. Hwy 3 continues east toward Salmo and Creston.

**Erie Lake Rest Area:** On Hwy 3, about 6km east of Hwy 3B junction. Small roadside lake. Good spot for kids to fish for bass and rainbow trout.

**Hwy 6:** At Salmo, 11km east of Hwy 3B junction. Hwy 6 goes north 40km to Nelson. To the south, Hwys 3 and 6 are the same road as far as Burnt Flat Junction, 15km south of Salmo.

**Salmo:** (Pop. 1,069). At junction of Hwys 3 and 6, 39km from Castlegar. Salmo is Latin for salmon, and the Salmo River was called the "Salmon" River as early as the 1850s. In those days, salmon used to run abundantly here, having travelled up the Columbia River. The teeming salmon runs ended with the construction of major dams, but fishing is still good here for the highly prized Dolly Varden.

Salmo started out as Salmon Siding, on the Nelson & Fort Sheppard Railway. The community flourished through the 1950s as both a mining (silver, lead, zinc, and gold) and forestry centre. Today, there are two small sawmills just outside town, and many residents are employed by Cominco in Trail. It is the Burlington Northern Railway that now carries freight, mostly lumber, through the community.

The streets and 1930s architecture of downtown Salmo are being revitalized to create a peaceful ambience for visitors. Particularly striking are the series of stone

*At Idaho Peak near New Denver in the "Silvery Slocan."*

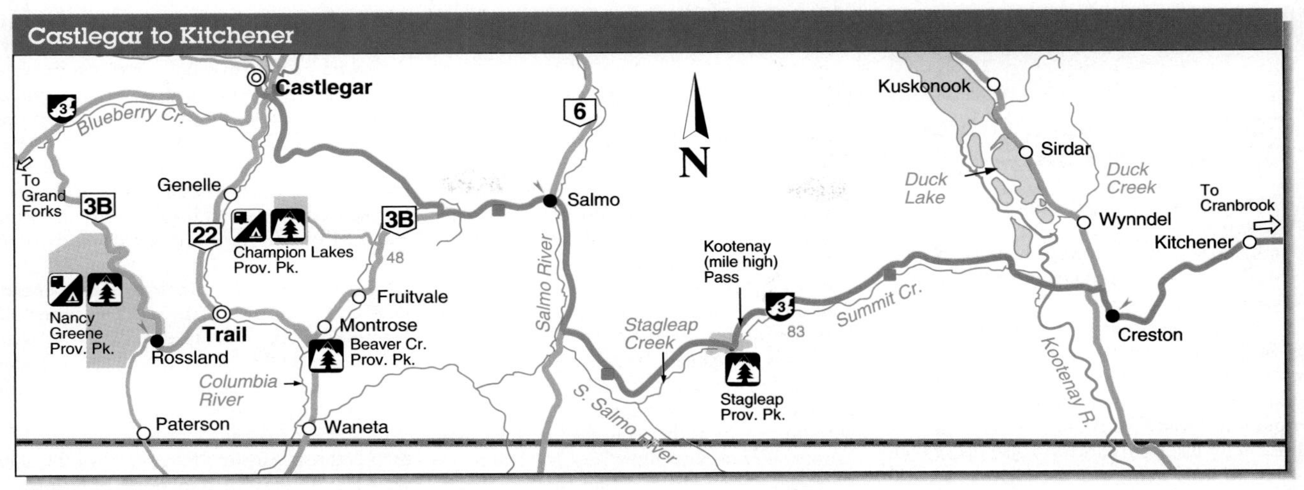


murals created by students at a newly started school of stone masonry in Salmo. These murals with a difference – made of locally quarried stone – have been mortared onto exterior walls of half a dozen buildings in downtown Salmo. More being added yearly with each class.

Ample facilities for travellers, including accommodation and campgrounds, restaurants, stores, banks, and service stations. Best of all, ask for a glass of Salmo's cold, clear water. And check out the great food in the Salmo Hotel.

**Salmo Information:** Infocentre, Salmo and District Chamber of Commerce, Box 400, Salmo, BC, V0G 1Z0. 357-9332. Outskirts of town on Hwy 3, marked by three flag poles. Daily early May - early Sept.

■ **Salmo Museum:** At corners of Railway Ave and Forest St.

■ **Kootenay Stone Masonry Training Institution and Kootenay Stone Centre:** Box 486, Salmo, BC, V0G 1Z0. Ask for Iris: 357-9515.

■ **World's Oldest Telephone Booth:** Carved into the trunk of a tree. Log in a few calls home.

■ **Salmo Golf Port:** On Airport Rd, about 5km south of Salmo. A combination airstrip and 9-hole golf course. Planes have priority – but they'll buzz the golf port before landing.

■ **Salmo Ski Hill:** About 1km up Ski Hill Rd on eastern outskirts of town. Vertical drop of 320m. T-bar and rope tow. Downhill, cross-country, and night skiing. Day lodge with restaurant, rental shop, ski school.

■ **Sheep Creek Mines:** About 8km south of Salmo, turn east on gravel Sheep Creek Rd. Along its first 15 to 20km are Kootenay Bell, Reno, Goldbelt, and Queens – abandoned mines. Also opportunities to see yet more wildlife, or cross-country ski. One of several such side roads in area. Ask locals.

**Burnt Flat Junction:** About 15km south of Salmo. Named for major fire in area about 1932. Hwy 6 continues south for 10.5km to BC/Washington border crossing at Nelway, BC. Hwy 3 runs east to Creston and Kitchener.

**Lost Creek Rest Area:** 2km east of Burnt Flat Junction.

**Avalanche Zone:** About 15km east of Burnt Flat Junction, Kootenay Pass can be seen rising in the distance as this part of the route becomes a roller-coaster ride. There are five cannons positioned to bring down prospective avalanches. In two trouble-spots, motorists are requested not to stop.

**Stagleap Provincial Park:** 1,133ha. On Hwy 3, 21km from Lost Creek Rest Area, 38km southeast of Salmo. At 1,774m summit of Kootenay Pass. Day-use. Picnic sites near Bridal Lake, at edge of highway. Hiking, cross-country skiing, outdoor nature display, and visitor centre.

Park is named for the large woodland cariboo that migrate through area. They are on the US endangered species list, and authorities in both Canada and the US are working to protect and enhance their small population.

**Kootenay Pass ("The Skyway"):** 38km southeast of Salmo. Often called Mile High Pass, best known as "The Skyway." At 1,774m, the highest paved road in Canada. Constantly maintained through winter, but subject to occasional avalanche precaution closures which may last a few minutes or a few days. As an alternate, travel from Salmo north to Nelson, across the free ferry to Kootenay Bay, returning south on east shore of Kootenay Lake to Creston. See *Nelson to Creston,* p.155.

**Blazed Creek Rest Area:** 20km east of Kootenay Pass (58km from Salmo). Old cedar stand by creek.

**Creston Valley Wildlife Management Area:** On Hwy 3, 17km from Blazed Creek, 75km east of Salmo (or 10km northwest of Creston). The Creston Valley is one of BC's few generously wide, flat valleys. Here is where the Kootenay River overflows its banks each spring.

The rich silt deposits are valued by farmers, and so some 9,000ha of this floodplain have been dyked to create fertile farmland. The remaining 6,880ha of wetland has been preserved, thankfully, as a bird and waterfowl refuge and outdoor education centre.

More than 250 bird species call it home. These include swans, Canada and snow geese, scaups, grebes, and many other waterfowl and upland birds. The area between Nelson and the US border has one of the world's highest densities of nesting ospreys. Other area residents are deer, moose, elk, and river otters.

Centre offers guided canoe trips, hikes, meadow walks, marsh crawls, forest walks, and lectures. Binoculars and telescopes are available, and use of a theatre and library is free.

**Summit Creek Campground:** 50 campsites operated by the wildlife area's management authority. Sani-station, showers, firewood, kitchen shelter with electrical outlets. A serviced base for people exploring the marshlands and taking part in the nature programs.

**Hwy 21:** Runs south from Hwy 3 near Creston, about 81km east of Salmo. About 13km to BC/Idaho border crossing at Rykerts, BC.

**Hwy 3A:** On outskirts of Creston. North off Hwy 3 for 79km to Kootenay Bay ferry terminal. Covered in *Nelson to Creston,* p. 155.

**Creston:** (Pop. 4,205). 83km beyond Salmo, on Hwy 3. Detail in *Nelson to Creston,* p.156.

**Erickson:** (Area pop. 441). 5km beyond Creston on Hwy 3. Farms, orchards, and roadside stands offering fruits and vegetables as they come in season in this lush valley.

**Kitchener:** (Pop. 218). 13.5km beyond Creston, on Hwy 3. Small service centre with store, pub, and restaurant. On boundary between BC's Kootenay Country and Rocky Mountain regions. Information in *Kitchener to Wasa,* p. 249.

# Cherryville to Nelson

## HIGHWAY 6, plus HIGHWAY 23 TO GALENA BAY

Cherryville is a small community on the border between the Okanagan-Similkameen and Kootenay regions. Hwy 6 actually begins in Vernon, about 52km west of Cherryville.

It is 290km from Cherryville to Nelson. Hwy 6 leads away from the dry rounded hills of the Okanagan to cross the Monashee Mountains into the moister, greener Kootenay region. Between Cherryville and Needles there are steep hills, slow corners, a few backwoods cafes. So little traffic that the highway is occasionally used to herd cattle. Get along little doggies.

At Needles, a free ferry crosses Lower Arrow Lake to Fauquier. Hwy 6 then runs north to Nakusp, then southeast through the Slocan Valley. South of Slocan, highway follows the Kootenay River to Nelson.

This *Log* also includes a side trip on Hwy 23 north from Nakusp to Galena Bay and the Galena Bay ferry.

All along, the people-scape oozes serenity. Here, back-to-the-landers and artists are hidden away in the forest, and on the shores of Slocan Lake and Slocan River. Not an easy place to make a living, but it offers other advantages.

**Cherryville:** A small centre on Hwy 6, 52km east of Vernon. Store, cafe, last gas station before Monashee Pass. Also known for its arts and crafts.

**Sugar Lake:** At Cherryville, turn north off Hwy 6 onto Sugar Lake Rd. 17km to outlet of lake. Gravel roads continue around lakeshores. Crystal-clear lake in the Monashees. Lake was much smaller before 1944 when the dam on the south end was built for irrigation purposes. In spring and fall when water's low, foundations of old farmsteads and cottages are visible.

**Monashee Provincial Park:** 7,513ha. North on Sugar Lake Rd at Cherryville. 35km drive to start of 12km walking trail to park. Write BC Parks, Okanagan District, Okanagan Lake Park, Box 318, Summerland, BC, V0H 1Z0. 494-0321. For topographic map, write: MAPS BC, 4th floor, 1802 Douglas St, Victoria, BC, V8V 1X4. 387-1441.

Wilderness park with spectacular mountain views, canyons, river valleys, waterfalls, alpine meadows, wildflowers, lakes, dense forests. Black bears, caribou, mule deer, ground squirrels, many birds.

**Kettle River Rd:** South off Hwy 6, 36km east of Cherryville. Beautiful back road along Kettle River, between Monashees on the east and Okanagan Highland on the west. 125km to Hwy 33 at Westbridge.

**Bench Creek Rest Area:** 46km east of Cherryville.

**Needles Ferry:** 86km east of Cherryville. 24 hours a day. 10 minutes. Crosses Lower Arrow Lake from Needles to Fauquier. 150 passengers, 28 cars.

Life has changed here since 1964-65 construction of Hugh Keenleyside Dam, some 85km south on Arrow Lakes (Columbia River) waterway. Some communities were flooded by the new reservoir. Others, like Fauquier and Burton, were reestablished on higher ground. Needles (now only a ferry dock) was abandoned. Needless to say, with all the changes, old-timers found much to grumble about. But there were a few roses to go with the thorns, as they conceded in their local history, *Whistle Stops Along the Columbia River Narrows*. They write: "The roads – THE BEAUTIFUL NO DUST Roads. Now a trip doesn't end with a cloud of dust billowing up ... as you walk along. The colour of the car in front of you can actually be seen ... And WOW! when you trade in a vehicle you needn't get red in the face and evasive about the area you're from."

**Arrow Lakes Provincial Park:** 72ha in four sites – near Edgewood, Fauquier, Burton, and Shelter Bay. To reach site near Edgewood turn south off Hwy 6 onto Edgewood Rd, 77.5km east of Cherryville. 10km to park site. Boat launch, fishing, swimming.

**Whatshan Lake:** Reached by secondary road from Needles ferry landing, 86km east of Cherryville. 7km to outlet of lake. Gravel roads continue around lakeshores. Camping on lakeshore. fishing.

**Fauquier:** (Pop. 159). Re-established after Hugh Keenleyside Dam's waters rose. Named for pioneer rancher and fruit grower who was government agent and Nakusp's first policeman in the 1890s. Some accommodation, restaurant.

**Arrow Lakes Provincial Park:** At Fauquier. Another of the three sites in this park.

**Burton:** (Pop. 162). About 21km north of Fauquier. Lakeside community with minimal tourist facilities.

**Arrow Lakes Provincial Park:** Burton site, about 21km north of Fauquier. Boat ramp, fishing, swimming.

**McDonald Creek Provincial Park:** 468ha; 10 campsites. 825-4421. 46km beyond Fauquier. Both sides of Upper Arrow Lake. Long beach, boat launching, swimming, fishing.

**Nakusp:** (Pop. 1,374). At junction of Hwys 6 and 23, 57km north of Fauquier. Name comes from Okanagan Indian word meaning "closed in," a safe place to land canoes. Town sits beautifully in a curve of Upper Arrow Lake, between Selkirks and Monashees. Tourism is a growing industry. Town has a new marina, a waterfront walk and park, 9-hole golf course, driving range, houseboat rentals, shops, restaurants, campgrounds, accommodation. Main attraction is the hot springs, located in the mountains a short distance northeast of town (see below). Old schoolhouse is of historic interest, also the Lord Minto Restaurant in former United Church.

**Nakusp Information:** Infocentre, Nakusp and District Chamber of Commerce, Box 387, Nakusp, BC, V0G 1R0. 265-4234. At 88-6th St (Hwy 23 in downtown Nakusp). In facsimile of a yellow sternwheeler's stern. 8am-6pm July-Labour Day. 9am-noon and 1-4pm Sept-June.

**Nakusp Airport:** East off Hwy 23 onto Hot Springs Rd, 3km north of Nakusp.

■ **Nakusp Museum:** On Hwy 23, in Nakusp Village Hall. Daily, June-Aug. Features Columbia River steamboats, logging, mining, and the Interior Salish Indians.

■ **Bonnington Arts Centre:** Corner of Hwy 23 and 4th St. Operated by Arrow Lakes Arts Council, which brings performing artists to Nakusp. Check with infocentre for events or write to the arts council at Box 895, Nakusp, BC, V0G 1R0.

■ **Kootenay Helicopter Skiing Ltd:** Based in Nakusp. Write to Box 717, Nakusp, BC, V0G 1R0. 265-3121 or 1-800-663-0100. Jan to mid-April. Heli-skiing in Selkirks and Monashees with deep powder runs up to 1,525m.

■ **Nakusp Centennial Golf Club:** Nine holes. 265-4531.

**Hwy 23:** In Nakusp. Hwy 6 continues southeast 46km to New Denver and Slocan Lake. Hwy 23 goes north 49km to Galena Bay ferry.

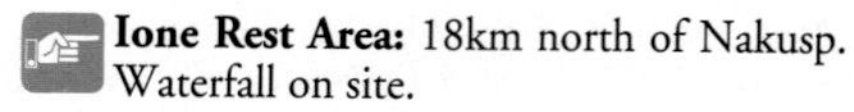

## SIDE TRIP

### to Galena Bay

Hwy 23 tracks the eastern shore of Upper Arrow Lake to the Galena Bay ferry terminal.

**Nakusp Hot Springs:** East off Hwy 23 onto Hot Springs Rd, 3km north of Nakusp. Paved 13km road to springs. Owned by village of Nakusp. Daily. Two steaming hot pools with temperatures between 39 and 44 degrees C. Particularly invigorating when it's snowing. Change rooms, showers, lockers. Cedar chalets and a campground.

**Ione Rest Area:** 18km north of Nakusp. Waterfall on site.

**St Leon Hot Springs:** East off Hwy 23, 24.5km north of Nakusp onto rough logging road. About 800m up steep hill then 1.5km on trail to spring. Undeveloped; on private property; please respect it. Temperatures up to 50 degrees C.

**Halfway River Hot Springs:** East off Hwy 23, 26km north of Nakusp. Follow logging road on south side of river for 10km then take trail to left about 100m to river. Springs downstream. Undeveloped. Crown land. Extremely hot, up to 60 degrees C.

**Halcyon Hot Springs:** On Hwy 23, about 34km north of Nakusp. Near roadside. Privately owned, undeveloped. Temperatures up to 50 degrees C.

**Hwy 31:** Intersects Hwy 23, 47km north of Nakusp. Hwy 31 is a 142km alternate route past Trout Lake to Kootenay Lake and Kaslo (see *Balfour to Galena Bay*, p.154). Hwy 23 continues from this junction for 2km to Galena Bay ferry terminal.

**Galena Bay:** 49km north of Nakusp. Crosses Upper Arrow Lake to Shelter Bay. Free. 20 minute. Hourly 6:30am-12:30am. 40 vehicles, 200 passengers. For continuation of Hwy 23, see *Shelter Bay to Mica Creek*, p.173.

## Return to Highway 6 at Nakusp

**Box Lake:** South side of Hwy 6, 10km south of Nakusp. Rainbow trout to 2.5kg. Good fly-fishing. Boat launching, camping. Restricted to electric motors.

**Summit Lake:** North side of Hwy 6, 17km southeast of Nakusp. Resort, camping. Skiing at Summit Peak. T-bar, clubhouse, run by local ski club.

**Rosebery Provincial Park:** 32ha; 36 campsites. 825-4421. On Hwy 6, 40.5km south of Nakusp (5.5km north of New Denver). On Wilson Creek near east shore of Slocan Lake.

**New Denver:** (Pop. 571). At junction of Hwys 6 and 31A, 46km southeast of Nakusp. Details in *Balfour to Galena Bay*, p.154.

**Hwy 31A:** East at New Denver. An extremely pleasant 46km route, past ghost towns and gold mines, to Kaslo on Kootenay Lake. Details in *Balfour to Galena Bay*, p.153.

From New Denver, the lovely Slocan Valley stretches south nearly 80km. Hwy 6 follows the lake, then the river, winding by small farms and homesteads. Because of its light traffic, Hwy 6 has been discovered by the bicycling fraternity as an excellent route for a challenging but quiet pedal.

**Slocan Lake:** New Denver sits near the northeast shore of Slocan Lake, a narrow 40km jewel in the deep valley between Valhalla and Slocan ranges of the Selkirks. Shores are a rugged combination of bluffs and boulders, with occasional pebble or white-sand beach. Native pictographs on shoreline rocks. Rainbow trout to 5kg and Dolly Varden char to 7kg.

Don't be misled by Slocan Lake's

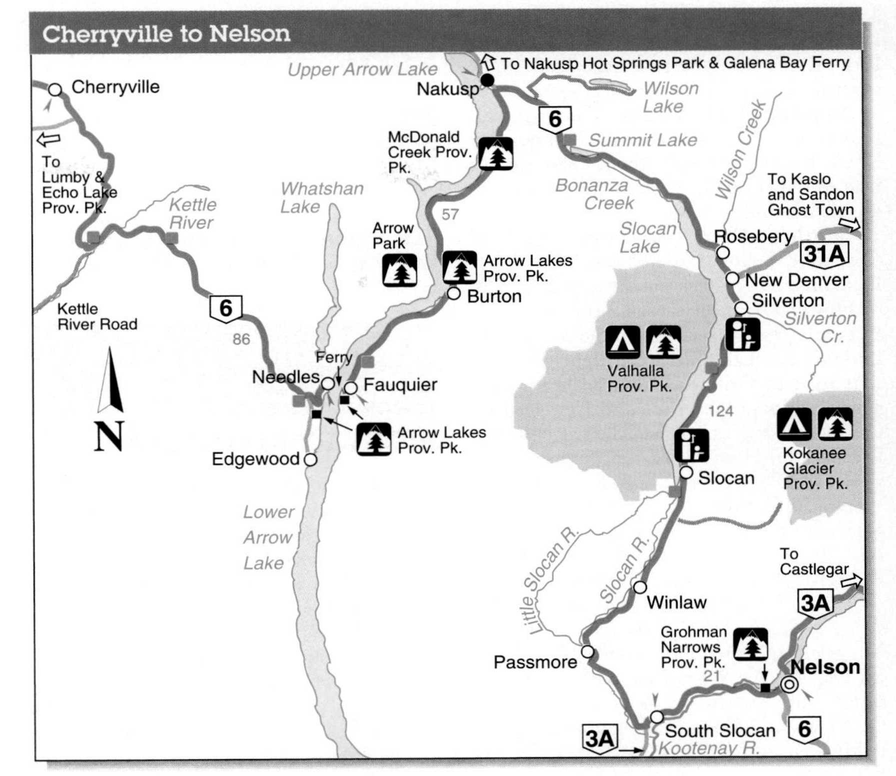


postcard-perfect placidness. Strong winds can funnel down between the mountains, whipping waters into frothy, dangerous whitecaps. Winds come with little warning: keep an eye over your shoulder.

**Silverton:** (Pop. 231). On Hwy 6, 4.5km beyond New Denver. Historic mining town. Has campground, and other accommodation.

- **Silverton Gallery:** Summer exhibitions of photography and work of local artists. Gallery Association operates the Valhalla Music Centre, annual retreat for performing artists. During this time Silverton hears some of the world's finest music.
- **Silverton Museum:** Honours the mining pioneers.
- **Silverton Resort:** Box 107, Silverton, BC, V0G 2B0. 358-7157. On shores of Slocan Lake.
- **Mistaya Country Inn:** Box 28, Silverton, BC, V0G 2B0. 358-7787. Trail rides and pack trips through the Selkirks.

**Slocan Lake Viewpoint:** On Hwy 6, 1.5km beyond Silverton. One of the most spectacular views in the West Kootenay. Fenced path around a 120m cliff.

**Kokanee Glacier Provincial Park:** See *Nelson to Creston*, p.155. Western edge of the park can be reached from Hwy 6 by turning east onto gravel road, 10.5km beyond Silverton.

**Cape Horn:** 22km beyond Silverton. This famous stretch, about 2km long, until just recently narrowed to one lane that clung in white-knuckle curves around a sheer mountainside. A $10 million project completed 1991 took some of the excitement out of the drive. 600,000m of rock were moved about to create a slope angle allowing a regular two-lane highway. A particularly terrifying 1400m stretch is still quietly missed by some locals. Change comes hard in the Slocan Valley.

**Slocan:** (Pop. 263). On Hwy 6, 27km beyond Silverton. In the heart of the "Silvery Slocan", town was one of several established after prospectors in the 1890s discovered the largest silver-lead deposits in BC. Mines around Slocan, New Denver, Silverton, and Sandon were worked until high production costs and low ore prices ended the boom. Slocan was incorporated in 1901 when its population was about 2,000 (at one time it reached 6,000). In 1958, Slocan was incorporated again, as a village. Logging and sawmills now the principal industries. Tourism, since establishment of Valhalla Provincial Park in 1983, has become important. Slocan has its own campground. Ask at infocentre about adventure tours.

**Slocan Information:** Infocentre, Village of Slocan, Box 50, Slocan, BC, V0G 2C0. 355-2277 year-round. Off Hwy 6 in town on Slocan St at Expo Park. Daily, mid-May to mid-Sept. Other times, check with village office located at Delaney Ave and Slocan St.

**Valhalla Provincial Park:** 49,800ha; wilderness camping.

825-4421. Includes western shore of Slocan Lake, and nearly all of the Valhalla Range. Park's Evans Creek-Beatrice Lake Trail can be reached from Slocan by a connecting trail.

**Northern End of Park**: Turn west off Hwy 6 onto gravel road at Hills, 2km north of Slocan Lake's north end. About 28km on dirt road to start of trails. (Terrain here is rugged; experienced hikers only).

**Southern Part**: Turn into Slocan and cross river. Follow Little Slocan River Rd to Passmore-Hoder Creek junction, then 18.5km to Hoder-Drinnon Creek Junction. Also accessible from the village of Slocan, via the Little Slocan Lake Rd. Keep right on rocky spur road to Drinnon Pass trail head. Boat ramps at Slocan, Silverton, and New Denver. Car-toppers also can be launched at Hills and Rosebery on Hwy 6. For topographic maps, write MAPS BC, Parliament Buildings, Victoria, BC, V8V 1X5. For info and a trail guide, write The Valhalla Wilderness Society, Box 224, New Denver, BC, V0G 1S0, or BC Parks, RR 3, Nelson, BC, V1L 5P6.

Peaks of the Valhalla Range dominate the shores of Slocan Lake. On southern boundary is a group of spired and castellated peaks – Mt Dag and the Wolfs Ears, both at 2,667m, Gimli and Asgard peaks at 2,758m, and Gladsheim at 2,827m. Among northern peaks is Mt Denver at 2,758m, with New Denver Glacier clinging to its northern slopes.

A park for climbers and hikers, with challenging rock walls and peaks, and trails that take a few hours or a few days. There is rugged terrain, and those venturing in should be in good shape, properly equipped, maps and compasses a must. It is suggested that anyone considering an extended or overnight hike might register first with the nearest RCMP detachment.

In Norse mythology, Valhalla was palace where slain warriors lived on under the leadership of the god Odin. The splendour of these dramatic peaks fits the heroic legend.

**Wintje's Farm:** Just beyond Slocan on Hwy 6. "Stop and look around, if not, smile as you drive by." A collection of antique farm equipment, bizarre sculptures.

**Kokanee Glacier Provincial Park:** See *Nelson to Creston*, p.155. Can be reached from Hwy 6 by turning east onto gravel road at Lemon Creek, 7.5km south of Slocan. 16km to park.

**Lemon Creek Rest Area:** 7.5km south of Slocan, at Lemon Creek.

**Winlaw:** (Pop. 180). On Hwy 6, 19.5km south of Slocan on Slocan River. John B Winlaw built a sawmill here around 1900. Accommodation and campgrounds.

From here, wilderness starts to give way to farmland, as Slocan River flows through its wide valley.

**Hwy 3A:** Intersects Hwy 6, 46.5km south of Slocan. Hwy 3A goes some 21km south to Castlegar. Hwy 6 continues east 21km to Nelson.

**Nelson:** (Pop. 8,760). Eastern end of Hwy 6. For details, see *Five-Town Loop*, p.145.

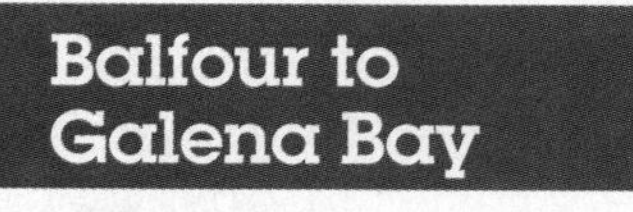


## HIGHWAY 31 and 31A

The 178km lakes and mountains route from Balfour to Galena Bay first follows Hwy 31 to Kaslo, the highway just a narrow ledge along the west side of Kootenay Lake. There's a spot or two where curves and bridges and scenery demand fullest attention and braking dexterity.

From Kaslo, there's a choice between continuing on Hwy 31 north past Duncan and Trout lakes to Galena Bay; or switching east on Hwy 31A to New Denver, and on up Hwy 6, then 23, to Galena Bay.

Surprisingly, the routes cover the same distance, both 142km. Yet there's a big difference in the experience. Hwy 31 is more of an adventure: it's rougher, very isolated, and portions are unpaved. Hwy 31A offers a totally stunning drive through the Selkirks, skirting ghost towns. Both routes are scenic; both are steeped in gold rush history; both are described below. Take your pick.

**Balfour:** (Area pop. 239). Western terminus for free ferry service across Kootenay Lake. For details of Balfour and east shore, see *Nelson to Creston*, p.155.

**Balfour Rest Area:** At ferry terminal. Pleasant beach.

**Pilot Bay:** Road offers view across lake to smoke stacks of smelter that treated ore from Bluebell mine – the discovery of galena here sparked the Slocan's silver rush.

**Coffee Creek:** One of five sites in Kootenay Lake Provincial Park. 71ha. On Hwy 31, 10km north of Balfour. Creek boils downs a narrow gorge, forcing highway into a very sharp switchback.

**Kokanee Glacier Provincial Park:** Reached from Hwy 31 by turning west on gravel road at Coffee Creek, 10km north of Balfour. 10km to park boundary. Described in *Nelson to Creston*, p.155.

**Ainsworth Hot Springs:** (Pop. 57). On Hwy 31, some 15km north of Balfour. Features a horseshoe-shaped cave that was a mine shaft, abandoned when drillers discovered more hot water than ore. Highest mineral content of any hot springs in Canada. Pool temperature 45 degrees C, and the view is fabulous, too. Year-round. At turn of century, Ainsworth supported five hotels: Silver Ledge Hotel remains.

Today you can explore a 20m lighted cave to spring's source, a steam bath with stalactites.

■ **Ainsworth Hot Springs Resort:** Box 1268, Ainsworth Hot Springs, BC, V0G 1A0. 229-4212.

■ **Mountain Trek Fitness Retreat & Health Spa:** Brand new. Box 1352, Ainsworth Hot Springs, BC, V0G 1A0. 229-5636.

**Cody Caves Provincial Park:** 63ha. West onto gravel road off Hwy 31, 3km north of Ainsworth Hot Springs. 15km to start of 20-minute trail to caves. Road usually passable for high-clearance vehicles June-Oct. GUIDED TOURS ONLY! For information, write to Kokanee Creek Provincial Park, RR 3, Nelson, BC, V1L 5P6. 825-4421. Except for a few ladders it's just as Henry Cody found it a hundred years ago. Nearly 1km of passages to explore: stalagmites, stalactites, soda straws, moonmilk, and bacon strips. Take rope, flashlight, rain gear, waterproof boots.

**Woodbury Resort and Marina:** On Hwy 31, 4km north of Ainsworth Hot Springs. Large resort and marina complex. Motel, chalets, campsites. Box 1262, Ainsworth, BC, V0G 1A0. 353-7717.

**Woodbury Mining Museum:** Across from Woodbury Marina. Daily, early July-early Sept. Tours. Blacksmith shop. Gold panning. Write Woodbury Mining Museum, Box 896, Kaslo, BC, V0G 1M0. 354-4470.

**Mirror Lake:** A private lake 15.5km beyond Ainsworth Hot Springs. An important ship-building site during the mining boom.

**Kaslo:** (Pop. 863). On Hwy 31, 5.5km north of Mirror Lake, 36km north of Balfour. Magnificently set on delta of the Kaslo River, between the Selkirks and the Purcells. Called "The Switzerland of the Americas."

A product of the silver bonanza of the 1890s, Kaslo has had its share of disasters. On February 25, 1894, fire broke out at the Bon Ton Restaurant, and swept through the lower half of Front St, destroying almost everything. Later that year Kaslo was struck by a hurricane that blew the front out of the Great Northern Hotel, and completely swept away the jail. 70 other buildings went, too. During the storm a bridge and a log jam gave way, and the rising Kaslo River roared through town, destroying even more. Somehow Kaslo rebuilt over the years. Tree-lined streets, vintage buildings. Also marinas, restaurants, stores, campgrounds, hotels, motels.

**Kaslo Information:** Kaslo & District Chamber of Commerce, Box 329, Kaslo, BC, V0G 1M0. 353-7323. Plans afoot to locate an infocentre, along with the Chamber and Economic Development Office, in the SS *Moyie* Interpretive Centre.

■ **SS *Moyie*:** Beached on Front St, the 49m ship was the last commercial sternwheeler to serve in BC. Daily tours from mid-April to mid-Oct. 353-2525. Sternwheelers played a major role in opening up the western frontier: their shallow draft and light construction let them nose up on beaches to unload people and freight. In olden days, every wharf on the lake was piled with boxes of apples, waiting for the boat. Life for the lakers beat to the rhythm of the friendly paddlewheel. Only two dozen sternwheelers left on the continent, six of them in Canada. Oldest is the "grand old lady of the lake", the *Moyie*, launched in Nelson in 1898, retired from service in 1957. Designated an historic site by the Historic Sites and Monuments Board of Canada.

■ **Langham Cultural Centre:** On A Ave, across from post office. Built in 1893 as a hotel for miners (it had a somewhat dubious reputation). Later successively occupied by Bank of British North America, Knapp Bottling Co, a land speculator, and about 80 interned Japanese-Canadians during World War Two. Now: two galleries, a theatre, studios, arts library, lounge and facilities for artists. Plus newly opened free museum and archival display on Japanese-Canadian internment years. 353-2661.

■ **Kaslo Golf and Country Club:** Nine challenging holes. 353-2262.

**Kaslo Bay:** 2ha. Part of Kootenay Lake Provincial Park. At Kaslo.

**Campbell Creek:** 25ha. Part of Kootenay Lake Provincial Park. Unorganized camping. Boat access only. On east side of lake, opposite Hwy 31, 4km north of Kaslo.

**Hwy 31A:** Up Main St in Kaslo and northwest, leading 47km to New Denver. Hwy 31 continues north, providing the 142km alternate route to Galena Bay via Trout Lake (see final section of this *Log*).

## Highway 31A to New Denver

Hwy 31A is brief and beautiful: a 47km link west across the Selkirks to New Denver. Watch for beavers dragging alders across highway. From New Denver, Hwy 6 runs northwest 46km to Nakusp. Last leg is Hwy 23, 49km to Galena Bay ferry terminal, covered in *Cherryville to Nelson*, p.150.

West off Hwy 31 at Kaslo onto Hwy 31A. Road is built on the old roadbed of narrow-gauge Kaslo and Slocan (K&S) Railway. For five years in the 1890s, the K&S carried ore and passengers up (and down) hair-raising grades on the 45km trip between Sandon and steamboats in Kaslo.

**Kokanee Glacier Provincial Park:** Described under *Nelson to Creston*, p.155. Can be reached by turning southwest off Hwy 31A, onto gravel road 6.5km west of Kaslo. 24km to trails from Joker Millsite.

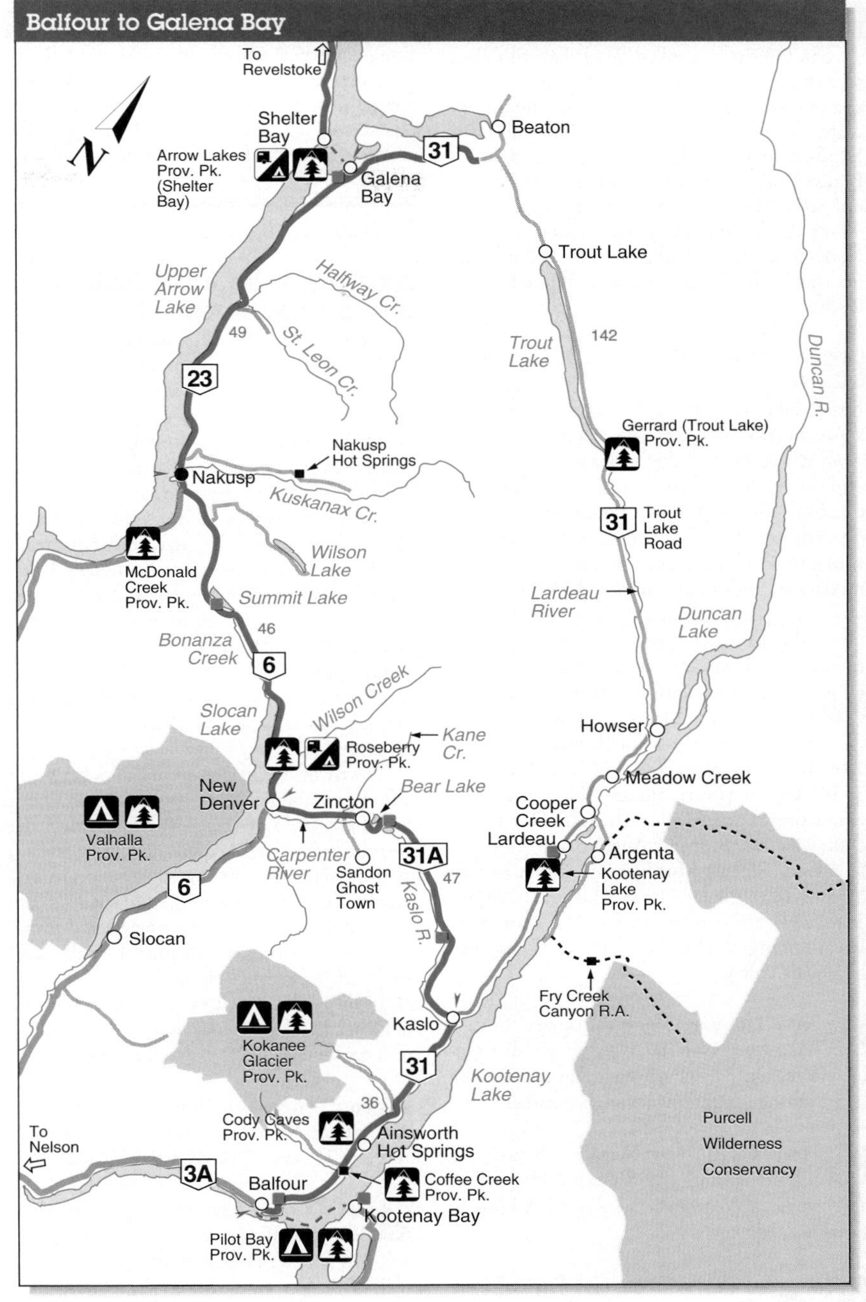


**Fish and Bear Lakes:** On Hwy 31A, beginning about 23km west of Kaslo.

**Retallack Ghost Town:** 27km beyond Kaslo. Area staked in 1892 for iron, but more valuable galena was found. There was an ore concentrator, hotel, and stores.

**Zincton Ghost Town:** 32km beyond Kaslo. Zinc mined here sporadically from 1892 to early 1950s.

**Three Forks Ghost Town:** 38km beyond Kaslo, at junction of Kane, Seaton, and Carpenter creeks, named after prospectors. Nothing left of the six hotels.

**Sandon Ghost Town:** South off Hwy 31A on Sandon Rd, just beyond Three Forks. 5km to town. One of five mining towns in the "Silvery Slocan" that have long been left to the elements. Founded in 1892 and spawned almost overnight by the silver rush, Sandon was a glittering Kootenay mining capital, with 24 hotels, 23 saloons, opera house, red light district. As Colonel Lowery, editor of the *New Denver Ledge*, put it in 1893: "Pumpkins, turnips and townsites are easily grown." Sandon even had electric power (before Vancouver and Victoria). Population was 5,000.

Today, there are just the sounds of Carpenter Creek, a few dilapidated or collapsed buildings from the past, and the tidy houses of hangers-on.

Sandon sits in a valley that is beautiful, but so narrow the towering mountains keep the sun out for much of the day. Museum is open daily, mid-June to mid-Sept. A 2km trail from Sandon leads through alpine meadow to **Idaho Peak Lookout**. Or follow 7km of the old K&S Railway bed between Sandon and Three Forks, near Hwy 31A. Ghost town of Cody is an hour's walk east of Sandon. The famous Noble Five mine was situated above Cody.

**New Denver:** (Pop. 571). At junction of Hwys 31A and 6, 47km northwest of Kaslo. New Denver, idyllically set on eastern shore of Slocan Lake, is a sleepy mountain town where the odd dog snoozes on the street, and stores have false fronts. But don't be deceived: town is a busy service centre for hikers, anglers, boaters, skiers, snowmobilers, with campgrounds, stores, restaurants, accommodation, and a golf course. Back in 1890s, was nearly called El Dorado, but New Denver never did produce gold. What it did have, though, was silver, lead, and zinc.

**New Denver Information:** Infocentre, Slocan and District Chamber of Commerce. Box 448, New Denver, BC, V0G 1S0. July and Aug: 358-7111. Off-season: 358-7906. In Silvery Slocan Museum at corner of 6th St and Marine Dr. May Day weekend, daily, late June-late Aug.

■ **Silvery Slocan Museum:** At corner of 6th St and Marine Dr. Late May-early Sept. 358-7111. Housed in old Bank of Montreal. Local mining and logging. History of Japanese in Slocan Valley.

**New Denver Glacier:** Across Slocan Lake from New Denver. 6km trail from lakeshore. Only patch of snow that remains on surrounding mountains through summer.

**Hwy 6:** In New Denver. South to Silverton and the Slocan Valley. See *Cherryville to Nelson*, p.151. *Log* takes Hwy 6 north to Nakusp.

**Rosebery Provincial Park:** 32ha; 36 campsites. 825-4421. On Hwy 6, 5.5km north of New Denver. On Wilson Creek near Slocan Lake's east shore.

**Summit Lake:** North side of Hwy 6, 29km northwest of New Denver. Resort, camping. Skiing at Summit Peak. T-bar, clubhouse, run by local ski club.

**Box Lake:** South side of Hwy 6, 36km northwest of New Denver. Rainbow trout to 2.5kg. Good fly-fishing. Boat launching, camping. Restricted to electric motors.

**Nakusp:** (Pop. 1,374). At junction of Hwys 6 and 23, 46km northwest of New Denver. Details in *Cherryville to Nelson*, p.150.

**Hwys 6 and 23:** 46km northwest of New Denver. Hwy 6 runs southwest along eastern shore of Upper Arrow Lake to Fauquier and Needles ferry. See *Cherryville to Nelson Log*, p.150. Hwy 23 travels north to Galena Bay and parts north. This leg of the journey is covered in *Cherryville to Nelson*, p.150.

## Return to Kaslo

### Alternate Route to Galena Bay on Highway 31

Hwy 31, between Kaslo and Galena Bay, is a 142km alternate route to Galena Bay, through the once-active Lardeau-Duncan valleys. The landscape is dominated by steep rugged mountains, fast-flowing rivers, long narrow lakes in narrow forested valleys. Northern section of the highway is gravel, and parts are very narrow (some tight squeezes if trucks come along). To start, old farmsteads on Shutty Bench overlook Kootenay Lake. Lakeside resorts, camping. Parts of road, overhung by rocky cliffs, are sometimes closed in winter to clear rock and snow slides.

Grey-green Kootenay argillite, used by Kootenay natives for knives, arrowheads, and scrapers can still be found along creek outwashes.

Towns of Trout Lake City and Ferguson were centres of activity: 200 claims had been staked by 1893. For a while it seemed the Lardeau region might equal the Silvery Slocan, but treacherous terrain made transportation a nightmare. Nevertheless, thousands made their way into the northern valleys, and towns such as Camborne, Poplar Creek, and Goldfields had a brief bloom.

Today the valleys are quiet. The Arrowhead and Kootenay Railway is gone; so are the sawmills at Gerrard and Howser.

**Lost Ledge:** 3ha; 10 primitive campsites. Part of Kootenay Lake Provincial Park. On Hwy 31, some 22km north of Kaslo.

**Davis Creek:** 5ha; 10 simple campsites, also part of Kootenay Lake Provincial Park. On southern outskirts of Lardeau, 30km north of Kaslo.

**Lardeau:** (Pop. 59). On Hwy 31, 30km north of Kaslo. Logging community on a point on Kootenay Lake's west shore. Arrowhead and Kootenay Railway Station has been restored.

**Duncan Dam:** East off Hwy 31 at Cooper Creek, 42km north of Kaslo. Road crosses Duncan River, runs north to Duncan Dam. East side of Duncan Lake, reservoir can be reached by continuing past the dam. Fishing for Dolly Varden char to 4kg and rainbow trout to 1kg. Camping, boating, paddling, swimming, windsurfing. West side can be reached from Howser, on Hwy 31, about 7km north of the turnoff to the Duncan Dam Access Rd at Cooper Creek.

**Purcell Wilderness Conservancy:** Described in *British Columbia Rockies* section, p.258. Can also be reached from Hwy 31 off Duncan Dam Access Rd. Turn south after crossing Duncan River. 5km to Argenta, where sign indicates a short logging road to a trail leading to conservancy.

**Fry Creek Canyon Provincial Recreation Area:** 550ha; unorganized camping. Continue on road south of Argenta for 16km. Excellent hiking along western slopes of Purcell Mountains. 10km trail.

**Meadow Creek:** (Pop. 83). On Hwy 31, 46km north of Kaslo. Store, service station, cafe. Site of Lardeau Lew Logger's Day, held on Labour Day weekend.

**Meadow Creek Spawning Channel:** Follow signs from Meadow Creek. Built to compensate for fish lost in construction of Duncan Dam in 1967. Channel is 9m wide and follows wide S-curves for 3.5km. BC's first kokanee spawning channel. Between 500,000 and 1.2 million return each fall.

**Selkirk Wilderness Skiing:** Snowcat skiing based at Meadow Mountain Lodge. Runs between 300 to 1,200 vertical metres. Snowcat transportation to 2,440m level. Write to Selkirk Wilderness Skiing Ltd, Meadow Creek, BC, V0G 1N0. 366-4424.

**Marblehead:** Just north of Meadow Creek. Quarry here manufactured tombstones and supplied much of the stone for Nelson's most impressive buildings. Closed about 1940.

**Gerrard Provincial Park:** 445ha; 13 campsites. 825-4421. At southeast end of Trout Lake, on Hwy 31 about 37km northwest of Meadow Creek.

**Trout Lake:** Narrow, 28km lake with good fishing for Dolly Varden char and burbot to 4kg, rainbow trout to 2kg. Boat launching at Gerrard or community of Trout Lake, at opposite end of lake.

**Trout Lake:** (Pop. 56). At northwest end of lake, 65km northwest of Meadow Creek. Nice views from road high above lake between Gerrard and Trout Lake.

■ **Great Northern Lodge and Great Northern Snow-Cat Skiing Ltd:** New (1990) 900-sq-m lodge, amid 130 sq km of wilderness ski terrain. Heated snowcats transport 15 passengers a time from lodge to upper alpine ridges of Great Northern and Thompson mountains. Mid-Dec to mid-April. Contact Box 220, Stn G, Calgary, AB. T3A 2G2. (403) 287-2267, or Trout Lake: 369-2227.

**Staubert and Armstrong Lakes:** 8km and 13km northwest of Trout Lake. Fishing for rainbow trout and whitefish.

**Beaton Rd:** North off Hwy 31, 15km northwest of Trout Lake. This is a great road for explorers, and an exciting way to drive back in time. It is certainly off the beaten track. The road goes 5km north to the ghost town of Beaton. Then about 10km farther to Camborne ghost town; and, for the inveterate adventurer, another 10km to Goldfields. Bonus points for Gunterman and Captain Soules falls.

**Hill Creek Spawning Channel and Hatchery:** West off Hwy 31, 9km west of Beaton Rd turnoff. Man-made 1.5km spawning channel. Mainly for kokanee, but also rainbow. Dolly Varden raised in hatchery.

**Hwy 23:** 140km north of Kaslo. Hwy 31 ends at this junction. North onto Hwy 23 for 2km to free **Galena Bay ferry**. Crosses Upper Arrow Lake to Shelter Bay. 20 minutes. Hourly 6:30am-10:30pm, plus one sailing at 12:30am. (June-Sept: Extra sailing at 11:30pm also.) 40 vehicles, 200 passengers. For continuation of Hwy 23, see *Shelter Bay to Mica Creek*, p.173.

# Nelson to Creston

## HIGHWAY 3

Highway 3A between Nelson and Creston is a leisurely, scenic, 113km drive along Kootenay Lake's east shores, between the southern Purcell and Selkirk mountains. From Nelson, Hwy 3A goes 34km to Balfour where free car-and-passenger ferry makes a 40-minute trip across Kootenay Lake. From Crawford Bay, a pretty but constantly twisting route hugs lakeshore 79km to Creston. Pleasant stops – beaches, galleries, and second-hand shops – along the way. The ambience is hard to define, but rarified, laid-back, and definitely special.

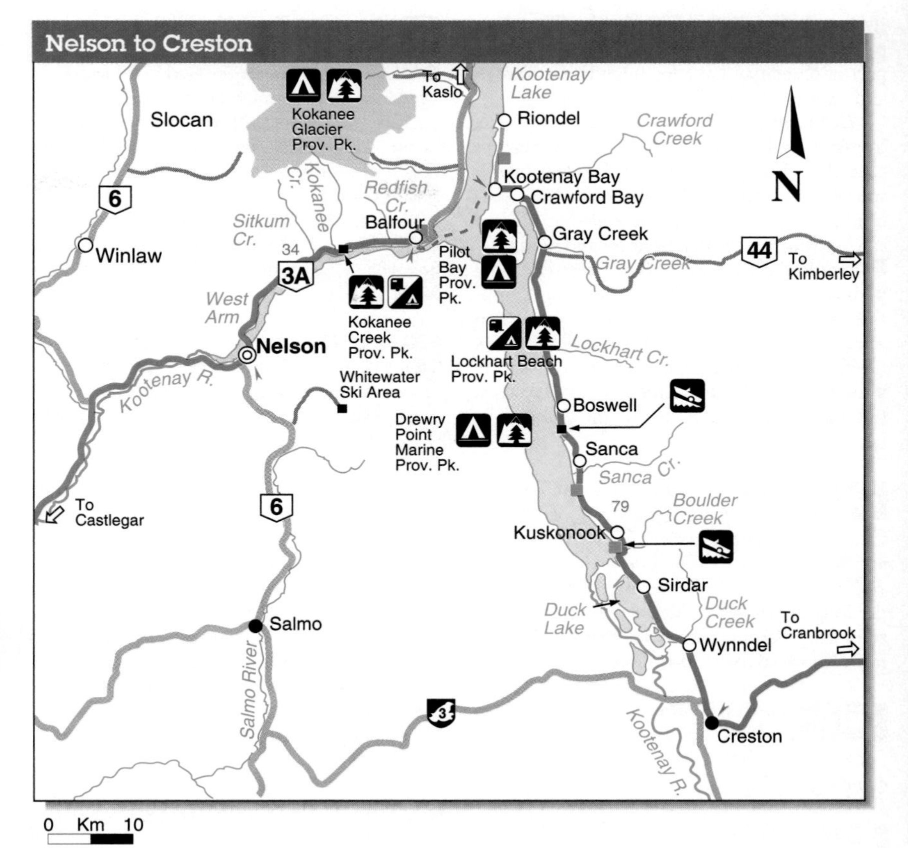

**Nelson:** Detail on Nelson in *Five-Town Loop*, p.145.

**Kokanee Creek Provincial Park:** 260ha; 112 campsites in two campgrounds, sani-station. 825-4421. On Hwy 3A, 21km east of Nelson. Excellent family vacation spot with long, sandy beaches, adventure playground, information centre. Guided tours of man-made spawning channel for kokanee, which return between mid-Aug and mid-Sept. Swimming, fishing, paddling, boating, water-skiing, windsurfing, hiking, visitor programs, photography. Photos especially of ospreys: area has one of the highest osprey (or fish-hawk) populations in North America.

**Kokanee Glacier Provincial Park:** 32,137ha. Information available at Kokanee Creek Provincial Park, RR 3, Nelson, BC, V1L 5P6. 825-4421. For topographic map write MAPS BC, Parliament Buildings, Victoria, BC, V8V 1X5; or Government Agent, 310 Ward St, Nelson, BC, V1L 5S4.

Like the centre of a pinwheel, Kokanee Glacier Park can be reached from a circle of access routes, from here near Nelson, also near Ainsworth, Kaslo, and the Slocan Valley (all described in appropriate *Logs*). All these routes are limited to appropriate vehicles (see below). Main access is reached by driving north off Hwy 3A from Kokanee Creek Provincial Park. 16km gravel road, unsuitable for low-slung vehicles, trailers, or RVs. Parking at Gibson Lake where a 2km nature trail encircles the lake. Also accessible from Hwys 6, 31, and 31A.

The park, in Slocan Range of Selkirk Mountains, is named for the glacier that clings to eastern and northeastern slopes of 2,774m Kokanee Peak, near park's centre. Undeveloped wilderness park with 30 high-elevation lakes, and an extensive network of trails. One of BC's finest hiking locations. Designated outback campsites, a few cabins and shelters. Park covers a variety of climatic zones, with vegetation ranging from dense forest to alpine grassland. Terrain is rugged and diverse. Mountain goats, deer, grizzly and black bears, hoary marmots, pikas, squirrels, and variety of birds.

Prospectors like Dirty Face Johnson and Dutch Charley were drawn to the area more than 100 years ago. Lead, silver, and zinc mines were cut into the rock. Only evidence of this boom left today are ghost towns and abandoned mine shafts.

**Balfour:** (Pop. 239). On Hwy 3A, 34km east of Nelson. Terminal for ferry across Kootenay Lake to Crawford Bay. Town was originally steamboat terminus for mining activities up and down lake. A resort community with accommodation, campgrounds, marinas, full range of fishing services. There's a pub right at the ferry dock, and local cafe offers quacker cwackers to feed the ducks.
■ **Balfour Golf Course:** New. Nine holes on the benchlands above Kootenay Lake. 229-5655.

**Redfish Creek Spawning Channel:** Off Hwy 3A near Balfour. Man-made spawning channel for kokanee. About 3,000 kokanee from mid-Aug to mid-Sept. Interpretive displays, self-guided trails.

**Hwy 31:** From Balfour ferry landing, Hwy 31 runs north to Kaslo, Duncan Lake, Trout Lake, and Galena Bay on Upper Arrow Lake. See *Balfour to Galena Bay*, p.154.

**Kootenay Lake:** Access at Balfour and other locations along lakeshore. More than 100km long, 2km - 6km wide. In the Columbia Mountains, between the Purcells and Selkirks. The West Arm runs 30km down to the city of Nelson, where it narrows into another fork of the Kootenay, eventually joining the Columbia River at Castlegar.

Fishing on this big lake, which doesn't freeze, is a year-round pastime. The lake has been known to yield rainbow trout to 16kg – world's largest – and Dolly Varden char over 10kg. Kokanee here are the largest in the world – over 4kg – and whitefish reach 2kg. Kokanee runs in the West Arm peak about third week in Aug, when they school up at the mouths of creeks. Near the end of July, rainbow trout 1-4kg move into the arm and feed near the surface, an irresistible invitation to fly-fishers. Rainbow fishing in the West Arm peaks about mid-Sept. Trolling in the main part of Kootenay Lake for huge Dolly Varden and rainbows is good from Oct-June.

At the south end of the lake, Duck Lake, Summit and Corn creeks, and the marshy sloughs of the Creston Valley are good spin-casting waters for largemouth bass, particularly April-May. A hot spot for kids to catch yellow perch with bobbers and worms.

■ **Provincial Marine Parks:** Accessible only by boat. Midge Creek Park (158ha; six campsites) is on west side of Kootenay Lake, 16km north of Creston Valley. Drewry Point Park (21ha; two campsites) is also on west shore, 4km north of Midge Creek. Pilot Bay Park (347ha; two campsites) is on east side of lake near ferry landing.

**Kootenay Lake Ferry:** At Balfour, on Hwy 3A, 34km east of Nelson. Car-and-passenger service between Balfour and Kootenay Bay. MV *Anscomb* and the MV *Balfour* ply the waters, offering what's billed as the longest free ferry ride in the world. 15-18 runs a day. Begins 6am from Balfour, 6:50am from Kootenay Bay. 40-minute, 9km crossing.

**Kootenay Bay:** (Pop. 38). 9km across Kootenay Lake from Balfour. Ferry landing has rest area. Restaurants and camping facilities.

**Riondel Rd:** North off Hwy 3A near Kootenay Bay ferry landing. About 9km to village of Riondel.

**Yasodhara Ashram:** North on Riondel Rd. Take Walkers Landing turn-off. Yoga retreat in mountain setting, established over 30 years ago. 227-9224.

**Riondel:** (Pop. 350). On east side of Kootenay Lake. Village with store, pub, restaurant, and community centre. 9-hole golf course overlooking lake. Historic walkway through mine site. Public beach. Riondel Historic Society operates a small museum, open daily, 2-4pm in July-Aug, in Riondel Recreation Building. Photos of sternwheelers, mining operations, and early history of Riondel, site of the Bluebell Mine. Mine closed in 1972. Riondel now a retirement centre – the community centre is in the former high school.

**Crawford Bay:** (Pop. 312). On Hwy 3A, 3.5km southeast of ferry dock. Stores, accommodation, marina. Home to a championship 18-hole golf course, and several unusual cottage industries, such as North Woven Broom and Kootenay Forge. Forge is a traditional blacksmith shop where visitors can watch craftsmen forge graceful, timeless items. Community named for "White Man Jim" Crawford, a prospector and trapper who died in 1914.

**Kootenay Lake Information:** No specific infocentre at the moment, so ask at local friendly stores. Or write Kootenay Lake Chamber of Commerce, Box 4, Gray Creek, BC, V0B 1S0. 227-9315.

**Crawford Bay Airstrip:** Maintained spring, summer, fall.

■ **Kokanee Springs Golf Resort:** In Crawford Bay. A celebrated 18-hole championship golf course. New luxury EE Moore Lodge, where every sundeck faces the Kokanee Glacier. Facilities include airstrip, cottages, campground. Box 96, Crawford Bay, BC, V0B 1E0. 227-9226.

■ **Wedgwood Manor:** Victorian era luxury. Box 135, Crawford Bay, BC, V0B 1E0. 227-9233.

**Gray Creek:** (Pop. 150). On Hwy 3A, 11km south of ferry dock. Beam us down, Scotty. A time-warp here. Gray Creek sets itself up as "metric free." Buy your gas by the gallon, and visit Sharon and Tom Lymbery's Gray Creek Store, where you can also pick up your food, fishing tackle, garden plants, chainsaws, and wood-burning stoves. Also campgrounds, laundromat, boat ramps, Tipi Camp. Sailing regatta on Labour Day weekend. And underwater, site of the famous sunken paddlewheeler, *City of Ainsworth.*

Also, "Gentle Adventures" – water taxi across to Pilot Peninsula, sleep in a tipi, enjoy a custom catered romantic gourmet dinner; or have a seminar or group retreat. Call Guiding Hands Recreation Society, 227-9555. Seasonal.

**Gray Creek-Kimberley Forestry (Hwy 44):** Just south of Gray Creek. Seasonal (June-Oct) gravel road east up Gray Creek and over Baker Pass 86km to Kimberley via St Mary River drainage. Steep, with some 14 percent grades on western side, but passable for RVs and trailers with clearance. East-west, takes an hour off the Calgary to Kootenay Lake trek. Scenic.

**Lockhart Beach Provincial Park:** 3ha; 18 campsites. 825-4421. On Hwy 3A, 13.5km south of Gray Creek (24.5km south of ferry). Hiking, fishing, swimming, boat ramp. Park in a forest of Douglas fir, western red cedar, ponderosa pine.

**Boswell:** (Pop. 200). Lakeside resort 5.5km south of Lockhart Beach (30km beyond ferry). Home of the East Shore Craft Faire, long weekend in Aug. Restaurants, store.

**The Glass House:** 7km south of Boswell, 37km south of ferry. Circular glass castle made by a retired funeral director from 500,000 square embalming fluid bottles.

**Sanca:** (Pop. 33). 41km south of ferry. Once a gold-rush town of 1,500 souls.

**Twin Bays Rest Area:** 44km south of ferry. Near public beach.

**Kuskonook:** (Pop. 43). 51km south of ferry. Thought to have come from Kutenai word meaning "end of the lake". It *is* at the end of the lake. Of course, it could mean something entirely different.

**Kuskonook Rest Area:** On Hwy 3A, 52km south of ferry. Pleasant beach with boat ramp, one of many lake accesses on Hwy 3A.

**Sirdar:** (Pop. 50). 58.5 south of ferry, on shores of Duck Lake. Named after Field Marshal Lord Kitchener who was Sirdar or Commander of Egyptian army in 1892. Sirdar General Store and Sirdar Pub (with home-made food) are both worth a linger.

**Wynndel:** (Area pop. 723). 8km beyond Sirdar (64.5km south of ferry). Known in the 1890s for its Duck Creek Hotel. Boasts one of the only three grain elevators in southern BC.

**Mountain Stream Trout Farm and Recreation Area:** 6.5km south of Wynndel (71km south of ferry). Eight trout ponds in woods overlooking Creston Valley. Fishing, hiking, barbecuing, tackle rentals.

**Bo-Fjords:** Just outside Creston, west of highway, small ranch breeding sturdy, dun-coloured Norwegian fjord horses. Manes are black in centre, white outside, bristling upright and cut in traditional crescent. Probably related to Asian wild horse, the Przewalski. Only 500 in Canada. Phone the Boes for a tour: 428-2181.

**Creston:** (Pop. 4,205). 79km south of Kootenay Bay ferry, on Hwy 3, near its intersection with Hwy 3A. 13km north of the BC/Idaho border. Creston overlooks a broad, fertile valley where the Kootenay River meanders between the Selkirk and Purcell mountains into Kootenay Lake. Known as the "Valley of the Swans," area visited or inhabited by more than 250 bird species. About 12,000ha have been reclaimed by a network of dikes, creating land which has been added to a natural habitat of about 9,000ha. This, and the rolling benchlands above, are important for orchardists, farmers, and hundreds of thousands of waterfowl and other birds that migrate and nest on the Pacific flyway.

Creston has a different history from the rest of the Kootenays, based as it is more on agriculture – dairy farms, orchards – than mining. Area has the mildest climate in BC's southeast, and spring arrives early. Blossom Festival in May celebrates that fact. Fruit stands line Hwy 3A near Creston, and in May, the entire valley is Lilac Heaven. There are only three grain elevators in southern BC: Creston has two, Wynndel, the third. All on the CPR line, these elevators, and the flat fields of alfalfa, give a prairie feel.

The Creston Valley Wildlife Management Area, about 10km northwest of Creston, is one of the area's highlights. It is covered in *Castlegar to Kitchener*, p.149.

During 1860s gold rush, Creston was a major transportation centre on historic Dewdney Trail from Hope to Fort Steele. Hwy 3 from here still follows much the same route. Creston is service centre for an area population of about 15,000.

Area from Creston east to Yahk is on

**Mountain Standard Time** year-round. During summer, when most parts of province move clocks ahead to Daylight-Saving Time, Creston, Kitchener, and Yahk make no changes. Their mountain time is already the same as Daylight-Saving Time.

**Creston Information:** Infocentre, Creston and District Chamber of Commerce, Box 268, Creston, BC, V0B 1G0. 428-4342. At 1711 Canyon St (Hwy 3), log cabin with locomotive in front. Open daily, 7 days a week, year-round. Ask here for brochures on the many trails: biking, hiking, walking, cross-country skiing, birdwatching.

**Creston Airport:** At Lister, about 8km south of Creston. Take Hwy 21 to Mallory Rd and turn east.

■ **Creston Valley Wildlife Centre:** On Hwy 3, 10km northwest of Creston. Detailed information in *Castlegar to Kitchener*, p.149.

■ **Creston Valley Museum (the "Stone House"):** 219 Devon St. 428-9262. Daily in summer, by appointment rest of year. Meticulously constructed of local stone (it took 15 years to build), on attractive grounds overlooking the valley. Has replica of world rarity, the (somewhat temperamental) Kutenai Canoe. "Sturgeon-nosed" canoe points down, under the water, at either end. Only other similar canoe in the world was made by Goldi peoples of Amur River Basin in Russia, suggesting migration across Bering Strait.

■ **The Murals:** Now there are six! The one that began it all is on McDowell's Department Store. Depicts Creston Valley's four seasons. By Stefan Bell. Others are around the town.

■ **Cresteramics:** 921 Railway Blvd. 428-7412. Ceramics workshop with store. Employment and training for handicapped. Mon-Sat, tours Mon-Fri.

■ **The Kootenay Candle Factory:** 1511 Northwest Blvd. 428-9785. Tours Mon-Sat, mid-May to Oct. Yesteryear candles in wax molds from antique glassware.

■ **Wayside Garden and Arboretum:** 2915 Hwy 3 at Erickson, eastern outskirts of Creston. Daily May-Oct. Roses, rhododendrons, and others, plus more than 200 trees and shrubs collected from temperate zones of the world. Mountain and orchard views.

■ **Creston Golf Club:** 18-hole course with omnipresent spectacular views of Creston Valley and Selkirk Mountains. 428-5515.

Hwy 3A ends at Creston. From here, Hwy 21 extends south 13km to Rykerts at US border. Open 8am-11pm. Hwy 3 (the Crowsnest) extends west and east. Pick up from Creston in *Castlegar to Kitchener*, p.149, or *Kitchener* to Wasa, p.249.

*The sternwheeler, SS* Moyie, *beached on Front St in downtown Kaslo, on Kootenay Lake.*

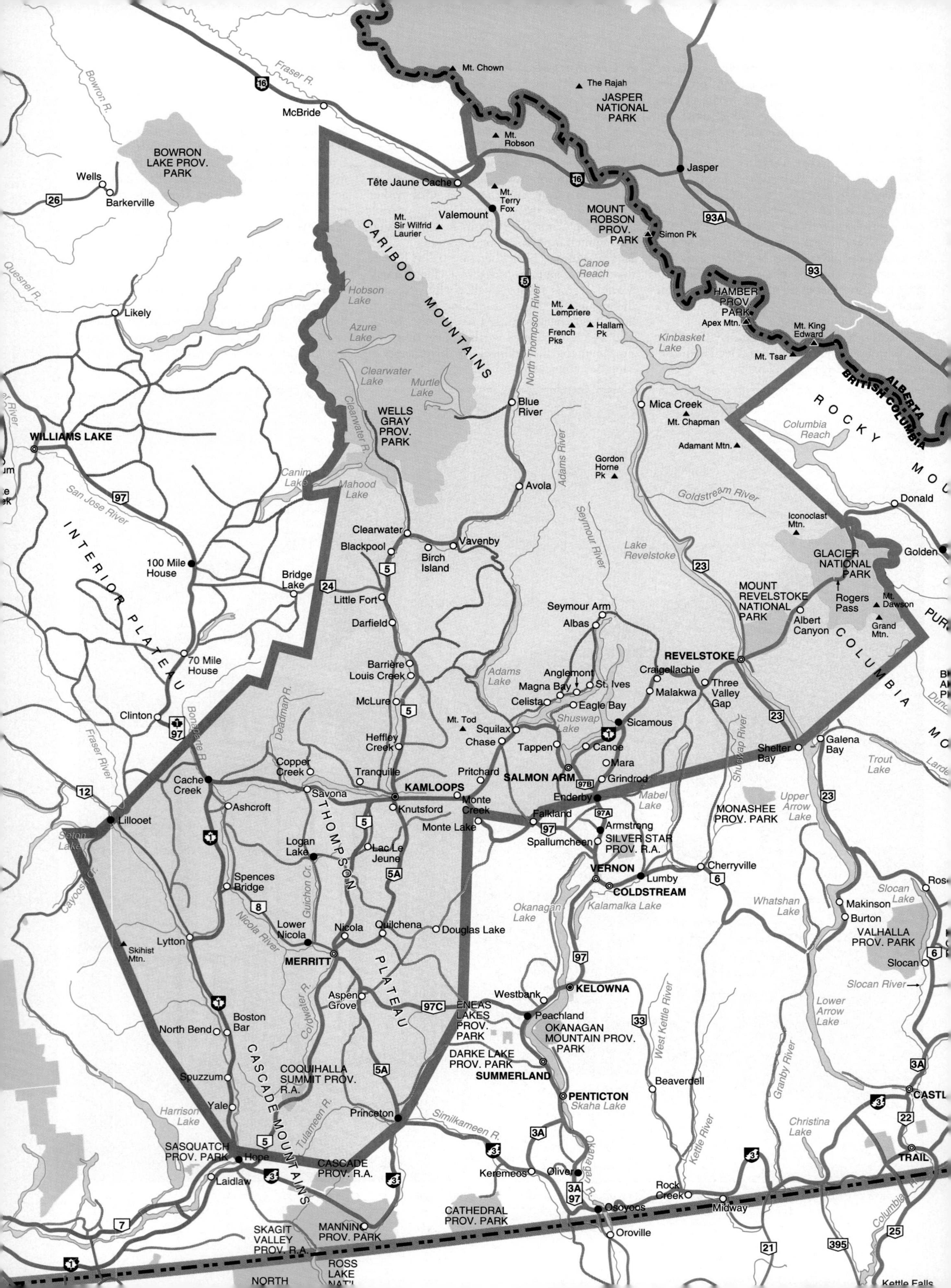

Mt. Chown
The Rajah
JASPER
NATIONAL
PARK
Fraser R.
Bowron R.
McBride
Mt.
Robson
BOWRON
LAKE PROV.
PARK
Wells
Barkerville
26
16
Tête Jaune Cache
Jasper
Mt.
Terry
Fox
Valemount
Mt.
Sir Wilfrid
Laurier
MOUNT
ROBSON
PROV.
PARK
93A
Simon Pk
CARIBOO
MOUNTAINS
Quesnel R.
Canoe
Reach
93
5
Hobson
Lake
HAMBER
PROV.
PARK
Apex Mtn.
Mt.
Lempriere
Hallam
Pk
French
Pks
Likely
Azure
Lake
North Thompson River
Kinbasket
Lake
Mt. King
Edward
Mt. Tsar
Clearwater
Lake
Murtle
Lake
ALBERTA
BRITISH COLUMBIA
Blue
River
Mica Creek
Mt. Chapman
ROCKY
MOU
WELLS
GRAY
PROV.
PARK
Clearwater R.
WILLIAMS LAKE
Adams River
Columbia
Reach
Adamant Mtn.
Gordon
Horne
Pk
Canim
Lake
Mahood
Lake
Avola
San Jose River
97
Goldstream River
Donald
Iconoclast
Mtn.
Clearwater
Blackpool
Vavenby
Birch
Island
Seymour River
Lake
Revelstoke
INTERIOR PLATEAU
100 Mile
House
GLACIER
NATIONAL
PARK
Golden
23
Bridge
Lake
24
Little Fort
MOUNT
REVELSTOKE
NATIONAL
PARK
Rogers
Pass
Mt.
Dawson
Grand
Mtn.
Albert
Canyon
Seymour Arm
Albas
Darfield
70 Mile
House
Barrière
Louis Creek
REVELSTOKE
Craigellachie
COLUMBIA
Adams
Lake
Anglemont
Magna Bay
St. Ives
Malakwa
Three
Valley
Gap
McLure
Celista
Eagle Bay
Clinton
Deadman R.
Bonaparte R.
Mt. Tod
Squilax
Shuswap
Lake
Sicamous
Fraser River
Heffley
Creek
Chase
Tappen
Canoe
Shuswap River
Galena
Bay
Shelter
Bay
Trout
Lake
Copper
Creek
Tranquille
Pritchard
Mara
12
Cache
Creek
SALMON ARM
Grindrod
KAMLOOPS
Savona
Monte
Creek
Enderby
Mabel
Lake
Upper
Arrow
Lake
Lillooet
Ashcroft
Knutsford
97B
97A
MONASHEE
PROV. PARK
Seton
Lake
THOMPSON
Monte Lake
Falkland
Armstrong
SILVER STAR
PROV. R.A.
Spallumcheen
Logan
Lake
Lac Le
Jeune
5A
VERNON
Cherryville
Spences
Bridge
Guichon Cr.
Lumby
COLDSTREAM
6
Slocan
Lake
Kalamalka Lake
Whatshan
Lake
Makinson
Cayoosh Cr.
8
Nicola River
Okanagan
Lake
Burton
Lower
Nicola
Nicola
Quilchena
Douglas Lake
VALHALLA
PROV. PARK
Skihist
Mtn.
Lytton
MERRITT
PLATEAU
Slocan
Westbank
KELOWNA
Slocan River
Coldwater R.
Aspen
Grove
97C
ENEAS
LAKES
PROV.
PARK
Peachland
West Kettle River
Lower
Arrow
Lake
North Bend
Boston
Bar
33
OKANAGAN
MOUNTAIN PROV.
PARK
DARKE LAKE
PROV. PARK
SUMMERLAND
Granby River
3A
CASCADE MOUNTAINS
COQUIHALLA
SUMMIT PROV.
R.A.
Spuzzum
Beaverdell
PENTICTON
Skaha Lake
Harrison
Lake
Yale
Tulameen R.
Princeton
Similkameen R.
Kettle River
Christina
Lake
22
SASQUATCH
PROV. PARK
Hope
CASCADE
PROV. R.A.
Okanagan R.
TRAIL
Laidlaw
3
Keremeos
Oliver
Rock
Creek
Columbia R.
CATHEDRAL
PROV. PARK
Osoyoos
Midway
7
MANNING
PROV. PARK
SKAGIT
VALLEY
PROV. R.A.
Oroville
21
395
25
ROSS
LAKE
NORTH
Kettle Falls

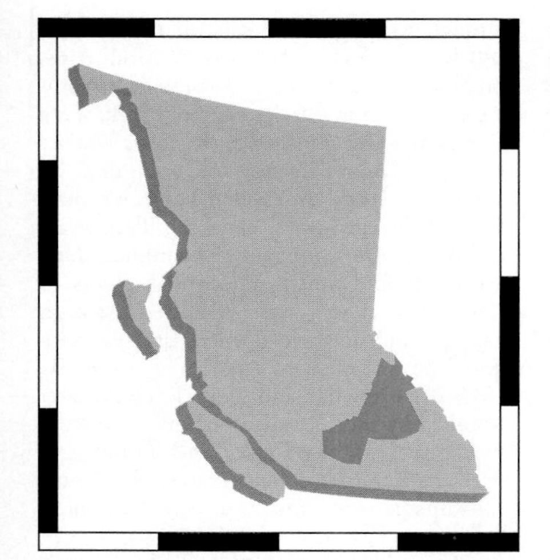

# High Country

## *Highways through Extremes*

Few regions are as diverse as British Columbia's High Country. From rolling grasslands in the west to the jagged peaks of the Rockies, it lacks only the salty sea air of the Pacific Coast. It's a region of extremes, with the glacier-green and deep blue waters of the Thompson River flowing from the forests of the Interior "wet belt", across a desertlike "dry belt" to the Fraser River. You can travel through in a single day, but you'd need a lifetime to explore the myriad lakes, mountain passes and peaks, and to absorb the history.

You'd have to return in every season to sample the endless array of activities these changing landscapes present. In summer you could view the shores of Shuswap Lake from the deck of a houseboat, or canoe the wilderness lakes of Wells Gray Provincial Park. You could hop on a horse and ride the ranges of the Nicola Valley or travel the trails of the Cariboo Mountains. You could splash down the Thompson, Fraser, Adams, Illecillewaet, or Clearwater rivers in a rubber raft, or windsurf on Stump Lake.

In winter you could take your downhill or cross-country skis to Lac Le Jeune, Tod Mountain, the Kane Valley, or Mt MacPherson. Board a helicopter at Revelstoke, Valemount, or Blue River to ski the Cariboos, Monashees, or Rockies. Snowmobile across fields and open ridges or climb the icy walls of Durrand Glacier. Huddle over a hole in a frozen lake and dangle a fishhook before the eyes of a hapless trout.

From spring to fall anglers from around the world come to test their piscatorial skills in more than 600 lakes and countless streams throughout the High Country region. It's known as one of the hottest fishing spots in Interior BC and angling here is big business. In spring and fall fly-fishermen catch rainbow trout, usually small, but occasionally up to 4.5kg. In summer, when rainbow fishing slackens with warmer weather, anglers switch to kokanee, small landlocked sockeye salmon. Many of the same waters are inhabited by Dolly Varden char, some as big as 9kg. Similarly sized lake trout are the prime quarry of deep-water anglers in Adams and Shuswap lakes. The Thompson and Nicola rivers are favourite fishing grounds between October and December, yielding steelhead trout weighing up to 4.5kg.

The High Country region is also superb for wildlife watching. The largest animals are moose, commonly spotted in winter and spring on the meadows beside Highway 5A, between Merritt and Kamloops, and farther north, along Hwy 5. You can watch for bighorn sheep between Lytton and Ashcroft, or on the Thompson River near Spences Bridge. Farther upstream on the Thompson you may see bighorns on Squilax Mountain near Chase, and by Tranquille Marsh on the north side of Kamloops Lake. If you scan the

*Revelstoke viewed from the top of 1,830m Mt Revelstoke, in Mount Revelstoke National Park.*

slopes in Mt Revelstoke and Glacier national parks you may see shaggy, sure-footed mountain goats. Black bears are extremely common, and if you're lucky you may focus your binoculars on a grizzly lumbering across a distant valley.

Bald eagles perch on snags along the Thompson River between Ashcroft and Sicamous, and also like the lakes along Hwy 5A between Merritt and Kamloops. Look for red-tailed hawks and kestrels on fence posts, and osprey on lofty stick nests on the shores of Kamloops Lake, Shuswap, and other large lakes. The hundreds of lakes and marshes are valuable spring and autumn stopovers as well as nesting grounds for thousands of waterfowl. Besides an incredible variety of puddle ducks, divers and dabblers, there are several large species that grace the High Country skies –trumpeter and whistling swans, Canada geese, snow geese, and pelicans.

The entire Thompson River system has always been important to wildlife. A major tributary to the Fraser River, the Thompson reaches almost all parts of the High Country region. Its course has also been one of the main transportation routes through the southern Interior since the early 1800s.

Before the Thompson's blue-green waters collide with the muddy Fraser River at Lytton, it cuts a course across the Thompson Plateau, the "dry belt," a gently rolling upland, 1,200 to 1,500m above sea level. This is cattle and horse country, with golden grasslands and sage, and some of Canada's largest cattle ranches – at Nicola, Quilchena, and Douglas Lake.

The North Thompson, flowing from the Cariboo Mountains, and the South Thompson, from Shuswap Lake, meet the Thompson River in downtown Kamloops. East and north of Kamloops is the Shuswap Highland, stretching east to the Monashee Mountains. These catch some of the moisture drifting across from the coast, creating an Interior wet belt.

The Monashees, along with the Selkirk ranges, with peaks over 3,200m, form part of the extensive Columbia River valley. This river has been dammed over several decades to become a major producer of hydroelectric power for both Canada and the US. The reservoirs in the High Country region – Arrow Lakes, Lake Revelstoke, and Kinbasket Lake – are among the province's largest lakes.

Long before the dams, the Columbia River was a highway to the sea for 19th-century fur traders. When gold was discovered in 1865 on the Columbia's Big Bend, north of Revelstoke, the region was flooded by treasure hunters. Most arrived, however, not by the Columbia, but by the Thompson system. By 1866 a mule-train route was established along the Thompson River from Cache Creek to Savona, at the western end of Kamloops Lake. Sternwheelers carried miners up the lake and along the South Thompson River to Salmon Arm, at the lake's south end. Seymour Arm, at the north end of the lake, became a thriving service depot as gold diggers, dropped by boats, set out on a trail across the Monashees to the Columbia River.

These routes were again used by railways after BC became a Canadian province in 1871. Under the terms of Confederation, the Canadian Pacific Railway brought its line through Kicking Horse Pass, in the Rockies, and Rogers Pass, in the Selkirk Mountains. Building through Rogers Pass, with its summit at 1,382m in Glacier National Park, was a formidable task. Construction crews worked in steep, unstable terrain, plagued by avalanches, rock slides, and harsh weather. West of the pass, which links the Illecillewaet and Beaver rivers, the railway continued along the Eagle and South Thompson rivers to Kamloops. It was later extended through Ashcroft and down to Spences Bridge, and a spur line was built to Merritt by 1906. By 1915 the Canadian Northern Railway, later absorbed by the Canadian National, ran from Vancouver up the Fraser and Thompson rivers to Kamloops. It then used the North Thompson route and continued through Yellowhead Pass.

Major highways to the High Country region today, with a few exceptions, use the same transportation corridors as the voyageurs and railway men of the last century did. The history along the highways and back roads here is part of the scenery – old churches and farmhouses, ancient orchards, rusting farm machinery, and weatherworn cabins. Some of the old country inns and other buildings have been restored and continue to operate as they have for many decades.

These remnants of pioneer life stir the imaginations of High Country travellers. And if you hike or paddle deep into the outback, or stand amid a colourful infinitude of alpine flowers, or simply lie on a hillside and watch the long, golden grass rippling in a summer breeze, you'll get the feeling that little has changed here in the last century, and you'll hope that little will change in the next one.

*Rogers Pass in Glacier National Park.*

## Information

**High Country Tourism Association:** Write #2-1490 Pearson Pl, Kamloops, BC, V1S 1J9, or call 372-7770. Fax: 828-4656. Addresses, telephone numbers, and hours of operation of local infocentres are shown in the *Logs* under write-ups on each community.

## Transportation

Airlines, buses, and railways provide transportation to High Country from major Canadian and American centres. Kamloops has a city bus service. A few small ferries provide river crossings and lake transportation. For telephone numbers of air, rail, and bus services, check the yellow pages of your telephone directory. Some companies have toll-free numbers, or numbers to call in the High Country region. Those numbers are shown below.

Infocentres provide transportation information, including names of small airline companies, car and RV rentals, canoe, kayak and boat rentals, packhorse outfitters, and local bus and taxi services.

### Airlines

Kamloops is the High Country's major centre and is served by several airlines.

■ **Canadian Airlines International:** In Kamloops, for reservations, 376-5721. For arrival and departure information, 376-3341.

■ **Air BC:** 360-9074.

■ **Air Canada:** 360-9074 or toll-free 1-800-663-3721.

■ **Canadian Airlines International:** Toll-free 1-800-663-3502.

### Railways

■ **VIA Rail:** Toll-free 1-800-561-8630. VIA Rail follows Hwy 1 from the Lower Mainland to Kamloops. From Kamloops, VIA Rail runs northeast along Hwy 5, the Yellowhead, through Valemount and the Rockies to Alberta via Jasper, and continues to Edmonton and Toronto. Departs Vancouver Mon, Thurs, Sat, 8pm.

■ **Rocky Mountain Railtours:** Great Canadian Rail Tour Company, Suite 104-340 Brooksbank Ave, Vancouver, BC, V7J 2C1. 1-800-665-7245. Sublimely, through the Rockies. Vancouver to Jasper, Vancouver to Banff, optional to Calgary. Travels only in daylight. Passengers going east or west spend the night in Kamloops. Continental breakfast, gourmet lunch, and hotel are included. Operates May-early Oct.

### Bus Lines

■ **Greyhound Lines of Canada:** In Kamloops, 374-1212. Travels the Trans-Canada, Coquihalla, and Yellowhead highways through High Country.

### Inland Ferries

The Ministry of Transportation and Highways operates a small fleet of inland ferries to complete the highway system where there are no bridges crossing the Fraser, Thompson, and Arrow Lakes waterways. These ferries are free of charge and carry both passengers and vehicles. Schedule information should be used only as a guideline since times can change on short notice.

■ **Shelter Bay to Galena Bay (Hwy 23):** Revelstoke, 837-7724, or New Denver, 358-2212. From Galena Bay, hourly sailings between 6:30am and 12:30am (except 11:30pm). From Shelter Bay, hourly sailings between 6am and midnight (except 11pm). 20 minutes. MV *Galena*: 40 cars, 200 passengers. Extra sailings in summer on MV *Shelter Bay*: 28 cars, 96 passengers. Some waits on busy weekends.

The provincial government also provides ferry service across the Fraser River at Lytton and across the North Thompson River at McClure and Little Fort.

■ **Shuswap Lake Ferry Service Ltd:** Box 370, Sicamous, BC, V0E 2V0. 836-2200. Runs two boats and a barge for passengers and freight on Shuswap Lake. Details under *Salmon Arm to Rogers Pass.*

## HIGH COUNTRY EVENTS

### Ashcroft

■ **Ashcroft and District Stampede:** Mid-June.

### Barrière

■ **Squam Bay Fishing Derby:** Early July.

■ **North Thompson Fall Fair and Rodeo:** Labour Day weekend.

### Cache Creek

■ **Graffiti Weekend and Old-Time Drag:** Early June.

### Chase

■ **Chase Daze, Mud Bog and Slowpitch:** Late June.

■ **Craftarama:** Mid-Aug.

### Clearwater

■ **Wells Gray Loppet:** Feb. Ski race.

■ **Wildflowers Wells Gray:** Late July.

■ **Raft River Riders Gymkhana and Horse Show:** Early Aug.

### Falkland

■ **International Dog Sled Races:** Jan.

■ **Falkland Stampede:** Late May.

■ **Daisy Daze:** Mid-Aug. Flea market, bed races, corn roast.

### Kamloops

■ **Kamloops Professional Indoor Rodeo:** Late April. At McArthur Island.

■ **Sagebrush Downs Horse Racing:** June-Sept.

■ **Kamloops Country Music-Bluegrass Festival:** Late July.

■ **Kamloops Rangeland Derby Days:** Late July.

■ **Tod Mountain Alpine Blossom Festival:** Late July.

■ **Kamloops International Air Show:** Early Aug.

■ **Kamloops Indian Powwow:** Mid-Aug. Kamloops Indian Reserve.

■ **Provincial Winter Fair:** Late Sept.

### Logan Lake

■ **Polar Carnival:** Feb.

■ **Lobsterfest:** Late May, early June.

■ **Little Britches Rodeo:** Late July, early Aug.

### Lytton

■ **Lytton Days:** May long weekend.

■ **Jelly Roll Days:** Aug. Slowpitch and Jelly Roll entertainment.

### Merritt

■ **Children's Festival:** Mid-April.

■ **Little Britches Rodeo:** June.

■ **Mountain Music Festival:** July.

■ **Nicola Valley Rodeo and Fair Days:** Labour Day weekend.

### North Shuswap

■ **Shuswap Lake Bluegrass Festival:** July.

■ **Adams River Salmon Run:** Oct.

### Revelstoke

■ **Snowfest:** 2nd weekend, Feb.

■ **Summer Live Entertainment:** Summer nights, Plaza Gazebo.

■ **Revelstoke Mountain Festival:** Early Aug.

■ **Pilgrimage to Eva Lake:** Mid-Aug. 12km Canadian Parks Service hike to Mt Revelstoke to see blooming wildflowers.

### Salmon Arm

■ **Sonnet Festival:** Late March.

■ **Shuswap Rodeo:** Late June.

■ **Strawberry Festival:** July.

■ **Pioneer Days:** Aug.

■ **Chariot and Chuckwagon Races:** Aug.

### Sicamous

■ **Reino Keski-Salmi Loppet:** Jan. Larch Hills.

■ **Shuswap-Mara Lake Regatta:** Late May.

■ **Moose-Mouse Days:** BC Day weekend.

■ **Adams River Salmon Run:** Sept-Oct.

### Sorrento

■ **Trappers Landing Days:** July 1. Fireworks, parade, fastball.

■ **Shuswap Lake Festival of the Arts:** July.

### Squilax

■ **Squilax Powwow:** Mid-July.

### Valemount

■ **Valemount Days:** Mid-June.

■ **Chinook Salmon Run:** Mid-Aug to Sept (Swift Creek).

**Logan Lake Information:** Infocentre, District of Logan Lake, Box 1060, Logan Lake, BC, V0K 1W0. 523-6322. On main road, near recreation centre. Daily, June-Sept.

**Mamit Lake Rd:** South off Highland Valley Rd, 3km west of Logan Lake. A paved, 40km alternate route to **Merritt** through open cattle country. **Ashcroft** can be reached by continuing west along Highland Valley Rd about 30km.

**Highland Valley Copper:** On Highland Valley Rd, about 15km west of Logan Lake. Largest open-pit copper mine in North America. Tours Mon-Fri, 10-1, early May-late Sept. 575-2443. Call ahead for large groups.

### Return to Highway 5

## SIDE TRIP
### to Lac Le Jeune

**Walloper Lake Provincial Park:** 55ha. Wilderness camping only. East off Hwy 5 on Lac Le Jeune Rd. Immediately past turnoff. Rainbow trout fishing, ice-fishing, cross-country skiing. Canoe and boat rentals, tackle, accommodation, camping, store.

**Lac Le Jeune Provincial Park:** 47ha; 144 campsites. 828-4494. East off Lac Le Jeune Rd, 7km northwest of Hwy 5. Good rainbow trout fishing. Visitor programs, wheelchair access, boat launch, sani-station, archaeological sites, swimming, cross-country skiing.

**Lac Le Jeune Resort:** Near provincial park. 100km of groomed cross-country trails. Also five downhill runs. 245m vertical drop. T-bar, handle tow. Day lodge and resort, ski school. Box 3215, Kamloops, BC, V2C 6B8. 372-2722.

**Stake-McConnell Lakes Provincial Recreation Area:** 189ha. 15 campsites. 3km north of turnoff to Lac Le Jeune Park. Excellent fly-fishing, boating, mountain biking, cross-country skiing, motorcycle ice-racing.

It is possible to reach **Kamloops** by continuing north on Lac Le Jeune Rd for 20km from McConnell Lake. Many lakes and streams.

### Return to Highway 5

**Hwy 1/97:** Short distance southwest of Kamloops town centre, 23km north of Lac Le Jeune-Meadow Creek roads junction. West to Cache Creek; east into Kamloops.

**Kamloops:** (Pop. 67,057). At the end of the Coquihalla Hwy, 200km northeast of Hope. The southern Interior's largest city, the province's 5th largest, and in terms of area, the vastest, occupying 310 sq km of Thompson River Valley. The old quarter of the city, with its dozen or so well-maintained turn-of-the-century brick buildings, sits on the low banks of the South Thompson River, fronted by a lovely sand-beach park. Greater Kamloops itself is an amalgamation of more than a dozen communities separated by the blue-green waters of the converging North and South Thompson rivers. The city takes its name from this convergence – *Kamloopa* is a Shuswap native word meaning "where the rivers meet."

The city is also junction of an important north-south valley and the only major east-west valley in southern BC.

Since its establishment as a fur-trading post in 1812, Kamloops has received travellers coming by packhorse and sternwheeler, by train, truck, and RV. It has always been a junction, an oasis for transient fur traders in the early 1800s, a depot for treasure hunters in the 1860s.

As the gold rush faded in late 1860s, way-worn miners preempted farmland and planted the roots of a community. By the time the Canadian Pacific Railway's first trans-continental train passed through in 1886, the government was already building a new courthouse and the locals were lobbying for Kamloops to be the new BC capital. On the old BC Fruitland estates (now North Kamloops), English gentlemen farmers and remittance men raised gamecocks to shoot. Scarlet-coated horsemen galloped about the hills to the sounds of hounds and hunting horns, chasing wild foxes. (In nearby Ashcroft, the quarry was the lowly coyote.) By 1893, when the city was incorporated, it was home to 1,000 people. When North Kamloops and Kamloops amalgamated in 1967, there were 20,000 residents.

Today, many of Kamloops' 70,000 residents are employed in the forest industry, in both logging and production of pulp and paper, plywood, and lumber. Large copper mines, south in the Highland Valley, are also major employers. The city is also something of a watering hole for the area's cowboys: the Thompson and nearby Okanagan valleys together support 1,100 ranches, most of them around Kamloops, where BC's cattle industry was born in the 1860s. See *Index* for historic ranches: Harpers, Douglas Lake Cattle Company, Quilchena.

This city, with so much growing space, has ambition. It touts itself both the Beef *and* Tournament Capital of Canada. Where else would you find enough room for 84 baseball diamonds, 73 soccer fields, five ice arenas, 40 gymnasiums, seven golf courses, 53 tennis courts, and the new 5,000-seat Riverside Coliseum built to accommodate Kamloops' biggest tournament yet, the Canada Summer Games, held in August 1993?

The rolling uplands surrounding the city are a mix of forests and grasslands, with the Coast Mountains in the distant west and the Shuswap Highland in the east. At hand are eerily shaped hills and hoodoos, scorched monoliths convey a feeling of otherworldly beauty.

There are about 200 lakes in the area, reckoned one of BC's best fishing centres, with steelhead, rainbow and eastern brook trout, Dolly Varden char, and kokanee. The most sought-after fresh-water fish is named after the city. The Kamloops, or rainbow trout, has enticed anglers from around the world. It has been introduced as a sport fish across North America and in New Zealand,

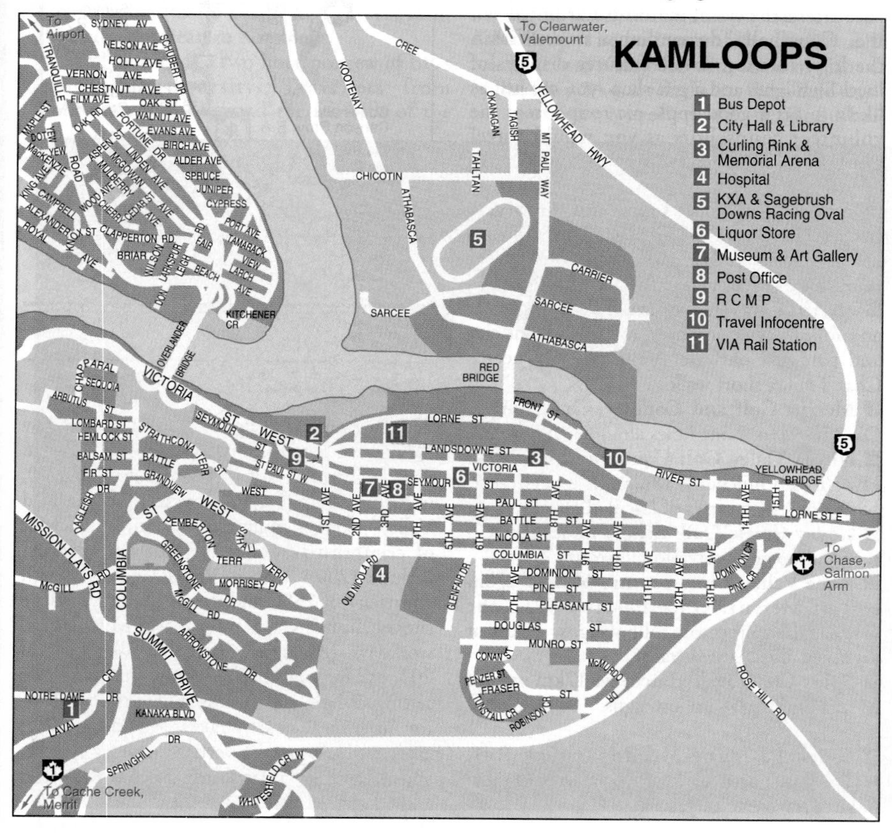

Africa, Australia, South America, Japan and southern Asia, Europe, and Hawaii.

Rainbow are stocked in lakes across BC and while the average size is .5kg, it is still fairly common for fishermen to land rainbows of about 2.5kg. These feisty fish are taken by all types of anglers, particularly fly-fishermen.

There are dozens of lodges and fish camps, and many operators belong to the BC Interior Fishing Camp Operator's Association, Box 3301, Kamloops, BC, V2C 6B9. Infocentres can help. Or write High Country Tourism Association, p.160.

Skiing is also popular. For info on Tod Mountain, 53km north of Kamloops, see *Kamloops to Jasper*, p.178.

Horseback-riding trips are offered by local stables. Check with infocentre.

**Kamloops Information:** Infocentre, 10-10th Ave, Kamloops, BC, V2C 6J7. 374-3377; toll-free 1-800-667-0143. Downtown near Thompson River. Mon-Fri, early Sept-June 30; open daily longer hours in July and Aug. Satellite infocentres at Hwy 1 west, and at Haltson Bridge Esso Station, Hwy 5 north.

**Kamloops Airport:** North side of Thompson River, 7km east of town centre. Served by major airlines.

■ **Kamloops Museum and Archives:** 207 Seymour St. 828-3576. 10-5, Tues-Sat; Sun, 1-5, except stat holidays. May 15-Sept 4, daily 10-9. History of the Kamloops region. Local native culture, fur trade, pioneer and Victorian life, industry and natural history.

■ **Kamloops Art Gallery:** 207 Seymour St (same building as museum). 828-3543. Daily. Monthly exhibits, local to international.

■ **Secwepemc Native Heritage Park:** 355 Yellowhead Hwy, Kamloops, BC, V2H 1H1. 828-9801 or 828-9781. On banks of South Thompson River, on Kamloops Indian Band reserve. 4ha of "living laboratory," museum, university, cultural and public education centre with mandate to bring Shuswap culture to the world. Shuswap is an English derivation of Secwepemc (pronounced she-kwe-pem), the people who have occupied the vast territory from Kamloops north to Soda Creek, east to the Rockies, and west to the Fraser River for at least 4,000 years. The Kamloops Band is one of 17 contemporary Secwepemc bands. The Heritage Park features an archaeological site – a winter village used by the Secwepemc people 1,200-2,400 years ago, and a reconstructed winter village showing housing over five periods, from 5,000 years ago to the late 19th century. There are also exhibits of native food plants, a salmon-fishing station, native song, dance, storytelling and theatre; salmon barbecues in a traditional summer lodge; indoor museum exhibits focussing on the Shuswap Nation; native arts and crafts sales and demonstrations. Opened Aug 1993.

The Kamloops Indian Band, a prosperous community of some 750, supervises industrial parkland, agricultural and grazing lands, historic and archaeological sites extending 11km up the North Thompson and 11km up the South Thompson (13,355ha) – immediately across the Red Bridge, due north of downtown Kamloops. The Shuswap language is taught in the local Sek'Lep School. In the new housing development, streets are named Haida Way, Chilcotin Street, Dené Drive. Stop signs say *Esti'l*.

■ **St Joseph's Church:** On Kamloops Indian Band reserve. 828-9700. July 1-Labour Day. This little Catholic church was built late in the 1800s. Cemetery adjacent.

■ **Riverside Park:** In town on south side of Thompson River. Tennis, swimming. Walking trails, rose gardens, and playground.

■ **MV *Wanda-Sue*:** 26m sternwheeler running worthwhile two-hour narrated cruises on Thompson River. 100 passengers. Licensed galley. Early May-Sept. Daily cruises, charters, group rates. Moored downtown near infocentre. Write 2472 Thompson Dr, Kamloops, BC, V2C 4L1, or call 374-7447, 374-1505, or Mobile: N412958YJ.

■ **Tranquille Marsh:** West on Tranquille Rd from North Kamloops. 10km to marsh. Very active waterfowl habitat, especially during spring and fall migrations. Hundreds of birds, many species (whistling and trumpeter swans, Canada and snow geese, pelicans). Viewing from road. Short drive beyond marsh, north up Red Lake Rd to see bighorn sheep.

■ **Weyerhaeuser Canada:** Modern pulp mill and sawmill on south side of the Thompson on Mission Flats Rd, across from airport. Daily tours at 10am, May-early Sept. Sawmill tours by arrangement. 372-2217. Long sleeves, pants, close-toed shoes required. Ages 12 and over.

■ **Kamloops Waterslide and RV Park:** 19km east of city on Hwy 1. May long weekend-Labour Day. Slides, hot tubs, wading pool, mini-golf. 85 RV sites, full hook-ups. 573-3789.

■ **Kamloops Wildlife Park:** 19km east of city on Hwy 1. Box 4666 Kamloops, BC, V2C 5L2. Open year-round. 573-3242.

■ **City of Kamloops Fire Dept Museum:** 1205 Summit Dr. 372-5131. By appointment only.

■ **Rocky Mountain Rangers Museum and Archives:** 1221 McGill Rd. 372-7424. Inside JR Vicars Armoury – fully operational reserve army regiment.

■ **Kamloops Old Courthouse Hostel:** 7 W Seymour St, Kamloops, BC, V2C 1E4. 828-7991. 60-bed international hostel in 1909 courthouse, with Gothic-style arches, stained-glass windows, judge's bench, jury seats, witnesses and prisoners boxes. Operated by Canadian Hostelling Association, BC Region.

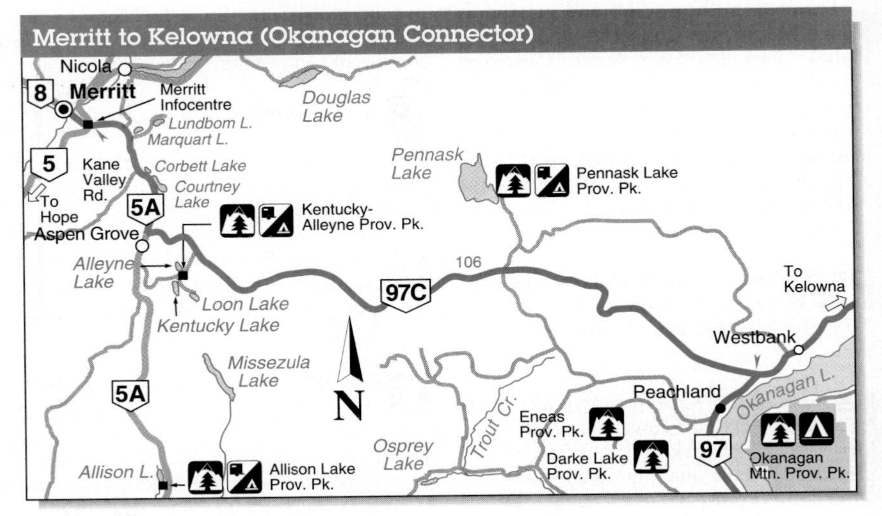


# Merritt to Kelowna

## OKANAGAN CONNECTOR (Highways 5A and 97C)

The 106km Connector between Merritt and Kelowna is the final phase of the Coquihalla freeway. It brings the Lower Mainland almost two hours closer to the Okanagan Valley. Greater Vancouver, bustling with its 1.5 million inhabitants, is now less than four hours from Kelowna. The Connector's first 24km trace Hwy 5A south from Merritt. Just before the vale of Aspen Grove, the Connector veers east, tracing Hwy 97C for 82km.

As the landscape unfolds, one thing becomes starkly apparent: this new highway is out of place. It's a long slab of asphalt rolled out over a wild middle of nowhere. It seems nature has lost another battle with the human race, surrendering to $225 million worth of pavement and fences.

This is a road for people with places to go, people to see. Though it is a particularly scenic route, it is not for dawdling sightseers. The speed limit is 110km-h (in winter, heavy snowfalls and fogs at higher altitudes will demand caution). Pullouts are scarce: the limited access is designed to minimize damage to the fragile alpine environment. The impact on wildlife has been softened with a $10.5 million protection system, featuring the continent's longest chain-link ungulate fence – 100km. There are 25 wildlife underpasses and an overpass for traveling deer, moose, and cattle. (The fence is expected to pay for itself by cutting insurance claims for accidents involving wildlife.)

From the rolling scrub and grasslands around Merritt, the Connector climbs across Pothole Creek into denser forests. Once over Pennask Summit, now BC's 2nd highest highway pass (highest is Kootenay Pass, Hwy 3), the road follows Trepanier Valley, possibly the most striking vista on the route. As the road descends towards Peachland, Okanagan Lake beckons, comfortably beneath Mt Acland and Okanagan Mountain.

**Hwys 5 and 5A/Merritt Infocentre:** 2.5km south of Merritt. 378-2281. Info about region, forestry, snack shop, curios.

**Kane Valley Cross-country Ski Area:** 14km beyond infocentre. 2km from highway to first parking lot, 2km to more parking. 14 trails totalling 40km. Also self-guided BC Forest Service Demonstration Forest, a 2.5km exploration of trees, plants, undergrowth.

**Corbett Lake:** 15km beyond infocentre. This reclaimed lake offers excellent trout fishing.

**Hwy 97C:** 24km beyond infocentre. The Connector continues eastward as 97C. Hwy 5A carries on south. It's a short distance to small community of Aspen Grove, 62km to Princeton.

**Loon Lake Rd:** 39km beyond infocentre. 3km to picturesque Loon Lake on good gravel road. This is the way to **Kentucky-Alleyne Provincial Park**, camping, swimming, boating, hiking to Quilchena Falls. See details, *Princeton to Kamloops*, p.182.

**Elkhart Rd:** 51km beyond infocentre. Leads to only food and accommodation between Aspen Grove and Hwy 97. Lodge with dining facilities, plus cross-country skiing, snowmobiling. Also a gas station for those who found the uphill climb rather draining.

**Sunset Main Rd:** 63km beyond infocentre. Seasonal road accessing some High Country highlights. Drive with caution, give right of way to logging trucks and forestry vehicles. 1.2km to wide spot in road, and short unmarked path to Sunset Lake. Farther along Sunset Main are Pennask, Headwaters, and Peachland lakes. A topographical map, good shock absorbers, and a full day are recommended for the journey. 24km from start, sometimes bumpy Trout Main Forest Service Rd leads 20km to Osprey lakes Rd, a gravel road cartographers have generously called Hwy 40. It links Princeton and Summerland. For details, see Summerland, in *Okanagan-Similkameen*, p.128.

**Pennask Summit:** (El 1,728m). 73km beyond infocentre. BC's 2nd highest highway pass, 46m lower than Hwy 3's Kootenay Pass.

**Brenda Mine:** 83km beyond infocentre. Brenda Mine Ltd operated open-pit copper and molybdenum mine here for 20 years, closing it in 1990. Smooth slope to the right is remains of tailing pond.

**Wildlife Overpass:** 99km beyond infocentre. Offering safe passage for pedestrians – mostly deer and moose of Trepanier Creek area. Deer seem to be having an easier time with the concept.

**Okanagan-Similkameen Information:** Okanagan-Similkameen Tourist Association infocentre. 102.5km beyond Merritt Infocentre.

**Hwy 97:** 106km beyond Merritt Infocentre. South leads to communities of Peachland, Summerland, and Penticton. See *Okanagan-Similkameen*, p.128. Continuing east leads to Westbank, Kelowna, and Vernon. See pp.129-132.

# Kamloops to Jasper

## YELLOWHEAD SOUTH HIGHWAY (Highways 5 and 16)

The Yellowhead (Hwy 16) is a major Canadian highway beginning far beyond the eastern boundary of BC at Portage la Prairie, Manitoba. It travels west across the prairies, through Saskatoon, Saskatchewan, and Edmonton, Alberta, entering BC by way of the Yellowhead Pass, 1,600km from its beginning. About 75km west of the pass, at Tête Jaune Cache, the Yellowhead splits, becoming Hwy 16 to the northwest and Hwy 5, southwest. Hwy 16 to the coast is known simply as the Yellowhead; Hwy 5 is the Yellowhead South.

Between Kamloops and Tête Jaune Cache, Hwy 5 runs 340km up the North Thompson River valley, from rolling grasslands through the forests of the interior wet belt, to the Rockies. It's a long but delightful drive, with many views of the green, swirling North Thompson, one of BC's great rivers. Scenic rest areas, like little parks, are found on the riverbanks, as are hamlets and villages, all worth a stop for local colour.

From the Yellowhead South, this *Log* continues with the 75km segment of Yellowhead 16, eastwards from Tête Jaune Cache to the Jasper National Park boundary.

**Kamloops:** (Pop. 67,057). See *Hope to Kamloops*, p.176.

Hwy 5 skirts Kamloops' core before crossing the South Thompson River about 2km east of its confluence with the North Thompson. It then swings along the western boundary of the Kamloops Indian Reserve before following the North Thompson and CNR tracks upcountry.

**Kamloops Indian Reserve:** (Pop. 730). Hwy 5 follows reserve's 11km western boundary. Home of the Shuswap or Secwepemc people. 13,355ha of rugged landscape dominated by the Dome Hills. See also *Hope to Kamloops*, p.177.

St Joseph's Church, a Roman Catholic Indian mission church from the 1880s, is located on the reserve. Restored circa 1900, open for viewing in summer. 828-9700.

**Secwepemc Heritage Park:** 355 Yellowhead Hwy. Culture of the Shuswap Nation. See *Hope to Kamloops*, p.177.

**Paul Lake Rd:** East off Hwy 5, some 5.5km north of Kamloops.

## SIDE TRIP

### to Paul Lake Provincial Park and Harper Mountain

Following Paul Creek, Paul Lake Rd (paved) runs through Kamloops Reserve to a provincial park, ski area, Pinantan Lake.

**Paul Lake Provincial Park:** 402ha; 111 campsites, sani-station. 828-4494. 18km east of Hwy 5. Popular summer camping spot in forests of Douglas fir and aspen. Wildflowers, swimming, boating.

**Harper Mountain:** South off Paul Lake Rd 14km east of Hwy 5. Downhill and cross-country skiing. Geared to family. 425m vertical drop. 11 runs, triple chair, two T-bars, handle tows. Day lodge, ski school. Night skiing. Write 2042 Valleyview Dr, Kamloops, BC, V2C 4C5; 372-2119.

**Pinantan Lake:** 7km beyond Paul Lake park. Accommodation, camping, fishing.

### Return to Highway 5

**Heffley-Louis Creek Rd:** Turn east off Hwy 5, 23.5km north of Kamloops.

## SIDE TRIP

### to Heffley Lake and Tod Mountain

Heffley-Louis Creek Rd (Tod Mountain Rd) leads to good fishing spots, ski area.

**Heffley Lake:** Resort and campground 20km east of Hwy 5. Narrow, 5km lake with island and several small bays. Good rainbow trout fishing. Ice fishing, skating, boat rentals, groceries.

**Tod Mountain:** 10km east of Heffley Lake. 47 ski runs totalling 28km from Top of the World Summit at 2,149m. A 945m vertical drop. Chair and platter lifts carry 2,800 skiers per hour. Skiing starts mid-Nov. B&B, RV hook-ups. Box 869, Kamloops, BC, V2C 5M8. Call 578-7222, or 1-800-663-2838.

### Return to Highway 5

**McLure Ferry:** 43.5km from Kamloops. Road off highway runs west to free reaction ferry. Crosses North Thompson River to Westside Rd which runs south to Kamloops, north to Barrière. Two cars, 12 passengers, 7am and 6:45pm. Doesn't operate in high water (June), when heavy ice flows, or when river is frozen.

**McLure:** (Pop. 273). 47.5km. Some tourist facilities, campground. Named for rancher John McLure, died 1933, age 84.

**Fishtrap Rest Area:** 48.5km from Kamloops. Here at Fishtrap Canyon rapids, natives once trapped spawning salmon.

**Overlanders:** 54km from Kamloops. Views over North Thompson River where Overlanders of 1862 made their arduous river voyage. This group of some 150 settlers travelled all the way from Ontario by ship, railway, Red River cart, and packhorse, with the assistance of native people over the Rockies, and finally, by perilous river raft. The only woman among these early settlers, Catherine O'Hare Schubert, brought her three children with her, and gave birth to her fourth just hours after reaching Kamloops.

**Louis Creek:** (Pop. 95). 59km from Kamloops. Lumber mill. Gas and food. Named after Louis Barrie, a prospector who found some gold here in 1860.

**Barrière:** (Pop. 1,653). A few hundred metres east off Hwy 5, 63km north of Kamloops. Farming and forestry town with nearby fishing, swimming, canoeing, hiking, rockhounding, snowmobiling, and ice fishing. Named in 1828, when French was the language of the fur traders, after rocks in river, which were a barrier to navigation.

**Barrière Information:** Infocentre, Barrière Chamber of Commerce, Box 228, 352 Lilley Rd, Barrière, BC, V0E 1E0. On Hwy 5 near turnoff to town centre. Daily late May-early Sept.

■ **North Thompson Museum:** 352 Lilley Rd, Barrière, V0E 1E0. Daily, early May to mid-Sept. 1930s forestry warehouse.

Hwy 5 crosses North Thompson River just north of Barrière, now tracing its west shores.

**Barrière Lakes:** Take Barrière Lakes Rd, east of Barrière. Leads to North, South, and East Barrière lakes. Excellent fishing. Cabins and campgrounds. 16km to fork in road. South leads to South Barrière Lake. Short distance beyond intersection, fork to the north leads to North Barrière Lake; main road continues to East Barrière Lake. All three within 12km of junctions.

**Dunn Lake Rd:** North from Barrière. A scenic 61km route, mainly gravel, between Barrière and Clearwater. Parallel Hwy 5, but on east side of North Thompson River. Windpass Rd, 33km north of Barrière, is an 8km side road west off Dunn Lake Rd, leading to reaction ferry at Little Fort. Dunn Lake Rd continues 27.5km north of Windpass Rd to Clearwater. Fishing in McTaggart, Dunn, Hallamore, and other lakes along the route. Dunn Lake has a Forest Service campsite at north end. Dunn Lake Resort is at south end. Road passes Thompson Valley Golf Course (par 3/4). Pavement for 14km from golf course into Clearwater.

**Westside Rd:** 65km from Kamloops. Secondary route to Kamloops. Unpaved forestry road with several recreation sites.

**Chinook Cove Rest Area:** 68km from Kamloops. Named for small community nearby.

**Drinking Water Pullout:** 73km from Kamloops. Natural spring water piped out of the mountain. Ice cold, pure, delicious.

**Darfield:** 80km from Kamloops. Farming community. Cattle graze peacefully as you drive by.

**Little Fort:** (Pop. 175). On Hwy 5, 92km from Kamloops. Accommodation, campground. Hudson's Bay Company trading fort, 1850-52. Local work in craft shop situated in Joan's Esso Station.

**Little Fort Ferry:** On Hwy 5 at Little Fort. Over North Thompson River to Dunn Lake Rd and Clearwater. On call between 7am and 6:45pm. Free. Five minutes. One of seven current-propelled ferries still operating in BC. Foot passengers use aerial tramway when ferry is out of service.

**Hwy 24:** West off Hwy 5 at Little Fort. Scenic 97km route through Interlakes District to Hwy 97, 10km south of 100 Mile House. Hwy 24 and side roads lead to dozens of lakes, including Thuya Lakes, Lac Des Roches, Bonaparte, Sheridan, Eagan, Burn, Fawn, Lesser, and Bridge lakes. Fishing resorts, campgrounds; provincial parks at Bridge Lake. See details in *Cariboo-Chilcotin*, p.191.

**Little Fort Rest Area:** Right at town of Little Fort.

**Blackpool:** Hamlet just before Clearwater. Main attraction is Lacarya Golf Course (Par 3/4), clubhouse and lounge.

**North Thompson River Provincial Park:** 125ha; 61 campsites. 587- 6150. On Hwy 5, 118km north of Kamloops. Headquarters for Wells Gray Provincial Park. At confluence of North Thompson and Clearwater rivers. Archaeological sites. Visitors' centre, programs, wheelchair access, sani-station.

**Clearwater:** (Pop. 244). On Hwy 5, 122km north of Kamloops. Service centre to population of 7,000 and gateway to Wells Gray Provincial Park. Full range of facilities. See infocentre about white-water river rafting, trail rides, canoe trips and rentals, hiking expeditions, back-country chalets. Good fishing, also snowmobiling, skiing. Note Caboose restaurant, east side of highway. Also the new Chuckwagon Restaurant and Swingin' Granny's Saloon, a dream realized by Iva Bonar, longtime Clearwater resident. Western in feeling. Home cooking.

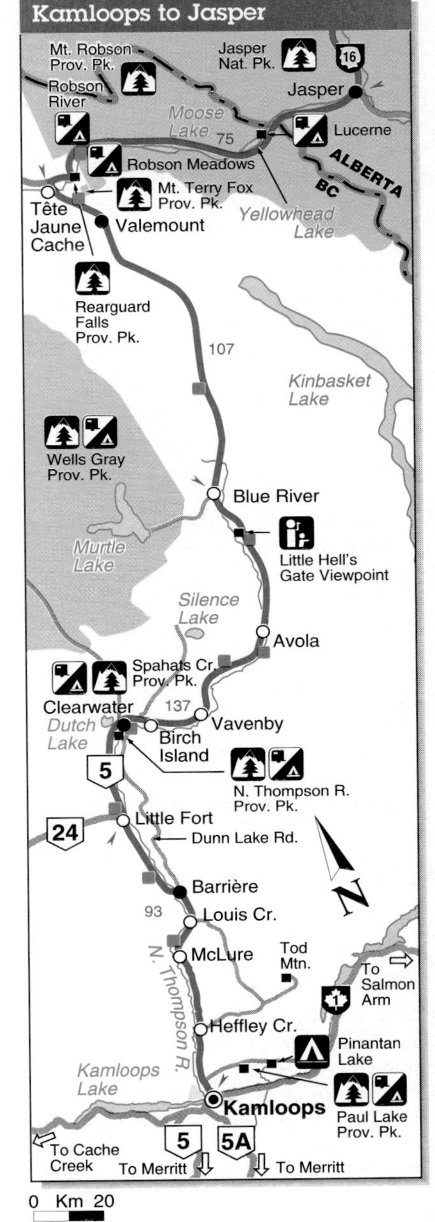


**Clearwater Information:** Infocentre, Clearwater and District Chamber of Commerce, Box 1988, RR1, Clearwater, BC, V0E 1N0. On Hwy 5 (west side) at Clearwater Valley Rd. Jerry the Moose stands outside. This infocentre, built by the Ministry of Parks, operated by the Chamber, rivals Merritt's as most imposing in all of BC. 674-2646. Mon-Sat, Labour Day-April 30; daily May 1-Sept. This is also infocentre for Wells Gray Provincial Park. Displays include "Windows on Wells Gray," antiques, depictions of the Overlanders' journey down the North Thompson River in 1862, Simpcw

(*Simcue*) natives. Topographical maps. Gift shop. Two good books: *Exploring Wells Gray Park*, by Roland Neave; and *Nature Wells Gray*, by Cathie Hickson and Trevor Goward.
■ **Clearwater Ski Hill:** On Dunn Lake Rd within town area. Vertical drop more than 300m, T-bar, night skiing.
■ **Dutch Lake Park:** In town. Swimming, playground, paddling, rainbow trout. Local anglers' club has built trout spawning channel onto the landlocked lake, putting over 100,000 fry back into it. Open for public viewing at Nordstrom's Resort and RV park.
■ **Yellowhead Museum:** From infocentre turn onto Clearwater Valley Rd (road to Wells Gray). 6km from highway follow sign. RR1, Box 1778, Clearwater, BC, V0E 1N0. 674-3660. On one of few original homesteads in area. Open by appointment. Pioneer and native artifacts, natural history displays. Good area information.
■ **Candlecreek Northern Miniature Railway:** 361 Candlecreek Rd, on Hwy 5. 674-3241. Weekends: May to mid-June, and Labour day-Sept 30. Tues-Sun, mid-June to Labour Day. Rides on "large-scale miniature railway." Railway memorabilia.

**Clearwater Valley Rd:** North off Hwy 5 at Clearwater. 36km, paved, to main entrance of Wells Gray Provincial Park at Hemp Creek.

# SIDE TRIP
## to Wells Gray Park

After leaving Hwy 5 and Clearwater, road climbs sharply up onto the Spahats Plateau before levelling out.

**Spahats Creek Provincial Park:** 306ha; 23 campsites. 587-6150. Enroute to Wells Gray Park, 10km north of Clearwater. From road into park you can see where Spahats Creek has carved a 122m deep canyon through layers of lava. Views of canyon walls and 61m Spahats Falls.

**Trophy Mountains Rd and Trophy Mountain Recreation Area:** 11.5km from Hwy 5. Turn east. Gravel road with steep grades. Watch for junction 4km from Clearwater Valley Rd. North leads 9km to Trophy Meadows Trail and Trophy Skyline Trail; straight ahead 9km more brings you to start of 88 Ridge Trail. En route, you will pass through a vast clearcut made in the '70s that has failed to regenerate.

**Wells Gray Ranch:** 27km. Trail rides, pack trips, canoeing, river rafting. 10 campsites. RR1, Box 1764, Clearwater, BC, V0E 1N0. 674-2792.

**Helmcken Falls Lodge:** 34km. Just before park entrance. Impressive 1948 log lodge is closely identified with park. 20 campsites. Hook-ups. Dining room, gift shop, rooms. Box 239, Clearwater, BC, V0E 1N0; 674-3657.

**Wells Gray Provincial Park:** 529,748ha; 117 sites in four campgrounds, 25 wilderness camping areas. 587-6150. Campsites are: Dawson Falls, 10 sites, 8km north of Hemp Creek park entrance; Clearwater Lake, 32 sites, 33km north of Hemp Creek entrance; Falls Creek, 41 sites, at Clearwater Lake; and Mahood Lake, 32 sites, 88km east of 100 Mile House (reached from Hwy 97). Accommodation and services here are provided by Helmcken Falls Lodge and Wells Gray Ranch. Visitors' centre, programs, boat launches, wheelchair access.

A vast wilderness, Wells Gray is one of BC's largest, most spectacular parks. High in the Cariboo Mountains, scenery includes alpine meadows and flowers, snow-capped peaks and glaciers, major lakes, rivers and waterfalls, small lakes and streams, extinct volcanos, lava beds, and mineral springs.

Hiking trails range from half-hour nature walks to week-long backpacking excursions. Extensive canoe trips on Clearwater, Azure, Mahood, and Murtle lakes.

**Wells Gray Provincial Park Information:** In Clearwater or write to BC Parks, Zone Supervisor, Box 70, Clearwater, BC, V0E 1N0. 674-2646. Topographic map of Wells Gray Provincial Park (PS-WG3) at a scale of 1:125,000 can be purchased at Clearwater Infocentre.

### *Wells Gray Park Highlights*

■ **Dawson Falls:** 5km north of Hemp Creek entrance. Murtle River, here 91m wide, drops 18m, miniature version of Niagara Falls. Short trail to viewpoints.
■ **The Mushbowl:** Short distance beyond Dawson Falls. Murtle River has carved huge holes in rock of a narrow gorge.
■ **Helmcken Falls:** Fourth largest waterfalls in Canada, park's most famous wonder. A few km downstream from Dawson Falls. Viewpoints at parking lot. Murtle River plunges over a sheer 137m precipice.
■ **Ray's Mineral Spring:** 18km north of Hemp Creek entrance. Trails to cold, clear springs and lava beds.
■ **Bailey's Chute:** Pullout 1km beyond Ray Mineral Spring marks start of trail to the chute, featuring a standing wave created by white water crashing into a broad pool. 10-minute walk. Chute named after Jim Bailey, who designed 1949 truss bridge over The Mushbowl. Bailey drowned in 1952 when his boat overturned in the chute.
■ **Murtle Lake Nature Conservancy:** Only accessible by vehicle from Blue River, 105.5km northeast of Clearwater on Hwy 5. By 26km rough gravel road, then a 2.5km portage from parking lot to Murtle Lake Lagoon, packing your canoe and camping gear in. Murtle Lake is stunning centrepiece of the conservancy (40 percent of park's area). Largest fresh-water lake in North America that forbids boat motors.

### *Return to Highway 5*

**Silence Lake Rd:** Northeast off Hwy 5, just east of Clearwater before Raft River Bridge. Winding 35km logging road along Raft River to Silence Lake.

**Birch Island Rest Area:** 12km from Clearwater. Turn south. Overlooks river valley.

**Birch Island:** (Pop. 221). 12.5km from Clearwater. Named after island in river.

Cross one-way bridge over North Thompson to take secondary route up river's south side to Vavenby. Called Lost Creek Rd, it's paved for its 14km distance. Nearing Vavenby, look for Molliet sheep ranch, one of the biggest in Canada. Visitors welcome.

**Vavenby:** (Pop. 396). South short distance off Hwy 5, 26km from Clearwater. Minimal services.

**McMurphy Rest Area:** 51km from Clearwater. Pictographs on a granite bluff, 60m west. Speculation that the burnt-red paintings on the creamy orange rock related to ancient puberty rite.

**Wire Cache Rest Area:** 54km from Clearwater. On North Thompson riverbank. Birch trees.

**Avola:** (Pop. 160). 68km from Clearwater. Service centre with accommodation. The Log Inn – you can't miss it, it's the only one there – bills itself "The Largest and Friendliest Pub in Avola". Pub is watering hole for loggers, rail workers, and farmers from around the area. A few steps up the street is another log structure, formerly a one-room schoolhouse, which now houses the Avola Library. Main street peters out along banks of North Thompson. Definitely a photogenic stop. Avola is named after a village in Sicily.

**Finn Creek Rest Area:** 84km from Clearwater. Pleasantly situated along the North Thompson river.

**Little Hell's Gate Viewpoint:** 85km from Clearwater. Follow signs. 3km off Hwy 5 to views of Upper North Thompson River where it narrows to a 4.5m gorge. Open May-Oct. Road *not* accessible to trailers.

**Messiter Summit:** 86.5km from Clearwater. Views of North Thompson River Valley. Highway between Avola and Valemount crosses countryside with a parkland feeling, despite the odd, jarring clearcut to remind you it isn't protected.

**Blue River:** (Pop. 283). On Hwy 5, 107km from Clearwater. A logging and tourism town, recently a base for heli-skiers flying into the Cariboo and Monashee mountains. Eleanor Lake, within the town, is site of a campground and Mike Wiegele Heli-Ski Village. Cross-country skiing and ice-fishing at Eleanor Lake. Swimming, hiking, and fishing in summer.

*Helmcken Falls, in Wells Gray Provincial Park.*

**Blue River Information:** No infocentre at Blue River, but help available from Eleanor Lake Campsite and Trailer Park, Box 13, Blue River, BC, V0E 1J0. 673-8316.

**Blue River Airport:** East off Hwy 5, 1km north of town centre.

**Wells Gray Provincial Park:** Murtle Lake, hiking and canoeing area, is reached by turning west onto rough gravel road, 1km north of Blue River. 45 minutes, 24km to parking lot at park boundary. Then up-and-down 2.5km trail to the lake.

**Thunder River Rest Area:** 122km from Clearwater. West into a delightful site: tables beside the rushing Thunder River, even a meadow.

**Valemount:** (Pop. 1,128). On Hwy 5, 195km from Clearwater. Valemount, where the Cariboo, Monashee, and Rocky mountains meet, is a logging village with good accommodation, campgrounds, and a range of facilities. Nearby is northern end of Kinbasket Lake's Canoe Reach, and start of an extensive boating area (see *Shelter Bay to Mica Creek*, p.173). Infocentre can help with fishing, trail riding, heli-skiing, and snowmobiling trips.

**Valemount Information:** Infocentre, Village of Valemount, Box 168, Valemount, BC, V0E 2Z0. 566-4846. On Hwy 5, south side of town. Seasonal.

**Valemount Airport:** On Hwy 5, about 1km north of village centre.

■ **Robert W Starratt Wildlife Sanctuary:** On Hwy 5 on south side of town centre. 200ha of marshland.

■ **George Hicks Regional Park:** On Hwy 5, across from business centre. Parking for RVs, buses, cars. Viewing bridge for chinook salmon run. Trails, picnics.

■ **Robson Helimagic Inc:** Hwy 5 N. Box 18, Valemount BC, V0E 2Z0. 566-4700. Heli-hiking, heli-skiing, heli-sightseeing. Standard or custom tours of Mt Robson, Cariboo Range, Robson Valley, and more.

**Mt Terry Fox Provincial Park:** 1,930ha. East off Hwy 5, 202.5km from Clearwater. Drive 2km to parking area and trail head for steep, strenuous, but worthwhile 7km hike. Spectacular alpine views. Undeveloped park with 2,650m peak named in honour of one-legged runner who died of bone cancer before completing his historic cross-Canada run.

**Mt Terry Fox Viewpoint and Rest Area:** West off highway 203km from Clearwater.

**Hwy 16 (Tête Jaune Cache):** At end of Hwy 5, 216km from Clearwater; 338km from Kamloops. *Log* now follows Hwy 16 east to Alberta border, which is also west boundary of Jasper National Park. (Yellowhead continues on to Portage la Prairie, Manitoba, a distance of 1,700km.)

Westward, the Yellowhead (Hwy 16) travels more than 1,000km to its end on the Queen Charlotte Islands (see *North by Northwest*).

For details on Tête Jaune Cache, see *North by Northwest*, p.212.

The 75km of Hwy 16 from Tête Jaune Cache to Jasper Park's boundary climbs the Rocky Mountain pass for which the highway is named. Although the Yellowhead Pass, 80km east of Tête Jaune Cache, reaches an elevation of 1,131m, the mountains that surround it exceed 3,000m. Scenery is extraordinary, with wintry peaks, glaciers, and cold, turquoise rivers. Journey takes in Mount Robson Provincial Park and Alberta's Jasper National Park.

A powerful visual experience awaits the traveller heading east from Tête Jaune Cache. As one rounds a bend near Mt Terry Fox Provincial Park, suddenly a titanic mountain rises up, blotting out the horizon and dwarfing neighbouring and otherwise impressive peaks. It's Mt Robson, biggest in the Canadian Rockies, and BC's most storied mountain.

**Tête Jaune Cache Rest Area:** 1km east of Tête Jaune Cache junction. Overlooks Fraser.

**Rearguard Falls Provincial Park:** 48ha. On Hwy 16, 4km east of Tête Jaune Cache junction. The 10m falls are final barrier to salmon that migrate about 1,200km up the Fraser River from the sea. Viewpoints, hiking, fishing.

**Mt Terry Fox Rest Area :** 7.5km east of Tête Jaune Cache junction. Provides telescope to view Mt Terry Fox in Selwyn Range of the Rockies. Some of the best views of Mt Robson.

**Mount Robson Provincial Park:** 219,829ha; 176 campsites in three campgrounds. 566-4325. Western entrance on Hwy 16, 14km east of Tête Jaune Cache junction. Eastern entrance at BC/Alberta border, 75km east of Tête Jaune Cache junction. Campsites are: Robson Meadows, 125 sites, and Robson River, 19 sites, both near western entrance, on Hwy 16, 17km east of Tête Jaune Cache; Lucerne, 32 sites, is on Yellowhead Lake about 10km west of the Alberta boundary.

Mt Robson, at 3,954m the highest peak in the Canadian Rockies, dominates the western entrance to the park. The park is bordered on the east by the Continental Divide and Jasper National Park. The rugged snow-capped mountains, wandering valleys, steep-sided canyons, glacier-fed lakes and streams are the birthplace of the Fraser, Canada's third-longest river, BC's longest. From its headwaters here the Fraser flows 1,370km to the sea at Vancouver.

Yellowhead Pass, el 1,131m, is the eastern entrance to the park. Much wildlife: moose, mountain goats, mule deer, elk, caribou, grizzly and black bears, pikas, marmots, squirrels, chipmunks, muskrats, beavers and more than 170 bird species. A hiker's paradise with an extensive network of trails – from a few hours to a few days – to good campsites and viewpoints. Visitor's centre, programs, wheelchair access, boat launch, sani-station.

**Mount Robson Provincial Park Information:** Visitor centre is at Mt Robson Viewpoint 2km from western entrance. Displays on natural and human history, audio-visual programs. Service station, café, and store adjacent. Daily mid-June to Sept. Write BC Parks, Park Supervisor, Box 579, Valemount, BC, V0E 2Z0. 566-4325.

**Moose Lake:** Boat launch and picnic facilities at east end, 43.5km from Tête Jaune Cache junction.

**Yellowhead Lake:** Boat launch, picnic facilities, and viewpoint at east end, 69.5km from junction.

**Yellowhead Pass:** El 1,131m. 77km from Tête Jaune Cache junction. BC-Alberta border, and division between Jasper National and Mt Robson Provincial parks.

**Time Zone:** 77km from Tête Jaune Cache junction. As you cross BC/Alberta border, set your time one hour ahead.

**Jasper National Park:** See *Alberta Rockies*, p.277.

## Princeton to Kamloops

### HIGHWAY 5A

Hwy 5A, running a total of 185km from Princeton to Kamloops, is often used by travellers from the south Okanagan. Those coming from the Lower Mainland, wanting to save the $10 toll on the Coquihalla Hwy, drive the Hope-Princeton (Hwy 3), then take Hwy 5A north to Kamloops. The route is 118km longer, but avoids the long, steep hills of the Coquihalla.

**Princeton:** (Pop. 2,796). See details in *Okanagan-Similkameen*, p.121.

**Hwys 3 and 5A:** Hwy 3 (the Crowsnest) from Princeton goes through Manning Provincial Park to Hope, then east to the south Okanagan. Hwy 5A joins Hwy 5, the Coquihalla, at Merritt, 40km north of Princeton. Hwys 5 and 5A continue on their respective journeys from Merritt to Kamloops.

**Coalmont Rd:** West off Hwy 5A, 1km north of Princeton. Alternate 70km back road toward, but not to, Merritt. Passes community of Coalmont and Otter Lake Provincial Park. Rejoins Hwy 5A about 36km south of Merritt.

## SIDE TRIP

### on Coalmont Road

**Coalmont:** (Pop. 83). On Coalmont Rd, 15km west of Princeton. Old mining town with a café and general store. Coalmont Hotel, established 1912, has a pub, restaurant, and rooms. Ask at store or hotel for info on nearby mine sites.

During the early 1900s Coalmont was a thriving mining community. In 1925, town produced 100,000t of coal, making it the region's largest producer. It held this title through 1936. By 1940, however, the mines were exhausted, and most of the 250 residents had moved. Today it's a sleepy little village.

**Otter Lake Provincial Park:** 73ha; 45 campsites. 828-4494. 7km northwest of Coalmont. Boating, swimming, hiking, gold panning.

### Return to Highway 5A

**Princeton Airport:** West off Hwy 5A, 2km north of Princeton. 3km to airport.

**Five Mile Chain Lakes:** East off Hwy 5A, 8km north of Princeton. A 34km backroad to chain of excellent trout-fishing lakes, including Chain, Link, Osprey, and Thirsk.

**One Mile Chain Lakes:** Five-lake chain (McCaffrey, Laird, Dry, Borgeson, and Allison) begins 18km from Princeton. Some have eastern brook trout. Several other small fishing lakes along Hwy 5A.

**Allison Lake Provincial Park:** 23ha; 24 campsites. 828-4494. 28.5km from Princeton.

**Missezula Lake:** 45km from Princeton, east off Hwy 5A, onto logging road. Winding 10km to small lakes and campsite at Missezula Lake. Trout and kokanee.

*Kamloops Lake, west of Kamloops, one of the large Interior lakes.*

**Coalmont Rd:** 52km from Princeton, west off Hwy 5A. Other end of 70km back road mentioned above. To Otter Lake Provincial Park.

**Kentucky-Alleyne Provincial Park:** 144ha; 61 campsites. 828-4494. East off Hwy 5A onto Loon Lake Rd, 55.5km from Princeton. Popular destination. Beautiful blue-green lakes, fishing, boating, hiking, swimming, waterfowl, birdwatching. Hike to Quilchena Falls through open grasslands.

**Corbett and Courtney Lakes:** 69km from Princeton. Site of 123ha ranch-turned-resort. Fishing, canoeing, hiking, trail riding, cross-country skiing. Boat launch nearby.

**Kane Valley:** West on Kane Valley Rd, a few hundred metres north of Corbett Lake. One of Interior BC's best cross-country ski areas. 14 trails totalling 40km.

**Marquart and Lundbom Lakes:** East off Hwy 5A, 77km north of Princeton. Just off highway. Snowmobile reserve with informal trails. Fishing and camping in summer.

**Sugarloaf Mountain:** East off Hwy 5A, 80km north of Princeton. Superb hiking around 1,364m peak. 4km to Hamilton Lake. For scenic back-road route to western end of Nicola Lake, take northwest turn just over 1km from Hwy 5A and drive about 9km. Mountain's sweet name derives from Douglas fir on its slopes which produced wild sugar or "Douglas fir" sugar. Thompson natives' name for this mountain meant "tree milk."

**Hwy 5:** Southwest off Hwy 5A, 84km from Princeton, Coquihalla Hwy runs 115km to Hope.

**Merritt:** (Pop. 6,253). On Hwy 5A, 89.5km from Princeton. See *Hope to Kamloops*, p.175.

**Hwy 8:** 65km route west from Merritt to Hwy 1 at Spences Bridge.

**Hwy 5 (Coquihalla):** 3km north of Merritt, Coquihalla Hwy runs north 80km to Kamloops. Hwy 5A continues past Nicola Lake to Kamloops, 91km.

**Nicola Lake Rest Area:** 15.5km from Merritt. Boat launch.

**Monck Provincial Park:** 87ha; 71 campsites, sani-station. 828-4494. Northeast off Hwy 5A at western side of Nicola Lake, 22km east of Merritt. Family vacation destination. Excellent beaches. Boating, fishing, swimming, paddling, hiking, windsurfing, nature programs.

**Quilchena:** (Pop. 24). On Hwy 5A, 23km from Merritt. Overlooking Nicola Lake in the rolling grasslands that were once considered to be Nicola Valley gold. The **Quilchena Cattle Company** is the largest working ranch in BC still accommodating guests. 378-2611. The **Quilchena Hotel**, established 1908 by the Guichon brothers, blends "elegance" with "unpretentious hospitality," maintaining its Old-West charm with a saloon (complete with brass foot rails, spittoons, antique cash register, and bullet hole – reputedly placed by a frustrated bar guest in 1912), sitting parlour, iron beds, washstands. General store nearby. Trail rides, hay rides, golf, fishing, hiking.

Ranching is still an important part of the local economy. There are dozens of ranches around here, and hundreds of people, real cowboys, who make their living by riding the range. During the summer months some of the cowboys, and most of the cows, are up in higher country taking advantage of the shadier woodlands. They come back down in the fall, and you're more likely to see them then.

**Douglas Lake Cattle Company:** Southeast off Hwy 5A, 27.5km from Merritt. 20km to ranch. Established 1884, Canada's largest cattle company, running up to 17,000 head of cattle over 200,000ha. Offers privately guided day-tours incorporating routine of company into itinerary. Also overview of ranch and exploration of back country, cow camps, areas of historic and scenic interest, wildflowers, wildlife. General store, and resort with boat rentals. Call ahead: 350-3344.

**Douglas Lake Rd:** A leisurely 80km back-country route from Nicola Lake to tiny community of Westwold on Hwy 97. Excellent fishing in Chapperon, Rush, and Salmon lakes.

**Peter Hope Lake:** East off Hwy 5A, 44km from Merritt. 7km to lake. Hiking, cross-country skiing. Trail circles lake. Accommodation, camping. Named for a prospector and guide of the 1860s.

**Stump Lake:** Northeast off Hwy 5A, 52km from Merritt. Cross-country skiing at Mineral Hill, overlooking lake. Site of annual Force Ten Summer Classic, a major sailing event. Windsurfing, ice fishing. Migration path: about 20 species of waterfowl, as many as 5,000 birds some days. Access to Stump Lake's northwest shore on Hwy 5A. First in a string of lakes: Tullee, Napier, Richie, Trapp, Shumway. All good fishing spots.

**Roche Lake:** East off Hwy 5A, 70km from Merritt. 10km to cluster of fishing lakes – Roche, Horseshoe, John Frank, Bulman, Frisken. Accommodation, camping.

**Kamloops City Limits:** 87km from Merritt. Pullout for visitors' map, right. Kamloops is a big city; you're still in the southern suburbs – Aberdeen to the west, South Sahali Summit to the east. See city details in *Hope to Kamloops*, p.176.

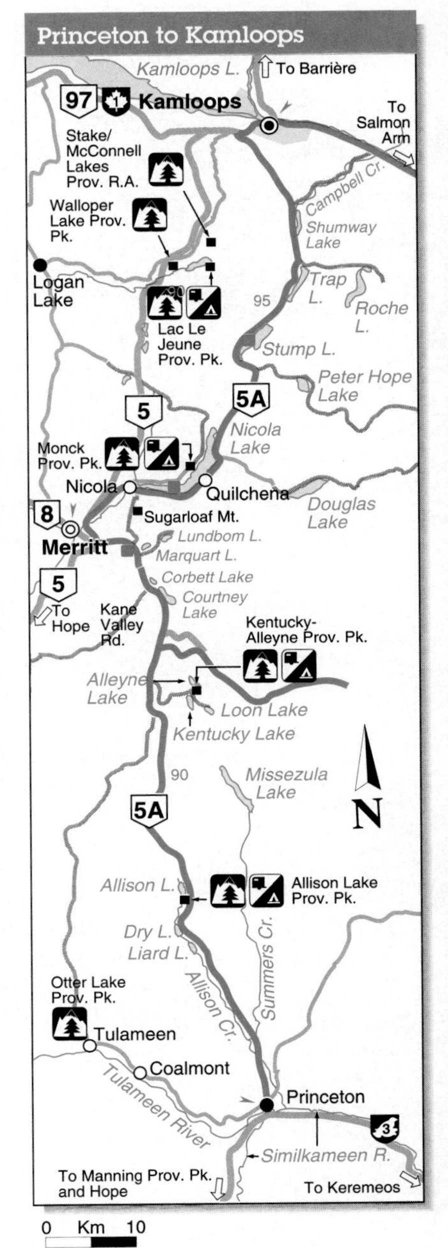


**Hwy 1/97:** 92km from Merritt, west off Hwy 5A. 6km to Hwy 5 (Coquihalla) and fast route south 200km to Hope. 78.5km on Hwy 1/97 to Cache Creek. See *Cache Creek to Salmon Arm*, p.175.

**Downtown Kamloops:** 95km from Merritt. From here, Hwys 1/97 lead east toward Shuswap Lake. See *Cache Creek to Salmon Arm*, p.175. Hwy 5, the Yellowhead, runs north to Tête Jaune Cache. See *Kamloops to Jasper*, p.178.

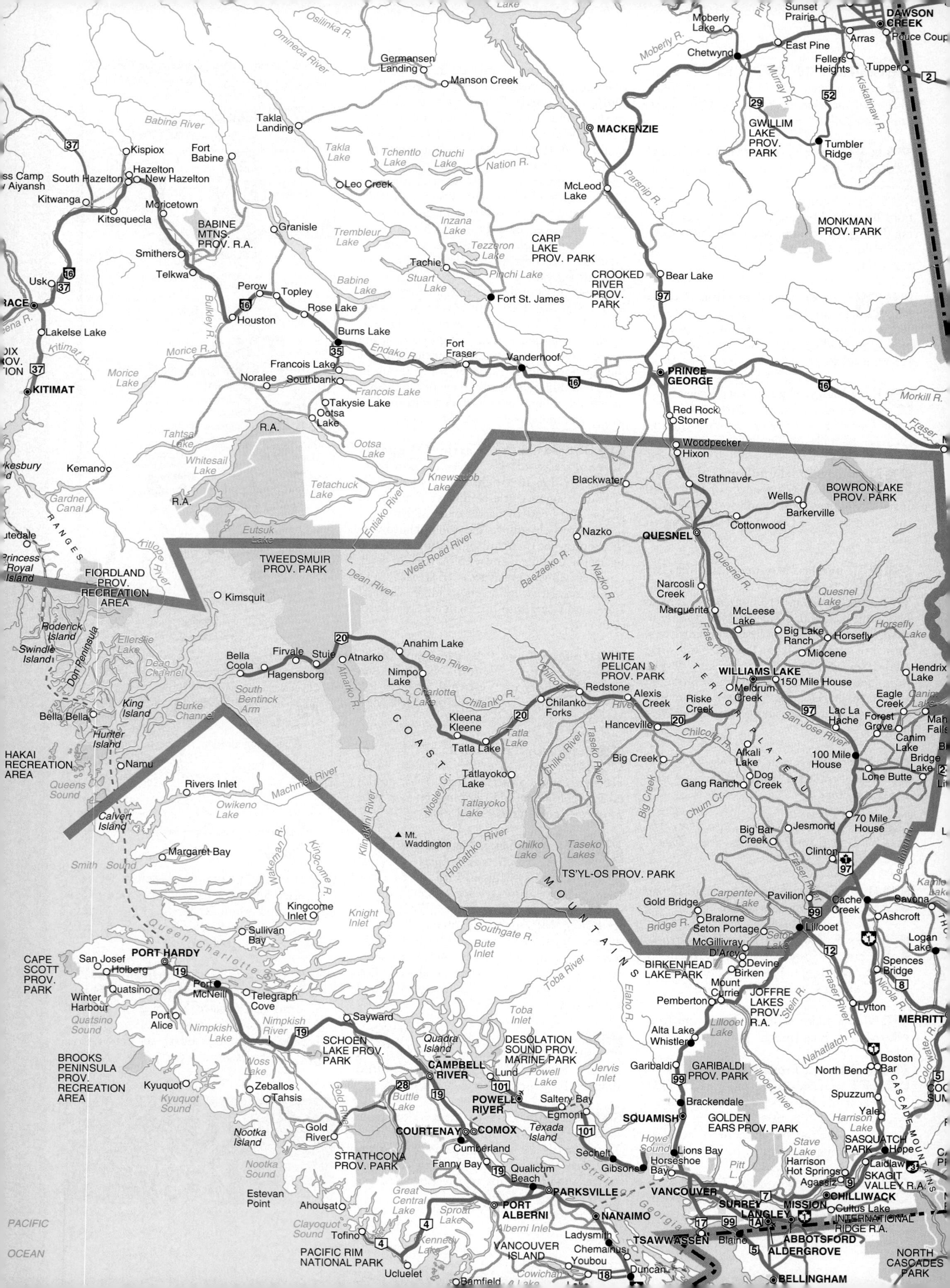

DAWSON CREEK
Sunset Prairie
Pouce Coupe
Moberly Lake
Chetwynd
East Pine
Arras
Fellers Heights
Tupper
Moberly R.
Murray R.
Kiskatinaw R.
GWILLIM LAKE PROV. PARK
Tumbler Ridge
MONKMAN PROV. PARK
Osilinka R.
Omineca River
Germansen Landing
Manson Creek
MACKENZIE
Babine River
Takla Landing
Takla Lake
Tchentlo Lake
Chuchi Lake
Nation R.
Parsnip R.
McLeod Lake
Kispiox
Fort Babine
Hazelton
South Hazelton
New Hazelton
Kitwanga
Kitsequecla
Moricetown
BABINE MTNS. PROV. R.A.
Leo Creek
Granisle
Trembleur Lake
Inzana Lake
Tezzeron Lake
CARP LAKE PROV. PARK
Smithers
Telkwa
Tachie
Pinchi Lake
Stuart Lake
Babine Lake
Usk
Bulkley R.
Perow
Topley
Houston
Rose Lake
Fort St. James
CROOKED RIVER PROV. PARK
Bear Lake
Lakelse Lake
Kitimat R.
Morice R.
Burns Lake
Endako R.
Fort Fraser
Vanderhoof
PRINCE GEORGE
Morkill R.
Fraser
KITIMAT
Morice Lake
Francois Lake
Noralee
Southbank
Takysie Lake
Ootsa Lake
Red Rock
Stoner
Woodpecker
Hixon
Kemano
Tahtsa Lake
Whitesail Lake
R.A.
Tetachuck Lake
Knewstubb Lake
Entiako River
Gardner Canal
Blackwater
Strathnaver
Wells
Barkerville
BOWRON LAKE PROV. PARK
Cottonwood
Nazko
QUESNEL
Eutsuk Lake
RANGES
Kitlope River
TWEEDSMUIR PROV. PARK
West Road River
Baezaeko R.
Nazko R.
Quesnel R.
Princess Royal Island
FIORDLAND PROV. RECREATION AREA
Kimsquit
Dean River
Narcosli Creek
Marguerite
McLeese Lake
Quesnel Lake
Roderick Island
Don Peninsula
Swindle Island
Ellerslie Lake
Dean Channel
Bella Coola
Firvale
Stuie
Hagensborg
Atnarko
Anahim Lake
Nimpo Lake
Dean River
Big Lake Ranch
Horsefly
Horsefly Lake
Miocene
WHITE PELICAN PROV. PARK
WILLIAMS LAKE
150 Mile House
Hendrix Lake
King Island
Burke Channel
South Bentinck Arm
Atnarko R.
Charlotte Lake
Chilanko R.
Chilcotin
Redstone
Chilanko Forks
Alexis Creek
Meldrum Creek
Riske Creek
INTERIOR PLATEAU
Eagle Creek
Lac La Hache
Forest Grove
Bella Bella
Hunter Island
COAST
Kleena Kleene
Tatla Lake
Hanceville
Chilcotin R.
San Jose River
Canim Lake
HAKAI RECREATION AREA
Namu
Chilko River
Taseko River
Big Creek
Alkali Lake
100 Mile House
Bridge Lake
Queens Sound
Rivers Inlet
Machmell River
Tatlayoko Lake
Mosley Cr.
Big Creek
Gang Ranch
Dog Creek
Lone Butte
Owikeno Lake
Calvert Island
Klinaklini River
Churn Cr.
70 Mile House
Mt. Waddington
Homathko River
Chilko Lake
Taseko Lakes
Big Bar Creek
Jesmond
Margaret Bay
Smith Sound
Wakeman R.
Kingcome R.
Clinton
TS'YL-OS PROV. PARK
Deadman R.
MOUNTAINS
Carpenter Lake
Pavilion
Cache Creek
Savona
Kingcome Inlet
Knight Inlet
Gold Bridge
Bralorne
Ashcroft
Bridge R.
Seton Portage
Seton Lake
Lillooet
Sullivan Bay
Queen Charlotte
Southgate R.
Bute Inlet
McGillivray
D'Arcy
Devine
Logan Lake
CAPE SCOTT PROV. PARK
San Josef
PORT HARDY
Holberg
Birken
BIRKENHEAD LAKE PARK
Spences Bridge
Toba River
Elaho R.
Quatsino
Port McNeill
Telegraph Cove
Mount Currie
Pemberton
JOFFRE LAKES PROV. R.A.
Stein R.
Fraser River
Nicola R.
Winter Harbour
Port Alice
Quatsino Sound
Nimpkish Lake
Nimpkish River
Sayward
Toba Inlet
Lillooet Lake
Lytton
MERRITT
BROOKS PENINSULA PROV. RECREATION AREA
SCHOEN LAKE PROV. PARK
Quadra Island
DESOLATION SOUND PROV. MARINE PARK
Alta Lake
Whistler
Nahatlatch R.
Woss Lake
CAMPBELL RIVER
Lund
Powell Lake
Jervis Inlet
Garibaldi
GARIBALDI PROV. PARK
Boston Bar
North Bend
Coldwater R.
Kyuquot
Zeballos
Tahsis
Kyuquot Sound
Gold River
Buttle Lake
POWELL RIVER
Saltery Bay
Egmont
Brackendale
Lillooet River
Spuzzum
CASCADE MOUNTAINS
SQUAMISH
Yale
Nootka Island
Gold River
COURTENAY
COMOX
Texada Island
GOLDEN EARS PROV. PARK
Harrison Lake
Cumberland
Sechelt
Howe Sound
Lions Bay
Stave Lake
SASQUATCH PARK
Hope
STRATHCONA PROV. PARK
Fanny Bay
Qualicum Beach
Gibsons
Horseshoe Bay
Harrison Hot Springs
Laidlaw
Nootka Sound
Strait
Pitt L.
Agassiz
SKAGIT VALLEY R.A.
Estevan Point
PARKSVILLE
VANCOUVER
CHILLIWACK
Ahousat
Great Central Lake
PORT ALBERNI
SURREY
MISSION
Cultus Lake
PACIFIC
Clayoquot Sound
Sproat Lake
NANAIMO
Georgia
LANGLEY
INTERNATIONAL RIDGE R.A.
Tofino
Kennedy Lake
Alberni Inlet
Ladysmith
TSAWWASSEN
Blaine
ABBOTSFORD
ALDERGROVE
OCEAN
PACIFIC RIM NATIONAL PARK
VANCOUVER ISLAND
Chemainus
Youbou
NORTH CASCADES PARK
Ucluelet
Duncan
Bamfield
Cowichan Lake
BELLINGHAM

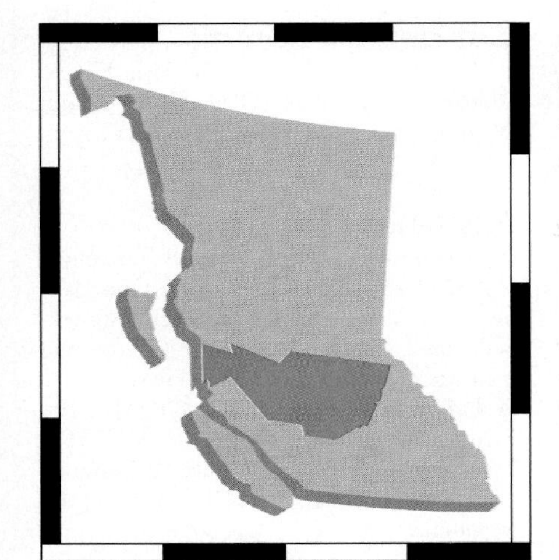

# Cariboo-Chilcotin

## *Riding into the Real West*

> *"We have art galleries and museums here, and musical performances and libraries. Please don't write about the Cariboo as the land of the gold pan and the cowboy in the big hat."*
>
> – Cariboo resident, 1988

Sorry, ma'am. Many a traveller has looked to the Cariboo-Chilcotin for riches or romance, but hardly a one for Shakespeare and sushi. It must be tiring to hear it all over again, but the image of the Cariboo-Chilcotin as a land where cowboys roam the plains, ghosts of gold panners haunt ghost towns, and settlers build dreams of independence and isolation is just too entrancing to abandon. It ain't the wild west, but it's our west, and we hope it stays that way.

The Cariboo-Chilcotin is three regions in one, stretching almost from the Alberta border all the way to the Pacific Ocean.

The Cariboo, land of lakes and evergreen forest, spreads west from the foot of the Cariboo Mountains to the Fraser River, north and south across eroded benchlands and deep-cut river canyons.

In the mountains, spruce and fir grow thickly and snow falls some years to a depth that reaches halfway up the houses. Farther west, vegetation is sparser and the climate drier. This is the beginning of cowboy country, and home to much of the region's population, grouped in towns and cities along a line midway between the mountains and the Fraser River.

Almost all of the region's industry – mainly logging and sawmilling, mining, and cattle ranching – is also concentrated along this line.

To the west, from the Fraser River to the Coast Mountains, is the Chilcotin. Named for the Chilcotin Indian words meaning "people of the young man's river," this is a region of rivers and lakes set in rolling bunchgrass hills. Some of the world's largest cattle ranches are in the Chilcotin, and some of BC's best freshwater fishing.

Still farther west, the land rises abruptly into the Coast Mountains, including the highest peak totally within BC, Mt Waddington at 4,016m. From the mountains then to the central coast, where deep fjords cut inland up to 70km from the Pacific to small coastal settlements set in a rain-forest wilderness.

Native peoples lived here for centuries before the arrival of Europeans. The coastal tribes – primarily the Heiltsuk and Kwakwala – lived from both land and sea, with cedar and salmon their main resources. They traded with the Dene tribes across the Coast Mountains, carrying the oily fish – the little eulachons – along routes that became known as "Grease Trails" to exchange for obsidian, furs, and other goods. These inland natives developed natural medicines that saved the lives of many a white intruder in later years.

When Alexander Mackenzie, an explorer for the North West Company in search of furs and an overland route to the Pacific, reached the Cariboo in 1792, it was a combination of river and grease trail he followed with his native Indian guides to become the first white man to cross the continent overland.

Over the next 50 years, fur traders built posts, brought trade goods and took away beaver and other pelts from the region they named New Caledonia.

They suffered from very mixed emotions, however, when their native acquaintances brought them shiny dust and pebbles from Cariboo rivers. They were delighted to get the gold, but horrified at the thought that hun-

*Autumn at Chilco Lake in the Chilcotins.*

dreds of prospectors might invade their carefully guarded territory.

By 1857, traders for the Hudson's Bay Company had collected some 800 ounces of gold, and the company was forced to send it to San Francisco. Reaction was immediate. Thousands booked passage north.

For five short years, prospectors, merchants, gamblers, farmers, hurdy-gurdy girls, and an assortment of flimflam men rushed from site to site, working their way ever closer to El Dorado, always seeking the mother lode.

Creek by creek, instant town to instant town, prospectors worked their way closer to the Cariboo Mountains. Finally, in 1861, miners sank shafts through the thick blue clay of an old creek bed, and the wild times on Williams Creek began.

Keithley, Antler, Lightning, Richfield – and finally, Barkerville. The richest vein in the Cariboo had been uncovered. Men dug out 675 ounces in a single day; some saved their money, some squandered it on liquor and ladies in the growing shantytown of Barkerville. By 1864, Barkerville boasted it was the largest town north of San Francisco.

James Douglas became governor of the new Crown Colony of British Columbia that was created because of the gold rush. In 1859, he set down-on-their-luck miners to work building a road to the Cariboo. Just as fast, all along this Cariboo Road, roadhouses went up to cater to the needs of travellers. Many of today's village names – from 70 Mile to 150 Mile House – date from that era.

By the 1880s, though, even most of the industrious Chinese miners had abandoned their riverbed workings. Gold continued to be mined, but by hydraulic or deep-pit methods out of the reach of individual miners, and yield was low. Prospectors rushed off to other promises of El Dorado, and the Cariboo slipped into quieter times.

However, some would-be miners had looked around and realized that the bunchgrass hills were ideal ranching country. They settled in to raise cattle. Others came and saw a place where they could escape from civilization. Eccentric British lords, refugees from smoky cities, European emigrants seeking homesteads, all found a haven in the wide land. They brought with them a desire to do as they pleased, and a determination to live outside the rules that governments imposed. The picture of the Cariboo-Chilcotin, as a land with room for every resident to live his or her own life, began to grow.

Richard Hobson, pioneer rancher on the western fringe of the Chilcotin, wrote that the Cariboo was "a land that drew me like a magnet into its soul," echoing and foreshadowing a thousand other settlers who were captured by the magic of the Cariboo-Chilcotin.

You need go no farther than a bookstore or a library to discover this corner of the world. The Cariboo-Chilcotin has inspired works of fiction and non-fiction, settlers' stories, tall tales, and biographies that try to capture this spirit, the way more fertile areas produce farm crops. Beware of visiting, however. Once you've been here, it's hard to leave, and it's impossible to stay away.

## Information

**The Cariboo Tourist Association:** Box 4900, Williams Lake, BC, V2G 2V8. 392-2226. Or, toll-free from BC, Alta, and US: 1-800-663-5885. Fax: 392-2838. Addresses and telephone numbers of local infocentres are provided in the *Log* under the write-up on each community.

## Transportation

Getting around in the Cariboo-Chilcotin is a matter of alternatives. If you want to drive paved roads and see the main sites, you can easily do so. If you want back-road adventure, it's there. If you are willing to try walking, horseback riding, flying in small planes, canoeing or rafting, you'll see the same Big Country that locals do.

### By Road

The Cariboo-Chilcotin is cut into neat packages by its two major roads. The only north-south artery is Hwy 97, the Cariboo Hwy; it runs 441km between Cache Creek and Prince George. A well-maintained, two-lane, paved highway, 97 is the Cariboo lifeline and all the region's major towns are located along it.

To reach Cache Creek from points east, travel west from Alberta on Trans-Canada Hwy 1. Hwy 97 joins the Trans-Canada at Sicamous; continue west to Cache Creek.

Travellers from places such as Edmonton and other northern places will find it easier to drive south on Hwy 97 from Prince George.

Those on their way to the Cariboo from southern BC can follow several routes: Hwy 1, the Trans-Canada, east and north from Vancouver along the Fraser Canyon to Cache Creek; Hwy 5 (the Coquihalla) north from Hope to Kamloops, then Hwys 1 and 97 west to Cache Creek; or, from Osoyoos, Hwy 97 north through the Okanagan, connecting with Hwys 1 and 97 at Monte Creek near Kamloops. Hwy 20, the Chilcotin or Bella Coola Road, is the other major road in the region. It is two paved lanes for close to two-thirds of the route, two lanes of gravel for the remainder. Both are well-maintained and usable by any vehicle that can negotiate the climb through the Coast Mountains. To reach Hwy 20, turn west at Williams Lake.

Back roads lead to many lakes, ranches and through the scenic back country. Almost all of these are gravel or dirt roads. Those described in the *Log* are usually fine for two-wheel drive vehicles. For large RVs, check locally before setting out.

The Cariboo is also criss-crossed by a fascinating variety of dirt roads, tracks, and trails that can be traversed by some vehicles in some weather. Always check locally on conditions, since bridges may be out or culverts collapsed. **Rule of thumb:** When you're in the Cariboo, always ask first, and never go in wet weather.

### Car and RV Rentals

Cars can be rented at 100 Mile House, Williams Lake, Quesnel, Bella Coola. RVs at Williams Lake: contact Chemo RV, 392-4451.

### Bus Lines

■ **Greyhound Bus Lines:** Call Vancouver 662-3222, or specific cities. Three times daily between Vancouver and Cache Creek, Williams Lake, Quesnel, Prince George, and intermediate points on Cariboo Hwy.

■ **Canim Lake Stage Lines:** Box 415, 100 Mile House, BC, V0K 2E0. 397-2562. Service from 100 Mile House to Noranda Mines, Canim Lake South, Hendrix Lake, and waypoints.

### Airlines

Scheduled air service is available in Williams Lake, Quesnel, Anahim Lake, Bella Coola, and Bella Bella.

■ **Air BC:** 688-5515. Scheduled service to Williams Lake and Quesnel.

■ **Pacific Coastal Airlines:** 273-8666 or 1-800-663-2872. Flights to Bella Bella, Ocean Falls, Rivers Inlet, from Vancouver International Airport's south terminal. Charters available.

■ **Harbour Airlines:** 627-1341. Coastal flights from Prince Rupert.

■ **Waglisla Airlines:** 278-3483, or 1-800-663-2875. Bases at South Terminal, Vancouver International Airport; and at Prince Rupert. Serves Bella Bella, Klempu, Powell River, Port Hardy, Massett.

■ **Wilderness Airline (1975) Ltd:** 276-2635 or 1-800-665-9453. Flights from Vancouver to Anahim Lake, Bella Coola, Dean River, Kimsquit.

### Railways

Passenger rail service is available from Vancouver to the Cariboo along a highly scenic route.

■ **BC Rail:** 984-5246; 631-3500. Departs 7:30am daily from North Vancouver's BC Rail station. Daily service to Prince George late June-mid-Sept. Rest of year on Wed, Fri, and Sun. The train reaches Lillooet (Mile Zero of Cariboo Wagon Road that carried gold rushers north), at about 1:05pm. Train divides at Lillooet: one Budd car returns to Vancouver, the other completes the 745km excursion to Prince George, with many stops including Clinton, 100 Mile House, Quesnel, Williams Lake, Prince George. Advance booking required.

# CARIBOO-CHILCOTIN EVENTS

## Alexis Creek

- **Pioneer Days and Fall Fair:** Late Aug. Parade, ranch games, canoe race, team roping, barbecue.

## Anahim Lake

- **Dean River Canoe Race:** May.
- **Anahim Lake Stampede:** Early July. One of the best-known, least-commercialized stampedes in BC. Write: Stampede, General Delivery, Anahim Lake, BC, V0L 1C0.

## Barkerville

- **International Hose Carriage Races:** Early Sept. Invitational. Local fire depts compete 1870s style.
- **Ghostly Tour:** Oct 31.

## Bella Bella

- **Waglisla Sports Day:** Late May.
- **Salmon Queen Festival:** July.

## Bella Coola

- **Oolichan Fishery:** April.
- **Bella Coola Rodeo:** July.
- **Fall Fair and Loggers' Sports:** Labour Day weekend.

## Bridge Lake

- **Rodeo:** July 1.

## Clinton

- **Clinton Ball:** Late May. Believed the oldest annual event in BC. In 1860s, *the* Cariboo social event. Held in the Clinton Hotel (originally 47 Mile House) until it burned down in 1958. Now in the Clinton Memorial Hall. Also includes a rodeo, but probably not in the ballroom.
- **Medieval Days:** Early Aug.
- **United Native Nations Rodeo:** Early Aug.

## Horsefly

- **Fishing Derby:** Early June.
- **Horsefly Fall Fair:** Late Aug.
- **Salmon Run:** Late Aug-Sept.

## 100 Mile House

- **Cariboo Cross-Country Ski Marathon:** Feb. 50km. Western Canada's largest. Competitors from BC, Canada, US, and Europe.
- **Little Britches Rodeo:** May.
- **South Cariboo Children's Festival:** June.
- **Great Cariboo Ride:** Late July. Six-day, 160km horseback ride.
- **Cariboo Open Golf Tourney:** At 108 Mile Ranch. Early Sept.

## Lac la Hache

- **South Cariboo Square Dance Jamboree:** June.
- **Country Music Festival:** On the lake. Early Aug.

## Lone Butte

- **Black Powder Shoot:** July.

## Likely

- **Black Powder Rendezvous:** July. Competitors from all over BC in shooting events.

## Lillooet

- **Only in Lillooet Days:** June. A weekend of the old west re-created, ending with Judge Begbie's Casino Night.
- **Lillooet Fall Fair:** Mid-Sept.

## Quesnel

- **Sled Dog Race Championships:** Jan.
- **Billy Barker Days:** Mid-July. Four-day event. Parade, fireworks, largest amateur rodeo in BC, white-water raft race. Billy Barker Days Society, Box 4441, Quesnel, BC, V2J 3J4.
- **Fall Fair:** Labour Day weekend. Draft horse pulling, dog pulling, agricultural delights, midway.

## Riske Creek

- **Frontier Days:** Aug.

## Seton Portage/Shalalth

- **Spring Skoot:** Off-road motorcycle rally. May 24 weekend.

## Wells

- **Heritage Festival:** Labour Day. Collectibles auction, hose carriage races in Barkerville.

## Williams Lake

- **Annual Bull Sale:** April.
- **Sugarcane Rodeo:** At Sugarcane Indian village. June.
- **Williams Lake Stampede:** Four-day event over the July 1 weekend. This is the big one, and the old one (getting on for 70 years), the major stampede of Cariboo cow country, with professional cowboys and cowgirls competing in saddle bronc riding, calf roping, team roping, Brahma bull riding. Native dancing, old-time fiddling, car races, and a parade.
- **Cariboo Fall Fair:** Sept. Stampede Grounds.
- **Wrestling Day:** The day after Boxing Day. At least it is in Williams Lake, where civic employees have been enjoying a paid holiday on Jan 2 since 1959. A day to wrestle with hangovers, it was thought.

*Calf roping at the Williams Lake Stampede.*

*Chilcotin back road south of Choelquoit Lake, with views of the Waddington Range.*

# Cariboo-Chilcotin Routes and Highlights

## TRAVELLER'S LOGS



## HIGHLIGHTS



## Cache Creek to Williams Lake

### THE CARIBOO HIGHWAY (Highway 97)

The Cariboo Hwy, Hwy 97 north, begins in Cache Creek, at the junction of Trans-Canada Hwy 1 and Hwy 97, and runs north 445km to Prince George. The section from Cache Creek to Williams Lake is 203km. To reach the Cariboo Hwy, head west from Kamloops on Hwy 1/97, or north from Hope on Hwy 1.

The Cariboo Hwy snakes through the ranch, plateau, and mountain country of the fabled Cariboo. To the east are the lakes and streams that yielded the gold that sparked the Cariboo Gold Rush.

To the west stretches the Chilcotin, a vast expanse of plain, plateau, and mountain, virtually uninhabited, much of it unreachable except on foot or horseback, or by boat or plane. Wherever water is available, there are stands of Douglas fir, lodgepole pine and aspens.

**Cache Creek:** (Pop. 1,007). For details, see *High Country*, p.166.

**Hwy 99:** 11km north of Cache Creek. Hwy 99 (formerly Hwy 12) comes in from the west, from North Vancouver via Whistler and Lillooet, to end at Hwy 97. It is 75km to Lillooet.

**Hat Creek Ranch:** At junction of Hwys 97 and 99. Daily mid-May to mid-Oct. 457-9722. 1861 ranch was roadhouse stopping place on original Cariboo Wagon Road. Restored by BC Heritage Trust. Guided tours, blacksmith, saddle maker, trail and wagon rides.

**Loon Lake Rd:** 21km north of Cache Creek turn east to Loon Lake. Paved all the way.

### SIDE TRIP to Loon Lake

**Loon Creek Hatchery:** About 10km along Loon Lake Rd. Kokanee salmon and rainbow trout. Best time to see fry is July-April. Write Loon Creek Hatchery, Loon Lake Rd, RR 1, Cache Creek, BC, V0K 1H0. 459-2454.

**Loon Lake:** A popular family fishing and resort area, 20km northeast of Hwy 97 junction, on Loon Lake Rd. Lake is nearly 12km long, only about 400m wide. Dependable stocks of rainbow trout.

**Loon Lake Provincial Park:** 3ha; 14 campsites. 398-4144. Midway on lake, nestled in a forest of Douglas fir and ponderosa pine.

### Return to Highway 97

**Carguile Rest Area:** 5km beyond Loon Lake Rd turnoff, 26km from Cache Creek.

**Cariboo Lakes:** Between Loon Lake and Clinton there are many small roadside lakes, some fresh, some alkaline. Fed by rainwater and runoff, they have no intakes or outlets, and most shrink to small pools in summer sun.

**Clinton:** (Pop. 662). 40km beyond Cache Creek. In gold-rush days, Clinton was at the junction of the two wagon roads leading to the gold fields, so was a major stopping place for merchants, ranchers, and would-be prospectors. Driving into Clinton today involves a time-warp: there's a pleasant feeling that nothing's changed very much. Clinton residents still seem to be prime examples of the pioneering, individualistic spirit of the Cariboo, routing motorcycle gangs (a famous incident in the '60s), and in general keeping the town the way they want it. That includes touches of the sublime and the absurd. Note Hickory Daiquiri Doc's office on the otherwise unprepossessing main street. Sign out front reads: "BONES SET – BLOOD LET – HOLES PATCHED – BABIES HATCHED." This is the real-life office of Dr. Frank Campbell. Read about him and others in Paul St Pierre's *Chilcotin Holiday.*

Clinton is called the Guest Ranch Capital of BC. Area ranches offer trail riding, hiking, fishing, barbecues. Some are open year-round for cross-country skiing, sleighing. (And hot tubbing.) All ranches have regular guest pick-up at BC Rail Station in Clinton.

**Clinton Information:** Infocentre, Clinton and District Chamber of Commerce, 1400 Cariboo Hwy, Clinton, BC, V0K 1K0. 459-2640. Daily June-Sept. In historic 1915 Pollard House.

■ **South Cariboo Historical Museum:** 1419 Cariboo Hwy. 459-2442. June-Aug. Originally an 1890s schoolhouse, built from

Cache Creek to Williams Lake

local, homemade bricks, now houses native, Chinese, and gold-rush artifacts.

■ **Wolf's Cry Inn:** 459-2610. New chef at this restaurant is drawing crowds.

**Pavilion Mountain Rd:** Southwest as you enter Clinton, leads 16km southwest to **Kelly Lake**. Paved to Kelly Lake, where road forks. **North fork** is the Jesmond Rd through to Jesmond and the Big Bar Ferry; see *Big Bar Rd Side Trip*, below. **South fork** leads about 15km over Pavilion Mountain to Pavilion on Hwy 99. Panoramic view of Coast Mountains, alpine flowers, and a cattle ranch perched on the mountaintop. Don't attempt to travel south of Kelly Lake if it has been raining, or even if it looks like rain. Muddy curves extremely treacherous in this usually bone-dry land. Check locally for conditions. For details from Pavilion on, see *Lillooet Road*, p.194.

**Downing Provincial Park:** 100ha; 25 campsites. 16km southwest of Clinton on Pavilion Mountain Rd. 398-4144. On shoreline of mountain-surrounded Kelly Lake. Rainbow trout, swimming, picnicking.

**Big Bar Rd:** Off Hwy 97, 9.5km north of Clinton. West to Chilcotin ranch country, gravel back roads and provincial park.

## SIDE TRIP
### on Big Bar Road

**Cross-country Ski Trails:** south off Big Bar Rd, 6km from Hwy 97. 60km of marked trails. Hiking and mountain biking in summer.

**Cariboo Rose Guest Ranch:** 14km west on Big Bar Rd; turn south on Hook Rd for 4km; then west 2km on Isadore Rd, and watch for signs. A small ranch (eight guests) in the Marble Mountains for dedicated horse people. Clinics, lessons for beginners, all-day rides. April-Oct. Box 160, Clinton, BC, V0K 1K0. 459-2255.

**Big Bar Lake Provincial Park:** 332ha; 33 campsites. 398-4144. June-Sept. On Big Bar Rd, 34km northwest of Hwy 97. Fraser Plateau landscape, created by ancient glacial action, with Marble Range to south. Glacial rubble formed eskers (long, snaking ridges of gravel), drumlins (tear-shaped hills), and other geological formations. Camping, swimming, fishing, boating, picnicking. Deer, bear, moose, squirrels, marmots. Rainbow trout.

**Rd to Meadow Lake Rd**: 10km north of Big Bar Lake, 44km from Hwy 97. T-junction. Right fork turns sharply northeast, 8km to Meadow Lake where it joins Meadow Lake Rd (see below). Big Bar Rd curves left or southwest toward Jesmond and Big Bar Creek.

**Big Bar Guest Ranch:** On Big Bar Rd, 4km west of Meadow Lake Rd fork, 48km from Hwy 97. Year-round, with skiing, gold panning, pack trips, riding lessons. 44 guests. Box 27, Jesmond, Clinton, BC, V0K 1K0. 459-2333.

*Barkerville Gold-Rush Town.*

**Jesmond Rd:** 5km from Big Bar Guest Ranch, 53km from Hwy 97. Jesmond Rd comes in from Kelly Lake to the south. Big Bar Rd turns northwest 19km to the **Fraser River**, **Big Bar Creek**, and **Big Bar Ferry**.

**Big Bar:** 19km from junction with Jesmond Rd. 35km downstream from the Gang Ranch. Current-driven ferry crosses the Fraser River. There has been a ferry in continuous operation at this point since 1894. When water is low or icy, an aerial tramway operates for passengers only. At times like this, ranchers leave a truck on either side. On demand 7am-7pm (except noon-1pm, 5-6pm). Five min.

Rock piles on the riverbanks show where Chinese miners painstakingly washed the gravel for gold. On the **West Bank**, there's a 4x4 road that goes all the way to **Lillooet**, 64km, three hours. Watch for California bighorn sheep near Big Bar Creek.

**Jesmond:** On Jesmond Rd, 1km south of turnoff to Big Bar Ferry. Behind the lilacs is the original ranch homesteaded by Phil Grinder in 1870. Ranch became an overnight stopping place for the Clinton to 150 Mile stage coach. Owned by the Coldwell family since 1911, run for years as a post office and store. Peter Coldwell wanted to call it "Mountain House," but that was thought too general. Post Office did approve the name Jesmond, after the town in England. Today a private residence. PO closed in 1965, store in 1970.

**Circle H Mountain Lodge:** On the Jesmond Rd 14km south of Jesmond. (Ranch is 40km from Clinton via Jesmond and Kelly Lake roads going south.) May-Oct. Box 7, Jesmond, Clinton, BC, V0K 1K0. 459-2565. First guest ranch in the area. Beautiful setting near Mt Bowman. Has a swimming pool, too.

**Cougar Point:** South on Jesmond Rd 10km from Circle H Mountain Lodge. At fork, take High Bar Rd 8km down in a stunning descent to the Fraser River. Chilcotin Plateau and panorama of ranches stretch out to the north and west. (This back road continues north along Fraser to Big Bar Creek.)

### *Return to Highway 97*

**Clinton Lookout and Big Bar Rest Area:** 9.5km north of Clinton on Hwy 97, just north of Big Bar Rd. From here to Prince George, BC Rail tracks parallel the Cariboo Hwy. Railway extends 745km from North Vancouver to Prince George. There are several stops thoughout the Cariboo. Freight lines carry on 823km to Fort Nelson.

**Meadow Lake Rd:** West off Hwy 97, 7km north of Big Bar Rd junction, 16.5km north of Clinton.

## SIDE TRIP

### on Meadow Lake Rd

Meadow Lake Rd offers an adventurous back road trip through the heart of the western Chilcotins, to Meadow Lake and the famous **Gang Ranch**, where Dog Creek Rd goes north 86km to Hwy 20 and Williams Lake. The whole area is laced with roads, most of them rough, some maintained by Forest Service, going thither and yon: ask as you go. Back roads maps available at infocentres.

**Meadow Lake:** About 46km west of Hwy 97 on Meadow Lake Rd. Even for locals, the lake is hard to find: it dries up somewhat in summer. But if you can see it, you know you're about halfway to the Gang Ranch.

**No-Name Rd:** Back road comes in from the south, where it connects 8km away with Big Bar Rd. Once you see this junction, you know you have just passed Meadow Lake (in case you missed it).

**Gang Ranch:** 100km west of Hwy 97 on Meadow Lake Rd. Travel 46km west of Meadow Lake junction (above) to Turn Creek Bridge, a suspension bridge; cross bridge, take right fork at top of the hill, then drive 4km in to the ranch.

For years, this was the largest ranch in North America, still one of the largest working ranches, covering some 400,000ha (a million acres) stretching south to the Chilcotin Mountains. Most of the ranch buildings – cookhouse, bunkhouse, post office, one-room school –are painted a distinctive red. It is no longer a guest ranch, but some rustic accommodation is available for independent-minded visitors. Gang Ranch Ltd, Gang Ranch PO, BC, V0K 1N0. 459-7923.

Thought to be named because Jerome and Thaddeus Harper, who started the ranch in the 1860s, were the first in the BC Interior to use the multi-bladed gang plough. Over the years, the ranch has had a romantic and sometimes troubled history as owners struggled with cattle market's ups and downs. Ranch is currently said to be co-owned by a Cessna-flying Alberta cattleman and a Saudi Arabian oil sheik. Nevertheless, cattle are still branded with a J and sideways T (called the "J lazy-T"), for Jerome and Thaddeus.

**Dog Creek Rd:** At Turn Creek Bridge turnoff to the Gang Ranch. Continues north 86km to Hwy 20 (Bella Coola Rd) near Williams Lake. Details in *Williams Lake to Bella Coola*, p.198.

**Dog Creek:** About 10km north of Turn Creek Bridge, on Dog Creek Rd. Site of ancient native settlement; a huge cavern under Dog Creek Dome contains rock paintings. Non-natives arrived in 1856; built the (now gone) Dog Creek Hotel and BC's first flour mill. Today, there's a two-storey log store and a one-room school.

**Alkali Lake:** 34km north of Turn Creek Bridge, on Dog Creek Rd. Home to white pelicans during spring and fall migrations. Also to other migrant birds. Indeed, a mecca for birdwatchers. **Alkali Lake Ranch**, said to be the oldest in BC, has red-roofed log buildings. **Alkali Lake Band** is part of Shuswap Nation, and the written Shuswap language may be seen on signs and buildings. Reserve is recognized as a leader in drug and alcohol treatment.

It is a further 27km to the community of Springhouse; 13km to junction with road from Chimney Lake (to the south); a final 12km to connect with Hwy 20.

### Return to Highway 97

**Chasm Provincial Park:** 141ha; open year-round. Day use. 5.5km north of Meadow Lake Rd, 22km north of Clinton, turn east on gravel road; 4km to park. Painted Chasm is a spectacular cut in lava bedrock, closed on three sides, about 1.5km long and up to 120m deep. Reveals the colours and textures of volcanoes active 12 to 25 million years ago. Chasm was cut by glacial meltwaters about 10,000 years ago.

**70 Mile House:** (Pop. 179). On Hwy 97, 9km beyond turnoff to Chasm Park, 31km north of Clinton (71km north of Cache Creek). Historic roadhouse location, one of first stopping places on the Cariboo Wagon Rd. Named because roadhouse was 70 miles on the Cariboo Wagon Road from Lillooet.

**Old Bonaparte Rd:** At 70 Mile House. Gateway to the South Cariboo lakes, goes east to **Green and Watch lakes** and others. 6km from 70 Mile, road forks at North Bonaparte, south fork leading through Bonaparte Valley to Bonaparte Lake. Many delightful smaller lakes within walking distance of Bonaparte Lake. Boating, hunting, fishing, riding, swimming, cross-country skiing. Resorts and guest ranches. North fork is North Green Lake Rd.

**Green Lake:** At the fork, take North Green Lake Rd. A warm, shallow, turquoise-green lake, 15km long, edged with fir, larch and whispering aspen. Greenish hue comes from algae and other microorganisms, though some say it's from the reflections of the trees. In any case, there's good swimming, fishing, and birding (particularly osprey and bald eagles). Many resorts and lodges.

**Flying U Ranch:** On north shoreof Green Lake, 6km from the fork. Box 69, 70 Mile House, BC, V0K 2K0. 456-7717. An 18,000ha working ranch dating back to 1849. Only resort ranch in BC where guests –provided with maps – can trail ride on their own. Run by the five Fremlin families. Has an airstrip, and its own BC Rail train stop, "Flying U."

**Green Lake Provincial Park:** 347ha; 121 campsites at five campgrounds. Sani-station. 398-4414. Year-round. 15km northeast of 70 Mile House, on Old Bonaparte Rd (paved). Water activities; winter sports.

**Rd at 83 Mile House:** 18km north of 70 Mile House, 89.5km north of Cache Creek. Leads southeast to Green Lake area.

**93 Mile House:** (Pop. 91). 103km north of Cache Creek. Scene of biggest robbery in Cariboo history, when BX stage coach was held up. Highwayman was caught, but the $15,000 in gold dust, nuggets, and bricks was never found.

**Hwy 24:** Just north of 93 Mile, 103.5km north of Cache Creek. Hwy travels east through Lakes Country.

## SIDE TRIP

### to Lakes Country

Hwy 24 offers a scenic, potentially fishful trip through South Cariboo lake country, continuing east 97km to small community of Little Fort on Yellowhead Hwy 5. See *High Country* p.179, for details on easterly portions of Hwy 24.

**Lone Butte:** (Pop. 71). 10km east of Hwy 97 on Hwy 24. Small settlement and BC Railway station. Has the line's last standing wooden water tower, from the age of steam. Named for the large flat-top hill to the east. Guest ranches in area.

**Interlakes District:** Hwy 24 leads to hundreds of lakes offering fishing, mainly for rainbow trout, also eastern brook trout, lake trout, burbot, and kokanee. Sheridan and Bridge lakes are favourites; Lac des Roches good for fly-fishing. Resorts throughout area provide facilities ranging from primitive to luxurious. Some stay open through winter for cross-country skiing.

**Bridge Lake:** (Pop. 16). 41km beyond Lone Butte, 51km east of Hwy 97. Tourist services, resorts. Bridge Lake Centennial Park for picnicking.

**Bridge Lake Provincial Park:** At Bridge Lake, off Hwy 24. 6ha; 20 vehicle/tent campsites; 13 walk-in campsites. 828-4494. May-Sept. Walking trail around Bridge Lake.

### Return to Highway 97

**100 Mile House:** (Pop. 1,866). 113km north of Cache Creek (90km south of Williams Lake). 100 Mile House was a stopping place on the Cariboo Road as early as 1861. Stagecoach from 1860s is exhibited at Red Coach Inn, north end of town. In 1930, Lord Martin Cecil (who became the Marquis of Exeter) arrived at 100 Mile House to manage his father's property, the Bridge Creek Ranch. 100 Mile House was well known around the world as headquarters of the

Emissaries of the Divine Light, a non-sectarian group headed by Cecil until his recent death.

100 Mile House is now a service centre for the central Cariboo, with a trading population of some 17,000. Major producer of log homes for North American and Japanese markets. Houses are completely finished, then dismantled and shipped off.

In winter, 100 Mile House is a centre for cross-country skiing and in early February hosts the Cariboo Marathon, a 50km race attracting over 1,000 participants from across the continent.

**100 Mile House Information:** Infocentre, South Cariboo Chamber of Commerce, Box 2312, 100 Mile House, BC, V0K 2E0. 395-5353. Daily May-Sept. Off-season: weekdays 9-5. On Hwy 97, right beside the **Giant Skis**: 12m-long replicas of racing cross-country country skis, flanked by 9m ski poles – reputed to be world's largest.

**Rd to Canim Lake:** 4km north of 100 Mile House, at top of hill. Stay on paved road. Goes east 36km to Canim Lake, and on to Mahood Falls.

## SIDE TRIP
### to Canim Lake

**Forest Grove:** Small community about 20km east of Hwy 97. Take north fork to **Ruth Lake**.

**Ruth Lake Provincial Park:** 30ha. 9km north of Forest Grove. April-Oct. 398-4144. Day-use area, small beach, picnicking. May-June are great months for Ruth Lake.

**Canim Lake:** (Pop. 64). 16km east of Forest Grove, 36km east of Hwy 97 junction. Canim means "canoe" in Shuswap language. A large lake – 37km long – and very beautiful, surrounded by mountains. Harbours large sport fish, the "laker" or char. Family-oriented resort community. Fishing, horseback riding, water activities, birdwatching. Road forks here, leading north to Eagle Creek and along north shore of lake, or east along south shore toward Mahood Falls. Tourist facilities along both roads.

**Canim Beach Provincial Park:** 6ha. 5km north of Canim Lake community, following north fork. Seven vehicle/tent campsites, nine walk-in beachfront sites. April-Oct. 398-4144. Gravel and pebble beach. Moose common.

**Hathaway, Sulphurous, and Horse Lakes:** Take east fork out of Canim Lake community. At 24km east of Canim Lake, turn southwest for these and other resort lakes. Road leads back to Hwy 97 at 100 Mile House.

**Canim River Falls, Mahood Lake, Deception Falls:** Take east fork out of Canim Lake community (as above). Travel 24km, to fork in road. Take northeast fork for 6km. Walk to Canim and Mahood falls, spectacular cascades between Canim and Mahood lakes. Mahood Lake is part of, and a secondary entrance into, **Wells Gray Provincial Park**. A store, resorts, and a wilderness campsite are located in area. Deception Falls are located on Deception Creek just above where it flows into Mahood Lake. For details, see *High Country*, p.180.

## Return to Highway 97

**108 Mile Ranch:** 13km north of 100 Mile House on Hwy 97. Once a large cattle operation. Now features history, and fine resorts.

■ **108 Heritage Site:** Contact 100 Mile House & District Historical Society, Box 2002, 100 Mile House, BC, V0K 2E0. 791-5288. Late May-Labour Day: daily 9am-6pm. Early 20th-century buildings at north entrance to 108 Ranch include rebuilt ranch building from 105 Mile, post house buildings from 108 Ranch, an ice house, and the Watson Clydesdale Barn, built in 1908 and restored (one of the largest log barns in Canada). Guided tours. Post House Gallery.

■ **Best Western 108 Resort:** 260ha all-season recreational resort with airstrip. Write Comp 2, 108 Ranch, BC, V0K 2Z0. 791-5211, 1-800-667-5233. Spa, heated pool, tennis, trail riding, 200km cross-country trails, and (believe it!) golf. The **108 Resort Golf Club** offers a demanding, 18-hole championship course.

■ **Hills Health & Guest Ranch:** C-26, 108 Ranch, BC, V0K 2Z0. 791-5225. Indoor pool, jacuzzis, saunas, aerobics, horseback riding, cross-country skiing.

**Lac la Hache:** (Pop. 420). 25km beyond 100 Mile House. Called the "Longest Town in the Cariboo," it stretches several km along a beautiful lakeshore. Lac la Hache, which translates as "Lake of the Axe," is, the story goes, named for an axe that an early French Canadian fur trader dropped through a hole in the lake ice. That perhaps wasn't all that he called it. Today there is still fishing (and ice fishing) – for kokanee, large lake trout. Also resorts, winter sports.

**Lac la Hache Information:** Contact 100 Mile House Infocentre, South Cariboo Chamber of Commerce, Box 2312, 100 Mile House, BC, V0K 2E0. 395-5353.

■ **Lac la Hache Museum:** Hwy 97, near the community hall. 396-7262. Daily July-Aug. In a former 1930s log school. Small schoolroom exhibit, tools, photographs.

**Rd to Timothy Lake:** To Timothy and other fishing lakes, east at Lac la Hache. Road partially paved. Many services.

**Lac la Hache Provincial Park:** 24ha; 83 campsites, sani-station. 398- 4414. 13.5km north of Lac la Hache, camping area on east side of highway, picnic sites on west beside lake. Beach, forest trails, winter recreation.

**Cariboo Provincial Nature Park:** 98ha. Year-round. 15km north of Lac la Hache, walk-in only. 398-4414. Set aside as a place to study nature. Beaver pond on San Jose River, waterfowl on Frog Lake. Tread carefully; don't disturb the wildlife.

**San Jose River:** West side of highway, which follows the river almost to Williams Lake. River drains Lac la Hache and winds its way gently, flowing into Williams Lake.

**To the Gold Fields:** Point-of-interest sign 27km north of Lac la Hache. Explains background of the 1860s gold rush.

**Mission Rd:** 45km north of Lac la Hache. West a short distance to site of **St Joseph's Mission**. Established by Oblates of Mary Immaculate, in 1866, for the Shuswap, Carrier, and Chilcotin Indians. Father James Maria McGuckin also operated a farm/ranch to provide income. Its OMI brand was the first registered in the Cariboo. A few old farm buildings and a small cemetery for natives and missionaries remain.

**Wetlands Conservation Project:** 48km north of Lac la Hache. Ducks Unlimited project to increase habitat for waterfowl.

**150 Mile House:** (Pop. 899). 50km north of Lac la Hache. Once an important junction where passengers changed stagecoaches before going west to the Chilcotin or east to the gold fields. Now a small service centre for surrounding region.

**Rd to Horsefly:** To community of Horsefly and Quesnel Lake. Turn east at 150 Mile House. Paved road to Horsefly. Gravel to lakes beyond. Through open pasture and rolling hills with Cariboo Mountains in background.

## SIDE TRIP
### to Horsefly, Quesnel and Other Lakes, and (Eventually) Likely

**153 Mile Store:** 5km east of 150 Mile House on Horsefly Rd. Country store dating from Wagon Road days. Ceased operating as a store in 1964 and is now a private museum, much of contents in tip-top condition. Mid-May to Sept. Call 296-3360 for appointment.

**Horsefly:** (Pop. 131). 51km east of store, 56km east of Hwy 97 and 150 Mile House. On the banks of the Horsefly River, an important salmon spawning stream. First called Harper's Camp, after one of the brothers who founded the Gang Ranch. Renamed when later settlers discovered one of the drawbacks to its location. Site of first gold discovery in the Cariboo, in 1859. Prospectors, still with stakes in the area, can sometimes be seen washing creek gravel.

■ **Jack Lynn Memorial Museum:** Campbell Ave, one block south of Horsefly town centre.

620-3304. July-Aug, Tues-Sat. Artifacts from Horsefly's mining, trapping, logging days.

**Rd to Lakes:** Bear right in Horsefly on paved road, links with gravel roads leading to lakes. 1.5km east, the road splits: north fork to **Horsefly and Quesnel lakes**; south fork to **Black Creek** and **Canim Lake**.

**Horsefly Lake Provincial Park:** 148ha; 22 campsites. May-Oct. 398-4414. 13km northeast of Horsefly. Follow lakes road to Horsefly Lake. Water activities. Good base camp for exploring.

**Quesnel Lake:** 36km northeast of Horsefly. Gravel road dead-ends on southern shores of Quesnel Lake. At 600m, Quesnel Lake is the deepest lake in BC, and second deepest in North America. If there are any lake monsters or Ogopogo cousins, they haven't shown up yet. But there are lots of resorts, good fishing, skiing.

**Rd to Likely:** Bear north past the schoolhouse in Horsefly onto Mitchell Bay Rd to Likely. Road passes along west end of Quesnel Lake, giving fine river and lake views. Resorts, campgrounds. Closed in winter. Check locally for road conditions, especially in wet weather. This is a good gravel road, but route is not recommended for RVs. A better route, north from 150 Mile House, is cited immediately below.

Continue to Likely on Quesnel Lake road, or return to Hwy 97 at 150 Mile House. A second paved road from 150 Mile House leads north to Big Lake Ranch, and around Morehead Lake, again to Likely.

**Quesnel River Hatchery:** Chinook salmon hatchery on road to Likely (2km south of Likely). 790-2266. Daily. Adult salmon Aug- late Sept. Fry: Jan to mid-May.

**Likely:** (Pop.268). 80km northeast of 150 Mile House. No, it's not named because gold was very likely there. John A ("Plato John") Likely, a 1920s gold miner who liked to consider the meaning of life, gave his name to this pretty community on the Quesnel River at its mouth on Quesnel Lake. The Likely area has witnessed some of the richest gold finds in the district; as late as 1922, some 20kg were taken out from a single mine in one year. Mineral exploration continues to be Likely's most important economic activity, but visitors appreciate its fishing, hunting, hiking, and history.

**Likely Information:** Infocentre, Box 79, Likely, BC, V0L 1N0. 790-2380. On Likely St. End of June-Aug.

■ **Cedar Point Park:** On Cedar Creek Rd in Likely. A pretty day-use park sporting some hefty mining artifacts, including one of the "Twin Giants," huge steam shovels weighing 10,000kg each.

**Rd to Quesnelle Forks:** Cross bridge over Quesnel River at Likely, continue on for 200m, then turn northwest onto Quesnelle Forks Rd.

**Quesnelle Forks:** About 8km beyond Likely. In 1859, this ghost town claimed fleeting fame as "the largest city on the mainland." The gold – and the fame –lasted five years, as miners, gamblers, storekeepers, and ladies of the evening crowded into the log buildings quickly built near the gold finds. Once home to 5,000 people, Quesnelle Forks shrank as the gold ran out. Today, greying log buildings are set amid fields of daisies. Quesnelle Forks is on the list for heritage restoration. To date, the cemetery has been restored, and there is a wheelchair accessible bathroom.

**Note: As with other Cariboo back roads, the road to Quesnelle Forks can be difficult in wet weather.**

**Bullion Pit:** 5km west of Likely, off the road back to Hwy 97. Simply called **"Hydraulic"** on some area maps. Billed as the world's largest gold-mining pit, the Bullion hydraulic mine pit sinks 90m into the ground, and is more than 3km long. Gold-mining operations took place from 1892-1942. From 1892 to 1898, gold worth $1.25 million was extracted. Abandoned after the original strike, the hydraulic area still produced almost $1 million in gold for the Chinese miners who stayed on. Later hydraulic operations drew on water carried in over 65km of canals. In 1938, the mine used more water each day than the city of Vancouver.

Here, in March 1988, pensioner-prospector George Williams unearthed a gold nugget the size of a turkey egg. It weighed 28gm, and was worth as much as $10,000. Williams had no plans to sell it.

## Return to Highway 97

**Williams Lake:** (Pop. 10,385). 15km north of 150 Mile House, 203km north of Cache Creek. Fastest-growing community in the Cariboo, and the only city between Hope and Quesnel. It's also Stampede Town. The famous Williams Lake Stampede, a four-day event over the July 1 weekend, was officially started in the 1920s, and is now a major professional rodeo.

Williams Lake did not share in the Cariboo gold bonanza, all because of a loan that was refused. Tom Manifee owned land now at the heart of the city. Asked by the Cariboo road contractors for a short-term loan so they could pay their workers, he refused. Refusal led to angry words, and angry words led the contractors to reroute the road through 150 Mile House, where the roadhouse owner was more than pleased to lend them money. Bypassed, Manifee's roadhouse got no more business, and Williams Lake did not come into its own until the Pacific Great Eastern Railway tracks arrived in 1920. In a reversal of fate, the coming of steel did in 150 Mile House, and established Williams Lake as area's commercial centre.

Community has a diversified economic base, with forestry, mining, and agriculture; and the most active stockyard in the province. It was probably named for pioneer William Pinchbeck, who bought land from the original native inhabitants, or for Chief William, of the Sugar Cane native tribe. All tourist facilities available.

**Williams Lake Information:** Infocentre, Williams Lake and District Chamber of Commerce, 1148 S Broadway (Hwy 97 at south end of town), Williams Lake, BC, V2G 1A2. 392-5025. Daily July-Aug. Weekdays Sept-June.

**Williams Lake Airport:** East 11km north of Williams Lake. Service to Vancouver, Prince George. Charters.

■ **Williams Lake Museum:** Near City Hall. 113 N 4th Ave, Williams Lake, BC, V2G 2C8. 392-7404. June-Sept, daily 11am-4pm. Interior Salish artifacts, grist mill equipment, printing press.

■ **Stationhouse Gallery:** At the foot of Oliver St. #1 N Mackenzie Ave, BC Rail Station, Williams Lake, BC, V2G 1N4. 392-6113. Year-round. In historic passenger train depot. Monthly shows, some local work, crafts.

■ **Scout Island Nature Centre:** On Scout Island at west end of Williams Lake, reached by a causeway. Turn off Hwy 97 east of city centre, follow signs. Centre is only .5km from Hwy 97. Area open year-round. Nature House seasonal: May-Aug, 9am-4pm. 398-8532. Nature house for adults and children, lots of hands-on exhibits. Trails along lakeshore.

■ **Williams Lake Golf and Tennis Club:** 104 Fairview Dr, five minutes from town. Box 4006, Williams Lake, BC, V2G 2V2. 392-6026. 18-hole championship course, night-lit tennis courts, restaurant.

**Hwy 20:** Hwy 20 comes into town at the traffic lights at the south end of the lake, goes straight through town to Oliver St, the town's centre. Turn west on Hwy 20, for Bella Coola. For details see *Williams Lake to Bella Coola*, p.198. Or continue north on Hwy 97 to Quesnel.

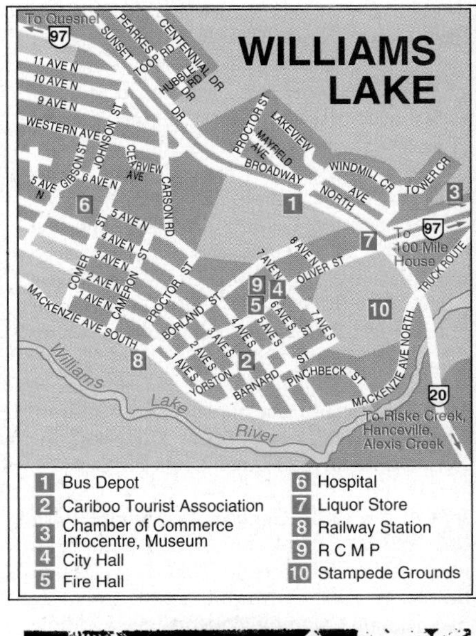

# Lillooet Road

## HIGHWAYS 99 and 12

The Lillooet Rd loops from a point on the Cariboo Hwy (Hwy 97) 11km north of Cache Creek and leads in a vaguely westerly fashion 75km to Lillooet (this part is an extension of Hwy 99 through from Whistler, and used to be called Hwy 12). Then the Lillooet Rd (here still called Hwy 12) continues southeast from Lillooet along the Fraser River another 64km to Lytton and Trans-Canada Hwy 1.

In terms of awesome scenery, this is perhaps the most underrated route in BC. As it follows the churning Fraser River, the road twists, climbs, and descends in hair-raising hair-pin bends. Often the river is pressed in by mountainsides, with the road carved into the cliffs high above. There are struggling pine trees and sagebrush. Intriguing homesteads appear in gaps between verticals. As you peer down and over the Fraser you might see a bench with an irrigated field on it – a deep green blotch in the vast brown. At one end of the ride, just as you pass the viewpoint where the blue waters of the North Thompson River blast out into the yellow-brown surge of the Fraser, you find yourself suddenly on a quiet residential street in Lytton. It's like being beamed down from the moon into a familiar backyard.

The Lillooet Rd gives access to the largely undeveloped wilderness beyond Bralorne and Bridge River, at the south end of the Chilcotin. Lillooet itself, the heart of one of the driest regions in BC, offers its Golden Mile of history, a rockhound's paradise and a healthful, insect-free climate attested to by the advanced ages noted on pioneers'tombstones.

The *Log* begins at the Hwy 99 turnoff from Hwy 97, and proceeds south.

**Hwys 97 and 99:** 11km north of Cache Creek. Hwy 99 (formerly Hwy 12) travels in a westerly fashion 75km to Lillooet.

**Hat Creek Ranch:** At junction of Hwys 97 and 99. Daily mid-May to mid-Oct. 457-9722. 1861 ranch was roadhouse stopping place on original Cariboo Wagon Road. Restored by BC Heritage Trust. Guided tours, blacksmith, saddle maker, trail and wagon rides.

**Pictograph:** 21.5km beyond beginning of Hwy 99, north side of road, 1km up a steep trail. Native rock paintings. No signs.

**Marble Canyon Provincial Park:** 335ha; 34 campsites. About 28km west of Hwy 99 junction. June-Sept. 1,000m limestone cliffs of Marble Canyon give the park its name. Camping, picnicking, paddling, swimming, fishing, hiking. Crown and Turquoise lakes. Trail to waterfall and Teapot Rock formation. Archeological sites and pictographs. Native plants include coyote willow, used by Interior Salish Indians for rope making; and soapberry, the berries whipped with water to make "Indian ice cream."

**Pavilion Lake:**About 30km west of Hwy 97 junction. A car-stopper.(Trout, too.)

**Pavilion Rd:** About 5km past Pavilion Lake, 35km west of Hwy 97. Leads north 31km to Clinton, over Pavilion Mountain. Main Cariboo road in the early 1860s, and the first wagon road in BC to be surveyed (in 1863, by Royal Engineer Sgt James McMurphy). Passengers used to have to push the coaches uphill, and freight wagons dragged logs as brakes on down grades. Spectacular views and the old Carson Ranch as well. Road is part gravel, part paved, and pretty narrow. May be closed in winter; check locally, and if there's been so much as a drop of rain, pass this one by. Muddy curves are treacherous.

**Note**: About 15km from Hwy 99, Pavilion Rd forks at **Kelly Lake**. Take right (northeast) fork 16km to Clinton; northwest is the Jesmond Rd connecting 39km north with Big Bar Rd. The Cariboo is laced with fascinating back roads like these. Details in *Cache Creek to Williams Lake*, p.190.

**Fraser Benchlands:** For next 40km, from Marble Canyon south to Lillooet, highway skirts the upper Fraser Canyon. Semi-desert benchlands high above the river are often irrigated to produce crops or pasture. Benchlands lie at the original level of the land in this region. The deeply incised cliffs that descend to the river are the result of centuries of erosion by water and weather. Here, the highway corkscrews in a long, dazzling descent to Lillooet.

**Rd to Lillooet:** 75km from Hwy 97 junction. West into Lillooet across Bridge of the 23 Camels.

**Bridge of the 23 Camels:** Built in 1981, crossing the Fraser River at Lillooet. Named for ill-fated beasts brought as freight carriers during Cariboo gold rush. In May 1862, the two-humped Bactrian camels arrived at Fort Douglas, at the head of Harrison Lake. By 1864 this Dromedary Express had been disbanded. The rocky landscape was too harsh for their large flat feet, but the stubborn camels also made it hard on themselves by refusing to fit in socially. Indiscriminate in their discrimination, they bit and kicked mules, oxen, and men. They ate everything including laundry, and their potent odour was so offensive that other pack animals bolted in fear. Some camels died in snow storms, others were shot and eaten.

**Lillooet:** (Pop. 1,782). 86km north and west of Cache Creek; 64km north of Lytton. Incorporated 1946, Lillooet dates back to the Cariboo Gold Rush, when it was terminus of the boat route north through Harrison and Anderson lakes, and beginning of the first Cariboo Road. By 1863, with a population of 15,000, it claimed to be the second largest town north of San Francisco. As oxen cannot be backed up, its main street was made wide enough to turn a double freight wagon hauled by the 10 yoke-spans of oxen required to pull 20 tonnes over the 2,000m Pavilion summit.

More recently, resident legend Ma Murray put Lillooet on the map. With her husband, George, Ma founded the *Bridge River-Lillooet News* in 1934, the liveliest weekly in the province. A tough-talking, down-to-earth editor who snorted snuff and smoked hand-rolled cigarettes as she pounded away on her old typewriter, Ma's pungent commentaries on politics and events were quoted across Canada.

In a 1975 interview with *Beautiful British Columbia* magazine, when she was 88 years old and still living in her big white house on Lillooet's main street, Ma Murray said: "We moved up here in 1933 with the children and everything, and, oh, we've been rewarded. It's like casting your bread on the waters and it comes back with nuts and raisins and cinnamon on it. It's a fabulous country and anybody would be a sap that ever got a chance to get into it that didn't stay. It couldn't help but fascinate anyone who ever came here. Lillooet just couldn't miss." Margaret Lally Murray died in 1982 at age 94.

**Lillooet Information:** Infocentre, Box 441, Lillooet, BC, V0K 1V0. 256-4308. 790 Main St. Shares former Anglican church with village museum. Daily July-Aug. Afternoons, shoulder months. Closed winter. Off-season: 256-4289.

■ **Mile 0 Cairn:** Main St, in the centre of Lillooet, marks beginning of first Cariboo Road. The towns and villages on the Cariboo Road that incorporate mileages into their names number from this point. Cairn is part of Lillooet's Golden Mile of History, with 15 historic points of interest along main streets of the town.

■ **Hangman's Tree:** On the benchland above Main St. Said to be one of the places where 1860s' "Hanging" Judge Matthew Baillie Begbie meted out justice: probably a slander on the name of a man strict but fair, who rarely sentenced anyone to die.

■ **Old Newspaper Office:** Main St. Former haunt of famed frontier journalist Ma Murray. Her newspaper guaranteed "a chuckle every week and a belly laugh once a month or your money back."

■ **Lillooet Museum:** With infocentre in former St Mary's Anglican Church. Box 441, Main St, Lillooet, BC, V0K 1V0. 256-4308. Seasonal. Daily July-Aug. Afternoons, shoulder months. Local pioneer and mining artifacts, First Nations relics, Chinese utensils, Ma Murray's printing press, and a new Ma Murray family video.

■ **Miyazaki Heritage House:** 6th Ave off Main St. Built in the 1890s, occupied by Dr Masajiro Miyazaki and family, after he was interned in wartime evacuation, then sent to provide medical care for Japanese evacuated to Lillooet area. Recipient of the Order of Canada for his pioneering medical work in this region.

■ **Rockhounding:** Lillooet area is one of BC's finest rockhounding areas, with jade, agate, and other semi-precious stones. Largest jade boulder found to date weighed more than 16t.

■ **Gold Panning:** Cayoosh Creek Park. Ask at infocentre.
■ **Archeological Sites:** About 350 sites, evidence of the history of Upper Lillooet Indians, exist in Lillooet region. Some include pictographs.
■ **Sheep Pasture Golf Course:** On Texas Creek Rd, 8km south of town. Local farmer Dave Jones has converted his 600ha sheep pasture to dual use. Now sheep must share their turf with golfers. "Never a baaaad round," Jones boasts. Fabulous views of Fraser River and mountains, especially from second hole.
■ **Chinese Rock Piles:** Two locations. On Main St below Hangman's Tree Park, and by old suspension bridge. Tailings left by Chinese miners are evidence of their tremendous efforts.
■ **Cariboo Chilcotin Helicopters Ltd:** Nugget Rd, Lillooet, BC, V0L 1V0. 256-4888. Also offices in Kamloops, Gold Bridge. Wilderness adventures, photo safaris.

**Bridge River Rd (Hwy 40):** West from Main St at north end of town, to Gold Bridge and Bralorne.

## SIDE TRIP

### to Gold Bridge and Bralorne

Bridge River Rd (Hwy 40), gravel, leads west 100km to Gold Bridge, 7km farther to Bralorne, skirting north shore of sinewy Carpenter Lake.

**Terzaghi Dam:** 47km from Lillooet, at the base of Mission Mountain near Carpenter Lake, at junction with Seton Portage Rd. Intake structures above the dam divert Bridge River through Mission Mountain via two long tunnels with a vertical drop of 326m down to powerhouses at Shalalth, on Seton Portage Rd.

**Seton Portage Rd:** 47km from Lillooet, at eastern tip of Carpenter Lake. Goes south 18km over spiralling Mission Pass down to Shalalth (pronounced "shalath") and Seton Portage on Seton Lake. Descent to Seton Lake is a dramatic 1300m. Road is gravel, safe for most vehicles, but trailers not recommended.

**Shalalth:** On Seton Portage Rd, 17km south of Hwy 40. Site of Bridge River hydroelectric complex, and powerhouses #1 and #2. Tours on request. Also picnics, boat launching site.

**Seton Portage:** (Pop. 96). Just 1km west along the lake from Shalalth, 65km beyond Lillooet. Seton Portage was site of first railway in BC, using wooden rails to portage supplies between Anderson and Seton lakes in gold-rush days. Each lake is some 210m deep. Today, a small spirited community. Holds off-road motorcycle races on May 24 weekend, called "Spring Skoot."

**Seton Portage and Shalalth Information:** Infocentre in BC Rail Caboose. Box 2066, Seton Portage, BC, V0N 3B0. 259-8383. July-Aug, 9am-5pm.

■ **Seton Portage Provincial Park:** 1ha. Beside Infocentre Caboose on Seton Portage Rd. May-Oct. Day use.

**Carpenter Lake:** Hwy 40 follows north shore of Carpenter Lake for 53km west from Seton Portage Rd junction and Terzaghi Dam to Gold Bridge. Several Forest Service recreation sites on Carpenter Lake.

**Tyaughton Lake Rd:** Turn north 90km beyond Lillooet. Tyaughton means "lake of the jumping fish." This is also home territory of cougar, black bear, mountain goat, and California bighorn sheep.
■ **Tyax Mountain Lake Resort:** 5km north of Hwy 40 on Tyaughton Lake Rd. Tyax Mountain Lake Resort, General Delivery, Gold Bridge, BC, V0K 1P0. 238-2221. Luxury resort includes a stunning lodge, said to be the largest log structure on the West Coast. Heli-skiing, tennis, riding, beach, canoes, sailboats, sauna, fitness centre.

**Gold Bridge:** (Pop. 68). 10km west of Tyaughton Lake Rd, 100km west of Lillooet. Resort community. Fishing, public gold panning on east bank of Hurley River, access to mountain snowmobiling, ski touring, hiking, riding. Guest ranches, lodges, Forest Service recreation sites all nearby.
■ **Cariboo Chilcotin Helicopters Ltd:** 238-2414 in Gold Bridge. Also offices in Lillooet and Kamloops. Fishing trips.

**Bralorne:** (Pop. 78). 7km beyond Gold Bridge. Home in 1920s to the Bralorne Pioneer Mine, the richest gold claim in Canada, producing over $145 million worth of gold before it closed in 1970. Historic area is now home to resorts featuring a variety of wilderness activities: fishing, trail riding, sailing, ghost town tours. Hiking and ski touring on Warner Pass Trail, Chism Pass Trail, and McGillivray Pass Trail, day-use trails near town site. Cross-country skiing, sleigh rides, snowshoeing.
■ **Bralorne Pioneer Museum:** 238-2240. July- early Sept, 12-4 daily. Mining equipment, photos of miners and families.

### Return to Lillooet and Bridge of the 23 Camels

**Duffey Lake Rd (Hwy 99):** At this point, the "Lillooet Road" continues south from Lillooet on Hwy 12, on the east bank of the Fraser River, and we leave Hwy 99 to its own devices.

For your information, what Hwy 99 does is cross the Fraser at the Bridge of 23 Camels, and travel south over Cayoosh Creek. From here it continues southwest to Seton Lake, Duffey Lake, Pemberton, and through to Whistler, Squamish, and Horseshoe Bay on the coast. It is an excellent recently paved road, now the official extension of Hwy 99. A circle tour from Vancouver is now possible using Hwy 99 (including the Duffey Lake Rd), Hwy 12, and Hwy 1. See *Horseshoe Bay to Lillooet*, p.102.

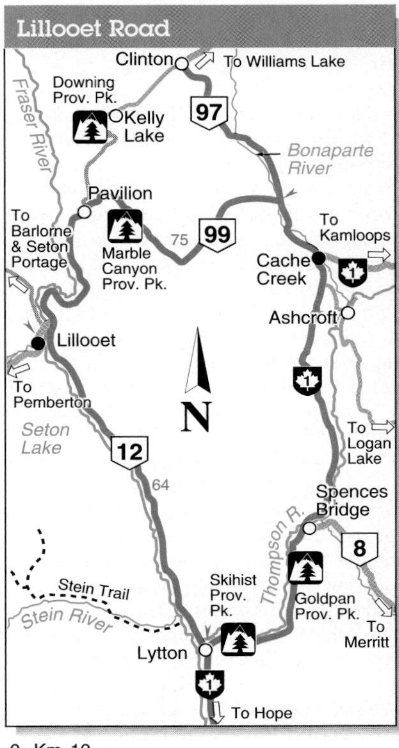


## Lillooet Road (Highway 12)

The following 64km between Lillooet and Lytton are exciting. "You're fine as long as you don't look up," advised the girl in the bakery in Lillooet. Another word of advice: don't look down either. Rocks can skelter down from above, especially in a rainstorm (rain is infrequent), and way below are the yellow-brown swirling waters of the Fraser Canyon. Just keep driving.

**Ginseng Farming:** 30km south of Lillooet. Stretching out over the Fraser benchlands are endless rows of mysterious crops shaded with black plastic screening. It's ginseng, and this area is the world's largest producer of North American ginseng. 77ha are under cultivation. "So much ginseng, so little time." The screening is polypropylene shade cloth. Ginseng requires deep shade for growth, and its water requirements must be strictly controlled, thus the attraction of this exceedingly dry region (ginseng is also being grown in the Merritt and Kamloops areaa). Seeds take at least 18 months to germinate. Exported to Asian markets as an aid to male sexual potency and staying power. Write Chai-Na-Ta Ginseng Products, 5965 205A St, Langley, BC, V3A 8C4.

**Lytton Ferry:** 61.5km southeast of Lillooet on Hwy 12. To Stein Trail and Lytton. Five-minute crossing. Reaction ferry carries 9t. Two vehicles or 20 passengers.

**Stein Heritage Trail:** Take Lytton Ferry off Hwy 12, turn north and drive about 6km to sign indicating start of Stein Heritage Trail. Turn west and take short drive to parking lot marked by a cairn. About 2km beyond turnoff to parking lot is picturesque mouth of Stein River, walking trails, and Indian pictographs.

**This is the last unlogged watershed in BC within reasonable driving distance of Vancouver.** The First Nation Peoples of Lytton and Mt Currie, with support from environmental groups and concerned people throughout the province, have been negotiating to save this wilderness watershed from logging. The two groups have made public their vision for a Stein Tribal Heritage Park, with a cultural interpretive centre and a system of lodge-to-lodge hiking along the Stein Heritage Trail. The government has yet to concur with the "tribal park" designation, and negotiations are still pending.

The trail is 75km long, and follows the pristine Stein Valley from an elevation of 460m, up the valley toward the Coast Mountains, where the headwaters lie at an elevation of 2,400m. There's good family hiking in the lower valley. Only the hale and hearty should attempt the nine-day trek into the rugged alpine regions. Three cable car crossings. Stunning scenery between Stein Mountain (2,774m) and Skihist Mountain (2,944m). This has long been regarded as a sacred place for the Lytton and Mt Currie native people. Pictographs here, which have aroused the curiosity of archaeologists from around the world, are thousands of years old. Virgin forests of pine, spruce, cottonwood, cedar. Wildflowers, lakes and streams.

**Lytton:** (Pop. 335). 2.5km south of Lytton Ferry, 64km south of Lillooet. For details, see *High Country*, p.165.

# Williams Lake to Prince George

## CARIBOO HIGHWAY (Highway 97)

From Williams Lake, the Cariboo Hwy (Hwy 97) continues north 238km to Prince George. On the northern fringes of the Cariboo, beyond Quesnel, the landscape changes, as evergreen forest closes in on road and river, and the lakes country is left behind. For the thousands of visitors interested: the turnoff to **Barkerville** is 5km north of downtown Quesnel, on Hwy 26.

**Williams Lake:** (Pop. 10,385). At Hwys 97 and 20. For details, see *Cache Creek to Williams Lake*, p.193. From here, it is 119km to Quesnel; and a further 119km from Quesnel to Prince George.

**Soda Creek Rd:** From main intersection of Hwys 97 and 20 in downtown Williams Lake, head west past the Stampede Grounds, then turn right at second set of traffic lights on Mackenzie Ave. This becomes Soda Creek Rd which runs, part-paved, part-gravel, north out of town along the east bank of the Fraser, parallel to Hwy 97.

## SIDE TRIP

### to Soda Creek

**Rudy Johnson's Bridge:** 20km north of Williams Lake. Built by an independent and annoyed west-side rancher who resented having to travel west on the Bella Coola Rd, then north up the Fraser west-side road in a time-consuming detour every time he wanted to go to town. The government refused to build a bridge, so in 1968 Johnson had one shipped down in pieces from Alaska. He erected it across the Fraser where government engineers had said a bridge was impossible, and ran it for 15 years as a private toll bridge, heavily used by logging trucks and ranch traffic. The government then took it over. It now operates as a free crossing.

Cross here to **Meldrum Creek Rd** on the west side, and continue north through ranchland and forest, to the Marguerite ferry. Or continue on the Soda Creek Rd.

**Soda Creek:** (Est. pop. 32). 33km north of Williams Lake. Creek bed, carbonate of lime, causes the water to bubble. This is the head of the upper Fraser River Canyon, and the beginning of 650km of navigable waters which is why the town became the gold-rush road terminus for sternwheelers. They were transported in pieces by road, and reassembled here to carry miners north to Quesnel. When the railway came through in 1920, the steamboats disappeared.

### Return to Highway 97

**McLeese Lake:** (Est pop. 300). A small community 43.5km north of Williams Lake. Resorts on lake, tourist facilities.

**McLeese Lake Rest Area:** 44.5km north of Williams Lake, at the north end of McLeese Lake. Haunted by restless loons.

**Likely Rd:** At north end of McLeese Lake, turn east on gravel road leading to Big Lake Ranch, Horsefly, and, just possibly, Likely. See *Cache Creek to Williams Lake*, p.193.

**Marguerite Rest Area:** 61.5km north of Wiliams Lake, east side of highway.

**Marguerite Ferry:** 62.5km north of Williams Lake. Usually April-Sept. Stops when the river freezes. Small, passenger-only aerial tram runs when ferry doesn't. One of the last reaction ferries crossing the Fraser. Runs on an overhead cable; power is supplied by the river current. Holds one RV, one car. Free. On call 7am-6:45pm (except 11:45am-1pm, 4:45pm-6pm.)

**Fort Alexandria Monument:** 66.5km north of Williams Lake. Was last post established (1821) by the North West Company west of the Rockies, and Alexander Mackenzie's farthest point south in his Fraser River descent, 1793.

**Australian Rest Area:** 83km north of Williams Lake, west side of highway. This farming area began as the "Australian Ranch" in 1863, when two wandering Aussies, Andrew Olsen and Stephen Downes, giving up on the gold fields, started a ranch on these rich alluvial benchlands.

**Kersley:** (Pop. 283). 98km north of Williams Lake. Named for early rancher, Charles Kersley, who supplied foodstuffs to the gold fields.

**Quesnel-Hydraulic Rd:** 114km north of Williams Lake. Paved in a loop around Dragon Lake and back to Hwy 97 just south of Quesnel. Dragon is a beautiful fishing lake. Fish here have been used to produce eggs for hatchery stock.

**Quesnel:** (Pop. 8,179). 119km north of Williams Lake, at confluence of Fraser and Quesnel rivers. Named after Jules Maurice Quesnelle, a member of Simon Fraser's exploration party. Downtown Quesnel is bridge-dependent: it lies on a rounded piece of land held between the Fraser and a great curve of the Quesnel River. This is exactly the point where gold rushers left the Fraser and headed east along muddy trails for Barkerville and Williams Creek.

Today Quesnel is a major lumber, pulp, commercial, and service centre for the north Cariboo. Also, Quesnel is the turnoff to one of the province's main attractions, the former ghost town (it's now pretty lively) of **Barkerville.**

**Quesnel Information:** Infocentre. At south entrance to town opposite BC Rail station, at museum. Open year-round with extended hours May-Sept. 992-8716.

■ **Gold Panning:** You can't pan or set up your sluice box in staked territory, but you can pick up a map at the Gold Commissioner's Office, Suite 102, 350 Barlow St, Quesnel,

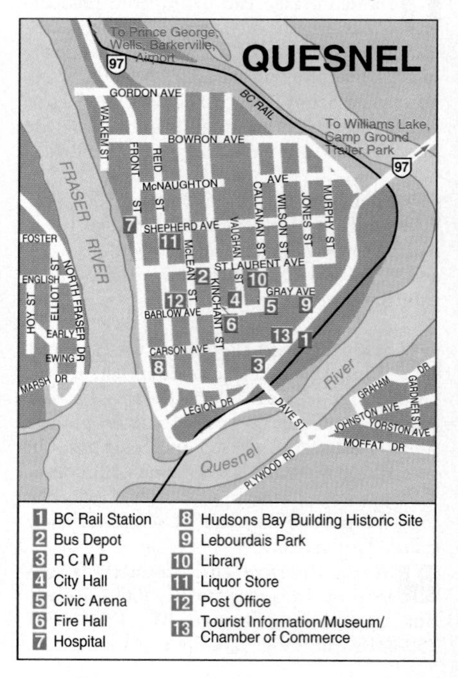

BC, V2J 2C1, or call 992-4301, to find some tiny corner that isn't staked. Or try your hand at panning in the Quesnel River where it joins the Fraser in Quesnel city limits; it's set aside for public hand panning. Check Gold Commissioner's office for details.

■ **Quesnel and District Museum:** South end of town at **LeBourdais Park** (Hwy 97 and Carson Ave). 992-9580. Open year-round with extended hours May-Sept. Historic Cariboo: artifacts of pioneers, native peoples, and Chinese. Note that LeBourdais Park has an outstanding flower garden, next to Pioneer Cemetery.

■ **Heritage Corner:** At Carson and Front streets, where Hwy 97 turns north for Prince George. Old Fraser bridge, built in 1929, is now a footbridge. New bridge was built in 1970. Remains of the steamer *Enterprise* from gold-rush days. Cornish waterwheel used in sluicing. Cairn commemorating the Overland Telegraph Line, which reached Quesnel in 1865, as part of a grandiose scheme to link North America and Europe via Asia. **Hudson's Bay Store**, a log building dating from 1882, is now a restaurant.

■ **Riverfront Trail Park:** Paved trail starts at Fraser River footbridge (Carson and Fronts streets), goes through the park, then along Quesnel River and past BC Railyards. **Riverboat trips** accessed from Riverfront Park.

■ **Alexander Mackenzie Trail Association:** 242 Reid St, Quesnel BC, V2J 2M2. 762-4241. For more information on this historic trail, see *Circle Trip* following.

■ **Quesnel Golf Course:** On 6 Mile Rd, 5.5km west of Quesnel across Fraser Bridge. 249-5550. 18 holes.

■ **Dragon Lake Golf Course:** 9-hole executive golf course. 747-1358.

There are several side trips from Quesnel leading west or south from West Quesnel over the Moffat Bridge. Cross bridge from Hwy 97 (Front St).

## CIRCLE TRIP

### to Bouchie Lake, Puntchesakut Lake, Nazko, Blackwater River, and the Mackenzie Trail

**Nazko Rd:** Across Moffat Bridge, then north on Elliott St to Bouchie Lake and Nazko. Road forks at **Bouchie Lake**, 11km northwest of Quesnel. **North fork**, the Blackwater Rd, takes the circle counterclockwise; **South fork**, the Nazko Rd, runs clockwise. Either way, the circle trip from Bouchie Lake to Bouchie Lake is 217km. The direction chosen here is the **South Fork**.

**Puntchesakut Lake Provincial Park:** 27km west of Bouchie Lake on Nazko Rd. 38ha. May-Oct. Picnicking, fishing, swimming.

**Nazko:** Small community 58km west of Puntchesakut Lake, 85km west of Bouchie Lake, on the Nazko river.

**Nazko River:** From Nazko, road follows the Nazko River north 47km to a junction with the Blackwater River (also called the West Road River) and Blackwater Rd. At this junction, a lesser road travels due west to the Alexander Mackenzie Trail past Moses and Pelican lakes.

**Alexander Mackenzie Heritage Trail:** Access for day trips at several places along Nazko Rd, along the old Blackwater Rd connecting with Nazko Rd, or near Bella Coola (see p.203). Horseback riding, fishing, hunting, wildlife, camping, snowshoeing, cross-country skiing.

Information available from Visitor Services Coordinator, BC Parks, 640 Borland St, Williams Lake, BC, V2G 1R8. Or contact Alexander Mackenzie Trail Association in Quesnel (see above).

The Alexander Mackenzie Trail is a 420km corridor from the mouth of the Blackwater River to Sir Alexander Mackenzie Provincial Park in the Dean Channel northwest of Bella Coola. Mackenzie made his historic trek from the Fraser to Pacific tidewater in 1793. Today's trail follows Mackenzie's route as closely as possible, via local wagon roads, highways, forestry access roads, rivers, and coastal waterways. About 300km is recreational trail; remainder is aboriginal footpath. The entire trail is for serious hikers only, and takes 18-24 days to traverse. Some is across Indian reserve or private property; please respect owners' rights.

**Blackwater and Nazko Roads:** 47km north of Nazko. Blackwater Rd travels east 19km to Boot Lake, then a final 66km east back to Bouchie Lake, passing Pantage Lake on the way back into Quesnel.

## SIDE TRIP

### to Pinnacles Provincial Park

**Baker Dr:** Depart Quesnel travelling west across Moffat Bridge, then north on Baker Dr to Pinnacles Park.

**Pinnacles Provincial Park:** 124ha. 8km west of Quesnel on Baker Dr. May-Oct. Unusual geological formations (pinnacles or hoodoos) formed by glacial erosion and weathering.

## SIDE TRIP

### on West Fraser Rd

**West Fraser Rd:** Depart Quesnel travelling west across Moffat Bridge, then south on Anderson Dr. Paved, then gravel road down west side of river to Marguerite and Meldrum Creek, and eventually connecting with Hwy 20 southwest of Williams Lake. For details on **Marguerite Ferry** and **Meldrum Creek Rd**, see previous page.

*Return to Highway 97*

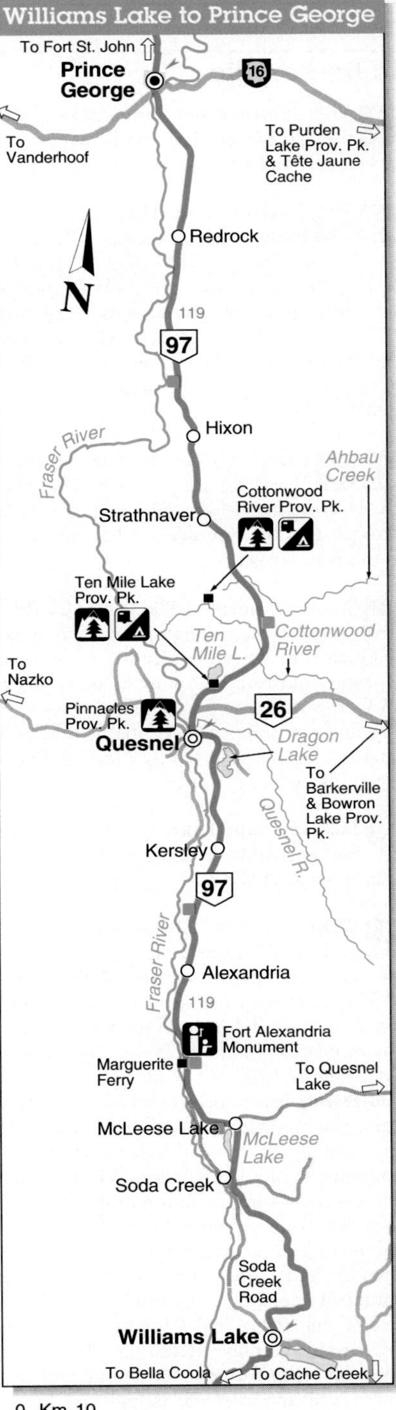


**Quesnel Forest Industry Observation Tower:** 3km north of Quesnel on Hwy 97. Year-round. Free. Observation Tower gives a bird's eye view of "Two Mile Flat" industrial area: four lumber mills, two pulp mills, related activities. Tours of mills and harvesting areas can be arranged.

**Barkerville Hwy (Hwy 26):** 5km north of downtown Quesnel, east to Cottonwood House, Wells, the Bowron Lakes, and Barkerville.

## SIDE TRIP

### to Barkerville

**Area Information:** Infocentre, run by the **Friends of Barkerville**, at junction of Hwys 97 and 26. Mid-June to early Sept.

**Cottonwood House Historic Park:** 11ha. 28km east of Hwy 97 on Hwy 26. On the old Cariboo Wagon Rd. 994-3209. Buildings open daily May-Sept. Grounds open year-round. Operated from 1874 to the 1950s by John and Janet Boyd and their children. Main house (from 1864), barns, sheds, animals, stagecoach ride. Excellent picnic site.

**Blessing's Grave Historic Park:** 1ha; 39km east of Hwy 97 on Hwy 26. Historic site. Marks the grave of Charles Morgan Blessing, murdered by a companion for his gold nugget.

**Stanley Cemetery:** Beside Stanley Rd, a short loop to the right, about 65km east of Quesnel on Hwy 26. Historic grave markers from gold-rush era, plus the open pits of 36 former Chinese graves. The bones were dug up and shipped to China to find their final resting place in family plots. Relics of ghost town of Stanley nearby.

**Jack of Clubs Lake:** Good fishing and family boating on south side of Hwy 26 near outskirts of Wells.

**Wells:** (Pop. 240). 80km east of Hwy 97 on Hwy 26. Dates from a gold rush, but not the Cariboo rush of the 1860s. In the 1930s, as depression set in and rumours abounded that the price of gold would soon rise, hundreds trekked to Wells. The Cariboo Gold-Quartz Mining Co set up shop at the gold-bearing quartz vein found by Fred Wells. Then the company planned the town, and very carefully, so it would have staying power. According to Gordon R Elliot, "The town was wheel shaped, with the hub on top of a knoll. Churches, banks, theatres, hospital, newspaper and recreation centres were located on the "spokes" and "rim." The mining company continued operating until 1967, so Wells did become (and remained) a bright spot in dark days. Architecturally interesting, the wooden sidewalks, false-fronted stores, and romantic names recall an earlier era. Skiing.

**Wells/Barkerville Information:** Infocentre, Wells and District Chamber of Commerce, Box 123, Wells, BC, V0K 1R0. 994-3237. Beside Hwy 26. Daily mid-June to early Sept. Ask about historical tours.

- **Wells Museum:** On Pooley St (Wells' main street). Box 244, Wells, BC, V0K 2R0. 994-3422. June-Sept. Daily 10am-8pm. Wells from 1931-1967.
- **Sunset Theatre:** June-Sept, Mon and Fri nights. Built in 1934, and still showing the same old flicks (some new ones, too).
- **Island Mountain Gallery:** Pooley St. Features local and other BC artists.
- **Island Mountain Arts Summer School:** End of July. 994-3466.

**Bowron Lakes Rd:** North from Hwy 26, 6km east of Wells. Leads to Bowron Lakes.

**Bowron Lake Provincial Park:** 121,600ha; 25 vehicle\tent campsites, 48 wilderness campsites. 29km from Wells; 23km north from Hwy 26 turnoff. 398-4414. One of the best canoe circuits in the province, 116km long, with portages between the six major lakes and other waterways in the chain. Trails, patrol cabins, and cooking shelters. Wildlife sanctuary. Seven-10 days, also day trips. Moose, deer, caribou, mountain goats, grizzly bear, beavers. Reservations mandatory for groups over six, and advised for groups six and under: 992-3111. Accommodation, equipment and canoe rentals at Bowron Lake. Information available from BC Parks at 540 Borland St, Williams Lake, BC, V2G 1R8.

**Bowron Lake Registration Centre:** At Bowron Lakes Park Headquarters. May 15-Sept 30.

**Barkerville Gold-Rush Town:** 2km southeast of turnoff to Bowron Lake Park, 8km from Wells, and 88km from Hwy 97. Box 19, Barkerville, BC, V0K 1B0. 994-3332. Daily year-round, historic programs mid-June to Labour Day.

One of BC's premiere attractions. Restored gold-rush town from the 1860s. In its prime, Barkerville seemed on its way to becoming the largest city west of Chicago and north of San Francisco. But the gold rush fizzled and Barkerville died. For about 75 years it was a ghost town.

Restoration of this significant site began in 1958. Today, businesses operate as they might have 120 years ago: bakery, restaurant, merchants, photographer, print shop. Gold panning. Over 40 restored pre-1900 structures; well-preserved cemetery. Events include performances at the **Theatre Royal** in historic costume, and 1860s style Dominion Day celebrations. Off-season: slide shows at administration building. Winter recreation: cross-country ski trail from Barkerville's main street to Richfield, the gold-rush ghost town where courthouse is located.

**Barkerville Provincial Park:** 55ha. Adjacent Gold-Rush Town. 168 campsites at three campgrounds, sani-station. 944-3332.

### Return to Highway 97

**Ten Mile Lake Provincial Park:** 241ha; 142 campsites. 11km north of Quesnel. 398-4414. Developed beach, boat ramp, hiking trails, cross-country ski trails, snowshoeing, ice fishing.

**Hush Lake Rest Area:** 25km north of Quesnel. Boat launch.

**Cottonwood River Provincial Park:** 66ha; 15 campsites. 29km north of Quesnel on old **Prince George Rd**. (Left off Hwy 97 just past drive-in theatre on northern outskirts of Quesnel.) Fishing, picnicking, in quiet setting.

**Strathnaver:** (Pop. 21). 43km north of Quesnel, at Naver Creek. **Old Prince George Rd** returns to Hwy 97 here.

**Hixon:** (Pop. 191). 56.5km north of Quesnel. Tourist facilities.

**Viewpoint:** 62km north of Quesnel. About halfway up (down) the hill. Excellent view westward into infinity, over the tops of millions of spruce trees.

**Woodpecker Rest Area:** 64.5km beyond Quesnel. Named for Woodpecker Landing, a sternwheeler dock once located near here.

**Stoner:** 76km beyond Quesnel. Small community.

**Red Rock:** About 88km beyond Quesnel. Another small community.

**Prince George:** (Pop. 69,653). 119km beyond Quesnel. For details, see *North by Northwest*, p.209.

## Williams Lake to Bella Coola

### BELLA COOLA ROAD (Highway 20)

Highway 20 traverses the Chilcotin Plateau and the Coast Mountains from the Cariboo Hwy to the head of a Pacific Ocean fjord. This Bella Coola Rd – the "Freedom Road" – begins at Williams Lake, at Hwy 97, and runs west 456km to Bella Coola.

It is only relatively recently – 1953 – that the two ends of the road finally met. For years there was a 60km gap in the road, that wild section through the towering Coast Mountains. In 1950, tired of waiting for an unenthusiastic government that felt that the feat couldn't be done, or at least not without an outpouring of millions, settlers on both sides of the gap took matters into their own capable hands. In three backbreaking years, they completed the road themselves. They called it the Freedom Road because, at last, Bella Coolans could drive from their homes to the outside world, and the outside world could visit them.

Today Hwy 20 is still a challenge. More than half is paved now: all the way from Williams Lake to west of Chilanko Forks; and two other portions, between Nimpo Lake and Anahim Lake; and east from Bella Coola into Tweedsmuir Provincial Park near Park Headquarters. The rest is gravel. And then there's the Big Hill. Well, this is not a road for speed demons.

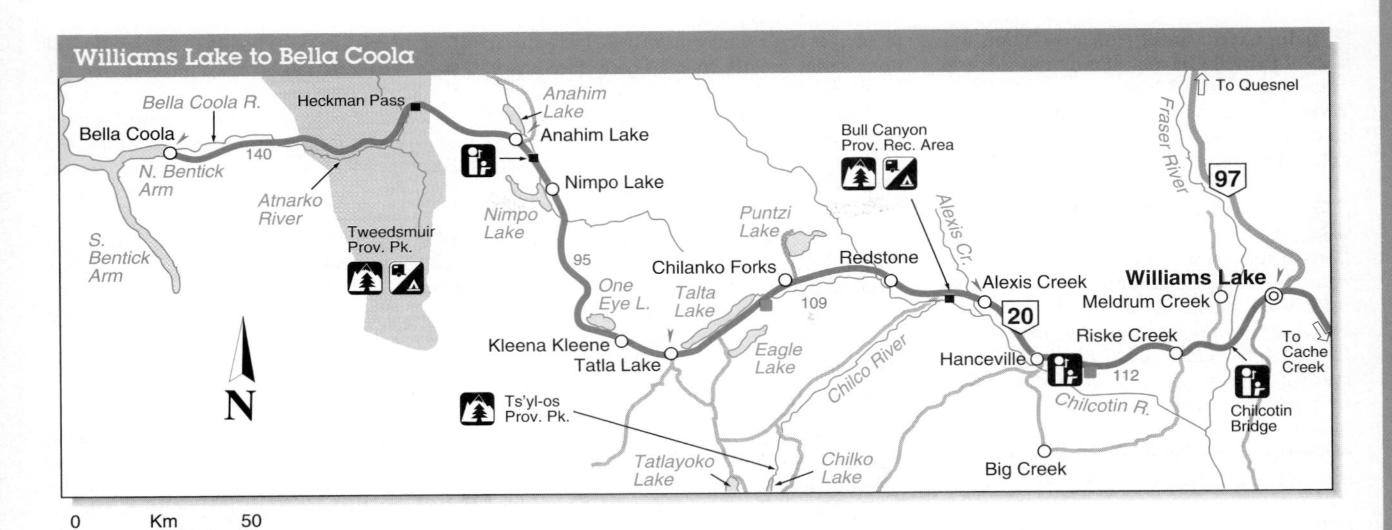


**The trek divides into four main portions:**

| | |
|---|---|
| **Williams Lake to Alexis Creek:** | **112km** |
| **Alexis Creek to Tatla Lake:** | **109km** |
| **Tatla Lake to Anahim:** | **95km** |
| **Anahim to Bella Coola:** | **140km** |

The eastern starting point of Hwy 20 is Williams Lake: turn west at the traffic lights just south of town.

Note that you won't see another set of traffic lights from here to Bella Coola. The Chilcotin is the last western frontier for the pioneer rancher: limitations on freedom of movement are scarce. There are rolling vistas of plateau backed by long, fish-filled lakes. In the rugged Coast Mountains, where horses outnumber cars, it seems rules are things to be ignored. One of the earliest European imports was, in fact, the horse, and herds of wild horses, obeying no man's rules, still roam the Chilcotins.

The Chilcotin peoples lived between the Fraser River and the Coast Mountains, trading with neighbouring Shuswap, Carrier, and Bella Coola peoples. Coastal peoples particularly traded the oily eulachons, little fish so oil-heavy they could be used as lamps. The routes they made have become known as the **"Grease Trails."** Chilcotin peoples in turn traded prized volcanic glass, or obsidian, used in making sharp weapons and tools.

When outsiders arrived, trading patterns changed. A Hudson's Bay Company trading post was established as early as 1828 at the confluence of the Chilko and Chilcotin rivers, near Alexis Creek. Native peoples then concentrated more on furs, in order to trade for guns, blankets, iron tools, rice, and flour.

The first cattle ranchers came in the 1860s, and small communities began. Names of many towns on Hwy 20 derive from these early traders and shopkeepers: Tom Hance (Hanceville Post Office); L W Riskie, who shipped bacon and butter to Barkerville (Riske Creek); Norman Lee (Lees Corner).

**Williams Lake:** (Pop. 10,385). At junction of Hwys 97 and 20. For details, see *Cache Creek to Williams Lake*, p.193.

**Big Bar Rd:** Turn south off Hwy 20 2km beyond Williams Lake for Dog Creek and Gang Ranch (70km). For details, see *Cache Creek to Williams Lake*, p.191.

**Upper Fraser River Canyon:** For the first 24km the road climbs sharply, then drops just as sharply into the upper Fraser River canyon. Use this section as a test area for brakes and engine.

**Viewpoint:** 24.5km from Williams Lake, north of highway. Views of upper Fraser canyon.

**Chilcotin Bridge:** Just beyond the viewpoint, 25km from Williams Lake, highway crosses the Fraser River, 500km from its mouth in the Fraser Delta.

**Chilcotin Country:** From the bridge, another long climb to the Chilcotin (or Fraser) Plateau. Boulder-strewn plains, distant snowy mountains, ranches, one-blink towns (blink and you miss it), crumbling log cabins, and the best general stores you'll ever find. Up on the plateau, watch for a flash of brilliant blue. That will be a bluebird. Nesting boxes are nailed in pairs to fence posts along the road. The birds are not only pretty, they also eat crop-threatening grasshoppers.

**Meldrum Creek Rd (or West Side Rd):** 33.5km beyond Williams Lake. Gravel road leads north to Quesnel, travelling on the west side of Fraser River. Details in *Williams Lake to Prince George*, p.196.

**Loran C Tower:** 35km west of Williams Lake, north of highway. With others in Alaska and Washington, this huge tower is part of a long-range marine navigation system that can locate precise positions within a 4,000km range. Tours can usually be arranged. 659-5611.

**Chilcotin Back Roads:** Back roads and trails criss-cross the central Chilcotins, and are the only access to many of area's most interesting places. However, roads are gravel or dirt, some challenging. And rain can turn roads to quagmires. Check road conditions locally before setting out.

**Farwell Canyon Rd:** 44.5km beyond Williams Lake, south of highway on a 95km loop via Farwell Canyon, Big Creek, and Hanceville. Back to Hwy 20 at Hanceville/Lees Corner (46km west of Farwell Canyon Rd junction).

## SIDE TRIP
### to Farwell Canyon

**Bighorn Sheep Reserve:** 15km south of Hwy 20. 5,300ha triangular plot at confluence of Chilcotin and Fraser rivers. This **Junction Wildlife Management Area (JWMA)** protects the habitat of some 500 California bighorn sheep. In early 1900s, there were only 2,000 bighorns left in North America; today, thanks to a long-term (begun in 1954) transplant program from the healthy JWMA herds, there are more than 9,000 of these spectacular animals alive and well in most of the historic ranges of the continent.

There are more than 40 species of butterflies in the JWMA area. Plus Lewis woodpeckers and other cavity-nesting birds attracted by the giant snags. Black bears feast on rose hips and berries. Rubber boas come out after dark and enjoy lying on the warm road. They're gentle creatures. Drive carefully.

**Farwell Canyon:** 19km from Hwy 20 junction, road crosses the Chilcotin River at Farwell Canyon. A spectacular bridge over a spectacular canyon. Chilcotin River cuts deeply through golden clay and limestone cliffs, forming groves of hoodoos on the rock walls. Active sand dune at top of cliffs changes form with wind currents. Early rock paintings can be seen on the overhang, south of bridge. Under the bridge are fish ladders. Summer and fall, native fishermen dip-net from riverbanks, then rack the salmon in the sun to dry.

River rafting, hiking trails. These are so-called **badlands**: note sagebrush, rabbit brush, and prickly pear cactus. Sit carefully.

**Big Creek:** Small settlement 41km west of Farwell Canyon. During this side trip, Farwell Canyon Rd loops over the Chilcotin River twice, and Big Creek once. There are trout in the creeks, steelhead in the river. In fall, sockeye return, heading for Chilko Lake.

**Hanceville:** (Pop. 68). 35km from Big Creek, just beyond second Chilcotin River bridge, near return to Hwy 20. Signs name the small community Hanceville, but it's always been called Lees Corners (see below). Hanceville was the post office at Tom Hance's (the "TH") ranch. Hance also had a trading post on the site as early as 1869. Certainly an historic settlement, once largest in area.

## Return to Highway 20

**Riske Creek:** (Pop. 181). 46.5km west of Williams Lake, 2km west of Farwell Canyon Rd junction. Farming here in open range country may well be risky, but name is for LW Riskie, 1870s Polish farmer in area. Drop in at the Riske Creek General Store.

**Riske Creek Rodeo Grounds:** 58km west of Williams Lake, north side of highway.

**Point of Interest and Rest Area:** 82km west of Williams Lake, south side of highway. Panoramic views over Chilcotin country, with first glimpses of Coast Mountains to the west. Plaque describes Norman Lee's ill-fated cattle drive to Dawson City in 1889. At least he survived, to set up shop at what is still known as Lees Corner.

**Lees Corner (Hanceville):** 90.5km west of Williams Lake, 44km west of Riske Creek. Site of historic Norman Lee Ranch (est 1893) and long-lived general store. Norman Lee himself ran the store until 1939. Current building is the fourth Lees Corner general store since opening day over a century ago. Help yourself to an ever-ready Chilcotin coffee. The general store is truly general: contains post office, snack bar, laundromat, liquor store, motel rooms, fishing licenses, cases of canned peas, meat, muffins, and books on how to build a log cabin.

**Chilcotin Lakes:** Side roads from Lees Corner lead to many fishermen's favourites. Smaller lakes are often at ends of rough side roads, impassable except by four-wheel drive. Maps of roads and campsites from local tourist offices, Ministry of Forests and Lands offices at 100 Mile House, Clinton, Quesnel, or Alexis Creek, or Recreational Section, Ministry of Forests and Lands, 540 Borland St, Williams Lake, BC, V2G 1R8.

**Ts'yl-os Provincial Park:** 233,240ha. Via Taseko Lake Rd, Tatla Lake, and Tatlayoko/Chilko Lake Rd, see below. 398-4414. New park, BC's sixth largest, encompasses spectacular 90km Chilko and Taseko lakes in Chilko Mountains. Managed by BC government and Nemiah Valley Band to protect wildlife, BC's third largest sockeye salmon run, and traditional First Nations cultural and economic activities.

**Chilcotin White Water:** Rafters, kayakers, and canoeists consider these rivers among the continent's best. Highest rated for rafters: the Chilko's Lava Canyon; for canoeists and kayakers, stretches of the Chilcotin and Taseko rivers. All are high-grade, white-water rivers. Check with local outfitters for info, rentals, and tours.

**Taseko Lake Rd:** South at Lees Corner, then southwest toward **Taseko Lake** and **Nemaiah Valley** after crossing Chilcotin River. Southeast fork is Farwell Canyon Rd described above. Road from Lees Corner to **Konni Lake**, 100km, is all-weather gravel. Beyond this, road continues to **Chilko Lake**, but suitable only for four-wheel drive.

**Chilko River**, flowing toward the Fraser, is a major river rafting destination. Many resorts, guest ranches, guiding operations.

*Chilcotin River through Farwell Canyon, west of Williams Lake.*

**Alexis Creek:** (Pop. 243). 112km west of Williams Lake, 21.5km west of Lees Corner. Service centre for eastern Chilcotin. Accommodation, Red Cross outpost hospital, RCMP station, gas, groceries, post office. BC Forest Service Office is a good source of info, Mon-Fri.

**White Pelican Provincial Park:** On Stum Lake, 34km northeast of Alexis Creek. No road access. Breeding sanctuary for once- threatened white pelicans. The good news is that the white pelican has been officially delisted by the Committee on the Status of Endangered Wildlife in Canada.

**Bull Canyon Provincial Park:** 123ha. 20 campsites. 398-4414. 9km west of Alexis Creek. Scenic spot by Chilcotin River, sheer rocks, caves. Site of an historic battleground, more recently a cattle round-up point.

**Redstone:** (Pop. 170). 54.5km west of Alexis Creek. Indian settlement and cemetery. Winter cold spot: to -50 C.

**Puntzi Lake Rd:** 60.5km west of Alexis Creek. Road leads north 7km to Puntzi Lake. Stocked with trout and kokanee. White pelicans now feed and rest on the lake (See *White Pelican Provincial Park*, above.) Many lakeside resorts, campgrounds. Hiking, riding. Fishing derby last weekend in June.

**Chilanko Forks:** (Pop. 123). On Hwy 20, about 1km west of Puntzi Lake Rd junction, 61.5km west of Alexis Creek. Service station, well-stocked traditional general store with accommodation, post office, crafts.

**And this will really be of interest – END OF PAVEMENT:** 8.5km west of Chilanko Forks, 70km west of Alexis Creek, the blacktop ends. Added in to the 112km from Williams Lake to Alexis Creek, that's 182km of beautiful blacktop so far. And the blacktop is being pushed a bit farther west all the time. The **gravel sections**, formerly such an ordeal, are much improved. The surface has been sealed with a sulphite pulp mill residue that cuts down dust. Grading and high-quality gravel have helped with the problem of oversized stones and potholes. Result: a well-maintained all-weather gravel surface.

**Polywog Rest Area:** 35.5km beyond Chilanko Forks, 97km west of Alexis Creek. Duck nesting ground.

**Tatla Lake:** (Pop. 52). 109km beyond Alexis Creek, 221km from Williams Lake. Considered a rough halfway mark on Hwy 20. Stop in at the Graham, have a coffee and some homemade pie, and discuss the matter. This is the western edge of the Chilcotin plateau, and a taking-off point for wilderness fly-ins, fishing/diving charters, and cross-country ski trails. Old buildings, homey food, accommodation.

**Tatla Lake Information:** At post office, in Tatla Lake Motel. 476-1113.

**Tatlayoko/Chilko Lake Rd:** South at Tatla Lake for Tatlayoko Lake. Bear southwest at fork for Horn and Bluff lakes; keep left at fork, 35km to Tatlayoko. Small community in dry-belt ranching country; basic services. Private campground. Turn right at Tatlayoko community hall for lake beyond town, in Coast Mountains. The Homathko River runs into Tatlayoko Lake, then drains it directly into the salt water of Bute Inlet, only 80km away. The valley sits in the Coast Mountains, with distant views of Mt Waddington, at 4,016m the highest peak totally within BC. For **Chilko Lake**, go east at Tatlayoko community hall, past **Choesiquoit Lake**, then south 25km along road, to Chilko River bridge. Just before the bridge, turn south, keeping to west side of Chilko River; Chilko Lake is 20km farther on. For **Tsuniah Lake**, cross the Chilko River bridge and follow signs to lake (20km).

Many ranches, resorts, and lodges. Local trail ride operators take visitors through the mountains to fishing lakes, ancient native sites, caves, fossils, and wildlife viewing (mountain goats, grizzlies, cougar). Also cross-country and alpine skiing in winter.

**Ranger Station:** On Hwy 20, at outskirts of Tatla Lake, marks beginning of climb into Coast Mountains. Open ranching country is replaced by pine forest and scattered lakes. Sadly, the lodgepole pines here have fallen prey to the pine beetle. Always endemic, the beetle is now epidemic. Forest is pockmarked with red and black dying and dead trees. Locals hope for a very hot summer or a killingly cold winter to wipe out the insects. Or wait for young trees, not susceptible to the beetle, to mature.

**Kleena Kleene:** (Pop. 92). 31km west of Tatla Lake. "One-honk" settlement, post office, and general store. Near here, the **Klinaklini River** flows into **One Eye Lake**. Wilderness and fly-in fishing resorts take visitors to truly remote spots. Name is native people's word for eulachon grease.

**Charlotte Lake Rd:** 65.5km beyond Tatla Lake, leads southwest some 15km to Charlotte Lake. Large rainbows. Resort accommodation.

**Nimpo Lake South Rd:** 71km west of Tatla Lake. Leads to Nimpo Lake's south end.

**Nimpo Lake:** (Pop. 164). 76.5km west of Tatla Lake. Scenic 12km lake, with Mt Kappan in background, is the floatplane capital of BC and centre for air charters to remote fly-in fishing spots. General store, motels, campgrounds. Six resorts on the lake, complete facilities. Rainbows!

■ **Note: Highway is paved between Nimpo Lake and Anahim Lake!**

**Chilcotin War:** 81.5m west of Tatla Lake. Historic site. In 1860s, Victoria merchant Alfred Waddington, a well-meaning dreamer, tried to build a road from Bute Inlet to Quesnel. Fearing for their lands, terrified by the threat of smallpox, some Chilcotin peoples killed 19 white people, many of them road workers, in a series of ambushes. The colonial governor dispatched troops. Chief Alexis assisted in the pursuit. Five men, including two chiefs called Klatsassin and Telloot, were found guilty and hung in 1864. Peace was restored, but the road was never finished. It had been unrealistic, from the start.

Waddington himself died in 1872 of smallpox, the white man's disease that had killed so many natives.

*Near Farwell Canyon, south of Riske Creek.*

**Anahim Lake:** (Pop. 260). 95km west of Tatla Lake, 316km west of Williams Lake. Largest settlement in the west Chilcotin. Expanded in 1940, when Ulkatcho native peoples abandoned remote villages and moved to town. The Anahim Lake Stampede happens here each July, a major social event and showcase for talent. Free coffee in the general store. Full tourist services; centre for outfitting, guides.

**Anahim Lake Airport:** Paved airport across highway from general store. Daily flights to Bella Coola and Vancouver. Fly-in charters to popular Dean River fishery.

**Lessard Lake Rd:** North at Anahim Lake, goes 18km to Lessard Lake and points north. Check road conditions first. Good gravel for 32km, along Dean River (famed for its downstream steelhead fishery); fair gravel for another 32km. Four-wheel drive or hiking beyond. Far Mountain and Tsitsutl peaks, extinct volcanoes, Rainbow Range, Alexander Mackenzie Heritage Trail. Hike or fly in to historic native villages at Iluak and Ulkatcho, and historic Home Ranch. **Iluak and Ulkatcho**, southern Carrier villages, are now abandoned; just cemeteries and old buildings.

**Home Ranch**: Early this century, Americans Pan Phillips and Richard Hobson rode in seeking ranchland, and established the Home Ranch on natural hay meadows. Cattle drives followed old Indian grease trails to Quesnel or Vanderhoof. Hobson's books, *Grass Beyond the Mountains* and *The Rancher Takes a Wife* made this area familiar to thousands. Lodge and original sod-roof log house and barns remain, deserted. Phillips' son operates a fishing/hunting camp nearby.

**Pavement Ends, Sorry:** 1km west of Anahim. Here begins no more than 61km (there may be less by the time you read this) of gravel as the highway leaves the Chilcotin Plateau and begins its climb through the Coast Mountains of Tweedsmuir Provincial Park. You'll do "The Hill" on gravel.

Until quite recently (the late '80s), trailers had to be left at Anahim; not nowadays, though. The road is wide enough, and there are many pullouts. If you're pulling a load, watch brakes for over-heating.

**Rainbow Range:** About 30km from Anahim Lake, multicoloured 2,500m peaks are visible from several pullouts on north side of Hwy 20. Heavily dissected shield volcanoes, like Hawaiian peaks but with different vegetation; bare rock bluffs and scree slopes brightly coloured by purple, red, and yellow mineralization. Accessible by hiking and horseback trails.

**Coast Mountains**: From 30km west of Anahim Lake all the way to Bella Coola. The highway climbs steadily, then drops to the Pacific fjord. Steep-sided valleys, rugged peaks with icefields and glaciers.

**Tweedsmuir Park Boundary Sign:** 36km west of Anahim Lake, 352km west of Williams Lake. Highway now enters the largest provincial park in BC, and stays in the park for 54km.

**Tweedsmuir Provincial Park and Recreation Area:** 994,246ha. 35 campsites, sani-station. 398-4414. Write BC Parks, 640 Borland St, Williams Lake, BC, V2G 1R8. **Park Headquarters** 28km west of park's east entrance. Park highway open year-round; campgrounds, picnic areas closed after first snowfall. Established 1937, named for Baron Tweedsmuir of Elsfield, then Governor-General of Canada. Hwy 20 cuts through the narrowing southern wedge of the park. Tweedsmuir is a wilderness park: bring suitable clothing, equipment, supplies, and maps. Grizzly bears along the Dean and Atnarko rivers in summer and fall; check with park headquarters or lodge operators for suitable precautions.

**Bella Coola Rd Summit and Heckman Pass:** Just beyond park entrance, 36km west of Anahim, highway clears Heckman Pass, 1,524m.

**Rainbow Range Trailhead and Picnic Ground**: 6km west of east entrance, 42km west of Anahim, north side of highway. On East Branch Creek. Trails lead 20km to Rainbow Range. Winter snowmobile-designated area (not permitted elsewhere).

**Descent to Atnarko Valley, or, "The Big Hill":** Descent starts about 7km from east entrance, continues for 19km. Steepest part of the 1,400m descent is known as "The Hill." Road was finally completed in 1953, not by the government, but by local people themselves. Plaque marks the spot where two bulldozers met – one from the east, one from the west – to complete the last link. They had conquered a double rise and fall. Heading west, road climbs to 1,600m, then drops to 1,000m at Young Creek, climbs back up to 1,300m, then makes its final precarious descent to 300m and the beginning of the Bella Coola Valley.

Widening has made the original hair-pin bends and precipitous dropoffs less hair-raising, but it's exciting all the same, and when you get to Bella Coola – and you will – everyone will want to know what you thought of "The Hill."

**Hurray! Foot of The Hill, and Pavement Begins Again:** 26km west of east entrance.

**Young Creek Picnic Site:** 26km west of east entrance, south side of highway. At the bottom of the hill.

**Upper Atnarko Valley:** From Young Creek picnic site, four-wheel drive tote road and trails head south along spectacular Upper Atnarko Valley. Hike to Hunlen Falls 29km from picnic site, one of highest single-drop waterfalls in Canada (260m) with an overall cascade series of 366m. Falls are at start of Turner Lakes chain, unique subalpine canoe route above Atnarko Valley; wilderness resort and fishing. High alpine hiking on Ptarmigan Trail and Panorama Ridge above lakes. Lonesome Lake is 30km from picnic site; Monarch Icefield is 70km. In 1912, Ralph Edwards endured a harsh climate and isolation to create a homestead and farm in dense forest on the east side of Lonesome Lake. Members of his family still occupy the farm, where trumpeter swans winter. Contact John Edwards at Box 308, Bella Coola, BC, V0T 1C0. Edwards' story was made famous through the best-seller *Crusoe of Lonesome Lake*, by Leland Stowe.

*Seacoast town of Bella Coola, at the head of North Bentinck Arm.*

**Atnarko River Campground:** 1.5km west of Young Creek picnic site, 27.5km from east entrance. 24 sites (two doubles). No reservations or hook-ups. RV sani-station.

**Tweedsmuir Provincial Park Headquarters:** .5km west of campground, 28km from park's east entrance (26km from park's west entrance). In the coastal valley. Not staffed full-time. Contact 398-4414. RV sani-station.

**Big Rock:** Picnic site 11km west of park headquarters, 39km from east entrance.

**Atnarko River Spawning Channels:** About 1km past Big Rock. Federal Government enhancement of Atnarko salmon spawning gravel beds. Viewing pool on crystal-clear Atnarko River. Beware of bears. They like watching salmon, too.

**Stuie:** Little settlement on the Atnarko River, 14km west of park headquarters, 42km from east entrance. Or, as locals put it, 16km west of the Bottom of the Hill.
Atnarko is Carrier Indian word for "River of Strangers." The strangers were the coast natives, and here is the historic meeting place of coast and Interior tribes. Unexcavated smokehouse, burial grounds, pictographs.
■ **Tweedsmuir Lodge:** Historic lodge (on site of original Stuie Lodge) run for 50 years by the Corbould family. Draws guests from around the world interested in fishing and hiking. Reservations required. 982-2402.

**Fisheries Pool:** 16km west of park headquarters, 44km from east entrance. Spawning channels, salmon-viewing pool. Resort, campground (14 sites), boat launch, picnic site.

**Burnt Bridge:** 26km west of park headquarters, at **Tweedsmuir Park West Entrance**. Picnic site south side of highway. Cairn commemorates federal-provincial agreement on the "Mackenzie Grease Trail." Scenic loop hiking trail (one-to-two hours) leads north, offers a view of Stupendous Mountain. Loop is part of Alexander Mackenzie Heritage Trail, described on next page.

**Tweedsmuir Provincial Park West Entrance:** 26km west of park headquarters, 54km from east entrance, 90km west of Anahim. Or 51km east of Bella Coola.

**Alexander Mackenzie Heritage Trail:** Access from Burnt Bridge. For details on entire trail, see also *Williams Lake to Prince George*, p.197. Trail descends from the north along Mackenzie's route on his historic trip in 1793. He was the first non-native to reach the Pacific overland. From here, trail follows the Bella Coola Valley. Arduous. Dedicated hikers only.

**Stupendous Mountain:** At 2,677m one of several massive mountains visible south of highway. Best viewed from loop trail (above). Mackenzie wrote in his journal, "Before us appeared a stupendous mountain, whose snow-capped summit was lost in clouds."

**Summer Trail:** 10.5km beyond park's west entrance, 40km east of Bella Coola. North from Hwy 20, one of several grease trails used up until 19th century for transport of eulachon oil and cedar from coast to Interior.

**Hagensborg:** (Pop. 606). 32km beyond west entrance to park, 18.5km east of Bella Coola. Non-native settlement of Bella Coola Valley began here in 1894, when Norwegians, attracted by the homelike settings of the fjords, moved here from their first settlements in Minnesota. Original settlement centred around Hagen Christensen's store, hence the name. Today the square-timbered, hand-adzed log barns and houses, as well as place names and surnames, reflect Norwegian heritage. 1,000 descendants left.

**Bella Coola Airstrip:** At Hagensborg. Chilcotin and Vancouver flights.

**Acwsalcta (Nuxalk Nation School):** On the highway, just west of Hagensborg. This magnificent school, called Acwsalcta, "the place of learning," was built by the Nuxalk Nation. Natural cedar walls are painted with native designs created by six Nuxalk under direction of artist Alvin Mack. Note the powerful eagle on the outside of the building. For more information on this and other artistic and cultural points of interest, contact the Band Office, or visit the Museum or information centre (see below).

**Snootli Creek Hatchery:** 4km beyond Hagensborg, 14.5km from Bella Coola. Established 1978 to enhance runs of chum and chinook salmon in the Bella Coola River system.

**Thorsen Creek Petroglyphs:** 10km beyond Hagensborg, 8km east of Bella Coola. A large petroglyph site, with more than 100 Indian rock paintings. Ask at Bella Coola for a guide to the site.

**Bella Coola:** (Pop. 705). Hwy 20 ends 456km west of Williams Lake. Bella Coola sits at the head of North Bentinck Arm, an inlet of the Pacific. Visited in 1793 by Alexander Mackenzie who came overland, and by Captain George Vancouver who came by water. The Hudson's Bay Company established a post here in 1869, but Company clerk John Clayton's house by the river is all that remains. Most non-native settlement occurred after 1894. Town was isolated until the Freedom Road was completed in 1953.

Beyond town are the docks where fishboats ride the milky turquoise waters of the Bella Coola River as it spills into the sea. Bella Coola is the major port between Vancouver Island and Prince Rupert. Its waterfront offers an interesting collection of fishing boats, pleasure boats, cannery sites, tidal flats, log-sorting facilities. A restaurant serves fresh salmon and halibut. But passenger boats and ferries call here no longer. The only way out is by air, by charter water transport, or by connecting with the ferry at Bella Bella. A BC Ferry stops at Bella Bella once a week, but Bella Bella lacks a ramp for unloading vehicles from the ferry. So if you have come by car, your only choice is to return by car, along the 456km of the Freedom Road.

Tourist facilities, commercial and sports fishing, government wharf. Native craft store. As well, Bella Coola gives access to a wide world of maritime excitement. See *Side Trips to Coastal Points*, below.

**Bella Coola Information:** Infocentre, Box 670, Bella Coola, BC, V0T 1C0. June-Sept. Located in Bella Coola Museum Anteroom. 799-5919. Off-season, ask at Senior Citizens' Centre next to Coop.

■ **Bella Coola Museum:** In schoolhouse and surveyor's cabin dating from 1800s, town centre. Items brought from Norway by early settlers, Hudson's Bay Company relics. June - Sept. Hours vary. 799-5919.

■ **Charters:** To Fjordland and Hakai provincial recreation areas. See Bella Bella, below, and ask at infocentre.

## SIDE TRIPS
### to Coastal Points

Although the highway ends at Bella Coola, there are a number of points of interest farther west. In fact the area, lately billed the "Cariboo Coast," is a spectacular archipelago melding land and sea, offering comfortable lodges, luxury resorts and vessels, good meals, and "guaranteed" fabulous fishing. Sea kayaking, diving, wildlife viewing, petroglyphs. The names are exotic: Hakai Pass, Fjordland, Ocean Falls, Shearwater, Klemtu, Namu, Kimsquit, Bella Bella. Places can be reached by air or boat charter from Bella Coola.

**Bella Bella:** (Pop. 1,104). Island village of Heiltsuk Band across Fitz Hugh Sound. Called Waglisla Village. BC Ferry makes scheduled stops for foot passengers. Remains of old Bella Bella site can be found near Shearwater on Denny Island.

■ **Heiltsuk Cultural Education Centre:** Secondary building of Bella Bella Community School. Mon-Fri. 957-2626 year-round. Display cases in school hallway contain archeological artifacts, work by Heiltsuk carvers, photos.

■ **Fjordland Provincial Recreation Area:** 91,000ha. Magnificent oceanscapes in one of the most scenic areas of the Pacific coast. No road access. Undeveloped. Four hours by boat north of Bella Bella. Info from BC Parks in Williams Lake, 398-4414.

■ **Hakai Provincial Recreation Area:** 122,998ha. Myriad islands surrounding some of the world's finest salmon fishing. No road access. Accommodation. Four hours by boat south of Bella Bella. BC Parks: 398-4414.

**Sir Alexander Mackenzie Provincial Park and Mackenzie Rock:** 5ha. 60km west of Bella Coola on Dean Channel. No road access. Western terminus of Alexander Mackenzie's voyage to the Pacific in 1793, and terminus of choice to many dedicated modern voyageurs, determined to finish the MacKenzie Trail, who are flown in or come by boat charter from the trail's end at Bella Coola.

Alexander Mackenzie was brought here by local Indians, and this is the spot where, in Mackenzie's words, he "mixed some vermillion in melted grease, and inscribed in large characters on the south-east face of the rock on which we had slept last night, this brief memorial: **'Alexander Mackenzie, from Canada, by land, the twenty-second of July, one thousand, seven hundred and ninety-three.'"** The words have since been engraved into the rock. Historic Sites and Monuments Board of Canada plaque.

**Ocean Falls:** (Pop. 29). On Fisher Channel west of Bella Coola. Former thriving pulp-mill town, now almost abandoned after mill closure. In the old company-town days even the light bulbs had Pacific Mills' name stamped on them. Now it's a base for fishing, hunting, and some local industries, one of which is the bottling of water from waterfalls and lakes in the area, for export around the world. Considered one of the few unspoiled spots on the globe: dolphins in the sea, eagles in the air.

**Rivers Inlet:** On coast, south of Bella Coola. Famed salt-water fishing locale with record-breaking tyee to 36kg. Coho and spring salmon, steelhead, scenery, reefs, coves, sea life. Don't look too hard for the rivers: inlet is named for Baron Rivers, 18th-century English writer and politician, characterized by Horace Walpole as "brutal and half-mad." Capt George Vancouver must have been running out of good names by the time he reached the inlet: Baron Rivers was a relation of a midshipman in his crew. About 12 salmon canneries were located here in the days before refrigeration.

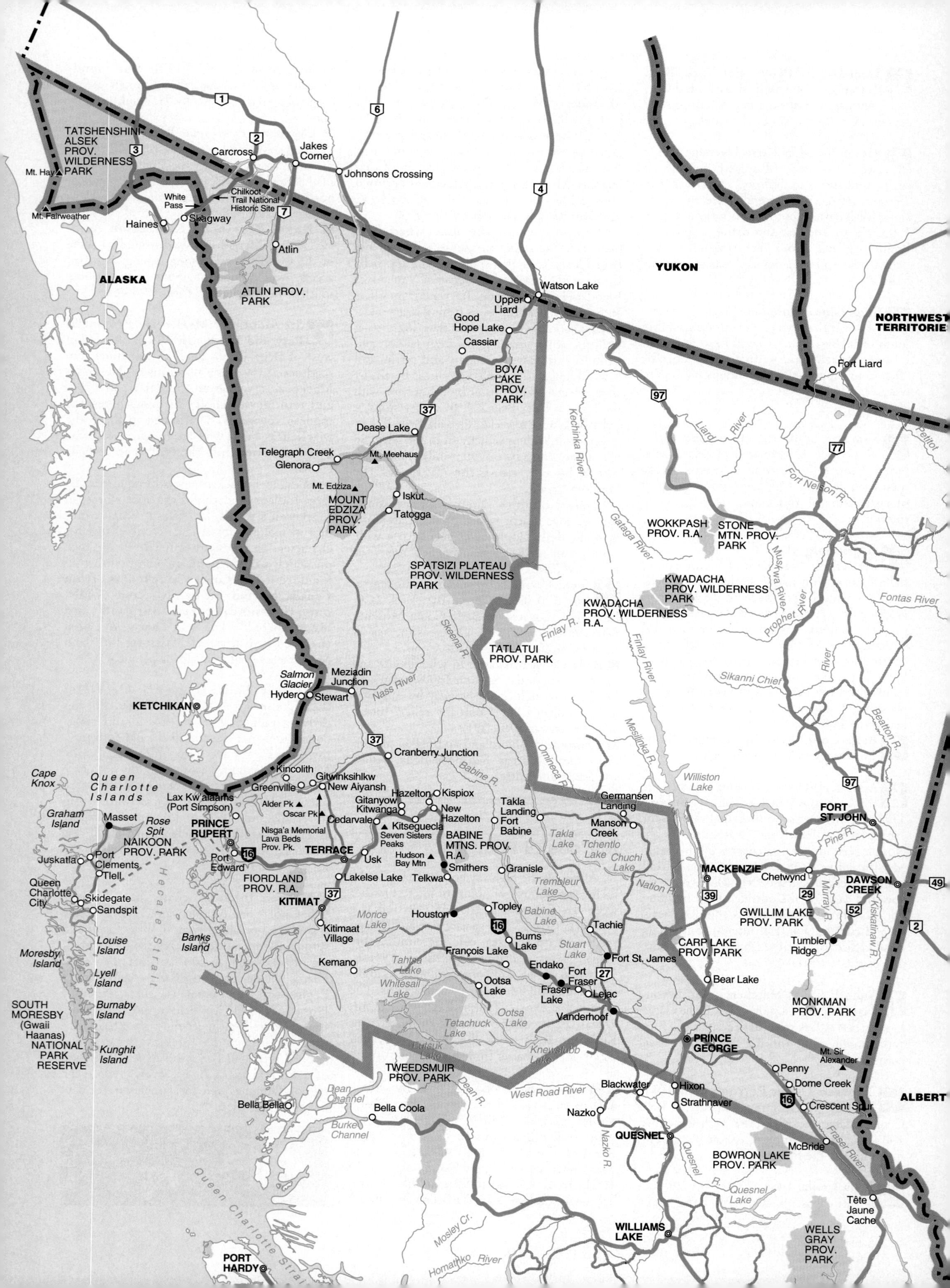

TATSHENSHINI-ALSEK PROV. WILDERNESS PARK
Mt. Hay
Mt. Fairweather
Haines
Skagway
White Pass
Chilkoot Trail National Historic Site
Carcross
Jakes Corner
Johnsons Crossing
Atlin
ALASKA
ATLIN PROV. PARK
YUKON
Watson Lake
Upper Liard
Good Hope Lake
Cassiar
BOYA LAKE PROV. PARK
NORTHWEST TERRITORIE
Fort Liard
Dease Lake
Telegraph Creek
Glenora
Mt. Meehaus
Mt. Edziza
MOUNT EDZIZA PROV. PARK
Iskut
Tatogga
SPATSIZI PLATEAU PROV. WILDERNESS PARK
Kechika River
Liard River
Fort Nelson R.
Gataga River
WOKKPASH PROV. R.A.
STONE MTN. PROV. PARK
Muskwa River
KWADACHA PROV. WILDERNESS PARK
KWADACHA PROV. WILDERNESS R.A.
Finlay R.
Prophet River
Fontas River
Petitot
Skeena R.
TATLATUI PROV. PARK
Finlay River
Sikanni Chief River
Beatton R.
Salmon Glacier
Meziadin Junction
Hyder
Stewart
Nass River
KETCHIKAN
Cranberry Junction
Mesilinka R.
Omineca R.
Babine R.
Williston Lake
Cape Knox
Queen Charlotte Islands
Kincolith
Gitwinksihlkw
Greenville
New Aiyansh
Lax Kw'alaams (Port Simpson)
Alder Pk
Oscar Pk
Hazelton
Kispiox
Gitanyow
Kitwanga
New Hazelton
Takla Landing
Fort Babine
Germansen Landing
Manson Creek
FORT ST. JOHN
Graham Island
Masset
Rose Spit
PRINCE RUPERT
NAIKOON PROV. PARK
Nisga'a Memorial Lava Beds Prov. Pk.
Cedarvale
Kitseguecla
Seven Sisters Peaks
BABINE MTNS. PROV. R.A.
Takla Lake
Tchentlo Lake
Chuchi Lake
Pine R.
Juskatla
Port Clements
Tlell
Port Edward
TERRACE
Usk
Hudson Bay Mtn
Smithers
Granisle
MACKENZIE
Chetwynd
DAWSON CREEK
Queen Charlotte City
Skidegate
Sandspit
Hecate Strait
FIORDLAND PROV. R.A.
Lakelse Lake
Telkwa
Trembleur Lake
Nation R.
Murray R.
KITIMAT
Morice Lake
Houston
Topley
Babine Lake
Tachie
GWILLIM LAKE PROV. PARK
Kitimaat Village
Burns Lake
Stuart Lake
CARP LAKE PROV. PARK
Tumbler Ridge
Kiskatinaw R.
Banks Island
Moresby Island
Louise Island
Kemano
Tahtsa Lake
François Lake
Endako
Fort St. James
Fort Fraser
Lyell Island
Whitesail Lake
Ootsa Lake
Fraser Lake
Lejac
Bear Lake
SOUTH MORESBY (Gwaii Haanas) NATIONAL PARK RESERVE
Burnaby Island
Vanderhoof
MONKMAN PROV. PARK
Tetachuck Lake
Ootsa Lake
Eutsuk Lake
Knewstubb Lake
PRINCE GEORGE
Kunghit Island
TWEEDSMUIR PROV. PARK
Dean R.
Mt. Sir Alexander
Penny
Dome Creek
Blackwater
Hixon
West Road River
Dean Channel
Bella Bella
Bella Coola
Nazko
Strathnaver
Crescent Spur
ALBERT
Burke Channel
QUESNEL
Nazko R.
Quesnel R.
McBride
Fraser River
BOWRON LAKE PROV. PARK
Queen Charlotte Strait
Quesnel Lake
Tête Jaune Cache
Mosley Cr.
WILLIAMS LAKE
WELLS GRAY PROV. PARK
PORT HARDY
Homathko River
1
2
3
4
6
7
16
27
29
37
39
49
52
77
97

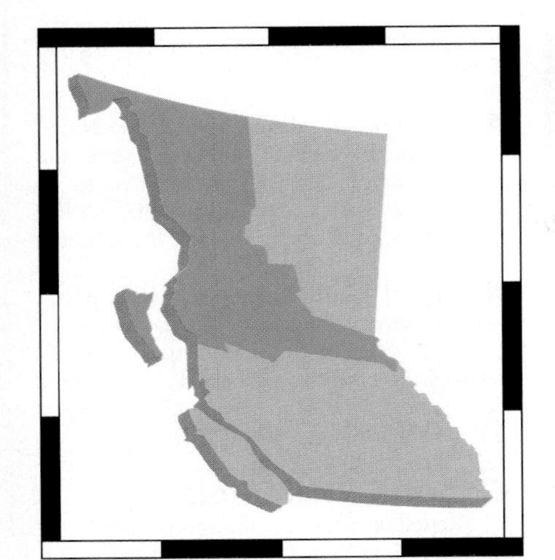

# North by Northwest

## *Endless Landscapes, Room to Roam*

> *"We would get a song from the whistling of the trees when the wind was blowing, from the rippling of the stream upon the mountainsides, from the great storm or tempest or from the singing of the birds and the voices of the animals. There is a song in everything."*
>
> – quoted in *It's God's Country* *by Rev FE Runnalls*

That simple statement from an unnamed north-coast First Nations citizen says much about the nature of this land North by Northwest. The quotation was collected by missionaries in the early 1900s. These men, driven by conviction, paddled canoes into island coves and took their message between mountain walls into deep, green Interior valleys. What they discovered must have impressed them as surely as it challenged their faith. The coastal native fishermen and interior nomadic hunters shared a mystical harmony with the land. Their songs, dances, and stories, their rituals and taboos flowed directly from the land and sea. The power of nature dominated their lives. Little wonder they heard a song in everything.

Today's visitors will still find an astonishing 317,000 sq km of relatively unpolluted land in the North by Northwest. The region's southern border stretches about 932km from the Rockies to the Pacific and the Queen Charlotte Islands. The region covers a third of BC.

Interior plateaus are densely forested with spruce, pine, and fir, and sprinkled with thousands of lakes, all clean and alive. In the deep, first-growth rain forests of South Moresby Island stand magnificent red cedar, 1,200 years old. The plateaus are separated by successions of mountain ranges. Fast, wild rivers rush from these places, gathering and combining forces to better slice through the Coast Mountains to the Pacific.

There are entire symphonies within those landscapes. For all its size and diversity, the region is not inaccessible. The Canadian National Railway and Yellowhead Hwy 16 share a route east-west from the Rockies to Prince Rupert. Stewart-Cassiar Hwy 37 links the Yellowhead with the Alaska Hwy to the north, following a sheltered route east of the Coast Mountains.

Where roads don't go, bush planes and helicopters do. Residents are as used to seeing small planes as southerners are traffic lights.

And yet ... much of the land remains the same wilderness that confronted the first Europeans here. In 1806, the intrepid Simon Fraser sailed two birch-bark canoes to Stuart Lake (Fort St James) where First Nations peo-

*Bear Glacier near Stewart, on the BC/Alaska border.*

ple had never before seen white men. They believed his tobacco smoke to be the spirits of dead ancestors escaping, and were alarmed when their women ate Fraser's soap and frothed at the mouth.

Fraser called the land New Caledonia, for the lakes and mountains of Scotland. But it was impossible for him at that time to comprehend its size and diversity. The region remained solely the domain of native peoples for many years after that.

The development of the area was galvanized with completion of the Grand Trunk Pacific Railway in 1914, linking the northwest coast with the rest of Canada.

Today the region is home to about 190,000 people, most close to railway or highway. Even in the largest cities, the back country starts just beyond the last street. In the Dease Lake-Atlin area, in the extreme northwest, there is one person for every 181 sq km.

The forests still sustain healthy wildlife populations. Black bears amble along roadsides, moose browse on the lakeshores. The city of Terrace has become famous for the beautiful white Kermode bear that is found only in that one area of the world. Lakes and rivers are an embarrassment of profusion. And hundreds of species of birds, from hummingbirds to eagles, peregrine falcons and trumpeter swans, inhabit the region.

People are aware today of a need to protect the wilderness and the magnificent range of experiences it allows. A large grizzly bear population now has sanctuary in the Khutzeymateen Valley north of Prince Rupert. But several rivers are under pressure. The salmon-bearing Nechako River will become a mere trickle of its former self if Alcan's stalled Kemano Completion hydroelectric power project survives economic and environmental reassessments. If the project proceeds as planned, water flows in the Nechako will be about 12 percent of the pre-1950 level when Alcan was permitted to build the Kennedy Dam, creating a vast reservoir to power its aluminum smelting operation at Kitimat.

Much farther north, with its headwaters in the Spatsizi Plateau Wilderness Park, the Stikine River attracted international attention when plans surfaced for a hydro dam in the river's 80km long "Grand Canyon". In 1987, the IUCN (International Union for the Conservation of Nature and Natural Resources) called for the entire Stikine to be designated an international park. Some "corridor" protection has been afforded and while renewed development plans are muted, friends of the Stikine remain vigilant.

In the far northeast corner of BC, abutting the Yukon's Kluane National Park, the Tatshenshini River, considered one of the 10 best wild rivers in the world; has just been spared. It allows white-water rafting beyond belief, past great mountains and glaciers, to icebergs, and finally the ocean.

Few places on earth have such a cornucopia of natural wonders. Even those who can't themselves visit the wild spots feel comforted knowing the space, the animals, the wilderness are there.

## Information

**The North by Northwest Tourism Association:** Box 1030, Smithers, BC, V0J 2N0; call 847-5227; Fax: 847-7585. Addresses and telephone numbers of local infocentres are in *Log* with write-ups on each community. New provincial parks are being planned for the North by Northwest region. For up-to-date information on park expansions or new park and wilderness areas, contact the North by Northwest Tourism Association.

## Transportation

The area is served by major and local airlines, railways, car and passenger ferries, and bus lines. There is also an extensive and well-maintained system of paved and secondary roads. Travel infocentres can provide information, and help with rentals of RV equipment, kayaks, houseboats, bicycles, skis, horses.

### Roads

The main access route from the east is the Yellowhead Hwy (Hwy 16), a designated scenic and interprovincial highway stretching 2,844km from the wheatlands of Manitoba to the misty Queen Charlottes. The BC portion is 1,073km.

Visitors from southern BC and the US can travel Hwy 5 to its intersection with the Yellowhead near Tête Jaune Cache, or via Hwys 1 and 97 to Prince George.

Prince George is very much a gateway to the region. Hwys 16 and 97 intersect here, less than 800km from Edmonton, Calgary, or Vancouver. Residents think nothing of driving that distance in a day. It's an easy two-day drive for vacationers.

The Stewart-Cassiar Hwy (Hwys 37 and 37A) is the newest and shortest route to Alaska, connecting the Alaska Hwy from a point near Watson Lake in the Yukon, to the Yellowhead Hwy near Kitwanga, 243km east of Prince Rupert. The road is paved for 448km of its 749km length.

Hundreds of logging roads are open to the public, unless otherwise posted. Of course, there are no gas stations. Some roads are not suitable for large RVs. Logging roads are built for industrial traffic, and care should be taken. Follow an empty logging truck: the driver can radio your location to other truckers. Or travel weekends, when most logging ceases. Check infocentres, or Forest Service offices for exceptions.

Drive with headlights on at all times, especially on dusty logging roads. Carry extra fuel, tires, supplies, a survival and first-aid kit. Friends or the RCMP should be notified in advance of any lengthy back-road excursions.

### Bus Lines

■ **Greyhound Bus Lines:** Vancouver 662-3222, or specific communities. Coaches stop daily at all communities along the Yellowhead Hwy from the Alberta border to Prince Rupert.

■ **Northland Buslines:** 996-8421. Daily, except Sun, service between Fort St James and Prince George.

■ **Farwest Bus Lines:** 624-6400. Service between Prince Rupert, Terrace, Stewart, and Smithers.

■ **Seaport Limousine:** 636-2622. Mon-Wed-Fri service, Stewart to Terrace.

Four cities in the region operate transit services. For information call Prince George 563-0011, Prince Rupert 624-6400, Terrace 635-6617, or Kitimat 632-3333.

### Car and RV Rentals

Rental agencies are at airports and downtown locations. Some RV rentals. Check infocentres for leads. Taxis available in all but the smallest communities. Cabs may be limited. Phone early.

### Railways

■ **VIA Rail:** 1-800-561-8630. A branch line completed 1914 connects Jasper with Prince Rupert. Trains leave Jasper Mon-Wed-Fri evenings. 928km, 22 hours, to Prince Rupert (14 hours from Prince George). Roomettes. Early reservations recommended in summer. Check for possible new schedule offering daylight service with overnight stop in Prince George. This allows visitors travelling both ways between Jasper and Prince Rupert to enjoy scenery. Also allows connections with BC Rail's passenger service to North Vancouver.

■ **BC Rail:** North Vancouver 984-5246 or Prince George 561-4033. Northern passenger terminus is Prince George. Leaves North Vancouver for Prince George daily June-Sept, otherwise Sun-Wed-Fri mornings, a leisurely 13-hour (745km) trip.

■ **White Pass and Yukon Route:** From northern BC, Yukon Territory, and Northwest Territories. 1-800-343-7373; from other places 907-983-2217. Box 435, Skagway, Alaska, USA, 99840. This is a narrow-gauge (36") privately owned railway, built in 1898 to accommodate gold rushers, linking Skagway, Alaska, on the coast, with the Interior. Reservations required. Summit excursion (Skagway to Canadian border and return); Skagway to Whitehorse excursion; and Chilkoot Trail hikers' shuttle.

### Airlines

Largest airports are in Prince George, Smithers, Terrace-Kitimat, Prince Rupert, and Sandspit. All offer daily jet flights to and from Vancouver.

■ **Air BC:** 360-9074. Connects Prince George and Vancouver with other interior communities.

■ **Canadian Airlines International:** Vancouver 382-6111, or centres listed above.

■ **Central Mountain Air:** Toll free 1-800-663-3905 or 847-4780 in Smithers. Serves Prince George, Smithers, Terrace, Prince Rupert, Vancouver, Edmonton, and small communities in northwest.

■ **North Coast Air Services:** 627-1351. Connects Prince Rupert with Port Simpson, Kincolith, Kitkatla, and Queen Charlottes.
■ **Northern Thunderbird Air Ltd:** Prince George 963-9611 or Mackenzie 997-3247. Scheduled service between Prince George and Mackenzie.
■ **Canadian Regional Airlines:** 1-800-663-1661 or regionally in Sandspit, Prince Rupert, Smithers, and Prince George.
■ **Waglisla Air Inc:** 626-5006, 1-800-663-2875. Scheduled service from Vancouver International Airport, Prince Rupert to Masset.

This is bush-plane country. Charter flights by fixed-wing and helicopter readily available. Most communities and some isolated work camps and resorts have small airstrips. Landings on grass, gravel, or water. Check with infocentres. Local sporting goods stores often provide leads.

## Ferries

■ **BC Ferries:** Vancouver 669-1211. Prince Rupert is northern terminus for Inside Passage route from Port Hardy on Vancouver Island. *Queen of the North* runs year-round. 491km, 15 hrs. In winter one sailing a week. In summer, the ship leaves Port Hardy one day, Rupert the next. Vehicle and cabin reservations essential.

Also reserve early for service between Prince Rupert and Skidegate on Graham Island in the Queen Charlottes. 172km, eight hrs. Up to five sailings a week in summer, three in winter.

MV *Kwuna* connects Skidegate Landing to Alliford Bay on Moresby Island. 12 sailings a day, year-round, 20 minutes.
■ **The Alaska Marine Highway System:** 1-800-642-0066 from the US; in Canada, 907-465-3941. Or write Alaska Marine Hwy System, Box 25535, Juneau, Alaska 99802-5535. Prince Rupert is southern terminus of Alaska Marine Hwy System. Ferries call at Alaska Panhandle communities, and terminate in Skagway, 789km north of Prince Rupert. 36-hour cruise. Vehicle reservations required.

A ferry leaves Hyder, Alaska every Mon, May-Sept, for Ketchikan. Hyder shares head of Portland Canal with Stewart, BC.

### Inland Ferries

BC's transportation and highways ministry operates free car-and-passenger ferries to complement the road network.
■ **François Lake to Southbank:** Hwy 35, 29km south of Burns Lake. 21 daily sailings aboard MV *Omineca Princess*, 25-minute turnaround. 32 cars.
■ **Hwy 16 to Usk across Skeena:** 20km east of Terrace. On demand. Five minutes, two vehicles.

## NORTH by NORTHWEST EVENTS

### Atlin
■ **Tarahne Day:** Aug, 1st Mon.

### Burns Lake
■ **Bluegrass Festival:** Early July.
■ **Tweedsmuir Park Days:** Early July.

### Fraser Lake
■ **Mouse Mountain Days:** July 1st weekend.

### Granisle
■ **Granisle Days:** Mid-June.

### Hazelton
■ **Pioneer Day:** Aug, 2nd Sat.

### Houston
■ **Pleasant Valley Days:** May long weekend. Horse show, loggers' sports, rodeo, chuckwagon races.

### Kispiox
■ **Kispiox Valley Rodeo:** Early June. The real thing.

### Kitimat
■ **July 1 Celebrations:** Parade, food festival, hill climb.
■ **Annual Coho Derby:** Labour Day weekend.

### McBride
■ **Yellowhead Loppett:** Cross-country ski race. Last weekend Feb.

### Manson Creek
■ **Gold Rush Days:** July.

### Prince George
■ **Dogsled Races:** Jan. Tabor Lake.
■ **Tree Planter's Picnic:** Early May.
■ **Canadian Northern Children's Festival:** May.
■ **Native Awareness Week:** July.
■ **Simon Fraser Days, International Food Festival:** Late July, early Aug.
■ **Sandblast:** Mid-Aug.

### Prince Rupert
■ **Sea Fest and Indian Cultural Days:** June, 2nd weekend.

### Queen Charlotte City
■ **Hospital Day:** Late June. Taking place for the better part of a century.

### Skidegate
■ **Singaay Laa Day:** Early June.

### Smithers
■ **Winter Festival:** Late Feb.
■ **Mid-summer Festival:** June.
■ **Bulkley Valley Rodeo:** Late June.
■ **Midnight Mardi Gras:** July.
■ **Bulkley Valley Exhibition:** Late Aug.

### Stewart
■ **Cabin Fever Days:** 2nd week Feb. A good 8m of snow by this time; everyone ready for a party.
■ **International Days:** July 1-4. Canada/US birthday celebration.

### Terrace
■ **Riverboat Days:** Late July.

### Vanderhoof
■ **Bull-A-Rama:** April. Bull riding championships.
■ **Vanderhoof International Air Show:** July, 3rd weekend. 567-3144.
■ **Nechako Valley Summer School of the Arts:** July 24-Aug 5. Day- and week-long art courses. Box 1438, Vanderhoof, BC, V0J 3A0. 567-3030.
■ **Rich Hobson Frontier Cattle Drive:** Mid-Aug.

*Mending nets at Prince Rupert.*

*'Ksan, model Gitksan village near Hazelton, northern BC.*

# North by Northwest Routes and Highlights

## TRAVELLER'S LOGS



## HIGHLIGHTS



## Prince George

### BC'S NORTHERN CAPITAL

**Prince George:** (Pop. 69,653). BC's geographical heart, situated midway on Hwy 97, a 2,260km north-south artery connecting Osoyoos on the US border with Lower Post bordering the Yukon. Also roughly midpoint on the 1,073km Yellowhead Hwy (Hwy 16) connecting Prince Rupert on the central west coast with Jasper National Park on the BC/Alberta border. Prince George is 786km northeast of Vancouver. Two major trans-provincial railways, BC Rail (south/north), and VIA Rail (east/west), intersect here as well.

Here, just 91km east of the province's geographical centre, two large rivers converge and only one lives to tell the tale. Prince George's downtown core has grown up in the bowl formed between the Nechako River gliding down from the west and the larger Fraser River flowing from the Rockies. The flat bottomed basin was once the bed of a lake during the glacial period. Distinctive cutbanks have emerged from that evolutionary tumble. Sandy cliffs topped with evergreens enwrap the north shore of the Nechako and the east flank of the Fraser. The cutbanks contribute to the city's character.

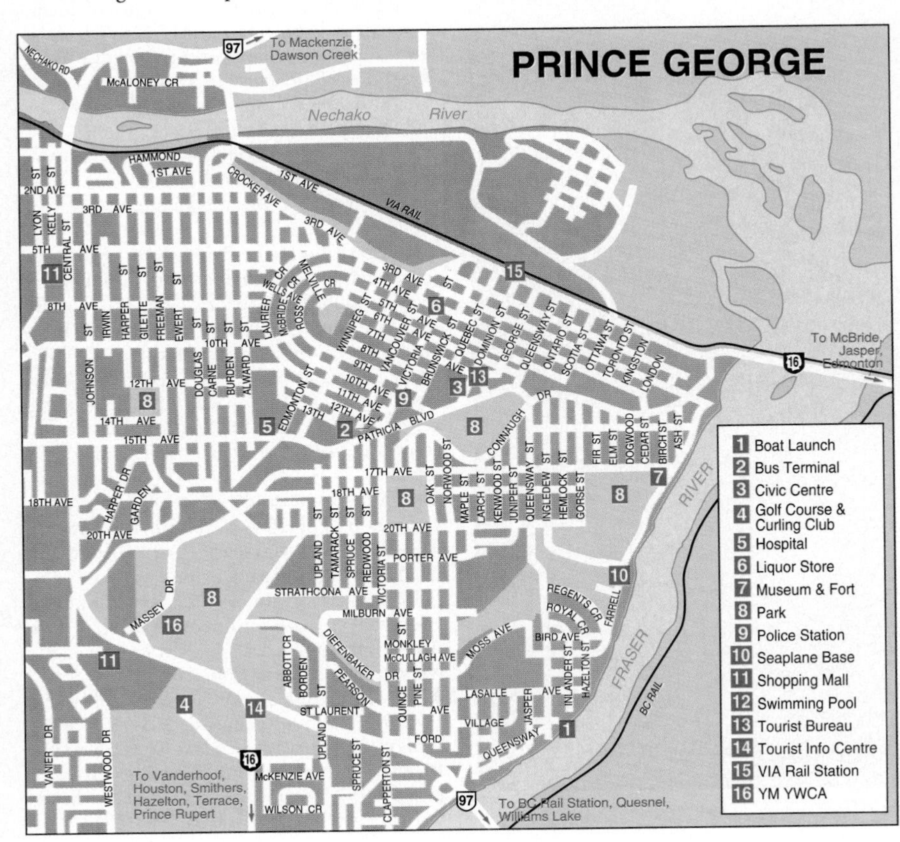


For hundreds, even thousands of years, native peoples – represented today by the Lheit-Lit'en Nation – have used the lands around where the two rivers meet. The first Europeans didn't arrive until June, 1793. Alexander Mackenzie, canoeing southward on the Fraser in early morning mists didn't notice the outpouring of the Nechako. He left it to Simon Fraser, 14 years later, to recognize this important river junction and name it Fort George after King George III. Fraser actually wintered over in the area in 1807-08, and built the tiny outpost at the confluence of the rivers. With the arrival of spring, he embarked on his famous journey down the river now bearing his name.

Fort George remained little more than a trading post until a century later when the Grand Trunk Pacific Railway found, through the Fraser and Nechako valleys, a feasible route for its line to Prince Rupert on the coast (now part of the CNR system). A wild wave of speculation accompanied the line's completion in 1914, and Prince George was officially incorporated in 1915. World War One brought this period of growth sharply to an end, and for two decades Prince George became a sleepy hollow again.

However, another destiny was in store for the city so pivotally situated. Completion of the John Hart Hwy between Prince George and Dawson Creek in 1952 opened access to the Yukon. The same year, the Pacific Great Eastern (now BC Rail) finally extended its line from Quesnel to Prince George. (It reached the Peace River in 1958 and Fort Nelson in 1970.)

Then there was a big change in the forest industry. In the '40s and '50s, about 600 tiny portable "gypo" sawmills dotted the surrounding forests, producing rough-cut white spruce for lumber. Better use of the trees changed the economy and the city forever. Pulp was the factor. Lumber mills could turn their leftovers into pulp, and that could be converted into paper products. In 1964, Prince George Pulp and Paper's $80-million mill was started. It was followed by Northwood Pulp and Timber, and Intercontinental Pulp, and together the three mills triggered a population boom. Prince George exploded from a comfortable little place of 14,000 people in 1961 to 50,000 in 1971. It is now the province's fourth largest city.

Prince George is no longer a rough-and-ready lumber town. At the heart of Canada's largest softwood lumber producing area, the city is home to some of the most sophisticated and efficient sawmills in the world. Silvicultural techniques to re-establish trees on logged areas and ways of managing forest lands for non-timber values have been pioneered here and continue to evolve.

Paralleling its industrial development, Prince George has become more of a cosmopolitan city with everything visitors require. It has more art galleries than pulp mills, more municipal parks than warehouses. There is, of course, a daily newspaper, the *Prince George Citizen.* For all its government, service, distribution, and transportation functions, Prince George plays a corresponding role in offering cultural, entertainment, recreational, and educational opportunities for visitor and resident alike.

Indeed, Prince George is enjoying a renaissance of growth and expression rivalling the excitement of the pulp mill building era. The University of Northern British Columbia's main campus is being built on Cranbrook Hill, overlooking the city. Canada's first autonomous university in the last 25 years becomes fully operational in September, 1994. The university's structure is based on programs of First Nations, environmental, international, northern, and women's studies. UNBC's impact is already being felt. An influx of people with different talents and fresh dreams have moved into the city. The university's presence has helped spur downtown rejuvenation with planned construction of a new civic centre/plaza and domed courthouse. New homes, shopping and recreational facilities and cappuccino shops are springing up in areas throughout the city.

And yet just an hour's drive in any direction from the city are lakes and rivers where the harried traveller will only have to share space with loons, and the occasional moose.

**Prince George Information:** Tourism Prince George, 1198 Victoria St, Prince George, BC, V2L 2L2. Year-round. 562-3700. Seasonal infocentre at Hwys 16/97 junction. May-Sept. 563-5493.

**Prince George Airport:** 10km southeast of downtown Prince George. Take Hwy 97 south across Fraser Bridge. At Sintich Rd turn left, follow signs for 5km.

■ **The Heritage River Trail System:** Peace and seclusion fringing downtown. Starts at Cameron St Bridge. Some 10km along Fraser and Nechako rivers, with viewpoints and signed nature trails. Check infocentres or City Hall (561-7633) for details.

■ **Forests for the World Park:** Atop Cranbrook Hill, an escarpment lying west of the city. The largest of the city's 117 parks. 106ha affording expansive views and containing a small lake with beavers and waterfowl. There are hiking, nature walks, and cross-country skiing trails through mixed hardwood/softwood forests. Learn about forest management techniques, and plant tree seedlings in an unusual "Leave Your Roots in Prince George" program.

■ **Cottonwood Island Nature Park:** Off River Rd 2km northeast of downtown Prince George, 32ha. A peaceful wooded sanctuary with trails skirting Nechako River, located close to junction of Fraser. Bring a bird identification book.

■ **Prince George Railway and Forest Industry Museum:** Adjacent Cottonwood Island Nature Park. 563-7351. Daily mid-May to early Sept. Revives the days of steam, including history of Grand Trunk Pacific Railway (now the CNR). Rolling stock, a complete station, and guards' lanterns, Grand Trunk Pacific reception car and workers bunkhouse. Also, the *Nechako Car,* a restored Grand Trunk Pacific reception car. Exhibits date to 1903.

■ **Fort George Park:** At the end of 20th Ave, running between l7th and 20th, and overlooking the Fraser. Site of small outpost built by Fraser for the North West Company in 1807. Now a popular picnic and meeting spot. Summer rides on a narrow gauge steam locomotive, Canada's smallest official railway. Weekends and holidays, May-Sept. Nearly 1ha of the park is the ancestral burial ground for local Lheit-Li'ten Nation. Evening entertainment at the band shell July and Aug.

■ **Elders' Salmon Camp:** 563-9909. Jet boat from Hudson's Bay Slough near Fort George Park, 29km down the Fraser to camp. Help catch and cook salmon and listen to elders' stories and legends while feasting. July-Sept.

■ **Fraser-Fort George Regional Museum:** In Fort George Park. 562-1612. Story of transportation from dugouts to sternwheelers, and the laying of steel. Museum shop, archives. Until May 14, open noon-5, daily, except Sun, Mon, and holidays. May 15-Sept 15: daily 10-5 (Tues 10-8).

■ **Connaught Hill Park:** Off Queensway on Connaught Dr. A plug of land rising above city hall, 360-degree views. Shady trees, flower gardens, and fresh air where downtowners come to "brown bag it."

■ **Prince George Art Gallery:** 2820-15th Ave. 563-6447. Daily in summer; off-season closed Mon. Regular exhibitions of local, regional, and provincial artists and craftsmen. Some travelling exhibits or thematic displays.

■ **Studio 2880:** Next to art gallery on 15th Ave. Year-round. 562-4526. Regular craft fairs and markets. Ticket office.

■ **Native Art Gallery:** 144 George St. Year-round. 564-3568. Coastal and Interior native art and crafts for sale. Often site of work in progress.

■ **Tours:** Tourism Prince George offers scheduled and self-guided tours during summer. 1-800-668-1646 or 562-3700. Forest industry tours, including Northwood Pulp and Timber operations. Northwood's Tree Farm Licence is to become one of 10 Model Forest Locations in Canada. Advance booking recommended. Contact Visitors Bureau for tours or motor coach step-on tour guide services.

■ **Huble Homestead:** 40km north of Prince George, 4km off Hwy 97 North, on Mitchell Rd. Daily late May-early Oct, 10-6. 563-9225. Living museum of homestead established 1905 at the Fraser River end of Giscome Portage, connecting Pacific and Arctic watersheds; declined 1919 when highway drew traffic away from river route.

■ **18-Hole Golf: Aspen Grove**, on Mile 9, Hwy 97 S, right at Leno Rd, 963-9650. **Pine Valley**, 2.5km west on Hwy 16, 562-4811. **Prince George Golf and Curling Club**, at Hwys 16/97 junction, 563-0357. **Yellowhead Grove**, Hwy 16W, Leland Rd, 964-8813.

*Boya Lake and the Cassiar Mountains, in northern BC.*

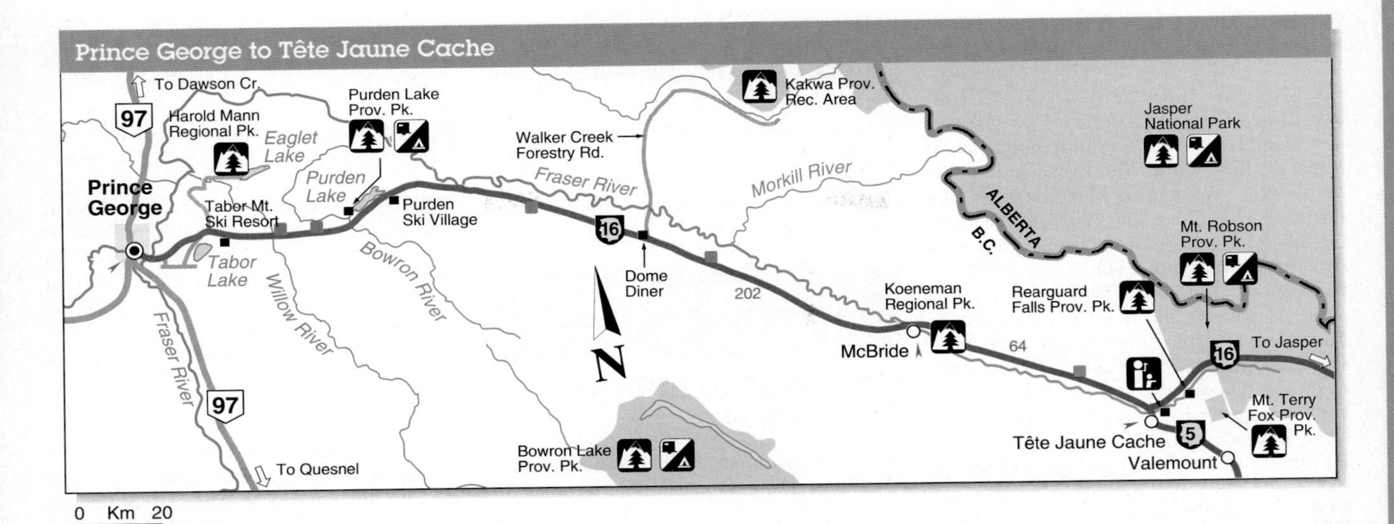


## Prince George to Tête Jaune Cache

### YELLOWHEAD HIGHWAY (Highway 16)

The Yellowhead Hwy (Hwy 16) leaves Prince George east of the city centre on First Ave. Tête Jaune Cache is 266km from here. Leave "the Bowl" area of Prince George by crossing the Fraser River on the new Yellowhead Hwy Bridge, 500m long and finally opened in 1987, to the relief of all Prince Georgians. Cause of relief is immediately upstream (north), a graceless but historic steel trestle bridge shared uncomfortably for 75 years by trains and two lanes of automobiles. There was no room for both cars and train, and the train had right-of-way. The bridge was completed by the Grand Trunk Pacific Railway in 1914, and engineered with a movable centre span for sternwheelers to pass through. However, the railway killed river traffic, and the bridge was never raised in earnest. Strictly for rail traffic these days.

The highway curves up Airport Hill after crossing the river, offering views of city's three pulp mills. Distances are measured from the east end of the Yellowhead Hwy Bridge.

**Tabor Lake:** Turn south 4km from Yellowhead Hwy Bridge in Prince George. Follow old Cariboo Hwy and Giscome Rd 7km to small, weedy lake. Consistent producer of pan-sized rainbow trout. RV park, restaurant.

**Harold Mann Regional Park:** 13ha. 563-9225. On Upper Fraser Rd, 17km beyond Prince George. Turn north for 30.5km. Duck habitat, fishing and boating on Eaglet Lake. Named for the man who brought in the first two logging trucks in 1934, putting horse loggers out to pasture.

**Tabor Mountain Ski Resort:** Access road 20km beyond Prince George. 963-7542. Full-service ski hill. Triple chair, T-bar, night skiing. Vertical drop 244m.

**Moose Viewing Area:** About 29km beyond Prince George. A raised platform five minutes' walk from a pullout on north side of highway. Area burned in 1961 Grove Forest fire. Now good moose habitat. Approach cautiously.

**Willow River Rest Area and Demonstration Forest:** 33km east of Prince George. Easy 2km 45-minute walk through mixed hardwood and softwood forest. Memorial cairn for eight teenage boys who died May 10, 1974 canoeing an "impassable canyon just downstream."

**Bowron River:** 55km east of Prince George. Day-use rest area, north side of highway. Guided white-water raft trips, May-June only. 962-6438. Upper Bowron River valley scene of intense salvage logging of trees killed or damaged by spruce bark beetle epidemics. Now the largest silviculture plantation in the world (53,000ha).

**Purden Lake Provincial Park:** 320ha; 78 campsites. 57km from Prince George. 565-6340. Large picnic area with sandy beach, rainbow trout. 7km of woodsy trails. Boat launching.

Purden Lake Resort is on south shore 3.5km from park. **Last gas service for about 145km.** Gas stations in small towns often close early.

**Purden Ski Village:** South off highway 60km from Prince George, drive short distance up a gravel road. Call mobile 565-9038. Full-service ski hill with double chair and T-bar. Vertical drop 335m.

From Purden Lake to McBride is the Yellowhead's loneliest stretch. The only settlements are the tiny Fraser River communities of Penny (pop. 10), Dome Creek (pop. 51), Kidd, Fraser, Urling, Loos (pop. 8), Crescent Spur, Goat River, Rider, Legrand, and Lamming Mills, located off the highway, and offering no travellers' services. The highway crosses many streams and passes through dense wet-belt cedar and hemlock forests. The stark beauty made an indelible impression on Alexander Anderson, a young English Hudson's Bay clerk on his first assignment to the area. "Indeed, after leaving Fort Assiniboine in the winter of 1835, not the vestige of a human inhabitant was met with, save a few recluses at Jasper's, until we reached the neighbourhood of Fort George. The whole was one trackless waste, save where occasionally the footprints of wild animals disturbed the snow."

**Sugarbowl Mountain Trail:** About 77.5km from Prince George. Steep access to alpine and 1,836m peak of Sugarbowl Mountain. Five hours. For information write Caledonia Ramblers, Box 26, Station A, Prince George, BC, V2L 4R9.

**Slim Creek Rest Area:** 118km east of Prince George, south side of highway.

**Coffee Break:** Dome Diner, about 123km from Prince George at junction of Hwy 16 and Bristow Rd. Home-cooked pies, muffins, tarts.

**Kakwa Provincial Recreation Area:** 127,690ha. 566-4325. A remote wilderness recreation area on BC/Alberta border, northwest of Mt Robson, along the Continental Divide. There is minimal road access on Walker Creek Forestry Rd, 133km from Prince George. It leads 87km north and is very rough. Travel is restricted by bridge washouts and high-water levels. There is also air-charter access. Visitors must be self-sufficient. Old guiding trails. Some designated campsites. Grand open valleys and stunning mountain peaks. Prime grizzly and black bear habitat. Also caribou and moose. Park ranger headquarters at south end of Kakwa Lake; cabins used only in summer, available for public in winter. Elevations: Mt Sir Alexander (3,270m), Mt Ida (3,180m).

Also accessible from Grande Prairie, Alberta, on Kakwa River Forestry Rd. Last section very rough: 4X4 trucks prohibited; only ATVs allowed, but are to be kept off mountainsides and alpine.

**Goat River Rest Area:** 166km east of Prince George. North side of highway.

**McBride:** (Pop. 580). 207km east of Prince George on fertile Fraser River benchlands. This was a railway boom town before the First World War, known as Railway Siding 39. Now named McBride after BC Premier Richard McBride (1903-15). Many of the 2,000 residents moved out with the construction crews. Those who stayed relied on farming or cutting cedar telegraph poles and posts. Agriculture and forestry still mainstay. McBride is a bustling little market town for a scattered population of about 2,500 who enjoy a laid-back rural lifestyle. It has all the basic tourist services, including good campsites. Back-country hiking and canoeing. Handmade lace and fabrics. A good checkout spot before going in to Kakwa (see above).

**McBride Information:** Infocentre, Railway caboose, Robson Square Shopping Centre. 569-3366. Off season: McBride Village Office, 569-2229.

**Koeneman Regional Park:** 7ha. About 1.5km beyond McBride. Drive or hike to Rainbow Falls and first of two lookouts on Dear Mountain. Views of Robson Valley and Cariboo Mountains. Named for homesteading family whose log house, built in 1939, is now used as theatre and special events gallery. In summer call 563-9225.

**Small River Rest Area:** 253km beyond Prince George, south side of highway.

**Hwy 5:** Leads south, just west of Tête Jaune Cache. 340km to Kamloops. Hwy 16 continues east from here, to Mt Robson Provincial Park and Jasper National Park. See *High Country*, p.178.

**Tête Jaune Cache:** (Pop. 143). 266km beyond Prince George. Turn south and cross one-way bridge over Fraser River. *Tête Jaune*, is French for "Yellow Head," the nickname of a golden-haired, dark-skinned, mixed-blood Iroquois trapper. Historians disagree on his surname. Man and legend have been brought to life in Howard O'Hagan's *Tay John*, a 1939 Canadian classic. A powerful story, not for the faint-hearted. Tête Jaune was reputed to have hidden or cached a fortune in furs somewhere between here and Yellowhead Pass.

Tête Jaune Cache, at the confluence of the Fraser and Robson rivers, was a major railway construction centre and head of navigation for sternwheelers on the Fraser. In its heyday early in the century, it was a booming shantytown of 5,000. Today, Tête Jaune's only visible "downtown" is a cluster of three small buildings and two gas pumps. One is the Yellowhead Trading Post, the area's general store. Its proprietors question Statistics Canada population figures, claiming nearly 300 people live here, scattered in homesteads throughout the woods.

Some 5.5km westward, down the Tête Jaune Cache Rd, there's a bend in the Fraser and remains of old pilings, a landing area for sternwheelers that hauled passengers and supplies up from Prince George. One wonders how boats so large – carrying 200 people and 200t of freight – could get this far upriver, where it's swift and narrow. Just upstream is a recreation site.

The river here is a beautiful green. As it broadens in its rampage to the coast, it becomes a silty yellow.

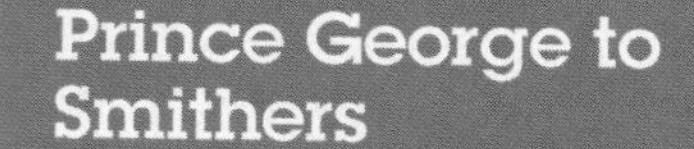

## Prince George to Smithers

### YELLOWHEAD HIGHWAY (Highway 16)

This section of the Yellowhead Hwy runs west 371km from Prince George to Smithers. It crosses the rolling Interior Plateau and an ever-changing landscape. Ranches and farms in pleasant, open country blend with extensive spruce, pine, and fir forests, near some of the largest natural lakes in BC. The Hazelton Mountains come into view approaching Houston and form an impressive backdrop to Smithers. This section begins at the Prince George Travel Infocentre, Hwys 16/97 junction.

**Prince George:** (Pop. 69,653). For details, see p.209.

**Blackwater Rd:** 9.5km from Prince George.

### SIDE TRIP
#### to Park and Canyon

**West Lake Provincial Park:** 256ha. 565-6340. On Blackwater Rd, 14km from Hwy 16 to park. Grassy picnic sites, sandy beaches, good swimming. Paddlewheel boat rides planned.

**Fort George Canyon Trail:** On West Lake Rd, 11km beyond park. 4.5km trail a naturalist's and photographer's delight. Some 56 species of flowers, almost as many shrubs. Trail ends where Fraser River boils in whirlpools and courses over jagged rocks through canyon. Small sternwheelers used to be winched up the canyon while passengers walked around. Cross-country skiing.

#### *Return to Highway 16*

**Bednesti Lake:** 39km from Blackwater Rd. Services and lake access.

**Cluculz Lake:** Several access routes south of highway, from 2.5km to 17km past Bednesti Resort. Prince George cottage country. Rainbow trout and some big char, uncatchable, lurk in lake.

**Cluculz Creek Rest Area:** 13km beyond Bednesti Lake Resort, on the south side of the highway.

**Sob Lake Rd:** 11km beyond rest area. Apparently named for an early homesteader who was, well ... cantankerous.

**The Geographical Centre of BC:** 9km beyond rest area. Cairn marks the spot.

**Vanderhoof:** (Pop. 4,023).10km beyond Geographical Centre, 97km west of Prince George, 129km east of Burns Lake. On Nechako River. In the early 1900s, pioneer Herbert Vanderhoof, an American publicist working for railway, had a recurring dream of a luxury riverside hotel amid spruce forests, a haven for writers and artists. (Writing was a vocation he pursued in his native Chicago.) The hotel was never built, and the writers were never rejuvenated. But Vanderhoof and district flourishes. Writers didn't stay, but ranchers did, lured by large and cheap acreages for raising beef and dairy cattle.

Vanderhoof today is a service centre for ranchers and loggers. Lots of cowboy boots and hard hats. Logging has provided access to many lakes, and resorts are plentiful. Fly in to remote locations. Check infocentre for details. Vanderhoof is also home to Canada's largest camp-in air show, attracting 25,000 people late July, annually. Airshow office, 567-3144. The Rich Hobson Frontier Cattle Drive has also become an annual event. In late Aug, over 200 participants and volunteers trace trails of pioneer cattle rancher, and author of such popular accounts as *Rancher Takes Wife*. Cattle Drive Office, 567-4664.

**Vanderhoof Information:** Infocentre one block north of Hwy 16, on Burrard St. Year-round. 567-2124. Off-season, Vanderhoof and District Chamber of Commerce, Box 126, Vanderhoof, BC, V0J 3A0. 567-2124.

- **Vanderhoof Heritage Village Museum:** On Hwy 16, West and Pine, on western perimeter of town. Daily May-Aug, except Mon. 567-2991. 11 reconstructed 1920s buildings, including OK Café. Tours.
- **Vanderhoof Bird Sanctuary:** 200ha along 5km of Nechako river bank. On north perimeter of town. Each spring and fall, skies are filled with sights and sounds of 50,000 migrating birds. Call Nechako Valley Sporting Association,Box 1077,Vanderhoof, BC, V0J 3A0.
- **Kenney Dam/Cheslatta Falls:** 96km southwest of Vanderhoof. Dam impounds Alcan reservoir, water from the spillway is directed over the Cheslatta Falls into Nechako River. Forestry recreation area with camping, picnicking, and falls.
- **Cross-country Ski Trails:** Three sets of maintained and tracked trails close to town – 6.5km Nechako Valley Sporting Association trail; 30km Water Lily Lake trail; 15km Mooney Pit trail. For details: Nechako Valley Sporting Association, Box 1077, Vanderhoof, BC, V0J 3A0.
- **Omineca Golf Course:** 1.5km north of Vanderhoof on Hwy 27. 567-2920. Nine holes.

**Hwy 27:** Turn north off Hwy 16 in Vanderhoof for Fort St James, 62km away.

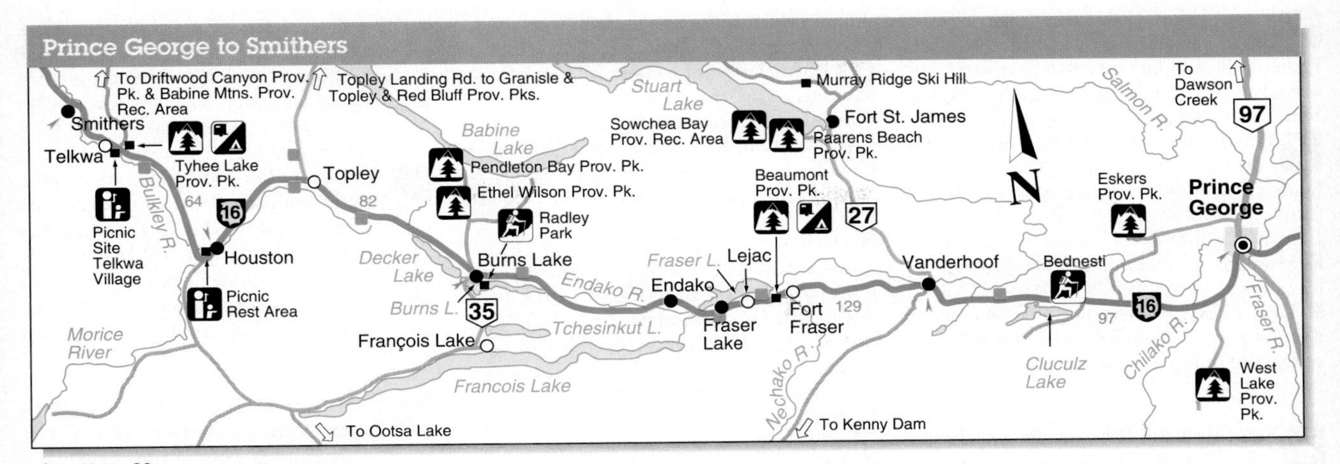


# SIDE TRIP

## to Fort St James

**Paarens Beach Provincial Park:** 43ha; 65 campsites. West off Hwy 27, 57km north of Vanderhoof, on Sowchea Rd. (15km west of Fort St James.) 565-6340. South end of 100km Stuart Lake. Fishing, boating, swimming, windsurfing. High winds and waves.

**Sowchea Bay Provincial Recreation Area:** 13ha; 30 campsites. On Sowchea Rd about 20km west of Fort St James, just past Paarens Beach. On Stuart Lake: boat launch, swimming, fishing. Watch for high winds and waves.

**Fort St James:** (Pop. 2,058). 62km north of Vanderhoof on Hwy 27. Founded by explorer Simon Fraser in 1806, headquarters of his "New Caledonia." Stunning lake and mountain setting, access to 300km chain of lakes and rivers. Not for neophyte navigators.

"The Fort" retains its pioneer feel. A busy, friendly little place with accommodation, stores, banks, and gas stations on the fringe of the great outdoors. Guiding, boat rentals.

**Fort St James Information:** Infocentre on Hwy 27 entering village. May-Sept. 996-7023 year-round. Or write Fort St James Chamber of Commerce, Box 1164, Fort St James, BC, V0J 1P0.

■ **Lady of Good Hope Church:** On Lakeshore Drive. Built 1873. BC's third oldest (Catholic) church.

■ **Junkers W-34 Replica:** In Cottonwood Park, on lakeshore, edge of town (walking distance). Memorial to "fly by the pants" bush pilots and the region's pioneer aviation history. The little park by the lake is a locals' favourite for picnicking and swimming.

■ **Russ Baker Memorial:** On Lakeshore Dr just north of town, .5km beyond old Catholic Church. For Frank Russel ("Russ") Baker who died Nov 15, 1958. In the 1930s he was one of area's first bush pilots. Before World War Two he founded Western Canada Airways here, and after the war, he started BC Airways, later Pacific Western Airlines.

■ **Fort St James National Historic Park:** 4ha on Chief Kwah Rd. 996-7191. Mid-May to late Sept. Splendidly restored Hudson's Bay Company fur-trade post on Stuart Lake. General warehouse and fur store (1888) and men's residence (1884); original buildings. Exhibits reveal harshness of life for early pioneers. Park staff in period costumes. Allow two good hours.

■ **Fort St James Hatchery:** At northern outskirts of village. Write Necoslie Indian Band, Box 1329, Fort St James, BC, V0J 1P0. 996-8575. Species here is chinook salmon; best time is mid-Sept to mid-April.

■ **Stuart Lake Golf Course:** Northwest of town on Stones Bay Rd, follow signs. Nine holes. Spectacular views of Stuart Lake.

■ **Mt Pope:** 5km northwest of town along Stones Bay Rd. Two-to-four-hour hike up, half that coming down. 996-7023. An old forestry lookout building at the top offers great view of Stuart Lake and other lakes around mountain.

■ **Native Pictographs:** On north shore of Stuart Lake between Fort St James and Pinchi Bay. Also on the shore facing Honeymoon Island. Accessible by boat only.

**Murray Ridge Ski Hill:** Follow main road about 1km north of Fort St James to Tachie Rd. Turn west and follow signs for 8km. 996-8513. Longest T-bar in North America (1,981m). Vertical drop is 518m. 20km cross-country ski trails.

**Takla Lake Marine Park:** About 160km northwest of Fort St James, west on Tachie Rd, then north on Leo Creek Forest Rd at Takla Narrows. 565-6340. Boat launching on cold deep Takla Lake. Good rainbow-trout fishing. Private resort, houseboat rental, BC's most isolated pub nearby.

Back on main road, Hwy 27 becomes known as the Omineca Mining Access Rd. Goes to some rugged country. Don't expect fast-food franchises and gas bars here. Gravel road is generally good; side roads may be difficult. Logging, guiding, prospecting, trapping are main activities.

**Manson Creek:** (Pop. 0). 180km north of Fort St James. Was temporary home to thousands during Omineca gold rush of early 1880s. Until recently, offered private accommodation, gas and diesel. General Store was source of all local knowledge. Now, it's small population has scattered hither and yon.

**Germansen Landing:** (Pop. 44). 27km beyond Manson Creek. Bridge across Omineca River. Fishing for large Dolly Varden. Boating. Emerald-coloured water. Mining area. Large deposits of jade at nearby Ogden Mountain. Omineca Mining Rd continues 220km to private mine site in Toodoggone River area.

## Return to Highway 16 in Vanderhoof

**Alternate Rd to Fort St James:** 7km west of Vanderhoof. Info sign.

**Sawmill:** 22km west of Vanderhoof on Hwy 16. Operated by Slocan Forest Products.

**The Last Spike:** 15km beyond sawmill. Plaque at south side of highway commemorates the last spike driven on the Grand Trunk Pacific Railway April 7, 1914.

**Fort Fraser:** (Pop. 370). Less than 1km from last spike. Trading post established by Simon Fraser in 1806 (4km west).

**Beaumont Provincial Park:** 191ha; 49 campsites; sani-station. On Fraser Lake, 4km west of Fort Fraser. 565-6340. Fine sandy beach. Saskatoons and huckleberries. Nautley River, north from park, flows less than 1km from lake to Nechako River.

**Drywilliam Lake Rest Area:** 4.5km beyond park. On lake.

**Lejac:** 6.5km beyond rest area, north side of highway. Site of old Indian Catholic residential school on First Nations Nadleh Whuten land. Former classroom building, and cemetery remain.

**Fraser Lake:** (Pop. 1,302). 5km beyond Lejac. Attractive lakeside setting. Bedroom community for sawmill at Lejac and Canada's largest molybdenum mine located southwest of here. Cattle ranching, tourism.

**Fraser Lake Information:** Infocentre on north side of highway. May-late Sept, hours vary. 699-8941. Off-season try Village Office 699-6257 or write Box 430, Fraser Lake, BC, V0J 1S0.

■ **Museum:** At infocentre. Tells the community's story.

■ **Lava Flows:** Flat top of Table Mountain, northwest of village. Remains of a volcanic cone 25 million years old. Gives hills their red tinge.

**François Lake Rd:** 4km west of Fraser Lake. Turn south down gravel road to resorts at east end of François Lake, 120km long, sometimes rough. Great lake views partly responsible for fairways missed at challenging Moly Hills Golf Course: 699-7761.

**Stellako River:** 4km from Fraser Lake. Premier fly-fishing stream for rainbow trout. Catch and release. Spectacular salmon-spawning run Aug-Sept.

**Endako Mine Rd:** 9km beyond Stellako River. Leads to Placer Dome Inc's molybdenum mine and alternate access to François Lake.

**Endako:** (Pop. 102). Just west of Endako Mine Rd. Divisional point on Grand Trunk Pacific Railway. During railway construction (1908-14), nearby tent town of Freeport housed 1,500 navvies, gamblers, and soiled doves.

**Savory Rest Area:** About 9km beyond Endako, south side of highway.

**Tintagel Cairn and Rest Area:** 43km beyond Endako, 11km east of Burns Lake. Contains a 45kg chunk of wall from King Arthur's Tintagel Castle in Cornwall, England. Symbolic tie to this tiny settlement of Tintagel.

**Burns Lake:** (Pop. 1,682). 129km west of Vanderhoof, 81km east of Houston. Far-flung populace of 8,000. Claim is: 4,828km worth of fishing in a 100km radius (17 or 18 lakes). Handsome carved-cedar trout displayed on village entrances.

Originally "Burnt Lake," after nearby forest fire. Building the Grand Trunk Pacific Railway (1908-14) ushered in stump farm and broadaxe era. Raising cattle in summer, cutting lodgepole-pine railway ties in winter.

Plethora of places to fish, camp, canoe, horseback ride, or explore, most within easy reach. Resorts for classic cross-country skiing, snowmobiling, and ice fishing.

Burns Lake is an access point to **Tweedsmuir Provincial Park**: 981,000ha. Call Smithers 847-7320 for information. This is BC's largest park and expansions are planned. Access only by boat (see *Side Trip to Ootsa Lake*, below), or floatplane. Visitors should be self-sufficient and wilderness-wise. Also see *Cariboo-Chilcotin*, p.202.

**Burns Lake Information:** Infocentre on Hwy 16 opposite William Konkin Elementary School. Year-round: winter weekdays 9-5; summer extended hours. 692-3773. Or write Burns Lake and District Chamber of Commerce, Box 339, Burns Lake, BC, V0J 1E0.

■ **Heritage Centre:** Includes Lakes District Museum with 1920s operating room, and logging paraphernalia. Weekdays in winter, extended hours in summer. 692-3773. 1943 forestry building houses arts centre. The "Bucket of Blood" is a fur-trading office turned gambling den and scene of a gruesome shooting.

**Hwy 35:** South off Hwy 16 at the eastern end of the village leads, ultimately, to Ootsa Lake.

## SIDE TRIP
### to Ootsa Lake

**Radley Park:** On Hwy 35, less than 1km from junction with Hwy 16. Small municipal park on Burns Lake. Boat launch.

**Eagle Creek Opal Deposits:** On Hwy 35, about 3km from junction. Turn west on Eagle Creek Rd. Rockhounders' delight. White and amber agates up to 5cm, and opals. Walking trails.

**François Lake Ferry:** 23km south of junction. Free ferry across lake to Southbank 21 times daily. Good fishing for rainbow and lake trout.

**Ootsa Lake:** 42km from François Lake ferry on sign-posted gravel road. Forest Service boat launch. Ootsa Lake is part of Nechako Reservoir and northern boundary of **Tweedsmuir Provincial Park**. Reservoir created in 1952 to power Aluminum Company of Canada's smelter at Kitimat. Shoreline of drowned forest and floating debris creates dangerous boating conditions.

**Wistaria Provincial Park:** 40ha. About 20km west of Ootsa Lake boat launch. 847-7320. Primarily boat launch ramp.

### Return to Highway 16 at Burns Lake

**Babine Lake Rd:** Follow signs from junction of Hwy 16 and 8th Ave in Burns Lake. Turn north from Yellowhead Hwy towards Babine Lake.

## SIDE TRIP
### to Babine Lake

**Ethel F Wilson Provincial Park:** 29ha; 10 campsites. On Pinkut Lake, 24km from Hwy 16 on gravel road. 847-7320. Park named for Ethel Wilson (1888-1980), author of novel *Swamp Angel*, about a woman escaping a troubled marriage and travelling to a remote lake in northern BC. Salmon spawning channels about 30km northeast of park on Babine Lake.

**Babine Lake:** Side roads of varying lengths lead to resorts and residences on lake. Main road leads 12km to Pendleton Bay Provincial Park. Longest natural lake in BC – slices 177km between mountain ridges. Creeks important for sockeye salmon spawning. Excellent summer lake fishing for large char and trout. Kokanee.

**Babine Provincial Marine Park System:** New provincial parks' initiative. Involves developing existing provincial parks on Babine Lake. 847-7320 or contact regional info centres for updates.

**Pendleton Bay Provincial Park:** 8ha; 20 campsites. Open May-Oct. 12km from Ethel Wilson Park. 847-7320. On Babine Lake. Has boat launch, and is popular spot for swimming and fishing.

**Pinkut Salmon Project:** About 50km from Burns Lake. Follow signs. Box 188, Burns Lake, BC, V0J 1E0. Radio phone: Burns Lake J-K, N622989. Sockeye salmon here: spawning in Sept.

### Return to Highway 16 at Babine Lake Road

**Carnoustie Golf Course:** 16km west of Babine Lake Rd. 698-7677. Open weather permitting. Nine holes on fairways carved out of the bush. Dining by reservation.

**Palling Rest Area:** 1km west of golf course, south side of highway.

**Burns Lake Airport:** 4km west of rest area. Landing strip adjacent highway.

**Six Mile (China Nose Mountain) Summit:** 20km beyond airport. El 1,423m. Gradual climb to highest point on Hwy 16. Offers splendid view of mountains and valley.

**Topley:** (Pop. 178). 10km down from Six Mile summit. Have a chin-wag with the locals in the café/store.

**Topley Landing Rd (Hwy 118):** Turn north in Topley for Granisle, 50km away.

## SIDE TRIP
### to Granisle

Road is paved, but drive slowly. Good chances of spotting moose, black bear, or coyotes.

**Finlay Falls Rest Area:** 7km north of Topley.

**Topley Provincial Park:** 12ha. Day use. Off Topley Landing Rd, 39km from Topley. 847-7320. A former Carrier native trapping and trading area. Private accommodation nearby. Fulton River flows into Babine Lake north of park. An easy 6.5km hike upstream to Millionaires Pool, below Fulton Falls. Bob Hope has fly-fished here.

**Fulton River Spawning Channels:** 40km from Topley. 697-2314. Box 9, Granisle, BC, V0J 1W0. Ask federal fisheries officers to explain how they're improving salmon egg survival 500 percent. Salmon return home late Aug.

**Red Bluff Provincial Park:** 75ha; 64 campsites. 5km beyond spawning channels. 847-7320. Named for iron-stained cliffs of ruddy hue. Good fishing and wildlife viewing, nature trails. Sandy beach, boat launch, swimming. Bald eagles.

**Granisle:** (Pop. 803). 50km north of Topley. Was copper mining town, but mines closed in 1992. Now outdoor recreation centre for Babine Lake. Adventure camping. Bones of extinct mammoth have been unearthed here – replicas at infocentre.

**Granisle Information:** At entrance to village. Year-round. 697-2428 or write Granisle Travel Information, Box 128, Granisle, BC, V0J 1W0.

■ **Old Fort and Fort Babine:** Native life here still conforms closely to traditional ways.

## Return to Topley on Highway 16

**Topley Rest Area:** 2km west of Topley, south side of highway.

**Houston:** (Pop. 3,628). 30km west of Topley, 64km south of Smithers. Started out in early 1900s as tie-cutting centre for Grand Trunk Pacific Railway. In the decades to follow, forest industry has kept Houston working.

But for play, there's the steelhead. Houston sports the world's largest fly-fishing rod, more than 18m long, with a reel 1m in diameter, a bright orange line, and 53cm long fly. A deft cast away from a nicely sculpted trout and salmon, suggesting scope of local angling.

Sitting in friendly clatter of a Houston coffee shop, talk is about clearcuts, cattle ranching, and probably fishing, breaking in new four-by-fours and going to the lake for the weekend. Young families everywhere. 70 percent of Houston's population is under 35. Day-long forestry tours can be reserved mid-June to Aug. 845-7640. Houston is at Bulkley-Morice rivers' junction, names to bring a lump to any dedicated steelhead fisherman's throat. Aug-Nov is prime steelhead time. Sockeye salmon run in summer. Wilderness canoeing on Nanika-Kidprice lake system.

Accommodation, two golf courses, groomed and natural cross-country skiing and hiking trails.

**Houston Information:** Infocentre on north side of Hwy 16 opposite Houston Shopping Centre, and under shadow of huge fishing rod. Year-round. 845-7640. Houston and District Chamber of Commerce, Box 396, Houston, BC, V0J 1Z0. Forest interpretation centre on site.

**Nadina River Salmon Project:** 3km west of Houston turn onto Morice Forest Rd. Follow past Owen Lake to Nadina Lake turnoff (Tahtsa Rd); follow Tahtsa Rd for 30km almost to Nadina Lake; signs lead to project. Sockeye salmon. Spawning peaks mid-Sept.

Leaving Houston, Hwy 16 crosses the Bulkley River and heads north. Watch for moose on road, particularly at night.

**Bulkley View Rest Area:** 43km west of Houston. Good leg-stretching spot.

**Telkwa:** (Pop. 959). On Hwy 16, some 49km beyond Houston. Picture-postcard village where the green Telkwa River meets the blue Bulkley. Community began in 1860s with arrival of Collins Overland Telegraph workers. Remained Bulkley Valley's economic centre until 1913 when railway diverted traffic. The river now remains an attraction for its salmon and steelhead pools. Novice and intermediate canoe runs. Scenic drive up Telkwa River Rd past old coal-mine workings.

**Telkwa Information:** Year-round from the Village Office, 846-5212. Box 220, Telkwa, BC, V0J 2X0.

■ **St Stephen's Anglican Church:** On Hwy 16. Built in 1910. Roofed English gate.

■ **Telkwa Museum:** On Hwy 16 next to post office. In a 1920 heritage building. Six days a week through summer. 846-5264. Self-guided heritage walk. Maps of 31 historic sites available at museum.

■ **Eddy Park:** On the Bulkley River, a pretty picnic spot.

*Bulkley River near Moricetown, north of*

**Telkwa High Rd:** About 1km west of village centre. Turn north and wind gently through farmlands of Glentanna and Driftwood on eastern benchlands of Bulkley River. Superb views of Hudson Bay Mountain. Rejoins Yellowhead at Moricetown, 35.5km north of Smithers.

**Tyhee Lake Provincial Park:** 33ha; 59 campsites; sani-station. 2km north of Telkwa off Telkwa High Rd. 847-7320. Long-lived pygmy whitefish. Family recreation. Marsh viewing platform to see common loons, red-necked grebes, ruffed grouse, beavers. Boat launch, swimming, hiking, wheelchair access.

**Another Rd to Babine Lake:** Turn east off Hwy 16, 9km beyond Telkwa, for Driftwood Canyon Provincial Park and Babine Mountains Recreation Area.

## SIDE TRIP
### to Babine Mountains

**Driftwood Canyon Provincial Park:** 23ha. 11km from Yellowhead Hwy. 847-7320. Fossils, 40-70 million years old, exposed in creek beds and canyon walls. Fernlike metasequoia, poplar, cranberry leaves. Occasional mosquito or fish fossils. Don't prospect in canyon walls, they are unstable. Removal of fossils prohibited.

**Babine Mountains Provincial Recreation Area:** 32,000ha. 4km beyond Driftwood Canyon Park. 847-7320. Telkwa High Rd also intersects this road to Babine Lake. Wilderness hiking and skiing into alpine country. Flowers at peak in Aug. ATVs restricted.

**Smithers Landing Provincial Park:** 90ha. On Babine Lake about 46km beyond Babine Mountains Provincial Recreation Area and 65km northeast of Smithers. 847-7320. New, undeveloped park with access to Babine Lake.

**Babine River Fish Counting Fence/ Fort Babine Salmon Enhancement:** 120km northeast of Smithers. Write Fort Babine Enterprises, Box 2292, Smithers, BC, V0J 2N0. Call Prince George Radio, Mt Dixon Ch, N693569. Sockeye, coho, pink, and chinook salmon. Prime fall steelhead fishing in Babine River. Camping.

## Return to Highway 16

About 11km beyond Telkwa, Hwy 16 crosses Bulkley River and enters Smithers. See *Smithers to Prince Rupert*, following.

# Smithers to Prince Rupert

## YELLOWHEAD HIGHWAY (Highway 16)

This section of the Yellowhead travels southwest, down into the land of 'Ksan. *'Ksan* means River of the Mists, Water of the Clouds – the Tsimshian native root of the river's now more common name, Skeena. The Skeena and its tributaries form a massive white-water system that drains more than 39,000 sq km of northwestern BC.

Perhaps it's the Skeena's misty, moody nature that has inspired the potent and still ascendant native culture here. Native peoples have travelled and used this area for at least 8,000 years, and have occupied it continuously for 4,000 years. The river has provided transportation and food. Cedar canoes 18m long once navigated between villages. Eulachon or candle fish, coho, chinook, sockeye, pink, and chum were and are still plentiful. The Kispiox River, a major tributary, is perhaps the world's most famous steelhead fishing stream.

In small native villages along Hwy 16, visitors are invited to witness both ancient and newly carved poles which stand singly or in clusters beside native homes. All that is asked is your appreciation and respect.

The *Log* starts in Smithers from the infocentre at the junction of Main St and Hwy 16. Smithers is halfway along the wide Bulkley River, the Skeena's major tributary. At Hazelton, the Bulkley adds its considerable volume to the Skeena, which then makes its way to the sea. The transition to lush cedar and hemlock forests indicates the influence of the Pacific Ocean. It is 354km to ferry terminals in Prince Rupert.

**Smithers:** (Pop. 5,029). 64km north of Houston, 68km south of New Hazelton. Centre of Bulkley Valley. Smithers' atmosphere is set by the commanding presence of Hudson Bay Mountain. The 2,621m classically shaped peak appears etched upon the sky. Elsewhere, a main street of Bavarianlike architecture, red brick sidewalks, and the statue of a man playing an alpenhorn, might seem contrived.

Grand Trunk Pacific Railway selected the town site in 1913. Legends of the Gitksan-Wet'suwet'en people tell of a shallow swampy lake where Smithers is now, extending east 212km to Fraser Lake. Perhaps that accounts for the fertile soils of the Bulkley Valley. Agriculture, forestry, mining, and tourism are key industries. Wet'suwet'en arts and crafts are available. Excellent outdoor recreation area.

**Smithers Information:** In Canadian National Railway parlour car on east side of Hwy 16. Sani-station. May-Sept. 847-9854. Off-season Smithers and District Chamber of Commerce, Box 2379, Smithers, BC, V0J 2N0.

■ **Riverside Recreation Centre:** On Bulkley River. Full-service RV park, golf course, restaurant.

■ **Central Park Building:** Municipal heritage structure built in 1925. At 1425 Main St behind infocentre. Houses Chamber of Commerce, Smithers Art Gallery, and Bulkley Valley Museum with some 5,000 artifacts. Art Gallery is year-round, 847-3898. Museum displays include minerals, fossils, railway memorabilia. 847-5322.

■ **Ski Smithers:** Premier downhill skiing from 1,676m Hudson Bay Mountain. 18 runs, gentle to challenging. Triple chair, two T-bars, full services. Vertical drop 530m. Day lodges, rentals, child-minding, lessons. Season Nov-late April. Access road 22.5km from downtown Smithers. 847-2058 or toll-free in BC: 1-800-665-4299.

■ **Smithers Golf and Country Club:** 1km west of Smithers on Hwy 16 (Scotia Rd). 847-3591. 18 holes overlooking Hudson Bay Mountain.

■ **Views:** From Ski Hill Rd. Bulkley Valley and access to alpine meadows.

■ **Forest Tours:** 847-2656 during summer.

**Kathlyn Lake Rd:** Turn west about 4km from Smithers.

## SIDE TRIP

### to Lake Kathlyn Glacier

**Municipal Campground:** On Kathlyn Lake Rd. Popular picnic spot.

**Glacier Gulch and Twin Falls:** Follow signs on Kathlyn Lake Rd. 2km-wide gulch has twin waterfalls cascading 152m down canyon walls. Easy .5km trail leads to base of south falls. Moderate hike to 120m thick Lake Kathlyn Glacier.

### Return to Highway 16

**Smithers Airport:** 5km west of Smithers, east off Hwy 16. Daily jet service to Vancouver, Terrace, Prince Rupert, and Prince George.

**Hudson Bay Rest Area:** 3.5km beyond road to airport. Excellent view of Hudson Bay Mountain Glacier.

**Adams' Igloo Wildlife Museum:** Beside rest area. Mounted displays.

**Moricetown:** (Pop. 680). 31.5km beyond Smithers. Native village named for Father AG Morice, missionary here, 1885-1904. Spring salmon have been caught here for 5,000 years. Bulkley River narrows to 15m at base of falls. Locals fish with gaffs, standing poised on rocks above the milling salmon. 57kg specimen speared in 1950s. Private campsite. Craft shop.

**Ross Lake Provincial Park:** 307ha. 30km from Moricetown. Day-use park. Canoeing, swimming, fly-fishing, hiking. No power boats.

**New Hazelton:** (Pop. 786). 67km northwest of Smithers. Dominated by Mt Rocher Déboulé, mountain of "rolling stone," named by the miners who explored its peak and were constantly threatened by landslides and large rolling boulders. To the native Gitksan and Wet'suwet'en people in this region, the mountain has always been Stii-Kyo-Din. They tell of the ancient city state, Dimlahamid or Tam-Lax-Aamid or Dzilke, stretching for miles where the Kitwanga Back Rd is now. Here all people lived together as one, until a flock of supernatural one-horned goats sent the peak of Stii-Kyo-Din hurtling down as punishment after mountain goats were killed for sport. Subsequent wars and ecological disasters led to the abandonment of what may very well have been one of the continent's greatest societies.

New Hazelton, 1914. The scene of a gunfight never matched in the Canadian West. Seven Russian anarchists, having once successfully stolen the railway's payroll, attempted to steal it again. Within two minutes of the hold-up, 200 bullets had zinged between townsfolk and thieves (police were nowhere). When all quieted down, three robbers were dead, three were wounded (later deported), and one escaped. *He* had the money.

**Hazelton Area Information:** At junction of Yellowhead Hwy and Hwy 62 north. Beside fibreglass statues of Jean Jacques Caux (Cataline, a legendary packer) and a generic miner and logger. Provides info for the three Hazeltons: New Hazelton, "Old Town" Hazelton, and South Hazelton. June-Sept. 842-6071. Off-season write New Hazelton Travel Infocentre, Box 340, New Hazelton, BC, V0J 2J0. 842-6571.

**Hwy 62:** Turn north off Yellowhead Hwy at infocentre in New Hazelton. In about 2km highway crosses Bulkley River Canyon on one-lane Hagwilget suspension bridge. River is a dizzying 76m below. Natives used to sway across the gorge on footbridge of poles lashed with cedar bark rope.

## SIDE TRIP

### to Hazelton and Kispiox

**Hazelton:** (Pop. 339). 6km northwest of New Hazelton on Hwy 62. Hazelton, at junction of Bulkley and Skeena rivers, is heart and soul of vibrant Gitksan culture. This is living, breathing stuff, past and present fused into 'Ksan. Seven communal houses recreated where villages have stood for 7,000 years.

White man is a new neighbour, arriving around 1866. Sternwheelers puffed up from the coast through misty Skeena shoals and canyons riverboat captains claimed were as capricious as a temperamental mistress. Initially boats carried supplies for telegraph link with Europe via Bering Strait. In the end, what they did was open up the Skeena Valley for settlers and agriculture. By 1910 they were bringing supplies for the building of Canada's second transcontinental railway which, of course, ended the steamboat era. The road came through in 1944.

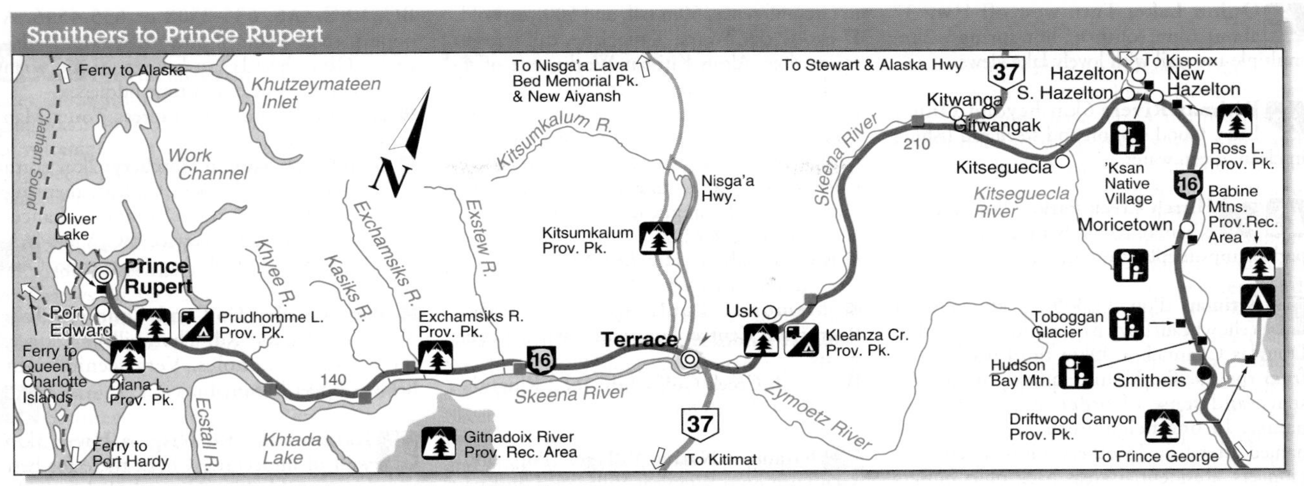


Old Town Hazelton could be a movie set with its Victorian buildings and the characters who once lived there. Cataline was a famed packer and guide with legendary stamina; and Simon Gunanoot was an accused murderer whose bush craft let him elude RCMP for 13 years.

**Hazelton Information:** Village office, 842-5991, or write Hazelton Infocentre, Box 340, New Hazelton, BC, V0J 2J0.

■ **'Ksan:** Native village and museum on High Level Rd. 842-5544. Reconstructed Gitksan village. 'Ksan dancers perform Fri evenings July-Aug. Gift shop and carving school open year-round.

■ **Northwestern National Exhibition Centre:** On 'Ksan grounds. Daily June-Aug; Thurs-Mon, Sept-May. Longhouse, Gitksan artifacts. 842-5723. Private campsite, good fishing.

■ **Hands of History Tour:** 113km loop tour between Hazelton and Kitwanga. About 14 historical plaques along route.

■ **Walking Tour of Hazelton:** Original steam donkey, paddlewheelers, and 100-year-old St Peter's Anglican church. Check with village office.

■ **Abandoned Gold and Silver Mines:** Ask at village office about hiking trails.

Hwy 62 leaves Hazelton and crosses the Skeena on its way to Kispiox.

**Kispiox:** (Pop. 532). 13km north of Hazelton on Kispiox Valley Rd, at junction of Kispiox and Skeena rivers. Traditional Gitksan village with Frog, Wolf, and Fireweed clans. Name means "people of the hiding place." Totem pole grounds are phenomenal. Locally operated salmon hatchery. Tours on request. 842-6384. Also, the Bent Box Gallery, featuring work of local artist Arthur Wilson, is usually open 10 - 4.

A world-renowned steelhead river, with fishing camps, guiding and rafting services. Check infocentre. Steelhead run Sept-Nov; coho salmon Aug-Sept.

**Kispiox Information:** Infocentre on south side after crossing Kispiox River. Next to Band Administration office. June-Sept. 842-5248. Off-season write Travel Infocentre, RR 1, Box 25, Kispiox, BC, V0J 1Y0. 842-5248.

## Return to New Hazelton on Highway 16

**South Hazelton Access Rd:** 3km west of New Hazelton. Turn north.

**South Hazelton:** (Pop. 654). Lodging, services. Road rejoins Hwy 16.

**Seeley Lake Provincial Park:** 24ha; 20 campsites. 10km west of New Hazelton. 847-7320. Secluded campsites. Use binoculars to spot old mine workings on flanks of Mt Rocher Déboulé. Cutthroat and rainbow trout fishing.

**Kitseguecla:** (Pop. 247). 16km beyond Seeley Lake Park on Kitseguecla River straddling Hwy 16. Native community with fine totem poles.

**Hwy 37 North (Stewart-Cassiar Hwy):** Near Kitwanga, 16km beyond Kitseguecla, 91km northeast of Terrace, leads a short distance to communities of Gitwangak, Kitwanga, and Gitanyow. It's 722km to Yukon border. For details, see *Stewart-Cassiar Hwy*, p.223.

**Seven Sisters Mountain Peaks:** 6km past junction with Hwy 37.

**Boulder Creek Rest Area:** 9km west of Hwy 37 junction.

**Skeena River Boat Passage:** 33km west of Hwy 37 junction. Where steamboats churned up the Skeena as early as 1866.

**Sanderson Point Rest Area:** 60km beyond Hwy 37 junction.

**Usk Ferry:** On Hwy 16, 12km from rest area. On-demand reaction ferry crosses Skeena to small community of Usk. Note tiny Usk Pioneer Chapel east of highway.

**Kleanza Creek Provincial Park:** 269ha; 23 campsites. 4km from Usk Ferry Rd (10km east of Terrace). 847-7320. Abandoned gold mine. But try panning: a 180g nugget was taken from creek in 1934. *Kleanza* is Gitksan word for gold. 4.5km Bornite Mountain trail starts in park. Canyon, waterfalls, fishing. Wheelchair access.

**Hwy 37 South:** 15.5km beyond Kleanza Creek Park turnoff, at outskirts of Terrace. 57km paved road south to Kitimat. Lake and mountain views.

## SIDE TRIP
### to Kitimat and Kitamaat

**Terrace-Kitimat Airport:** Turn west on access road 5km south of Hwy 37/16 junction. Daily jet service to Vancouver, Prince Rupert, Smithers, and Prince George.

**Lakelse Lake Provincial Park:** 362ha; 156 campsites, also group camping. Park headquarters 9km south of airport. Campground at Furlong Bay 4.5km beyond. 798-2277.

In local Tsimshian language, *Lakelse* means freshwater mussel. Fishing is great. Natural beaches. Twin Spruce self-guiding nature trail. Mature forests. Williams Creek is spawning stream for sockeye salmon end of Aug. Moose, wolf, bear, and cougar. Trumpeter swans winter over. Amphitheatre, visitor program, showers, boat launch, swimming, fishing, wheelchair access. Commercial resorts.

**Lakelse Hot Springs:** A few km beyond park headquarters. Odourless mineral hot springs. Nine very hot pools (from 42 to 72 degrees C). Most pools inaccessible, and too hot for bathing, but their water has been channelled into resorts here since 1910. Today's place to soak is **Mount Layton Hot Springs Resort**. Year-round. Waterslides into hot pools. $1-million ozone treatment plant. Motel, Splashdown Lounge, coffee shop. 798-2214, or 1-800-663-3862.

Hwy 16 hugs coast north of Skidegate with views across Hecate Strait. Look for California grey whales breaking water late April-June. Rainbows are extraordinary.

**Tlell:** (Pop. 138). 36km north of Skidegate. Picturesque grassy estuary of Tlell River. First homesteaded by Mexican Tom, in 1904. Coho salmon, migrating shore birds late summer. Richardson Ranch, oldest working ranch in Charlottes (1919). The sea is not far away – mile after mile of sand dunes and driftwood. The people are welcoming. Ask Dorothy Bellis, at the Bellis Lodge and Hostel, about the Haida chief who paddled his chair across the sea. Also info on fishing, berry picking, and what's interesting about the neighbours.

**Naikoon Provincial Park:** 72,641ha covering almost entire northeast corner of Graham Island. 36 campsites at Agate Beach Campground on the north end; 30 sites at Misty Meadows near Tlell. Wheelchair access. Also primitive campsites throughout park. 557-4390 or 847-7320. Park headquarters at Tlell on Yellowhead Hwy. Access to southern end is at Tlell; to northern end 25km, mostly gravel, from Masset causeway.

Naikoon is an intriguing combination of low-lying swamps, stunted pine and cedar, lakes, sand dunes, beaches. *Nai-Kun* is the Haida word meaning "long nose of the Nai," for Rose Spit at the park's far north end.

■ **Pesuta:** (or *Pezuta*). South-end access. Shipwreck in Naikoon Park is about 5km west of Tlell River bridge through forest and sand. Half-buried hull of 1928 log carrier.

■ **Tow Hill:** North-end access. Trail leads 15 minutes from parking lot through heavy rain forest to top of hill for views of mainland and Alaska. Site was largest of Haida villages within park boundaries. Tow Hill's 109m basalt cliff is the most prominent landmark on northeast coast. Visit nearby blowhole. Agates on beach.

■ **Rose Spit:** North-end access. 17km along beach from parking lot. Rose Spit is an ecological reserve.

■ **East Beach Hike:** 94km of sand dunes, driftwood, and deer, from Tlell to Tow Hill. Takes 4-6 days. Limited water but no dangerous headlands. Some shelters.

Yellowhead Hwy swings abruptly northwest from the coast, leaving Tlell.

**Port Clements:** (Pop. 483). 21km northwest of Tlell on Masset Inlet, between the Kumdis and Yakoun rivers. Centre of World War One airplane building industry using wood from huge spruce trees. Logging still main industry. Bedroom community for MacMillan Bloedel's operations at Juskatla. Call 557-4212 before using logging roads. Nearly the whole town gathers at dock to see purse seiners in action when season opens.

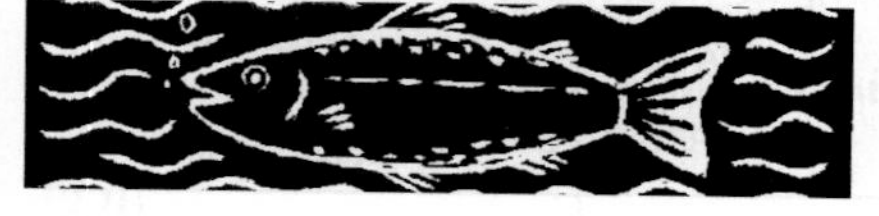

**Port Clements Information:** Village of Port Clements, Box 198, Port Clements, BC, V0T 1R0.

■ **Port Clements Museum:** 45 Bayview Dr (main road into town). Open each afternoon except Mon, June-Sept. Winter hours depend on availability of volunteers. 557-4576.

■ **Golden Spruce:** Watch for marker in pullout about 5.5km south of Port Clements on Juskatla Rd. Ten-minute walk on trail to river, then look across and up at genetically unusual spruce whose needles are bleached by the sun. Scientific world still puzzled by phenomenon of this spectacular golden tree. Experts are trying to reproduce it.

■ **Haida Canoe:** On east side of Juskatla Rd 8km from Golden Spruce trail marker. Short walk on trail. Old cedar dugout canoe abandoned before it was completed, more than a century ago. Not much left but one gets the idea. Bow of canoe points to stump of tree it was taken from. Discovered by loggers in Yakoun Valley. Largest Haida canoes were 23m long with a 2m beam and could carry 40 people.

■ **Marie Lake Salmon Hatchery:** 40km south of Port Clements on logging road. Write Masset Indian Band, Box 189, Masset, BC, V0T 1M0. Chinook, coho, sockeye.

Watch for black-tailed Sitka deer along roadside north of Port Clements.

**Pure Lake Provincial Park:** 130ha. North of Port Clements. Day use. Warm lake for swimming. Canoeing, fishing.

**Masset:** (Pop. 1,476). 40km north of Port Clements. Masset, on Masset Sound, is largest community in Charlottes. At terminus of Hwy 16. Canadian Forces base here. All travellers' services. RV park open year-round. Road access to north end of Naikoon Provincial Park on Tow Hill Rd. Fishing trips for salmon, halibut, abalone, and crab. Beachcombing. Restaurants, accommodation, groceries.

**Masset Information:** Travel infocentre, About 400m from the "Welcome to Masset" sign on the east side of the highway. 626-3982. Daily June-late Aug. Off-season, Chamber of Commerce, Box 420, Port Clements, BC, V0T 1R0. 557-4600.

■ **Delkatla Wildlife Sanctuary:** 554ha in Masset. Haven for weary wings on Pacific flyway for migratory birds. Some 113 species identified.

**Old Masset:** (Pop. 700). About 2km north of Masset at entrance to harbour. Largest Haida village in Charlottes. On site of three ancient Haida town sites. Artists' galleries are also their homes.

■ **Ed Jones Haida Museum:** Haida artifacts, photos, map showing ancient village sites, in old schoolhouse. Staff can tell you about Old Massett, pointing out houses where chiefs and artists live.

## Moresby Island

Visitors arrive on Moresby by ferry from Graham Island or by air.

**Sandspit:** (Pop. 702). About 13km from Alliford Bay, Moresby Island terminus for ferry sailings to Skidegate Landing on Graham Island.

**Sandspit Airport:** Main airport for Queen Charlotte Islands. Scheduled flights to Vancouver (Time Air), and Prince Rupert (Trans-Provincial Airlines). Charter operators for visits to South Moresby.

Most logging roads on North Moresby are controlled by Fletcher Challenge Canada Ltd. Before travelling visit their office on Beach Rd about 3km from airport or call 637-5323. Forest tours available.

**Gray Bay:** BC Forest Service/MacMillan Bloedel campsites about 21km southeast of Sandspit. Hard sand and gravel beaches. It really is peaceful.

**Mosquito Lake Park:** 11 rural campsites, about 44km southwest of Sandspit. Operated by Western Forest Products and BC Forest Service. Named for the Second World War mosquito bombers. Sitka spruce for building bombers was harvested from area, and is still treasured for making fine pianos and guitars.

**Pallant Creek Hatchery:** About 46km southwest of Sandspit. Chum, pink, coho. Spawning mid-Sept to Oct. See adult chum Feb-May, juvenile coho March-June. Write Box 225, Sandspit, BC, V0T 1C0.

**Moresby Camp:** 2km beyond Pallant Creek. Boat-launching site for exploring Cumshewa Inlet and Moresby Islands.

## South Moresby

*Gwaii Haanas*, or South Moresby, about 15 percent (147,000ha) of the Queen Charlotte archipelago's land mass, was formally declared a national park reserve in July 1988. This is a wilderness area, there are no roads or shore facilities. Environment Canada info offices in Queen Charlotte City, 559-8818, and Sandspit, 637-5362. Also check with infocentres or boat charter operators for up-to-date information.

There are several abandoned Haida villages that can be visited on South Moresby; however they are all remote, and only accessible by boat or air. Visit Skidegate Band Council office for permission.

**Anthony Island:** 140ha. Site of Ninstints ancient Kunghit Haida native village in South Moresby. The island was tragically abandoned in the 1880s after massacres by American fur traders, and a smallpox plague in the 1860s. Not one Kunghit remains today. Ninstints was declared a UNESCO world cultural heritage site in 1981.

Visit by permission of parks branch and Skidegate Indian Band Council. Call Haida Gwaii Watchmen, in Skidegate,559-8225. Access by boat or helicopter, is difficult and weather dependent.

## Stewart-Cassiar Highway

### HIGHWAY 37

The Stewart-Cassiar Hwy runs north linking Yellowhead Hwy 16 with the Alaska Hwy, 725km. It leaves the Yellowhead near Kitwanga, and joins the Alaska Hwy 23km west of Watson Lake, 432km east of Whitehorse.

Most of the Stewart-Cassiar is paved. Less than 200km remains gravel. The highway is being continuously improved but rough and broken pavement sections require that care be taken. Distances are great, communities and travellers' services few. Keep the gas tank topped up and carry spare tires. Local people are friendly and informal. Native communities of Gitwangak and Gitanyow offer chances to experience native culture.

The scenery is spectacular and varied. Wildlife is abundant. The highway, built in sections over many years and completed in 1972, is becoming increasingly popular as a destination in itself. Travel *Log* starts where Yellowhead Hwy 16 intersects Stewart-Cassiar Hwy 37, 35km west of Hazelton.

Hwy 37 crosses the Skeena River immediately north of its junction with the Yellowhead.

**Gitwangak:** (Pop. 424). East off Hwy 37, .5km north of Hwy 16 junction. Less than 2km down a narrow road. Name means Land of the Rabbits; long ago there was an abundance. The three village clans are Eagle, Wolf, and Frog, each with a hereditary chief and its own fishing and hunting territory.

Visitors are encouraged to stroll through, take photographs of the tall totems (at least one was erected as early as 1875), and ask questions. Drive carefully in village.

■ **St Paul's Anglican Church:** Opposite totems. Built 1893. Stained-glass windows travelled from England. Services held regularly, visitors welcome. Gitwangak tourist information may also be available here.

The Gitwangak road rejoins Hwy 37 almost 4km from the Yellowhead Hwy.

**Kitwanga:** (Pop. 30). South-access road is 4km north of Yellowhead Hwy 16. Basic travellers' services. Sawmilling main occupation. Pretty village with great views of 2,900m peaks of Seven Sisters Mountains. School playground good vantage point for photographs. Try Mill Pond for swimming, Bard's Hole, on Kitwanga River, for fishing. Ask if local craftsmen have work for sale.

**Kitwanga Information:** Kitwanga Community and Association, Box 98, Kitwanga, BC, V0J 2A0.

■ **Kitwanga National Historic Site:** On Kitwanga Valley Rd. Year-round. Known locally as Battle Hill or *Ta'awdzep*. Nearly 200 years ago, a warrior, Nekt, bedecked in an armour of grizzly bear skins and slate, used the 13m hill as stronghold to control fishing and trade routes. Self-guiding trail. Call Fort St James National Historic Park : 996-7191.

**Kitwanga Rd North:** 2.5km north of south access. Alternate route to Kitwanga.

**Grease Trail:** Hwy 37 north of Kitwanga parallels route taken by Coastal natives to trade greasy eulachons (tiny saltwater fish) with Interior tribes.

**Gitanyow:** (Pop. 308). 14km north of Kitwanga north access, just west of Hwy 37. Formerly **Kitwancool**, meaning "people of a small village." Depleted over a century ago by disease and warfare, Kitwancool has recently reclaimed its former name, Gitanyow, "awesome warrior people." Here are 18 major poles, including the oldest, "Hole in the Ice" or "Hole in the Sky." This powerful totem, dramatically perforated with a large oval opening, is about 140 years old. Some poles may be removed for repairs. Carvers work in shop nearby. Visitors are encouraged to ask them about their work.

**Gitanyow Information:** Infocentre, Gitanyow Band Council, Box 340, Kitwanga, BC, V0J 2A0. 849-5222. Centre is on 1st Ave, main road into village, next to Pentecostal Church. Open late June-Sept.

**Gitanyow Rd North:** About 5km beyond south access. Alternate route to Gitanyow.

**Moonlit Creek Rest Area:** About 4.5km from Gitanyow north access. East side of highway. Route Map.

**Kitwancool Lake:** Access about 2km north of rest area and again about 8km. Lake, sometimes referred to as Kitwanga Lake, is off old highway to the west and below Hwy 37. Roads often in poor condition.

**Nass River Forest Service Rd:** About 40km beyond Kitwancool Lake; 74km north of Hwy 37/16 junction, just before the second crossing of the Cranberry River. The Nass or Cranberry Rd turns west off Hwy 37 leading 160km to Terrace. Active logging road: take care. Small Forest Service Campground 45km from Hwy 37, at Dragon Lake. Good salmon fishing in Cranberry River. Watch for bears. For info on **Nisga'a Memorial Lava Bed Park**, see *Smithers to Prince Rupert*, p.218.

**Fasten Seat Belts:** Highway becomes an airstrip about 47km beyond Nass River Forest Service Rd. Highway also doubles as an emergency airstrip about 27km north of 1st crossing of Bell-Irving River, see below. Aircraft have right of way.

**Nass River Bridge:** 65km north of Nass River Forest Service Rd; 138km north of Hwy 16. Rest area east side of highway. Crosses 122m-wide Nass River gorge. One-lane bridge, opened in 1972, was final link completing Hwy 37.

**Meziadin Fish Ladders:** Turn west about 300m beyond bridge. More than a quarter million salmon, mainly sockeye, use these ladders July to mid-Sept en route to spawning streams.

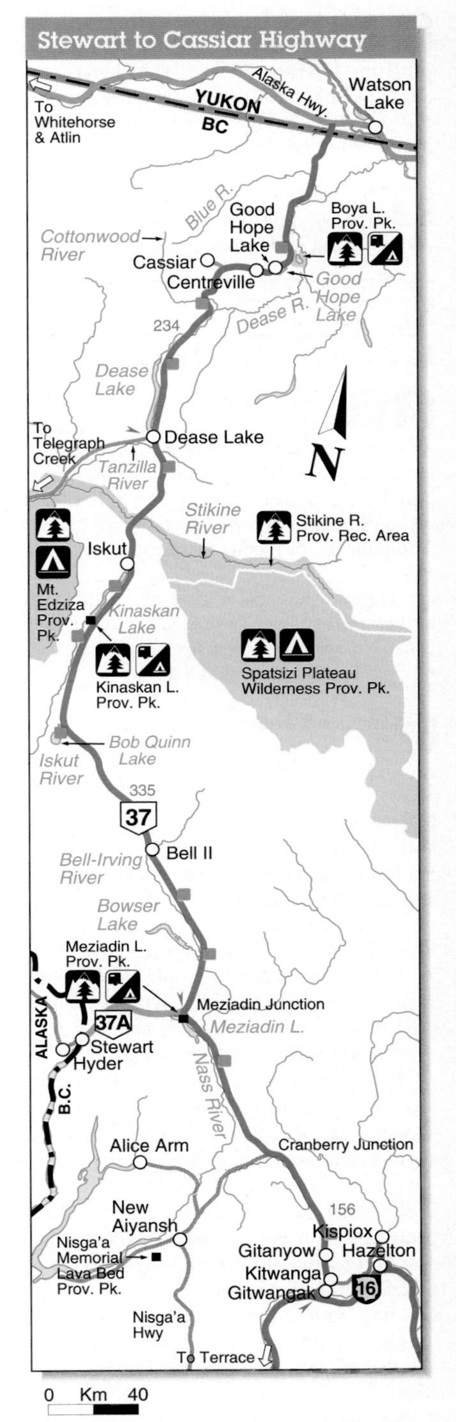


**Meziadin Lake Provincial Park:** 335ha; 46 campsites. 12km beyond Nass River bridge. 847-7320. Popular spot with boat launch, canoeing, wildlife viewing. Wheelchair access. Extremely busy July-Aug.

**Meziadin Junction:** (Pop. 7). 1.5km beyond road to park. From here 160km south to Hwy 16, 570km north to Alaska Hwy. Small community: accommodation, food, gas, repairs.

**Meziadin Information:** Infocentre is log building on north side of highway at junction of Hwys 37 and 37A. Late June-Sept. No phone. Off-season write Stewart Historical Society, Box 402, Stewart, BC, V0T 1W0 or call 636-2568.

**Hwy 37A:** Paved road heads west 62km to Stewart. A "Will you look at that!" drive between walls of rock, forest, and ice.

## SIDE TRIP

### to Stewart and Hyder

**Strohn Lake:** About 24km beyond Hwy 37A junction. Lake created by melting Bear Glacier, still retreating. It's grubby from glacial debris on top, but incredibly blue inside crevices. Glows at night. Rest area on south side of highway, 1km before glacier. Also pullouts for picture taking.

Highway and glacial river plunge through narrow Bear Canyon, a year-round active slide zone. **No stopping.** When road widens, scan mountainsides for mountain goats.

**Clements Lake:** About 22km past Bear Glacier. Pretty Forest Service recreation site and hiking trail on south side of highway.

**Stewart:** (Pop. 1,151). 62km southwest of Meziadin Junction, on BC/Alaska border. Canada's most northerly ice-free port, at head of Portland Canal.

Stewart's fortunes have varied with those of hard-rock gold, silver, and copper miners. In 1910, some 10,000 people lived in the area. The town was built on pilings above tidal flats, its remains are still visible. Locals take boom-and-bust cycles in stride.

Something always turns up, like in the movies. Three major movie producers have chosen Stewart's rugged mountains, limitless snow, and frontier atmosphere. Tour old mining areas and movie locations. Moderately difficult hiking trails, some rewarded by icefield panoramas. Bus tours to **Salmon Glacier**. See *below.* Excellent salt-water fishing in Portland Canal. Need separate licences for Canada and US. Boat rentals. Campsites, accommodation, stores, restaurant, gas station. Ferry to Ketchikan, Alaska, leaves every Monday, May-Sept.

**Stewart Information:** Infocentre in former fire hall, now museum, at 6th and Columbia. Open late June-Sept. 636-2111. Off-season write District of Stewart, Box 460, Stewart, BC, V0T 1W0. 636-2251.

■ **Museum:** At infocentre. 1910 building has mining, logging, transportation, and wildlife exhibits. Stewart Historical Society: 635-2568.

■ **Salmon Glacier:** Spectacular. First views are about 90km from Stewart via gravel road into US – and out again: the road leads northeast, back into Canada. Glacier is well worth the trip, but the road is unmarked, and rough.

**Hyder, USA:** (Est pop. 70). 3km from Stewart in Alaska. Border marked with stone storehouse built in 1896. No customs office either side, but RCMP conduct spot checks. Canada Customs regulations posted.

Hyder's claim to fame today is its two bars. Take a shot glass of pure grain alcohol in a gulp to become formally "Hyderized".

■ **Fish Creek:** 5km beyond Hyder. Becomes choked with spawning chum salmon late July, early Aug. Bald eagles and black bears feast. Don't get close to bears.

### Return to Highway 37 at Meziadin Junction

Pavement ends just beyond junction. Use headlights at all times. Road strikes north through wild country with Coast Mountains to west and Skeena Mountains, east.

**Bell-Irving River Crossing No. 1 Rest Area:** 31km north of Meziadin. Bear country.

**Hodder Lake Rest Area:** 57km beyond Bell-Irving No.1 crossing.

**Bell-Irving River:** Highway crosses again, 3km beyond Hodder Lake rest area. First services in a while. Food, lodging, gas, minor repairs. Dominion Telegraph Line (1889-1901) ran along river's north side.

**Ningunsaw Pass:** 25km north of Bell-Irving River. Summit 466m. Divide between Nass and Stikine river drainages. Try deep bankside pools of Ningunsaw River for Dolly Varden.

**Bob Quinn Airport and Lake:** 22km north of Ningunsaw Summit. New landing strip, not shared with highway traffic. Just west is attractive, mountain-fringed Bob Quinn Lake.

**Iskut Burn Rest Area:** 21km beyond Bob Quinn Lake. 31,566ha destroyed in 1958. Growing in well with pine, spruce, deciduous species.

**Eastman Creek Rest Area:** About 28km beyond Iskut Burn rest area.

**Trail to Natadesleen Lake:** About 12km from Eastman Creek rest area. 1km walk. Fishing for rainbow trout.

**Kinaskan Lake Provincial Park:** 1,800ha; 50 campsites. 8km from Natadesleen Lake trail. 847-7320. Camp at lake's south end. Easy boat launching, good rainbow trout fishing. Boat required to reach head of Mowdade Trail from Kinaskan Park. Trail leads northwest 24km into **Mount Edziza Provincial Park**. Not for the inexperienced. For access information, check guides and outfitters in Iskut area, north about 56km. See continuation of *Log.* For full details on Mount Edziza Park *Side Trip to Telegraph Creek,* below.

**Tatogga Lake:** About 25km beyond Kinaskan Lake Park. Resort, gas, food, information. Tatogga Lake is a southern extension of Eddontenajon Lake.

**Ealue Lake Rd:** Turns northeast off Hwy 37 about 2km north of Tatogga Lake Resort. Follow past private campsite at Ealue Lake. Road crosses the Klappan River and intercepts abandoned BC Rail bed 22km from Hwy 37. Turn southeast along bed. Parallels southwestern boundary of Spatsizi Plateau Wilderness Park for 60km. Bed is rough, narrow, and may be impassable in bad weather. Check before leaving Hwy 37. Access is only to trail heads leading into park. No direct road access.

## SIDE TRIP

### to Spatsizi Park

**Spatsizi Plateau Wilderness Provincial Park:** 656,785ha. No road access. Located 300 air km north of Smithers. 847-7320. Write BC Parks Skeena District Office, Bag 5000, 3790 Alfred Ave, Smithers, BC, V0J 2N0.

One of Canada's largest and most significant parks. Quintessential wilderness, Spatsizi encompasses rolling Spatsizi Plateau and glaciated Skeena Mountains. Only for experienced hikers and campers.

Large wildlife populations, including woodland cariboo. Spatsizi, in Dene language, means red goat, for goat's habit of rolling in iron oxide dust. Gladys Lake ecological reserve for study of Stone sheep and mountain goats. Over 140 species of birds, including gyrfalcons.

"From the time of creation, slowly and inevitably this tiny segment of our world had heaved, erupted, and finally been scraped by the ice until it won its present glory. No wonder mountain people are moved to simple prayer in the natural cathedral of an unaltered wilderness," wrote Tommy Walker, one of the first to call for Spatsizi's protection.

Floatplanes can be chartered from Hwy 37 communities or Smithers and Terrace. Local guides and outfitters on Hwy 37 offer horseback trips. Air sightseeing tours. Eight cabins, sauna, and cookhouse for public use at Cold Fish Lake, year-round, first-come, first-served basis. Riverboat and canoe trips can also be arranged. Look for the book *Spatsizi,* by TA Walker.

**Tatlatui Provincial Park:** 105,826ha. No road access. A magnificent wilderness that adjoins Spatsizi Park. Similar to Spatsizi in landscape and wildlife, great for anglers. Floatplanes most common access. 847-7320.

### Return to Highway 37

**Eddontenajon Lake Rest Area:** About 4km north of Ealue Lake Rd. Boat launch here provides only access to lake.

**Iskut:** (Pop. 300). 9km from rest area; 15km beyond Tatogga Lake.

**Iskut Information:** The Iskut Band Administration Office, stores, resorts, gas stations, and outfitters happy to provide information. Community strung out along lakes bordering Hwy 37. Information about Klastline-Eddontenajon Trail to Mount Edziza Provincial Park. See also *Side Trip to Telegraph Creek*, following.

**Morchuea Lake:** Turn west about 20km beyond Iskut. Forest Service recreation site. Mt Edziza views. Canoe launch.

**Stikine River Provincial Recreation Area:** 217,000ha. 847-7320. Southern boundary nearly 4km beyond Morchuea Lake turnoff. A corridor on both sides of Stikine River from Spatsizi Park along the Grand Canyon to Telegraph Creek and border of Mount Edziza Park. No east-west road access.

Hwy 37 begins a switchbacking descent into Stikine River valley. Drivers: watch road, not scenery.

**Stikine River:** About 12km from Morchuea Lake turnoff. A magnificent wild river with as many moods as twists and turns. Pullout for canoeing trips starting in Spatsizi Park. Weather and water conditions change rapidly. Downstream of the bridge, the Stikine enters its dangerously unnavigable Grand Canyon. Its waters surge 80km between sedimentary and volcanic walls 305m high.

**Upper and Lower Gnat Lakes:** 17km beyond northern boundary of Stikine River Recreation Area.

**Tanzilla River Rest Area:** 15km beyond Upper Gnat, on sparkling Tanzilla River, flowing southeast toward Dease Lake, but never reaching the community. The Arctic-Pacific divide (820m) abruptly diverts its course southwest toward the Stikine.

**Dease Lake:** (Pop. 271). On south end of Dease Lake, 9km from rest area. About 490km north of Kitwanga on Hwy 16, 234km south of Alaska Hwy. Government supply centre for region. Scheduled air service to Terrace. Full travellers' services, guides and outfitters. Near site of Hudson's Bay Company fort and trading post built in 1837 and a gold rush in 1873 on Dease and Thibert creeks. Mining exploration remains active. Sip a cool one in the Tanzilla pub.

**Dease Lake Information:** Any store or business glad to help.

**Telegraph Creek Rd:** Southwest off main road through Dease Lake, about 1.5km from Hwy 37. From here it's 113km to Telegraph Creek. No trailers or large RVs. Or drivers subject to vertigo. This route, punched through in 1922, twists like a serpent, switchbacking in and out of deep canyons on rough, narrow roadbed with up to 20 percent grades. Check with highways department before leaving.

## SIDE TRIP

### to Telegraph Creek

Road starts off benignly traversing Tanzilla Plateau through an old burn punctuated by small creeks. Expansive view.

**Mount Edziza:** 63km beyond Dease Lake, volcanic cone visible to southeast.

**Deep Breath Time:** Road leaves plateau and enters canyon about 80km from Dease Lake. Switchback begins down to Tuya River. Passing oncoming vehicles requires cooperation. Native fish camps.

**Windy Point Rest Area and Viewpoint:** 88km from Dease Lake by Stikine River. Expansive views, picnic tables at cliff's edge.

**Lower Grand Canyon of the Stikine:** 93km from Dease Lake. Breathtaking views from 15m-wide ridge of lava supporting the road. Drop offs 122m either side. Road spirals down bare, sandy side cuts of adjoining canyon to swift, blue Tahltan River.

**Telegraph Creek:** (Pop. 300). 113km from Dease Lake, 260km upriver from Wrangell, Alaska. As the crow flies, less than 60km from Alaska's border. It's the only town on the 600km Stikine River. Tahltan First Nations community sits atop the hill, non-native village is one terrace down: both overlooking the Stikine. A delightful spot.

Telegraph Creek has been continuously settled by non-native peoples since placer gold was found a few km downstream in 1861. As the farthest navigable point on the Stikine for steamships, the community was well situated for such enterprises as Western Union's overland telegraph to link New York and Paris. Telegraph Creek may have been the Northwest's great communications centre by 1866 if the transatlantic cable, completed the same year, had not made the overland line redundant. Less than a decade later, Telegraph Creek was rejuvenated as a gateway to the Cassiar gold rush and, in 1897, gateway to Klondike. In 1901 another telegraph line, linking Klondike with the south, was strung into Telegraph Creek, but brought few changes to the village. Benefits came after 1928 with improvements to the road east to Dease Lake, and during World War Two, with the construction of the Alaska Hwy.

More recently, the community has been, simply, a refuge for people who prefer fewer links with the world beyond. Another mini-boom is looming, though. Gold again, 100km south, between the Scud and Iskut rivers, and the mining companies are moving in.

Gas, food, and lodging (by appointment Oct-May). **RiverSong Café**, general store, lodge, and restaurant, is where you'll meet nearly everyone in town at some point or another. Riverboat and aircraft charters. Guided river-raft trips. Limitless hiking. Take a gold pan. Sawmill Lake a convenient camp spot. Enjoy locally grown vegetables and Stikine salmon.

**Mount Edziza Provincial Park and Recreation Area:** 230,000ha. About 500km north of Kitwanga on Hwy 16. 847-7320. Write BC Parks, Prince George District, Box 2045, 4051-18th Ave, Prince George, BC, V2N 2J6. 565-6340.

The park begins across the Stikine from Telegraph Creek. Call in advance to select suitable access. Guided hiking and pack-horse trips arranged in Telegraph Creek, Dease Lake, and Iskut areas.

The eruptions creating Mt Edziza (el 2,787m,) began four million years ago. Smaller eruptions only 1,300 years ago produced an eerie landscape of perfectly symmetrical cone and craters. Five major lakes in park and Spectrum Range with purple, yellow, and red rocks have been affected by lava flows.

No road access or services. Trails difficult to follow, especially in bad weather. Edziza is not for the ill-equipped or inexperienced.

**Forest Service Recreation Camping:** Two pleasant sites between Telegraph Creek and Glenora. Watch closely for signs. Tahltan fish camps nearby.

**Glenora:** 19km beyond Telegraph Creek. Once a thriving tent city of 10,000. Hudson's Bay Company moved its headquarters to Telegraph Creek after 1900, and Glenora was soon a ghost town.

### *Return to Highway 37*

Hwy 37 continues north with views of Dease Lake.

**Rabid Grizzly Rest Area:** 28km beyond townsite, turn west for easy access to deep cold waters of Dease Lake. Big char. Gold-rush ghost towns of Laketon and Porter Landing.

**Dease River Bridge:** New structure 37km from Rabid Grizzly Rest Area. Grayling fishing. Convenient start point for canoe trips.

**Pine Tree Lake:** About 9km beyond Dease River bridge. Series of narrow lakes and meandering Dease River.

**Wildfire Sign:** Burned areas start near Cotton Lake, just beyond Pine Tree Lake. Caused by abandoned campfire.

**Cottonwood River Rest Area:** 7km beyond Wildfire Sign.

**Simmons and Twin Lakes:** 7km and 10.5km respectively from rest area. Small lakes deep in mountain folds, surrounded by spires of spruce.

**Jade City:** About 9.5km past Twin Lake. Locally mined jade. Souvenirs and rock cut to order. Services.

**Cassiar Junction:** At Jade City. 116km north of Dease Lake, 119km south of Alaska Hwy. Road takes sharp west off Hwy 37. 14km paved road to Cassiar.

**Cassiar:** 133km from Alaska Hwy, tucked into an impressive mountain valley. Late in 1992, this thriving community of 1,500 souls became another BC ghost town. Cassiar was created 40 years ago to help satisfy the postwar need for asbestos. Now, because it's too costly to develop new underground mines and transport the asbestos to world markets, the townsite has been returned to the mountain sheep. Mining equipment has been auctioned off; the houses, sold – many to become vacation homes around Vancouver. Even the coffins (empty, of course) went away with a bargain-hunting undertaker from "up north." The town's new $6.4-million school has been relocated, the church knocked down.

**Centreville:** (Pop. 2). About 14km north of Cassiar Junction on Hwy 37. In mid-1870s, hundreds of miners clustered in this gold camp working up and down McDame Creek. A massive 2kg gold nugget was found near here in 1877.

**Good Hope Lake:** (Pop. 100). 21km beyond Cassiar junction. Attractive lake, Tlingit native village.

**Boya Lake Provincial Park:** 4,597ha; 45 campsites. Take access road 33km from Cassiar Junction; 13.5km beyond Good Hope Lake. Turn east 2.5km from Hwy 37. 847-7320. Retreating ice sheets have left maze of eskers and kettle lakes. About 22 islands and convoluted shoreline. Swimming, boat launching, canoeing. Fishing best on cloudy days when surface is ruffled. Water clearer than a municipal swimming pool. And chlorine free. Wheelchair access.

**Beaver Dam Rest Area:** 11km from Boya Lake access road. Information sign.

Hwy 37 moves onto Liard Plateau. Dry sandy soils and small pine trees. Horseranch Mountains on eastern horizon date to pre-Cambrian era.

**Blue Lakes:** 46km beyond rest area. Little picnic spot for weary travellers, by clear blue water.

**60th Parallel:** 22km from lakes. Boundary between BC and Canada's Yukon Territory. 4km to Alaska Hwy. **Road is now Yukon Hwy 16.**

**Alaska Hwy:** 3.5km north of 60. 722km north of Hwy 16. Alaska Hwy goes east 23km to town of Watson Lake. West to Atlin in BC, Whitehorse in the Yukon, and Alaska, US.

This travel guide does not take the visitor into the Yukon Territory or Alaska. For brief information on some of the highway options, see *The True North, Peace River-Alaska Highway*, p.242. Contact Yukon Territorial Government, Tourism Branch, at (403) 667-5340. Or Watson Lake Chamber of Commerce, (403) 536-2240.

## SIDE TRIP
### to Atlin

**Atlin:** (Pop. 506). Located in northwest corner of BC, 96km by winding, scenic, gravel road south from Jakes Corner on Alaska Hwy. Last 22km are paved. Jakes Corner is 84km south of Whitehorse.

Atlin sits midway on eastern shores of the long finger that is Atlin Lake, glacier-fed, and BC's largest natural lake. Coast Mountains are a dramatic backdrop to the town, and also protect it from the worst of Pacific storms. Atlin enjoys warm summers with long hours of daylight.

Atlin is unfairly beautiful with a moody presence. Visitors quickly discover what residents prize, a magical quality of life that seems to evoke spiritual journeys and creative endeavour. It's a place where people go to get their lives on track. Like Machu Picchu. Photographers, artists, naturalists, scientists, soul-searchers, and Tom Sawyers gravitate to Atlin. Many stay.

This was a gold-rush town with about 10,000 people at turn of century – 5,000 in Atlin and 5,000 in Discovery, some 10km from here, where gold was first discovered. The rush is over, but visitors can still pan for colour at provincial government placer lease on Spruce Creek, 8km from town. Check infocentre for directions.

There are lakeshore cottages, log buildings, and the 1918 gas-powered vessel *Tarahne* (hosting tea July 1 weekend). Atlin Lake spreads over 795 sq km of bays, arms, and channels. Houseboat rentals, charter aircraft. The lake can get rough. Cartop boats should stay near shore. Try fly-fishing for grayling where streams enter lake. Lake trout are huge. One hotel, cottages, B&Bs, RV parking. Atlin runs Pine Creek Campground (no hook-ups) about 1.5km south of town. Service station, grocery store, hardware, craft and gift shops.

**Atlin Information:** Infocentre, Atlin Visitors Association, Box 365, Atlin, BC, V0W 1A0. 651-7522. At Third and Trainor, in Atlin Historical Museum. Look for building with artifacts outside. Late June-early Sept.

**Aircraft Landing Strip:** Just over 1km east of town.

■ **Atlin Museum:** Third and Trainor. 651-7522. Daily late June-early Sept. By appointment rest of year. In 1902 schoolhouse. Collections of gold-rush artifacts, Tlingit exhibits, early transportation displays. Walking tour.

■ **Atlin Mineral Springs:** Located at Warm Bay, 24km south of Atlin close to lake. Clear, odourless mineral water 29 degrees C. Meadow campground nearby.

■ **Atlin Pioneer Cemetery:** Used from 1898 to 1948. Restored by Atlin Historical Society. Located near airport.

■ **Atlin Centre for the Arts:** July-Aug, Box 207 Atlin, BC, V0W 1A0. 651-7659. Rest of year, 19 Elm Grove Ave, Toronto, Ont, 416-536-7971. Centre is 5km from the village. Three-to-four week programs such as "Art Through Experiencing", "Idea and the Creative Process", "Writing From the Edge", for artists, art students, art educators.

**Atlin Provincial Park:** 271,140ha. 847-7320. No road access. Wilderness/walk-in campsite. In Tagish Highlands of Coast Mountains, surrounding bottom half of Atlin Lake. Total wilderness area, no facilities, access only by boat or plane. One-third of park glacier covered. Meltwater from Llewellyn Glacier carries sediment giving the lake its aquamarine colour. Outstanding wildlife photography, climbing, fishing, birdwatching. Consult guides and outfitters.

## SIDE TRIP
### to Chilkoot Trail – Dyea, Alaska to Bennett, BC

In 1897, more than 100,000 adventurers travelled through fledgling Victoria, Seattle, and San Francisco to the northern gold fields. Hundreds perished – starved, or froze to death while lost on perilous routes through BC and Alaska. Some 50 stampeders are buried at the trailhead of the best-known of these routes, the Chilkoot Trail, "the cussedest trail this side of hell."

When the White Pass and Yukon Route Railroad opened in 1900, the trail's destiny changed.

Today, this 53km trek from Dyea, Alaska to Bennett, BC, the gateway to the Klondike (Canada's Yukon Territory), is an international hiking trail and wilderness preserve managed jointly by the Canadian Parks Service and the US National Parks Service. Departure point is Skagway, Alaska. Hundreds of hikers from around the world come to experience the dramatic scenery of coastal rain forest, lofty summits and high alpine lakes; the life of the stampeders – the trail is still strewn with well-preserved debris cast off by stampeders when their feverish dreams encountered cold reality; abandoned boom towns; mosquitos, muscle-wrenching climbs, weather.

For information on preparedness, transportation, recommended reading, and regulations: Superintendent, Yukon National Historic Sites, Canadian Parks Service, 205-300 Main Rd, Whitehorse, Yukon, Y1A 2B5. 403-668-2116. Also see White Pass and Yukon Railway hikers' shuttle, under *Transportation,* p.206.

## SIDE TRIP

### to Tatshenshini-Alsek Wilderness Provincial Park

For those who think, "So that was the Chilkoot, what's next?" The "Tat", by raft. The 260km journey starting from Dalton Post, in the Yukon, is for serious adventurers only. The "Tat" traverses a new 958,000ha wilderness park in that knob of BC northwest of the Chilkoot, separating Alaska from the Yukon. The area is known as the "Haines Triangle", for the highway forming its eastern boundary. Midst the St Elias Mountains – North America's highest peaks, ranging from 3,000-4,000m, and among some 350 glaciers forming part of the largest non-polar icecap on earth – this has been called a Lost Horizon, a rare, "unspoiled" place on earth. (It has been pointed out, however, that with 1,100 and more wilderness river rafters a year, enthusiasm for beauty is already putting some pressure on this not-so-Lost Horizon.)

The Tatshenshini-Alsek watershed was recently spared from the greater threat of a mining scheme that would have converted the peak of Windy Craggy Mountain into a gigantic open pit. Conservationists declared the Tat "the wildest river on the continent" and, until the Class A – no development, ever – park was announced, they said it was "the second most endangered [river], after the Colorado."

The region supports a valuable salmon fishery and a rare diversity of wildlife, including half of BC's population of Dall sheep, grizzlies, and what may be Canada's only glacier bears.

Linked up with existing Canadian and US national parks in the Yukon and Alaska, the parkland becomes one of the largest international protected areas in the world – 8.5 million hectares. The region is to be nominated a UN World Heritage Site.

For information on rafting: Registrar of River Rafting, c/o BC Parks, 800 Johnson St, Victoria, BC, V8W 1X4. 387-4427. Or travel infocentres. Info on the river: 1-800-667-5527.

*Totem poles at Ninstints, ancient Kunghit Haida village, on Sgan Gwai (Anthony Island), in the Queen Charlottes.*

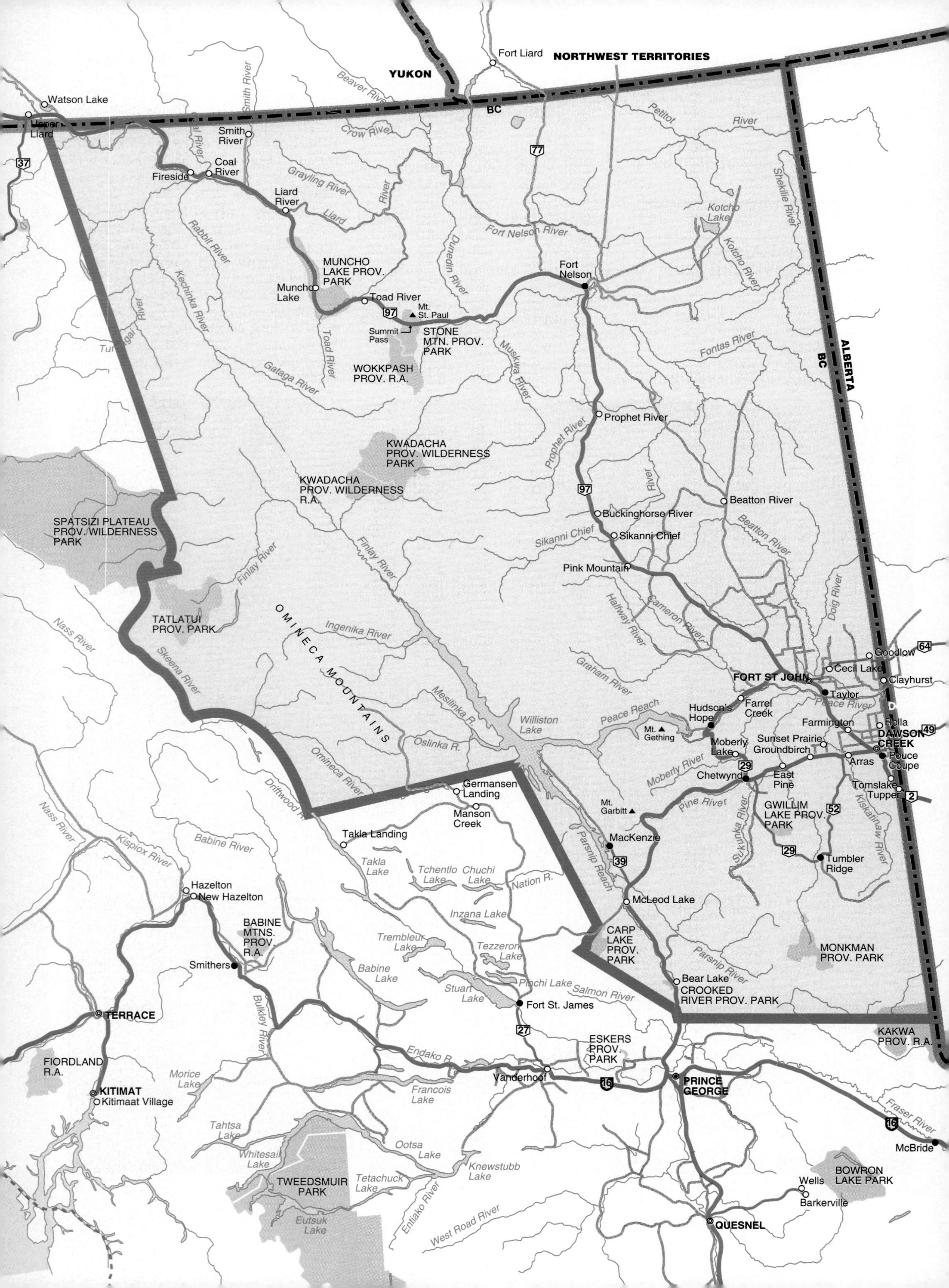

YUKON
NORTHWEST TERRITORIES
Fort Liard
Watson Lake
Upper Liard
BC
37
Smith River
Beaver River
Crow River
Petitot
River
77
Coal River
Fireside
Grayling River
Liard River
Liard
River
Rabbit River
Fort Nelson River
Kotcho Lake
Shekilie River
Kotcho River
Dunedin River
MUNCHO LAKE PROV. PARK
Muncho Lake
Toad River
Fort Nelson
Kechika River
Mt. St. Paul
97
Summit Pass
STONE MTN. PROV. PARK
Toad River
Muskwa River
WOKKPASH PROV. R.A.
Gataga River
Fontas River
BC
ALBERTA
Prophet River
Prophet River
KWADACHA PROV. WILDERNESS PARK
KWADACHA PROV. WILDERNESS R.A.
97
Beatton River
Buckinghorse River
SPATSIZI PLATEAU PROV. WILDERNESS PARK
Sikanni Chief
Sikanni Chief
Beatton River
Finlay River
Finlay River
Pink Mountain
Doig River
TATLATUI PROV. PARK
OMINECA MOUNTAINS
Halfway River
Cameron River
Nass River
Ingenika River
Goodlow
64
Skeena River
Graham River
Cecil Lake
FORT ST JOHN
Clayhurst
Taylor
Peace River
Mesilinka R.
Hudson's Hope
Farrel Creek
Williston Lake
Peace Reach
Mt. Gething
Farmington
Rolla
DAWSON CREEK
49
Moberly Lake
Sunset Prairie
Groundbirch
Pouce Coupe
Oslinka R.
Omineca River
Moberly River
29
East Pine
Arras
Chetwynd
Tomslake
Germansen Landing
Tupper
2
Driftwood R.
Manson Creek
Mt. Garbitt
Pine River
GWILLIM LAKE PROV. PARK
52
Nass River
Kispiox River
Babine River
Takla Landing
MacKenzie
Kiskatinaw River
Sukunka River
29
Tumbler Ridge
39
Takla Lake
Tchentlo Lake
Chuchi Lake
Parsnip Reach
Hazelton
New Hazelton
Nation R.
McLeod Lake
Inzana Lake
BABINE MTNS. PROV. R.A.
Trembleur Lake
Tezzeron Lake
CARP LAKE PROV. PARK
MONKMAN PROV. PARK
Smithers
Babine Lake
Parsnip River
Pinchi Lake
Bear Lake
Stuart Lake
Salmon River
CROOKED RIVER PROV. PARK
Bulkley River
TERRACE
Fort St. James
27
KAKWA PROV. R.A.
ESKERS PROV. PARK
Endako R.
FIORDLAND R.A.
Morice Lake
Vanderhoof
16
PRINCE GEORGE
KITIMAT
Kitimaat Village
Francois Lake
Fraser River
16
Tahtsa Lake
Ootsa Lake
McBride
Whitesail Lake
Knewstubb Lake
BOWRON LAKE PARK
TWEEDSMUIR PARK
Tetachuck Lake
Wells
Entiako River
Barkerville
Eutsuk Lake
West Road River
QUESNEL

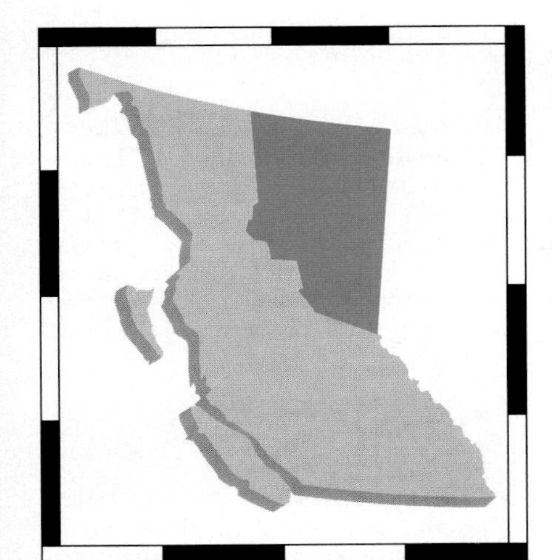

# Peace River - Alaska Highway

## *Exploring a Land of Gigantics*

Nothing is half measure in the Peace River-Alaska Highway region of northeastern British Columbia. The landscape and man's impressions upon it are painted with broad, bold brush strokes. The widely varied and wildly beautiful region between the Rocky Mountains and the Alberta border inspires awe.

When the first white explorer, Alexander Mackenzie, came here in 1793 obsessed with reaching Canada's western ocean, he encountered and struggled to overcome the turbulent Peace River that blocked his passage and challenged his resolve.

Nearly 150 years later, in 1942, another visionary undertaking of epic proportions was completed with the wilderness trail that is today's Alaska Highway.

Starting in the 1960s, the Peace River – Mackenzie's old nemesis – was twice dammed and tamed, leaving as a legacy a huge and ugly reservoir. The 164,600ha Lake Williston is like a little inland sea infiltrating the Rocky Mountain Trench.

The land of the Peace has been submerged and reemerged from water before. About 100 million years ago, the rich prairie soils that comprise the Peace today were coated with warm swampy forests. Browsing within them were placid families of plant-eating dinosaurs. Their fossilized remains, dinosaur tracks, and evidence of other ancient creatures were discovered during construction of the WAC Bennett and Peace Canyon dams near Hudson's Hope.

But the natural world has always practised recycling. Through the eons, the organic material from those prehistoric forests has metamorphosed into coal, oil, and gas. Yesterday's verdant, subtropical landscapes are today's economic mainstay. Along with agriculture and forestry, these fossil fuels sustain the people of the region.

The northern Rocky Mountains – geological adolescents a mere 160 million years old – angle northwest through the region. The land to their east gradually flattens into the vast Interior plains that stretch halfway across the continent.

The result is a region of remarkable contrasts.

Fertile farmlands surrounding the Peace River valley are prodigious producers of grains, grasses, and seeds. They fatten all kinds of livestock from cattle to domesticated reindeer. Yet not far away, between Fort St John and Fort Nelson, are stretches of muskeg – boggy, water-saturated soils where trees have trouble rooting. And in the mountains, ah, in the mountains, there's grandeur, and loneliness and magnificence enough to soothe anyone's troubled soul.

*Canola field near Dawson Creek.*

The many rivers in the northern half of the region twist and turn as they cut their valleys and course toward their destiny in the Liard River. The Liard, unlike the Peace to its south, is unfettered by dams, although covetous eyes have been cast at its formidable hydroelectric potential.

The Liard lazily and obligingly swings south of the 60th parallel that forms the border between BC and the Northwest Territories, collecting the water that cascades off the Rockies and saunters from the plains.

And in the Liard valley, more than 700km up the Alaska Highway, is another enigma. Super warm, mineral-rich water seeps through faults in the sedimentary rocks to create the Liard River Hot Springs and a little world unto itself. One that missed the last smothering effect of glaciation and now supports flora not normally encountered in the northern boreal forest.

The Peace River was so named after a peace pipe was smoked around 1790, settling a territorial dispute between the First Nations Cree and Beaver people. They went their separate ways. The Peace Region has in a similar manner gone its separate way from the rest of BC. Its topography, climate and transportation network was more closely aligned with Alberta than BC. The John Hart Hwy connecting the Peace River country with the rest of the province wasn't completed until 1952. Its communities were small and few. Settlement today is on or contiguous to Hwy 97, and the largest city is Fort St John with a population of about 14,000 residents.

But it is another highway that has had the most profound effect on the region: the 2,400km Alaska Hwy between Mile Zero in Dawson Creek and Fairbanks, Alaska. Originally a military supply route, it was constructed in response to the bombing of Pearl Harbour in 1941, and the invasion of two Aleutian Islands in southwestern Alaska. The inland route was considered less vulnerable to Japanese planes.

This highway was, quite simply, an amazing achievement. Construction began in earnest February, 1942, well before winter snows began to melt. Some 11,000 US soldiers and 16,000 civilians, including 3,700 Canadians, built 8,000 culverts and 133 bridges over an endlessly winding route. Overcoming a morass of logistic nightmares, workers completed the road in eight months and 12 days.

The economic impact of the highway has been immeasurable. The social ramifications equally so, especially for the native population. The white man from the south introduced diseases like dysentery and jaundice to which the natives had no immunity. The serpentine ribbon of mud and gravel shattered the native's traditional lifestyle, and introduced new religions and alcohol from which these people are still reeling.

But around the world, the Alaska Highway struck a cord. It appealed to a latent pioneering instinct and millions have responded, challenging the dust, the potholes, and the unknown in cathartic pilgrimages.

The Alaska Highway is paved now, but its mystique endures, part of a potent fascination with the north. Much of its appeal is in the proximity of abundant wilderness and wildlife, the kinds of things most people only see in television documentaries. There are few places, indeed, where visitors can step from a motor home and be face-to-snout with a Stone sheep.

Venture off the highway and become a modern-day Alexander Mackenzie. Backcountry parks like Wokkpash, Kwadacha, and Monkman are Meccas to committed outdoors lovers. They're as untouched and unmarred as areas can be these days.

That's one reason why this land known as the Peace River-Alaska Highway region always leaves its visitors with powerful and indelible impressions.

*Moose at a mineral lick.*

## Information

**Peace River-Alaska Highway Tourist Association:** Write Box 6850, Fort St John, BC, V1J 4J3, or call 785-2544 for information on all highway communities in the region. Fax: 785-4424. Addresses and telephone numbers of local infocentres are shown in the *Log* with the write-ups on each community.

## Transportation

People travel the Peace River-Alaska Highway region on a good paved highway system and via the air. Major centres enjoy the same public transportation amenities as cities farther south with regularly scheduled bus and air services. Access to the vast hinterlands is usually by air. Northerners take to bush planes and helicopters with the alacrity southerners jump in a truck. That's why it's not difficult to find aircraft available for charter in the smallest whistle stops. It pays to shop around. Help is available at the travel infocentres throughout the region and most places along the highway; where ever the door's open and the coffee's on.

### Airlines

Fort St John has the region's largest airport. Also regularly scheduled service to Dawson Creek and Fort Nelson.

■ **Air Canada:** 1-800-661-3936.
■ **Canadian Airlines International:** 1-800-663-3502. Serves Fort St John.
■ **Air BC:** 360-9074. Serves Dawson Creek.
■ **Canadian Regional Airlines:** 1-800-663-1661. Serves Fort St John and Fort Nelson.
■ **Central Mountain Air:** 1-800-663-3905. Serves Fort St John.

### Bus Lines

■ **Greyhound Bus Lines:** 1-800-661-8747 or specific communities. Daily service to communities along Hwy 97 and Alaska Hwy.
■ **Peace Coaches Inc:** 785-5945 in Fort St John. Daily service between Fort St John, Hudson's Hope, and Chetwynd.

Two cities in the region operate transit systems. For information call Dawson Creek, 782-INFO, and Fort St John, 787-RIDE.

### Car and RV Rentals

Rental agencies at airports and downtown in Dawson Creek, Fort St John, and Fort Nelson. Some RV rentals. Check infocentres for leads. Also classified sections of local newspapers. Taxis available in Dawson Creek, Fort St John, Tumbler Ridge, and Fort Nelson. Cabs may be limited. Phone early.

### Driving

Most visitors drive into the region. "Doing" the Alaska Hwy is an irresistible draw for urban pioneers worldwide. The highway is paved now but distances are great, northern weather is unpredictable and common sense should accompany every driver: little things like keeping the gas topped up, carrying serviceable spare tires, keeping headlights on at all times when driving. Remembering to turn them off when parked. Service stations aren't plentiful, but most stay open year-round.

The highway's always going to be under repair and reconstruction. Obey signs. Don't be afraid of gravel sections, but don't use them as speedways.

Winter driving requires more preparation. Roads are well maintained, but vehicle and driver should be in good condition to adjust to often rapidly changing driving conditions. Obviously the vehicle must have good winter tread tires and be thoroughly winterized with a block heater. Don't take anything for granted. Remember, this isn't downtown. It's wise to stow an emergency kit of items like first aid supplies, shovel, axe, matches, emergency food, spare clothes, and sleeping bag. Chances are good it won't be needed. But if it is, it could save your own or someone else's life.

### Sour Gas

The Peace River region is BC's oil patch. Oil and natural gas wells are in production and exploration for new finds continues. Activity stretches from the Monkman area south of Tumbler Ridge into the Interior plains near Fort Nelson. At a few well sites, the danger of hydrogen sulphide gas exists. These sites are identified by signs, and warnings must be heeded. High-level exposure to the "rotten egg" smell of hydrogen sulphide gas can kill. For further information call the Ministry of Energy, Mines and Petroleum Resources, in Charlie Lake, at 787-3450.

### Where are We?

Sometimes when driving the Alaska Highway, it's hard to tell exactly where you are. The original wooden mileposts were traded in for kilometre posts, but because the highway has been improved and shortened since then, they no longer always reflect the true distances between points. Your *Travel Guide* has done its humble best to provide accurate distances.

Historic ties confuse the matter further. Towns are often referred to by their old milepost numbers. To many, Fort Nelson will forever be Mile 300.

Also, in 1992, BC, the Yukon, and Alaska cooperated in an historic milepost project to commemorate the highway's 50th anniversary. They identified 183 sites with historic mileposts where significant construction-related events occurred. Some sites also have a sign, and 38 of the most important ones have an interpretive panel. These historic posts use original highway mileage, and may not have been restored in the exact location.

## PEACE RIVER - ALASKA HIGHWAY EVENTS

### Chetwynd

- **Moberly Lake Bathtub Races:** Early Aug. Dawson Creek
- **Mile Zero Days:** Late May-June. Beef barbecues. Street entertainment.
- **Fall Fair and Rodeo:** Mid-Aug.

### Fort Nelson

- **Trappers Rendezvous:** March.
- **Andy Bailey Days:** Aug, BC Day weekend.
- **Canadian Open Dog Sled Races:** Dec.

### Fort St John

- **World Class Dog Sled Races:** Jan. At Charlie Lake.
- **Annual Outhouse Races:** June.
- **North Peace Light Horse Association Rodeo:** Early July.

### Hudson's Hope

- **Rodeo and Parade:** Early June.
- **Dinosaur Paddlers Raft Race:** Late Aug.

### Mackenzie

- **Winter Carnival:** Feb. Miss Mackenzie Pageant, bed races, baby crawl, Oldie Wed Game.
- **Bluegrass Festival:** Mid-Aug.

### Moberly Lake

- **West Moberly Days:** Late July. Native skills, like Pugeesee.

### Muncho Lake

- **Trout Derby:** June.

### Pouce Coupe

- **Pouce Coupe Hospital Barbecue Day:** July 1. Parade, gymkhana, games, dance.

### Taylor

- **Gold Panning Championships:** Aug, BC Day weekend.

### Tumbler Ridge

- **Tumbler Ridge Days:** 3rd weekend Aug. Fair and rodeo.
- **Grizzly Valley Days:** Aug.

### Wonowon

- **Gymkhana:** July

*Andy Bailey Lake, south of Fort Nelson.*

*Azouzetta Lake and the Rockies' Hart Range, at Pine Pass Summit in northern BC.*

# Peace River - Alaska Highway Routes and Highlights

### TRAVELLER'S LOGS



### HIGHLIGHTS



## Prince George to Dawson Creek

### HART HIGHWAY (Highway 97)

The Hart Highway is an extension of Hwy 97 which starts near the US border at Osoyoos and traverses the Okanagan and Cariboo regions to Prince George. North of Dawson Creek it becomes the famous Alaska Highway.

This *Log* is measured from the John Hart bridge in Prince George, where Hwy 97 crosses the Nechako River. Prince George itself is covered under *North by Northwest*, p.209. The paved highway angles northeast 406km to Dawson Creek. Farmlands north of Prince George gradually give away to rolling forested terrain. The road climbs after crossing the Rocky Mountain trench into the wild Hart Range of the Rockies. Once it has twisted its way through the mountains, the highway unwinds into attractive foothills country. By Dawson Creek, it's a prairie landscape with grain elevators and expansive skies.

The highway is named for John Hart, BC premier, 1941-47.

**Eskers Provincial Park:** 1,603ha. Day use. 565-6340. 10km north of John Hart Bridge, west onto Chief Lake Rd, 28km then north 1km to park featuring several lakes between glaciated ridges or eskers. Hiking, wildlife viewing, cross-country skiing. Some areas wheelchair accessible.

**Salmon River:** 23km beyond John Hart Bridge. Refreshing swimming holes.

**Giscome Portage Regional Park:** 22ha. 13km beyond Salmon River on unpaved road. East 4km to peaceful park on bench above Fraser River. 563-9225. Day use. Features 1912 Huble Homestead. Guided tours daily mid-May to early Oct. Hike and cross-country ski 8km of Giscome Portage Trail between Pacific and Arctic watersheds.

**Summit Lake:** About 3.5km beyond Mitchell Rd. South and north access roads to community west of Hwy 97. Cottage country. Char and rainbow trout fishing. Location of **Arctic-Pacific Divide**. Waters to north drain into Arctic, those south to the Pacific. The Crooked River flows north from Summit Lake paralleling Hwy 97. Good for canoeing. Boats restricted to 10 horsepower motors. Lots of squawfish.

**Crooked River Provincial Park:** 1,016ha; 90 campsites, sani-station. 565-6340. 20km beyond northern Summit Lake access road. Open year-round. Excellent sandy beaches at Bear Lake. Swimming and boating (no power boats). Three other lakes – Skeleton, Hart, and Squaw – offer fine swimming and fishing for rainbow and brook trout, Dolly Varden, grayling, and Rocky Mountain whitefish. Good fishing in the Crooked River as well. Hiking trails, including 9km trail around Bear and Squaw lakes. Winter activities: cross-country skiing, snowshoeing, ice fishing. Paddlewheel boat rides are planned.

**Bear Lake:** (Pop. 270). East side of Hwy 97, 2.5km from park. Services.

**Tacheeda Lake Rd:** 13km beyond Bear Lake, turn east on gravel road for rainbow trout fishing and forest service recreation sites. Watch for industrial traffic. Also route of BC Rail's 129km branch line to Tumbler Ridge, Canada's first electrified heavy freight railway. 99-unit coal train line electrified to eliminate ventilation of 9km and 6km tunnels under Rocky Mountains.

**Crooked River Rest Area:** 21.5km beyond Tacheeda Lake Rd. West side of highway. Trumpeter swan viewing close by.

**Whiskers Point Provincial Park:** 52ha; 69 campsites, sani-station. 565-6340. 15km from rest area. West side of highway. A pleasantly forested park with campsites on McLeod Lake. Good swimming, fine sandy gravel beaches, play area. Rainbow trout, char, and grayling. Boat launch. Wonderful sunsets. Nature trail.

**McLeod Lake:** (Pop. 51). 11km beyond Whiskers Point Park. From here, local Sekani people traversed a trail to the Fort St James area. Services. Simon Fraser established Trout Lake Fort here in 1805. First European settlement west of Rockies. Commemorative cairn.

**Rd to Carp Lake:** West off highway. 1km north of McLeod Lake. Gravel.

## SIDE TRIP
### to Carp Lake

**War Falls and Lake:** In Carp Lake Provincial Park about 26km from McLeod Lake. Campground and small boat launch. War Falls tumbles 18m in two cascades divided by 100m of white water. About 8km to Carp Lake and park HQ.

**Carp Lake Provincial Park:** 19,344ha; 102 campsites and wilderness tenting campsites on five of Carp Lake's 20 islands. 565-6340. May-Oct. 32km from McLeod Lake on narrow road: can be rough, especially during spring break-up. Carp Lake trout fishing big draw. Fish from here kept Simon Fraser and his men alive in 1806. Swimming, canoeing, hiking including McLeod River Trail. Moose and black bears seen in park. Keep campsites clean.

### *Return to Highway 97*

**Tudyah Lake Provincial Park:** 87ha; 36 campsites. 565-6340. On Hwy 97, 8km beyond community of McLeod Lake. North of highway. Fishing, boating, and swimming. This park marks western edge of the **Rocky Mountain Trench**, between the Hart Ranges on the east and Nechako Plateau on the west. The steep-sided trench, probably formed by a combination of volcanic and glacial action, varies from 3-16km wide. In Canada, it parallels the western edge of Rocky Mountains for over 1,440km.

**Parsnip River:** Hwy 97 crosses river 7.5km beyond park. Named for the wild parsnips growing along its banks. Before the creation of Williston Lake, the Parsnip joined the Finlay River to form the Peace. Good grayling and Dolly Varden fishing in fall.

**Hwy 39:** 500m north of Parsnip River bridge. Summer infocentre at junction. 750-4497.

# SIDE TRIP

## to Mackenzie

Hwy 39 provides access to Mackenzie, back country, and recreation onWilliston Lake, the largest manmade reservoir on the continent. At 164,600ha, it's also the most expansive freshwater body in northern BC.

**Mackenzie:** (Pop. 5,796). North off Hwy 97. On paved Hwy 39, 29km from junction. Area was wilderness until 1965 when town was built near southern end of Williston Lake as a centre for pulp, paper, and lumber manufacturing.

Town is named for Alexander Mackenzie, who camped near the townsite on his 1793 epic journey as the first white person to reach Canada's Pacific coast by land. A centre for fishing, hiking, swimming, waterskiing, and wilderness adventure, Mackenzie has the amenities of a larger town. Logging roads fan out from the community, offering year-round access to wilderness back-country camping. (Roads must be driven with care; keep lights on at all times.) For information on access and restrictions contact BC Forest Service, Mackenzie District Office, Bag 5000, Mackenzie, BC, VOJ 2CO. 997-2200.

**Mackenzie Information:** Travel Infocentre, Mackenzie Chamber of Commerce, Box 880, Mackenzie, BC, V0J 2C0. 750-4497. Located at Hwys 97 and 39 junction. Daily May-Sept. Chamber of Commerce open year-round, 997-5459.

**Mackenzie Airport:** Mill Rd, short distance south of town. 1,555m runway. Scheduled service to Prince George.

**Morfee Lake Float Plane Base:** 2km east of Mackenzie, on Centennial Dr.

■ **Mackenzie Museum:** At Community Centre in John Dahl Park, heart of town. 997-3021. Limited hours off-season. Can call, though, to be let in. John Dahl Park has hiking trails, picnic tables, view of Morfee Lake.

■ **Morfee Lake:** 2km east of town, on Centennial Dr. Swimming and boating.

■ **Morfee Mountain:** (El 1,817m). For an endless view of Williston Lake and Rockies. Turn right about 3km north of town. Drive right up mid-summer.

■ **World's Largest Tree Crusher:** On Mackenzie Boulevard. Weighs 178t. Cleared forested land when WAC Bennett Dam was built.

■ **Mackenzie Municipal RV Park:** 20 campsites, sani-station. In town. Free.

■ **Mackenzie Golf Course:** Just south of town. 997-4004. May-Sept. Nine holes.

■ **Recreation Complex:** In town. Pool, arena, library.

■ **Demonstration Forest:** Along the 29km of Hwy 39 between Hwy 97 and Mackenzie. Signs to several trails through replanted forest.

## *Return to Highway 97*

The Misinchinka River soon flows into view on east side of Hwy 97. Rugged valley views.

**Bijoux Falls Provincial Park:** 40ha. About 31km beyond Hwy 39 junction. May-Oct. Day use. Park named for sparkling waterfall that spills 40m through the spruce forest. *Bijoux* means jewel in French. Don't feed the bears.

**Powder King Ski Village:** 6.5km beyond park. Box 2405, Pine Pass, BC, V0J 2C0. 561-1776. Fine powder skiing. 640m vertical drop, longest run 2,650m. 23 runs, one triple chair, two T-bars. RV hook-ups, on-mountain accommodation.

**Pine Pass Summit and Viewpoint:** (El 933m). 2.5km from ski village. View of Azouzetta Lake; name means flying grizzly bear in local native language.

**Pine River:** Hwy 97 crosses the Pine for the first time about 3.5km beyond summit. Watch it gather strength from its tributaries as it flows through the Rocky Mountains to the rolling plains of the Peace River Valley.

**Time Zone:** On Hwy 97, about 10km beyond Pine Pass Summit. No changes in summer, when daylight-savings time is in effect elsewhere in BC. But from late Oct-April, set your time one hour ahead for **Mountain Standard Time**.

**West Pine Rest Area:** 30km beyond Pine Pass River bridge by railway underpass. Good fossil collecting and fishing on river.

**Heart Lake Campground:** Across highway from rest area. Take gravel road 3km east. Pretty spot. Forest service recreation sites.

**Willow Flats:** About 29km from Heart Lake turnoff. Rural community. Access to Westcoast Transmission's natural gas pumping station.

**Rest Area:** 3km beyond Willow Flats. Picnic tables.

**Peace Foothills Area Map:** 9km beyond rest area, near Hassler Flats.

In 1935 the provincial government sponsored a search for oil. First producing well was drilled at Commotion Creek near here in 1940.

**Chetwynd:** (Pop. 2,843). 28km beyond foothills map. Once known as Little Prairie, the town changed its name to honour the late Ralph Chetwynd, BC highways minister, son of an English baronet. A fast-growing community that depends on forestry, mining for oil and gas, farming, and tourism. At Chetwynd, BC Rail tracks divide: one line goes to Dawson Creek, the other to Fort St John. (Both are freight lines only. The passenger service from North Vancouver ends at Prince George.) This is a bustling little place with poplar trees and chain-saw sculptures decorating streets and businesses.

**Chetwynd Infocentre:** At Chetwynd Chamber of Commerce, North Access Rd, Box 1000, Chetwynd, BC, V0C 1JO. Year-round, daily July-Aug. 788-3345, or 788-3655.

**Chetwynd Airport:** Charter service only. Also heli-pad.

■ **Little Prairie Heritage Museum:** 2km west of town, in old post office. Little Prairie was Chetwynd's name until 1959. Open June-Sept. 788-3358. 788-3345 year-round. Trapping and farming implements. Pioneer bedroom with antique quilt made by the residents. And caboose, which displays railway artifacts.

■ **The Little Giant:** Adjacent museum. Statue of The Little Giant of Big Peace, the town logo.

■ **Old Baldy Hill:** Within town. A gentle hike up. Sit on the benches and look over the community.

■ **Chetwynd Municipal Campground:** West of Hwys 97/29 junction. 15 sites, sani-station, firewood. Stream runs through campground. Free.

**Hwy 29 North:** In Chetwynd. North to **Moberly Lake**, **Moberly Lake Provincial Park**, **Spenser Tuck Provincial Park**, **Hudson's Hope**, **Peace Canyon Dam**, and **WAC Bennett Dam**. Hwy 29 rejoins Hwy 97 (the Alaska Hwy) 13km north of Fort St John. See *Fort St John to Tumbler Ridge*, p.236.

**Hwy 29 South:** 3km beyond Chetwynd. South to **Sukunka Falls, Gwillim Lake** Provincial Park**.** 90km to **Tumbler Ridge**. For details see *Fort St John to Tumbler Ridge*, p.237.

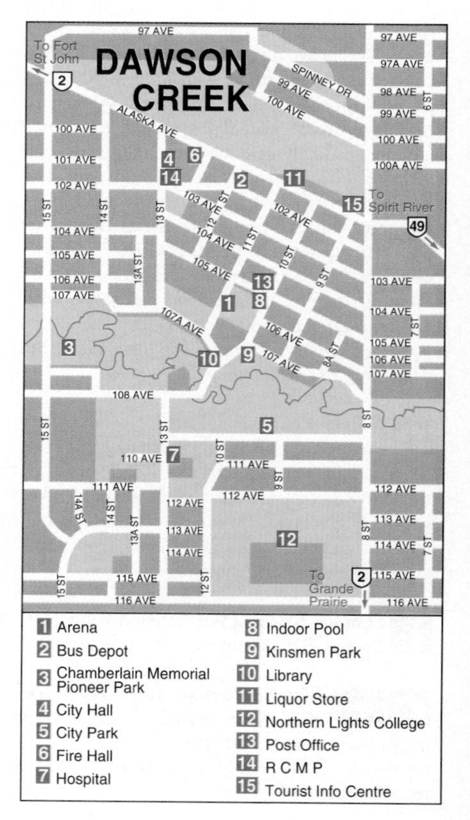

Hwy 97 travels through pleasant open country punctuated by broad ridges of deciduous trees. About 31km beyond Chetwynd, the road takes a broad sweep down the terraced valley of the Pine River.

**East Pine Provincial Park:** 14ha. South of highway at bridge. Year-round, day-use. At junction of East Pine and Murray rivers. Good fishing and canoeing, boat launching.

**Pine River**: At access to East Pine Provincial Park, Hwy 97 crosses Pine River bridge and BC Rail tracks.

**Groundbirch Store:** About 21km beyond Pine River crossing. Source of all local knowledge. Check the **Bruce Groner Memorial Museum**.

**Rd to Sunset Prairie:** North about 10km from store. Gravel road to small rural community joins Hwy 97 north of Dawson Creek.

**Hwy 52:** About 13km beyond road to Sunset Prairie. This paved and gravel Heritage Highway leads south 98km to Tumbler Ridge. See *Fort St John to Tumbler Ridge*, p.237.

**Arras:** Small community 2km beyond Hwy 52 junction.

**Rd to Farmington:** 2km beyond Arras. Road, bypassing Dawson Creek, travels north to rejoin Hwy 97 (Alaska Hwy) at small town of Farmington.

**Hwy 97N (Alaska Hwy):** 17km beyond Arras. Leads north 73km to Fort St John. See *Dawson Creek to Fort Nelson*, p.238.

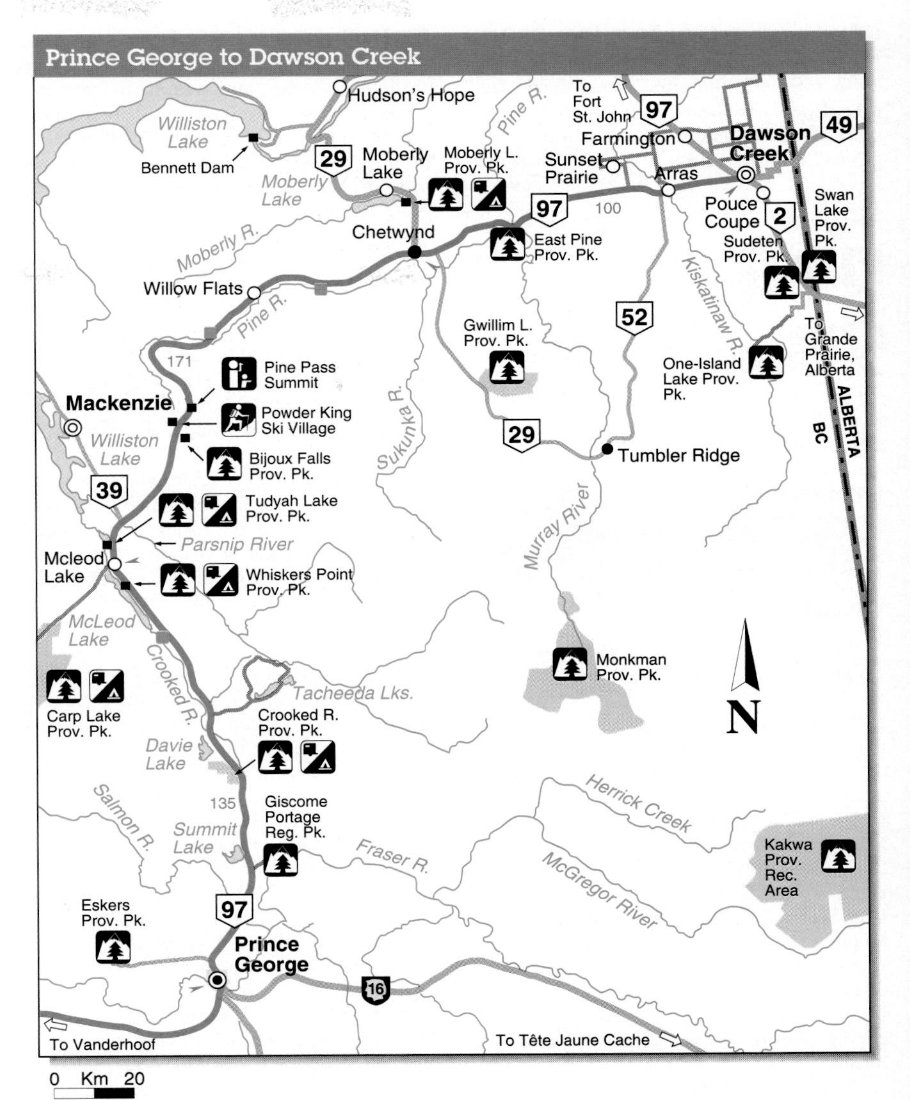


**Dawson Creek:** (Pop. 10,981). At crossroads of Alaska and Hart Hwys, and Hwys 49 and 2 to Alberta. Dawson Creek is 663m above sea level, and operates on Mountain Standard Time year-round. City boasts 125 frost-free days.

Dawson Creek is the major transportation centre in the Peace River area, and serves an extensive agricultural area. There has been recent diversification into game farming: reindeer and plains bison (buffalo). Located on what was once called the Beaver Plains, its grain elevators are a visual link with the prairie provinces. Main settlers came here in 1912. The town was named for George Mercer Dawson, of the Geological Survey of Canada, whose meticulous geological and natural history reports on this region, and much of Canada, have rarely been improved upon.

Dawson Creek is a friendly, laid-back city with every visitor service. It is famous as Mile Zero of the legendary Alaska Hwy. A post to commemorate this is located in the heart of the city, a popular spot to be photographed before setting off on adventures north. The community is also the terminus of the Northern Alberta Railway (NAR). The first passenger steam train arrived Jan 15, 1931, and the last steam train left Dawson Creek in 1974. The NAR Station, handsomely restored in its original location, received the Canada Built Heritage Award in 1984. Dawson Creek is still a railway town, served by BC Rail (freight only) and Canadian National Railway.

Wander about and find the teahouse, period photo studio, old-time general store, and printing press.

**Dawson Creek Information:** 900 Alaska Ave, Dawson Creek, BC, V1G 4T6. 782-9595. Dawson Creek and District Chamber of Commerce, 102-816 Alaska Ave, Dawson Creek, BC, V1G 4T6. 782-4868. At Northern Alberta Railroad Park on Alaska Ave at 10th St. Daily 8-8, May-Aug; Tues-Sat, 9-5 in winter.

**Dawson Creek Airport:** On Hwy 2, southeast of town. Scheduled and charter aircraft.

■ **Farmer's Market:** Sat, May-Oct. NAR Park. See *below*.

■ **Northern Alberta Railway Station Park, or the NAR Park:** On Alaska Ave near the traffic circle in centre of city. Site of several interesting exhibits, including a turn-of-the-century rail car and restored 1949 grain elevator. Walking tours of Dawson Creek start here. Ask at infocentre.

■ **The NAR Station Museum:** In restored NAR Station, in NAR Park. Daily June-Aug; Tues-Sat, Sept-May. 782-9595. Wildlife exhibits. Huge mammoth tusks. Beaver First Nations artifacts.

■ **Dawson Creek Art Gallery:** Housed in Alberta Wheat Pool Elevator Annex of NAR Park. June-Aug, daily 10-5. Sept-June, Tues-Sat, 9-5. 782-2601. Local arts and crafts.

■ **Walter Wright Pioneer Village:** At Hart/Alaska Hwys junction. 782-7144. 99 June-Aug. Off-season, 782-9595. Restored buildings on site commemorate 1940s. Dinner theatre.

■ **Buffalo Barbecue:** Every week at Pioneer Village, days TBA.

■ **Dawson Creek Golf and Country Club:** 782-7882. May-Oct. 18 holes.

Dawson Creek is a jumping-off spot for the spectacular **Monkman Provincial Park** 130km to the southwest. Access is by air from Dawson Creek, or jet boat from Tumbler Ridge. Also, the north end of the park is accessible by a 35km two-lane forest service gravel road from the **Tumbler Ridge** mining site

(60km south of town of Tumbler Ridge). Kinuseo Falls campground, opened there 1992, offers 42 campsites, picnic shelter, and special needs facilities. Viewing platform for 60m falls. 24km hiking trail leads from campground to further back-country explorations. 787-3407. Also see *Fort St John to Tumbler Ridge*, p.237.

**Hwy 49:** To province of Alberta, 89km to Spirit River.

**Hwy 2:** To Alberta via Pouce Coupe, Toms Lake, Tupper.

For continuation of Hwy 97 north to Fort Nelson, see *Dawson Creek to Fort Nelson*, p.238.

## Fort St John to Tumbler Ridge

### HIGHWAY 29

Hwy 29 from Fort St John south to Tumbler Ridge is one of BC's most scenically varied. It parallels the Peace River for more than 70km, sliding through rolling hills and plains patchworked with farms and ranches. The drive's a treat any time of year. This area produces more grain, forage, seed, and honey than any other in the province, and is also the main sheep-farming valley.

Manmade marvels have also added to the attraction of the area. The WAC Bennett Dam represents an incredible engineering feat; building the Peace Canyon Dam involved rerouting part of the Peace River and revealed dinosaur prints and the tracks of ancient birds in the canyon bedrock. Both dams have fascinating visitor centres, and should not be missed.

South of Chetwynd, Hwy 29 moves into the Rocky Mountain Foothills scoured by deep valleys. Tumbler Ridge is attractively located away from the coal mines it serves.

**Fort St John:** On Hwy 97, 387km south of Fort Nelson; 73km north of Dawson Creek, 13km east of Hwy 29. Details in *Dawson Creek to Fort Nelson*, p.240.

**Hwy 29:** Leads west 13km north of Fort St John, from Hwy 97 opposite turnoff to **Charlie Lake Provincial Park**. See *Dawson Creek to Fort Nelson*, for park and lake. Hudson's Hope is 75km beyond.

**Lakepoint Golf and Country Club:** At Charlie Lake. 785-5566. May-Oct. 18 holes overlooking lake.

About 12km beyond Hwy 97 junction, Hwy 29 switchbacks down Bear Hill's 10 percent grades. Lovely views for passengers. Below, the Peace River is studded with islands, a home for Canada Geese.

The highway and Peace River now wind for about 63km through serene mix of bottom lands and hills. Good chance to spot deer; bear and moose not uncommon.

**Halfway River:** 35km beyond junction. Good fishing for rainbow trout, Dolly Varden, grayling, and whitefish from the bridge. River is about "halfway" between Fort St John and Portage Mountain, 1,429m, overlooking Hudson's Hope. Before the Peace Canyon Dam was built, canoes were portaged along this turbulent section of the Peace, hence the mountain's name.

**Hudson's Hope:** (Pop. 985). On Hwy 29 some 75km beyond Hwy 97 junction. The Peace River was the main transportation route early in the 1900s, when sternwheelers plied the river. From Hudson's Hope to Vermilion Chutes in Alberta, 917km away, the fare was $52; this included use of bedding and bathroom.

Hudson's Hope is a charming little town perched 61m above the Peace River. One version of the name is that a prospector called Hudson was hopeful of striking it rich here. Explorer Simon Fraser founded a trading post on the Peace River here in 1805, supporting the town's claim to being BC's third oldest community. Remains of the original settlement, named Rocky Mountain Portage, can be seen in town. Excellent cross-country skiing and hiking trails around the community; maps and information at infocentre. Town calls itself "Playground of the Peace: Land of Dinosaurs and Dams." A friendly place.

**Hudson's Hope Information:** 783-9154, or contact District of Hudson's Hope, Box 330, Hudson's Hope, BC, VOC 1VO. 783-9901. In Beattie Park on Hwy 29. Daily 8-8, mid-May to Sept.

**Hudson's Hope Airport:** About 5km beyond junction on Dam Access Rd. Charter service.

■ **Hudson's Hope Museum:** 10506-105th Ave, opposite infocentre. Daily May-early Sept. Weekends only in winter. 783-5735. On north bank of Peace River, overlooking the spot where Simon Fraser wintered 1805-1806.

Museum is on the first parcel of land ever surveyed on the north side of the Peace, in 1899, in original Hudson's Bay Company store. Displays range from dinosaurs to trappers. Exhibits dinosaurs of prehistory. Ask about ichthyosaur. Also native crafts, Peace gold mining equipment, early pioneers. Gift shop.

■ **St Peter's Church:** Beautiful log church beside museum, built 1938. Open for viewing during museum hours. Regular Sunday services.

■ **Alwin Holland Park:** 3km beyond town on banks of the Peace. Fantastic view. Also trout, grayling, whitefish.

■ **King Gething Park and Campground:** At edge of town. Mid-May to Sept. Sani-station, cook house, showers. By donation.

**Dam Access Rd:** West off Hwy 29, 39km beyond Halfway River.

## SIDE TRIP

### to Bennett Dam

**Dunlevy Provincial Recreation Area:** 110ha; day use. West 15km on Dam Access Rd and northwest 20km on road along north side of Williston Lake. April-Oct. Pretty park on north shore of Williston Lake's Peace Reach. Boat launch. Good fishing. Watch for floating debris on lake.

**WAC Bennett Dam Viewpoint:** West side of highway. 22km along Dam Access Rd. Good view of dam, the countryside, and Muskwa Range of the Rockies.

**WAC Bennett Dam:** West 24km along Dam Access Rd. Dam is on eastern tip of Williston Lake, which is 362km long. BC's largest reservoir, it took five years to fill. 183m high and 2km across, it is constructed with rocky debris from a glacial moraine left from last ice age. This moraine blocked the original valley of the Peace, and the river cut a new course. Today the river is again dammed by the same material that blocked it 15,000 years ago.

**Visitors Centre of the WAC Bennett Dam and Gordon Shrum Generating Station:** Daily, with free tours of powerhouse May-Oct. Tours by reservation only in winter. 783-5211. Information on the generation of electricity. Summer snack bar.

**Peace Canyon Visitor Centre:** Daily Mid-May to Oct, 8-4. Weekdays only in winter when tour reservations are necessary. 783-9943. Engrossing information about area from the time when dinosaurs roamed the shores of a vast inland ocean. Life-size models of dinosaurs, and casts of their footprints from the canyon bedrock.

### *Return to Hudson's Hope*

**Peace Canyon Dam and Generating Station:** East side of Hwy 29, 7km beyond Hudson's Hope. Second hydroelectric project to harness the Peace River. This dam, at the outlet of the Peace River Canyon, is 23km downstream from the WAC Bennett Dam and reuses the same water. Behind the dam is a small reservoir, 800ha in size, 21km long, called Dinosaur Lake, that has flooded over part of the canyon.

**Dinosaur Lake Campground:** On Dinosaur Lake. By donation. Boat launch, hiking trails.

**Peace River Bridge:** 1km beyond Peace Canyon Dam, highway crosses Peace River's only suspension bridge. Rainbow trout and Dolly Varden. Pullouts at each end facilitate admiration of unusual concrete totem poles.

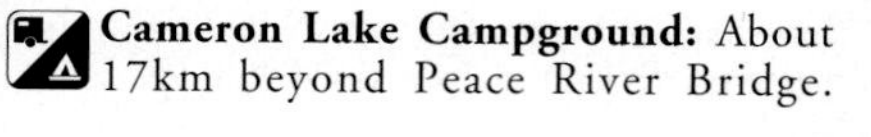

**Cameron Lake Campground:** About 17km beyond Peace River Bridge.

Swimming and playground. No motor boats. By donation.

**Spencer Tuck Regional Park:** 4ha; day use. April-Oct. South side of highway, 26km beyond Peace River bridge. Picnic spot on north shore of Moberly Lake. Good swimming, fishing.

**Moberly Lake:** (Pop. 242). South, 5km beyond Spencer Tuck Park. This community on north shore of Moberly Lake is named for Henry Moberly, trader, trapper, and prospector who lived on lakeshore 1865-1868. Cree people moved to the area after Riel Rebellion.

Keep an eye open for Moberly Dick, a lake monster allegedly lurking in the depths.

■ **Moberly Lake Golf Club:** 788-3880. Nine holes overlooking lake.

**Moberly Lake Provincial Park:** 98ha; 109 campsites, sani-station. 787-3407. Also try 788-9322 May 1-Oct 30. South side of highway, 8km from community of Moberly Lake, then west 3km along gravel road to lake's south shore. Excellent day-use park. Moose and black bear come for the berries.

**Chetwynd:** About 20km beyond Moberly Lake. See *Prince George to Dawson Creek*, p.234.

**Hwy 97 (Hart Hwy):** At Chetwynd. East 100km to Dawson Creek. Southwest 306km to Prince George. See *Prince George to Dawson Creek*, p.233.

For Hwy 29 south to Tumbler Ridge, head east on Hwy 97.

**Hwy 29S:** South, 3km beyond Hwy 97 junction. Leads 90km southeast to Tumbler Ridge.

**Sukunka River:** 12km beyond Hwy 97, Hwy 29 crosses river. Dolly Varden, grayling.

**Sukunka Falls Provincial Park:** 360ha; no development. 22km beyond Hwy 97 junction, then south off Hwy 29 onto Sunkunka forest service road for 25km. Sukunka Falls are actually a sequence of 3m tumbling cascades. Good hiking along unmarked trails. Park straddles Sukunka River (good fishing).

**Gwillim Lake Provincial Park:** 9,199ha; 49 campsites. 787-3407. 48km from Chetwynd, then east off Hwy 29. Paved access. Year-round. Deep blue waters beneath Mt Meikle. Wooded campsites. Good boating but water choppy when windy. Popular ice fishing lake. Viewpoint, trails, playground facility, horseshoe pits, picnicking.

**Bullmoose Mine:** Access road 20km from Gwillim Lake Park. 90-minute tours Tues and Thurs at 10am. Mid-June to late Aug. 242-4702.

**Tumbler Ridge:** (Pop. 4,650). 37km south of Bullmoose Mine road. Incorporated in 1981; well planned in attempt to avoid the instant-town image and architecture. Home to the people who work at the two computerized coal mines nearby. Developing the mines, and building Tumbler Ridge and the transportation infrastructure has been BC's largest industrial undertaking.

Facilities cluster around the town centre on Main St. Tumbler Ridge is an excellent centre for outdoor recreation year-round, offering easy access to hiking, fishing, hunting, snowmobiling, cross-country skiing, and horseback riding. Also nine-hole golf course, recreation and aquatic centre.

Jet-boat charters to Monkman Provincial Park may be available. Contact Chamber of Commerce.

**Tumbler Ridge Information:** Travel Infocentre and Chamber of Commerce now in new building on Southgate and Front streets. Box 606, Tumbler Ridge, BC, V0C 2W0. Weekdays year-round, weekends also July-Aug. 242-4702. Also try District of Tumbler Ridge, 242-4242.

■ **Quintette Mine Tours:** Ask at or call infocentre. Scheduled tours in summer. Off-season by arrangement.

**Monkman Provincial Park:** 32,000ha; 42 campsites. 787-3407. **Kinuseo Falls Camground** is 35km from Tumbler Ridge mining site on gravel-surfaced Murray River forest service road (60km south of town). Watch for industrial traffic. Opened 1992.

No road access to rest of park. Air, hiking, or horseback access only. Park is on eastern flank of Rockies in Hart Range. Fine wilderness hiking. Fascinating geological structures. Stirring alpine views and crystal-clear lakes. Prime grizzly habitat.

Park named for Alex Monkman, trapper and homesteader who envisioned a route along old Indian trails to connect Peace River country to BC coast. Alas for Monkman, the Pine Pass route to the west was selected instead.

Return via Hwy 29 to Chetwynd. Hwys 52N and 52E are alternative routes back to Hwy 97.

**Hwy 52:** East of Tumbler Ridge, Hwy 52N (Heritage Highway) winds 98km through foothill country to join Hwy 97 at Arras, 17km west of Dawson Creek. Mainly gravel.

A longer scenic route to Hwy 2 and Dawson Creek, or to the Province of Alberta, is Hwy 52E, also known as Boundary Rd. The mainly gravel highway circles east, then north about 146km from Tumbler Ridge to join Hwy 2 at Tupper on BC/Alberta border.

## SIDE TRIP
### on Highway 52E

After turnoff to Quintette Mine, about 13.5km south of Tumbler Ridge, the highway becomes a good quality gravel road used by oil, gas, and forest industries. Lonely, wild country. Respect sour-gas warnings on some side roads. Forest service recreation sites at Flatbed Creek East (about 34km from Tumbler Ridge), Stoney Lake (56km), Red Willow (79km), and Thunder Creek (82km).

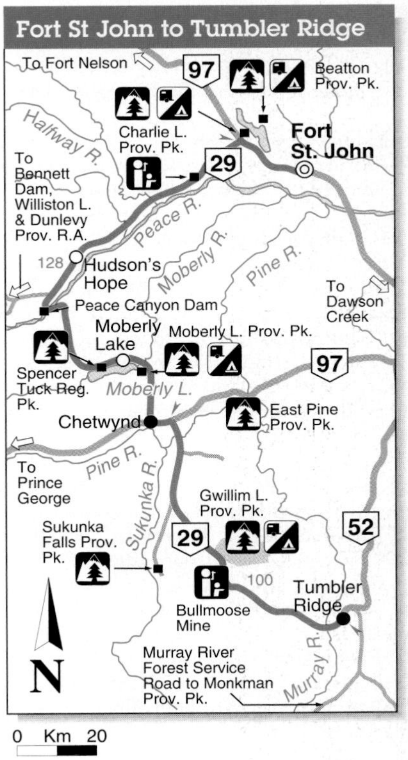

**One Island Lake Provincial Park:** 61ha; 30 campsites. 787-3407. Take One Island Lake Rd north off Hwy 52E about 136km beyond Tumbler Ridge, or from Hwy 2 south, 30km rough road access. In the gently undulating Rocky Mountain foothills. Chance of large rainbow, brook trout. Boat launch.

**Hwy 2:** About 10km beyond Hwy 52E junction with One Island Park Rd. This *Log* travels northwest 36km to Dawson Creek via Pouce Coupe. Southeast leads 2km to Alberta.

**Tupper:** (Pop. 33). Off Hwy 2, 1km beyond junction with Hwy 52. Seeking refuge from Hitler, a group of Sudetens (Czechoslovakians named for the Sudetes mountain range on the Czech/Polish border), settled in this attractive area in the late 1930s. Services.

**Swan Lake Provincial Park:** 67ha; 41 campsites. 787-3407. East off highway about 2km beyond Tupper. Access on 3km gravel road. May-Nov. Attractive park with beautiful beach, excellent swimming and boating on 5km Swan Lake. Recently stocked, the lake offers good fishing for pike and some perch. This, the third oldest provincial park in BC, celebrated its 75th birthday in 1993. There is a baseball diamond, horseshoe pits, picnic shelter.

**Fort St John to Tumbler Ridge**

0 Km 20

**Sudeten Provincial Park:** 5ha; 15 campsites. Day use in pastoral setting. 787-3407. West off Hwy 2, 3km beyond Swan Lake park. Picnic shelter, playing field.

**Pouce Coupe:** (Pop. 832). A serene little community overlooking the Pouce Coupe River, 20km beyond Sudeten Park. Pioneer Peace River community looks like a movie set. Locals pronounce it "Poose Coop" – those affecting French accents pronounce it "Poose Coo-pay." Said to be named for a Sekanni trapper who lost a thumb in a gun accident: means, literally, "thumb cut off."

Hector Tremblay, a French-Canadian en route to the Yukon to seek his fortune, stopped instead at Pouce Coupe in 1898 and became the first settler in the area. This was once the seat of government in Peace River country, but most departments have now moved to Dawson Creek, 10km north.

**Pouce Coupe Travel Information:** Village of Pouce Coupe, Box 190, Pouce Coupe, BC, V0C 2C0. Infocentre on Main St, one block off Hwy 2. Daily mid-May to mid-Sept. 786-5555; off-season 786-5794.

■ **Pouce Coupe Museum:** On 49th Ave. Daily May 15-Sept 15. 786-5555. Exhibits, housed in former Northern Alberta Railway Station (1931).

**Dawson Creek:** 10km beyond Pouce Coupe, at Hwy 2/97 junction. See *Prince George to Dawson Creek*, p.235.

## Dawson Creek to Fort Nelson

### THE ALASKA HIGHWAY (Highway 97)

Within the first year after its construction in 1942, the Alaska Highway had earned a reputation as an arduous drive. It was "a tortuous little trail barely wide enough to allow one vehicle to work its way through the trees," declared a 1943 issue of *National Geographic* magazine. "We drove through deeply rutted bogs which required the lowest gear and four-wheel drive...the major and I were thrown from side to side and beaten about as if we were in a small boat on a rough sea."

During that same year Canadian and American contractors began upgrading the supply road for year-round use. Bridges were built, stretches of road were straightened and widened, surfaces gravelled. After the war, on April 1, 1946, the Canadian government took over the highway in exchange for certain concessions, such as right of way.

Civilians were denied the rigours of travelling the Alaska Highway until 1948. Soon after its public opening, the journey's reputation as "tough and challenging" was upgraded, or downgraded, to "suicidal." It was closed. And re-opened again in 1949, but flat tires and empty gas tanks continued to plague persistent drivers.

Today, more than 360,000 people worldwide, lured by its legendary status, travel the Alaska Hwy from May-Sept (though it remains open year-round.) An omniscient view reveals a black ribbon of pavement, now 2,288km, running just less than 1,000km through BC, more than that across the Yukon, and 320km in Alaska.

Still, this remains a road to adventure. The forests, the mountains, and all the encompassing wilderness stir the spirit and the adrenalin. See introduction to this region, p.229, for more of the Alaska Highway story.

The section from Dawson Creek slices 73km through rolling farmlands, crossing the Peace River at Taylor, and on to Fort St John. From there, it's 387km to Fort Nelson. The mood of the land becomes more rugged and wild, the views more camera-defying. To the west, the Rocky Mountains shimmer. There are a seductive prelude to what awaits farther north.

**Dawson Creek (Mile 0):** A junction point for Alaska/Hart/49/2 Hwys. For details on city, see *Prince George to Dawson Creek*, p.235.

**Farmington:** (Pop. 79). 19km beyond Dawson Creek (Alaska/Hart junction). A secondary highway from Farmington leads south, joining Hwy 97 at Arras, 17km west of Dawson Creek. East of Farmington, Sweetwater Rd leads to Rolla and Clayhurst.

**Kiskatinaw Provincial Park:** 58ha; 28 campsites. 787-3407. Turn east 4km from Farmington, 3km in on old Alaska Hwy leads to well-treed riverside park.

**Kiskatinaw River Bridge:** Just beyond park entrance. River cuts a deep canyon. Bridge across it is a curved, three-span wooden trestle built 1943. The old highway goes on to rejoin Alaska Highway.

**Peace River Valley Viewpoint:** On Hwy 97, 22km north of Kiskatinaw Park turnoff.

**Taylor Landing Provincial Park:** 2ha. East side of highway, 5km from viewpoint, 25km beyond Kiskatinaw Park turnoff. Day use. Boat launch. Boaters take care, the river here is downstream from Bennett and Peace Canyon dams; water levels can fluctuate rapidly.

**Peace Island Park:** 17.5ha; 20 campsites, four group sites (one with shelter). On the west side of highway, across from Taylor Landing park. May 15-Sept 4. 789-3392. Has playground. Also beaver, geese, moose, deer. And this is home to World Gold Panning Championships in Aug.

**Peace River Bridge:** 500m beyond Peace Island Park. Built 1960. Its predecessor, known as Galloping Gerdie, collapsed 1957. On east side of highway is the natural gas pipeline, which looks like a bridge itself. From here to Fort St John, gas pipelines run beneath fields, and gas-processing plants are many.

**Taylor (Mile 35):** (Pop. 821). Begins at Peace River Bridge. Community is built on a broad plateau above the river. Alexander Mackenzie, describing the area in 1793, wrote: "The land above the spot where we are encamped, spreads into an extensive plain and stretches onto a very high ridge. The country is so crowded with animals as to have the appearance, in some places of a stall-yard from the state of the ground. The soil is black and light. We this day saw two grisly and hideous bears."

Town takes its name from DH "Herbie" Taylor, in 1906 the area's first homesteader. Taylor – its economy based on lumber, pulp, oil and gas – is deep in the river valley, surrounded by lightly forested hills of poplar, cottonwood, and spruce. Fall colours are wonderful. Wildlife is plentiful, but Mackenzie's "hideous" bears are seldom seen. Try delicious sweet corn from local garden markets.

**Taylor Information:** Infocentre, May-late Oct. 789-9015. District of Taylor, Box 300, Taylor, BC, VOC 2KO. 789-3392.

■ **Church of the Good Shepherd:** Little 1932 structure was built as memorial by father of four daughters who drowned in a boating accident on the Peace.

■ **World's Largest Golf Ball:** Marks location of Taylor Golf and Country Club adjacent Alaska Hwy. Ball, once an old fuel tank, is 12.8m in diameter and weighs 37t.

**Fort St John (Mile 47):** (Pop. 14,156). 19km beyond Taylor. Fort St John, the "Energy Capital of BC," is also the "Land of the New Totems," referring to the huge oil derricks on the horizon. It's a bustling, modern city with a sparkling library and arts centre, a daily newspaper, and a thriving economy dependent on oil and gas, agriculture, and lumber.

**FORT ST JOHN**

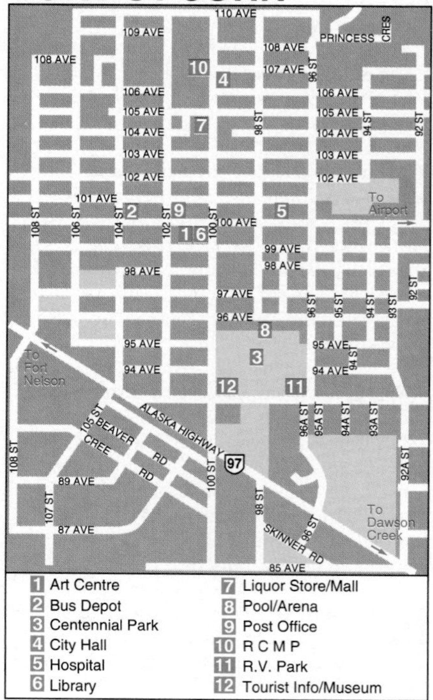

Some 10km upstream on the Peace River is site of Rocky Mountain Fort. It was built by the North West Company in 1794, making it the oldest white settlement on BC's mainland. Since then, Fort St John has moved four times, but is likely to stay put now.

**Fort St John Information:** Fort St John Chamber of Commerce, 9323-100th St, Fort St John, BC, V1J 4N4. 785-3033. In North Peace Museum, behind the huge oil derrick clearly seen from Hwy 97, open year-round.

**Fort St John Airport:** 8km southeast toward Taylor. Scheduled and charter airlines.

■ **Monument to Alexander Mackenzie:** Located in Fort St John Centennial Park on Mackenzie St.

■ **Fort St John-North Peace Museum:** Behind 46m oil derrick. Daily May-Sept, Mon-Sat rest of year. Reconstructed schoolhouse. Pioneer artifacts. Trapper's cabin. Exhibit on Alaska Hwy. Gift shop and unique Peace River crafts.

■ **North Peace Cultural Centre:** 100th and 100th. 785-1992. Houses art gallery, library, and theatre.

■ **Peace River Lookout:** South end of 100th St. Wonderful view of river valley. Picnicking.

■ **Fish Creek Community Forest:** 785-8906. 2km northeast of town, off 100th St. Guided or self-guided forest walks year-round.

**Beatton Provincial Park:** 312ha; 37 campsites. 787-3407. 6km north of Fort St John. Year-round. Camping May-Oct. Turn north off Hwy 97. 10km on paved road to park entrance, then turn west on gravel. Aspen-lined trails lead to 300m developed beach on Charlie Lake. Boating, hiking, walking trails. Fishing for walleye and northern pike. Playing field. Winter activities: cross-country skiing, ice fishing, snowshoeing. Warm-up huts.

**Charlie Lake:** 7km north of Fort St John. Services. Was Mile Zero on army tote road. Some locals insist this is true beginning of Alaska Highway construction. It was also here, on May 14, 1942, that 11 soldiers drowned when their cargo barge sank.

**Hwy 29:** 13km north of Fort St John. Leads south 75km to Hudson's Hope, rejoining Hwy 97 at Chetwynd, 100km west of Dawson Creek. See Fort *St John to Tumbler Ridge*, p.236.

**Charlie Lake Provincial Park:** 92ha; 58 campsites, sani-station. 787-3407. Located at Hwys 29/97 junction. May-Oct. A destination for walleye fishermen. Also boating and hiking. Heavily treed park, with berries in autumn. Snowshoe hare and ruffed grouse commonly seen. Charlie Lake can be thick with algae in the summer which makes it one of the most productive lakes in BC. Playground, picnic shelter, boat launch.

**Rest Areas:** 18km and 40km from Hwy 29/97 junction. Both on highway's west side.

**Wonowon (Mile 101):** (Pop. 84). 76km from Hwy 29/97 junction. Tourist facilities. Wonowon used to be known as Blueberry, for the Blueberry River that flows on the east side of highway. Was a 24-hour military checkpoint during war years.

North of Wonowon the highway starts climbing through dense forests intersected by arrow-straight seismic lines. 360 degree vistas as highway breaches ridges.

**Pink Mountain (Mile 143):** (Pop. 19). 62km beyond Wonowon. Tourist facilities. Moose often seen, sometimes caribou, too. Highway has steadily climbed to 1,100m. Now, descends steeply into the Beatton River Valley.

**Suicide Hill:** About 8km from Pink Mountain; Historic Milepost 148. Prepare to meet thy maker. "I rolled her along 'till I reached the drop they now call suicide hill. As I inched her down with squeaking brakes, it was a horrible thrill." Words of Gene Wilkinson who trucked perishables to work camps during Alaska Highway construction, and lived to write about it. Today, the hill's a breeze.

**Time Zone:** About 4km beyond Suicide Hill. No changes in summer, when daylight-savings time is in effect elsewhere in BC. But from late Oct-April, set your clock back one hour as you move from Mountain Standard to **Pacific Standard Time**.

**Sikanni Chief River Bridge (Mile 162):** 21km from Suicide Hill. (30km from Pink Mountain.) 5km descent into valley to bridge. Reasonable summer fishing for pike, grayling, and whitefish.

**Buckinghorse River Provincial Park (Mile 173):** 55ha; 30 campsites. 787-3407. 22.5km beyond Sikanni Chief River. Park at edge of Rocky Mountain foothills. Cast a fly at grayling. Moose wintering area. Services across road.

About 4km north of park, the highway was rerouted around Trutch Mountain in 1987. Heavy vehicles had problems climbing 1,260m summit. The military chose the high route rather than contend with muskeg at lower elevations. The new stretch of road follows the side hill of Minnaker River Valley.

This is a scenic stretch, with mountain and river valley views, and moose.

**Prophet River Provincial Recreation Area (Mile 217):** 115ha; 36 campsites. 787-3407. 73km beyond Buckinghorse River park. May-Oct. Park overlooks, but is not on, Prophet River. Heavily wooded with poplar. A rough trail leads to river, but the banks are eroding and it is dangerous. Excellent birdwatching. Wood warblers nest in poplar trees. Check small pond on way in for ducks. Watch for bears. Natural spring water.

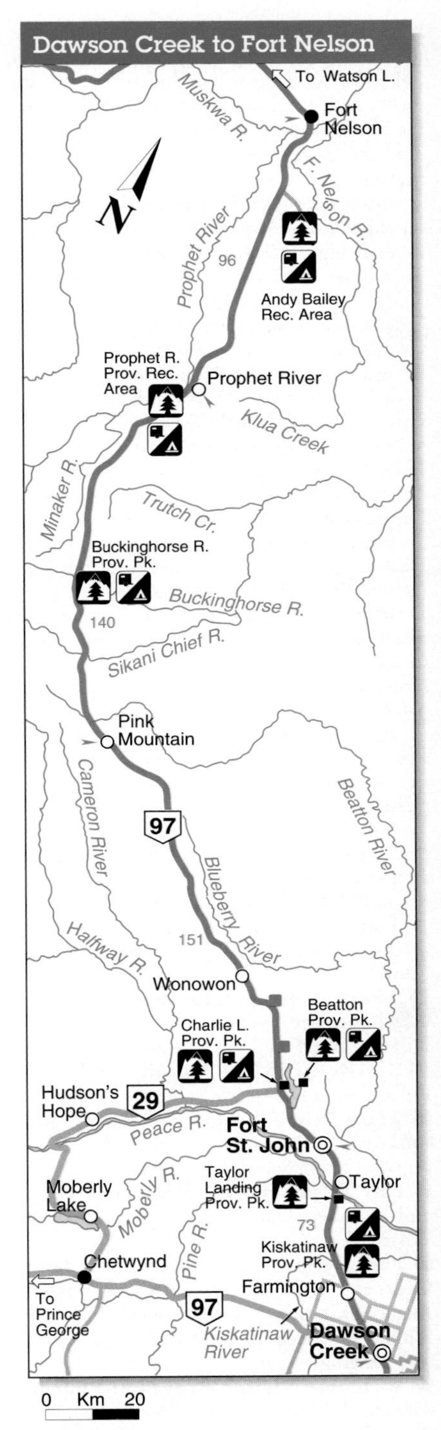


**Prophet River (Mile 233):** (Pop. 77). 15km north of Prophet River Provincial Recreation Area. Services, school, little wooden church with tin roof and no bell.

**Curve Cutting:** The Adsett Creek realignment project completed in 1992 removed 132 arm-aching curves from about 66km of highway.

**Andy Bailey Provincial Recreation Area (Mile 265):** 174ha; 12 campsites. 787-3407. Turn east 65.5km north of Prophet River, and 12km on dirt road.

Named for pioneer who cut the original access road. May-Oct. Long sandy beach on Jackfish Lake. Because most northern beaches are rocky, sand has been imported. Good fishing for northern pike. Swimming, boat launch. The spruce forests here encourage insects. Marshy.

From here it's 25km to the lowest point on the Alaska Hwy, 307m, at the Muskwa River Bridge. *Muskwa* is the Cree name for black bear.

**Fort Nelson (Mile 300):** (Pop. 3,804). 31km beyond road to Andy Bailey Recreation Area. Fort Nelson is presumed to have been named after British naval hero, Lord Nelson. A North West Company post built here in 1805 was destroyed by natives in 1813. Four more trading posts were built, and destroyed, between 1813 and 1890. Fort Nelson is on site of fifth post.

Near here, the Muskwa, Prophet, and Sikanni Chief rivers meet to create the Fort Nelson River, which flows into the Liard.

In the 1920s Fort Nelson's economy was based on the fur trade. In 1942, it was home to 2,000 troops "working on the highway." Now the city thrives on lumber and the oil patch.

Area is heavily forested with marketable white spruce and lodgepole pine, supporting the world's largest chopstick manufacturing plant.

Fort Nelson has a large gas-producing plant, and a byproduct, sulphur, is shipped around the world. Here is the northern terminus of BC Rail's freight-only line.

Fort Nelson also offers the easiest access into the Kwadacha Wilderness Park. See below.

**Fort Nelson Information:** Travel Infocentre, Fort Nelson-Liard Regional District, Bag Service 399, Fort Nelson, BC, V0C 1R0. 774-6400. Daily May-Aug. Off-season call 774-2541.

**Fort Nelson Airport:** 6km east of town. Airport Dr leads right from Hwy 97 in centre of town. Scheduled and charter.

■ **Fort Nelson Historical Museum:** North end of town. Daily 10am-9pm May-Aug. 774-3536.

■ **Fort Nelson-Liard Native Friendship Centre:** 774-2993. On 49th Ave, next to Anglican Church. Local native crafts for sale: mukluks, moccasins, and moosehair-tufted wall hangings.

■ **Welcome Visitor Program:** Phoenix Theatre. Mid-May to mid-Aug. Evening stories, talks and demonstrations by residents about anything and everything to do with the area, from flowers to native legends to horseback riding. Details at infocentre.

■ **BC's Most Northerly Grass Greens Golf Course:** Poplar Hills Golf Club. Mile 304 Radar Rd. On highest point in Fort Nelson, the old DEW Line radar site. Nine holes.

**Kwadacha Wilderness Provincial Park:** 158,475ha. 787-3407 for maps and information. Roughly 160km southwest of Fort Nelson. No road access. Most visitors fly in, but guided horseback riding or hiking access can be arranged. Open all year, wilderness campsites. Excellent climbing and hiking, but few marked trails. For wilderness-wise visitors only.

*Kwadacha*, the Sekanni native word for white water, describes the milky colour of the Kwadacha River, which is heavy with glacial debris leached from the Lloyd George Icefield, one of the most spectacular features of this rugged park. Kwadacha is carefully preserved as BC's truly total wilderness park. Grizzlies are common, hikers beware. Among the sky-reaching limestone peaks are thickly wooded valleys, flower-studded alpine meadows, and turquoise lakes. Here, too, are hoodoos – castellated rock sculpted by the elements. A great diversity of habitats is reflected in wildlife populations. Elk are abundant, as are bears, timber wolves, wolverines, mountain goats, and many smaller mammals. Park is also a bird refuge. More than 70 bird species have been identified, including peregrine falcons, golden eagles, and the red-throated loon.

For continuation of Alaska Hwy see *Fort Nelson to Watson Lake*, following.

## Fort Nelson to Watson Lake

### THE ALASKA HIGHWAY (Highway 97)

This section is everything the Alaska Hwy is supposed to be. A mountain lover's dream. The highway climbs and curls through 525km of the most diverse landscape imaginable. The rugged peaks of the northern Rocky Mountains, with their convoluted rock formations, present spectacular views at each twist of the road. Occasional remains of log cabins are a reminder of the prospectors, explorers, and trappers who lived in this splendid isolation. Some still do.

The region contains lakes of crystal clarity but perhaps most unlikely of all are the relaxing waters of Liard Hot Springs where moose munch algae and carnivorous plants await their prey.

The highway from Fort Nelson starts benignly enough through mixed forests and patches of muskeg. Then it winds up into the mountains. The stretch through Stone Mountain and Muncho Lake parks is arguably the most scenic in North America. After conquering the mountains, the highway follows the Liard River to the BC/Yukon border.

**Fort Nelson (Mile 300):** (Pop. 3,804) On Alaska Hwy (97 North), 460km north of Fort St John. And 525km southeast of Watson Lake. See *Dawson Creek to Fort Nelson*, above.

**Hwy 77 (Liard Hwy):** 27km beyond Fort Nelson. Leads north off Alaska Hwy, 137km to BC/NWT border. There it becomes Hwy 7. The first settlement north of the border is tiny Fort Liard, about 42km away. In all, the Liard Hwy travels nearly 400km through to its junction with the Mackenzie Hwy near Fort Simpson. This wilderness highway is very much like the old Alaska Hwy: it's a gravel road, with few facilities and travel should be undertaken with care. The Liard Hwy is also part of a 2,240km loop drive along the Alaska, Liard, and Mackenzie Hwys, passing through BC, Alberta, and the Northwest Territories.

**Maxhamish Provincial Park:** 520ha. West of Hwy 77 (Liard Hwy) near NWT border. No road access; fly in only. Sandy beaches and solitude.

**Steamboat Mountain (Mile 351):** (Pop. just 3). 57km beyond Liard Hwy junction. Road clings to valley side. Services. Locals call this "steamboat country." One story says it is named by a homesick Scot who, used to looking down on the loch steamboats from his hikes among Scottish hills, decided the mountain here resembled a steamboat.

**Rd to Vista:** North off Hwy 97 1km from Steamboat Mountain "community". A rough, narrow road leads up Steamboat Mountain, 1,067m. Wonderful views of the Rocky Mountains.

**Indian Head Mountain:** 14.5km from Steamboat. View of the mountain shaped, someone thought, like the classic native profile.

**Teetering Rock:** 2.5km beyond Indian Head, north side of highway, start of 12.5km hiking trail to a glacial erratic.

**Tetsa River Provincial Park:** 115ha; 25 campsites. 787-3407. About 6km beyond Steamboat Mountain. 1km south off Hwy 97 on dirt road. April-Oct. Good fishing for grayling. Check fishing regulations. Pleasant, short hikes through poplar trees along river. Braided river channels. Pleasant, private campsites.

**Tetsa River Services:** 17km beyond Tetsa River Park. Jet-boat rides.

**Stone Mountain Provincial Park:** 25,691ha. Boundary about 22km from Tetsa River Services; straddles highway for 14km. 787-3407. Park offers landscapes of extensive alpine tundra and long, U-shaped valleys beneath sweeping, bare mountain peaks. Dramatic stuff. Erosion pillars or hoodoos. Turquoise sub-alpine lakes and waterfalls. Park is home to mountain caribou and Stone sheep (relative of Dall sheep). Also watch for elk, deer, bear, and moose. Stone Mountain offers limitless wilderness hiking. Much of it strictly for experienced backpackers as distances are great, terrain rugged and marked trails few. A feature is the 6km Flower Springs Lake Trail.

**Summit Lake (Mile 392):** (Pop. 50). About 3km beyond park boundary. BC Parks Summit Lake campground. 28 sites. Services. Summit Lake, 1,295m, is the highest point on the Alaska

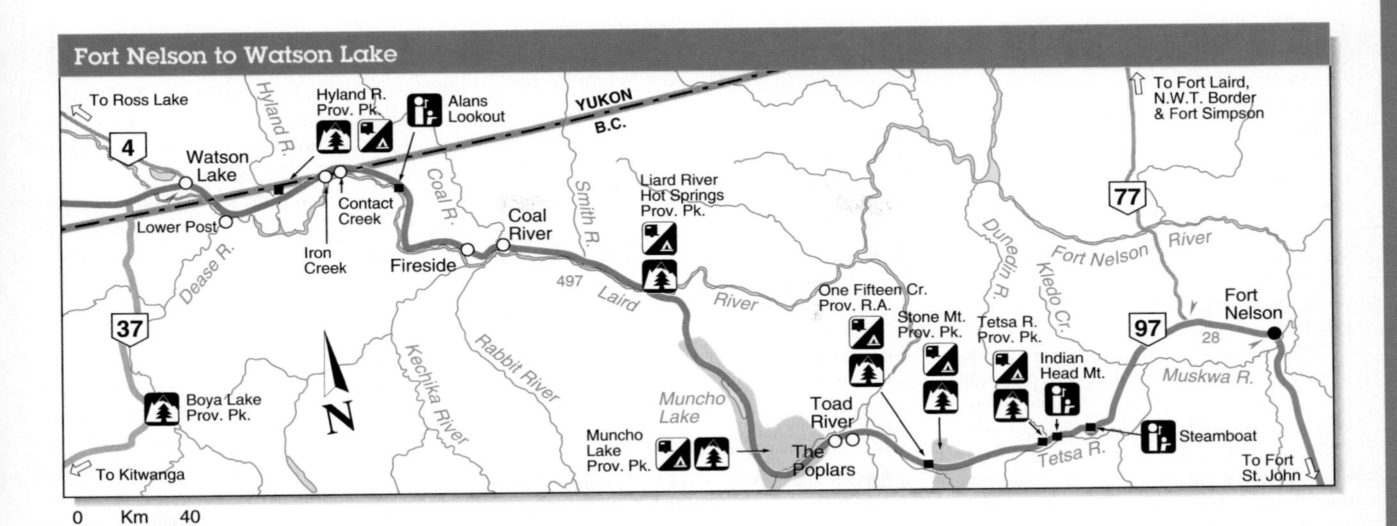


Hwy. The timberline, where spruce and dark firs give way to scrub willow and birch, is only a few hundred metres above the road. It can snow here at any time of year.

**Trails:** Summit Lake campground is starting point for some great walks. Just west of campground, a 10-minute trail to two hoodoos; legend has it they are the heads of devils. Just north, an arduous 5km hike through spruce forests to alpine near **Summit Peak**. And just south of the campground, four-wheel-drive trail leads to microwave tower and stunning views. **Flower Springs Lake Trail** leads 6km return trip to enchanting aquamarine tarn. Reasonably easy going. A memorable way to introduce children – or grandparents – to alpine country. But stay on the trail, the land's as fragile as it is beautiful.

**Wokkpash Provincial Recreation Area:** 37,800ha; wilderness camping. No facilities. 787-3407. Adjoins southwestern boundary of Stone Mountain Park.

Access trail starts at Churchill Mine Rd, about 15km west of Summit Lake campsite. Bridge washed out. This 70km (five-to-seven-day) loop recommended only for experienced hikers. Hikers can rejoin Alaska Hwy just west of Summit Lake, or retrace steps, but it is strongly recommended the hike is completed at campground. Flash flooding on MacDonald Creek – a braided stream up to 1km wide – can render the creek impassable, stranding hikers for several days.

Within this wilderness valley is the spectacular Wokkpash Gorge, also called Forlorn Gorge, 5km of which is lined on both sides with 30m hoodoos, or erosion pillars. The gorge is a miniature Grand Canyon, only 25m wide, but 150m deep, giving a rocky record of millions of years of the earth's upheavals. Trail crosses the Stony Mountains section of the Rockies before descending to Summit Lake campsite. Share wilderness with caribou, mountain goats, Stone sheep, and moose.

Highway parallels MacDonald Creek and the next few km offer views of the Stone Range to the northeast and the Muskwa Ranges of the Rockies to the west.

**Deadly Mix:** Graphic red signs depicting dead sheep and crumpled cars urge motorists to slow down in areas frequented by Stone sheep. Pull well off road to photograph animals.

**Northern Boundary:** End of Stone Mountain Provincial Park about 11km beyond Summit Lake campground.

**One-Fifteen Creek Provincial Recreation Area:** 51ha; eight campsites. 787-3407. South side of highway, 18km beyond Summit Lake campground. A series of big, old beaver dams and ponds are just two minutes' walk behind the park. Trails.

**Racing River Wayside Area:** Hwy 97 crosses this bridge 25km from One-Fifteen Park. Good fishing for grayling and Dolly Varden in late summer. River access is at south end of bridge. A natural hot spring pool is about 10km hike north to junction of Toad and Racing rivers.

**Toad River (Mile 422):** (Pop 60). 5km from the Racing River Bridge. Home of a collection of 2,500 hats, one for every mile of the highway from the southern US border to the Alaska border. Services, airstrip, school.

**The Poplars (Mile 426):** (Pop. 4). 5km beyond Toad River. Services.

**Muncho Lake Provincial Park:** 88,416ha; 30 campsites. 787-3407. Southern boundary of park is 2km beyond the Poplars. Canada's northern Rocky Mountains at their spectacular best. Fortunately for today's visitors, they're on view because highway surveyors wanted to avoid the Grand Canyon of the Liard. They chose to route the highway 82km along the Toad and Trout river valleys. In between, the highway skirts the eastern shore of Muncho Lake – meaning Big Lake in Kaskan native dialect. It looks longer than its 12km, probably because it pops up unexpectedly from the tight quarters of the mountains. And because these jade-green waters that change tone with the light have the visual impact of a sledgehammer. The colour originates from copper dioxides deep down in the lake's bedrock.

Wildlife loves the park, although several species are near the northern limit of their range. Watch for loons, grebes or mergansers, as well as black bear in spring. Check locally for best photo opportunities. Serendipity helps.

**Folded Mountain:** 4km from southern boundary of Muncho Lake Park. A mountain with wrinkles. One of several peaks tortured by tectonic folding and faulting; pastel colour coordination in exposed rock.

**Centennial Falls:** Attractive waterfall about 8km beyond Folded Mountain.

**Strawberry Flats Provincial Campground:** 29km from falls. 15 sites on gravel fan overlooking Muncho Lake. Popular spot in summer, with imposing lake and mountain views. Admire, but don't pick the wildflowers.

**Muncho Lake (Mile 456):** (Pop. 24). About 8km beyond Strawberry Flats. Services. One of the few Canadian towns inside a provincial park. Ask about lake tours June-Sept.

**MacDonald Provincial Campground:** 15 sites. 2km from Muncho Lake.

**Muncho Lake Park Northern Boundary:** 28km from MacDonald campground. Gradually, the highway leaves the Rockies behind and descends into the Liard River valley. *Liard* is French for cottonwood tree.

**Liard River Bridge (Mile 496):** About 25km beyond northern boundary of Muncho Lake Park. Services.

**Liard River Hot Springs Provincial Park:** 668ha; 52 campsites. 787-3407. 2km beyond Liard River Bridge. North off Hwy 97. Two hot, soothing, mineral water pools creating their own luxuriant micro-climate. Access to Alpha and Beta pools by wooden boardwalk across warm water swamps. Look for tiny chub skittering about. Water temperatures range 38-49 degrees C. Using shampoo or soap in pools is not permitted. Nor is liquor. Prolonged lounging may not be safe for some medical conditions. Plan to stop early in day; it's a very popular spot in summer. Informative visitor programs including nature walks. In winter, hot springs are transformed into a mystical oasis of steam and hoarfrost.

When homesteader John Smith lived here in the 1920s, word spread of a tropical valley in the northern wilderness – images of monkeys and parrots frolicking in banana groves. Well, not quite – but the hot springs proved a most welcome "discovery" to highway building crews in 1942, although women in the construction camps were only granted the privilege of relaxing in them once a week.

The hot springs increase humidity and raise temperatures about 2 degrees C from regional annual averages. That allows plants to grow here in profusion farther north than their normal range. Moose, bear, and many bird species share this haven.

A few km north of the hot springs is the southern boundary of a June 1982 forest fire. BC's second largest, it burned 182,725ha. Two separate fires, the Eg and Cran, were sparked by lightning and then joined. The worst of the burned area has been covered by low scrub and wildflowers.

**Smith River Falls:** About 27km north of Liard Hot Springs, 2km off Hwy 97. Pleasant picnic spot. Good fishing for Dolly Varden and grayling in river beneath falls.

**Coal River (Mile 533):** (Pop. 8). About 30km north of road to Smith River Falls. Services. In wet weather before highway was paved, vehicles emerged from this section splattered in black from coal in the road's surface.

**Whirlpool Canyon Viewpoint:** Nearly 9km beyond Coal River. Viewpoint, south side of highway, where Liard River makes sweeping right-hand turn between three rocky-rimmed channels.

**Fireside (Mile 543):** (Pop. 4). 7km beyond Whirlpool Canyon. Stark reminders in all directions of devastation caused by forest fires.

**Alans Lookout (Mile 570):** About 40km beyond Fireside. Great view of Liard River and Goat Mountain.

**Contact Creek (Mile 590):** (Pop. 4). 27km beyond Alans Lookout. Services. Construction crews working from north and south on Alaska Hwy, met here, September 24, 1942. Tourist facilities 3km beyond. *This is the Yukon.* Highway flip-flops across the BC/Yukon border seven times before the official border about 63km away.

**Iron Creek (Mile 596):** (Pop 4). 10km north of Contact Creek. South side of highway. Services.

**Hyland River Bridge:** Kilometre Post 1,000. About 14km from Iron Creek. Dolly Varden and grayling.

**Lower Post Rd (Mile 620):** 21km beyond Hyland River Bridge. South off Hwy 97. Road does not loop through village. Lower Post was a Hudson's Bay Company trading post and native community. No services for visitors now. Lower Post derived its name from Upper Post on McDame Creek, on the Dease River. The Liard and Dease rivers meet here.

**BC/Yukon Territory Border (Mile 627):** 17km beyond Lower Post junction. The Alaska Hwy crosses the 60th parallel as it enters Yukon Territory. The town of **Watson Lake**, 12km north of the border, is famous for the Sign Post Forest, a symbolic display of the construction crew's isolation and loneliness. It was initiated in 1942 by US army soldier Carl Lindley. Soon after he posted the first carved sign of his home town, Danville, Illinois, others followed suit. Travellers still carry out the tradition; there are more than 9,000 signs and licence plates from all sorts of places.

From the border, Alaska Hwy 97 becomes Alaska Hwy 1, and veers east. The Cassiar Mountains to the southwest, are now visible. The highway dips back into BC one more time just before Teslin Lake, then continues on to Whitehorse.

## ROADS TO THE KLONDIKE

The lure of the north still exists; the desire to go to the end of the road, or the earth, still grips the wanderer. First the gold fields of the Cariboo beckoned, then the Omineca Mountains north of Prince George, and the Cassiar Mountains. Beyond that the Pelly Mountains north of Whitehorse, and the Ogilvies nestling Dawson City. The Klondike coaxes the traveller onward, as much now as 100 years ago. The fever is no longer fuelled by gold, but there's always a dream.

The highways to BC's northern border take the traveller through some of the province's most spectacular scenery. It's like sitting on top of the world.

There are five highways crossing from BC into the Yukon. The Alaska Hwy (Hwy 97) leads northwest to Lower Post, crossing the border near Watson Lake, and joining Hwy 1 as it begins its westward journey to Alaska's border. About 23km west of Watson Lake, just past Upper Liard, is Hwy 1's junction with Hwy 37. The Stewart-Cassiar Hwy 37 connects the Alaska Hwy with Hwy 16, 725km to the south. For details on Hwy 37, see *North by Northwest*, p.223.

From its junction with Hwy 37 on the BC/Yukon border, Hwy 1 travels west for 299km to Johnsons Crossing (in the Yukon), and another 48km west to Jakes Corner. From here it is 98km south to Atlin, BC, on mainly unpaved Hwy 7.

There are two short scenic highways travelling north from Lynn Canal in southern Alaska, which cross a small portion of northern BC before joining with the Yukon's Alaska Hwy 1 heading west to the Alaska border. They link the Alaska Marine Hwy System (*North by Northwest*, p.207) with the Yukon and Alaska proper, and follow two historic gold-rush routes used by miners and adventurers bound for the Klondike gold fields in 1898. Both the Haines and South Klondike Hwys offer breathtaking passage north, but drivers should be prepared. In winter, northbound and southbound travellers on both highways should check road conditions before leaving. These are heavy snowfall areas, and services are scant. International border stations are open 8am-12pm. Identification is required.

The Haines Hwy, a 256km mainly paved road connects Haines, Alaska, a port on the ferry system, with Haines Junction in the Yukon. It follows the Dalton Trail route to the gold fields. The first 65km climb from lush coastal valley to Canada Custom's Pleasant Camp. For the next 74km the highway flanks the St Elias Mountains in glorious open alpine country. The highest point in BC is in the St Elias Range. Mt Fairweather, el 4,663m, is tucked away in range's southwest on the BC/Alaska border. From the Chilkat Pass, 1,065m, the highway gradually descends into interior valleys of the Yukon basin. The highway's Yukon section provides access to Kluane National Park. Haines Junction, the park headquarters, is 126km west of Whitehorse.

The paved South Klondike Hwy stretches 180km from Skagway, Alaska to Whitehorse, Yukon. Skagway is one ferry stop north from Haines up an inlet of Lynn Canal. About 30,000 would-be miners hauled their possessions over the Chilkoot and White Pass routes from Dyea and Skagway. Many never made it to the gold-fields. (See Chilkoot Trail, *North by Northwest*, p.226) The White Pass and Yukon Route Railway was completed in 1900. It recently reopened to take travellers between Skagway and Fraser, the Canada Customs post. (See *Railways*, p.206.) The Alaska/BC border is 23.5km from Skagway in a glaciated subalpine landscape. Gradually, forests return and the highway hugs the shores of deep, wild lakes.

The BC/Yukon border is 81km from Skagway, 95km south of Whitehorse. Abandoned mine workings and discarded timbers litter the route to Carcross, the only community on route. Carcross is 69km south of Whitehorse.

*Alaska Hotel across from Mile Zero, start of the Alaska Highway, in Dawson Creek.*

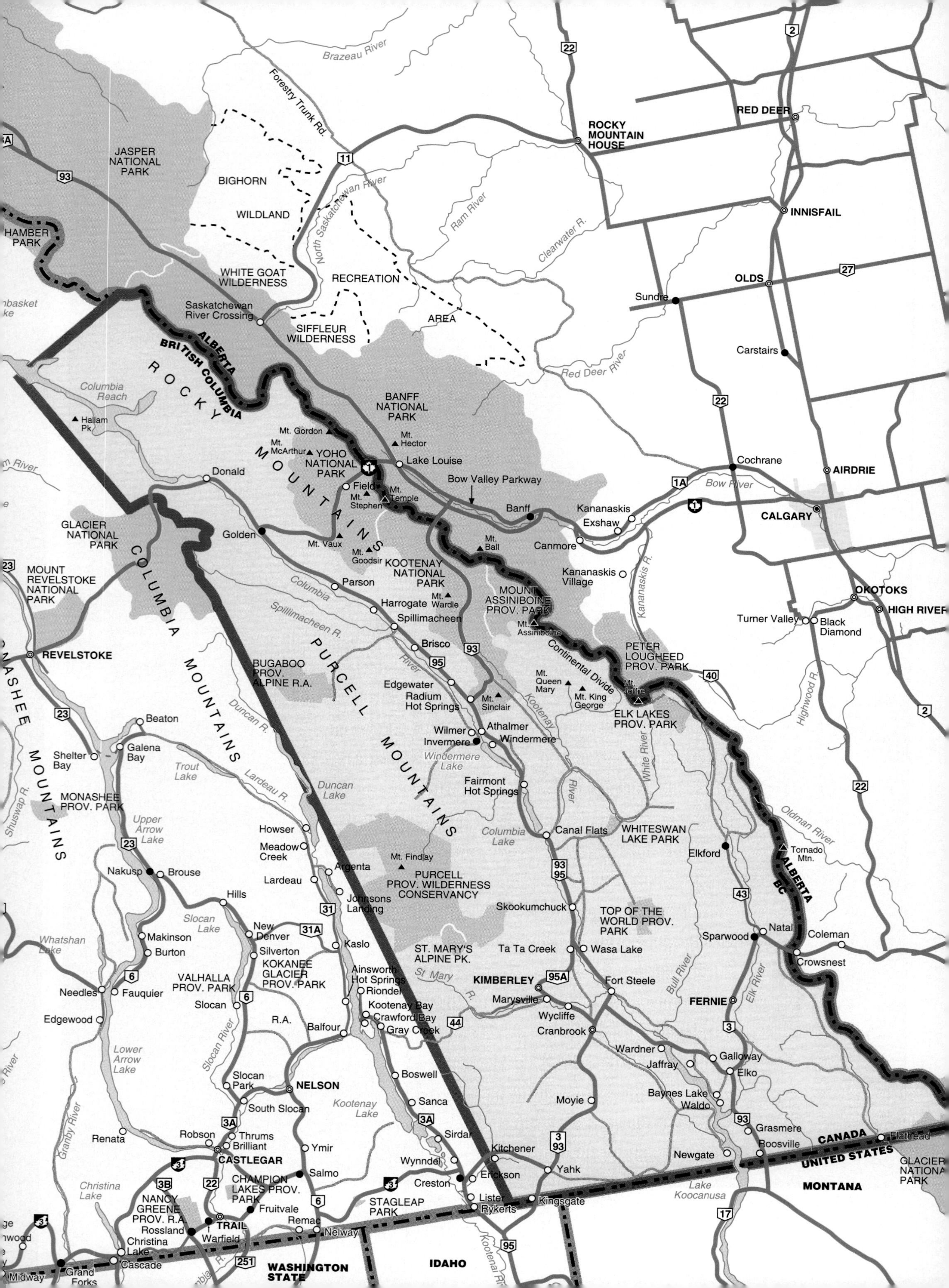

Brazeau River
Forestry Trunk Rd.
22
2
RED DEER
ROCKY
MOUNTAIN
HOUSE
11
JASPER
NATIONAL
PARK
93
BIGHORN
WILDLAND
North Saskatchewan River
Ram River
Clearwater R.
INNISFAIL
HAMBER
PARK
WHITE GOAT
WILDERNESS
RECREATION
OLDS
27
Sundre
Saskatchewan
River Crossing
SIFFLEUR
WILDERNESS
AREA
Carstairs
ALBERTA
BRITISH COLUMBIA
ROCKY
Red Deer River
Columbia
Reach
Hallam
Pk
BANFF
NATIONAL
PARK
Mt. Gordon
Mt.
Hector
Mt.
McArthur
YOHO
NATIONAL
PARK
Lake Louise
Cochrane
AIRDRIE
Donald
MOUNTAINS
Field
Mt.
Stephen
Mt.
Temple
Bow Valley Parkway
1A
Bow River
Banff
Kananaskis
Exshaw
CALGARY
GLACIER
NATIONAL
PARK
Golden
Mt. Vaux
Mt.
Goodsir
Mt.
Ball
Canmore
23
MOUNT
REVELSTOKE
NATIONAL
PARK
COLUMBIA
Columbia
KOOTENAY
NATIONAL
PARK
Parson
Kananaskis
Village
Kananaskis R.
OKOTOKS
Harrogate
Mt.
Wardle
MOUNT
ASSINIBOINE
PROV. PARK
HIGH RIVER
Spillimacheen R.
Spillimacheen
Mt.
Assiniboine
Turner Valley
Black
Diamond
REVELSTOKE
MOUNTAINS
Brisco
93
Continental Divide
PETER
LOUGHEED
PROV. PARK
BUGABOO
PROV.
ALPINE R.A.
PURCELL
95
River
40
Edgewater
Radium
Hot Springs
Mt.
Sinclair
Mt.
Queen
Mary
Mt. King
George
Mt.
Joffre
ELK LAKES
PROV. PARK
Highwood R.
2
Duncan R.
Athalmer
Beaton
23
Wilmer
Windermere
Invermere
MOUNTAINS
Kootenay
Shelter
Bay
Galena
Bay
Windermere
Lake
White River
Trout
Lake
Lardeau R.
Fairmont
Hot Springs
River
22
Oldman River
Duncan
Lake
MONASHEE
PROV. PARK
Upper
Arrow
Lake
Columbia
Lake
Canal Flats
WHITESWAN
LAKE PARK
Shuswap R.
MOUNTAINS
Howser
Meadow
Creek
23
Tornado
Mtn.
Elkford
Mt. Findlay
Nakusp
Brouse
Argenta
PURCELL
PROV. WILDERNESS
CONSERVANCY
93
95
ALBERTA
BC
Lardeau
Hills
Johnsons
Landing
43
Slocan
Lake
31
Skookumchuck
TOP OF THE
WORLD PROV.
PARK
New
Denver
31A
Whatshan
Lake
Makinson
Silverton
Natal
Sparwood
Coleman
Burton
Kaslo
ST. MARY'S
ALPINE PK.
Ta Ta Creek
Wasa Lake
Crowsnest
KOKANEE
GLACIER
PROV. PARK
Ainsworth
Hot Springs
6
VALHALLA
PROV. PARK
St Mary
KIMBERLEY
95A
Fort Steele
Bull River
Elk River
Needles
Fauquier
Riondel
Slocan
6
R.
Marysville
FERNIE
Kootenay Bay
Wycliffe
Edgewood
R.A.
Crawford Bay
44
Cranbrook
Balfour
Gray Creek
3
Slocan River
Lower
Arrow
Lake
Wardner
Galloway
Jaffray
Elko
Boswell
Slocan
Park
NELSON
Granby River
Baynes Lake
Waldo
Sanca
Moyie
South Slocan
Kootenay
Lake
3A
93
Grasmere
3A
Sirdar
3
93
CANADA
Renata
Robson
Thrums
Flathead
Brilliant
Roosville
Ymir
Kitchener
CASTLEGAR
Newgate
GLACIER
NATIONAL
PARK
Wynndel
UNITED STATES
Yahk
Salmo
Christina
Lake
3B
22
CHAMPION
LAKES PROV.
PARK
Erickson
Creston
Lake
Koocanusa
MONTANA
NANCY
GREENE
PROV. R.A.
Fruitvale
STAGLEAP
PARK
Lister
Kingsgate
Rykerts
17
TRAIL
Remac
Rossland
Warfield
Nelway
Christina
Lake
95
Cascade
251
WASHINGTON
STATE
IDAHO
Kootenai R.
Midway
Grand
Forks

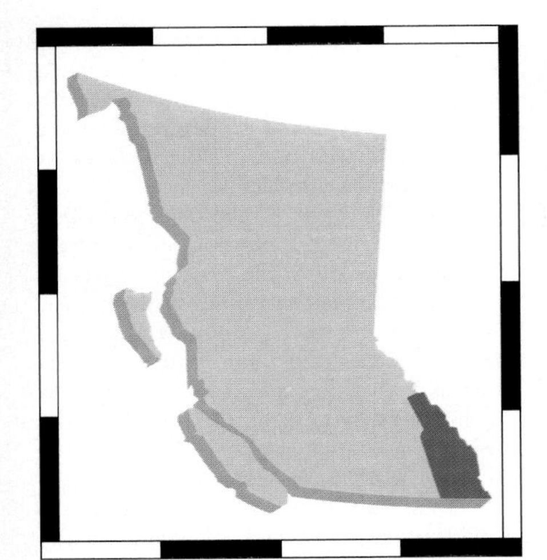

# British Columbia Rockies

## *Entrenched in the Wilds of Beauty*

> *"My first trip through what is now known as the Crows Nest Pass was an ideal one – a picnic in a country full of new interests.... The Elk River country was full of game, the river full of fish."*
>
> Michael Phillipps, explorer of the Crowsnest Pass in 1873, from an interview with the *Cranbrook Herald*, 1904.

It is surprising that an early trailblazer through this massive and forbidding region could find anything frivolous to say about the experience. A hundred years ago, BC's southeastern corner was considered impenetrable, barricaded by mountain ranges on both sides, one of the last parts of southern Canada to be explored. Early nation-builders despaired of ever finding an east-west route to unite the country.

The Purcell Mountain range starts modestly in the south, with treed summits at about 2,100m. Farther north, the peaks increase to 3,000m, active glaciers still clinging to the higher mountains. The Rockies to the east are arranged in rugged, elongated ridges with steep slopes and deep narrow valleys.

The land is sublimely beautiful, to be sure, and no matter how arduous those early journeys, the glory of the country seemed to eclipse the difficulties. Phillipps himself endured many rough journeys, suffering "days of endless toil, nights of unutterable misery" blazing trails for gold commissioner William Fernie and others. (He found no gold, but noted great seams of coal through the Elk Valley.) But he never left the East Kootenays. He stayed for the duration, dying on June 22, 1916, aged 74, on his ranch near the Elk River.

Then as now, the Rockies were a kind of paradise, if not always a picnic, nevertheless a land of plenty amidst the peaks. The heart of the region is not the great mountain ranges, but the Rocky Mountain Trench, the broad valley running parallel, flanked by the Rockies on the east, the Purcells on the west. The Trench, or "the Valley," is geologically unique. Visible from space, it is a significant feature of the planet. Over 1,600km long, the Trench is about 3km wide at the north, broadening to 16 km in the south. It was this rich valley that lured travellers through the mountains. It was also a natural transportation corridor – north to south – once you got there, and its open wooded grasslands were filled with game.

For 9,000 years, perhaps even 12,000, the Kootenay (or Kutenai) peoples have lived in this area, mainly in the hospitable region of the Trench. At some point they acquired horses, enabling them to make regular trips over the Rockies to hunt buffalo. They knew all the secret passes through the mountains. But it was not until 1807 that David Thompson of the fur-trading North West Company struggled over Howse Pass in the Rockies and down to the Columbia River, becoming the first white man to cross the Canadian Rockies. Travelling with eight men, his Indian wife, and three small children, he established Kootenay House on Lake Windermere. From this post, he set out on the many hard jour-

*Canoeing on Emerald Lake, Yoho National Park.*

neys that would become the basis for his remarkably accurate maps of the Northwest. He was called "the Star Man" by his Indian friends who felt he was superhuman.

Some 30 years later, a most unlikely and bizarre figure could be seen plodding resolutely along through the wilderness passes. It was the Jesuit priest, Father Pierre (or Pieter) Jean De Smet, far from his comfortable mission near Missoula, Montana, in love with the land, and intent on bringing God's grace to the "savages" he loved so well. He was spectacular in his way, past middle age, roly-poly, joyfully experiencing all hardships, fording rivers, and climbing through brush, his black robe trailing behind him.

He was absolutely ecstatic at his first sight of the valley. "It resembles a large basin," he wrote in 1845, "surrounded by lofty mountains which form a vast amphitheatre and present a picturesque sight." The rivers thrilled him, too – "the sweet murmur of their falls ... their succession of cascades." De Smet baptized hundreds of the Kootenay people and said dozens of outdoor masses in God's own country. In 1846 he actually crossed the Rockies at the "Great Pass" (the Athabasca Pass in the north), though he had to fast for a month first because he had been warned he was too fat to manage the journey. As it was, he kept tumbling about in "somersets."

This was the same year that the Oregon Treaty established the 49th parallel as the Canada-US border. The wilderness was starting to get organized.

In 1859, De Smet left the Kootenays for the last time, leaving in his journal the prophetic comment that he knew this country was a treasure trove of mineral wealth, and that within a few years the area would be inundated with hordes of white men motivated by greed, who would totally disrupt the lives of his beloved converts. That was indeed about to happen.

Gold was discovered in Wild Horse Creek in 1863. It was actually called Stud Horse Creek, but changed early on for propriety, though it was so wild in Wild Horse Creek that it's a wonder anyone thought much of propriety. Just 8km northeast of present Fort Steele, it yielded more gold than all the other placer creeks in the East Kootenays combined. On one day alone, early prospector Robert Dore sluiced nearly eight kilograms of gold from the bars of the creek. Interest in the area surged, just as De Smet had said it would, and mining became the key to history, to the flowing and ebbing fortunes of the early towns.

Wild Horse Creek, where it all started, is a perfect case in point. In 1864, scarcely a year after gold was found, an instant town of 1,500 souls bustled on the bank of the river. This was Fisherville. Then gold was discovered in the gravel underlying the town. In the stampede to sluice the gravel, buildings were torn down, some were moved up the hill, some were burnt. Fisherville was literally washed up. Its remains were revived upstream and renamed Wild Horse.

At first the town's fortunes looked so promising that Edgar "the Friendly Giant" Dewdney was persuaded to extend his original Hope-Princeton trail all the way to the gold-rush site. The trail was needed to protect Canadian sovereignty and give the Kootenays access to the coast. As it was, Americans were piling in over the border, not paying duties or license fees, certainly not paying the head tax, nor the hated export tax on gold. They had to be presented with a set of rules.

Dewdney completed his trail in 1865, in a remarkable seven months, but it was already too late. Fewer than 400 had wintered over; the others had drifted away, lured by new rumours; and what was left of the town had been destroyed by floods and fires.

So much for Wild Horse. Not far away, the Galbraith brothers, John and Robert, had started a cable ferry service across the Kootenay River at the present site of Fort Steele. The little settlement was called "Galbraith's Ferry," later renamed Fort Steele to honour charismatic Superintendent Sam Steele of the North-West Mounted Police who peaceably settled a dispute with the St Marys Indian band in 1887.

Fort Steele grew. Kimberley's North Star Mine opened in 1893, began shipping its lead, zinc, and silver down the Kootenay River by sternwheeler to smelters south of the border. Fort Steele became a commercial centre. Beautiful homes were built by townsfolk settling into what they hoped was a prosperous life in the pretty town on the bluff above the river.

Then, in 1898, the CPR came through the Crowsnest Pass. Fort Steele, it was assumed, would be the vital divisional point. But the railway bypassed the town and went to fledgling Cranbrook. Kimberley ore was shipped to Trail, and Fort Steele residents began moving to Cranbrook. In 1904 the government offices moved, and the life of the town was snuffed. Gold, and the magic rails, had shaped history once again.

Now, nearly a century later, Kimberley is still producing lead and zinc (though dwindling ore reserves will force permanent closure of its mine by 2000), the Elk Valley is the main coal producer of the province, Cranbrook is the largest city in the region, and Fort Steele is a heritage town where the past has been given new life. For a rip-roaring history, pick up David Scott and Edna Hanic's paperback, *East Kootenay Chronicle.* It's a wonderful read.

Other things are still much the same. "The sea of mountains" is virtually untouched, the beauty unchanged. The open parklands of the trench still merge into forested mountain slopes, with lodgepole pine, western larch, and trembling aspen. In autumn, the larches still turn golden yellow before losing their needles, a colour contrast in the evergreens.

Even today, the Rocky Mountain region is one of the prime ungulate (hoofed animal) habitats on the continent – it's called the Serengetti of the West; biologists believe about half of BC's elk population lives here. The Trench is also an important flyway for migratory birds, and the marshlands along the Columbia River provide fine habitats for waterfowl, herons, osprey, eagles. More than 60 percent of BC's bird species may be seen in the East Kootenays.

Choices for the visitor are many: guest ranches; luxury resorts with hot springs and golf; alpine wilderness backpacking; canoe trips down the Columbia; bird-watching in the marshes; white-water rafting. Four major winter resorts offer downhill and cross-country skiing, or – the ultimate thrill – heli-skiing into the world famous Bugaboos of the Purcell Range.

In the end, though, nothing can equal just sitting around the campfire, fresh trout sizzling in the pan, watching the alpenglow on the mysterious Rockies, as the sun sinks, slowly, behind the Purcells. Nothing.

*Mountain goats at a mineral lick, Kootenay National Park.*

## Information

Rocky Mountain Visitors Association: Box 10, Kimberley, BC, V1A 2Y5. 427-4838. Fax: 427-3344. The office is located at 495 Wallinger Ave in downtown Kimberley. Addresses and telephone numbers of local information centres are given with the details on each community.

## Transportation

### By Road

There are four main highway routes through the region; all are two-lane and offer good driving conditions year-round. Winter snow storms or icy conditions can cause temporary problems; however, roads are promptly plowed and sanded.

This region is interlaced with an incredible number of back-country roads not recommended for the average traveller. Many are designed only for four-wheel-drive, radio-equipped vehicles. In this regard, the Rocky Mountain region is still truly a frontier, tamed only on the strips of highway that ribbon their way through.

The approximate distance by road from Vancouver to Cranbrook and Kimberley is 855km. From Calgary, Alberta, it is 405km. From Spokane, Washington, it is some 310km.

### By Bus

- **Greyhound Bus Lines:** Call Vancouver 662-3222 or specific cities. Twice daily service through the region in each direction via alternate routes. One service follows Hwy 3 from Fort Macleod, Alberta; the other follows Hwy 1 from Calgary through Banff to Radium.
- **Dewdney Trail Stages:** Call Cranbrook 426-4662. Service daily except Sun. Cranbrook to Golden and return.

### By Train

- **Rocky Mountain Railtours:** Great Canadian Rail Tour Company, Suite 104 - 340 Brooksbank Ave, Vancouver, BC, V7J 2O1. 1-800-665-7245. Vancouver to Jasper, Vancouver to Banff, optional to Calgary. Travels only in daylight. Passengers going east or west spend the night in Kamloops. Hotel, continental breakfast, gourmet lunch, included. May-early Oct.

### By Air

Major air terminal is the Cranbrook-Kimberley Airport, on Hwy 95A, 20 minutes from both Cranbrook and Kimberley. The area is serviced from both Calgary and Vancouver.

- **Canadian Regional Airlines:** 1-800-665-1177.
- **Air BC:** 1-800-663-3721.

### Car Rentals

Cars can be rented at Cranbrook-Kimberley Airport and in the city of Cranbrook.

## BRITISH COLUMBIA ROCKIES EVENTS

### Cranbrook

- **Cranbrook Wintertainment:** Late Jan. Snowmobile, cross-country ski races, snogolf.
- **Sam Steele Days:** Mid-June. Parade and loggers' sports to celebrate Superintendent Sam Steele's arrival in Fort Steele in 1887. (He established the first North West Mounted Police Post west of the Rockies.)
- **Pro Rodeo:** Mid-Aug.

### Elkford

- **Snowarama:** Feb. Snowmobile fund raiser.
- **Wildcat Days:** Beginning of July. Pay tribute to such pioneers as occasionally cantankerous Charlie Weigert, or Wildcat Charlie.

### Fernie

- **Griz Days:** Feb.
- **Power, Pedal, Paddle Relay Race:** April. Skiing, biking, canoeing/kayaking.
- **Fernie 500 Celebrity Golf Classic:** mid-July. Raising funds for the handicapped.

### Fort Steele Heritage Town

- **Pepsi Hose Reel Race, Harvest Festival, Halloween, Thanksgiving:** Historic celebrations throughout the year.

### Golden

- **Willy Forest Days:** Feb. Winter festival to banish cabin fever.
- **Columbia River Raft Race:** In May (maybe).
- **Golden Rodeo:** Labour Day weekend.

### Invermere

- **Visitor Appreciation Day:** July.
- **Windermere Loop Triathlon:** Aug.
- **Fabulous Inflatable Fish Festival:** Aug.

### Kimberley

- **International Accordion Championship:** early July.
- **Elk Bugling Contest:** Late Aug.

### Radium Hot Springs

- **Radium Days:** Late May.

### Sparwood

- **Coal Miner Days:** Third weekend in June.
- **Fall Fair:** Early Sept.

### Yahk

- **Yahk Raft Race:** First weekend in June, on Moyie River.

*History lives on at Fort Steele Heritage Town.*

*Sinclair Canyon near Radium Hot Springs, Kootenay National Park.*

# British Columbia Rockies Routes and Highlights

## TRAVELLER'S LOGS



## HIGHLIGHTS



## Kitchener to Wasa Lake

### CROWSNEST HIGHWAY (Highway 3 and 95A)

This is one of the main corridors for travellers from the coast and the US heading for the Rocky Mountains' national parks. It's a wild and lovely route, much of it following the winding Moyie River as it cuts through the gentler slopes of the Purcell Range.

Hwy 3 (the Crowsnest) enters the region from Creston in the Kootenays. Hwy 95 crosses the US border at Kingsgate. At a junction south of Yahk, these two highways join to become Hwy 3/95, which continues north to Cranbrook. North of Cranbrook, Hwy 95A breaks off from Hwy 3/95, and makes a westerly loop through Kimberley and Ta Ta Creek, north 137km to a junction at Wasa.

The stretch of Hwy 3 between Creston and Yahk is on **Mountain Standard Time** year-round. During summer, when most parts of the province move clocks one hour ahead to daylight-savings time, Creston, Kitchener, and Yahk make no changes. Their Mountain Time is already the same as Pacific daylight-savings time. **This is the only time-change-free area in the province.**

**Kitchener:** (Pop. 156). 13.5km east of Creston on Hwy 3. Small settlement near the Goat River, with store, pub, restaurant. On boundary between BC's Kootenay and Rocky Mountain regions.

**Kidd Creek Rest Area:** 23.5km east of Creston, on north side of highway.

**Hwy 95:** 38km beyond Creston. South 11km to BC/Idaho border crossing at Kingsgate/ Eastport. Customs open 24 hours a day. North, Hwy 95 joins Hwy 3 to become Hwy 3/95.

**Yahk Provincial Park:** 9ha; 26 campsites. 3.5km north of junction on Hwy 3. A pleasant wooded campsite on the bank of the Moyie River, near services in town of Yahk. Good fishing for dollies May-June.

**Yahk:** (Pop. 173). 4km beyond Hwy 3/95 junction, bordering the park. A prosperous lumber town with 400 inhabitants in early 1900s. Town's fortunes and population declined in 1930s depression, but the town has survived. Today, the main export is "I've Been to Yahk and Back" T-shirts, and Fiddlers Restaurant features Bigyahkattack Burgers. "Yahk" may be Kootenay people's word for "bow in the river."

**Ryan Rest Area:** 7.5km beyond Yahk on Hwy 3/95. Attractive picnic site on the ubiquitous Moyie River.

Hwy 3/95 follows Moyie River north to what else but Moyie Lake. Moose feed along river. Also, mule deer with the giveaway large ears (they're a subspecies of black-tailed deer). Highway follows the east shore of Moyie Lake.

**Time Zone:** On Hwy 3, 15km east of Yahk. In daylight-savings time (early April to mid-autumn) set your watch ahead one hour. You are leaving Mountain Standard Time and entering Mountain daylight-savings time. During Standard Time (the winter months) there is no time change. Yahk is always on Mountain Standard Time.

**Rest Area:** 15.5km beyond Yahk. North side of highway

**Moyie:** (Pop. 169). 33km north of Yahk, 31km south of Cranbrook. Exceptionally pretty, on a slight hillside overlooking Moyie Lake, and boasting some character buildings. Name thought to come from the French *mouille,* for "wet or soggy," which is how the early explorers found themselves after dragging through the pass from Cranbrook.

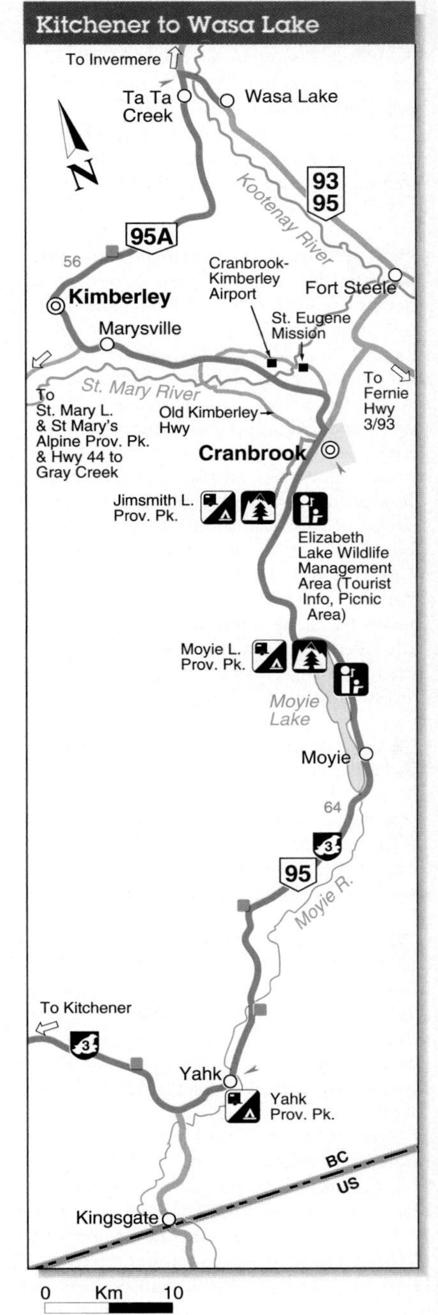


Moyie was for a time site of one of the richest lead-silver mines in the province. Ore body was discovered by Pierre, a Kootenay native from St Eugene Mission near Fort Steele. He guided Father Coccola and miner James Cronin to the location where they staked claims. Pierre and Father Coccola sold their claims to Cronin's mining company, which started the St Eugene Mine. The priest used his share to build churches in Moyie and at the St Eugene Mission (between Cranbrook and Kimberley).

In 1898 the CPR's Crowsnest line was extended around Moyie Lake, to Kootenay

Lake. A steamboat operated on Moyie Lake for two seasons, but the railway took over its job. Moyie's population was over 800 while mine operated, but when it closed after 17 years, people moved away.

South of present townsite, some of the old mine structures, a slag heap, and an old graveyard, are reminders of town's history. Original fire hall still stands.

**Moyie Lake Provincial Park:** 90ha; 104 campsites, sani-station. 46km north of Yahk, 1km off hwy. 422-3212. Popular wooded campground on lake's north shore giving good access for water sports. Area used by local sailing club for regattas. Showers, sani-station, fishing, swimming, boat launch, playground, hiking, picnics, interpretive programs.

On May 29, 1808, explorer David Thompson passed through on his arduous search for a fur-trade route from Rockies to Columbia River mouth. Arriving at the peak of spring floods, Thompson found the surging channels of the Moyie River almost impassable. After many attempts to span the river with felled trees (quickly swept away by the torrent), losing valuable furs and goods in the process, they finally advanced.

**Jimsmith Lake Provincial Park:** 12ha; 28 campsites. 422-3212. 62km north of Yahk, 2km west of Cranbrook. West on paved road 4km to park. Wooded campsite on lake shore. Year-round. Swimming, boating (no powerboats), fishing; cross-country skiing, skating, ice fishing.

**Cranbrook:** (Pop.16,447). 64km beyond Yahk on Hwy 3/95. Rocky Mountain region's major city, sited magnificently on a broad, generous plain with a stunning view of the Rockies east and south, Purcells to the west. At this point, the Rocky Mountain Trench is a good 16km wide, and "big sky" is what you see.

Present site of Cranbrook was used by Kootenay peoples as a camp and pasture land. Originally called Joseph's Prairie, the land was first owned by the Galbraiths who operated the ferry at Fort Steele. Then it was bought by Colonel James Baker, member of the BC Legislature, 1886 to 1900, who perhaps had something to do with the CPR's bypassing Fort Steele in favour of Cranbrook in 1898. Cranbrook became the divisional point of the railway, and therefore the new "capital" of the region. (Fort Steele was ruined.) Named after Baker's birthplace in England, Cranbrook grew as Fort Steele declined. City was incorporated in 1905.

Billed as "A Place to Live as well as a Place to Make a Living," Cranbrook offers attractions both natural and cultural: 20 parks within the city itself, an 18-hole golf course, the **East Kootenay Commmunity College**, and a new, 600-seat, performing arts centre called the **Key City Theatre**. Things tend to come together at the oblique angled "corner" of Van Horne and Baker streets, where the tall brick Post Office Clock Tower awesomely holds its own in Baker Square; and on Sam Steele Days in June, otherwise sane citizens can be seen racing outhouses on wheels down the city streets.

**Cranbrook Information:** Infocentre, Chamber of Commerce, Box 84, Cranbrook, BC, V1C 4H6. 489-5261 or 426-5914. Two locations: main office, 2279 Cranbrook St North, on Hwy 3/95, north side of city, year-round; summer office on Hwy 3/95, at Elizabeth Lake Sanctuary, June-Sept.

**Cranbrook-Kimberley Airport:** Off Hwy 95A, 12km north of Cranbrook. Airport is 3km off Hwy 95A. For more info, see below.

■ **Canadian Museum of Rail Travel:** 1 Van Horne St South, Cranbrook, BC, V1C 4H9. On Hwy 3 at Baker St, city centre. 489-3918. Daily year-round, afternoons in winter. Nine original cars from the CPR Trans-Canada Limited of 1929 (which provided luxury service between Montreal and Vancouver). As far as is known, the only integrated set in the world, designed at the time as a nine-car travelling hotel. Also a caboose, and CPR station from 1900. The cars, last of their type built in Canada, represented epitome of railway technology and decor. Luxurious by any standard, with inlaid Honduran mahogany and black walnut woodwork, brass fixtures, and plush or leather upholstered furniture. Fully restored, the dining car even features CPR silverware, glassware, china.

Includes dining car, *Argyle* (often open for tea); solarium car, *River Rouge;* deluxe sleeping cars, *Rutherglen, Glen Cassie,* and *Somerset*; combination baggage and sleeping car (housing a display on restoration process); day parlour car 6751; baggage car; and superintendent's business car, *British Columbia*, in completely original condition.

Gift shop, reception area, library, archives, and offices. Daily year-round.

■ **Cranbrook Heritage Tour:** Map of heritage buildings at infocentres or Railway Museum: Imperial Building, City Hall, Fire Hall, Mt Baker Hotel, Masonic Temple, Rotary Clock Tower, Colonel Baker's home.

■ **Cranbrook Golf Club:** 2700 2nd St S, Cranbrook, BC, V1C 4H8. 426-5455. Sunny, in-town, 18-hole course with backdrop of stunning Mt Baker.

■ **Elizabeth Lake Sanctuary (Confederation Park):** On Hwy 3/95, south side of Cranbrook. Location of **Summer Infocentre**. Also ball fields, and bird sanctuary. This 113ha marsh was preserved in 1972 through the Ministry of Environment and Ducks Unlimited. In the Rocky Mountain Trench migration corridor, marsh attracts Canada geese, mallard, teal, ringneck, scaup, redhead, goldeneye, bufflehead, and ruddy ducks. Also coots, grebes, black terns, and various songbirds; plus white-tailed deer, moose, muskrats, and painted turtles. Picnic while you watch.

**King St West/Wycliffe Rd (the Old Kimberley Hwy):** King St W intercepts Van Horne St (Hwy 3/95) in downtown Cranbrook. Take King St W north; it eventually turns into Wycliffe Park Rd, ending at Hwy 95A near Wycliffe Regional Park, 8km north of Hwys 3/95 and 95A junction.

**Hwys 3/95 and 95A:** On north edge of Cranbrook, 4km from city centre, Hwy 95A loops northwest through Kimberley; *Log*

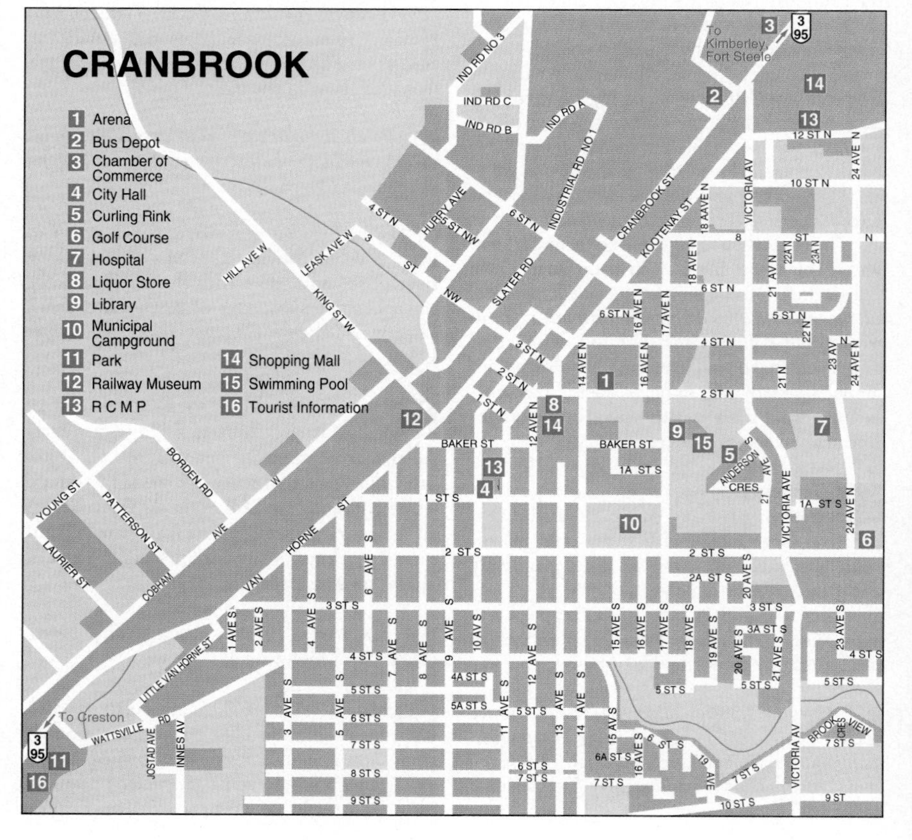

follows 95A. For Hwy 3/95 and 3/93 through Fort Steele, see *Elko to Invermere*, p. 255.

## *Highway 95A*

**Mission Rd to Kimberley (Old Airport Rd):** 1km north of junction with Hwy 3/95. Rd runs east of Hwy 95A, is scenic and blacktopped but seldom used. Leads through **St Mary's Indian Reserve** and **St Eugene Mission**, past **Cranbrook-Kimberley Airport**, returning to Hwy 95A 11km north.

**St Eugene Mission and Church:** Located on St Mary's Indian Reserve, on Mission Rd. The restored church was built in 1897 by Father Coccola from proceeds of his share in St Eugene Mine in Moyie. Finest Gothic-style mission church in the province, with hand-painted Italian stained and leaded glass, scalloped louvres, blind windows, and pinnacles and buttresses at each corner. Complete exterior renovation was done in 1985, by the St Mary's Band and East Kootenay Historical Association. Summer tours by reservation: 489-2464.

Northern portion of Mission Rd passes by airport, continues 3km to junction with Hwy 95A (see below).

**Wycliffe Park Rd (Old Kimberley Hwy):** 5km north of junction with Hwy 3/95. Road travels west of Hwy 95A (the New Kimberley Hwy) in a loop joining Hwy 95A again at Wycliffe. About 5km along is Bill Dove's **Raptor Rescue and Rehabilitation Society (RRRS)** developed to aid injured or orphaned birds of prey – hawks, falcons, osprey, eagles, and owls. Tours are offered to the public in summer, but by appointment only. Contact Bill Dove, c/o RRRS, at SS3, Site 19 - A0, Cranbrook, BC. V1C 6H3. 489-2841.

**St Mary River:** 7km north of 3/95 junction, Hwy 95A crosses pretty river.

**Cranbrook-Kimberley Airport Rd:** 12km beyond junction of Hwy 3/95, 16km south of Kimberley. East side of highway. 3km to airport. Daily flights to Vancouver and Calgary.

**Wycliffe Regional Park:** At junction of Hwy 95A and Airport Rd (see above), west of highway. Small local park with ball park, picnic facilities. Serves farming area of Wycliffe.

**Marysville:** 21km beyond Hwy 3/95 junction, 7km south of Kimberley. On southern outskirts of Kimberley, and incorporated into that city. Marysville is site of original smelter built in 1903 for Sullivan Mine. Ore was difficult to process, and the mine and smelter closed after four years.

■ **Marysville Falls:** Sign and parking area in town. Short walk along Mark Creek to waterfalls.

**Road to St Mary Lake and St Mary's Alpine Provincial Park:** On north edge of Marysville, 22km from Hwy 3/95 junction.

# SIDE TRIP
## to St Mary Lake

**St Mary Lake:** Lies 17km from junction with Hwy 95A on part-paved, part-gravel road. Fishing. No tourist facilities.

**Gray Creek-Kimberley Forestry Rd (Hwy 44):** West of St Mary Lake and overland, so to speak, to Kootenay Lake, on new grade A gravel road over Baker Pass. In all, 86km, Kimberley to Gray Creek. Steep, with some 14 percent grades on the western side, but OK for RVs with good clearance. Open seasonally only; will cut an hour off the journey around. Scenic, too.

**St Mary's Alpine Provincial Park:** 9,146ha. Wilderness area, no facilities. 28km north of St Mary Lake on rough gravel logging road. Extreme caution: watch for logging trucks. 422-3212. Beautiful wilderness park in Purcell Mountains. Peaks as high as 2,900m surround the many lakes. Seven main creeks, some with spectacular waterfalls. No designated campsites, no maintained trails.

## *Return to Highway 95A*

**Kimberley:** (Pop. 6,531). (El. 1,113m) 28km north of Hwy 3/95 junction (32km north of Cranbrook), 27km south of Wasa. Canada's highest city, Kimberley has always been a mining townl in fact, it was named after Kimberley, South Africa, though instead of gold and silver, it harboured silver, lead, and zinc. In 1892, Joe Bourgeois and James Langill staked the North Star silver-lead claim. Later the same year a second group staked the Shylock and Hamlet claims (which became the Sullivan Mine). The North Star Mine started in 1893, and Kimberley grew up nearby. Ore was hauled by wagon to Fort Steele, then shipped by riverboat to Jennings, Montana. After the Crowsnest Railway was pushed through, the ore was shipped to the smelter at Trail.

Kimberley was always a one-industry town. Everyone worked in the Sullivan Mine. Now, with depleting ore reserves, Cominco has announced permanent closure of the mine by the year 2000. Like another little BC "town that did," Kimberley is rising high to the occasion. If one mountain can't do it any more, perhaps another can. Hopes are now pinned on North Star Mountain, already becoming a major ski destination. If resourceful Kimberleyites can't work the mines, they'll work the slopes.

In keeping with its status as the highest city in Canada, Kimberley has adopted an appealing Bavarian alpine theme. Stores have gingerbread fronts and bright painted shutters. The pedestrian-only downtown shopping area known as "the Platzl" holds the world's largest operating cuckoo clock. Befitting BC's new Oom-pah-pah capital, a minstrel wanders amidst footbridges, fountains, and flowerbeds, entertaining on the accordion. For golfers, there are two 18-hole courses.

**Kimberley Information:** Infocentre, 350 Ross St, Kimberley, BC, V1A 2Z9. 427-3666.

■ **Kimberley Heritage Museum:** In the Platzl. Mon-Sat. Winter, afternoons only. 427-7510. Historical displays and artifacts, hockey and skiing.

■ **Cominco Gardens:** Footpath from the Platzl. Extensive, beautifully landscaped flower garden. Teahouse. 427-4885.

■ **Bavarian City Mining Railway:** 2km from downtown at Happy Hans Campground. Authentic train used in underground mining takes visitors on a 2.5km scenic ride, which rambles through a tunnel and over a trestle. Commentary. Mini-golf.

■ **Kimberley Ski and Summer Resort:** 4km from downtown via Gerry Sorenson Way. Summer: chairlift to mountaintop, alpine slide, tennis, mini-golf, bumper boats, go-carts, mountain biking. Winter: vertical 701m; longest run, 6.5km; three chairs, one T-bar, three handle tows. Longest lit run in North America. Nordic skiing. Indoor tennis. Info and reservations: 427-4881.

■ **Kimberley Golf Club:** Oldest course in the region, a very playable mountain course just off the cliffs of the St Mary's River. Tee times: 427-4161.

■ **Trickle Creek Golf Resort:** New 18-hole course cut into the forested slopes of North Star Mountain. Accommodations adjacent. 427-5171.

**Cherry Creek Rest Area:** 11.5km beyond Kimberley on Hwy 95A.

**Ta Ta Creek:** (Pop. 114). 24km beyond Kimberley on Hwy 95A. Stories about how it got its name are legion and lengthy. The one we like involves a bank robber who left the local constable behind, nicely roped up. "Ta ta," was his cheerful farewell.

**Junction of Hwy 93/95:** 27.5km north of Kimberley, 59.5km north of Cranbrook. North on Hwy 93/95 to Canal Flats, Fairmont Hot Springs, and Invermere. South to Wasa Lake (2km), Fort Steele, Elko, and US Border. See *Elko to Invermere*, p.255.

*The Paint Pots, Kootenay National Park.*

# Roosville to Crowsnest Pass

## HIGHWAY 93, CROWSNEST HIGHWAY 3, HIGHWAY 43

Hwy 93 provides easy access to BC's Rocky Mountain region from Montana at the Roosville border crossing. The valley in the border area is known as Tobacco Plains, home to the Kootenay peoples for hundreds of years. From here it's 36km to the junction at Elko where Hwy 93 veers west toward Kimberley. This *Log* veers east, following the Crowsnest Hwy 3 for 80.5km through the gorgeous Elk River valley to the Crowsnest Pass in the Rockies at the BC/Alberta border.

Crowsnest Pass takes its name from the unusual rounded mountain which stands alone at 2,730m above the rolling hills just into Alberta. Nomadic Cree peoples passing through named the mountain *Kah, Ka-coo-wut-tskis-lun*, meaning "nesting place of the raven." The pass for centuries served as an access route for the Kootenay peoples who made three trips a year to hunt buffalo in the Alberta foothills.

The first white man to traverse the pass, at least from the west, was Michael Phillipps in 1873 (see *Introduction to Rockies*). Phillipps worked for the Hudson's Bay Company, and was one of the first real settlers in the East Kootenays. His early efforts to build a trail through the pass were thwarted by Colonel Baker and William Fernie, who were busy sniffing out coal deposits in the Elk Valley and possibly wanted to keep the area under wraps until their claims were staked in the name of the Crow's Nest Coal Company.

**Roosville:** (Pop. 40). At BC/Montana border. 119km north of Kalispell on US Hwy 93. Customs open 8am-midnight. Fred Roo was postmaster here from 1899. The border town on US side is called Port of Roosville.

**Grasmere:** (Pop. 147). On Hwy 93, 12km north of border. Named by James Lancaster, an early settler, who was reminded of lovely Grasmere in the English Lake District. A one-store town on the edge of a Tobacco Plains Indian reserve.

**Elk River:** 23km north of border, Hwy 93 crosses this beautiful river.

**Jaffray-Baynes Lake Rd:** 26.5km north of US border. 23km paved back road to the east; rejoins Hwy 3/93 at Jaffray.

## SIDE TRIP

### to Kikomun Creek

**Kikomun Creek Provincial Park:** 682ha; 104 campsites, sani-station. 7km off Hwy 93 on Jaffray-Baynes Lake Rd. 422-3212. On east shore of Lake Koocanusa (Libby Reservoir), 110km long, formed by Libby Dam on Kootenay River in Montana. Lake level fluctuates substantially. Name is combo of Kootenay, Canada, USA. Park also contains smaller Surveyors and Hidden lakes. Boat launch, playground, swimming, hiking, fishing. Interpretive programs (summer).

## Return to Highway 93

**Caithness Rest Area:** 29km north of US border, by Caithness Creek.

**Crowsnest Hwy 3:** 36km north of US border. Northwest on Hwy 3/93 to Cranbrook (65km), Kimberley, and Fort Steele. Northeast on Hwy 3 to Elko, Fernie, Sparwood, and Alberta border (80.5km).

**Elko:** (Pop. 165). On Hwy 3 just east of junction, 36km north of border. On a bench above the Elk River. Large sawmill is main employer. Town was more robust early in the century; today, it offers only limited services.

**The Elk Valley:** From Elko to Sparwood, Hwy 3 follows Elk River through the Elk Valley with mountain ranges close on either side. From Sparwood, Hwy 43 follows the river north to Elkford and Elk Lakes Provincial Park.

This beautiful valley was pretty much unsettled until the CPR line was put through the Crowsnest to Cranbrook in 1898. Then the rich coal deposits began to be exploited, people moved into the area, and the *Fernie Free Press* reported in 1901 that the population had reached 3,000. Smaller mining communities such as Hosmer, Michel, Natal, and Corbin sprang up, though most have now virtually disappeared.

Fortunes of the region have fluctuated with the coal markets; mining activity was reduced to almost nil at times. Recently a number of major open-pit mines have been developed, mainly for export of coking coal to Japan and other Asian countries. Mine tours available; contact local infocentres.

The Elk Valley was named for the herds of 100 or more elk frequently seen by early explorers. Area is unique in North America in its capability of supporting large populations of big game. Elk are still the most common large animals, but just from the highway, visitors may also see mule and whitetail deer, bighorn sheep, black bears. Farther from the beaten track: moose, mountain goats, wolves, grizzlies. Alpine meadows have vivid blue larkspur, red paint brushes, buttercups, and white bunch berry.

In 1969, a Canadian Land Inventory Survey evaluated Elk Valley as *the* prime recreational area of North America. There have been fears that the area might be torn apart for its coal; revegetation on areas that have been strip-mined is very slow (at certain elevations, it is calculated to take 1,000 years to rebuild 2.5cm of topsoil).

The region offers access, mainly by logging roads, to huge unpopulated areas such as the **Flathead Valley** and the **Akamina-Kishinena Provincial Recreation Area**. Roads vary greatly: they may be heavily travelled by logging trucks; some are restricted to two-way-radio equipped vehicles. Travellers should gain as much local information as possible, and carry topographical maps. (Beware that some of these may be quite out of date

*The Platzl in downtown Kimberley.*

and roads shown may not be accurate.) BC Forest Service in Cranbrook can advise on road conditions and restrictions, and has brochure on Forest Service campsites.

**Morrissey Provincial Park:** 5ha. 16.5km beyond Elko on east side of highway. Picnic area along the Elk River. Fishing.

**Rest Area:** 21km north of Elko, east side of highway.

**Fernie Snow Valley Ski Area:** 25km beyond Elko, west of highway. Impressive Lizard Range forms backdrop. Vertical drop 640m; longest run, 5km. Double, triple, and new quad chairlifts, two T-bars, rope tow, hanger tow. Cross-country trails. Stay at Griz Inn.

**Mount Fernie Provincial Park:** 259ha; 38 campsites. 28km beyond Elko, west of hwy. 422-3212. Picnic and day-use area, hiking. Lizard Creek, with waterfall, flows through wooded park.

**Fernie:** (Pop. 5,012). 31.5km north of Elko, 49km east of Alberta border. Named after William Fernie, who was instrumental in developing area's coal mines. The community sprang up at turn of the century along new railway through the broad, sheltered Elk Valley. Fernie was built in a loop on the Elk River: Hwy 3 enters and exits the town over bridges. Nearby Coal Creek Mine was economic impetus for the city which suffered serious trials in its early years.

Tobacco Plains peoples' legend has it that William Fernie wheedled information about a coal deposit from an Indian maiden, promising her marriage. Then Fernie jilted her, invoking the wrath of her father, who placed a curse on the name of Fernie. The events that followed are more than legend.

In 1902, an explosion in the Coal Creek Mine killed at least 128 men. In 1904 there was a fire. Four years later, another fire destroyed whatever was left, leaving 6,000 people homeless. Floods have ravaged the town. Finally, in 1964, in an elaborate and dramatic ceremony, Chief Red Eagle of the Tobacco Plains Band, last of the native men in this area to wear braids, lifted the curse on Fernie. That same year, he died.

Fernie today has a great deal of charm. Scars on the landscape are being erased, the beauty of the valley is returning.

**Fernie Information:** Infocentre, Fernie Chamber of Commerce, Hwy 3 and Dicken Rd, Fernie, BC, V0B 1M0. On north edge of city, beside huge oil derrick. 423-6868.

■ **Historic Oil Derrick and Drilling Equipment:** Next to infocentre. An exact reconstruction of derrick and drilling equipment used in Flathead Valley southeast of Fernie from 1914 - 1920. Includes a new 21m wooden derrick, restored metal drilling equipment, and steam engine of the original well. In working order.

■ **Fernie and District Historical Museum:** At corner of 5th Ave and 5th St. 502 - 5th Ave, PO Box 1527, Fernie, BC, V0B 1M0. 423-7016. Weekdays 1-5pm, July-Aug. Group tours year-round, by arrangement: 423-6512. 1905 museum building was originally a Roman Catholic rectory.

■ **Heritage Buildings and Walking Tour:** Map of city available from infocentre shows heritage building locations including 1906 brick courthouse and 1904 city hall. Some wonderful old stone buildings.

■ **Fernie Golf and Country Club**: World-class 18-hole course, flanked by expansive mountains. East end of 2nd Ave. 423-7773.

■ **Ghost Rider:** Every summer evening just before sunset, ghost of the Indian princess rides across the slopes of Hosmer Mountain. She is led by her father, in his never-ending search for William Fernie.

**Rd to Mine:** This road through town leads 5km to abandoned Coal Creek Mine where remnants of the operation still exist. Ask in Fernie for directions.

**Rest Area:** On Hwy 3, 7km past Fernie, east of highway.

**Hosmer:** (Pop. 271). On Hwy 3, 11.5km north of Fernie. Former mining town, heritage sites. Limited services.

**Olson Rest Area:** 16km beyond Fernie, north side of highway. Great view of the Rocky Mountains.

**Sparwood:** (Pop. 4,211). On Hwy 3, 28km northeast of Fernie; 21km west of Alberta border. Sparwood was incorporated in 1966 to replace the blackened twin towns of Michel and Natal which had existed since the turn of the century. These had reached a peak population of about 2,000 in 1920, but their proximity to the mine, and the amount of coal dust deposited on them, made them an environmental nightmare. They were bulldozed. Most residents moved to the new town of Sparwood when the mine was bought by Kaiser Resources in 1968. In '69, Kaiser opened its new Balmer open-pit mine at Harmer Ridge across highway from the old underground mine.

Operation was bought by the BC government in 1980; now named Westar Mining. New buildings were constructed on sites of old towns of Michel and Natal. Tours July-Aug; group tours off-season. On site is the largest dump truck ever manufactured, the 350t Terex Titan. Call infocentre for tours: 425-2423.

Sparwood has modern residential neighbourhoods, an impressive leisure centre, shopping mall, golf course.

**Sparwood Information:** Infocentre, Chamber of Commerce, Box 1448, Sparwood, BC, V0B 2G0. Aspen Dr, adjacent Hwy 3, with 3m statue of coal miner in front. Year-round. 425-2423.

■ **Henry Volkmann Memorial Leisure Centre:** Corner of Red Cedar and Pine Ave. Pool, whirlpool, sauna, racquetball, weight room, curling, arena, restaurant. 425-0552.

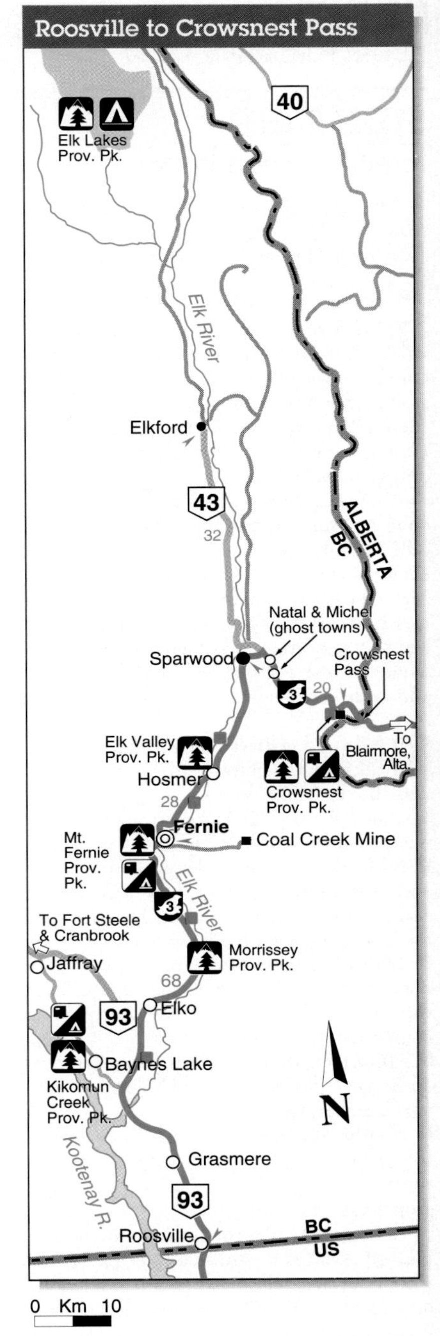


■ **Sparwood Community Campground:** South entrance to town on Hwy 3. 30 campsites, unserviced, some pull-throughs. Adjacent golf course.

■ **Sparwood Golf Club:** Hwy 3. Nine holes on challenging mountain course. 425-2612.

■ **Heritage Murals:** Historic Michel, Natal, come to life.

■ **Rocky Mountain High Adventures:** North of Sparwood, just off Hwy 43. Horseback riding, hay rides, buggy rides. 425-2399.

**Elk Valley Regional Airport:** North of Sparwood on Hwy 43. Charters.

**Hwy 43:** Travels north from Sparwood 32km to Elkford, and a further 87km to Elk Lakes Provincial Park.

## SIDE TRIP
### to Elkford and Park

Hwy 43 follows the Elk River north, and passes the Line Creek Mine 13km north of Sparwood. This open-pit coal mine was developed in 1980.

**Elkford:** (Pop. 2,846). On Hwy 43, 32km north of Sparwood. Elkford is another new town, incorporated in 1970 shortly after work had started on Fording Coal Mine 29km north of the town site. Tours of Fording Coal's open-pit mine are offered only during annual Wild Cat Days, early July. In 1982 Westar Mines developed its Greenhills open-pit mine 6km north of town. Elkford calls itself the Wilderness Capital of BC, and enjoys a spectacular Rocky Mountain setting. Many wilderness walking trails start just minutes from town. Wildlife is of prime interest: here is one of the largest bighorn sheep populations on the continent. Amenities include a golf course, shopping, parks, a new aquatic centre.

**Elkford Information:** Infocentre, Elkford Chamber of Commerce, Box 220, Elkford, BC, V0B 1H0. In the mall at Michel Rd. 865-2241. Year-round (winter, weekdays only, 10am-1pm).

■ **Elkford Municipal Campground:** 80 RV and tent sites. On Hwy 43 at junction of Michel Rd. Call 865-2241. Full services, hook-ups, sani-station, hiking trails.

■ **Elkford Interpretive Trail System:** More than 40km of trails present hikers and skiers with diverse forest ecosystems. Infocentre has maps and info.

■ **Mountain Meadows Golf Club:** On Hwy 43 in town. 865-7413. Nine holes, mountain vistas, rentals, restaurant.

■ **Wapiti Ski Hill:** On Natal Rd, very near town. 865-2020. Open winter weekends, some evenings. One T-bar, night skiing, groomed cross-country track.

Two adventure roads lead north from Elkford. One is a continuation of Hwy 43, which terminates at Alberta border. This paved highway runs northeast of Elkford along Fording River to Greenhills and Fording Coal mines. 5km beyond Elkford a parking lot offers access to the series of hiking trails mentioned above, including trails to Josephine and Fording falls. Some townspeople hope that eventually Hwy 43 will be extended across the border to connect with Alberta's Hwy 40 and Kananaskis country. For now, the area stands in magnificent isolation. Others want to keep it this way.

The other road north out of Elkford is Elk Lakes Forestry Rd going to remote Elk Lakes Recreation Area and Elk Lakes Provincial Park. This is a secondary gravel road maintained June-Sept for two-wheel- drive access to the park gate. At all other times, strictly 4x4 country.

About 44km north of Elkford, Forestry Rd crosses the Elk River, joining the Kananaskis Power Line Rd. It is 43km from this crossing to the park.

**Elk Lakes Provincial Recreation Area:** 11,700ha. Wilderness area adjoining Elk Lakes Provincial Park, taking in Abruzzi and Cadorna valleys. Only development is old seismic road closed to vehicle traffic.

**Elk Lakes Provincial Park:** 5,625ha. 18km beyond Elk Lakes Recreation Area on Elk Lakes Forestry Rd. Walk-in camping only. 422-3212. Subalpine wilderness park with hiking trails leading to Elk Lakes (head waters of Elk River) and Petain Creek. Another trail leads to Elk Pass over the Continental Divide and into Kananaskis Lakes area in Alberta. Elk Lakes are surrounded by mountains and glaciers named in honour of French leaders in the First World War, such as Mt Petain, Mt Nivelle, Mt Joffre, and Mt Foch. Lakes and streams offer fishing for cutthroat, Dolly Varden, and whitefish. Many mountain goats. Check locally about road conditions before departing. This is a true wilderness area without supplies or equipment of any kind.

### *Return to Highway 3 at Sparwood*

**Westar Mines:** 4km beyond Sparwood Hwy 3 passes through Westar Mining operation. Mine is on west side of road; office and service buildings on the east. This is site of old towns of Michel and Natal. Three of the old buildings remain, the **Michel Hotel** (still in use) and two abandoned buildings dating from 1907 and 1908. Westar operates the largest surface mine in Canada. Its annual output is 5.6 million tonnes.

About 3km beyond the Michel Hotel, where the railway crosses highway, sign points out road to **Byron Creek Collieries**. This mine 29km south of Hwy 3 is just beyond the old mining community of Corbin. The original mine was closed after a strike and riot in 1935. The remains of a few of the old buildings still survive.

**Crowsnest Provincial Park:** 46ha. 20km east of Sparwood, 400m west of Alberta border. Rest area, picnics, interpretive signs. 422-3212. Right in the middle of the Crowsnest Pass.

The Crowsnest Pass is, by the way, a relatively easy 1,357m pass through the Rockies. It was used for centuries as an easy travel route by native peoples. Hwy 3 crosses the BC/Alberta border in the pass, just beyond the park, and carries on through the Alberta coal mining towns of **Coleman** and **Blairmore** to **Fort Macleod**.

# Elko to Invermere

## HIGHWAY 3/93, HIGHWAY 93, HIGHWAY 93/95

This 176km stretch begins on Hwy 3/93 leading northwest from the Elko junction. Junction is 63.5km east of Cranbrook, 31.5km west of Fernie, and 36km north of the BC/Montana border. Hwy 3/93, which becomes Hwy 93 (just for a short 8km-segment west of Fort Steele), and then 93/95, joins the Kootenay River near Wardner and follows its shores closely to Canal Flats. The river flows south, the *Log* flows north. This portion of the Rocky Mountain Trench is quite flat – some woodland, some open grass-

*The Aquacourt at Radium Hot Springs.*

land – and it is clear why this was used as a transportation corridor by the first travellers. Finally, Hwy 93/95 skirts the long and lovely Columbia and Windermere lakes en route to Invermere.

**Jaffray:** (Pop. 375). 16.5km beyond Elko. Basic tourist services.

**Baynes Lake-Jaffray Rd:** At Jaffray. Goes south 11km to Kikomun Creek Provincial Park. Details in *Roosville to Crowsnest Pass*, p.252.

**Wardner-Fort Steele Rd:** 28km north of Elko, on northeast side of Kootenay River. Alternate (paved) 33km route to Fort Steele via Bull River, Kootenay Trout Hatchery, Norbury Lake Park.

## BACK ROADS TRIP

### to Fort Steele

**Bull River:** (Pop. 18). 5km beyond Hwy 3/93, on Wardner-Fort Steele Rd. **Bull River Inn**, some houses, are reminders of busier days as lumber town for the CPR. Town shrank after 1900.

**Kootenay Trout Hatchery:** 8km beyond Hwy 3/93 junction, on Wardner-Fort Steele Rd. Hatchery raises 6 million trout annually (rainbow, brook, and cutthroat), 75 percent released in Kamloops, Cariboo, and Prince George areas, 25 percent in the Kootenays. Daily 8-4, year-round. Tours by appointment: 429-3214.

**Norbury Lake Provincial Park:** 97ha; 46 campsites. 16km along Wardner-Fort Steele Rd, 17km south of Fort Steele. 422-3212. Below spectacular Steeples Range, includes Peckhams Lake and fronts Norbury Lake. Swimming, fishing, boat launch (no power boats).

Near Fort Steele junction, road follows, then crosses, **Wild Horse Creek**. This is the creek that precipitated the largest gold rush in the Rocky Mountain region. See *Introduction* to region.

### Return to Highway 3/93 and Wardner-Fort Steele Road

**Wardner Bridge:** Just north of junction with Wardner-Fort Steele Rd, 28km north of Elko, Hwy 3/93 crosses point at which the Kootenay River becomes Lake Koocanusa (Libby Reservoir). Koocanusa is a combo of Kootenay, Canada, and USA.

**Wardner Provincial Park:** 4ha. South of highway, across bridge from junction. Small park on shore of Lake Koocanusa. Swimming, fishing (no boat launch).

**Wardner:** (Pop. 195). Off Hwy 3/93 2km beyond Wardner Provincial Park. Founded in 1895, once site of a large sawmill.

**Rampart Rest Area:** 49km beyond Elko, south of highway.

**Hwy 3 and Hwy 93:** A T-intersection 4.5km beyond rest area, 53.5km north of Elko. Here, Hwy 3/93 divides to become Hwy 93 leading north 8km to Fort Steele; and Hwy 3 leading southwest 6km to Hwy 95, then 4km to downtown Cranbrook. *Log* veers northeast with Hwy 93 to Fort Steele and Invermere.

**Fort Steele Heritage Town:** 150ha. On Hwy 93, 8km north of Hwy 3/93 junction. 489-3351. Sitting high above Kootenay River is turn-of-the-century gold boom town of Fort Steele, very much alive with the presence of the past.

At confluence of Kootenay and St Mary rivers, Fort Steele should have been major city of the region. Accident and skulduggery gave the nod to Cranbrook, reduclng Fort Steele to ghost status (see *Introduction*, p.245).

Fort Steele is a perfect heritage town today, precisely because it was abandoned in such thriving condition, young and promising, and left pretty much alone for a long time. It was never completely abandoned, though: the Kershaw, and Carlin & Durick stores were open till the 1950s.

In 1961, the provincial government saw Fort Steele's historic importance, and began reconstruction. More than mere renovation, the town has almost been reborn. There are some 50 buildings, including some from the original town and North-West Mounted Police camp, some old buildings moved in from other towns, and some replicas. The Prospector Printing Office prints souvenir copies of old newspapers, Kershaw's Family Store sells pioneer goods once again, and staff and volunteers in costume carry on wheel making, horseshoeing, baking, and quilting.

Town also raises popular Clydesdale horses, and offers free wagon rides every 20 min (horses take time out 1:30pm-2:10pm). A steam train takes a scenic loop to a lookout over the valley. Special events include a Fire Hose Reel Race, Harvest Day, Halloween and Thanksgiving Celebrations.

In his book, *Fort Steele: Here History Lives*, resident historian Derryll White comments on the "vast quantities of physical energy" expended in the 1800s just to survive, let alone prosper; even just to housekeep when the house is "constantly under siege from coal dust, dirt and kerosene lamp residue," was a heavy daily task. It is this feeling for the everyday quality of people's lives – as pioneers at the turn of the century –that one gains so strongly from a visit to Fort Steele. A 1904 order at Carlin's Store requests "1000 lbs. cabbage, 1 ton potatoes, 1000 lbs. of mixed Carrots & Turnips," and adds, "As we are entirely out we would like to have this shipment at once." The order was dated October 17, and with winter coming on, and no potatoes, it could have been rough. This is history one can really understand.

Grounds open year-round, dawn to dusk; activities mostly mid-June to early Sept. Admission fee in peak season. Museum,

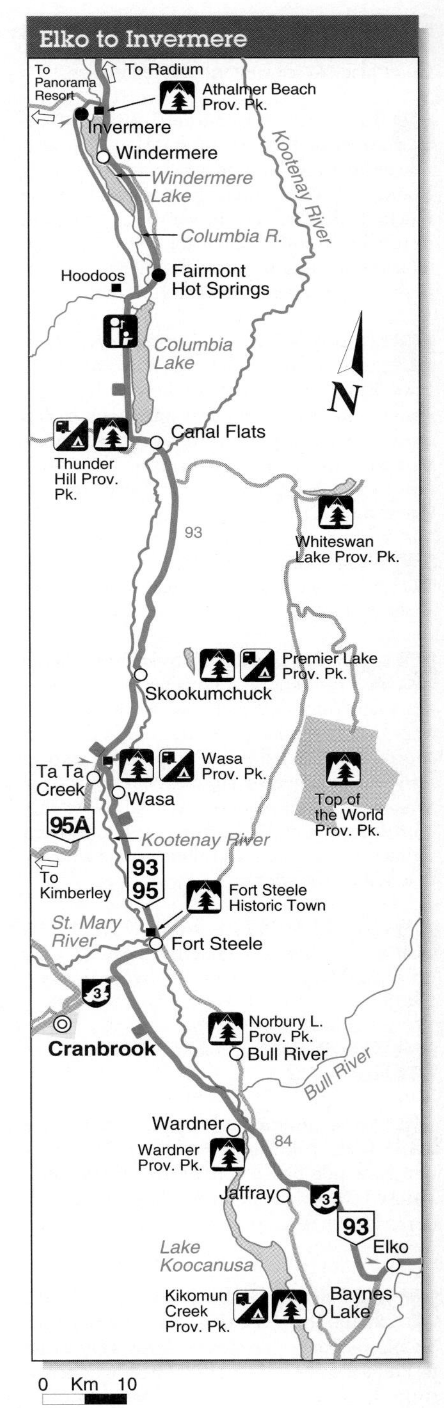


International Hotel Restaurant, Prospector Print Shop, City Bakery, Kershaw's General Store, Mrs Sprague's Confectionery, Wildhorse Theatre, Opera House Mondays.

**Wild Horse, Fisherville, and Last Mile of the Dewdney Trail:** Just north of Fort Steele on Hwy 93 at junction of Wardner-Fort Steele back road. Ask at campground. Two-hour walk up Wild Horse Creek to see remnants of historic gold-rush ghost towns, and the last portion of Dewdney's 1.2m-wide trail that was blazed east from Hope in seven months during 1865.

**Campbell-Meyer Rest Area:** 3.5km north of Fort Steele, east side of highway. Good place to see western painted turtles.

**Bummers Flats:** Small pulloff 9km north of Fort Steele on Hwy 93, west side of highway. Nesting area in marshes along Kootenay River. Potholes have been created by Ducks Unlimited and provincial government to provide nesting habitat for waterfowl. Also look for mountain bluebirds, pileated woodpeckers, meadowlarks, turkey vultures.

**Slough Wildlife Sanctuary:** 14km beyond Fort Steele, northward along Hwy 93 for 4km. Sanctuary borders highway, visible from road. Home to waterfowl, eagles, osprey, herons, turkey vultures. Canada geese nest on top of muskrat houses. (Muskrats don't eat the eggs, would be foolish to try. Geese are fierce.)

**Wasa Lake:** (Pop. 384). On Hwy 93, 20km beyond Fort Steele. On popular Wasa Lake, shallow and warm for swimming.

**Wasa Lake Provincial Park:** 144ha; 104 campsites, sani-station. On road which loops around town and lake. 422-3212. Popular for swimming and water sports, less for fishing. Playground, nature trail, interpretive programs. Winter sports. Wasa is a glacier-made kettle lake. Note that both Osoyoos and Christina lakes have been claimed the warmest, but there's folks who say that Wasa's the winner.

**Hwy 95A:** 2km beyond Wasa. Leads south 27km to Kimberley. Hwy 93 joins up with Hwy 95 north, to become Hwy 93/95.

**Wasa Rest Area:** about 1.5km north of Hwy 95A.

**Skookumchuck:** (Pop. 25). On Hwy 93/95, 13km north of Hwy 95A junction, east side of Kootenay River. Crestbrook Forest Industries operates a large pulp mill here. Name is Chinook jargon for "strong water."

**Premier Lake Provincial Park:** 662ha; 55 campsites. Just north of Skookumchuck, gravel road leads 16km east to Premier Lake. 422-3212. Wheelchair accessible. Premier and four smaller lakes offer good fishing, summer and winter. Bighorn sheep, elk, and deer. Display of fish trap near campground shows how eggs are collected for Kootenay Trout Hatchery. Swimming,fishing, boat launch, hiking; also winter recreation area

**Elk Viewing:** Cleared hills are likely elk-spotting areas, especially in spring. Fence wires are flagged to make them more visible to wildlife when crossing the road.

**Whiteswan Lake Rd:** 36km beyond Hwy 95A junction. Leads east to Whiteswan Lake and Top of the World provincial parks.

## SIDE TRIP
### to Provincial Parks

**Whiteswan Lake Provincial Park:** 1,994ha; 88 campsites in four campgrounds located 17.5km-33km off Hwy 93/95 on fairly rough gravel road. This logging and mining road frequently narrows to one lane, edged by cliffs, and drivers must use caution –there's always the chance that an ore truck is bearing down around the corner. Trucks have right of way! The experience is worth it: just know what you're facing before setting out and be prepared. 422-3212.

Park is on a scenic plateau in the Kootenay ranges, includes Whiteswan and Alces (Moose) lakes, part of White River, many small creeks. Lakes stocked annually since 1961 with rainbow trout. **Alces Lake**: fly-fishing only, no powerboats. *Alces* is Latin for "moose," seen in and around the lake. These are Shiras moose, a subspecies whose Canadian range is confined to this corner of BC.

Campgrounds are at Alces Lake (one), and Whiteswan Lake (three). **Lussier Hot Springs** (undeveloped natural hot springs) are located at park boundary (km 17.5). Swimming, fishing, boat launch; winter recreation. 8km hiking trail on north shores of the two lakes.

**Lussier River Rd:** 22km beyond Hwy 93/95, just inside Whiteswan Lake Park at Alces Lake. Road leads south 31km to Top of the World Provincial Park.

**Top of the World Provincial Park:** 8,791ha. Walk-in camping only. 422-3212. On Lussier River Rd, 31km south of junction with Whiteswan Lake Rd. Watch for logging and ore trucks. An alpine wilderness park of great beauty. Mt Morro, highest peak, reaches 3,002m. Archaeological sites. Trails from parking area lead to five camping sites. Most popular hike (two-hour) is along Lussier River to Fish Lake; tent sites and one cabin accommodating up to 24 people on first-come first-served basis. Good lake fishing for cutthroat and Dollies. Winter: Good fishing, ski touring.

This wilderness has a long history of human use: natives were here at least 9,000 years ago, mining the area's top-of-the-line chert (a flint-like quartz.) Artifacts found on summit of Mt Morro suggest the mountain was an important spiritual destination. Visitors are asked to respect this place as a living museum – take only photographs and leave only footprints.

### *Return to Highway 93/95*

**Canal Flats:** (Pop. 685). On Hwy 93/95, 41km north of Hwy 95A junction. Between Kootenay River and south shore of Columbia Lake. Logging, sawmill.

Canal Flats is centre of one of the continent's most interesting geographical areas, sitting on a 2km strip of land separating Columbia Lake (headwaters of the northward-flowing Columbia River), from the southward-flowing Kootenay River. Details on the surprising flow charts of these rivers in *Introduction to Kootenay Country.*

These two river systems have been focus of much history. David Thompson, first European to visit, came up the Columbia from the Golden area in 1807, called the site McGillivray's Portage.

Today's name, Canal Flats, originates from an extraordinary scheme devised in the 1880s by one William Adolph Baillie-Grohman, to dig a canal through the narrow strip of earth separating Kootenay River and Columbia Lake. His intention was to drain much of the Kootenay River into the Columbia system, thus preventing the annual flooding of valuable farmland along the Kootenay near today's Creston. There were strong objections from residents of the Columbia Valley, needless to say, and also from the CPR, which feared rail washouts. Undauntable Baillie-Grohman altered his plans, said his new purpose was to help navigation through the river systems.

The canal was completed in 1889, but the lock was so narrow and dangerous that only two boats ever passed through it, the *Gwendoline* in 1894, and the *North Star,* in 1902, the latter completely wrecking the locks in the process. (Baillie-Grohman's career was one bizarre disaster after another, often with a silver lining: completing his absurd canal actually netted him a provincial land grant of more than 12,000ha. Not so lucky on a bear hunt, he shot a neighbour's prize boar.)

The idea of a canal or diversion of the Kootenay River at Canal Flats was revived in the 1970s by BC Hydro, to provide more electrical generating capacity in the Columbia River system. Plan met substantial opposition and has not proceeded.

**Canal Flats Provincial Park:** 3ha. 3km north of Canal Flats. Access from the town (not from Hwy 93/95); take northeast road. On east shore of Columbia Lake. Manicured grounds, picnic, boat launch, windsurfing. Here you may view the remains of the Baillie-Grohman Canal.

**Thunder Hill Provincial Park:** 115ha; 23 campsites. 3km north of Canal Flats on Hwy 93/95, west shore of Columbia Lake. 422-3212. Small campground overlooking lake. Saw-whet owls may be heard in spring and early summer.

**Coy's Hill Rest Area:** 15km beyond Canal Flats.

**Dutch Creek Hoodoos:** 20km beyond Thunder Hill Park. Strangely shaped formations of earth resulting from erosion, at north end of Columbia Lake, near bridge over Dutch Creek. Kootenay peoples' legend explains that, back in the mists of time, an enormous fish tried to make its way along the Rocky Mountain Trench. It was a difficult journey. Finally the fish gave up and died at Canal Flats. As its flesh decomposed, the ribs fell apart. Half became the hoodoos here, other half the hoodoos farther south, near Fort Steele.

**West Side Rd:** 22km north of Canal Flats, just past hoodoos, 26km paved back road offers an alternate route to Invermere on west side of Windermere Lake. Not much traffic: it's a great road for cycling, sometimes used for cycling races.

**Columbia River:** 23.5km north of Canal Flats, Hwy 93/95 crosses the Columbia as it begins its 2,000km journey to the Pacific Ocean.

**Fairmont Hot Springs:** (Pop. 249). On Hwy 93/95, 25km north of Canal Flats. In the shadow of the Rockies, with the Purcells across the valley to the west.

**Fairmont-Panorama Airport:** Across hwy from Fairmont Hot Springs Resort. Planes as large as Boeing 737s can land. Charters through Fairmont Glacier Tours: 345-6611.

■ **Fairmont Hot Springs Resort:** Established 1922. Box 10, Fairmont Hot Springs, BC, V0B 1L0. 345-6311. Or 1-800-663-4979. In Calgary: 264-6061. Kootenay peoples long ago discovered the curative powers of these waters, odourless and without sulphur. The springs were named in the late 19th century by Sarah Galbraith, wife of John, first white woman in Galbraith's Ferry (Fort Steele). The flowing hot waters have always intrigued. An English manufacturer from Manchester, W Heap Holland, and then his son, owned the property from the early 1900s, running it as a ranch and resort.

Brothers Lloyd and Earl Wilder, modern pioneers, came out from Saskatchewan after Second World War, operated a sawmill near Radium. They bought the property in 1957; by mid-'60s, had sold the sawmill and begun expansion of the resort. Earl retired, Lloyd carried on. Resort has expanded steadily; in fact, plans have been projected past the year 2000. Lloyd's great interest was the Charolais cattle from France, the "silver cattle with the golden future." He won the first medal given to a breeder outside France, for the bull "Demos." But finally ranchland was sacrificed for Fairmont's new jet airstrip. Twenty years of breeding was auctioned off at a World Sale at Fairmont in 1986. A painting of one of the grand silver sires hangs near the resort's lobby.

■ **The Hot Pools:** Resort's 1,000-square metre swimming and diving pools offer natural mineral waters ranging from 35 to 45 degrees C. 8am-10pm daily.

■ **Fairmont Ski Hill:** Vertical drop of 304m; longest run 1.5km; one triple chair, one platter lift. Cross-country trails.

■ **Mountainside Golf Course at Fairmont Hot Springs Resort:** 18-hole course popular for over 25 years. Unique crowned greens are a challenge; the scenery is splendid. Resort offers packages including unlimited golf on both courses. 345-6311, or 1-800-663-4979.

■ **Riverside Golf at Fairmont:** Exciting new 18-hole course, playing along 4km of frontage on the Columbia's headwaters. Mediterranean-style clubhouse, with white stucco and red-tile roof, features ethnic foods. Accommodation packages are available cooperation with Fairmont Hot Springs Resort.

*Takakkaw Falls in Yoho National Park.*

Tee Times: 345-6346 or 1-800-663-4979.

Along with golf and skiing, Fairmont offers hiking (ask about Kutenai Indian "Spirit Trail" that goes all the way to Canal Flats), trail riding, and small- aircraft and helicopter tours to the Bugaboos and Lake of the Hanging Glaciers.

**Windermere Lake:** A few kilometres beyond Fairmont Hot Springs, Hwy 93/95 follows lake's east shore. A popular resort area.

**Windermere:** (Pop. 821). 17km beyond Fairmont. East side of Windermere Lake. Bald eagles congregate at mouth of Windermere Creek to feed on spawning kokanee (landlocked salmon) Sept-Oct. Plenty of tourist facilities.

In Windermere, visible for all to see, is loot taken from BC's biggest robbery – the whole of **St Peter's Anglican Church**. Church is perched where the thieves left it, atop a knoll with views of both Purcells and Rockies. Back in 1887, St Peter's began life in railway town of Donald, 209km away. Ten years later, when the CPR moved operations westward, most of Donald's inhabitants trundled off, too, to the burgeoning town of Revelstoke. But Rufus and Celina Kimpton were moving east, to Windermere, and they wanted to have a church. They loaded St Peter's onto a railway flatcar.

Alas, somewhere en route the Kimptons discovered the 270kg bell was gone. When citizens of Revelstoke realized that their church was in Windermere, the Windermerians learned that their bell was in a church steeple in Golden. Justice, of a sort.

■ **St Peter's Church:** On Kooteney Ave. Box 205, Windermere, BC, V0B 2L0. 342-9400.

■ **Windermere Valley Golf Course:** New 18-hole course cut into the mountain's edge. 342-3004.

**Rd to James Chabot Beach Provincial Park, Invermere, and Panorama Resort:** 6km beyond Windermere, west off Hwy 93/95. Turn at the Black Forest Restaurant.

**James Chabot Beach Provincial Park:** 13ha. 2km west on road to Invermere. On lake's north shore. Sandy beach, playground, boat launch. Good swimming, windsurfing, sailing, fishing. Wheelchair ramp into swimming area.

**Invermere on the Lake:** (Pop. 2,207). 2km west of the park, 10km beyond Windermere. David Thompson, first European into the area, crossed the Rockies in 1807 and travelled up the Columbia River to Windermere Lake. With his Indian wife and children, and eight others, he built the region's first trading post, near present Invermere, and called it Kootenae House.

A lively tourist area, with Windermere Lake the centre of summer activities, and the ski slopes at Panorama Resort the focus for winter. The area is so popular with Albertans that a Calgary radio station has a satellite radio transmitter here.

Established as the shopping centre of the Windermere Valley, Invermere has unique shops, a full range of services, and that special kind of holiday ambience that money can't buy. Just go there.

**Invermere Information:** Infocentre, Invermere Business Association, Box 2605, Invermere, BC, V0A 1K0. 342-6316. Year-round.

■ **Windermere Valley Museum:** 622-7th Ave. 342-9769. May-Sept. Winter, by appointment. Mining and railway history, in heritage buildings.

■ **Pynelogs Cultural Centre:** On lakeshore next to Kinsmen Beach Park. Historic building constructed in 1915 by Lieutenant-Governor of BC, The Hon Robert Randolph Bruce and his wife, Lady Elizabeth. Now features exhibits, theatre, concerts, workshops, music events. Hosts the Fabulous Inflatable Fish Festival in Aug.

■ **Invermere Ostrich Farm:** On West Side Rd, on southern skirts of Invermere. 342-6255. Petting zoo and ostriches.

**Panorama Resort:** 17.5km west from downtown Invermere, on Toby Creek Rd. Panorama Resort, Panorama, BC, V0A 1T0. 342-6941. Or 1-800-663-2929. At 1050m, it's a sky-high resort, described as "deluxe wilderness." All-season, all-family, alpine activities. Summer: swimming in pool, tennis, riding, white-water rafting, hiking. Winter: heli-skiing, or simply downhill. Vertical drop is 1,158m; longest run 3.5km. Three chairs, T-bars, platter lift, rope tow, quadvilla lift. Cross- country trails, hot tubs.

**Purcell Wilderness Conservancy:** 131,500ha. Walk-in camping only. 150km of trails. Mechanized access prohibited. For Earl Grey Pass Trail drive 32km on Toby Creek Rd from downtown Invermere. Gravel road can be busy with logging and ore trucks. Get directions in Invermere. Leads to Earl Grey Pass, el. 1,070m, maximum el. 2,256m; suggested hiking time, three days. Check Invermere public library for Mary Ann Romback's *With Only the Goosebumps of Gladness Remaining: A Collection of Mountain Hikes.* Earl Grey Pass Trail is also accessible from town of Argenta on northeast shore of Kootenay lake. For more info, write BC Parks, District Manager, Wasa Lake Provincial Park, Box 118, Wasa, BC, V0B 2K0. 422-3212.

## Invermere to Golden

### HIGHWAY 93/95 and HIGHWAY 95

This 117km stretch follows the Columbia River north from Invermere to Golden. Here the Columbia River and Hwy 95 meet the Trans-Canada Hwy (Hwy 1). Beyond Radium, the Rocky Mountain Trench narrows, the mountains become higher and more rugged. To the west, the river winds through extensive marshlands, a superb wildlife habitat. It is interesting to contemplate that 100 years ago, there was no easily passable route through this area at all, though in 1885 the Canadian Pacific Railway had been completed. The railway had reached Golden to the north, and Fort Steele to the south, but there was nothing connecting the two except the Columbia River, and Windermere and Columbia lakes.

There were attempts to provide water links between the rail lines. Frank Armstrong, enterprising fellow, put the first steamboat on the Columbia one year after the railway came in. He built the *Duchess* out of scrap lumber and began to transport goods and passengers between Golden and Lake Windermere. Low water levels and moving sandbars presented problems. Passengers and crew were frequently required to get into the water and push when boat ran aground. Passengers were also called upon to go ashore and cut wood to fuel the steam engine.

Problems with the water link farther south, necessitating portages and at one point a horse-drawn tramway, made the dream less than an easy reality. With the building of the Crowsnest Pass Railway in 1898, steamboat service in the south quickly ended. North, on the Columbia River, however, steamers operated until 1914, for a total of 28 years. In all, 15 different boats were used in the Columbia River service. Eventually, completion of the Kootenay Central Railway, and the building of better highways in the area, spelled the demise of the riverboats.

Hwy 95 may not be as romantic as being right on the river, but no one will be asked to cut wood for the engine, or to get into the water and push.

**Invermere:** (Pop. 2,207). On western shores of Windermere Lake, 4km off Hwy 93/95, on Athalmer Rd. Athalmer Rd junction with Hwy 9 3/95 is 6km north of Windermere. See *previous page.*

**Dry Gulch Provincial Park:** 29ha; 25 campsites. 8km north of Invermere junction, then 1km east off highway on gravel road. 422-3212. Wooded site at foot of Stanford Range.

**Viewpoint:** 11.5km beyond Invermere junction. Panoramic view over the Columbia Valley.

**Redstreak Campground:** In Kootenay National Park. 242 campsites, some hookups, showers, sani-station. Mid-May to early Sept. 347-9615. East off highway at south edge of Radium Hot Springs, 13km from Invermere junction, before Hwy 93/95 junction. Walking trail (30 min) to hot springs. See **Kootenay National Park**, below; also *Radium Hot Springs and Kootenay National Park*, p.262.

**Radium Hot Springs:** (Pop. 395). 13km north of Invermere junction, 104km south of Golden. The springs, named for their relatively high radioactivity, surface at temperatures from 35 to 47 degrees C. Radium Hot Springs provides services for visitors to nearby Aquacourt, campgrounds, and Kootenay National Park. A small Parks Canada book, *Nipika: A Story of Radium Hot Springs,* sells in local stores; well worth the $1.

**Radium Hot Springs Information:** Infocentre, Radium Business Association, Box 225, Radium Hot Springs, BC, V0A 1M0. At junction of highways 93 and 95. 347-9331. May-early Sept. Winter afternoons only.

**Radium Hot Springs Airstrip:** (El 1,800m). Just north of Radium Hot Springs on Hwy 95. No scheduled flights.

■ **Radium Hot Springs Aquacourt:** On Hwy 93. Operated by Canadian Parks Service, offers both hot and cool outdoor pools in a gorgeous mountain setting. A delicious moment in any trip. Year-round.

■ **Our Lady Queen of Peace Shrine:** The Twelve Stations of the Cross on hillside behind Roman Catholic Church. Project started by local sculptor.

■ **Radium Hot Springs Resort and Golf Course:** A complete retreat, with 18-hole showpiece course. Located 1.5km south of the town. Box 310, Radium Hot Springs, BC, V0A 1M0. 347-9311. Or 1-800-665-3585.

■ **The Springs at Radium Golf Course:** 18 holes in panoramic setting with views of Columbia River Valley, the Purcells and the Rockies. Box 430, Radium Hot Springs, BC, V0A 1M0. 347-6444. Golf packages including accommodation and use of other courses: 1-800-667-6444.

**Hwy 93:** In Radium Hot Springs, Hwys 93 and 95 separate. Hwy 93 goes northeast to **Aquacourt**, **Kootenay National Park**, and **Banff National Park**. Details in *Radium Hot Springs and Kootenay National Park*, p.262. Hwy 95 travels north 104km to Golden.

**Kootenay National Park:** 140,600ha; 401 campsites. **West Gate** is 1km north of Hwy 93/95 junction at Radium. West Gate Information Centre: 347-9505 (June-Sept). Year-round: 347-9615. Details in *Radium Hot Springs and Kootenay National Park*, p.262.

Next section of the *Log* follows Hwy 95 north along the Columbia through marshland that is prime wildlife habitat, breeding and staging area for ducks and geese, as well as for water-dependent birds such as bald eagles, osprey, and herons. More than 270 species of birds have been recorded.

Marshes are also home to aquatic animals such as beaver, muskrat, painted turtles. Abundant elk and deer, along with smaller populations of bighorn sheep, moose, black bear, cougar, bobcat.

**Edgewater:** (Pop. 518). 11km beyond Radium. On the "edge" of the Columbia River. Attractive community supported by agriculture and logging. Area is Christmas tree farming land, also excellent grazing range for ungulates (hoofed animals).

**The Cauliflower Tree:** 21km beyond Radium, west of hwy. Strange-looking Douglas fir may have been afflicted by a virus, causing its deformity. Hard to describe, but you'll know it when you see it. Just beside the road.

**Brisco:** (Pop. 138). 28km beyond Radium, on Hwy 95. Named for Captain Arthur Brisco who accompanied Captain John Palliser to this area on the Palliser Expedition (1857-60) for the Royal Geographical Society, gathering information on the expanse from Lake Superior to BC's Okanagan Valley.

**Brisco Rd:** Leads west to Columbia Wildlife Area and Bugaboos.

## SIDE TRIP

### to Wildlife Area and Bugaboos

**Columbia Wildlife Area:** 1.5km west off highway at Brisco. Sloughs on both sides. One covered by pond lily has little attraction for waterfowl; the other is good habitat for Canada geese, wood ducks, redheads, green-winged teals, cinnamon teals, pintails, shovelers, buffleheads, ruddy ducks, American wigeons. Snow geese and Wilson's phalaropes pass through. Many songbirds nest here.

**Bugaboo Glacier Provincial Park:** 25,274ha. 48km west of Hwy 95 at Brisco, on Brisco Rd. Caution: logging trucks. Walk-in camping; commercial heli-skiing lodge near park entrance. 422-3212.

An alpine wilderness park with the largest glaciers in the Purcells, formed long before the Rockies. Erosion has long since worn away the softer rocks leaving exposed the solid granite cores. Ranges should only be climbed by the experienced. Hiking trails, one alpine hut.

## *Return to Highway 95*

Area from here north to Golden is rustic, natural, and un-touristy. Small communities are set with precision in the expanse of valley between mountains and marsh. There are many lovely homesteads on the sloping benchlands. Australian cattledogs (blue heelers) seem to be popular here, and on ranches throughout the area.

**Great Blue Heron Rookery:** 31.5km beyond Radium on Hwy 95. Look for nests in tall poplars along riverside. The 300 pairs of herons nesting here make it the second largest concentration in western Canada.

**Spillimacheen Rest Area:** 34km beyond Radium.

**St Mark's Anglican Church:** 36km beyond Radium. East of hwy, on the hill, old log cabin church is one of province's smallest.

**Spillimacheen:** (Pop. 77). 40km beyond Radium. An access point to the Columbia River, name comes from Indian word meaning "swift running water."

**Harrogate:** (Pop. 37). 52.5km beyond Radium. Named after a fashionable summer resort in Yorkshire. Before trains, a food and rest stop for stagecoaches.

**Nesting Platforms and Marshes:** Along the way, between 62km and 103km north of Radium. River and marshes are near highway, good viewing. Platforms provide safe nesting sites for Canada geese.

**Parson:** (Pop. 84). 70km beyond Radium. Logging community, good base for fishing, and there's still gold being panned in Canyon Creek. Town was named after the Parson brothers, who owned the hog ranch.

**Braisher Creek Rest Area:** 75km north of Radium.

**Nicholson:** (Pop. 1,057). 96km beyond Radium. Named after Swedish homesteaders. Now residential community for Golden, easy access for skiing in Selkirks.

**Golden:** (Pop. 3,721). 104km beyond Radium. See *Glacier National Park to Lake Louise*, following.

**Trans-Canada Hwy (Hwy 1):** At Golden. Leads west to Revelstoke, east to Yoho and Banff national parks. For continuation of Trans-Canada Hwy, see *Glacier National Park to Lake Louise*, following.

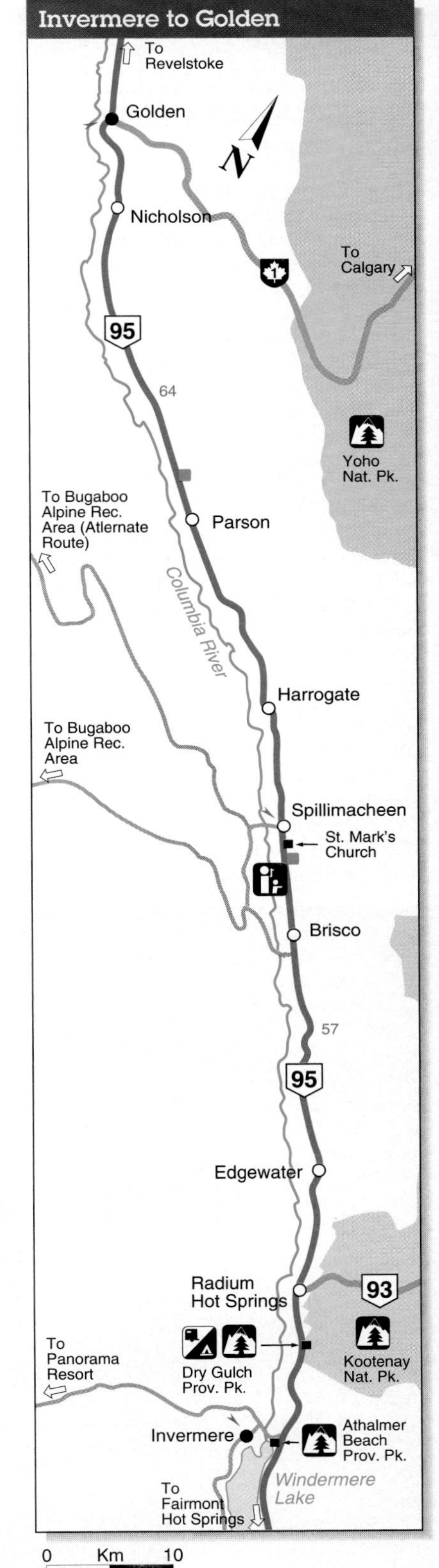

## Glacier National Park to Lake Louise

### TRANS-CANADA HIGHWAY (Highway 1)

From Glacier National Park East Gate, the Trans-Canada Hwy leads east through the city of Golden and then Yoho National Park, to Banff National Park and Lake Louise, a total of 139.5km. Hwy 1 descends from Rogers Pass out of Glacier Park, into the Rocky Mountain Trench, and follows the Columbia River. At Golden, the Kicking Horse River joins the Columbia, and here Hwy 1 takes up with the Kicking Horse, following it into spectacular Yoho National Park and up toward the Continental Divide. For details on Glacier National Park, see *High Country*, p.172.

In 1985, Canada's four Rocky Mountain national parks – **Jasper, Banff, Kootenay,** and **Yoho** – received distinguished designation as **World Heritage Sites** by the United Nations Educational, Scientific, and Cultural Organization. The parks are separate, but share common boundaries and appear as one enormous wilderness area. Yoho is the smallest, with 131,300ha (compared with Jasper's 1,087,800ha).

■ **Time Zone Change**: The transition point from Pacific to Mountain Time occurs 80km east of Revelstoke, within the boundaries of Glacier National Park. Eastbound watches should be set one hour ahead.

**Redgrave Rest Area:** 24.5km east of Glacier National Park East Gate. Both sides of highway.

**Donald Station:** (Pop. 101). 36km east of Glacier National Park East Gate. Named for Donald Smith, CPR director. Town was situated at the point of CPR's first crossing of the Columbia River.

**Doyle Creek Rest Area:** Nearly 44km from East Gate, west side of highway.

**Burges and James Gadsden Provincial Park:** 352ha. 50km from East Gate, west of highway. Encompasses much of the Moberly Marsh along the Columbia west of Golden. The marsh is an important nesting area and migration stopover. The Gadsdens were a pioneer family in the area. Day-use only.

**Hwy 95:** 61.5km east of Glacier Park, at edge of Golden. Leads south 117km to Invermere. See *Invermere to Golden*, p.258.

**Golden:** (Pop. 3,721). At junction of hwys 1 and 95, 61.5km east of Glacier Park East Gate, 78km west of Lake Louise. A town to delight anybody who has ever counted cars in a train: it's train city, a transportation link, at confluence of Columbia and Kicking Horse rivers. Golden only began to develop with the coming of the transcontinental CPR in 1884-85. Town then became terminus for steamboat traffic up the Columbia, linking railway with communities to the south.

Golden epitomizes the region: like many East Kootenay towns, it rose with the boom, then survived the bust because of its breathtaking mountain location, between the massive Rockies and the towering Columbias. And it's not only the mountains, it's the rivers, too: Golden sits at the mouth of the turbulent Kicking Horse, where it joins the Columbia. Golden today is an outdoor city. There is virtually everything for the sports enthusiast, from heli-skiing, ice-climbing, hang gliding, and mountaineering, to horseback riding, river rafting and kayaking.

**Golden Information:** Infocentres, Golden Chamber of Commerce, Box 677, Golden, BC, V0A 1H0. 344-7125. Summer (mid-May to Sept): the tepee on Hwy 1. Year-round: 500 10th Ave (Hwy 95), downtown.

■ **Golden Airport:** West side of town. 1220m runway. "Flightseeing" tour base.

■ **Golden and District Museum:** 1302-11th Ave and 13th St, Golden, BC, V0A 1H0. 344-5169. Weekdays May, June, Sept. Daily July-Aug. Area's history. Others buildings: an early log school, and a blacksmith shop.

■ **Golden Municipal Campground:** 70 sites. 344-5412 (seasonal). Beside the Kicking Horse River, walking distance from town. Showers, close to outdoor pool. Hook-ups.

■ **Golden Golf and Country Club:** Box 1615, Golden, BC, V0A 1H0. 344-2700. Was considered the most extraordinary 9-hole course in BC; now the back nine holes are complete, so it's doubly wonderful. West side of the Columbia amid deer and mountains.

■ **Whitetooth Ski Area:** West side of the

*Howser and Pigeon spires in the Bugaboo Mountains.*

Columbia, 13km from Golden. PO Box 1925, Golden, BC, V0A 1H0. 344-6114. Great powder snow. Day lodge, double chair, T-bar, ski school. Vertical 530m.

■ **Purcell Lodge:** On the eastern border of Glacier National Park. No road in. Accessed by a 15-min helicopter trip from Golden, or summer hiking trail. Contact ABC Wilderness Adventures, Box 1829, Golden, BC, V0A 1H0. 344-2639. Newest, some say finest, remote mountain lodge in North America. High comfort level (balconies, showers, flush toilets) at a high altitude (2,400m) amid unspoiled beauty.

■ **Natural Pursuits Adventure Brokers:** Box 2526, Golden, BC, V0A 1H0. 344-2543. Creative custom trips or packages.

The Trans-Canada Hwy (Hwy 1) continues east following the Kicking Horse River for 26km to Yoho National Park West Gate.

**Yoho Rest Area:** 12.5km east of Golden on Hwy 1.

**Yoho National Park:** 131,300ha; 262 campsites. Western boundary is 26km east of Golden. It is 45km from west to east across the park. All distances within Yoho Park are given from the park's west boundary. Left turns off Trans-Canada Hwy are restricted in the park; some picnic sites and viewpoints are not accessible to eastbound traffic.

Yoho is thought to be a Kootenay peoples' word expressing awe. Kicking Horse has a longer story behind it. Sir James Hector led the Palliser Expedition through Vermilion Pass in 1858. Expedition members continued west to the Kicking Horse River near Wapta Falls. Hector was kicked in the chest trying to rescue a horse from the river, and so the Kicking Horse River was named. We don't know what happened to the horse, but Hector's party followed the river east and returned to the prairies through Kicking Horse Pass.

When CP Rail began building its transcontinental line, Major AB Rogers surveyed a route through the Kicking Horse Pass, and the railway arrived in 1884.

The new railway's 4.5 percent grade between the pass and the small town of Field was known as **the Big Hill**, the steepest railway grade in North America. Four extra engines were required to push trains up the hill, and several runaway spur lines were required for downhill traffic. Still, accidents were frequent, and the remains of one wrecked train can be found near the Kicking Horse campground. After 20 years this "temporary" route was replaced by the **Spiral Tunnels**. From a viewpoint on the highway (see p.262), visitors can watch trains climbing out of Field disappear into a circular tunnel inside Mt Ogden on north side of highway. Train emerges from the 890m tunnel, passes under the highway, and circles through a 992m tunnel inside Cathedral Crags on the south side of the highway. The tunnels lengthen the route by about 10km, but decrease the grade to about 2.2 percent.

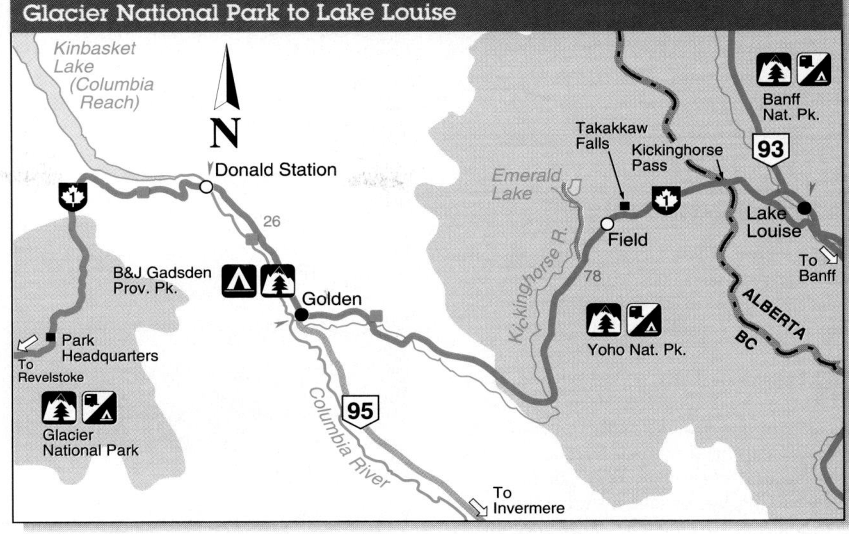


Early tourists came to the Yoho area by rail: highway was not built until 1927.

In addition to the three road-access campgrounds, Yoho National Park has two easily accessible walk-in campgrounds and a number of primitive back-country campsites. Park-use permits are required for overnight camping; check at park infocentre.

**Yoho Park Information:** At junction of Hwy 1 and Field, 29km beyond west boundary (16km from east boundary or BC/Alberta border). Year-round. 343-6324.

**Wapta Falls Rd:** South, off Hwy 1, 4.5km east of west boundary. Gravel road leads 2.5km past Leanchoil Marsh (wildlife viewing) to parking area. Walk 2.5km to Wapta Falls on Kicking Horse River.

**Chancellor Peak Campground:** 58 campsites. 5.5km beyond west boundary. North 1km off hwy. May to mid-Oct. Great setting on the banks of the Kicking Horse River, with views of Chancellor Peak (el 3,280m), Mt Vaux (el 3,320m), and Mt Ennis (el 3117m). Watch for parasitic dwarf mistletoe in great bunches in the trees.

**Hoodoo Creek Campground:** 106 campsites, sani-station. 7km beyond west boundary, just across Kicking Horse River, south of hwy. Late June-end of Aug. Steep 3km hiking trail to Leanchoil Hoodoos.

Beyond campground, Hwy 1 follows the Kicking Horse River. Three picnic sites (following) are on river side (north) of hwy, but restricted left turns limit access for eastbound traffic.

**Faeder Lake Picnic Area:** 8km beyond western boundary, north of highway.

**Finn Creek Picnic Area:** 13km beyond western boundary, on the north side of the highway.

**Ottertail Picnic Area:** 20km beyond west boundary, north of highway. Three little picnic tables.

**Emerald Lake:** 26.5km beyond west boundary, road leads 1.5km to **Natural Bridge** eroded out of solid rock by the Kicking Horse River. Short side road leads from Natural Bridge parking lot past animal lick to picnic site on river bank. It's 6km beyond Natural Bridge to stunning Emerald Lake. Lake was discovered in 1882 by CPR surveyor Tom Wilson, who was amazed by the gorgeous colour of the water. (He also named Lake Louise "Emerald Lake," but it was renamed later to honour Queen Victoria's daughter.)

■ **Emerald Lake Lodge:** Original lodge built in 1902 became a tourist destination for the adventurous early in century. Lodge still in use, with its massive stone fireplaces and hand-hewn timbers. Reopened 1986 with full recreational and conference facilities. 762-2400, or 1-800-661-1367.

**Yoho Park Information:** Located in a new building, at junction of Hwy 1 and Field, 29km beyond west boundary (16km from east boundary or BC/Alberta border). Year-round. 343-6324.

**Alberta Tourism:** Shares the same building. 343-6446.

**Field:** (Pop. 237). 29km beyond west boundary, just south of Hwy 1, across Kicking Horse River. Town grew during railway construction in 1884, and remained for a time an important railway centre because of the problems with the Big Hill and subsequent construction of the Spiral Tunnels. This is a pleasant place to stop for coffee and a look around.

Field is gaining popularity as a base for outdoor adventure, especially mountain climbing. The air is fresh: elevation of Field is 1,242m.

**Yoho Valley Rd:** 33km beyond west boundary. Leads north to Kicking Horse Campground, Takakkaw Falls, and Takakkaw Falls Campground. **Warning:** Very tight switchbacks on this road: see note below.

## SIDE TRIP
### to Takakkaw Falls

**Kicking Horse Campground:** 86 campsites, showers, sani-station, interpretive programs. Trails to railway historic sites. Near infocentre on Yoho Valley Rd.

**Takakkaw Falls:** 15km beyond Hwy 1 on Yoho Valley Rd. Very tight switchbacks prohibit vehicles with trailers or large RVs from using this road. Spectacular 254m falls (second highest in BC) can be viewed from parking lot, or take a short hike to foot of falls. From Cree peoples' word meaning "it is magnificent." Stunning example of "hanging valley falls" (where falls spill from one slightly higher valley into a deeper one).

**Takakkaw Falls Campground:** 35 walk-in campsites a short hike from parking lot.

### *Return to Highway 1 at Kicking Horse Campground*

**Spiral Tunnel Viewpoint:** 36.5km beyond west boundary. View of famous Spiral Tunnels built to avoid the treacherous Big Hill. Near viewpoint stands an old bridge which was part of the original track on the Big Hill. First train attempting to descend the Big Hill plummeted out of control and derailed, killing three men.

**Wapta Lake:** 40km beyond west boundary. Headwaters of Kicking Horse River. Picnics, waterfowl viewing. *Wapta* is "river" in Stoney peoples' dialect.

**Hwy 1A:** 42km beyond west boundary. Alternate route to Lake Louise. Also leads to Lake O'Hara Rd and Lake O'Hara.

## SIDE TRIP
### to Lake O'Hara

A beautiful mountain lake with an extensive series of hiking trails. Hwy 1A leads about 200m across railway tracks to junction with Lake O'Hara Rd. Lake O'Hara is 13km southwest. No private vehicles allowed. Walk in, or call Lake O'Hara for bus service: 343-6433.

**Lake O'Hara Campground:** 30 walk-in campsites, alpine hut, commercial accommodation. 13km south of Hwy 1A on Lake O'Hara Rd. Reservations required for bus transportation and overnight stays: 343-6433 (May-Sept); 343-6324 year-round. Reserve two months ahead.

**Eastern boundary of Yoho National Park and The Great Divide:** 45km beyond park's west boundary. This is also the Continental Divide, and the boundary of BC and Alberta. Banff National Park begins at this point. See *Alberta Rockies*, p. 265.

**Lake Louise:** (Pop. 355). 7km east of BC/Alberta border. Details on p.271. From Lake Louise, turn north to Jasper on the Icefields Parkway (p.276); or south to Banff on Hwy 1 (p.271), or Hwy 1A (p.275).

# Radium Hot Springs and Kootenay National Park

## HIGHWAY 93

Hwy 93, the "Banff-Windermere Parkway," offers a leisurely, scenic trip from Radium at the junction of Hwy 95, through Kootenay National Park to Hwy 1, in Banff National Park. It is 92.5km from West Gate to East Gate of Kootenay National Park; a further 10km to junction with Hwy 1; and from there, it is an equal 28km on Hwy 1 either north to Lake Louise, or south to Banff. Total distance, Radium to Lake Louise or Banff, is 131.5km. This magnificent stretch offers one of the greatest concentrations of stunning scenery in the Rockies parks.

**Radium Hot Springs:** (Pop. 395). Town lies outside gates of Kootenay National Park. See *Invermere to Golden*, p. 258.

**Hwys 93 and 95:** In Radium Hot Springs. Hwy goes south as 93/95 to Invermere junction, 13km, and Cranbrook, 142km. Hwy 95 travels north to Golden, 104km. See *Invermere to Golden*, p.258.

**Redstreak Campground:** 242 campsites, some hookups, showers, sani-station. Mid-May to early Sept. 347-9615. On a bench above the village of Radium. Campground is actually in Kootenay Park, but vehicle access is only possible from Hwy 93/95 on the south edge of Radium Hot Springs. Walking trail (30 min) to hot springs.

**Kootenay National Park:** 140,600ha; 401 campsites. **Administration**: write the Superintendent, Kootenay National Park, Box 220, Radium Hot Springs, BC, V0A 1M0. 347-9615 (year-round). **West Gate Information Centre**: 347-9505 (June-Sept). All distances are given from the park's West Gate 1km out of Radium Hot Springs. It is 92.5km to the park's East Gate in Vermilion Pass.

Present-day Kootenay Park has been used by local Indian tribes as a travel corridor for thousands of years. Like the travellers of today, the Indians liked to gather at the hot springs. Early European visitors were explorers and fur traders looking for transportation routes through the Rockies. These included Sir George Simpson, governor of the Hudson's Bay Company, who went through in 1841. In 1854 John Sinclair lead a party of settlers from Fort Garry through the canyon that now bears his name. Sir James Hector and the Palliser Expedition were looking for new routes in 1858 when they discovered Vermilion Pass.

In 1920 the park area was given by the Province of British Columbia to the Government of Canada in return for a road through the central Canadian Rockies. (It was completed in 1923.) In 1985, Kootenay National Park, with the other Rockies parks – Banff, Jasper, and Yoho – was declared a World Heritage Site as a highly significant and valuable representation of the Rocky Mountain landscape. More than 1.2 million visitors enter Kootenay National Park annually, second in numbers to Banff and Jasper parks.

The park road tracks through the Kootenay and Vermilion river valleys, flanked by such peaks as Mt Harkin, 2,935m, Split Peak, 2,926m, Mt Wardle, 2,810m, and Storm Mountain, 3,161m. Milky-green streams and waterfalls tumble from these mountains as the road climbs toward Vermilion Pass, at 1,651m one of BC's highest. Here, on the border between Banff and Kootenay parks, North America splits along the Continental Divide.

Kootenay National Park has more than spectacular mountain scenery: it is extremely varied, the only national park with both cactus and glaciers. There is excellent wildlife viewing. Elk, deer, bighorn sheep, mountain goats, moose, and black bear may be seen along hwy. Coyotes, wolves, and grizzly bears also inhabit the park, but stick mainly to the park's remote areas. More than 200km of hiking trails offer access to back-country areas. Park permits required for back-country camping. Free back-country guide at infocentres.

**Kootenay National Park West Gate and Information:** Infocentre, 1km north of Hwy 93/95 junction at Radium. Seasonal: 347-9505. Year-round: 347-9615.

**Radium Hot Springs Aquacourt (or Pools):** 2km beyond West Gate. Operated by the Canadian Parks Service. Natural hot and cool outdoor pools – temperatures to 38 degrees Celsius – in a gorgeous mountain setting. Some 350,000 bathers loll about here every year. Year-round. Restaurant May-Oct. Trails from here to Sinclair Canyon Viewpoint and Redstreak Campground.
■ **"The Infinite Field Trip":** Interactive video on laser disk. At the Aquacourt. Answers an infinite number of questions about the park. But holds back when asked to give out secret fishing spots. Voice says: "I'm sorry. I'm afraid I can't do that." Developed by park naturalist Larry Halverson.

**Bighorn Sheep:** 4km beyond West Gate. Seen along road spring and fall.

**Sinclair Creek Picnic Site:** 9km beyond West Gate. In Sinclair Creek valley.

**Olive Lake Picnic Site:** 11km beyond West Gate. On shore of unusual, olive-coloured lake. Site of one of first campgrounds in the park: note rustic picnic shelters. Brook trout easily seen, perhaps not so easily caught.

**Kootenay Valley Viewpoint:** 15km beyond West Gate. Sweeping view of valley, and Stanford and Mitchell mountain ranges.

**Settlers' Rd:** 18km beyond West Gate. Follows Kootenay River south out of park. Caution: logging and ore trucks have right of way. Extensive network of logging roads. Get info before venturing forth.

**Kootenay River Picnic Site:** 22.5km beyond West Gate. 1km trail to Nixon Lake.

**McLeod Meadows Campground:** 98 campsites, sani-station. 26.5km beyond West Gate. Late June-early Sept. On the banks of Kootenay River. Good jumping-off point for canoeists, and a good spot for elk, deer, coyotes, occasionally black bears, moose. At least four kinds of orchids bloom here in early summer: calypso, sparrow's egg, white bog, and rare round-leafed orchid. Trail (2.4km) leads to Dog Lake. Picnics.

**Dolly Varden Picnic Site:** 35km beyond West Gate. Winter camping, fishing.

**Kootenay Crossing Bridge:** 42.5km beyond West Gate. Warden station. Hwy crosses the Kootenay River (takes up 20km north with the Vermilion River which it follows to East Gate.) At the crossing. there is a hiking trail (9.7km) goes northwest to park boundary.

**Hector Gorge Viewpoint:** 46km from West Gate. Named after Dr James Hector of the Palliser expedition (he whose horse was the Kicking Horse).

**Hector Gorge Picnic Site:** 48km from West Gate.

**Mountain Goats:** 50km beyond West Gate. Goats are often seen on the banks west of highway at the base of Mount Wardle, if they are not actually right on the roadside.

**Wardle Creek Picnic Area:** 52km from West Gate.

**Animal Lick:** 54.5 beyond West Gate, east of hwy. Natural mineral lick. With patience and luck, travellers might see elk, moose, or mule deer.

**Simpson Monument and Trail to Mount Assiniboine Provincial Park:** 55.5km beyond West Gate. Commemorates journey of Sir George Simpson, governor of Hudson's Bay Company, who explored area in 1841. Simpson River Trail leads 32km to **Mount Assiniboine Provincial Park**, nestled between the southern reaches of Kootenay and Banff national parks, with no road access. Extensive trails, walk-in campsites. 42,000 visitors hike in each year through fragile alpine meadows. This is a special place. Be gentle.

**Vermilion River Crossing:** 62km beyond West Gate, where highway crosses the Vermilion River. Picnic site, fishing. Lodge and services during summer. Trailhead for Verdant and Verendrye Creek trails.

**Floe Lake-Hawke Creek Rd:** 70km beyond West Gate. Trail 10km west to one of the few "berg" lakes in the Rockies, named for the mini-icebergs which break off from Floe Glacier and float on the lake.

**Numa Creek Picnic Site:** 79km beyond West Gate. Scenic falls on Vermilion River.

**Paint Pots:** 83km beyond West Gate. Picnics. Self-guiding trail (.8km) to ochre beds once a source of vermilion paint used by first peoples as body and tepee paint. Cold mineral springs served as a spiritual meeting place for the Stoney and Kootenai peoples. Here they processed the red clay or ochre into a powder, later mixed with water and grease.

Access from Paint Pots to major trails in park's northwest section, and also some of the park's most spectacular sights: Goodsir and Ottertail passes, Tumbling Glacier, Valley of the Ten Peaks, Panorama Ridge, the Rock Wall (a towering limestone barrier), 300m Helmet Falls.

**Kootenay National Park Information:** Marble Canyon Infocentre. 85.5km from West Gate, 7km from East Gate at Vermilion Pass. Late June-Sept. 500m from campground, west of highway.

**Marble Canyon and Tokumm Creek:** At infocentre, 85.5km from West Gate. Picnic site. Short trail (.8km) along rim of extremely narrow canyon cut deep by bright blue mountain stream. Only 3 - 18m wide, but in places, the canyon cuts 39m deep into the limestone. Some limestone has metamorphosed into marble (actually a dolomite), hence the name. Access to Kaufmann Lake and Tokumm Creek trails.

**Marble Canyon Campground:** 61 campsites, sani-station. 85.5km from West Gate, 7km from East Gate. Just 500m from infocentre, east of Hwy 93. Late June-early Sept.

**Trail to Stanley Glacier:** 89km from West Gate. Spectacular four-hour (4.8km) hike to a hanging valley and alpine glacier.

**Vermilion Pass, East Gate, and Continental Divide:** (El 1,651m). Stop of interest at Continental Divide. To the west all water flows to the Pacific Ocean, to the

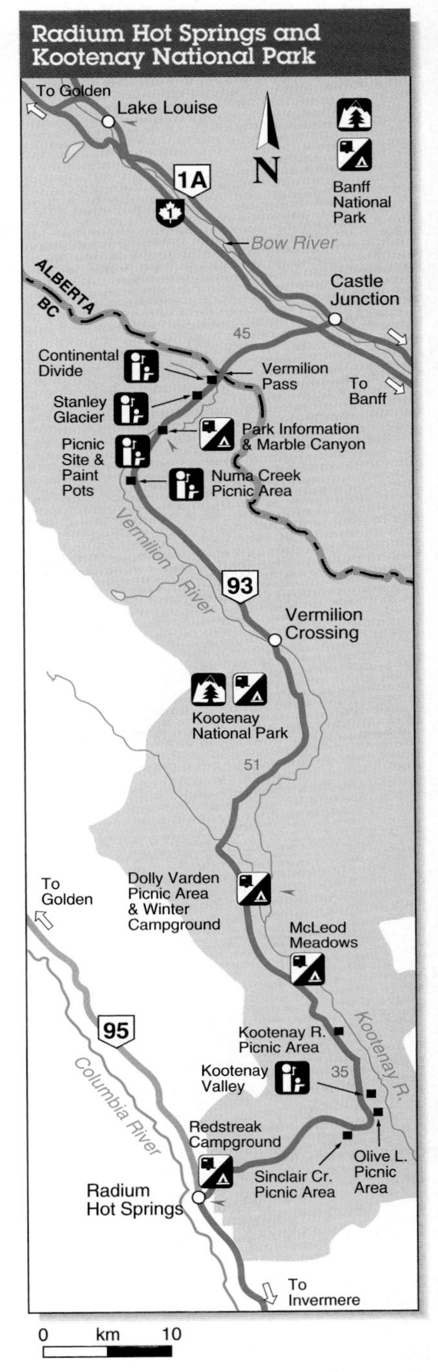


east it flows to Hudson Bay. The Divide marks the boundary between Alberta and BC, and between Banff and Kootenay national parks. At the Divide, take the **Fireweed Trail**, a short self-guiding nature trail, to see "the Vermilion Pass Burn," result of a 1968 forest fire.

From Vermilion Pass, Hwy 93 descends east 10km to Castle Mountain Junction, where it ends in a T-junction with Trans-Canada Hwy 1. (It is picked up by Alberta's Hwy 93 north of Lake Louise.) Following the lovely Bow River, Hwy 1 goes north 28km to Lake Louise, or south 28km to Banff. Castle Mountain Junction is exactly midway. For details, see *Lake Louise to Banff*, p.271.

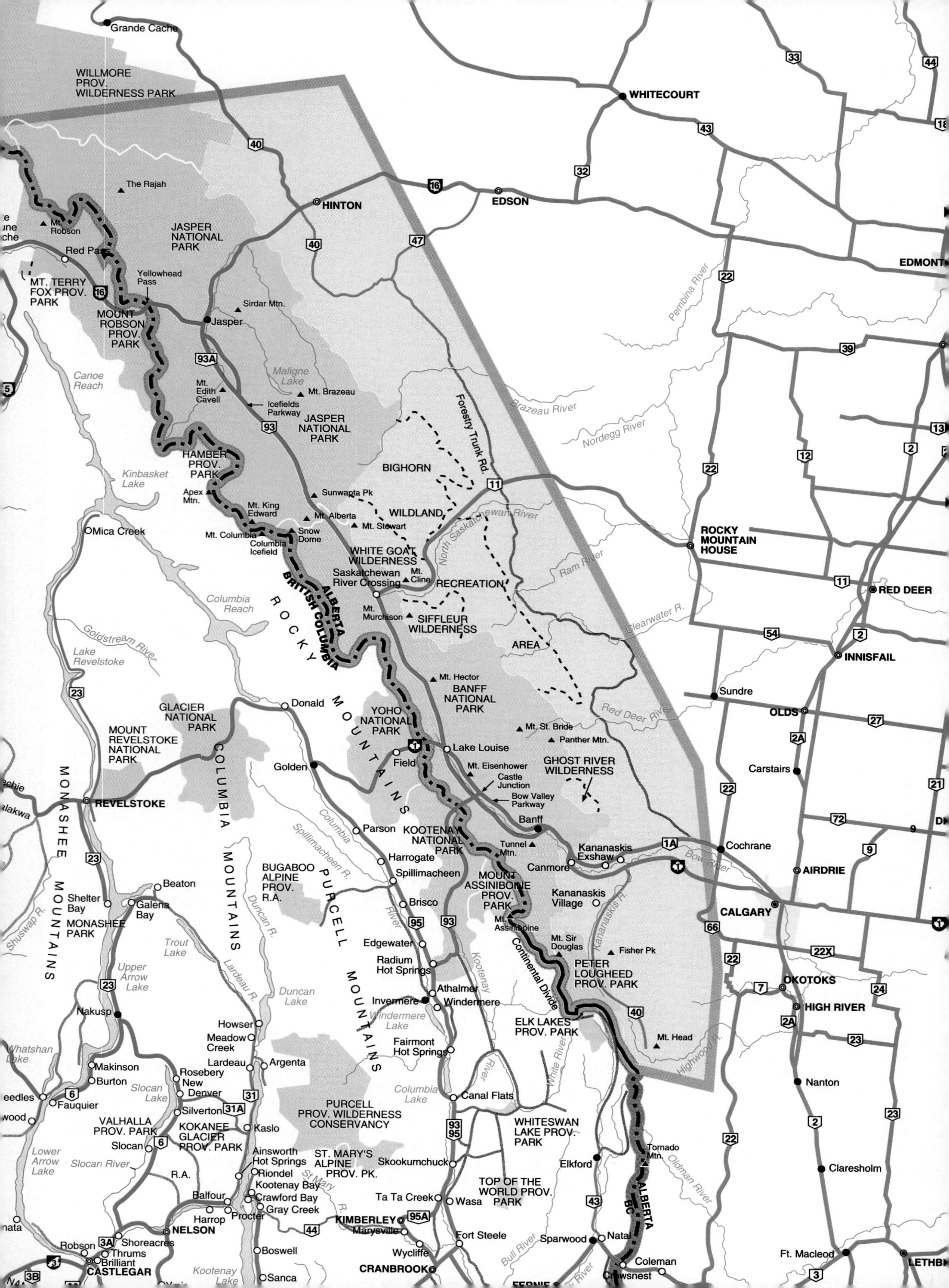

Grande Cache
WILLMORE PROV. WILDERNESS PARK
WHITECOURT
33
44
43
18
40
32
The Rajah
16
EDSON
HINTON
Mt. Robson
JASPER NATIONAL PARK
40
47
Red Pass
Yellowhead Pass
MT. TERRY FOX PROV. PARK
16
22
Pembina River
MOUNT ROBSON PROV. PARK
Jasper
Sirdar Mtn.
93A
39
Canoe Reach
Maligne Lake
Mt. Brazeau
Mt. Edith Cavell
Icefields Parkway
Forestry Trunk Rd.
Brazeau River
93
JASPER NATIONAL PARK
Nordegg River
13
2
12
HAMBER PROV. PARK
BIGHORN
22
Kinbasket Lake
Apex Mtn.
Sunwapta Pk
11
Mt. King Edward
Mt. Alberta
WILDLAND
North Saskatchewan River
Mt. Stewart
Mica Creek
Mt. Columbia
Columbia Icefield
Snow Dome
ROCKY MOUNTAIN HOUSE
WHITE GOAT WILDERNESS
North Saskatchewan River
Ram River
Saskatchewan River Crossing
Mt. Cline
RECREATION
11
RED DEER
ALBERTA
BRITISH COLUMBIA
Columbia Reach
ROCKY
Mt. Murchison
SIFFLEUR WILDERNESS
Clearwater R.
54
2
Goldstream River
Lake Revelstoke
AREA
INNISFAIL
Mt. Hector
BANFF NATIONAL PARK
Sundre
23
Donald
MOUNTAINS
Red Deer River
OLDS
27
GLACIER NATIONAL PARK
YOHO NATIONAL PARK
Mt. St. Bride
Panther Mtn.
2A
MOUNT REVELSTOKE NATIONAL PARK
1
Field
Lake Louise
Carstairs
Golden
Mt. Eisenhower
GHOST RIVER WILDERNESS
Castle Junction
22
21
REVELSTOKE
COLUMBIA
Bow Valley Parkway
72
MONASHEE MOUNTAINS
Banff
9
9
Columbia
Spillimacheen R.
Parson
KOOTENAY NATIONAL PARK
Tunnel Mtn.
Kananaskis
Exshaw
1A
Cochrane
23
Harrogate
Canmore
1
Bow River
AIRDRIE
BUGABOO ALPINE PROV. R.A.
PURCELL
Spillimacheen
MOUNT ASSINIBOINE PROV. PARK
Beaton
Kananaskis Village
Kananaskis R.
Shelter Bay
Galena Bay
MOUNTAINS
Brisco
CALGARY
Shuswap R.
MONASHEE PARK
Duncan R.
River
95
93
Mt. Assiniboine
66
1
Trout Lake
Edgewater
Mt. Sir Douglas
Fisher Pk
22X
22
Upper Arrow Lake
Radium Hot Springs
Kootenay
Continental Divide
PETER LOUGHEED PROV. PARK
OKOTOKS
23
Lardeau R.
Athalmer
7
24
Duncan Lake
Invermere
Windermere
HIGH RIVER
Nakusp
MOUNTAINS
Windermere Lake
40
2A
Howser
ELK LAKES PROV. PARK
23
Meadow Creek
Fairmont Hot Springs
Mt. Head
Whatshan Lake
White River
Highwood R.
Lardeau
Argenta
Makinson
Rosebery
River
Burton
New Denver
Slocan Lake
Columbia Lake
Nanton
6
31
Fauquier
Silverton
31A
Canal Flats
PURCELL PROV. WILDERNESS CONSERVANCY
VALHALLA PROV. PARK
KOKANEE GLACIER PROV. PARK
Kaslo
93
95
WHITESWAN LAKE PROV. PARK
2
23
Slocan
6
22
Lower Arrow Lake
Slocan River
Ainsworth Hot Springs
ST. MARY'S ALPINE PROV. PK.
Tornado Mtn.
R.A.
Riondel
Skookumchuck
Elkford
Oldman River
Claresholm
Kootenay Bay
St Mary
TOP OF THE WORLD PROV. PARK
Balfour
Crawford Bay
Ta Ta Creek
Wasa
43
ALBERTA
BC
Harrop
Procter
Gray Creek
R.
KIMBERLEY
95A
44
NELSON
Marysville
Fort Steele
Robson
3A
Shoreacres
Bull River
Sparwood
Natal
Thrums
Ft. Macleod
Brilliant
Wycliffe
Coleman
3
CASTLEGAR
Boswell
CRANBROOK
3B
Kootenay Lake
Sanca
Crowsnest
3

# Alberta Rockies

## *Pinnacle of the Wild Rose Province*

Lying like a holster along the leg of the Rockies, Alberta, the cowboy province, is two-thirds the size of BC, three times larger than the United Kingdom, and about the same size as the Lone Star state of Texas, with which it is often compared.

Both have cowboy roots and cowboy boots, vast ranches and farms, oil wells, and clusters of glass skyscrapers towering above sprawling young cities. One thing that Texas does not have is the Rockies, and they are the focus of this section.

The scope of this *Travel Guide* does not take us east of the Alberta Rockies, so offered below is only a tantalizing introduction to BC's flamboyant neighbour, Alberta, famed for its stampede and dinosaurs, its oil, and its tremendous hospitality. The *Log* sections of the *Alberta Rockies* will cover in detail Banff National Park and Jasper National Park, ending at the East Gates of the two parks. Beyond the mountains, may Alberta unfold for you like a wild prairie rose at dawn.

### The Lay of the Land

Alberta sprawls out over 644,390 sq km of land and 16,800 sq km of fresh water, covering a total of 661,190 sq km, making it Canada's fourth largest province. It is 2,400km long, 1,250km wide at the top, narrowing to 600km wide on the US border, giving the province its holster shape. The Continental Divide along the Rocky Mountains is a natural western border. In the south, the 49th parallel forms the boundary with Montana.

From the province's highest point, 3,747m Mt Columbia in Jasper National Park, Alberta rolls east and north from the Rockies, to just 200m above sea level along the Slave River in the far northeast corner. Alberta's river systems go with this flow. The Hay, Peace, and Athabasca river systems of northern Alberta drain north into the Arctic Ocean. Most of southern Alberta is the watershed of the North and South Saskatchewan river systems, flowing east to Hudson Bay. Meltwaters from the Columbia Icefield feed, eventually, the Arctic and Atlantic oceans; and the Milk River watershed, in the extreme south, actually drains into the Mississippi and the Gulf of Mexico.

### Badlands, Goodlands, and Others

Alberta offers a rich tapestry of distinct biophysical regions.

The Rockies roll into the foothills, which roll down onto the plains; the north woods – a swath of boreal forest called *taiga* in Russia – thin into aspen parklands; they in turn disappear into semi-arid grasslands of the south. Out into the foothills of southern Alberta is the round northern tip of the Great Plains. Cactus-studded, short-grass prairies cover the

*Peyto Lake, Banff National Park.*

driest southeast, with tall-grass prairies farther north and west.

Along the Red Deer River, especially near Drumheller and in Dinosaur Provincial Park, water and wind have carved eerie badlands from the colourful, fossil-filled clay soils. On the Milk River, at Writing-on-Stone Provincial Park, there are sandstone hoodoos etched with the largest collection of native rock "writing" on the North American plains.

## Rocky Mountains

Hauntingly beautiful as most of Alberta is, the province's most obvious and famous attraction is the Rocky Mountains. For the last two million years, glaciers and streams and winds have been busy sculpting, slicing, and polishing the Rockies into their present spectacular shape.

Hikers in the Rockies are often astonished to find marine fossils imbedded in peaks now 3,000m above sea level. For most of the past 1.5 billion years, Alberta was at the bottom of shallow seas stretching from the Arctic Ocean to the Gulf of Mexico, steadily blanketed by sinking sediments that in time became layers of sandstone, limestone, shale, and most of Canada's coal, oil, and natural gas.

About 75 million years ago, the North American continental plate, drifting west across the earth's molten basement, collided with the north bound Pacific plate. The earth's crust buckled where they met, pushing the young Rockies up and a new continental divide farther east. As the land lifted, the sedimentary layers on the eastern slope broke up into massive slabs, which tilted as they were pushed eastward, rippling up foothills in their wake.

So came the Rockies. And since their expansion 14,000 years ago, the glaciers have retreated to the peaks, and vegetation, wildlife, and people have moved into the landscape.

## Albertosaurus and Edmontosaurus

Long known as a rich source of fossil fuels, Alberta has now been recognized as one of the world's richest deposits of dinosaur fossils. Scientific interest, and the recent dino-craze, have made Alberta, and the Tyrrell Museum of Paleontology near Drumheller, a mecca for both fossil-hunting paleontologists and the tourists sharing their fascination.

Thirty-five different species of dinosaur (the word means "terrible lizard") have been found in Dinosaur Provincial Park, near Brooks, and many other species have been unearthed elsewhere, including a major new find of horned dinosaurs near Grande Prairie. Most of Alberta's dinosaurs lived between 100 and 64 million years ago, when the province was a vast swampy sea. Three local favourites were albertosaurus (a fierce carnivore, cousin to tyrannosaurus), edmontosaurus (a duck-billed plant eater that moved about in herds some 73 million years ago), and edmontonia (a vegetarian protected with armoured plates).

## The First Peoples

Alberta was one of the first parts of North America to be inhabited. Crossing the land bridge between Siberia and Alaska 12,000 to 28,000 years ago, the first aboriginal peoples may have moved south through eastern Alberta along the ice-free corridor that ran between the western and eastern continental icecaps. When the ice sheets receded again 14,000 years ago, Paleo-Indians began colonizing the plains. Several sites show evidence of early human activity: artifacts at Vermilion Lakes near Banff; flint quarries at Crowsnest Pass; pictographs near Canmore; ancient campsites in Waterton Lakes National Park.

In the early to mid 1700s, two factors revolutionized Alberta native life. From the southeast came the first horses, traded north from tribe to tribe after being acquired from the Spanish in Mexico in the early 1500s. Horses dramatically transformed the lives of the plains tribes. From the northeast, along the waterways of beaver country, came the fur trade. Long before the first white traders arrived, tribes from the east, primarily the Cree, armed with guns gained through fur trading on their eastern Canadian homelands, began to push west into northern Alberta to exploit the rich furs. The still unarmed Beaver and Slavey tribes were pushed farther north, the Sarcee farther west, the Blackfoot farther south. But in the late 1700s, the locals finally got their own firearms, held the line, and joined in the lucrative fur trade.

*Athabasca Falls, Jasper National Park.*

The horse and the fur trade brought brief prosperity to the native peoples of Alberta, but in the end, the contact with European civilization proved disastrous. Diseases wiped out healthy tribes, missionary zeal crushed ancient cultures, alcohol destroyed individual and family spirits. The story was far less wild and bloody than in the United States, especially in northern Alberta where the native peoples were partners in the fur trade.

However, nothing can mitigate the overall tragedy. In 1837, smallpox killed two-thirds of the Blackfoot nation. Today, some reserves have become wealthy from energy and real estate developments, but others are still seeking settlement for outstanding claims.

## Fur Traders and Map Makers

In 1754, Hudson's Bay Company explorer Anthony Henday, escorted by Cree traders, ascended the North Saskatchewan and Battle rivers, and became the first white man to see Alberta and the Rockies. He wintered near today's Edmonton and traded with local Indians for the first furs exported from Alberta. In 1792, looking for the legendary river west to the Pacific, "Nor'Wester" Alexander Mackenzie crossed northern Alberta up the Peace River on his way to becoming the first white person to cross North America to the Pacific.

About the same time, Peter Fidler, Hudson's Bay Company scout and surveyor, began 14 years of exploration. Alberta's first map maker, he opened up the north. The fur companies raced in to establish trading routes, clients, and posts: at Edmonton in 1795, Rocky Mountain House in 1799, Dunvegan in 1805 (all of which are now fascinating historic sites).

## Trains, Grains, Home on the Range

About the time the Mounties were establishing law and order, the first ranchers were eyeing the ocean of grass now all but empty of buffalo, which were slaughtered in the millions by white men. Sir Sanford Fleming began surveying possible routes for the promised transcontinental railway. The CPR finally pushed across southern Alberta to the Rockies below Kicking Horse Pass in 1883, creating Medicine Hat, Calgary and, indirectly, two years later, Canada's first national park, at Banff. Among the first to cash in were the big ranchers who quickly laid claim to the southern foothills. They exported their beef east to market from the Calgary - "Cow Town" railhead.

In 1888, the railway brought the first transcontinental tourists to the Banff Springs Hotel. The fame and fortune of the Canadian Rockies followed.

## Buried Treasure

In 1870, a Geological Survey of Canada crew noticed oil and natural gas seeps in what is now Waterton National Park. This went largely ignored amid reports of huge deposits of coal elsewhere. In 1886, local homesteader "Kootenai" Brown reread the old report, began collecting seeping oil, selling it to local ranchers for lamp fuel and lubricant. In 1902, Alberta's first successful oil well was drilled on Cameron Creek, but the deposit was small.

*Elk loitering about in residential Banff.*

In 1914, oil in quantity was finally found at Turner Valley in the foothills. This first major oil find in the British Empire created great excitement, but didn't pan out. Finally, in 1947, just south of Edmonton at Leduc, patient Imperial Oil drillers finally hit the long sought black mother-lode, and oil began heating up Alberta's economy.

## The People Today

More than half of the 2,545,553 Albertans live in the five largest urban centres: Edmonton (616,741), Alberta's capital and gateway to the north; Calgary (710,677), Canada's oil capital; Red Deer (58,134); Lethbridge (60,974); and Medicine Hat (43,625).

Calgary and Edmonton are typical Canadian cities, each with a rich multicultural mix. East of Edmonton is the "Dr Zhivago goes to Quebec" portion of Alberta, punctuated by tall spires of Roman Catholic churches and round domes of Russian Orthodox churches, with coffee shop conversations in English, French, Ukrainian, and Cree. The central parklands were homesteaded by Scandinavians, Icelanders, Germans, Poles. The far south, by Ukrainians, and Mormons from Utah, who brought irrigation to the parched prairies. Canada's only Mormon temple is in Cardston. The mountain parks were developed by British and American interests, and became home to many Swiss, who originally arrived as mountain guides.

The province's economy today is built on fossil fuels, agriculture, and tourism. With 75 percent of Canada's conventional oil, and 86 percent of its natural gas, the "oil-patch" province is in the unique position of having no retail sales tax. Alberta does, however, have a five percent room tax, and, along with the other provinces, enjoys paying the federal seven percent goods and services tax, or GST.

# Tourist Information

The Area Code for the province of Alberta is (403).

**Alberta Tourism:** Write Box 2500, Edmonton, AB, T5J 2Z4. 427-4321. Fax: 427-0867. Canada and United States: 1-800-661-8888. Alberta Tourism is the central service for all visitor information, and runs a network of information centres province-wide. Centres in Canmore, Edmonton, Jasper, Lloydminster, Milk River, Oyen, Sentinel, and Walsh are open year-round; also year-round, in Field (BC), and West Glacier (Montana). Others mid-May to Sept.

### *Events*

For general information on Canada's holidays, see *Introduction to British Columbia.* First Monday in August is Alberta Heritage Day, celebrated in almost every community, small and large, and revealing the diverse heritage of the province. Every summer weekend somewhere in Alberta there are ethnic festivals, art and music festivals, regattas, country fairs, First Nations powwows, and *lots* of rodeos, from small town "Howdy neighbour" events to the Big One at Calgary (the Calgary Stampede). It doesn't stop there. Throughout the year there are autumn harvest festivals, winter carnivals, spring ski parties, and "hurray-we-made-it-through-the-winter" parties. Perhaps because of their roots on the big, lonely land, Albertans like to get together and have a good time.

### Emblems

Alberta's provincial wildflower is the wild rose, and the great horned owl is the provincial bird. The emblem of the Sunshine Province sums it up – snowy mountains, green foothills, golden wheat fields, and evergreen forests under a deep blue sky.

### Parks

Alberta has more land in national parks than any other province. Banff, Jasper, and Waterton in the Rockies, Elk Island near Edmonton, and Wood Buffalo in the north, together cover more than 20,000 sq km. There is also one national historic site at Rocky Mountain House. Hunting and firearms are not allowed. Contact Canadian Parks Service, Western Regional Office, Room 520, 220 - 4th Ave SE, Box 2989, Station M, Calgary, AB, T2P 3H8. 292-4440.

There are more than 100 provincial parks and recreation areas representing landscapes and wildlife native to every part of the province. Alberta Parks also manages three Wilderness Areas –White Goat, Siffleur, and Ghost River – adjacent to Banff National Park, for maximum resource protection. Foot travel only; no hunting, fishing, or trapping. Contact Environmental Protection, Alberta Parks Service, Standard Life Centre, 10405 Jasper Ave, Edmonton, AB, T5J 3N4. 427-7009.

### Forest Reserves

In western Alberta, if the land is forested and it's not a national or provincial park, it's probably a forest reserve. Ten reserves cover more than 388,500 sq km. Most are multi-use areas, managed for timber, grazing, watersheds, wildlife, and recreation. Map of provincial forest areas is available from Alberta Forest Service, Forest Land Use Branch, Recreation Section, 6th Floor, 9920-108th St, Edmonton, AB, T5K 2M4. 427-3582.

### Natural Areas

There are more than 100 Natural Areas in Alberta, managed by the Alberta Forest Service to preserve (usually) small parcels of land with unique, distinctive, or rare flora, fauna, or physical features. Low- impact recreation (hiking, cross-country skiing, birding, photography) is allowed in many, but others have use restrictions to ensure protection of rare or fragile features. Contact Natural Areas Program, Alberta Forest Service (above).

*Lake Louise and the Victoria Glacier, Banff National Park.*

## Accommodation and Camping

Alberta has a complete range of travellers' accommodation: luxurious hotels (including some of the world's most famous mountain resort hotels: the Banff Springs, Chateau Lake Louise, Jasper Park Lodge), motels, hostels, ski resorts, guest ranches, vacation farms, fly-in fishing lodges, B&Bs, super-deluxe RV campgrounds, primitive tent sites.

The Alberta Hotel Association publishes annually a campground guide and a comprehensive accommodation guide that includes alternative accommodation (B&Bs, fishing lodges, farms, ranches, hostels) and adventure tours, as well as hotels, motels, and resorts. To get these free, extremely useful publications, contact Alberta Tourism, address above.

### Hostels

Visitors young and old, single or with family, can enjoy the economy and ambience of hostel accommodation. Open to members and non-members. There are several hostels in Banff, Lake Louise, and in Jasper. Contact: Southern Alberta Hostelling Assn, #203 - 1414 Kensington Rd NW, Calgary, AB, T2N 3P9. Reservations for Southern Alberta: 1-800-363-0096 (within BC, AB, Sask). For Lake Louise, 522-2200.

For Jasper, contact Northern Alberta Hostelling Assn, 10926 88 Ave, Edmonton, AB, T6E 0Z1. 439-3089.

There are YMCA and YWCA hostels in Calgary (YW), Edmonton (YM and YW), Banff (YW), Lethbridge (YW).

For info on their back-country huts and the Canmore Clubhouse, contact the Alpine Club of Canada, Box 2040, Canmore, AB, T0L 0M0. 678-3200.

### National Parks

Alberta's five national parks, and one national historic site (Rocky Mountain House) between them offer a full range of camping opportunities. No reservations. Contact Canadian Parks Service, Western Regional Office, Room 520, 220 - 4th Ave SE, Calgary, AB, T2P 3H8. 292-4440.

For local headquarters:

- Banff National Park: 762-1550.
- Jasper National Park: 852-6176.

### Provincial Parks

There are more than 100 provincial parks and recreation areas throughout the province providing primitive to deluxe, fully serviced campgrounds. Many take reservations for individual or group camping: contact Alberta Tourism, or local infocentres.

### Highway Campgrounds

Alberta Transportation maintains 100 roadside campgrounds. They are free, and offer basic services (pit toilets, tables, pump water, firewood, garbage disposal).

### Forest Service Campgrounds

On public forest lands, usually accessible by gravel road, often in prime lakeshore or riverside spots in western and northern Alberta. These have from five to 100 primitive sites (pit toilets, tables, pump water, firewood, bear-proof garbage cans, some boat launches). For map and info, contact Alberta Forest Service, Forest Land Use Branch, Recreation Section, 6th Floor, 9920 108th St, Edmonton, AB, T5K 2M9. 427-3582.

### Back to Basics

Camping is restricted to designated areas to protect adjacent areas from being crushed or trampled. Firewood is provided to save the campground trees. Garbage cans are there to keep the site clean and, in bear country, maintain the peace. Please use the campsites.

## Transportation

### By Road

Thousands of kilometres of highways criss-cross Alberta. The main north-south route (Hwy 2) links the Peace River and Edmonton, to Calgary and south to Fort Macleod. Most other major roads radiate from it. The most popular scenic route is the Icefields Parkway (Hwy 93) running north-south, through Jasper and Banff national parks. Alberta's favourite back-road route, the Forestry Trunk Rd (Hwy 40/940), runs 1,017km along the Rockies from Hwy 3 in Crowsnest Pass to Hwy 2 at Grande Prairie.

Alberta Motor Association provides travel services to AMA, CAA, AAA, and affiliated overseas auto club members. Head offices are in Calgary (240-5300) and Edmonton (430-5555). Emergency: 430-7700.

### Bus Lines

■ **Greyhound Bus Lines:** Across Canada: 1-800-661-8747. Edmonton: 421-4211. Calgary: 265-9111. Jasper: 852-3926. Cover the province; check phone book for other communities.

■ **Brewster Transportation and Tours:** Across Canada: 1-800-661-1152.

■ **Red Arrow Express:** Edmonton: 424-3339. Calgary: 531-0350. Red Deer: 343-2356. Fort McMurray: 791-2990. Serves these four cities. Within Alberta: 1-800-232-1958.

■ **Charters, Tours, Airport Services:** Offered in major cities and tourist centres like Banff and Jasper. Call Alberta Tourism: 1-800-661-8888.

### Airlines

Major airlines listed below have scheduled flights into Calgary International Airport (292-8477), fourth largest airport in Canada, and/or Edmonton International Airport (890-8382). Edmonton Municipal Airport (428-3991) is served by Air BC, NW Territorial, and Canadian Regional Airlines.

Most other cities and towns in Alberta have scheduled flights or airstrips. No commercial flights to Banff or Jasper. For info on charters, contact local sources or the Alberta Aviation Council, 67 Airport Rd, Edmonton, AB, T5G 0W6. 451-5289.

■ **Air Canada:** Within AB: 1-800-332-1080.

■ **America West:** Canada/US: 1-800-247-5692.

■ **Canadian International:** Within AB: 1-800-372-9508.

■ **Continental Airlines:** Canada/US: 1-800-231-0856.

■ **Delta Air Lines:** Canada/US: 1-800-843-9378.

■ **KLM:** Calgary: 236-2600.

■ **Lufthansa:** Within Canada: 1-800-563-5954.

■ **United:** Canada/US: 1-800-241-6522.

### Railways

■ **VIA Rail:** 1-800-561-8630. First-class transcontinental service on board *The Canadian*: routed from Vancouver through Jasper to Edmonton, and other points east to Toronto. The two-and-a-half-day trip originates from Vancouver at 9pm, to allow daylight travel in the Rockies.

■ **Rocky Mountaineer Railtours:** Great Canadian Railtour Company, #104 - 340 Brooksbank Ave, North Vancouver, BC, V7J 2C1. Canada and US: 1-800-665-7245. Sublimely, through the Rockies. Vancouver to Jasper, Vancouver to Banff, optional to Calgary. This train travels only in daylight, for maximum mountain viewing. Passengers going east or west spend the night in Kamloops, BC. Continental breakfast, lunch, and hotel included. May-early Oct.

### Car and RV Rentals

Rental cars are available at airports, major hotels, and other agencies in most towns and all cities. RV rentals available in Edmonton and Calgary.

For information on customs, motoring regulations, and emergencies, see appropriate sections in *Introduction to British Columbia*, where the same information applies.

*Moraine Lake, Banff National Park.*

*Maligne River carving out Maligne Canyon, Jasper National Park.*

# Alberta Rockies Routes and Highlights

## TRAVELLER'S LOGS



## HIGHLIGHTS



## Lake Louise to Banff

### BANFF NATIONAL PARK (Highway 1)

This 80km section of Hwy 1 passes through arguably the most famous and exciting cluster of mountain landscapes in the world. There surely is more intensity per kilometre here than in any other stretch of the Trans-Canada Highway. This *Log* follows the pearl-blue Bow River from Lake Louise through Banff, but note that Hwy 1 actually follows the river all the way into Calgary, 193km from the BC border. (Sections east of Canmore are not covered in this *Travel Guide*.)

For those seeking a quiet alternative, the original highway, Hwy 1A, parallels the entire route from the BC border to Calgary. The section running through Banff National Park is known as the Bow Valley Parkway; see *Log* following. The Canmore to Calgary lap of the old highway is called the Bow Valley Trail.

Much of the divided highway through Banff National Park is lined with fencing to keep wildlife off the road. Watch for animals on the road, particularly at night, on any unfenced sections.

**Great Divide Rd (Hwy 1A):** 2km west of BC border, south off Hwy 1. This, the original highway, is now a narrow, less- travelled alternate route to Lake Louise. It is 14km to Hwy 1 junction at Lake Louise. Road also leads to **Lake O'Hara**. See *Glacier National Park to Lake Louise*, p.262.

**The Great Divide:** Boundary between BC and Alberta, and Yoho and Banff national parks. Also marks the crest of the Rockies, and the continental watershed. All waters west of this point flow into the Pacific Ocean; those east of here empty into the Saskatchewan River system, eventually into Hudson Bay. Views of Bow Range's northern peaks: Mt Niblock (2,976m), Narao Peak (2,913m).

**Banff National Park:** 6,641 sq km. General info and campgrounds: 762-1550. Banff National Park Visitors Centre: 762-1550. Or write Superintendent, Box 900, Banff, AB, T0L 0C0. Established in 1885 as an early tourist mecca to help support the new Canadian Pacific Railway, Banff is the oldest and most visited of Canada's national parks. It is second-largest of the four parks straddling the Continental Divide, which together have been designated a World Heritage Site. There are 25 peaks over 3,000m, glaciers and glacial lakes – Louise, Moraine, Bow, Peyto – hoodoos, hot springs, canyons, wild rivers, wildlife, 1,100km of hiking trails, ski trails and hills, gondolas, accommodation from wilderness huts to palatial hotels. The Icefields Parkway traverses the northern half of the park (see *Lake Louise to Jasper*, p.276); Hwy 1 and Hwy 1A access south.

Banff National Park attracts more than 3.5 million visitors a year from all over the world. They come for the great outdoors, and also the great indoors, the unique combination of natural wilderness and civilized pleasure that dates back to the park's birth over a century ago. These days, the busiest times to visit are June-Labour Day, long weekends, holidays. Feb-April are best months for skiing; spring and fall for wildlife watching.

**Banff National Park Campgrounds:** 762-1550. 14 Canadian Parks Service campgrounds offer 2,504 sites: four areas with 214 sites on Hwy 93, Icefields Parkway; three areas with 264 sites on Hwy 1A, Bow Valley Parkway; two areas with 405 sites off Hwy 1 near Lake Louise; five areas with 1,621 sites off Hwy 1 near Banff. No reservation system. Campgrounds vary in the services provided and fees charged, from the simplest with drinking water and pit toilets, to elaborate grounds with full hook-ups. They open and close on a staggered schedule from early May-late Sept.

Winter camping is permitted at Lake Louise I and II, Mosquito Creek, and Tunnel Mountain Village II.

Back-country camping is free, but permits required. Obtain from Park Ranger stations or infocentre, 224 Banff Ave.

**Viewpoint:** 5.5km east of BC border on Hwy 1. Overlooks Bath Creek where Major AB Rogers, chief CPR surveyor, took an accidental bath while fording the stream on horseback in 1881.

**Bow River Bridge:** 6km east of border. Bow River is small here, only 32km south of its source in Bow Lake on Hwy 93.

**Icefields Parkway (Hwy 93):** 7km east of border, leading north along eastern side of Great Divide 230km to Jasper. One of the continent's most spectacular scenic drives.

**Bow Valley Parkway (Hwy 1A):** 3km south of Hwy 93 junction; east 500m from Lake Louise exit, then south onto Hwy 1A, an alternate scenic route to Banff along east side of Bow River. See *The Bow Valley Parkway*, following. Turn east here also to Lake Louise Gondola and ski area.

**Lake Louise Village:** (Pop. 355). 10km east of border, 58km west of Banff. CP Railway reached this point in 1883, at a station called Laggan, where there was a pause before the push westward over Kicking Horse Pass. A trail was cut up the western side of the valley to the just-discovered jewel of the Rockies, Lake Louise, and the railway was soon bringing tourists to this mountain playground, hiring Swiss guides to help the more adventurous climb the local summits. In 1930, skiers built Skoki Lodge east of the village, foreshadowing development of the huge ski area now on the east slope of the Bow Valley.

In the past decade, the village of Lake Louise has undergone major expansion (within National Park limits) to handle the expanding influx of both summer and winter tourists. There is new accommodation, a new mall and Canadian Parks Service Information Centre, major expansion and renovation of Chateau Lake Louise, lifts and facilities at the ski area.

**Lake Louise and Area Information:** Canadian Parks Service Visitors Centre: 522-3833. In the village. Year-round. Hours vary. Park Warden Office in Banff: 762-4506 (24 hours). Avalanche Report: 762-1460 or 762-4506 (24 hours).

**Canadian Alpine Centre and International Hostel of Lake Louise:** In the town site. 522-2200. New 105-bed facility built in 1992 by the Alpine Club of Canada and the Southern Alberta Hostelling Assoc.

**Lake Louise (the lake):** 4.5km west of Hwy 1. With a setting that seems too good to be true, the "Mona Lisa of the Mountains" is officially the most famous landmark of the Canadian Rockies. Despite summer crowds, Louise is a "must-see." Reflected in the usually calm waters – which change from emerald green to aquamarine – is a spectacular amphitheatre of high peaks, crowned by Mt Victoria (3,464m), and the Victoria Glacier on the crest of the Great Divide. Scenery-stunned visitors are often brought to their senses by the rumbling of ice crashing down the glacier in summer.

Known as the "Lake of Little Fishes" to the local First Peoples, Louise was discovered for the western world by CPR survey scout Tom Wilson in 1882 when the natives guided him there. (He named it "Emerald Lake." It was later renamed Lake Louise to honour Queen Victoria's daughter.)

■ **Chateau Lake Louise:** 522-3511. The year after Wilson found the lake, a trail was cut to it from the railway below, bringing in the first tourists and prompting the CPR to build rough accommodation on the lake's shore in 1890. This burned down, was replaced by a larger, "Swiss style" chalet, then another, until the first two wings of today's Chateau Lake Louise were completed in 1928. It remained largely unchanged, open summers only, until the last decade when the grand hotel's latest chapter began. It opened year-round, added the third wing in 1988 (from the original plan, complete with copper roofs, giving the hotel 515 rooms), and developed major convention facilities. A variety of shops and dining rooms; even a special breakfast for early birds to watch the Victoria Glacier blush at dawn.

■ **Lake Louise Trails:** Popular lakeshore trail continues to the Plain of Six Glaciers teahouse, and beyond, if you're a mountaineer, across the divide to Lake O'Hara basin in Yoho National Park. Another charming log teahouse on Lake Agnes trail. Above lake's south shore, Fairview Mountain lookout gives exceptionally fair views.

■ **Moraine Lake:** From a junction 3km up Lake Louise access road, then 12km on Moraine Lake Rd. Panoramic views en route. Set below the **Valley of Ten Peaks**, Moraine Lake rivals Lake Louise in beauty and in fame (it's the scene on the back of the Canadian $20 bill). Named for the pile of rock which dammed the valley, creating the lake. First thought to be a terminal moraine (rock pushed along by a glacier), but now believed to be debris from a landslide down the Tower of Babel peak to the south; or both. Highly recommended: the short self-guiding interpretive trail to magnificent views at top of the moraine. Golden-mantled ground squirrels (like giant chipmunks); pikas (rock rabbits). Harlequin ducks and dippers along the creek.

■ **Moraine Lake Trails:** Hiking trail along west shore to Valley of the Ten Peaks; Larch Valley trail (popular in autumn when larches turn golden); Paradise Valley loop around Mt Temple and back to a trailhead below on Moraine Lake Road; a gentle trail south to Consolation Lake.

■ **Moraine Lake Lodge:** Accommodation, restaurant, canoe rentals. Recent major renovation and expansion includes new lodge, designed by Arthur Erickson, famed Canadian architect of the UBC Museum of Anthropology, and the new Canadian embassy in Washington, DC.

■ **Lake Louise Ski Area:** East of Lake Louise village exit. 522-3555 or 256-8473. Within Alberta: 1-800-661-4141. Western Canada and Northwest US: 1-800-567-6262. One of the largest ski areas in Canada: 50 runs, three quad, three double, twp triple chairs, one T-bar, one platter, three day lodges. Snow Nov-May.

■ **Cross-country Skiing:** Suitable terrain, popular trails. Easy runs on frozen Lake Louise and on Moraine Lake Road. Whitehorn and Pipestone (with cosy Skoki Lodge) trail systems are east of the village.

■ **Lake Louise Gondola:** East of Lake Louise village exit (at ski hill). 522-3555. The "Friendly Giant" offers panoramic views of Bow Valley. Restaurant, trails on top. Daily June - mid-Sept.

■ **Lake Louise Campground:** 500m west of Hwy 1, offers 384 sites. Mid-May to mid-Sept.

■ **Trail Rides:** Brewster Lake Louise Stables, 522-3872 (stable), or 762-5454;
or Timberline Tours, 522-3743.

■ **Alpine Club of Canada:** Box 2040, Canmore, AB, T0L 0M0. 678-3200. Huts serving as bases for climbing can be booked by members. Huts at Abbot Pass above Lake Louise, above Moraine Lake, on Castle Mountain, and others.

■ **Canadian Parks Service Shelters:** 762-1550. Reservations and back-country use permits required from Banff Infocentre.

■ **Skoki Lodge:** 14.5km hike/ski from Lake Louise Ski area. 522-3555. Beautiful 1930 log lodge and cabins in a legendary retreat. Open Christmas-April, June-Sept.

## Back on Highway 1

**Mt Temple Viewpoint:** 7.5km south of Lake Louise. West, Mt Temple (3,544m) is highest in area, third-highest in Banff Park. Reddish brown Cambrian rocks laid down as sediment in a shallow sea over 500 million years ago. Imposing peak named for British scientist Sir Richard Temple, who came here in 1884. First climbed in 1894.

**Taylor Creek Picnic Area:** 17.5km south of Lake Louise. Picnic area and angler's trailhead for 7km hike up to Taylor and O'Brien lakes. Forest here, and along highway between Lake Louise and Banff, is mainly even-aged stands of lodgepole pine, result of many fires 100-60 years ago. Spruce will eventually take over as the forest matures.

**Hwy 93 South (Castle Junction):** 28km south of Lake Louise. West on Hwy 93 South (Banff-Windermere Parkway) to Vermilion Pass, BC border, Kootenay National Park, Radium Hot Springs (102.5km). East 500m to Bow River, 1km to Bow Valley Parkway (Hwy 1A).

**Altrude Creek Picnic Area:** Just south of Castle Junction, west of highway. Altrude Creek flows from Great Divide on Vermilion Pass 10km to west. 5km hike to Arnica Lake, 8km to Twin Lakes, 11km to Gibbon Pass.

**Copper Lake:** 500m south of junction. Hidden just west of highway, the little fishing hole is named for Copper Mountain (2,795m) to the south, where copper claims were worked in 1880s. Views of Castle Mountain.

**Castle Mountain Viewpoint:** 9km south of Castle Junction. One of the best views of Castle Mountain (2,766m), aptly named peak of layered rock weathered into turrets and towers. Named in 1858 by Sir James Hector, geologist of the Palliser Expedition and first white man in area. Castle was renamed Mt Eisenhower after the Second World War, but in 1979, common sense and local pressure prevailed, and the original name was reinstated. First tower is called Eisenhower Peak.

**Redearth Creek Picnic Area:** 10km south of Castle Junction.

**Redearth Creek Trail:** 11km south of Castle Junction. Hiking, skiing, backpacking to Shadow Lake (14.5km), and to high alpine meadows around Egypt Lake. Check with park warden office for current regulations for this high-use hiking area.

**Sawback Range Viewpoint:** 16km south of Castle Junction. Horizontal when formed 350 million years ago, layers of grey limestone were tilted almost vertical during uplifting of the Rockies 75 million years ago. Erosion of the vertical layers created distinctive smooth-walled, sawtooth summits, topped by 2,908m Mt Ishbel on north end of the range. See Hole-in- the-Wall Cave on Mt Cory to the south.

**Wolverine Creek Picnic Area:** 17km south of Castle junction.

**Bourgeau Lake Trail:** Trailhead 18km south of Castle Junction. Classic 8km hike up Wolverine Creek to Bourgeau Lake: forest, waterfalls, high alpine meadow at base of 2,931m Mt Bourgeau.

**Divided Highway:** 20km south of Castle junction. Divided four-lane highway begins here, continues beyond Calgary. From here to park's East Gate, highway is fenced to keep animals, particularly elk, off roads. They still cross via a series of specially designed underpasses.

**Sunshine Rd:** 21km south of Castle Junction. West 8km to Sunshine Village.

**Sunshine Village Ski Resort:** Box 1510, Banff, AB, T0L 0C0. 762-6500. Alberta: 1-800-372-9583. Canada and US: 1-800-661-1363. 8km west on Sunshine Rd, then 20-minute gondola to village at 2,160m.

The only on-mountain accommodation in Canadian Rockies. Tons of all-natural snow in winter. 12 lifts, 62 runs, high-speed quad chairlift, gondola, one triple chair, four double chairs, three T-bars, two beginner tows, ski school, groomed trails, lots of untracked powder. Mid-Nov to May 31.

**Bow Valley Parkway (Hwy 1A):** 24km southeast of Castle Junction. Alternate scenic route along Bow Valley. See *Bow Valley Parkway*, p. 275.

**Vermilion Lakes Viewpoint:** 28km south of Castle Junction. Three lakes just west of Banff town site. Recent archaeological digs nearby revealed that this prime wildlife area first attracted human hunters at least 10,000 years ago.

Rocky Mountain sheep and mule deer often seen above; elk, coyotes, bald eagles, osprey, and waterfowl below.

East to west, dominant landmarks are Tunnel Mountain (1,692m), the low, rounded "mountain" behind Banff (called the "sleeping buffalo" by the First Peoples, renamed for the tunnel the CPR never built); Mt Rundle (2,949m), an enormous titled chunk of the earth's crust; the "castle," the Banff Springs Hotel, at the bottom of the Spray Valley; pine-carpeted Sulphur Mountain (2,451m), source of Banff's hot sulphur springs.

**Banff Town Site West Access:** 30km southeast of Castle Junction. South 1km to town. 5km north up steep winding road to views of Banff and Mt Norquay Ski Area.

**Banff:** (Pop. 5,688). Banff is 38km east of BC border on Hwys 1 and 93, 128km west of Calgary. It's 404km to Edmonton; 848km to Vancouver.

Summer visitors to Banff will agree that the setting is beautiful, but the town is very busy. To the thousands of Japanese who visit each year (10 percent of international visitors are Japanese), it may seem placid, compared to a Tokyo subway, but anyone expecting a rustic, "mountain-town" atmosphere will be very surprised. Banff is an irresistible paradox. In the heart of a national park sits an island of condensed urban civilization, holiday-style. Most visitors love the choices it presents.

It has been this way ever since Banff, the town and the park, was established a century ago. It began in 1883 with the arrival of the

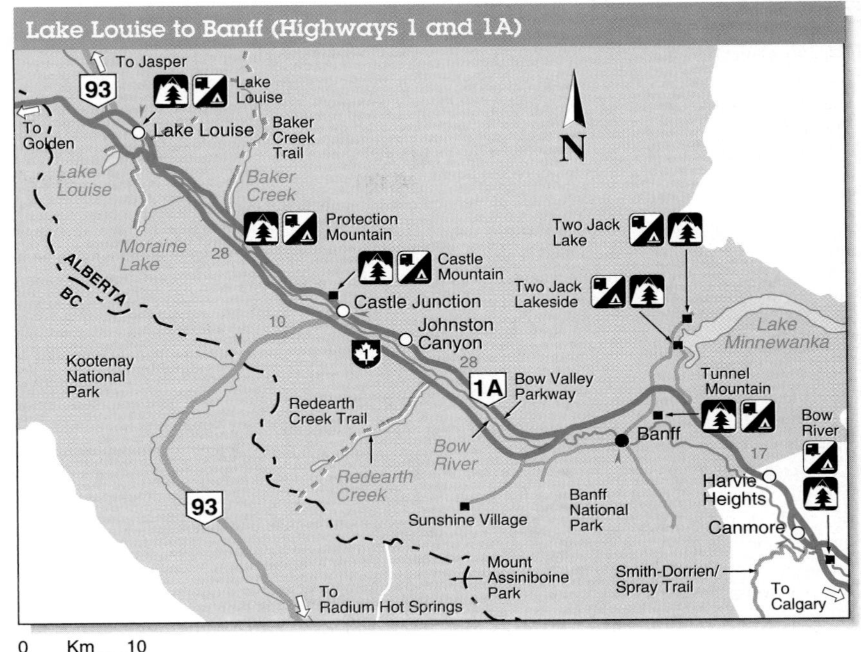


CPR. Prospecting on their days off, two railway construction men stumbled upon the hot springs at the base of Sulphur Mountain. They had hoped to stake a claim and eventually create a spa, but the federal government won the option, and in 1885 declared the springs and 10 surrounding miles the Hot Springs Reserve. In 1887, the area was enlarged, and the name changed to Rocky Mountains Park. This became Banff National Park in 1930, the start of the Canadian national park system. This was not entirely a noble, farsighted act to preserve the springs for everyone. The government was then heavily dependent on the financial success of the new railway, and Banff and other parks were created as CPR tourist attractions. (Cars were not allowed in the park until 1916.) The hot springs and the scenery were lures to bring tourists across on the new line (and install them in soon-to-be-built luxury CPR hotels).

Regardless, the tourism-minded planners who laid out the town site a century ago could hardly have done a nicer job. The town sits beside the Bow River at the base of Sulphur and Tunnel mountains. Towering a vertical mile above the town, Cascade Mountain (2,998m) to the north, Mt Rundle (2,949m) to the east, dominate the views.

No one could have foreseen the numbers of visitors that come here now, filling the compact town to the brim. There are signs in English, French, German, and Japanese. The nearby Parks Canada campgrounds and 3,500 hotel and motel rooms are packed through the summer.

But nature is always close at hand. Elk browse residential shrubbery or graze on the Banff Springs Golf Course. Beavers fell trees along the river, coyotes prowl the alleys at night. Side streets are aptly named: Squirrel, Fox, Beaver, Muskrat.

In 1990, after 105 years of distant government by the Canadian Parks Service, Banff became a semi-self-governing municipality (within its mandate as a park service centre). Locals now tackle the problems of parking shortages and winter leftovers, some world-class potholes.

**Banff Information: Banff Visitor Centre:** 224 Banff Ave. 762-1550. Year-round, displays, AV programs. Write Banff National Park, Box 900, Banff, AB, T0L 0C0. **Banff Park Warden Office:** between Hwy 1 and town site. Open 24 hours. 762-4506. 24-hour avalanche report: 762-1460. **Banff/Lake Louise Chamber of Commerce:** Also at 224 Banff Ave. Write Box 1298, Banff, AB, T0L 0C0. Daily 762-8421. Administration: 762-3777.

■ **Accommodation Reservations:** Book ahead through Banff Central Reservations, Box 1628, Banff, AB, T0L 0C0. For both Canada and US: 1-800-661-1676.

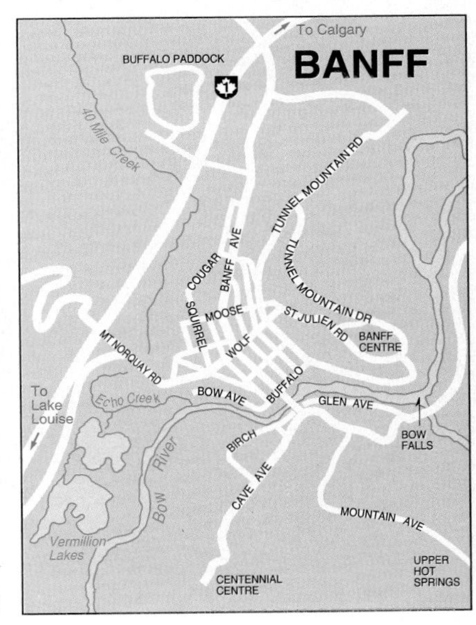

**■ Hostel Information and Reservations:** Within BC, AB, Sask: 1-800-363-0096.

**■ Campgrounds:** 762-1550. 1,621 sites in five campgrounds near town, most open mid-May to Sept. (See Tunnel Mountain and Two Jack Lake campgrounds, below.)

**■ Cave and Basin Historic Site:** On Cave Ave. 762-1557. Birthplace of Canada's first national park. Hotspring cave, historical and interpretive displays. Short self-guiding Discovery Trail (history and geology); Marsh Trail (plants, wildlife, including the tropical fish which, via someone's aquarium in 1960s, now call the spring's warm outflow home.) Swimming pool open July - Labour Day. Exhibits (free) 10-5 year-round.

**■ Sundance Canyon:** 2km beyond Cave and Basin, two-hour hike. Lower trail along Bow River is paved and wheelchair accessible.

**■ Upper Hot Springs:** 3km from downtown on Mountain Ave. 762-1515. If you like it hot, soak in mineral springs up to 43 C. Outdoor pool keeps you warm *apres ski* even on coldest winter day. Have a massage. Open daily year-round.

**■ Banff Springs Hotel:** On Spray Ave, 500m from downtown Banff (across bridge). Box 960, Banff, AB, T0L 0C0. 762-2211. Canada and US: 1-800-441-1414. CPR built first 250-room hotel here in 1888, above the confluence of the Bow and Spray rivers, and piped in water from the Sulphur Mountain hot springs for their guests. The current "castle," a blend of Scottish baronial and French chateau, was completed in 1928. It was the kind of place "where men would fish and golf, and women would change their clothes." Like who? Winston Churchill, the King of Siam, Paul Newman, Marilyn Monroe, Lassie. Some 50 feature-length motion pictures have been set in the Canadian Rockies, and the Banff Springs Hotel has very often been in the picture, certainly a home for celebrities. Hotel staff claim that ghosts, too, have drifted amidst their lovely furniture.

Still owned and operated by Canadian Pacific, the once ultra-exclusive hotel now serves a more "broad-based" clientele, including tour groups from the US and Japan (use of the hotel as a setting for a famous Japanese soap opera has made it something of a mecca), and lots of skiers. Hotel has undergone expansion to 829 rooms to accommodate its growing popularity abroad. Convention centre (with 1,600-person ballroom) completed in 1992. Presidential Suite, with private glass elevator, rents for $3,000 a night, Canada's most expensive accommodation. Public is welcome to wander through the parlours, smoking rooms, and lounges, tread on Persian carpets, admire stained-glass windows and gargoyles, recline on Gothic courting chairs or Jacobean hall seats. Restaurants, sushi bar, coffee shops, lounges, night club, some 30 shops. Also a 27-hole golf course, with sensational new clubhouse, tennis courts, swimming pool, trail rides, bowling alley, and a miniature version of the golf course.

**■ The Banff Centre:** St Julien Rd. For info: 762-6100. Tickets: 762-6300. Unique institute with schools of fine arts, management, and artists' colony. Music, theatre, opera, dance, drama, readings, videos, films. Summer Showcase and Festival of the Arts. Winter film series. Early Nov, Banff Festival of Mountain Films.

**■ Walter Phillips Gallery:** The Banff Centre, St Julien Rd. 762-6283. Noon-5 daily. Contemporary art exhibitions.

**■ Whyte Museum of the Canadian Rockies:** 111 Bear St. 762-2291. Archives of the Canadian Rockies, heritage collection of local human history and galleries with exhibits. Year-round, hours vary with season.

**■ Heritage Tours and Programs:** Guided tours of Banff's heritage homes and galleries. Various times. Summer: Tues-Sun. Winter: weekends. Contact Whyte Museum, 762-2291.

**■ Banff Park Museum:** 93 Banff Ave. 762-1558. Declared a National Historic Site in 1985, this unique 1903 "museum of a museum" houses animal exhibits dating back to 1860. Year-round. Hours vary. Closed Tues in winter.

**■ Luxton Museum:** Cave Ave (just across Banff bridge, then left). 762-2388. Fine collections and displays of Plains Indians artifacts. Summer: 9am-9pm. Winter: 11:30am-4:30pm. Guided tours available.

**■ Natural History Museum:** 112 Banff Ave. 762-4747.

**■ Cascade Gardens:** At south end of Banff Ave, around the stone park administration building (also known as "The Kremlin"). Splendid formal gardens with waterfalls, gazebos. Viewpoint below provides classic Banff Ave/Cascade Mountain photo opportunity.

**■ Sulphur Mountain Gondola:** Near Upper Hot Pool, Mountain Ave. 762-2523. Eight minutes, great view, restaurant.

**■ Bow Falls:** Short drive along Spray Ave (turn down golf course road just before Banff Springs Hotel), or 30-minute hike along river from the bridge on Banff Ave.

**■ Buffalo Paddock:** Off Hwy 1 between east and west Banff exits. May-Oct. Small herd of wood bison roam an enclosed area. Last native bison known in the park were killed in 1858. Drive through to view. **Do not leave vehicle!** Animals highly dangerous.

*Castle Mountain and Bow River, Banff National Park.*

■ **Lake Minnewanka:** Motorboating, fishing for lake trout, scuba-diving to submerged town, hiking trails, lots of bighorn sheep. Glass-enclosed boats make 90-minute tours to Devil's Gap, late May-Sept. 762-3473. Food outlet, boat rentals, fishing tackle and licenses.
■ **Bankhead:** 8km from Banff on Lake Minnewanka Rd. Historic site at ruins of early 1900s coal-mining town. 45-minute self-guiding walk. Base of Cascade Mountain.
■ **Hoodoos:** Above the Bow River, 4km from Banff on Tunnel Mountain Rd. Pillars of glacial till.
■ **Fenland Trail:** Off Banff west exit road just west of CPR station. Self-guiding trail (brochures at trailhead) through wetland and forest. Prime beaver spot.
■ **Mystic Ridge and Norquay Ski Area:** 5km up from Hwy 1, Banff west exit. 762-4421. The area's oldest resort, Mt Norquay has been totally redesigned to world-class standards. 25 runs, one express quad chair, two double chairs, one surface lift. Great views of Banff. Dec to mid-April.
■ **Cross-country Skiing:** Some hiking paths make good ski trails, some don't. Parks brochures and maps help. Every level possible, from a meander around the golf course, to a week's camping on a glacier. Close to town: Cascade Fire Rd, Carrot Creek, golf course, Tunnel-Hoodoos Loop, Spray River Trail. For above-tree-line experience without the effort of getting there, take a gondola to Sunshine Village, ski the vast meadows, often into May. Trails track-set.
■ **Fishing:** Park licence required. Minnewanka tours: 762-3473 for lake trout on Minnewanka; Banff Fishing Unlimited (762-4936) for Bow River, mountain lakes. Or go on your own. No fish hogs please.
■ **Boating:** Powerboats allowed only on Lake Minnewanka. Rentals available.
■ **Canoeing:** Rentals at Two Jack Lake, on Bow River in town site.
■ **Windsurfing:** On Vermilion and Two Jack lakes. No rentals.
■ **White-water Rafting:** On Bow River. Rocky Mt Raft Tours. 762-3632.
■ **Cycling:** Several rental outlets. Mountain bikes restricted to designated trails. Call park infocentre at 762-1550 for details, brochures.
■ **Golf:** 762-2211. Challenging and beautiful 27-hole course with clubhouse at the Banff Springs Hotel. Public welcome.
■ **Horseback Riding:** Local outfitters offer short "dude" rides and major pack trips. Brewster Mt Pack Trains: 762-5454; Timberline Tours: 522-3743; Holiday on Horseback: 762-4551. Carriage tours and sleigh rides in season.
■ **Tennis:** Culture and Recreation Dept, Town of Banff, has outdoor courts. 762-1200. Summer only. Courts at Banff Springs Hotel.
■ **Banff International Hostel:** On Tunnel Mt Rd 3km southeast. 762-4122. Or 1-800-363-0096. Sleeps 154, including families. Cafeteria, kitchen, laundry. Reservations accepted.
■ **Banff YWCA:** 102 Spray Ave. 762-3560.

**Tunnel Mountain Campgrounds:** 3km east of town. Three campgrounds, 1,163 sites including 320 hook-up sites, 200 year-round. Showers, programs.

**Two Jack Lake Campgrounds:** 13km northeast of town on Lake Minnewanka Rd. Two campgrounds, 458 sites.

**Hwy 1:** 2km north of town on Banff Ave. Straight 5.5km to Lake Minnewanka and Two Jack Lake. Turn west to Lake Louise, and 2km to Buffalo Paddock. East 13km to Banff National Park East Gate; 17km to Canmore.

**Anthracite Ghost Town:** 3km from Banff east access. To the north, outcrops of shale and sandstone containing anthracite coal. Just opposite Cascade Power Plant, and invisible to all but the practiced eye, are remains of a small coal-mining town called Anthracite, which flourished from 1886 till 1904, when Bankhead took prominence.

**Cascade Power Plant:** 3km from Banff east access. Hydroelectric generator is driven by water channelled down from Lake Minnewanka, leaving the Cascade River, across the railway tracks, usually dry.

**Valleyview Picnic Area:** 8.5km from Banff east access. Eastbound lane access only. From Banff, the highway sweeps around face of Mt Rundle, which dominates the southern horizon all the way to Canmore.

**Carrot Creek:** 11km from Banff east access. Eastbound travellers must continue 2.5km to park's East Gate and return west for access to trail parking lot. Hike or ski through aspen groves. Home to elk, deer, coyotes, songbirds, wildflowers.

**Banff National Park East Gate:** 13km from Banff east access. Congested area.

**Canmore West Access:** 16.5km from Banff east access.

**Canmore:** (Pop. 5,681). On Hwy 1, 17km east of Banff. A mountain playground area, boasting a $15 million Olympic Nordic Centre. From here, it is 111km east on Hwy 1 to Calgary.

# Bow Valley Parkway

## BANFF NATIONAL PARK (Highway 1A)

Hwy 1A from Lake Louise to Hwy 1, 5.5km west of Banff, is an excellent choice for touring motorists and cyclists. Running parallel to Hwy 1 on the opposite side of the Bow River Valley, Hwy 1A follows the route of the original 1920 road, climbing and winding, allowing views of the peaks at a leisurely pace. Access back to Hwy 1 at Castle Junction, about midway, if desired. There are campgrounds, commercial bungalow camps, youth hostels, and picnic areas, plus viewpoints, trails, displays, and an historic site. This is the perfect place to see wildlife – elk, deer, bighorn sheep, coyotes, and rarely, black bear and wolves. From Lake Louise to Castle Junction, the forests are even-aged stands of lodgepole pine; the southern section has more meadows, aspen groves, riverbottom and mountainside, and is the best area to see wildlife.

**Whitehorn Rd:** 1km east of Lake Louise. 1km to Lake Louise Gondola and Ski Area. Turn south onto Hwy 1A.

**Lake Louise Gondola:** 2km east of Lake Louise. 522-3555. 3km gondola ride to 2,040m on Whitehorn Mountain. Daily mid-June to mid-Sept. Fabulous views of ice-age glaciers, Continental Divide, Lake Louise. At top, hiking trails, restaurant. One of Canada's largest ski areas. Details in Lake Louise section, p.272.

**Bow Valley Parkway Exhibit:** 1.5km from Lake Louise. Explains area's history and geology.

**Corral Creek Picnic Area:** 3.5km from Lake Louise. Quiet spot in forest.

**Mt Temple Viewpoint:** 5km from Lake Louise. Spectacular Mt Temple (3,544m) is third highest peak in the park, quartzite and limestone formed 500 million years ago.

**Baker Creek Picnic Area:** 12km from Lake Louise. Panorama Ridge to west, Protection Mountain to east. Trail to alpine meadows and good skiing. Resort, bungalows, nearby.

**Protection Mountain Campground:** 15.5km from Lake Louise. 89 sites. Mid-June to mid-Sept. View of the rugged Bow Range.

**Castle Mountain Lookout Trail:** 21.5km from Lake Louise. 4km hike through pine forest on fire road to meadow high on side of Castle Mountain. Expansive views.

**Storm Mountain Viewpoint:** 24km from Lake Louise. This is as far as glacial ice advanced during last major glaciation 8,000 years ago. Look across to Vermilion Pass.

**Castle Cliffs Viewpoint:** 25.5km from Lake Louise. Look up to red-brown ramparts and turrets of 2,766m Castle Mountain. Named in 1858 by Dr James Hector, surgeon and geologist of Palliser Expedition, first white man to see this natural castle.

**Castle Junction:** 26.5km from Lake Louise, approximately midway between Lake Louise and Banff. Turn west for 1km to cross Bow River and rejoin Hwy 1.

**Castle Mt Village:** At Castle Junction. Quaint chalet resort with store, service station, accommodation. Year-round.

**Castle Mountain Youth Hostel:** Adjacent Castle Junction. Newly renovated, sleeps 36. Reservations: 1-800-363-0096.

**Rockbound Lake Trail:** Adjacent Castle Junction. 8km hike up to Rockbound and Tower lakes in a hanging valley. 15-minute hike to beautiful Silverton Falls.

**Castle Mountain Campground:** .5km southeast of Junction. 44 sites. June-Sept.

**Silver City:** 2km southeast of Castle Junction. Site of a mining town that sprang to life in 1883 with arrival of railway. In its two-year lifespan, boasted a population of 2,000, several hotels and stores. Became a ghost town overnight when copper and lead deposits didn't pan out.

**Moose Meadows:** 4km southeast of Castle Junction. Open shrub meadows inhabited by everything but moose. They're rarely seen here now due to general habitat changes, and effects of giant liver fluke, an internal parasite which is widespread, largely benign to elk, but fatal to moose. View of spiky Pilot Mountain (2,954m).

**Johnston Canyon Resort:** 7km southeast of junction. Restaurant, store, gas, rustic cottages. 762-2971. May-Sept.

**Johnston Canyon Trail:** 7km southeast of Castle Junction. One of the most travelled trails of the Rockies snakes up through a spectacular canyon to mountain meadows. 1km to Lower Falls; 3km to Upper Falls; 6km to the Ink Pots. Extraordinarily engineered trails and boardwalks.

Watch for dippers, plump grey birds that can walk underwater along stream bottoms, and nest under waterfalls. Also, the rare black swift: this is one of two nesting colonies in Alberta. The Ink Pots are seven cold-water springs bubbling into clear pools in an open, scenic meadow.

**Johnston Canyon Campground:** 7.5km southeast of Castle Junction. 140 sites.

**Pilot Pond:** 10km southeast of Castle Junction. 400m trail leads down to beautiful hidden lake popular with float- tubing anglers. Formerly called Lizard Lake for the long-toed salamanders that used to breed here in large numbers, until lake was stocked with trout, which ate them!

**Hillsdale Meadows Viewpoint:** 12km southeast of Castle Junction. Aspen-lined meadows were a traditional native hunting camp at turn of the century. Grand view of sawtooth peaks of Sawback Range, whose layers were pushed almost vertical by geological mountain building activities. Highest is 2,877m Mt Ishbel, down whose slopes came a gigantic rockslide. Because of divided highway, only westbound travellers can see exhibit at Hillsdale Slide. Trail leads up to top of Johnston Canyon trail.

**Tree-in-the-Road:** 14km southeast of Castle Junction. Used to be a huge spruce tree in the middle of the road, a famous landmark spared by the earliest road engineers. It blew over in early 1980s.

**Sawback Picnic Area:** 15km southeast of Castle junction. Wildlife exhibit, showing bark scars on aspen from hungry elk.

**Experimental Range Study Plot:** 16km southeast of Castle Junction. Compare vegetation that has been browsed on, to vegetation fenced-off since 1944.

**Muleshoe Picnic Area:** 21km southeast of Castle Junction. Named for horseshoe-shaped backwater of Bow River. Steep trail east of road leads to open views. East and 600m up is the **Hole-in-the-Wall Cave** on Mt Cory. Some 30m deep, it was dissolved from bedrock by action of glacial ice and meltwater when glaciers filled the valley. Burned areas on mountain were deliberately set by wardens to recreate natural ecosystem of park that was drastically altered by decades of forest fire control. In doing this, habitat was improved for grazing wildlife.

**Backswamp Viewpoint:** 24km southeast of Castle Junction. South across valley to Sundance Range; west to 2,931m Mt Bourgeau; farther west to 2,984m Mt Brett, and 2,435m Massive Mountain. River swamp is home to beaver, muskrat, nesting waterfowl, ospreys, songbirds, and a beautiful little carnivorous plant, the purple-flowered common butterwort, which feeds on swamp insects. In winter, best place to watch for wolves. Also bighorn sheep and, in early spring, mountain goats, on Mt Cory above.

**Bow Valley Parkway Exhibit:** 26km southeast of Castle Junction. Introduces westbound travellers to Bow Valley.

**Fireside Picnic Area:** 26.5km southeast of Castle Junction. Just .5km east off Hwy 1A to creekside picnic site. Steep trails lead 4.5km to Edith Pass or 6km to Cory Pass; a loop hike if you're energetic. Grand views.

**Hwy 1:** 27km southeast of Castle Junction, 53km from Lake Louise. Hwy 1 leads east 5.5km to Banff.

## Lake Louise to Jasper

### ICEFIELDS PARKWAY (Highway 93)

The Icefields Parkway (Hwy 93) provides a direct link from Trans-Canada Hwy (Hwy 1) near Lake Louise, 229km north to Jasper. It also connects with the David Thompson Hwy (Hwy 11) east to Rocky Mountain House and Red Deer.

For most travellers, however, where Hwy 93 leads is beside the point. The Icefields Parkway is a narrow manmade corridor through a vast unspoiled wilderness. Touring here is precisely where they want to be: on a world-famous stretch of spectacular Canadian Rockies scenery with sky-slicing peaks, icefields, glaciers, shockingly blue lakes, forests and wildflower meadows, wilderness, wildlife, and, in summer, *lots* of people! Be prepared: peak season driving and camping can be challenging. Note: few facilities and services.

One pleasant paradox of Hwy 93 is that, although it passes through extremely rugged terrain, the route is an easy drive. It follows a line between the Main Ranges on the west, and the Front Ranges to the east. The Main Ranges – Continental Divide – have most of the glaciers, including the vast Columbia Icefield sprawling beneath Mt Columbia, at 3,747m, Alberta's highest peak. The Front Ranges in places are tipped like huge dominoes, the result of the earth's forces that formed them.

Hwy 93 traverses two passes, the 2,069m Bow Pass 44km north up the valley from Hwy 1. Then, following the North Saskatchewan River for 36km, the highway climbs steeply 11km up a side valley to 2,035m Sunwapta Pass near the Columbia Icefield.

Passing through everything from wet and dry valley bottoms to dense mountain forests, from alpine meadows with permafrost, to rock, ice, and lichens, Hwy 93 is a naturalist's dream. Large mammals are often seen early and late in the day. Elk are most common, but moose, mule and white-tailed deer, wolves, coyotes, grizzly and black bears can be seen almost anywhere along the route. Bighorn sheep and mountain goats are found around the icefield; goats are regulars at mineral licks 40km south of Jasper. The rare woodland caribou is occasionally seen north of the icefield near Beauty Creek. Birds to watch for include ptarmigans, rosy finches, and golden eagles above the timberline, boreal owls and white-winged crossbills in high forests, and dippers and harlequin ducks on the streams.

Columbian and golden-mantled ground squirrels ("gophers" and "giant chipmunks") and two grey and black birds – the short-billed gray jay (alias "whiskey jack") and the brash, long-billed Clark's nutcracker – are frequent beggars at roadside stops.

There are 11 Canadian Parks Service campgrounds on the parkway, four in Banff and seven in Jasper. Also, picnic areas, displays, viewpoints, hiking trails. Eight hostels are operated by the Alberta Hostelling Association, three in the Banff National Park section of the parkway, five in Jasper's (see below). Private accommodation and most basic roadside services are available in summer, 39km north of Lake Louise at Bow Lake (no gas); 79km north at Saskatchewan River Crossing; 127km north at Columbia Icefield; and 176km north at Sunwapta Falls in Jasper National Park. No vehicle services in winter.

**Icefields Parkway Hostel Information:** For hostels south of the Icefields, contact Southern Alberta Hostelling Assoc, #203 - 1414 Kensington Rd NW, Calgary, AB, T2N 3P9. 1-800-363-0096. For hostels within Jasper National Park, contact Northern Alberta Hostelling Assoc, 10926-88th Ave, Edmonton, AB, T6E 0Z1. 439-3139.

**Hwy 1:** Junction of Trans-Canada Hwy and Hwy 93 (Icefields Parkway) 2km north of Lake Louise village overpass. From Lake Louise, drive north 2km to this junction. On Icefields Parkway (Hwy 93), it is 76km to junction of David Thompson Hwy (Hwy 11) at Saskatchewan River Crossing; 121km to the Columbia Icefield; 229km to Jasper.

**Herbert Lake:** Recreation area is at the north end of lake, 3km north of Hwy 1 on Hwy 93. Picnics, fishing, canoeing, and swimming (this is the only lake around that gets reasonably warm). Superb views south to the cluster of peaks around Lake Louise, crowned by 3,544m Mt Temple.

**Hector Lake:** 25km north of Hwy 1. Named for Palliser Expedition geologist Dr James Hector who found it in 1858. It sparkles below the Waputik (Stoney Indian for "white goat") Icefield and Range, and 3,246m Mt Balfour. Trail access only.

**Mosquito Creek Campground:** 25km north of Hwy 1, near Hector Lake. 32 campsites, day use, winter camping. Youth Hostel nearby. Along Bow River flats, mosquitoes can be ferocious. 10km trail west to Molar Pass.

**Crowfoot Glacier:** 34km north of Hwy 1. First glacier on the parkway, named for its distinctive shape. East side of highway, parking lot and trailhead to Dolomite Pass (and Siffleur Wilderness Area), home of Banff Park's only woodland caribou. From here to Bow Summit, watch for grizzlies.

**Bow Lake:** 36km north of Hwy 1. Source of the Bow River, this very cold, blue lake is fed by Bow Glacier, a tongue of the Wapta Icefield straddling the Great Divide. Beautiful picnic area on the lake's south shore. The Num-Ti-Jah Lodge, a 1920s, red-roofed log structure on the lake's north shore, was built by pioneer guide and outfitter, Jimmy Simpson. Meals, trail rides, accommodation, still offered. A 5km hiking trail from north viewpoint parking lot along lakeshore to Bow Glacier Falls (and beyond to an alpine hut below the glacier for serious hikers).

**Peyto Lake/Bow Summit:** 42km north of Hwy 1. At 2,069m Bow Summit, turn west on access road. 400m walk through fragrant subalpine spruce and fir forest opens to outstanding view over Peyto Lake – maybe the bluest blues in the Rockies – and north down Mistaya River valley. *Mistaya* is Cree for "grizzly bear." Lake was named for Bill Peyto, early guide and outfitter, one of Rockies' most colourful characters.

**Waterfowl Lake Campground:** 57km north of Hwy 1. 116 campsites. Day use, wheel-chair facilities, interpretive theatre, canoeing, fishing, trails, birdwatching. In lodgepole pine forest on southeast shore of Lower Waterfowl Lake. 3,307m Mt Chephren to west, 3,290m Howse Peak south, masterworks of glacial sculpting. Migrating and nesting waterfowl.

**Mistaya Canyon:** 71km north of Hwy 1 on Hwy 93. A short 300m hike to see a slot canyon carved through the limestone.

**North Saskatchewan River:** 77km north of Hwy 1. A natural path through the mountains, this valley, and Howse Pass just west, was used in 1807 by explorer David Thompson. In 1984, 49km of this river was nominated for inclusion in Canada's Heritage River System. The braided channels and gravel bars mark a young river, shifting each year with spring floods in search of a permanent channel. On south side, water below the bridge is usually green and clear, flowing in from the lake-filtered Mistaya River outlet; on the north, main river runs grey-green, loaded with glacial silt.

**Hwy 11 (David Thompson Hwy):** 79km north of Hwy 1. East 246km on Hwy 11 to Red Deer on Hwy 2. Kootenay Plains Natural Area, Rocky Mountain House National Historic Site, and Sylvan Lake en route.

**Saskatchewan River Crossing:** At Hwy 11 junction. Services here May-Nov.

**Rampart Creek Campground:** 12km north of Saskatchewan River Crossing on Hwy 93. 50 campsites, day use, wheel-chair facilities. June-Sept. Below ramparts of Mt Wilson, a magnificent 3,240m massif topped by quartzite peaks. Some of the best black bear habitat in Banff National Park. Hostel situated below highway.

**Cirrus Mountain Campground:** 29km north of Saskatchewan River Crossing. 16 campsites. Hiking trails. June-Oct.

**Weeping Wall:** 31km north of Crossing. Viewpoint. Meltwaters spill over a huge, sheer, grey Devonian limestone cliff at base of Cirrus Mountain, freezing in winter to become an international mecca for ice climbers.

**The Big Bend:** 37km north of Crossing. Source of North Saskatchewan River is the Saskatchewan Glacier, southern toe of the Columbia Icefield, just out of sight but due west. Highway switchbacks east and climbs steeply around Parker Ridge. Gear down!

**Parker Ridge:** 41km north of Crossing. A short, steep hike (about 5km round trip) leads up onto 2,100m Parker Ridge for a look at life above tree line. Mountain goats and ptarmigan often seen, and despite the Arctic conditions, a host of beautiful flowers and shrubs. Also fossil coral, here on top of the changing world. Prime spot for winter ski touring.

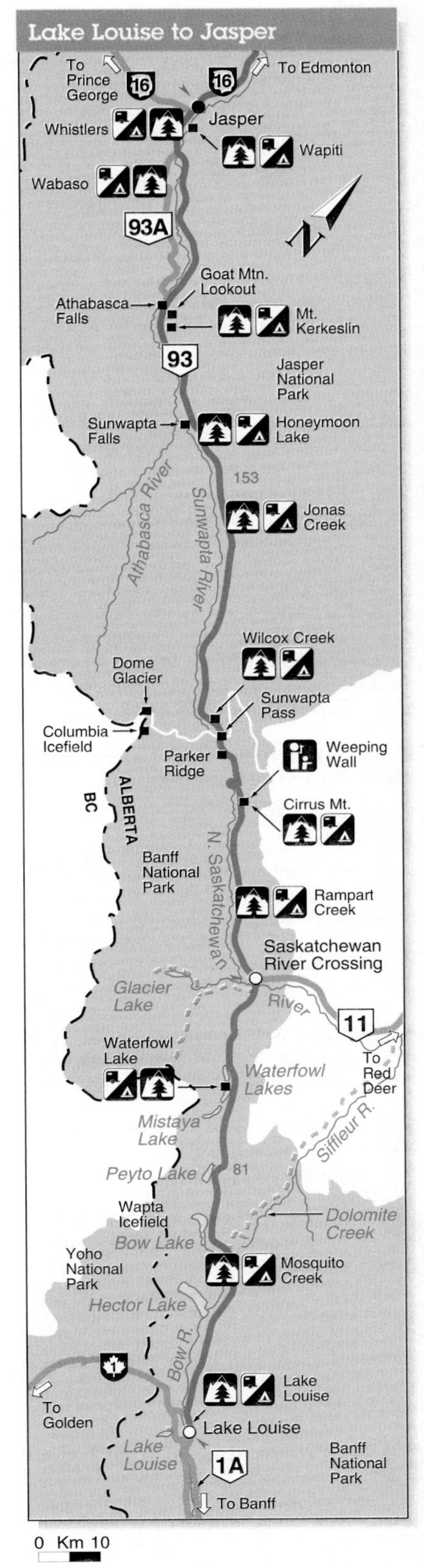

**Jasper National Park:** 1,087,800ha (10,878 sq km). Canadian Parks Service in Jasper: 852-6176. Or contact Superintendent, Jasper National Park, Box 10, Jasper, AB, T0E 1E0, 852-6161. Two infocentres: one in Jasper, on Connaught Drive, across from CNR station, daily year-round; one at Columbia Icefield, Hwy 93, 105km south of Jasper, daily, late May-early Oct. Slide shows, displays, park publications, maps.

Established 1907. 45km north of Saskatchewan River Crossing on Hwy 93 (108km south of Jasper). Western entrance at BC border, 77km east of Tete Jaune Cache. Eastern entrance 56km northeast of Jasper (306km west of Edmonton). Largest of Canada's four Rocky Mountain national parks. Parks were declared a World Heritage Site by UNESCO in 1985. Together they enclose a 20,238 sq km wilderness area straddling the Great Contintental Divide.

Jasper is a hiker's paradise, from day trails to 10-day wilderness treks. Popular hikes include 45km Skyline Trail from near Jasper to Maligne Lake; and 42km Tonquin Valley loop. Park-use permits are required by back-country hikers, and the number of hikers for more popular trails is limited by regulations. Reservations can be made for some hikes. Check with park infocentres.

**Jasper National Park Campgrounds:** 852-6161. 10 campgrounds, 1,772 campsites. No reservations.

From the Columbia Icefield, one of the park's most famous attractions, Hwy 93 follows Sunwapta then Athabasca River valleys to Jasper, the park's geographic and cultural centre, 108km north. There are seven Canadian Parks Service campgrounds (and some private) along the Icefields Parkway.

**Wilcox Creek Campground:** 2km north of Sunwapta Pass on Hwy 93. 46 campsites, programs, hiking trails.

**Columbia Icefield Campground:** 4km north of Sunwapta Pass on Hwy 93. 33 campsites (tents only), hiking trails.

**Columbia Icefield Access:** 4.5km north of park boundary (103km south of Jasper) on Hwy 93. A congested area. The bright-red lodge offers gas, food, lodging. Bighorn sheep, tame to brazen, are often seen here. Adjacent is Canadian Parks Service Icefield Centre and office for Columbia Icefield Sno-Coach Tours. All services here available May-Oct only.

**Road across Hwy 93 from Icefield Centre:** 1km to parking lot at Sunwapta Lake, and short trail to toe of Athabasca Glacier. This ice age remnant is receding; note dated posts marking glacier's retreat. **Do not walk on the glacier: very dangerous, many unmarked crevasses.**

**Icefield Information:** Infocentre, 4.5km north of park boundary on Hwy 93, across from Icefield access road. Area displays (including relief model of icefield), weather info, back-country camping permits. Late May-Sept.

**Columbia Icefield Sno-Coach Tours:** Office near Icefield Centre or call Banff 762-6735. Unusual tour onto Athabasca tongue of Icefields. Summer only.

**Columbia Icefield:** 325 sq km. Up to 350m thick. Only the tip of the icefield is visible here: southeast shore of vast 325 sq km icecap that sprawls 60km north along the Continental Divide. The Athabasca Glacier, beneath 3,491m Mt Athabasca to the west, and the Dome Glacier, spilling down 3,475m Mt Kitchener to the north, are edges of the largest icecap south of the Arctic Circle. They feed river systems flowing to the Pacific, Atlantic, and Arctic oceans. There are dangerous crevasses and the icefields are recommended only for experienced, equipped mountaineers. Most visitors take Sno-Coach tour. Professional guided hiking tours available. Contact Peter Lemieux, Athabasca Glacier Icewalks, Box 2067, Banff, AB, T0L 0C0.

**Sunwapta Canyon Viewpoint:** 6km north of Icefield Centre on Hwy 93. View of 3,475m Mt Athabasca. Mountain sheep and goats. Use caution around this congested viewpoint. Road descends sharply for next 4km north.

**Tangle Falls:** 7km north of Icefield Centre. A waterfall spills down steps of half-billion-year-old limestone. Another hangout for street-smart bighorn sheep.

**Stutfield Glacier Viewpoint:** 9km north of Icefield Centre. The Stutfield tongue of the icefield hangs off the northern side of 3,475m Mt Kitchener.

**Woodland Caribou:** Small herds of this rare animal, depicted on the Canadian 25-cent piece, summer high in the ranges east of Hwy 93, and are often seen along highway in Beauty Creek area late fall to spring.

**Jonas Creek Campground:** 31km north of Icefield Centre (77km south of Jasper). 25 campsites. May-Oct.

**Sunwapta Falls:** 49km north of Icefield Centre (54km south of Jasper). Turn west 600m to Sunwapta Falls parking lot. Short walk to 9m falls. *Sunwapta* is Stoney Indian word for "roaring river," and it does that. Also trailhead to Fortress Lake in BC's Hamber Provincial Park. **Sunwapta Falls Resort** on Hwy 93 has restaurant, groceries, gas. Seasonal. 852-4852.

**Honeymoon Lake Campground:** 35 lake- shore campsites. 53km north of Icefield (50km south of Jasper). June-Oct.

**Athabasca River:** 69km north of Icefield Centre (34km south of Jasper). Viewpoint, picnics. Great views of river valley. Mountain goats along road or river, attracted by minerals in the white glacial soils. Watch for kids on the road! 168km of Athabasca River in Jasper National Park nominated for inclusion in Canadian Heritage Rivers System.

**Mt Kerkeslin Campground:** 42 campsites. 72km north of Icefield Centre (36km south of Jasper) on Hwy 93. May-Sept.

**Hwy 93A:** 76km north of Icefield Centre. Access to Athabasca Falls, Wabasso Campground, and famed beauty spot below Mt Edith Cavell. A parallel 24km scenic drive on opposite side of Athabasca River. Rejoins Hwy 93, 23km north.

## SIDE TRIP

### to Athabasca Falls, and Mt Edith Cavell

**Athabasca Falls:** 400m west on Hwy 93A to parking lot. Short walk to high pressure 12m falls roaring through narrow canyon – awesome with spring runoff.

**Wabasso Campground:** 238 campsites, sani-station. 14km north of Hwy 93 on Hwy 93A (16km south of Jasper on Hwy 93A). Playground, wheelchair facilities. In lodgepole pine forest along Athabasca River. Mid-June to Sept.

**Mt Edith Cavell Rd:** 18km north of Hwy 93 on Hwy 93A. A narrow, winding, 15km road to lake. Short hike leads to classic views of 3,363m **Mt Edith Cavell** reflected in Cavell Lake, Jasper's Lake Louise. Also head of popular hiking and horseback riding trail 20km to Tonquin Valley, Jasper's most famous back-country area. Road open June-Oct (no bicycles allowed).

**Marmot Basin:** 20km north of Hwy 93 on Hwy 93A (12km south of Jasper). Jasper's downhill ski area. 852-3816. 701m vertical, six lifts; even mix of novice, intermediate, and expert terrain; longest run 5.6km. Dec-May.

## *Return to Highway 93*

**Wapiti Campground:** 103km north of Columbia Icefield (5km south of Jasper). 366 campsites, showers, winter camping.

**Whistlers Rd:** 105km north of Icefield Centre (3km south of Jasper) on Hwy 93; to Whistlers Campground and Jasper Tramway. The "whistlers" in question here are hoary marmots, huge alpine woodchucks with loud whistle alarm calls.

**Whistlers Campground:** West on Whistler Rd 100m, then south 300m on access. 781 campsites. Some fully serviced sites, showers, sani-station. May-Sept.

**Jasper Tramway:** 4km up and west on Whistlers Rd. 852-3093. A reversible tram ride to 2,265m alpine meadows, and a fantastic view of the area. Longest and highest tramway in Canada.

**Jasper:** (Pop. 3,269). On Hwy 16 in Jasper National Park, 101km east of Tête Jaune Cache, 153 km north of Saskatchewan River Crossing (Hwy 11).

As capital of Jasper National Park, Jasper is a kind of twin sister to Banff. The two used to have a sibling rivalry dating back to the two railways (CN and CP) which created the towns (and to a large degree, the parks) and their associated grand resorts, the Jasper Park Lodge and the Banff Springs Hotel. Competition is not so relevant today, especially since the recent acquisition of Jasper Park Lodge by Canadian Pacific Hotels.

Jasper is quieter and more relaxed than Banff, with more original mountain community charm intact than its busy, developed southern sister. This does not reflect on Jasper's relative beauty or attractions, but rather on the simple fact that while Calgary is little more than an hour from Banff, on Trans-Canada Highway, Jasper is a good four hours from Edmonton on a quieter highway. (Note, however, that Hwy 16 to Edmonton has recently been twinned from Hinton to Edmonton, cutting down the former five-hour trip to the current four. This more efficient highway may have an impact.) An historical factor is that Jasper is a major railway town, a third of its residents employed by the CNR. It is not, therefore, so preoccupied with tourism as Banff.

Nevertheless, on a busy summer day in Jasper, the streets are bustling with tourists, shopping for souvenirs or Inuit art, gathering park information and supplies for camping trips, booking raft trips, trail rides, golf games, bus tours or ski trips. With hotels, motels, B&Bs, and campgrounds filled with visitors, plus summer staff to service them, as well as summer cottagers, the town's population seasonally soars to over 10,000. Full range of tourist services, but no commercial airport (nearest is in Hinton, 77km east).

**Jasper Information:** Jasper Tourism and Commerce, Box 98, Jasper, AB, T0E 1E0. 852-3858. 632 Connaught Dr. Mon-Fri year-round. Daily April-Oct. Info for travellers to both BC and Alberta. Books for sale.

■ **Jasper Walking Tour:** Delightful introduction to Jasper's people, past and present, offered by an innovative, cooperative association called "Parks & People." Guided walks four days a week, July-Aug. 852-4767. A useful book, *Jasper: a Walk in the Past,* is available in shops and park infocentres.

■ **Jasper Yellowhead Museum and Archives:** 400 Pyramid Lake Rd, Box 42, Jasper, AB, T0E 1E0. 852-3013. Summer: 1-9pm. Winter: varies. Operated by the Jasper Yellowhead Historical Society.

■ **Mt Edith Cavell:** From Hwy 93A about 12km south of Jasper, then up narrow, winding 15km Mt Edith Cavell Rd, open June-Oct. Superb views of 3,363m Cavell, self-guided interpretive trail, hiking trail to Angel Glacier, Cavell Meadows. Mountain named for British nurse executed for helping Allied troops in First World War.

■ **Pyramid and Patricia Lakes:** From Connaught Drive in Jasper, turn north on Pine Ave, follow to Pyramid Lake Road, then 8km of winding road to lakes. Great views of colourful 2,733m Pyramid Mountain. Picnicking, fishing, canoeing, hiking, water sports. Boat rentals: 852-3536. Trail rides: 852-4581.

■ **The Den Wildlife Museum:** 852-3361. Jasper's wildlife museum, downtown in the Whistlers Inn, 105 Miette Ave. Daily. More than 100 specimens in natural settings.

■ **Rafting:** Raft trips down the Athabasca River. Jasper Raft Tours, 852-3613, or Whitewater Rafting (Jasper) Ltd, 852-7238. Or down the Maligne River: Rocky Mountain River Guides, 852-3777. In winter, Maligne Canyon Tours, 852-3370 (visit the ice-covered canyon).

## *Highway 16 from Jasper*

**Maligne Lake Rd:** 2km northeast of Jasper on Hwy 16. To Lake Annette (2km), Jasper Park Lodge (3km), Maligne Canyon (6km), Medicine Lake (21km), and Maligne Lake (44km).

## SIDE TRIP
### on Maligne Lake Road

**Lake Annette:** Just west of Athabasca River bridge, turn south on Jasper Park Lodge road; 1km to signed access road.

Annette offers (surprise!) warm water plus beach, picnics, hiking trails, and paved wheelchair path around lake.

**Jasper Park Lodge:** Just west of Athabasca River Bridge on Maligne Lake Rd, turn south onto 2km access road. 852-3301. World-class resort built in Roaring '20s by CN Railway as an exclusive mountain resort to compete with CP's Banff Springs. On beautiful Lac Beauvert, guests stay in bungalows and guest houses arranged on neatly landscaped mini-streets on spacious grounds around the main lodge (built 1953). Unique room service with staff on bicycles. Outstanding 18-hole golf course (the late Bing Crosby's favourite), trail rides, bike, canoe, and paddle-boat rentals, gift shops, restaurants. Cross-country ski trails. Year-round. Recently acquired by CP Hotels, $25 million has been spent on development and renovation. New Beauvert Promenade includes 13 boutiques, nightclub, lounge, new dining room. Meeting rooms and almost all guest rooms renovated.

**Maligne Canyon:** A steep-walled canyon sliced 50m into limestone by the Maligne River. Self-guiding trail, facilities. Maligne Canyon Tours: 852-3370.

**Medicine Lake:** 6km lake with two picnic areas. Drains into underground channels. Lake levels fluctuate. Motor boats allowed.

**Maligne Lake:** Largest lake in Canadian Rockies, second largest glacial lake in the world. A famous attraction. 36km cruises to Spirit Island in summer. Restaurant, boat rentals, fishing (record 9.3kg rainbow trout caught here in 1980), horseback-riding trails. Premium cross-country skiing.

## *Return to Highway 16*

**Snaring River Campground:** On Hwy 16, 10km east of Jasper. 66 sites.

**Jasper House:** Plaque 34km east of Jasper. Named for Jasper Hawes who arrived in 1817 to take over four-year-old North-West Company post across the valley.

**Miette Rd:** 48km northeast of Jasper. Southeast 2km to **Pocahontas Campground**, 140 sites, wheelchair facilities, interpretive programs. Punchbowl Falls nearby. Mid-May to Sept.

A further 15km southeast to **Miette Hot Springs**, hottest (54 degrees C) hot springs in the Canadian Rockies. Scenic pool, picnic area, as well as commercial services. May-early Sept.

**Jasper National Park East Gate:** 56km east of Jasper on Hwy 16. From here, it is 306km to Edmonton.

*Columbia Icefield, Jasper National Park.*

Index

# A



# B

# E



# F



# G

# H



# I



# J



# K

## L



## M

# N



# O



# P

# Q



# R



# S

# T

# U



# V



# W



# X



# Y



# Z